Spain

R. Mazin/DIAF

The icy crests of the Pyrennes
stretched east to west,
flashing in the sun like broken glass
on a wall, while
before me, to the south,
was what I had come to see –
range after range of little step-like
hills falling away to
the immensities of Spain.

Laurie Lee

As I Walked Out One Midsummer Morning

Travel Publications

38 Clarendon Road - WATFORD Herts WD1 1SX - U.K.
Tel. (01923) 415 000
www.michelin-travel.com
TheGreenGuide-uk@uk.michelin.com

Manufacture française des pneumatiques Michelin

Société en commandite par actions au capital de 2 000 000 000 de francs
Place des Carmes-Déchaux – 63000 Clermont-Ferrand (France)
R.C.S. Clermont-Fd B 855 200 507

© Michelin et Cie, Propriétaires-éditeurs, 2000
Dépôt légal novembre 2000 – ISBN 2-06-000010-6 – ISSN 0763-1383

Printed in France 01-01/4.2

Compogravure : MAURY Imprimeur S.A., Malesherbes
Impression et brochage : AUBIN, Ligugé.

Cover design : Carré Noir, Paris 17e

THE GREEN GUIDE:
The Spirit of Discovery

The exhilaration of new horizons,
the fun of seeing the world, the
excitement of discovery: this is what
we seek to share with you. To help you
make the most of your travel experience,
we offer first-hand knowledge and turn
a discerning eye on places to visit.
This wealth of information gives
you the expertise to plan your own
enriching adventure. With THE GREEN
GUIDE showing you the way, you can
explore new destinations with confidence
or rediscover old ones.
Leisure time spent with THE GREEN
GUIDE is also a time for refreshing
your spirit, enjoying yourself,
and taking advantage of our selection
of fine restaurants, hotels
and other places for relaxing.
So turn the page and open a window
on the world. Join THE GREEN GUIDE
in the spirit of discovery.

Contents

Using this guide
Key
Map of principal sights
Map of touring programmes
Map of places to stay

Introduction

Regions and landscapes	14
Government	21
Historical table and notes	22
Life in Spain	29
Art and architecture	30
ABC of architecture	40
Gardens of Spain	50
Literature	52
Music	53
Cinema	54

Handicrafts   5.
Traditions and folklore   5(
Food and wine   5(

Sights   6.

Aguilar de Campóo 64 – Parque Nacional d
Aigüestortes y lago de Sant Maurici 64
Alacante 66 – Alarcón 68 – Albacete 68
Albarracín 68 – La Alberca 69 – Alcalá d
Henares 70 – Alcántara 71 – Alcañiz 72 –
Alcaraz 72 – Almagro 72 – Almansa 73 –
Almería 74 – Castillo de Almodóvar del Rí
75 – Las Alpujarras 75 – Alquézar 76 –
Cuevas de Altamira 77 – Principality of And
orra 78 – Andújar 79 – Antequera 79 –
Aracena 80 – Aranjuez 81 – Arcos de la
Frontera 83 – Astorga 84 – Ávila 84– Bada
joz 87 – Baeza 88 – Bayona 90 – Barbastro
90 – Barcelona 91 – Béjar 113 – Belmonte
114 – Betanzos 114 – Bilbao 115 – El Burgo
de Osma 119 – Burgos 120 – Cáceres 126
– Cádiz 128 – Calatrava Castle-Monastery
130 – Cangas de Narcea 130 – Caravaca
de la Cruz 131 – Cardona 131 – Carmona
132 – Cartagena 132 – Sierra de Cazorla
133 – Celanova 134 – Ceuta 135 – Chinchón 135 – Ciudad Rodrigo 136 – Castillo
de Coca 136 – Córdoba 137 – Coria 144 –
A Coruña/La Coruña 144 – Costa Blanca
146 – Costa Brava 148 – Costa de Cantabria
151 – Costa de la Luz 152 – Costa del Sol
154 – Costa Vasca (Basque Coast) 155 –
Costa Verde 159 – Covadonga 161 – Covarrubias 162 – Cuenca 163 – Serranía de
Cuenca 165 – Daroca 166 – Donostia/San
Sebastián 167 – Parque Nacional de
Doñana 169 – Écija 169 – Elx/Elche 170 –
Empúries/Ampurias 171 – El Escorial Mona-
stery 172 – Estella – Figueras/Figueres 175 –
Frómista Church 176 – Gandía 177 –
Gasteiz/Vitoria 177 – Gibraltar 180– Straits

R. Mazin/DIAF

Like a pilgrim on the Way of Saint James...

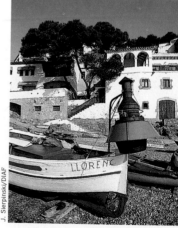

J. Sierpinski/DIAF

You may take a boat at Begur...

of Gilbraltar 182 – Girona/Gerona 183 – Granada 187 – Palacio de La Granja de San Idefonso 196 – Sierra de Gredos 197 – Guadalajara 197 – Guadalupe 198 – Sierra de Guadarrama 200 – Guadix 201 – Hondarribia/Fuenterrabía 202 – Huesca 203 – Iruñea/Pamplona 204 – Jaca 207 – Jaén 209 – Jerez de la Frontera 210 – Jerez de los Caballeros 212 – León 212 – Leyre Monastery 215 – Lizarra/Estella 217 – Lleida/Lérida 218 – Lorca 219 – Lugo 219 – Madrid 221 – Málaga 252 – Marbella 253 – Medina de Rioseco 254 – Melilla 254 – Mérida 255 – Mojácar 256 – Mondoñedo 256 – Montblanc 257 – Sierra de Montseny 259 – Sierra de Montserrat 259 – Morella 260 – Murcia 261 – Valle del Navia 263 – Olite 264 – Olivenza 265 – Oñati/Oñate 265 – Parque Nacional de Ordesa y Monte Perdido 266 – Orreaga/Roncesvalles 268 – Santa María la Real de Oseira Monastery 269 – Osuna 269 – Orense 269 – Oviedo 271 – El Pardo 275 – Pedraza de la Sierra 276 – Peñafiel 276 – Peñaranda de Duero 277 – Peñíscola 277 – Picos de Europa 278 – Piedra Monastery 282 – The Pyrenees in Aragón 282 – The Catalan Pyrenees 284 – Plasencia 290 – Poblet Monastery 291 – Ponferrada 294 – Pontevedra 294 – Port Aventura 296 – Priego de Córdoba 298 – Puebla de Sanabria 298 – White Villages of Andalucía 298 – Puente Viesgo 300 – Reinosa 300 – Rías Altas 301 – Rías Bajas 302 – La Rioja 304 – Ripoll 306 – Ronda 307 – Sagunt/Sagunto 309 – Salamanca 311 – Santuario de San Ignacio de Loyola 318 – San Juan de la Peña Monastery 319 – San Martín de Valdeiglesias 320 – Santa María de Huerta Monastery 321 – Santander 321 – Sant Cugat del Vallès Monastery 323 – Santes Creus Monastery 323 – Santiago de Compostela 325 – Santillana del Mar 334 – Sant Joan de les Abadesses 336 – Santo Domingo de la Calzada 337 – Santo Domingo de Silos Monastery –

Segovia 340 – La Seu d'Urgell/Seo de Urgel 344 – Sevilla 345 – Sigüenza 357 – Sitges 358 – Solsona 359 – Soria 360 – Sos del Rey Católico 362 – Tarragona 363 – Terrassa/Tarrasa 366 – Teruel 367 – Toledo 369 – Tordesillas 379 – Toro 380 – Tortosa 380 – Trujillo 382 – Tudela 384 – Tui/Tuy 385 – Úbeda 386 – Uclés 388 – Ujué 388 – Valdepeñas 389 – Valencia 389 – Valladolid 396 – Valle de los Caídos 399 – Verín 399 – Vic 400 – Villafamés 401 – Villena 401 – Xátiva/Játiva 401 – Zafra 402 – Zamora 402 – Zaragoza 404

The Islands 408

Balearic Islands 410

Mallorca 412 – Menorca 422 – Ibiza 425 – Formentera 429

Canary Islands 430

Tenerife 432 – Gran Canaria 442 – Fuerteventura 451 – La Gomera 453 – El Hierro 454 – Lanzarote 455 – La Palma 459

Practical Information 462

Travelling to Spain 464
Travelling in Spain 465
General information 467
Accommodation 468
Useful addresses 469
Tourist information 469
Eating out 470
Sports 470
Further reading 472
Vocabulary 473
Calendar of events 475
Admission times and charges 478
Index 518

Stop to meditate in Grenada...

Or discover the magic of Sevilla

Y. Travert/DIAF

G. Guittot/DIAF

Maps and plans

COMPANION PUBLICATIONS

Atlas España/Portugal (Michelin map 1460)

– a practical, spiral-bound atlas with maps on a scale of 1:400 000, with a complete index and 49 city and town plans

Michelin map 990 España/Portugal

– the Iberian Peninsula on a scale of 1:1 000 000

Michelin maps to the regions of Spain on a scale of 1:400 000

– 441 North-West
– 442 Northern
– 443 North-East & Balearics
– 444 Central
– 445 Central & Eastern
– 446 Southern

Canary Islands

– 220 Gran Canaria + 7 town plans
– 221 Fuerteventura/Lanzarote 6 town plans
– 222 Ténérife + 11 town pans

And Michelin City Plans with street index and enlargement of the city centre

– 41 Barcelona (1:12 000)
– 42 Madrid (1:12 000)
– 2042 Madrid spiral bound atlas

and if you are driving to Spain

Michelin Road Atlas to Europe: main road atlas with full index; Western Europe at 1:1 000 000; Eastern Europe at 1:3 000 000; 74 town and city plans

– 1136 Small Spiral
– 1129 Large Spiral
– 1135 Paperback
– 1133 Hardback

www.michelin-travel.com

– personalised route plans
– Michelin mapping on-line
– Addresses of hotels and restaurants featured in The Red Guides
– Practical and tourist information

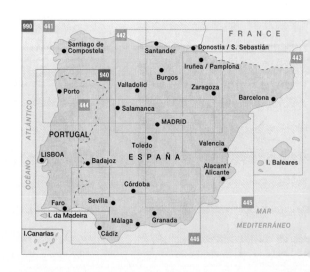

LIST OF MAPS AND PLANS

Thematic maps

Regions and landscape	15
Administrative organisation	21
The Christian reconquest	22
The Empire of Charles V	25
The Way of Saint James	328
Maritime connections between the Canary Islands	432

Town plans

Alacant/Alicante	66
Ávila	86
Baeza	89
Barcelona:	100
city centre	102
Bilbao	116
Burgos	123
Cáceres	128
Cádiz	129
Córdoba	142
A Coruña/La Coruña	146
Cuenca	165
Donostia/San Sebastián	168
Elx/Elche	170
Gasteiz/Vitoria	179
Girona/Gerona	183
Granada	188
Iruña/Pamplona	205
Jerez de la Frontera	211
León	213
Lugo	220
Madrid:	234
city centre	236, 240
old town	232
metro	230
Málaga	252
Montblanc	258
Murcia	262
Ourense/Orense	270
Oviedo	271
Pontevedra	295
Ronda	309
Salamanca	315
Santiago de Compostela	333
Segovia	341
Sevilla	350
Soria	360
Tarragona	363
Teruel	368
Toledo	374
Trujillo	384
Úbeda	386
Valencia	392
Valladolid	398
Zamora	403
Zaragoza	406
The Islands	
Palma de Mallorca	416
Eivissa (Ibiza)	428
Santa Cruz de Tenerife	438
Las Palmas de Gran Canaria	447
Vegueta and Triana (Gran Canaria)	449

Monuments and sites

Burgos Cathedral	122
Mosque-Cathedral, Córdoba	140
Alhambra, Granada	192
Guadalupe Monastery	199
Poblet Monastery	292
Santiago de Compostela Cathedral	331
Cloisters of the Santo Domingo de Silos Monastery	339
Sevilla Cathedral	352
Toledo Cathedral	373

Touring maps

Costa Brava	148
Basque Coast	156
Costa Verde	160
Sierra de Guadarrama	201
Excursions from Jaca	208
Parque Nacional de Ordesa y Monte Perdido	266
Picos de Europa	278
Pirineos Aragoneses	283
Pirineos Catalanes	286
Rías Bajas	303
The Islands	
Mallorca	412
Menorca	422
Ibiza	426
Tenerife	434
Gran Canaria	442
Fuerteventura	451
La Gomera	454
El Hierro	454
Lanzarote	456
La Palma	460

Using this guide

● The summary maps on the following pages are designed to assist you in planning your trip: the **Map of principal sights** identifies major sights and attractions, the **Touring programmes** propose regional driving itineraries and the **Places to stay** map points out pleasant holiday spots.

● We recommend that you read the **Introduction** before setting out on your trip. The background information it contains on history, the arts and traditional culture will make your visit more meaningful.

● The main towns and attractions are presented in alphabetical order in the **Sights** section. In order to ensure quick, easy identification, original place names have been used. The blue pages in this section provide a selection of suggested hotels, restaurants and entertainment. The clock symbol ☉, placed after monuments or other attractions, refers to the **Admission times and charges** section at the end of this guide.

● The **Practical information section** offers more useful addresses for planning your trip, seeking lodging, enjoying sports and leisure activities, dates of traditional fiestas and special events.

● The **Index** lists attractions, famous people and events and other subjects covered in this guide.

Let us hear from you. We are interested in your reaction to our guide, in any ideas you have to offer or good addresses you would like to share. Send your comments to Michelin Tyre PLC, Michelin Travel Publications, 38 Clarendon Road, Watford Herts WD1 SX, U.K. or thegreenguide-uk @ uk.michelin.com

F. Bouillot/MARCO POLO

Key

★★★ **Worth a journey**

★★ **Worth a detour**

★ **Interesting**

Tourism

ⓥ	Admission Times and Charges listed at the end of the guide	►►	Visit if time permits
➡	Sightseeing route with departure point indicated	AZ B	Map co-ordinates locating sights
✝ 🏛 ✝	Ecclesiastical building	🛈	Tourist information
Synagogue – Mosque		Historic house, castle – Ruins
🏠	Building (with main entrance)	Dam – Factory or power station
■	Statue, small building	Fort – Cave
✝	Wayside cross	Prehistoric site
◎	Fountain	Viewing table – View
Fortified walls – Tower – Gate		▲	Miscellaneous sight

Recreation

Racecourse		🏃	Waymarked footpath
Skating rink		◊	Outdoor leisure park/centre
Outdoor, indoor swimming pool		Theme/Amusement park
Marina, moorings		Wildlife/Safari park, zoo
Mountain refuge hut		Gardens, park, arboretum
Overhead cable-car		Aviary, bird sanctuary
Tourist or steam railway			

Additional symbols

Motorway (unclassified)		Post office – Telephone centre
Junction: complete, limited		Covered market
Pedestrian street		Barracks
Unsuitable for traffic, street subject to restrictions		Swing bridge
Steps – Footpath		Quarry – Mine
Railway – Coach station		B F	Ferry (river and lake crossings)
Funicular – Rack-railway		Ferry services: Passengers and cars
Tram – Metro, Underground		Foot passengers only
rt (R.)...	Main shopping street	③	Access route number common to MICHELIN maps and town plans

Abbreviations and special symbols

D	Provincial council (Diputación)	**POL.**	Police station (Policía)
G	Central government representation (Delegación del Gobierno)	**T**	Theatre (Teatro)
H	Town hall (Ayuntamiento)	**U**	University (Universidad)
J	Law courts/Courthouse (Palacio de Justicia)	ⓐ	Hotel
M	Museum (Museo)	ⓟ	Parador (hotel run by the State)

Esp. ang. 1 bis

Principal sights

Equestrian statue of Philip III, Plaza Mayor, Madrid

Introduction

Regions and landscape

The Iberian Peninsula (581 000km²/224 325sq mi), which is separated from the rest of Europe by the Pyrenees, is made up of continental Spain and Portugal. Spain covers an area of 505 000km²/194 980sq mi, including the Canary Islands and Balearic Islands, and is the fourth largest European country after Russia, the Ukraine and France. The population is nearing 40 million. Spain's position in Europe is unique due to its geographical isolation, its contrasts of relief and extremes of climate. The southernmost tip of the country is less than 15km/9mi from Africa.

A mountainous country – The average altitude in Spain is 650m/2 100ft above sea level and one sixth of the terrain rises to more than 1 000m/3 300ft. The highest peak is Mulhacén (3 482m/11 424ft) in the Sierra Nevada.

The dominant feature of the peninsula is the immense plateau at its centre. This is the **Meseta**, a Hercynian platform between 600m/2 000ft and 1 000m/3 300ft high which tilts slightly westwards. The Meseta is surrounded by long mountain ranges which form barriers between the central plateau and the coastal regions. All these ranges, the **Cordillera Cantábrica** of the northwest (an extension of the Pyrenees), the **Cordillera Ibérica** in the northeast and the **Sierra Morena** in the south, were caused by Alpine folding. Other mountains rising here and there from the Meseta are folds of the original, ancient massif. They include the **Sierras de Somosierra, Guadarrama** and **Gredos**, the **Peña de Francia** and the **Montes de Toledo**. The highest massifs in Spain, the **Pyrenees** (Pirineos) in the north and the **Sierras Béticas**, including the **Sierra Nevada**, in the south, are on the country's periphery, as are Spain's greatest depressions, those of the Ebro and Guadalquivir rivers.

A varied climate – The great diversity of landscapes in Spain is partly due to the variety of climates that prevail over the peninsula. The Meseta has a **continental** climate with extremes of temperature ranging from scorching hot in summer to freezing cold in winter. On the north coast where mist often develops into drizzle, the climate is **mild and very humid**. The east and south coasts have a **Mediterranean** climate verging on a desert climate in the Almería region.

For each of the regions described below, the respective autonomous communities are given, together with the provinces when appropriate, or otherwise the capital. See the administrative map on p 21.

ATLANTIC SPAIN

País Vasco/Euskadi

Provinces: Álava, Guipúzcoa, Vizcaya
Area: 7 261km²/2 803sq mi
Population: 2 109 009

Cantabria

Capital: Santander
Area: 5 282km²/2 039sq mi
Population: 530 281

Galicia

Provinces: A Coruña, Lugo, Ourense, Pontevedra
Area: 29 500km²/11 390sq mi
Population: 2 720 445

Principado de Asturias

Capital: Oviedo

Area: 10 565km²/4 079sq mi
Population: 1 098 725

País Vasco, Cantabria, Asturias: a kind of Switzerland by the sea – The mountain chain that borders the northern edge of the Meseta emerged in the Tertiary era and now runs through each of the coastal provinces. The **Montes Vascos**, secondary limestone ranges, continue westwards from the Pyrenean foothills and rise to 1 500m/4 900ft. The **Cordillera Cantábrica** further west forms an imposing barrier which has given the province of Cantabria the name of La Montaña. The range rises above 2 500m/8 200ft in the **Picos de Europa**, less than 50km/31mi from the sea.

The **País Vasco** (Basque Country) is a markedly undulating region with small villages and isolated farms nestling in the valleys. Local architecture is very distinctive: half-timbered houses with broad whitewashed fronts. The middle land sandwiched between the mountains and the sea in **Cantabria** and **Asturias** is very hilly. Roads wind along valley floors hemmed in by lush meadows, cider apple orchards and fields of maize and beans. Dairy produce is a major source of livelihood, especially in Cantabria. Maize, originally imported from America, has since become an important crop, judging by the large number of *hórreos* or squat drying sheds, so typical of Asturian villages.

The coast is indented by deep inlets or *rías* and lined by low cliffs in many places. There are beautiful beaches, particularly in Cantabria.

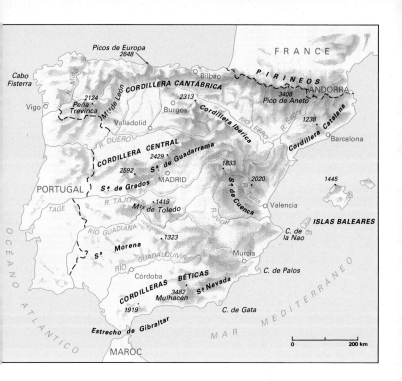

Galicia – This remote region fronting the Atlantic on its northern and western borders is reminiscent of Ireland, Wales or Brittany. Galicia is an ancient eroded granite massif that was displaced and rejuvenated as a result of Alpine folding. Although peaks on the massif rise to 2 000m/6 600ft (that of Peña Trevinca is 2 124m/6 968ft high) the average altitude is less than 500m/1 600ft. Yet the overall impression of Galicia is that of a hilly and mountainous region.

The coast, cut by deep **rías**, is more densely populated than the interior. It is Spain's chief fishing region where most of the produce is used for canning. Other activities include the timber industry and shipbuilding in the *rías* of Ferrol and Vigo.

The interior is primarily an agricultural region where mixed farming is the norm: maize, potatoes, grapes and rye. The Orense province produces beef for export.

The climate is strongly influenced by the sea: temperatures are mild and vary little (the annual average is 13°C/55°F), and rainfall is abundant.

THE PYRENEES AND THE EBRO REGION

Aragón

Provinces: Huesca, Zaragoza, Teruel
Area: 47 669km²/18 405sq mi

Population: 1 221 546

Navarra

Capital: Iruñea/Pamplona
Area: 10 421km²/
    4 024sq mi
Population: 523 563

La Rioja

Capital: Logroño
Area: 5 034km²/
    1 944sq mi
Population: 267 943

The Pyrenees (Pirineos) – **Alta (Upper) Aragón** embraces the Pirineos Centrales, a region of mountain valleys and piedmont vales, spring waterfalls (Parque Nacional de Ordesa) and villages of rough stone houses with slate roofs. The main source of livelihood is farming around Huesca and stock-raising in the valleys. There are some industries in Zaragoza.

In **Navarra** the Pyrenees are watered by Atlantic rain. They rise regularly from the 900m/2 953ft of Mont La Rhune to the 2 504m/8 215ft of the Pic d'Anie (both peaks just over the French border). East of Orreaga/Roncesvalles, the terrain becomes more mountainous and the harshness of the climate becomes visible in the ruggedness of the forest cover and the steeply sloped slate roofs and stone fronts of the houses. Resemblance to the Basque provinces is apparent west of Roncesvalles where small parcels of land grow alternate fields of pasture or maize and the houses have tiled roofs with half-timbered whitewashed fronts. Beyond the limestone range of the Andía, Urbasa, Navascués and Leyre *sierras* the land drops away to the Ebro basin.

The Ebro depression – This clay basin was formerly a gulf that has since been filled in. The terraces on either side of the river are deeply ravined, a feature even more pronounced in the Monegros desert in Aragón with its saline outcrops. In contrast, the lower valley has been transformed by irrigation into lovely green *huertas*.

The Arán Valley

Cereals predominate in the Cuenca region, also known as the Pamplona basin, in **Navarra**. Western **Ribera**, a continuation of the famous **Rioja**, is a wine-growing area, while the well-irrigated eastern part of the province around Tudela has become a prosperous horticultural region growing and canning asparagus, artichokes and peppers. Tall brick houses are typical of the architecture in this area.

Cordillera Ibérica – The clay hills bordering the Ebro basin in **Bajo Aragón** (Lower Aragón) around Piedra, Daroca and Alcañiz are planted with vineyards and olive groves. Brick villages and ochre-coloured houses merge in with the tawny shade of the deeply scored hillsides. The plateaux surrounding Teruel form part of the massive spread of the **Montes Universales**, one of Spain's great watersheds where the Cabriel, Turia, Júcar and Tajo (Tagus) rivers rise. The climate is harsh.

THE MESETA

Castilla y León

Provinces: Ávila, Burgos, León, Palencia, Salamanca, Segovia, Soria, Valladolid, Zamora.
Area: 94 147km²/36 350sq mi
Population: 2 562 979

Castilla – La Mancha

Provinces: Albacete, Ciudad Real, Cuenca, Guadalajara, Toledo.
Area: 79 226km²/30 589sq mi
Population: 1 651 833

Comunidad Autónoma de Madrid

Capital: Madrid
Area: 7 995km²/3 087sq mi
Population: 5 030 958

Extremadura

Provinces: Badajoz, Cáceres
Area: 41 602km²/16 063sq mi
Population: 1 056 538

The Meseta accounts for 40% of the surface area of the Iberian Peninsula. Its horizons appear infinite, broken only here and there by a rock-brown village clustered at the foot of a castle, or by the indistinct outline of **páramos** (bare limestone heights).

The northern Meseta – The Castilla y León region (Old Castile) in the north consists almost entirely of the Duero basin. This area is about 1 000m/3 300ft above sea level and is ringed by the Montes de León in the northwest, the Cordillera Cantábrica in the north, the Cordillera Ibérica in the east and the Cordillera Central in the southeast. As the Tertiary sediment on the Meseta resists erosion in different ways, there are different landscape features such as wide terraced valleys dotted with rock pinnacles, narrow defiles and gently rolling hills. In spite of these variations, the general aspect is one of a sparsely populated plateau with only the occasional village breaking the endless horizon. Cereal growing predominates everywhere; wheat on the better land, oats and rye elsewhere. Only the southwest peneplains near Salamanca are used for stock-raising; sheep on small properties and fighting bulls on larger ones of often over 500ha/1 200 acres.

The southern Meseta – This comprises the whole of Madrid-Castilla-La Mancha (New Castile) and Extremadura. It is a vast tableland slightly tilted towards the west, watered by two large rivers – the Tajo (Tagus), which cuts a deep gorge through the limestone Alcarria region, and the sluggish Guadiana. The terrain is flatter than in Castilla y León and rises to an average altitude of less than 700m/2 300ft compared to between 800m/2 600ft and 1 000m/3 300ft in the north. The aridity of the region is particularly apparent in summer and the name La Mancha comes from the Arab *manxa*, meaning dry land. Despite this there is considerable cultivation and a sweeping look across the Meseta would take in wind-ruffled cereal fields, stretches of saffron turned purple in the flowering season, and straight lines of olives and vines. This is Spain's leading vineyard for popular modestly-priced wines, with vintages such as Manzanares and Valde-peñas. The famous La Mancha cheese known as *queso manchego* is also produced here.

The bare, eroded and virtually uninhabited Montes de Toledo separate the Tajo basin from that of the Guadiana, while the other massifs in the region ring the borders. The **Cordillera Central** runs along the northern edge (Sierras de Gredos and Guadarrama), the **Sierra Morena** is in the south, and the **Serranía de Cuenca**, a limestone plateau pitted with swallow-holes (*torcas*) and cut by gorges (*hoces*), lies to the northeast. The **Alcarria** further north is a region of remote villages where the Tajo and its tributaries flow through deeply eroded gullies. Its upper mountain slopes grow aromatic plants such as thyme, rosemary, lavender and marjoram from which a well-known honey is produced.

The rural character of the region persists; small towns look more like large villages with the arcaded *Plaza Mayor* still acting as the nerve-centre.

Extremadura in the southwest is a schist and granite Hercynian platform that levels off at about 400m/1 300ft. The immense plateaux of the region are used for sheep grazing but lie deserted in summer when the animals are moved to higher pastures. Cork provides supplementary income as does traditional pig farming. The population is concentrated along the rivers that supply irrigation for a variety of crops including tobacco, cotton and wheat as well as market-garden produce. The Badajoz Plan that controls the flow of the Guadiana by means of a series of dams has made it possible to reafforest a large area and to develop high-yield crops such as maize, sunflowers, market-garden produce and above all animal fodder.

THE MEDITERRANEAN REGIONS

Catalunya/Cataluña

Provinces: Barcelona, Girona, Lleida, Tarragona
Area: 31 930km²/12 328sq mi
Population: 6 115 579

Comunidad valenciana

Provinces: Alacant/Alicante, Castellón, Valencia
Area: 23 305km²/8 998sq mi
Population: 3 923 841

Región de Murcia

Capital: Murcia
Area: 11 317km²/4 369 sq mi
Population: 1 059 612

Comunidad Autónoma de las Islas Baleares

Capital: Palma de Mallorca
Area: 5 014km²/1 936sq mi
Population: 745 944

Catalunya – Catalunya is a triangle of varied landscapes between the French border, Aragón and the Mediterranean. In the north, the eastern stretch of the Pyrenees, between Andorra and the Cabo de Creus headland, is a green wooded area with peaks over 3 000m/9 800ft high. The **Costa Brava** between France and Barcelona is a rocky area with many bays and inlets. It has a Mediterranean climate as does the **Costa Dorada** (Gold Coast) further south with its vast sandy beaches. The hinterland, separated from the coast by the Catalan *sierras*, is a drier region with harsh winters. The Pyrenean foothills resemble the *sierras* in Aragón and the houses here are like *mas*, the farmhouses in the south of France. The southern part of the triangle is composed of green hills sloping down to an intensively cultivated plain around the lower Ebro and its delta. Although fertile (cereals, vines, olives and market-garden produce), Catalunya is primarily an industrial region with its main activities centred around Barcelona.

Levante – The whole of the Levante, including Valencia and Murcia, comprises a narrow alluvial plain between the Mediterranean coast and the massifs of the interior (the Cordillera Ibérica in the north and the Sierras Béticas in the south). The coast, called **Costa del Azahar** (Orange Blossom Coast) near Valencia and the **Costa Blanca** (White Coast) around Alicante and Murcia, consists of dunes and offshore sand bars which form pools and lagoons.

Benidorm

The climate is Mediterranean but drier than average in this area. Little rain falls except during the autumn months when the rivers flood. Thanks to an ingenious system of irrigation *(acequias)* developed since Antiquity, the natural vegetation, of olives, almond and carob trees and vines, has gradually been replaced, and the countryside transformed into **huertas** (irrigated areas), lush citrus orchards and market gardens, with orange trees between Castellón and Denia and lemons near Murcia. The prosperous *huertas* are among the most densely populated areas in Spain. There are palm groves around Elche and Orihuela in the south and rice is grown in swampy areas.

The region's industry, based on mineral deposits (lead, zinc and copper) and backed by its ports, is well-developed and includes metallurgy, steel, oil refining, paper and shoes. Finally, tourism is booming on the coast where there are resorts like Benidorm.

Balearic Islands (Islas Baleares) – The Balearic archipelago consists of two groups of islands; Mallorca and Menorca on the one hand, Ibiza and Formentera, known as **Pityuses** in Antiquity, on the other.

The limestone hills, none of which exceed 1 500m/4 900ft, differ in origin. Ibiza and Mallorca are an extension of the Cordillera Bética in Andalucía while Menorca belongs to the submerged massif from which Corsica, Sardinia and the Catalan cordilleras rise.

The lush vegetation produced by the autumn rains is one of the sunny islands greatest attractions. Pines shade the indented shores, junipers and evergreen oaks cover the upper hillsides, while almonds, figs and olives cloak the plains.

The three larger islands differ considerably in character although they share the same contrast between the tranquillity of the hills inland and the bustling tourism along the coast. Their beaches are washed by a wonderfully calm, clean sea.

ANDALUCÍA

Provinces: Almería, Cádiz, Córdoba, Granada, Huelva, Jaén, Málaga, Sevilla.

Aria: 87 268km²/33 694sq mi

Population: 7 040 627

Andalucía was formerly known as *Baetica* by the Romans and *Al Andalus* by the Arabs. Although it comprises a wide variety of geographical regions, Andalucía's character has been strongly marked by its houses. Its villages and old quarters are usually lined by white houses adorned with wrought-iron grilles opening onto cool flowery *patios*.

Sierra Morena – This mountain chain separates the Meseta from Andalucía. It is rich in minerals and thickly covered by a scrub of oaks, lentisks (mastic trees) and arbutus (strawberry trees). Jaén province's extraordinary landscape consists of row upon row of olive trees as far as the eye can see.

The Guadalquivir depression – This Quaternary basin, a former gulf, opening broadly onto the Atlantic, is one of the richest agricultural areas in Spain. Cereals, cotton, olives and citrus fruit are grown on the plains, and rice and vines (around Jerez) on the coast where fighting bulls are also bred. The centre of the region is Sevilla, Spain's fourth largest city. The whole area is a vast tract of cultivated land divided into large properties known as **fincas**.

Cordilleras Béticas – The **Sierra Nevada**, which includes Spain's highest peak, Mulhacén (3 482m/11 424ft), is continued westwards by the **Serranía de Ronda** and **Sierra de Ubrique**. The range's snow-capped heights dominate a series of basins like the wide *vega* plain of Granada.

In spite of a sub-desert climate, the extremely touristic **Costa del Sol** (Sun Coast) produces citrus and early fruit and vegetables which are grown on irrigated land.

J.Begg/STOCK PHOTOS

Olive groves

World
Heritage List

In 1972, the United Nations Educational, Scientific and Cultural Organization (UNESCO) adopted a Convention for the preservation of cultural and natural sites. To date, more than 150 States Parties have signed this international agreement, which has listed over 500 sites "of outstanding universal value" on the World Heritage List. Each year, a committee of representatives from 21 countries, assisted by technical organizations (ICOMOS – International Council on Monuments and Sites; IUCN – International Union for Conservation of Nature and Natural Resources; ICCROM – International Centre for the Study of the Preservation and Restoration of Cultural Property, the Rome Centre), evaluates the proposals for new sites to be included on the list, which grows longer as new nominations are accepted and more countries sign the Convention. To be considered, a site must be nominated by the country in which it is located.

The protected cultural heritage may be monuments (buildings, sculptures, archeological structures etc) with unique historical, artistic or scientific features; groups of buildings (such as religious communities, ancient cities); or sites (human settlements, examples of exceptional landscapes, cultural landscapes) which are the combined works of man and nature of exceptional beauty. Natural sites may be a testimony to the stages of the earth's geological history or to the development of human cultures and creative genius or represent significant ongoing ecological processes, contain superlative natural phenomena or provide a habitat for threatened species.

Signatories of the Convention pledge to cooperate to preserve and protect these sites around the world as a common heritage to be shared by all humanity.

Some of the most well-known places which the World Heritage Committee has inscribed include: Australia's Great Barrier Reef (1981), the Canadian Rocky Mountain Parks (1984), The Great Wall of China (1987), the Statue of Liberty (1984), the Kremlin (1990), Mont-Saint-Michel and its Bay (France, 1979), Durham Castle and Cathedral (1986).

UNESCO
World Heritage sites included in this guide are:

Alcalá de Henares: University and historic quarter
Altamira: Cave
Ávila: Old Town and Extra-Muros Churches
Barcelona: Parque Güell, Palacio Güell and Casa Milà
Burgos: Cathedral
Cáceres: Old Town
Córdoba: Historic Centre
Cuenca: Historic Walled Town
Doñana: National Park
El Escorial: Monastery and Site
Garajonay: National Park
Granada: Alhambra, Generalife and Albaicín
Guadalupe: Royal Monastery of Santa María
Mérida: Archeological Site
Oviedo: Churches of the Kingdom of the Asturias and historic town centre
Poblet: Monastery
Salamanca: Old City
Santiago de Compostela: Old Town
Santiago de Compostela: Pilgrims' Way of St James
Segovia: Old Town and Aqueduct
Sevilla: Cathedral, Alcázar and Archivo de Indias
Teruel: Mudéjar Architecture
Toledo: Historic City
Valencia: La Lonja de la Seda

Government

POLITICAL ORGANISATION

The Spanish Constitution, which was approved by referendum on 6 December 1978, defines the political status of the Spanish State as a constitutional monarchy in which national sovereignty rests with the Spanish people. This political system can be broken down as follows: a **Head of State**, in the shape of the King, the **Cortes Generales** (Parliament), and a **Government**. The *Cortes* are elected by universal suffrage every four years. These are divided into two chambers: the **Congreso de los Diputados**, consisting of a minimum of 300 MPs and a maximum of 400, and the **Senado**, both of which represent the Spanish people, and with whom legislative power rests. The Government *(Gobierno)* performs executive functions and comprises a head of government *(Presidente del Gobierno)*, vice-presidents and ministers. Judicial power is an independent authority administered by judges and magistrates. The Supreme Court acts as the highest court in the land.

Territorially, Spain is organized into municipalities *(municipios)*, provinces *(provincias)* and autonomous communities *(comunidades autónomas)*.

ADMINISTRATIVE ORGANISATION

Spain can be broken down into the following administrative divisions:

– **Autonomous communities**: Spain is divided into 17 *Comunidades Autónomas*. These communities may comprise a single or several provinces. The leading political figure in these is the *Presidente de la Comunidad*, who is elected by universal suffrage every four years. The transfer of decision-making to autonomous bodies has yet to be fully achieved; however, the system of autonomy developed in Spain is one of the most advanced in Europe.

– **Provinces:** The need for greater administrative efficiency led the governments under Isabel II (in the 19C) to establish an initial division of the country into provinces. At present, Spain has 50 provinces, which are themselves grouped into autonomous communities.

– **Municipalities:** This is the smallest territorial division, comprising a town hall *(ayuntamiento)* headed by a mayor *(alcalde)*. The latter is also elected by universal suffrage every four years. Historically, this political body has the deepest roots within the country.

Given the new adminstrative system now operating within Spain, communities and municipalities are better able to administer the territory under their control.
(See the map below and the chapter on regions and landscape on p 14).

Historical table and notes

From Antiquity to the Visigothic kingdom

11-5C BC	Phœnician and Greek trading posts founded on the eastern and southern coasts of Spain, inhabited by **Iberians** and **Tartessians** respectively. In the 9C, the central-European **Celts** settle in west Spain and on the Meseta, intermingling with the Iberians (forming **Celtiberians**).
3-2C BC	The **Carthaginians** take over the southeast after conquering the Greeks and Tartessians. The capture of **Sagunto** by Hannibal leads to the Second Punic War (218-201 BC). Rome expels the Carthaginians and begins the conquest of peninsular Spain (with resistance at **Numancia**).
1CBC-1CAD	Cantabria and Asturias are finally pacified in AD 19. Spain is now known as *Iberia* or *Hispania*. Christianity spreads there during the 1C AD.
5-6C AD	Early Suevi (Swabian) and Vandal invasions are followed by those of the **Visigoths** (411) who estabish a powerful monarchy with Toledo as capital. The peninsula unites under King Leovigild (584).

THE CHRISTIAN RECONQUEST OF THE IBERIAN PENINSULA

Kingdom of Asturias C 750

Recovered territory

C 1040 — C 1270 — C 850 — C 1150 — Between 1270 and 1492

Christian victories — Muslim victories — Muslim strongholds

Muslim Spain and the Reconquest

8C	Moors invade and annihilate the Visigothic kingdom after the **Battle of Guadalete** in 711. Pelayo's victory at **Covadonga** in 722 heralds a 700-year-long Christian War of Reconquest. The first Muslim invaders are subjects of the Umayyad Caliphate in Damascus. **Abd ar-Rahman I** breaks with Damascus by founding an independent emirate at Córdoba in 756.
9C	Settlement of uninhabited land by Christians.
10C	Golden age of the emirate of Córdoba, which is raised to the status of a caliphate (929-1021) by **Abd ar-Rahman III**. A period of great prosperity ensues during which the expansion of Christian kingdoms is checked. Fortresses are built in the north along the Duero river.
11C	Christian Spain now includes the kingdoms of León, Castilla, Navarra, Aragón, and the County of Barcelona. On the death of al-Mansur in 1002, the Caliphate of Córdoba disintegrates into about 20 *taifa* (faction) kingdoms (1031). Alfonso VI conquers Toledo (1085), and the area around the Tajo river is resettled by Christians. The *taifa* kings call upon the **Almoravids** (Saharan Muslims) for assistance and in a short time the tribe overruns a large part of Spain. Pilgrims begin to tread the Way of Saint James of Compostela. **El Cid** conquers Valencia (1094).

<table>
<tr><td>12C</td><td>Dissension stemming from a second age of taifa kingdoms assists the Reconquest, especially in the Ebro Valley (Zaragoza is taken in 1118, Tortosa in 1148 and Lleida in 1149), but after Yacoub al-Mansur's victory in Alarcos (1195), the Almohads (who routed the Almoravids) recover Extremadura and check Christian expansion towards the Guadiana and Guadalquivir rivers.
Sevilla, with Córdoba under its control, enjoys great prosperity.
Great military Orders are founded (Calatrava, Alcántara, and Santiago).
Unification of the kingdoms of Aragón and Catalunya (1150).</td></tr>
<tr><td>13C</td><td>The taifa kingdoms enter their third age. The decline of the Muslims begins with the Battle of Las Navas de Tolosa (1212). Muslim influence is reduced to the Nasrid kingdom of Granada (modern provinces of Málaga, Granada and Almería) which holds out until its capture in 1492.
Unification of Castilla and León under Ferdinand III (1230).
The Crown of Aragón under James I, the Conqueror (1213-76), gains control over considerable territory in the Mediterranean.</td></tr>
</table>

All names in the family tree appear in Spanish. Where these names are referred to in the text, the Spanish appears in brackets.

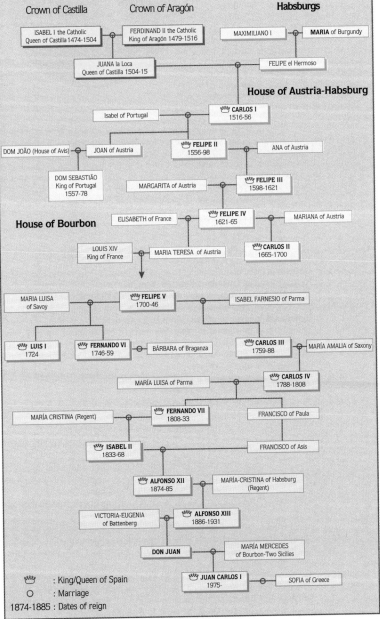

1492

If there were only one important date to remember in Spanish history, it would be 1492. That year, after 781 years of Muslim occupation, the Reconquest ended with the fall of Granada on 2 January. This was also the year that the Jews were expelled, the Spaniard Rodrigo Borja (Borgia) became Pope Alexander VI and on 12 October, Christopher Columbus discovered America.

Christopher Columbus (Cristóbal Colón) **(?1451-1506) and the discovery of America** – Born in Genoa, the son of a weaver, Columbus began his seafaring career at an early age. He travelled to Lisbon in 1476 where he developed a passion for mapmaking on discovering Ptolemy's *Geography* and the Frenchman Pierre d'Ailly's *Imago Mundi*. Convinced that the Indies could be reached by sailing west, he submitted a navigation plan to João II of Portugal and to the kings of France and England. He ultimately managed to gain the support of the Duke of Medinaceli and that of the Prior of the Monasterio de La Rábida, Juan Pérez, who was Isabel the Catholic's confessor. The Catholic monarchs agreed to finance his expedition, and if he succeeded, to bestow upon him the hereditary title of Admiral of the Ocean and the viceroyship of any lands discovered.

The Catholic monarchs

On 3 August 1492, heading a fleet of three caravels (the *Santa María*, under his command, and the *Pinta* and the *Niña* captained by the Pinzón brothers), he put out from Palos de la Frontera. On 12 October, after a difficult crossing, San Salvador (Bahamas) came into sight and a short time later Hispaniola (Haiti) and Cuba were discovered. On his return to Spain on 15 March 1493, Christopher Columbus was given a triumphant welcome and the means with which to organise new expeditions. This marked the beginning of the great Spanish discoveries of the New World.

The Catholic monarchs (1474-1516) and the unity of Spain

1474	Isabel, wife of Ferdinand of Aragón (Fernando II), succeeds her brother Henry IV to the throne of Castilla. She has to contend with opposition from the supporters of her niece Juana la Beltraneja until 1479.
1478-79	The court of the **Inquisition** is instituted by a special Papal Bull and **Torquemada** is later appointed Inquisitor-General. The court, a political and religious institution directed against Jews, Moors and later Protestants, survives until the 19C. Ferdinand becomes King of Aragón in 1479 and Christian Spain is united under one crown.
1492	**Fall of Granada** marks the end of the Reconquest. Expulsion of Jews. **Christopher Columbus** discovers America on 12 October.
1494	The Treaty of Tordesillas divides the New World between Spain and Portugal.
1496	Juana, daughter of the Catholic monarchs, marries Philip the Handsome (Felipe el Hermoso), son of Emperor Maximilian of Austria (Maximiliano I).
1504	Death of Isabel. The kingdom is inherited by her daughter Juana the Mad (Juana la Loca) but Ferdinand governs as regent until Juana's son Charles (b 1500), future Charles V, comes of age.
1512	The Duke of Alba conquers Navarra, thus bringing political unity to Spain.

Spain's Golden Age

16C	Spain flourishes under the rule of the Austrian Habsburgs – **Charles V** (Carlos V, 1516-56) and **Philip II** (Felipe II, 1556-98). American colonies are conquered.
1516	On the death of Ferdinand, his grandson becomes Charles I (Carlos I) of Spain. Through his mother, Charles inherits Spain, Naples, Sicily, Sardinia and American territories. Cardinal Cisneros governs until the new king arrives for the first time in Spain in 1517.

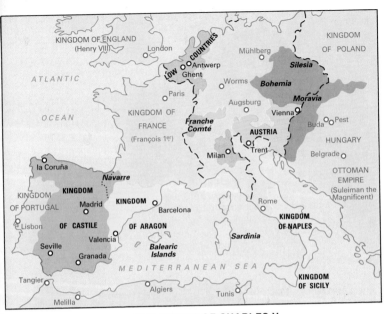

THE EMPIRE OF CHARLES V

▢ Burgundian inheritance	▢ Austrian inheritance
▢ Spanish inheritance	▢ Charles V's conquests
	▢ Other possessions
	– – – The Holy Roman Empire

1519	On the death of Maximilian of Austria, Charles I is elected Holy Roman Emperor under the name of **Charles V** (Carlos V). He inherits Germany, Austria, the Franche-Comté and the Low Countries.
1520-22	The Spanish, incensed by Charles V's largely Flemish court advisers and the increasing number of taxes, rise up in arms. The emperor quells **Comuneros** and **Germanías** revolts.
1521-56	Charles V wages five wars against France in order to secure complete control of Europe. In the first four he conquers François I (imprisoned at Pavia in 1525) and in the fifth he routs the new French king, Henry II, and captures Milan. The **conquistadores** move across America. **Núñez de Balboa** discovers the Pacific; **Cortés** seizes Mexico in 1521; **Pizarro** and **Diego de Almagro** subdue Peru in 1533; **Francisco Coronado** explores the Colorado river in 1535; **Hernando de Soto** takes possession of Florida in 1539, then Chile in 1541.
1555	Charles V signs the Peace of Augsburg with the Protestants in Germany after failing to suppress the Reformation.
1556	Charles V abdicates in favour of his son and retires to a monastery in Yuste. **Philip II** becomes king, inheriting Spain and its colonies, the Kingdom of Naples, Milan, the Low Countries and the Franche-Comté, but not Germany and Austria which are left by Charles to his brother Ferdinand I of Austria. Philip II turns his attention to Spain and the defence of Catholicism. He chooses Madrid as capital in 1561. Spain goes through a serious economic crisis.
1568-70	Revolt of the *Moriscos* (Muslims who converted to Christianity) in Granada.
1571	The Turks are defeated in the **Battle of Lepanto** by a fleet of ships sent by the Pope, the Venetians and the Spanish, under the command of **Don Juan of Austria**, the king's natural brother. The victory seals Spain's mastery of the Mediterranean.
1580	The King of Portugal dies without an heir. Philip II asserts his rights, invades Portugal and is proclaimed king in 1581.
1588	Philip II sends the **Invincible Armada** against Protestant England, which supports the Low Countries. The destruction of the fleet marks the end of Spain as a sea power.
1598	Philip II dies, leaving a vast kingdom which, in spite of huge wealth from the Americas, is crippled by debt after 70 years of almost incessant war and monumental building projects like El Escorial.

1598-1621	**Decline** – The last Habsburgs, **Philip III** (Felipe III, 1598-1621), **Philip IV** (Felipe IV, 1621-65) and **Charles II** (Carlos II, 1665-1700), lack the mettle of their forebears. Paradoxically, Spain enjoys a **golden age** of art and culture. Philip III entrusts the affairs of State to the Duke of Lerma who advises him to expel the *Moriscos* in 1609. 275 000 Moors leave Spain with disastrous consequences for agriculture.
1640	Under Philip IV (Felipe IV), the Count-Duke of Olivares adopts a policy of decentralisation which spurs Catalunya and Portugal to rebellion. The Portuguese proclaim the Duke of Braganza, King John IV, but their independence is not recognised until 1668.
1618-48	Spain wastes her strength in the **Thirty Years War**. In spite of victories like that of Breda (1624), the defeat in the Netherlands at Rocroi (1643) signals the end of Spain as a European power. The **Treaty of Westphalia** gives the Netherlands independence.
1659	The **Treaty of the Pyrenees** ends war with France. Philip IV arranges the marriage of his daughter María Teresa to Louis XIV of France.
1667-97	Spain loses strongholds in Flanders to France during the **War of Devolution** (1667-68). The Dutch Wars (1672-78) end with the **Treaty of Nijmegen**. The **Treaty of Ryswick** (1697) concludes the war waged by the Confederation of Augsburg (Spain is a member) against France.

The Bourbons; Napoleon and the War of Independence (1808-14)

1700	Charles II dies without issue. He wills the crown to Philip, Duke of Anjou, grandson of his sister María Teresa and Louis XIV. Emperor Leopold, who had renounced his rights to the Spanish throne in favour of his son, the Archduke Charles, is displeased, but the appointment of the Bourbons to the Spanish throne stabilises the balance of power in Europe.
1702-14	**War of the Spanish Succession** – England, the Netherlands, Denmark and Germany support the Archduke of Austria against France and Philip of Anjou. Catalunya, Valencia and Aragón also side with the Archduke and war spreads throughout Spain (1705). By the **Treaty of Utrecht**, Spain forfeits Gibraltar and Menorca (taken by the English) and many of her Italian possessions. **Philip V** (Felipe V) is proclaimed King of Spain (1714-45).
1759-88	The reign of **Charles III** (Carlos III), an enlightened despot, is the most brilliant of those of the Bourbons. He is assisted by competent ministers (Floridablanca and Aranda) who draw up important economic reforms. Expulsion of the Jesuits in 1767.
1788	**Charles IV** (Carlos IV) succeeds to the throne. A weak-willed king, he allows the country to be governed by his wife María Luisa and her favourite, Godoy.
1793	On the death of Louis XVI, Spain declares war on France (then in the throes of the Revolution).
1796-1805	Spain signs an alliance with the French Directory against England (Treaty of San Ildefonso, 1796). **Napoleon** enters Spain with his troops on the pretext that he is going to attack Portugal. The renewed offensive against England in 1804 ends disastrously with the **Battle of Trafalgar**.
1805-08	Napoleon takes advantage of the disagreement between Charles IV and his son Ferdinand to engineer Charles IV's abdication and appoint his own brother Joseph, King of Spain. The Aranjuez Revolt takes place in March 1808.
2 May 1808	The Madrid uprising against French troops marks the beginning of the **War of Independence** (The Peninsular War) which lasts until Napoleon is exiled by Wellington in 1814. During the war there are battles at Bailén (1808), Madrid, Zaragoza and Girona.
1812	The French are routed by Wellington in the Arapiles Valley; King Joseph flees from Madrid. Valencia is taken by the French general, Suchet. Spanish patriots convene the Cortes (parliament) and draw up the liberal **Constitution of Cádiz**.
1813-14	Anglo-Spanish forces expel Napoleon after successive victories. Ferdinand VII (Fernando VII) returns to Spain, repeals the Constitution of Cádiz and so reigns as an absolute monarch until 1820. Meanwhile, the South American colonies struggle for independence.

The 19C Disturbances

1820-23	The liberals oppose the king's absolute rule but their uprisings are all severely quelled. The 1812 constitution is reinstated after a **liberal revolt** led by **Riego** in Cádiz in 1820, but only for three years. In 1823 Ferdinand VII appeals to Europe for assistance and 100 000 Frenchmen are sent in the name of St Louis to re-establish absolute rule (which lasts until 1833).
1833-39	On the death of Ferdinand VII, his brother Don Carlos disputes the right to the throne of his niece Isabel II, daughter of the late king and Queen María Cristina. The traditionalist Carlists fight Isabel's liberal supporters who, after six years, win the **First Carlist War** (Convention of Vergara). In 1835, the minister **Mendizábal** has a series of decrees passed which do away with religious orders and confiscate their property **(desamortización)**.
1840	A revolutionary junta forces the regent María Cristina into exile. She is replaced by General Espartero.
1843-68	Queen Isabel II comes of age. The **Narváez uprising** forces Espartero to flee. A new constitution is drawn up in 1845. The **Second Carlist War** (1847-49) ends in victory for Isabel II but her reign is troubled by a succession of uprisings on behalf of progressives and moderates. The **1868 revolt** led by General Prim puts an end to her reign. Isabel leaves for France and General Serrano is appointed leader of the provisional government.
1869	The Cortes passes a progressive constitution which however envisages the establishment of a monarchy. Amadeo of Savoy is elected king.
1873	The **Third Carlist War** (1872-76). The king abdicates on finding himself unable to keep the peace. The National Assembly proclaims the **First Spanish Republic**.
1874	General Martínez Campos leads a revolt. The head of the government, Cánovas de Castillo, proclaims Isabel's son Alfonso XII, King of Spain. The Bourbon **Restoration** opens a long period of peace.
1885	Death of Alfonso XII (at 28). His widow María Cristina (who is expecting a baby) becomes regent.
1898	Cuba and the Philippines rise up with disastrous losses for Spain. The United States, which supports the rebel colonies, occupies Puerto Rico and the Philippines, marking the end of the Spanish Empire.
1902	**Alfonso XIII** (born after the death of his father Alfonso XII) succeeds to the throne at 16.

Fall of the monarchy; The Second Republic (1931-36)

1914-18	Spain remains neutral throughout the First World War. A general strike in 1917 is severely put down.
1921	Insurrection in Morocco; General Sanjurjo occupies the North (1927).
1923	**General Miguel Primo de Rivera** establishes a **dictatorship** with the king's approval. Order is restored, the country grows wealthier but opposition increases among the working classes.
1930	In the face of hostility from the masses, Primo de Rivera is forced into exile and General Berenguer is appointed dictator.
1931	April elections bring victory to the Republicans in Catalunya, the País Vasco, La Rioja and the Aragonese province of Huesca. The king leaves Spain and the **Second Republic** is proclaimed.
June 1931	A constituent Cortes is elected with a socialist republican majority; a Constitution is promulgated in December. Don Niceto Alcalá Zamora is elected President of the Republic. Agrarian reforms, such as compulsory purchase of large properties, meet strong right-wing opposition.
1933	**Falange Party**, against regional separation, founded by **José Antonio Primo de Rivera**, son of the dictator. The army plots against the régime.
Oct 1934	Catalunya proclaims its autonomy. Miners in Asturias spark off a revolt against the right-wing government and are brutally repressed.
Feb 1936	The Popular Front wins the elections, precipitating a revolutionary situation. Anarchy hits the streets and the right promptly retaliates.

The Civil War (1936-39)

17 July 1936	The Melilla uprising triggers off the Civil War. The army takes contro and puts an end to the Second Republic. Nationalist troops based in Morocco and led by **General Franco** cross the Straits of Gibraltar and make their way to Toledo which is taken at the end of September. Franco is proclaimed Generalísimo of the armec forces and Head of State in Burgos. Nationalists lead an unsuccessfu attack against Madrid. While Madrid, Catalunya and Valencia remain faithful to the Republi cans, the conservative agricultural regions – Andalucía, Castilla anc Galicia – are rapidly controlled by the Nationalists. These latter outnumber the Republicans tenfold and the Republicans themselves are torn by dissension between anarchists and communists within their own ranks. They do, however, receive assistance from Internationa Brigades.
1937	Industrial towns in the north are taken by Nationalist supporters in the summer (Guernica is bombed by German planes). The Republican Government is moved to Barcelona in November. In the battle of **Teruel** in December the Republicans try to breach the Nationalist front in Aragón and thereby relieve surrounded Catalunya. Teruel is taken by the Republicans and recaptured by the Nationalists soon after.
1938	The Nationalist army reaches the Mediterranean, dividing Republican territory into two parts. The **Battle of the Ebro** lasts from July to November: the Republican army flees eastwards and Franco launches an offensive against Catalunya which is occupied by the Nationalists in February 1939.
1 April 1939	The war ends with the capture of Madrid.

The Franco Era

1939-49	Spain becomes a monarchy with Franco as Head of State and remains neutral in the Second World War. Period of diplomatic isolation.
1952	Spain joins UNESCO.
1955	Spain becomes a member of the United Nations.
1969	Prince Juan Carlos is appointed Franco's successor.
20 Dec 1973	Prime Minister Carrero Blanco is assassinated.
20 Nov 1975	**Death of Franco. Juan Carlos I** becomes **King of Spain**.

Democracy

15 June 1977	General elections – **Adolfo Suárez** is elected Prime Minister. A new constitution is passed by referendum in 1978. Statutes of autonomy are granted to Catalunya, the País Vasco (Euskadi) and Galicia.

Opening ceremony of the Barcelona Olympic Games

1981-82	Suárez resigns. There is an attempted military coup on 23 February 1981. The general elections on 28 October 1982 are won by the Socialist Party and **Felipe González** becomes Prime Minister.
1 Jan 1986	Spain joins the **European Economic Community**.
11 March 1986	Spain's continued membership of NATO is voted by referendum.
11 June 1986	General elections - Felipe González, leader of the Socialist Party (PSOE), is re-elected Prime Minister.
Oct 1989	General elections again won by the Socialists under Felipe González.
1992	Barcelona hosts the 1992 Summer Olympics, and Sevilla Expo 1992.
3 March 1996	General election is won by the Popular Party; **José María Aznar** becomes Prime Minister.

Life in Spain

EVERYDAY SIGHTS AND SOUNDS

Mealtimes – The morning **(mañana)** in Spain lasts until 2pm, when it is time for lunch **(almuerzo** or **comida)**. After that there's the siesta, and the afternoon **(tarde)** begins at about 5pm. At 8pm people begin thinking about having a drink and so the evening **(noche)** begins. Dinner **(cena)** is served from 9pm and the evening may continue well into the night.

The Plaza Mayor – There's no town, large or small, nor village in Spain, without its main square, lined, for the most part, by a covered arcade. This rarely serves as a main crossroads; rather it is enclosed and accessible from adjoining streets only through arches beneath one or more of the surrounding houses. It is the hub of community life (often acting as a forecourt to the *Ayuntamiento*, or town hall) and is the setting for public festivities and great occasions. In the 18C, entrances would be blocked so that the square could serve as a bullring - a practice still observed in villages without an arena but determined to hold a *corrida*.

The street – Large towns generally have an old quarter of pedestrian streets where shops have retained their charm and their old-fashioned fronts. This is where whole families go out for a stroll, where one can do one's shopping or buy a lottery ticket from one of the many ticket sellers working for the *Once* (an association for the blind).
The great street event is the evening **paseo**. As the sun begins to set everyone meets in the main street to join the streams of people walking slowly up and down; people take a stroll *(pasear)* to enjoy the last light and the cool of the evening. Groups of girls and boys saunter along the street, laughing and chatting, while the older generation looks on from pavement cafés.

Bars – Bars are popular meeting places where one goes for an aperitif **(chateo)** at lunchtime, a well established tradition, to drink a glass of wine with friends and try the **tapas** or **raciones** which may be anything from olives to seafood to chips with mayonnaise. Televisions are ubiquitous as are the one-arm bandits that invariably play the theme tune from *The Third Man*. Then it's time for coffee: black is *café solo* or simply *café*; white *café con leche* or *café cortado*.
After work comes the **tertulia** or virtually informal club hour when men gather and, over a glass, discuss the news, politics and football (the latest feats of teams like Atlético, Real Madrid or F.C. Barcelona) or tell jokes **(chistes)**. The end of the afternoon is when people often have a *café con leche* or, in summer, a **horchata de chufas**, a refreshing cold drink made from the tiger-nut rhizome, and **churros**, delicious twisted fritters traditionally served with thick, hot chocolate.

National holidays – **Christmas** is a religious family holiday when *cestas de Navidad*, large traditional hampers containing bottles of wine, hams, sugared almonds, nougat *(turrón)* and marzipan, are given by friends. **New Year's Eve** is celebrated out of doors: in Madrid the crowds gather at the Puerta del Sol to eat a grape at each stroke of the clock at midnight - a custom observed in every Spanish home. At **Epiphany** there is a family exchange of presents and the Twelfth Night cake or **roscón** is eaten. (The person who draws the charm hidden in the cake is supposed to have a surprise that day.)

To choose a hotel or a restaurant in Spain,
to find an auto mechanic,
consult the current edition of the Michelin Red Guide España & Portugal.

Art and architecture

Prehistoric art – Prehistoric inhabitants of the Iberian Peninsula have left some outstanding examples of their art. The oldest are the Upper Paleolithic (40000-10000 BC) cave paintings in Cantabria (Altamira, Puente Viesgo) and the Levante (Cogull, Alpera). Megalithic monuments like the famous Antequera dolmens were erected during the Neolithic Era (7500-2500 BC) or Stone Age, while in the Balearic Islands strange stone monuments known as *talayots* and *navetas* were built by a Bronze Age people (2500-1000 BC).

First millennium BC – Iberian civilizations produced gold and silverware (treasure of Carambolo in the Museo Arqueológico in Sevilla), and fine sculpture. Some of their work such as the Córdoba lions, the Guisando toros and, in the Museo Arqueológico in Madrid, the *Dama de Baza* and the *Dama de Elche*, is of a remarkably high standard. Meanwhile, Phoenician and in turn Greek colonisers introduced their native art: Phoenician sarcophagi in Cádiz, Punic art in Ibiza and Greek art in Empúries.

Roman Spain (1C BC-5C AD) – Besides roads, bridges, aqueducts, towns and monuments, Roman legacies include the Mérida theatre, the ancient towns of Italica and Empúries, and the Segovia aqueduct and Tarragona triumphal arch.

The *Dama de Elche* (in the Museo Arqueológico, Madrid)

H. Stierlin, Ginebra

The Visigoths (6C-8C) – Christian Visigoths built small stone churches (Quintanilla de las Viñas, San Pedro de la Nave) adorned with friezes carved in geometric patterns with plant motifs. The apsidal plan was square and the arches were often horseshoe shaped. The Visigoths were outstanding gold and silversmiths who made sumptuous jewellery in the Byzantine and Germanic traditions. Gold votive crowns (Guarrazar treasure in Toledo), fibulae and belt buckles adorned with precious stones or *cloisonné* enamel were presented to churches or placed in the tombs of the great.

HISPANO-MOORISH ARCHITECTURE (8C-15C)

The three major periods of Hispano-Moorish architecture correspond to the reigns of successive Arab dynasties over the Muslim-held territories in the peninsula.

Caliphate or Córdoba architecture (8C-11C) – This period is characterised by three types of building: **mosques**, built to a simple plan consisting of a minaret, a courtyard with a pool for ritual ablutions and finally a square prayer room with a *mihrab* (prayer-niche marking the direction of Mecca); **alcázares** (palaces), built around attractive patios and surrounded by gardens and fountains; and **alcazabas** (castle fortresses), built on high ground and surrounded by several walls crowned with pointed merlons and dominated by a watchtower or *Torre de la Vela* as in Málaga. The most famous monuments from this period are in Córdoba (the Mezquita and the Medina Azahara palace) and in Toledo (Cristo de la Luz) where, besides the ubiquitous horseshoe arch which virtually became the hallmark of Moorish architecture, other characteristics developed including ornamental brickwork in relief, cupolas supported on ribs, turned modillions, arches with alternating white stone and red-brick voussoirs, multifoil arches and doors surmounted with blind arcades. These features subsequently became popular in Mudéjar and Romanesque churches.

The Umayyads brought a taste for profuse decoration from Syria. As the Koran forbids the representation of human or animal forms, Muslim decoration is based on calligraphy (Cufic inscriptions running along walls), geometric patterns (polygons and stars made of ornamental brickwork and marble) and lastly plant motifs (flowerets and interlacing palm leaves).

Almohad or Sevilla architecture (12C-13C) – The religious puritanism of the Almohad dynasty, of which Sevilla was the capital, was expressed in architecture by a refined, though sometimes rather austere, simplicity. One of the characteristics of the style consisted of brickwork highlighted by wide bands of decoration in relief, without excessive ornamentation (the Giralda tower in Sevilla is a good xample). The style was later used in the Mudéjar architecture of Aragón. Other eatures that emerged at this time include *artesonado* ceilings and *azulejos*. Arches f alternate brick and stonework disappeared, the horseshoe arch became pointed nd the multifoil arch was bordered by a curvilinear festoon (ornament like a arland) as in the Aljafería in Zaragoza. Calligraphic decoration included cursive flowing) as well as Cufic script to which floral motifs were added to fill the spaces etween vertical lines.

Nasrid or Granada architecture (14C-15C) – This period of high sophistication, of which the **Alhambra** in Granada is the masterpiece, produced less innovation in actual architectural design than in the decoration, whether stucco or ceramic, that covered he walls.

Surrounds to doors and windows became focal points for every room's design and he spaces between them were filled by perfectly proportioned panels. Arch outlines were simplified – the stilted round arch became widespread – while detailed lacework ornamentation was used as a border.

Mudéjar architecture – This is the name given to work carried out by Muslims while under the Christian yoke, yet executed in the Arab tradition. It was fashionable from the 11C to the 15C in different regions depending on the area recovered by the Reconquest, although some features, like *artesonado* ceilings, continued as deco-rative themes for centuries.

Court Mudéjar, developed by Muslim artists (in buildings ordered by Peter the Cruel n Tordesillas and Sevilla, and in synagogues in Toledo), was an extension of the Almohad or contemporary Nasrid style. Popular Mudéjar, on the other hand, was produced by local Muslim workshops and reflects marked regional taste: walls were decorated with blind arcades in Castilla (Arévalo, Sahagún and Toledo) and belfries were faced with *azulejos* and geometric strapwork in Aragón.

The decorative arts – Extremely rich and varied decorative artefacts from this period include geometric wood strapwork, brocades, weapons, ceramics with metal lustre decoration and small ivory chests.

PRE-ROMANESQUE AND ROMANESQUE ARCHITECTURE (8C-13C)

Asturian architecture – A highly sophisticated style of court architecture, characte-rised by sweeps of ascending lines, developed in the small Kingdom of Asturias between the 8C and the 10C. Asturian churches (Naranco, Santa Cristina de Lena) followed the precepts of the Latin basilica in their rectangular plan with a narthex, a nave and two aisles separated by semicircular arches, a vast transept and an east end divided into three. Decoration inside consisted of frescoes, and borrowings from the east including motifs carved on capitals (strapwork, rosettes and monsters) and ornamental openwork around windows. Gold and silversmiths in the 9C and 10C produced rich treasures, many of which may be seen in the Cámara Santa in Oviedo Cathedral.

Iglesia de San Martín

Mozarabic architecture – This term is given to work carried out by Christians livir under Arab rule after the Moorish invasion of 711. Churches built in this sty especially in Castilla (San Miguel de Escalada, San Millán de la Cogolla), brought ba Visigothic traditions (horseshoe arches) enriched by Moorish features such as ribb cupolas and turned modillions.

Illuminated manuscripts provide the earliest known examples of Spanish mediev painting (10C). They were executed in the 10C and 11C by Mozarabic monks and ha Moorish features such as horseshoe arches and Arab costumes. They portra St John's Commentary on the Apocalypse written in the 8C by the monk **Beatus** **Liébana**, after whom the manuscripts were named.

Catalunya, home of the earliest Romanesque style in Spain – Cataluny was largely closed to Mozarabic influences but had intimate links with Italy ar France and consequently developed an architectural style strongly influence by Lombardy from the 11C to the 13C. This evolved in the Pyrenean valley isolated from the more travelled pilgrim and trade routes. Sober little churche were built often accompanied by a separate bell-tower decorated with Lombar bands. Interior walls in the 11C and 12C were only embellished with fresco which, in spite of their borrowings from Byzantine mosaics (heavy blac outlines, rigid postures, and themes like Christ in Glory portrayed within mandorla), proved by their realistic and expressive details to be typically Spanish Altar fronts of painted wood, executed in bright colours, followed the same theme and layout.

European Romanesque art along the pilgrim routes to Compostela – Northwes Spain opened its gates to foreign influence during the reign of Sancho th Great of Navarra early in the 11C. Cistercian abbeys were founded and Frenc merchants allowed to settle rate-free in towns (Estella, Sangüesa and Pan plona). Meanwhile, the surge of pilgrims to Compostela and the fever to buil along the routes, brought about the construction of a great many religious bu dings in which French influence was clearly marked (characteristics from Poito in Soria and Sangüesa, and from Toulouse in Aragón and Santiago de Compostela) The acknowledged masterpiece of this style is the cathedral of Santiago d Compostela.

In Aragón, Romanesque art was particularly evident in sculpture. The artists wh carved capitals in the manner of their leader, the Maestro de San Juan de la Peña had a seemingly clumsy style because their emphasis was more on symbolism that realistic portrayal. Disproportionate faces with bulging eyes were the means b which the sculptor illustrated the soul, while gestures such as outstretched hand: conveyed religious meaning.

In the early 12C, reform of the Cistercian order with emphasis on austerity brough an important change to architecture. The Transitional style which heralded th Gothic (intersecting ribbed vaulting, squared apses) was introduced and the profusion of Romanesque decoration disappeared. Examples of this style may be seen in the monasteries of Poblet, Santes Creus, La Oliva and Santa María de Huerta.

THE GOTHIC PERIOD (from the 13C onwards)

Architecture, the early stages – French Gothic architecture made little headway into Spain except in Navarra where a French royal house had been in power since 1234. The first truly Gothic buildings (Roncesvalles church, Cuenca and Sigüenza cathedrals) appeared in the 13C. Bishops in some of the main towns in Castilla (León, Burgos, Toledo) sent abroad for cathedral plans, artists and masons. An original style of church, with no transept, a single nave (aisles, if there were any, would be as high as the nave), and pointed stone arches or a wooden roof resting on diaphragm arches, developed in Valencia, Catalunya and the Balearic Islands. The unadorned walls enclosed a large, homogeneous space in which there was little carved decoration, and purity of line supplied a dignified elegance.

Civil architecture followed the same pattern and had the same geometrical sense of space, used with rare skill particularly in the *lonjas* or commodity exchanges of Barcelona, Palma, Valencia and Zaragoza.

Development of the Gothic style – During the 14C and 15C in Castilla, the influence of artists from the north such as **Johan of Cologne** and **Hanequin of Brussels**, brought about the flowering of a style approaching Flamboyant Gothic. As it adapted to Spain, the style developed simultaneously in two different ways: in one, decoration proliferated to produce the Isabelline style; in the other, structures were simplified into a national church and cathedral style which remained in favour until the mid 16C (Segovia and Salamanca).

The last of the Gothic cathedrals – Following the example of Sevilla, the dimensions of Gothic cathedrals became ever more vast. Aisles almost as large as the nave increased the volume of the building, while pillars, though massive, retained the impression of thrusting upward lines. A new plan emerged in which the old crescendo of radiating chapels, ambulatory, chancel and transept was superseded by a plain

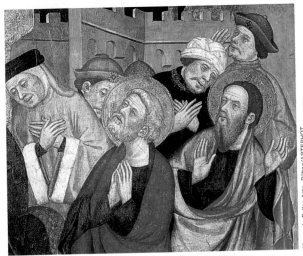

Museo de Bellas Arte, Bilbao/ARTEPHOT

Gothic painting, Altarpiece by Pedro Serra

rectangle, a vast space in which the only part that remained of the original cruciform plan was the transept crossing – set off by a lantern – between the *capilla mayor* and the *coro*. In contrast to this severity, specifically Gothic decoration accumulated around doors, on pinnacles and in elaborate star vaulting; a style echoed in some Andalusian cathedrals.

Painting – Artists in the Gothic era worked on polyptyches and altarpieces which sometimes reached a height of more than 15m/50ft. The Primitives, who customarily painted on gold backgrounds, were influenced by the Italians (soft contours), the French and the Flemish (rich fabrics with broken folds and painstaking detail). Nonetheless, as they strove for expressive naturalism and lively anecdotal detail, their work came across as distinctively Spanish.

There was intense artistic activity in the states attached to the Crown of Aragón, especially in Catalunya. The Vic, Barcelona and Valencia museums contain works by **Ferrer Bassá** (1285-1348) who was influenced by the Sienese **Duccio**, paintings by his successor **Ramón Destorrents** (1346-91), and by the **Serra** brothers, Destorrents' pupils. Among other artists were **Luis Borrassá** (c 1360-1425) who had a very Spanish sense of the picturesque, **Bernat Martorell** (d 1452) who gave special importance to landscape, **Jaime Huguet** (1415-92) who stands out for his extreme sensitivity and is considered to be the undisputed leader of the Catalan School, and finally **Luis Dalmau** and **Bartolomé Bermejo**, both influenced by Van Eyck (who was sent on missions to Spain by the Duke of Burgundy).

In Castilla, French influence predominated in the 14C and Italian in the 15C until about 1450 when Flemish artists like **Roger Van der Weyden** arrived. By the end of the 15C, **Fernando Gallego** had become the main figure in the Hispano-Flemish movement in which **Juan of Flanders** was noted for his appealingly delicate touch.

Sculpture – Gothic sculpture, like architecture, became more refined. Relief was more accentuated than in Romanesque carving, postures more natural and details more meticulous. Decoration grew increasingly abundant as the 15C progressed and faces became individualised to the point where recumbent funerary statues clearly resembled the deceased. Statues were surmounted by an openwork canopy, while door surrounds, cornices and capitals were decorated with friezes of intricate plant motifs. After being enriched by French influence in the 13C and 14C and Flemish in the 15C, sculpture ultimately developed a purely Spanish style, the Isabelline.

Portals showed a French influence. Tombs were at first sarcophagi decorated with coats of arms, sometimes surmounted by a recumbent statue in a conventional posture with a peaceful expression and hands joined. Later, more attention was paid to the costume of the deceased; with an increasingly honed technique marble craftsmen were able to render the richness of brocades and the supple quality of leather. In the 15C, sculptors produced lifelike figures in natural positions, kneeling for instance, or even in nonchalant attitudes like that of the remarkable Doncel in Sigüenza Cathedral. Altarpieces comprised a predella or plinth, surmounted by several levels of panels and finally by a carved openwork canopy. Choir stalls were adorned with Biblical and historical scenes or carved to resemble delicate stone tracery.

The Isabelline style – At the end of the 15C, the prestige surrounding the royal couple and the grandees in the reign of Isabel the Catholic (1474-1504) provided a favourable context for the emergence of a new style in which exuberant decoration covered entire façades of civil and religious buildings. Ornamentation took the form of supple free arcs, lace-like carving, heraldic motifs and every fantasy that imagination could devise *(see VALLADOLID)*.

The diversity of inspiration was largely due to foreign artists: **Simon of Cologne** (son of Johan) – San Pablo in Valladolid, Capilla del Condestable in Burgos; **Juan Guas** (son of the Frenchman, Pierre) – San Juan de los Reyes in Toledo; and **Enrique Egas** (nephew of Hanequin of Brussels) – Capilla Real in Granada.

THE RENAISSANCE (16C)

In the 16C, at the dawn of its golden age, Spain was swept by a deep sense of its own national character and so created a style in which Italian influence became acceptable only when hispanicised.

Architecture – **Plateresque** was the name given to the early Renaissance style because of its finely chiselled, lavish decoration reminiscent of silverwork *(platero: silversmith)*. Although close to the Isabelline style in its profusion of carved forms extending over entire façades, the rounded arches and ornamental themes (grotesques, foliage, pilasters, medallions and cornices) were Italian. The Plateresque style predominated during the reign of Charles V and was brought to a climax in Salamanca in the façade of the Universidad and that of the Convento de San Esteban. Among architects of the time were **Rodrigo Gil de Hontañón** who worked at Salamanca (Palacios de Monterrey

and Fonseca) and at Alcalá de Henares (university façade), and **Diego de Siloé**, the main architect in Burgos (Escalera de la Coronería). Together with **Alonso de Covarrubias** (d 1570) who worked mainly in Toledo (Alcázar and Capilla de los Reyes Nuevos in the cathedral), Diego de Siloé marked the transition from the Plateresque style to the Classical Renaissance. **Andrés de Vandelvira** (1509-76) was the leading architect of the Andalusian Renaissance (Jaén cathedral). His work introduces the austerity which was to characterise the last quarter of the century.

The Renaissance style drew upon Italian models and adopted features from Antiquity such as rounded arches, columns, entablatures and pediments. Decoration became of secondary importance after architectonic perfection. **Pedro Machuca** (d 1550) who studied under Michelangelo, designed the palace of Charles V in Granada, the most classical example of the Italian tradition. Another important figure, **Bartolomé Bustamante** (1500-70), built the Hospital de Tavera in Toledo.

The greatest figure of Spanish Classicism was **Juan de Herrera** (1530-97) who gave his name to an architectural style characterised by grandeur, austerity and geometric effect. He was the favourite architect of Philip II. The king saw in him the sobriety that suited the Counter-Reformation and in 1567 entrusted him with the task of continuing work on El Escorial, his greatest achievement.

The Plateresque Style,
Universidad de Salamanca

Sculpture – Sculpture in Spain reached its climax during the Renaissance. In the 16C, a great many choir stalls, mausoleums and altarpieces (also known as retables or reredos) were still being made of alabaster and wood. These latter were then painted by the **estofado** technique in which gold leaf is first applied, then the object is coloured and finally delicately scored to produce gold highlights. Carved altarpiece panels were framed by Corinthian architraves and pilasters.

The sculptures of **Damián Forment** (c 1480-1540), who worked mainly in Aragón, belong to the transition period between Gothic and Renaissance styles. The Burgundian **Felipe Vigarny** (d 1543) and the architect **Diego de Siloé**, who was apprenticed in Naples, both worked on Burgos Cathedral. **Bartolomé Ordóñez** (d 1520) studied in Naples and carved the *trascoro* (choir screen) in Barcelona Cathedral, the mausoleums of Juana the Mad, Philip the Handsome (Capilla Real in Granada) and Cardinal Cisneros (Alcalá de Henares).

The home of the Renaissance School moved from Burgos to Valladolid in the mid 16C by which time the Spanish style had absorbed foreign influences and Spain's two great Renaissance sculptors had emerged. The first, **Alonso Berruguete** (1488-1561), who studied in Italy under Michelangelo, had a style which drew closely on the Florentine Renaissance and reflected a strong personality. He sought strength of expression rather than formal beauty and his tormented fiery human forms are as powerful as those of his master (statue of San Sebastián in the Museo de Valladolid). The second, **Juan de Juni** (d 1577), a Frenchman who settled in Valladolid, was also influenced by Michelangelo and founded the Catalan School of sculpture. His statues, recognisable by their beauty and the fullness of their forms, anticipated the Baroque style through the dramatic postures they adopted to express sorrow. Many of his works, such as the famous Virgen de los Siete Cuchillos (Virgin of the Seven Knives) in the Iglesia de las Angustias in Valladolid and the Entombments in the Museo de Valladolid and Segovia Cathedral, were subsequently copied.

Most of the finely worked wrought-iron grilles closing off chapels and *coros* (chancels) were carved in the 15C and 16C. Members of the **Arfe** family, Enrique, Antonio and Juan, stand out in the field of gold and silversmithing. They made the monstrances of Toledo, Santiago de Compostela and Sevilla cathedrals respectively.

Painting – Under Italian Renaissance influence, Spanish painting in the 16C showed a mastery of perspective, a taste for clarity of composition and glorification of the human body. These features found their way into Spanish painting mainly through the Valencian School where **Fernando Yáñez de la Almedina** and **Fernando de Llanos** introduced the style of Leonardo da Vinci, while **Vicente Macip** added that of Raphael and his son **Juan de Juanes** produced Mannerist works. In Sevilla, **Alejo Fernández** painted the famous *Virgin of the Navigators* in the Alcázar. In Castilla, the great master of the late 15C was **Pedro Berruguete** (c 1450-1504) whose markedly personal style drew upon all the artistic influences in the country. His successor, **Juan de Borgoña**, specialised particularly in landscape, architecture and decorative motifs. Another artist, **Pedro de Campaña** from Brussels, used chiaroscuro to dramatic effect while **Luis de Morales** (c 1520-86), a Mannerist, gave his work a human dimension through the portrayal of feelings. Ordinary people with religious sentiments responded favourably to the spiritual emotion expressed in his paintings. At the end of the 16C, Philip II sent for a great many Italian or Italian-trained artists to paint pictures for El Escorial. During his reign he introduced portrait painting under the Dutchman **Antonio Moro** (1519-76), his disciple **Alonso Sánchez Coello** (1531-88) and **Pantoja de la Cruz** (1553-1608). **El Greco**, on the other hand, was scorned by the court and settled in Toledo.

BAROQUE (17C-18C)

Spanish art reached its apogee in the mid 17C. Baroque met with outstanding success in its role as an essentially religious art in the service of the Counter-Reformation and was particularly evident in Andalucía, then enriched by trade with America.

Architecture – Architects in the early 17C were still under the influence of 16C Classicism and the Herreran style to which they added decorative details. Public buildings proliferated and many continued to be built throughout the Baroque period. Public buildings of the time in Madrid include the Plaza Mayor by **Juan Gómez de Mora**, built shortly before the Ayuntamiento (town hall), and the most significant building of all, the present Ministerio de Asuntos Exteriores (Ministry for Foreign Affairs) by **Juan Bautista Crescenzi**, the architect of the Panteón de los Reyes at El Escorial. Church architecture of the period showed greater freedom from Classicism. A style of Jesuit church, with a cruciform plan and a large transept that served to light up altarpieces, began to emerge. Madrid has several examples including the Iglesia de San Isidro by the Jesuits Pedro Sánchez and **Francisco Bautista**, and the Real Convento de la Encarnación by Juan Gómez de Mora. In the middle of the century, architects began to look for alternatives to the austerity of El Escorial and so changed plans and façades, broke up entablatures and made pediments more elaborate. A good example of this Italian Baroque style is the Iglesia Pontificia de San Miguel (18C) in Madrid. A new feature, the *camarín*, was introduced: at first simply a passage behind the high altar leading to the retable niche containing a statue venerated by the faithful, it developed into a highly ornate chapel. Decoration of this kind may be seen in Zaragoza's Basílica de Nuestra Señora del Pilar designed by **Francisco Herrera the Younger** (1622-85). The Clerecía in Salamanca is a magnificent Baroque creation with a patio that anticipates the audacity and super-abundant decoration characteristic of the Churrigueresque style.

The Churrigueresque style – In this style, named after the Churriguera family of architects (late 17C), architecture became no more than a support for dense concentrations of ornament covering entire façades. The style is typified by the use of *salomónicas* or barley sugar columns entwined with vines, and *estípites*, or pilasters arranged in an inverse pyramid. Early examples of this extravagance, the altarpiece of the Convento de San Esteban in Salamanca and the palace in Nuevo Baztán near Madrid, were by **José de Churriguera** (1665-1725) who was the instigator of the style but did not make any architectural changes. His brothers **Joaquín**

(1674-1724) and especially **Alberto** (1676-1750) who designed the Plaza Mayor in Salamanca, took greater liberties in their work. **Pedro de Ribera** (1683-1742), a Castilian architect who worked mainly in Madrid, surpassed the Churriguera brothers in decorative delirium. The other great Castilian, **Narciso Tomé**, is remembered for the façade of the Universidad de Valladolid (1715) and particularly for the *Transparente* in Toledo Cathedral (1720-32).

Regional variations – The popularity of the Baroque spread countrywide, differing from province to province. In **Galicia**, where the hardness of the granite precluded delicate carving, Baroque took the form of bold lines and decorative mouldings. The best example of the style and the masterpiece of its designer, **Fernando de Casas y Novoa**, is the Obradoiro façade of Santiago de Compostela Cathedral (1750).

In **Andalucía**, Baroque attained its utmost splendour, especially in decoration. Undulating surfaces characterised the façades of palaces (Écija), cathedrals (Guadix), and the doorways of countless churches and mansions (Jerez) in the 18C. As well as sculptor and painter, **Alonso Cano** was the instigator of Andalusian Baroque and designed the façade of Granada Cathedral. The major exponent of the style was, however, **Vicente Acero**, who worked on the façade of Guadix Cathedral (1714-20), designed Cádiz Cathedral and built the tobacco factory in Sevilla. Mention should also be made of **Leonardo de Figueroa** (1650-1730) for the Palacio de San Telmo in Sevilla and **Francisco Hurtado** (1669-1725) and **Luis de Arévalo** for La Cartuja in Granada; Hurtado worked on the monastery's tabernacle and Arévalo on the sacristy, the most exuberant Baroque works in Andalucía.

In the **Levante**, Baroque artists used polychrome tiles to decorate church cupolas and spires like that of Santa Catalina in Valencia. In the same town, the Palacio del Marqués de Dos Aguas by **Luis Domingo** and **Ignacio Vergara** is reminiscent of façades by Ribera, although its design is more like French Rococo. The cathedral in Murcia has an impressive façade by **Jaime Bort**.

The Golden Age of Spanish painting – This was characterised by the rejection of the previous century's Mannerism and the adoption of naturalism. The starting point was Caravaggio's tenebrism, powerful contrasts of light and shade, and his stern realism. Painters took up portraiture and still life *(bodegón)*, while allegories on the theme of vanitas (still-life paintings showing the ephemerality of life) reflected a philosophical purpose by juxtaposing every-day objects with symbols of decay to illustrate the transience of wealth and the things of this world and the inevitability of death. Among 17C artists were two from the Valencian School – **Francisco Ribalta** (1565-1628), who introduced tenebrism into Spain, and **José de Ribera** (1591-1652), known for his forceful realism.

Some of the greatest Baroque artists worked in Andalucía. One was **Francisco Zurbarán** (1598-1664), master of the Sevilla School; light in his paintings springs from within the subjects themselves. Other artists included **Murillo** (1618-82), who painted intimate, mystical scenes, and **Valdés Leal** whose powerful realism clearly challenged earthly vanities. **Alonso Cano** (1601-67), architect, painter and sculptor, settled in Granada and painted delicate, reserved figures of the Virgin.

The Castilian painters of the century, **Vicente Carducho** (1575-1638) and the portraitists **Carreño de Miranda** (1614-85) and **Claudio Coello** (1642-93), all excellent artists, nonetheless pale beside Velázquez. His aerial perspective and outstanding sense of depth are beyond compare.

Sculpture – Spanish Baroque sculpture was naturalistic and intensely emotive. The most commonly used medium was wood, softer than marble. To enhance their realism, sculptures were painted in oils, rather than *estofado*, and given crystal eyes and tears. While altarpieces continued to be carved with simpler designs, **pasos** or statues specially made for Semana Santa processions proved a great novelty.

The two major schools of Baroque sculpture were in Castilla and Andalucía. **Gregorio Hernández**, Juni's successor, worked in Vallodolid, the Castilian centre. His style was a lot more natural than that of his master, and his Christ Recumbent for the Convento de Capuchinos in El Pardo was widely copied. Sevilla and Granada were the main centres for the Andalusian School. **Juan Martínez Montañés** (1568-1649) settled in Sevilla and worked exclusively in wood, carving a great many *pasos* and various altarpieces. Alonso Cano, Granada's illustrious artist, became famous for the grace and femininity of his Immaculate Conceptions while his best-known disciple, **Pedro de Mena**, produced sculptures of great dramatic tension which contrasted with his master's understated style. The statue of Mary Magdalene (Museo Nacional de Escultura Policromada, Valladolid), St Francis (Toledo Cathedral) and the Dolorosa (Monasterio de las Descalzas Reales, Madrid) are telling examples of his work.

In the 18C, the great Murcian, **Francisco Salzillo** emerged as an imaginative sculptor, developing a spectacular, dramatic style inspired by Italian Baroque.

Churrigueresque excess in sculpture took the form of immense altarpieces which reached the roof. These huge constructions surrounding a central tabernacle took on such grand proportions that they began to be designed by architects. Their statues seemed smothered by decoration, lost in an overabundance of gilding and stucco.

BOURBON ART

Austrian imperialism was succeeded by enlightened Bourbon despotism which resulted in artistic as well as political change in the 18C. Henceforth the rules of art were to be governed by official bodies like the Academia de Bellas Artes de San Fernando.

Architecture – During the first half of the century architecture still bore the stamp of Spanish Baroque, itself influenced at the time by French Rococo. The king and queen had palaces built in a moderate Baroque style (El Pardo, Riofrío, La Granja and Aranjuez) and began work on Madrid's Palacio Real modelled on Versailles. These buildings sought to ally French Classical harmony with Italian grace and to this end most of the work was entrusted to Italian architects who generally respected the traditional quadrangular plan of *alcázares*, so typically Spanish. The vast gardens were given a French design.

Excavations of Pompeii and Herculaneum contributed to the emergence of a new, neo-Classical style which flourished between the second half of the 18C and 19C. It repudiated Baroque excess and aspired to Hellenistic beauty through the use of Classical orders, pediments, porticoes and cupolas. The kings of Spain, Charles III in particular, set about embellishing the capital by building fountains (Cibeles, Neptune), gates (Alcalá and Toledo), and planting botanic gardens.

The first Spanish neo-Classical architect, **Ventura Rodríguez** (1717-85), who was actually apprenticed in Italian Baroque, quickly developed an academic neo-Classical style. His works include the façade of Pamplona Cathedral, Paseo del Prado boulevard in Madrid and the Basílica de Nuestra Señora del Pilar in Zaragoza. **Sabatini** (1722-97), whose style developed along similar lines, designed the Puerta de Alcalá and the building that now houses the Ministerio de Hacienda (Ministry of Finance) in Madrid. The leading architect was without doubt **Juan de Villanueva** (1739-1811), schooled in Classical principles during a stay in Rome. He designed the façade of the Ayuntamiento in Madrid, the Casita del Príncipe at El Escorial and most importantly, the Museo del Prado. Two notable town planners emerged during the 19C: **Ildefonso Cerdá** in Barcelona and **Arturo Soria** (1844-1920) in Madrid.

Painting – Bourbon monarchs took pains to attract the greatest painters to court and grant them official positions. In 1752 Ferdinand VI founded the Academia de Bellas Artes de San Fernando where it was intended that students should learn official painting techniques and study the Italian masters. Leading artists of the time were **Anton Raffael Mengs** (1728-79) from Bohemia and the Italian **Gian Battista Tiepolo** (1696-1770), both of whom decorated the Palacio Real. There was also **Francisco Bayeu** (1734-95) from Aragón, who painted a great many tapestry cartoons, as did his brother-in-law **Francisco Goya** (1746-1828). Goya's work, much of which may be seen in the Prado, Madrid, was to dominate the entire century.

Painters working in the post-Goya period did not follow in the master's footsteps as academic neo-Classical influences and Romanticism took over; Goya's legacy was not taken up until the end of the 19C. The following stand out among artists of the academic Romantic trend: **Federico de Madrazo**, representative of official taste in royal

The Second of May. Goya

portraits and historical scenes, **Vicente Esquivel**, portrait-painter, and lastly **Leonardo Alenza**, and **Eugenio Lucas**, the spokesmen for **Costumbrismo** which had attained full status as a genre. (This was a style of painting illustrating scenes of everyday life which gradually developed from the simply anecdotal to a higher calling, the evocation of the Spanish soul). Historical themes became very popular in the 19C with works by José Casado de Alisal, Eduardo Rosales and Mariano Fortuny.
Impressionist features began to appear in naturalist paintings by **Martí Alsina** and in post-Romantic landscapes by **Carlos de Haes**. The style secured a definitive hold in the works of **Narciso Oller**, **Ignacio Pinazo**, the best Valencian Impressionist, **Darío Regoyos** and lastly, **Joaquín Sorolla**, who specialised in light-filled folk scenes and regional subjects. The Basque artist **Ignacio Zuloaga** (1870-1945) expressed his love for Spain in brightly-coloured scenes of everyday life at a time when Impressionism was conquering Europe.

The decorative arts – Factories were built under Bourbon rule to produce decorative material for royal palaces. Philip V founded the Alcora tile factory in 1727, but this was soon superseded by the Buen Retiro works founded in 1760 by Charles III where ceramics for the famous Salón de Porcelana in the royal palaces of Aranjuez and Madrid were made. The factory was destroyed during the Napoleonic invasion. In 1720, Philip V opened the Real Fábrica de Tapices de Santa Bárbara (in Madrid), the equivalent of the French Gobelins factory in Paris. Some of the tapestries were of Don Quixote while others depicted scenes of everyday life based on preparatory cartoons by Bayeu and Goya.

20C ART

From Modernism to Surrealism – The barren period that Spanish art in general experienced at the end of the 19C was interrupted in Catalunya by a vast cultural movement known as **Modernism**. This was particularly strong in architecture, with outstanding work by **Antoni Gaudí, Lluís Domènech i Montaner** and **Josep María Jujol**.
In the field of sculpture, **Pau Gargallo** broke new ground through the simplicity of his shapes, the attention he gave to volume and the use of new materials like iron.
Painting was varied and prolific. The following stand out among the many artists of the time: **Ramón Casas**, the best Spanish Impressionist, whose works are suffused with an atmosphere of grey melancholy, **Santiago Rusiñol, Isidro Nonell**, instigator of Spanish Expressionism, and **Pablo Ruiz Picasso** (1881-1973), the dominant figure whose innovations were to mark the entire history of 20C painting.
Picasso's attention was first devoted to academic naturalism (Science and Charity). He subsequently became a Modernist and social Expressionist. Later, once he had moved to Paris (1904), his style developed through the successive blue and rose periods to Cubism (Les Demoiselles d'Avignon), Surrealism and Expressionism (Guernica), which in turn led to a totally personal and subjective lyrical style (La Joie de Vivre).
In the 1920s a movement began to emerge that was influenced by Cubism and more particularly, by Surrealism. Its sculptors were **Angel Ferrant, Victorio Macho, Alberto Sánchez** and lastly **Julio González**, who strove towards abstract Expressionism through the use of iron and simple shapes. Painters of the movement included **Daniel Vázquez Díaz**, Juan Gris, Joan Miró and Salvador Dalí. **Juan Gris** (1887-1927), the most faithful analytical Cubist, worked in Paris. The works of **Joan Miró** (1893-1983), champion of Surrealism, are characterised by childlike spontaneity and an original attitude to everyday objects. Miró used very bright colours and magic symbols in all his paintings. **Salvador Dalí** (1904-89), a quasi-Surrealist, dreamed up his own creative method which he called the paranoic critical. Some of his best paintings were a result of his interest in the subconscious and his vision of a dream world. All his works attest to an excellent drawing technique and many show an attention to detail worthy of the best miniaturists.

Post-war art – Spanish art was crucially affected by the Civil War in two ways: firstly, the fact that several artists went into exile meant that the country suffered cultural loss, and secondly, official taste in architecture developed a penchant for the monumental. This is clearly apparent in a number of colossal edifices. Many government buildings, all in Madrid, were designed in the manner of El Escorial, including the Ministerio del Aire, the Museo de América, the Arco del Triunfo and the Consejo de Investigaciones Científicas. The most striking example is the monument of the Valle de los Caídos (Valley of the Fallen) outside Madrid. However, among exponents of the nationalist style, there were several innovative architects like **Miguel Fisac**.
In 1950 the first signs of a new style, based on rational and functional criteria, began to emerge. Examples abound in Barcelona – the Vanguardia building by **Oriol Bohigas** and **José María Martorell**, the residential block by **Ricardo Bofill** in Carrer de Nicaragua – and in Madrid – the Colegio Monfort by **A Fernandez Alba** and the Maravillas secondary school (gimnasio) by **Alejandro de la Sota** and the Torres Blancas (White Towers) by **F Javier Sáenz de Oíza**.
Post-war sculpture and painting are basically academic but there are some notable artists such as **José Gutiérrez Solana**, whose paintings are full of anguish, and the landscape painters **Benjamín Palencia**, who glorifies the country and light of Castilla, and **Rafael Zabaleta**, who is more interested in painting the region's country folk.

Antoni Tàpies – *Llibre-mur*

vant-garde painters also began to emerge after the war. The first post-war surrealists are members of a group called **Dau al Set** including **Modest Cuixart, Antoni Tàpies** and **Juan José Tharrats**. Tàpies is a veritable pioneer, one of the major abstract artists. In the 1950s two abstract groups, with different qualities but with the common aim of artistic innovation, were formed. They are the **El Paso** group in Madrid with **Antonio Saura, Manuel Millares, Rafael Canogar, Luis Feito, Manuel Viola** and **Martín Chirino**, representatives of what is known as action painting, and the **El Equipo 57** group in Cuenca with **Duart, Ibarrola, Serrano** and **Duarte**, who are more interested in drawing. Among the movement's sculptors are **Jorge Oteiza, Andréu Alfaro** and lastly **Eduardo Chillida**, who works in iron and wood and strips his sculptures of any figurative suggestion.

ABC of architecture

Ground plan

BARCELONA – Cathedral (13C-15C)

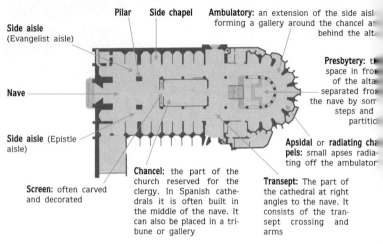

Side aisle
(Evangelist aisle)

Pilar

Side chapel

Ambulatory: an extension of the side aisl forming a gallery around the chancel a behind the alt.

Nave

Presbytery: t space in fro of the alta separated fro the nave by som steps and partitio

Side aisle (Epistle aisle)

Apsidal or **radiating cha pels:** small apses radia ting off the ambulator

Screen: often carved and decorated

Chancel: the part of the church reserved for the clergy. In Spanish cathedrals it is often built in the middle of the nave. It can also be placed in a tribune or gallery

Transept: The part of the cathedral at right angles to the nave. It consists of the transept crossing and arms

Cross-section of a church

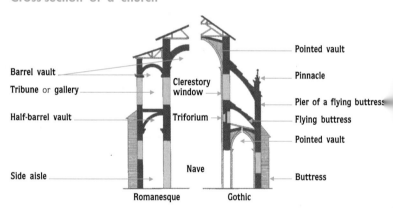

Barrel vault

Tribune or gallery

Half-barrel vault

Side aisle

Clerestory window

Triforium

Nave

Romanesque

Pointed vault

Pinnacle

Pier of a flying buttress

Flying buttress

Pointed vault

Buttress

Gothic

Retable or altarpiece

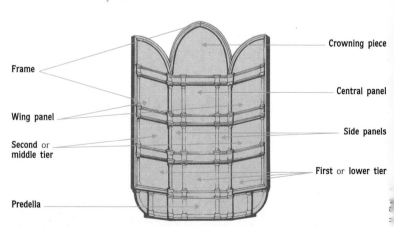

Frame

Wing panel

Second or middle tier

Predella

Crowning piece

Central panel

Side panels

First or lower tier

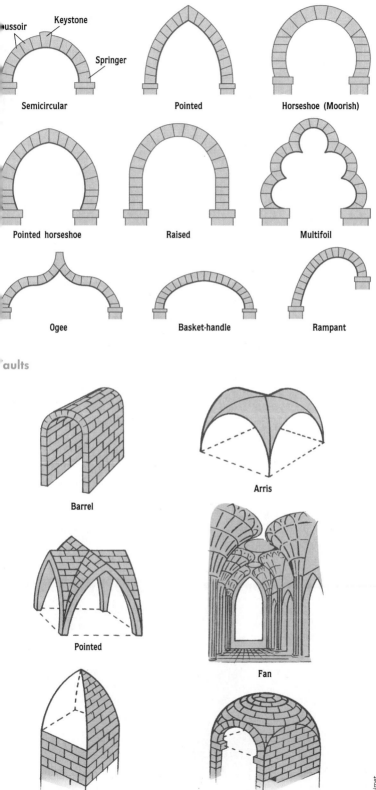

Keystone

ussoir

Springer

Semicircular

Pointed

Horseshoe (Moorish)

Pointed horseshoe

Raised

Multifoil

Ogee

Basket-handle

Rampant

Barrel

Arris

Pointed

Fan

Cylindrical

Oven

H. Choimet

CORDOBA – Mezquita: Puerta de Alhakem II (10C)

Eight centuries of Moorish rule in Spain had a fundamental influence on Spanish art.

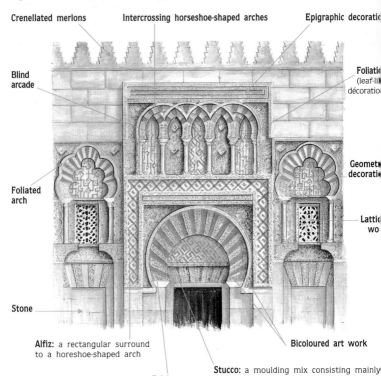

Crenellated merlons

Intercrossing horseshoe-shaped arches

Epigraphic decoratic

Blind
arcade

Foliatic
(leaf-li
décoratio

Foliated
arch

Geomet
decoratic

Lattic
wo

Stone

Alfiz: a rectangular surround
to a horeshoe-shaped arch

Bicoloured art work

Brick

Stucco: a moulding mix consisting mainly
of plaster and glue (sometimes includes
powdered marble)

GRANADA – La Alhambra (14C)

Mocárabes: decorative motifs of Muslim architecture formed by assembled prisms ending in concave
surfaces. Used to adorn vaults, arches and cornices

A panel of **azulejos** with epigraph
and geometric decoration

SANTIAGO DE COMPOSTELA – Cathedral: Interior (11-13C)

Santiago cathedral is a typical example of a Spanish pilgrimage church and shows clear French influence.

Tribune: a gallery above the side aisle and of a similar width

Paired arch: arches grouped in twos

Barrel vault

Barrel arch: formed of a single curved member, with no diagonal ribs

Organ

Wall arch: an arch parallel to the length of the nave, separating it from the side aisle

Abacus: the uppermost slab of a capital or column

Corinthian capital

Raised round arch

Pillar with engaged columns

H. Choimet

LEÓN – Cathedral: side façade (13C-14C)

In Gothic architecture, light was considered the essence of beauty and the symbol of truth. León cathedral is the brightest and most delicate of all the major Spanish cathedrals and is viewed as the best example of this concept. The beauty and magnificence of its stained glass attracts the admiration of its many thousands of visitors every year. French influence is clearly evident in its ground plan (Reims) and sculptures (Chartres).

Pinnacle

Gable: ornamental triangular feature with solid or ornamental decoration

Rose window

Gargoyle: projecting roof gutter normally carved in the shape of a grotesque animal

Buttress: a pillar built into a wall to reinforce those points subject to greatest stress

Tracery: decoration formed by geometric motifs, particularly used in rose windows and Gothic ogives

Flying buttress

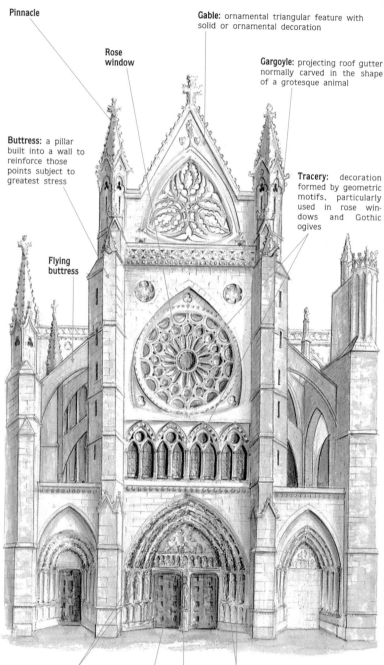

Pier: a vertical structure, often finely decorated, supporting a door or a wall

Archivolt: ornamental moulding on the outer edge of an arch

Tympanum

Mullion: a vertical feature which divides in two the opening or span of a portal or window

H. Cholmet

Plateresque

SALAMANCA – University: façade (16C)

Although the exuberant decoration used to cover the entire façade is somewhat Gothic in style, the motifs used are Classical.

Cresting: the ornamental ridge crowning an architectural work

Frieze: decorative horizontal band

Pilaster: pillar attached to the wall

Golden Fleece: an ornamental collar and symbol of the Order of the Golden Fleece often seen on the the the escutcheon of Charles V

Medallion: an oval or circular decorative relief moulding

Scallop shell: scallop-shaped moulding used as an ornamental feature

Escutcheon

Bust

Grotesque: decoration combining foliation, imaginary creatures and animals

Basket-handle arch

Renaissance

TOLEDO – Hospital Tavera: patio (16C)

The sense of proportion, visible on both the ground and first floors surrounding the double patio of this hospital, is a typical feature of pure Renaissance style.

Triglyph: three vertical bands separated by V-shaped grooves (characteristic of Doric frieze)

Spandrel or **pendentive** decorated with a rosette

Ionic column

Arris vault

Balustrade

Metope: the triglyphs alternate with plain or sculpted panels

Doric column

Superimposing of orders according to a **classical plan** (Doric on the lower gallery, Ionic on the upper gallery)

Base

Shaft

H. Cholmet

45

Baroque

MADRID – Museo Municipal (Antiguo Hospicio): portal (18C)

The Baroque retable or altarpiece, which reached new architectural heights in Spain, was created occasionally on the façade of a building, rather than inside it.

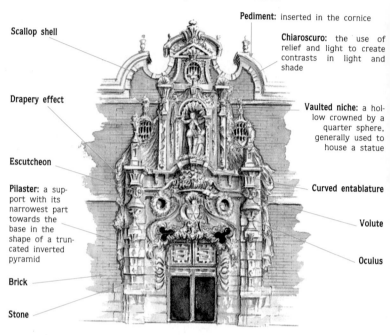

Scallop shell

Pediment: inserted in the cornice

Chiaroscuro: the use of relief and light to create contrasts in light and shade

Drapery effect

Vaulted niche: a hollow crowned by a quarter sphere, generally used to house a statue

Escutcheon

Pilaster: a support with its narrowest part towards the base in the shape of a truncated inverted pyramid

Curved entablature

Volute

Oculus

Brick

Stone

Neo-Classical

MADRID – Observatório Astronómico (18C)

This small building designed by Juan de Villanueva is a model of simplicity and purity which shows clear Palladian influence in its proportions and design.

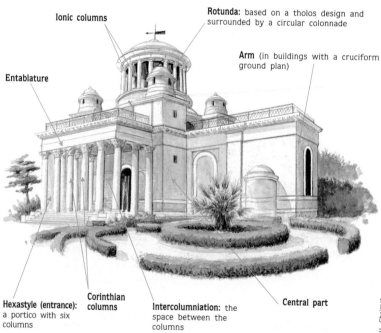

Ionic columns

Rotunda: based on a tholos design and surrounded by a circular colonnade

Arm (in buildings with a cruciform ground plan)

Entablature

Hexastyle (entrance): a portico with six columns

Corinthian columns

Intercolumniation: the space between the columns

Central part

H. Choimet

46

BARCELONA – Casa Batiló (Antoni Gaudí: 1905-1907)

Modernism is a colourful, decorative and sensual style which recreates organic forms in a world dominated by curves and reverse curves.

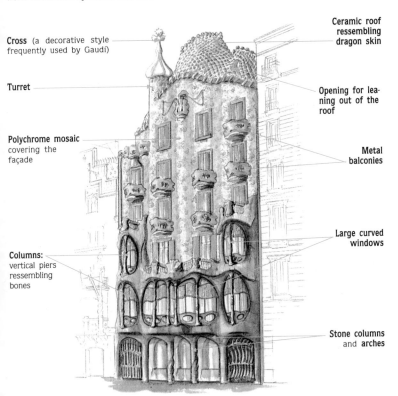

Cross (a decorative style frequently used by Gaudí)

Turret

Polychrome mosaic covering the façade

Columns: vertical piers ressembling bones

Ceramic roof ressembling dragon skin

Opening for leaning out of the roof

Metal balconies

Large curved windows

Stone columns and arches

BARCELONA – Fundació Joan Miró (JL Sert: 1972-1975)

The building consists of a series of inter-related architectural features and open spaces in which natural light plays a fundamental role.

Skylights

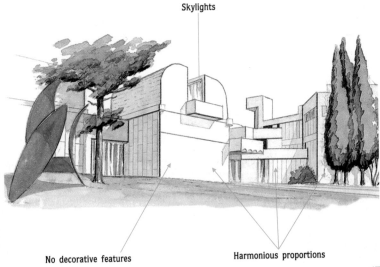

No decorative features

Harmonious proportions

H. Cholmet

ARCHITECTURAL TERMS

(Spanish words are printed in blue)

Ajimez: paired window or opening separated by a central column.

Alfarje: wooden ceiling, usually decorated, consisting of a board resting on cross beams (a feature of the Mudéjar style).

Alfiz: rectangular surround to a horseshoe-shaped arch in Muslim architecture.

Alicatado: section of wall or other surface covered with sheets of ceramic tiles *(azulejos)* cut in such a way as to form geometric patterns. Frequently used to decorate dados (a Mudéjar feature).

Aljibe: Arab word for cistern.

Altarpiece: also retable. Decorative screen above and behind the altar.

Apse: far end of a church housing the high altar; can be semicircular, polygonal or horseshoe.

Apsidal or radiating chapel: small chapel opening from the apse.

Arch: *See illustrations p 41.*

Archivolt: ornamental moulding on the outer edge of an arch.

Artesonado: marquetry ceiling in which raised fillets outline honeycomb-like cells in the shape of stars. This particular decoration, which first appeared under the Almohads, was popular throughout the country, including Christian Spain, in the 15C and 16C.

Ataurique: decorative plant motif on plaster or brick which was developed as a feature of the Caliphate style and was subsequently adopted by the Mudéjar.

Azulejos: glazed, patterned, ceramic tiles.

Barrel vaulting: vault with a semicircular cross-section.

Caliphate: the architectural style developed in Córdoba under the Caliphate (8C-11C) of which the finest example is the mosque in that town.

Churrigueresque: in the style of the Churrigueras, an 18C family of architects. Richly ornate Baroque decoration.

Estípite: pilaster in the shape of a truncated inverted pyramid.

Gargoyle: projecting roof gutter normally carved in the shape of a grotesque animal.

Groined vaulting: vault showing lines of intersection of two vaults or arches (usually pointed).

Grotesque: typical Renaissance decoration combining vegetation, imaginary beings and animals.

Kiblah: sacred wall of a mosque from which the *mihrab* is hollowed, facing towards Mecca.

H. Cholmet

Lacerías: geometric decoration formed by intersecting straight lines making star-shaped and polygonal figures. Characteristic of Moorish architecture.

Lombard bands: decorative pilaster strips typical of Romanesque architecture in Lombardy.

Lonja: commodity exchange building.

Mihrab: richly decorated prayer-niche in the sacred wall *(kiblah)* in a mosque.

Minaret: tower of the mosque *(mezquita)*, from which the muezzin calls the faithful to prayer.

Minbar: pulpit in a mosque.

Mocárabes: decorative motifs of Muslim architecture formed by assembled prisms ending in concave surfaces. They resemble stalactites or pendants and adorn vaults and cornices.

Mozarabic: the work of Christians living under Arab rule after the Moorish invasion of 711. On being persecuted in the 9C, they sought refuge in Christian areas bringing with them Moorish artistic traditions.

Mudéjar: the work of Muslims living in Christian territory following the Reconquest (13C-14C).

Naveta: megalithic monument found in the Balearic Islands, which has a pyramidal shape with a rectangular base, giving the appearance of an upturned boat.

Plateresque: term derived from *platero* (ie silversmith); used to describe the early style of the Renaissance characterised by finely carved decoration.

H. Cholmet

Predella: the lower part of an altarpiece.

Sebka: type of brick decoration developed under the Almohads consisting of an apparently endless series of small arches forming a network of diamond shapes.

Seo or **seu**: cathedral.

Soportales: porticoes of wood or stone pillars supporting the first floor of houses. They form an open gallery around the *plaza mayor* of towns and villages.

Star vault: vault with a square or polygonal plan formed by several intersecting arches.

Stucco: type of moulding mix consisting mainly of plaster, used for coating surfaces. It plays a fundamental role in wall decoration in Hispano-Muslim architecture.

H. Cholmet

Talayot: megalithic monument found in the Balearic Islands, which takes the form of a truncated cone of stones.

Taula (*mesa* in the Mallorcan language): megalithic monument found in the Balearic Islands, which consists of a monolithic horizontal stone block placed on top of a similar vertical stone block.

Triforium: arcade above the side aisles which opens onto the central nave of a church.

Tympanum: inner surface of a pediment. This often ornamented space is bounded by the archivolt and the lintel of the doors of churches.

Venera: scallop-shaped moulding frequently used as an ornamental feature. It is the symbol of pilgrimages to Santiago de Compostela.

Yesería: plasterwork used in sculptured decoration.

Plan and furnishings of a Spanish church

The following are Spanish architectural terms and their translations used in the guide. Some words like coro *are kept in the original Spanish as there is no equivalent in English.*

Cabecera: the east or apsidal end of a church.

Camarín: a small chapel on the first floor behind the altarpiece or retable. It is plushly decorated and very often contains a lavishly costumed statue of the Virgin Mary.

Capilla Mayor: the area of the high altar containing the retablo mayor or monumental altarpiece which often rises to the roof.

Coro: a chancel in Spanish canonical churches often built in the middle of the nave. It contains the stalls *(sillería)* used by members of religious orders. When placed in a tribune or gallery it is known as the **coro alto**.

Crucero: transept. The part of a church at right angles to the nave which gives the church the shape of a cross. It consists of the transept crossing and arms.

Girola (also *deambulatorio*): ambulatory. An extension to the aisles forming a gallery around the chancel and behind the altar.

Presbiterio: the space in front of the altar. (The presbytery is known as the *casa del cura*).

Púlpito: pulpit.

Sagrario: chapel containing the Holy Sacrament. May sometimes be a separate church.

Sillería: the stalls.

Trasaltar: back wall of the *capilla mayor* in front of which there are frequently sculptures or tombs.

Trascoro: the wall, often carved and decorated, which encloses the *coro.*

Consult the Places to Stay map at the beginning of this guide to select the a stopover or holiday destination. The map offers the following categories:
  Short holidays
  Weekend breaks
  Overnight stops
  Resorts

Depending on the region, this map also shows marinas, ski areas, spas, centres for mountain expeditions, etc.

THE GARDENS OF SPAIN

Spanish gardens are proof of the country's cultural wealth and its ability to adapt to its varied climate. Spanish landscape gardening has inherited a great European tradition, which itself has its origins in Greco-Roman culture. In Spain, this tradition was substantially enriched during the period of Moorish occupation.

The Generalife (14C) Granada

The Moors were truly gifted gardeners. The Generalife is *the* Moorish garden par excellence, despite the alterations it has undergone over the centuries. As a result of its extraordinary position it is a magnificent balcony, but above all it has been able to preserve an intimate, sensual character which was such a feature of Muslim gardens.

A Moorish garden is always an evocation of paradise; it is a feast for the senses and a harmonious whole which avoids grandiloquence. Nothing has been left to chance: the colour of the plants and flowers, their scent, and the omnipresence of water combine to create a serene ambience full of intimate charm.

The Generalife has been laid out on several levels to ensure that the trees in one garden do not interfere with the views from another. In fact, the Generalife is a series of landscaped areas and enclosures each with its own individuality yet part of an overall design. The garden's architectural features and vegetation, reflected in the water channels, blend together to create a perfect whole.

J.Helsing/STOCK PHOTOS

La Granja (18C) -La Granja de San Ildefonso- Segovia

Once he came to the Spanish throne, Philip V, the grandson of Louis XIV, chose a beautiful spot in the Segovian countryside at the foot of the Sierra de Guadarrama to create these magnificent Baroque gardens. They bring to mind those of Versailles, where the monarch spent his childhood. Philip V was to make La Granja his personal retreat.

Although the Versailles influence is clearly evident, the differences are also obvious. Because of its position, hemmed in by the mountains, the grandiose perspectives of Versailles are not to be found at La Granja. The rigidity of the French garden is also lost here as there is no clear central axis; instead, La Granja consists of a succession of parts each with a certain independence, thus adopting hints of Moorish design. Although the gardeners brought with them a variety of species from France, they were able to adapt perfectly to the features of the local landscape and to preserve the somewhat wild appearance which gives it an undoubted charm. Magnificent fountains and sculptures scattered in small squares and along avenues add a theatrical touch.

Pazo de Oca (18-19C) - La Estrada- La Coruña

A *pazo* is a Baroque-style manor typically found in Galicia. These large rustic residences are built on plots of land which generally comprise a recreational garden, a kitchen garden and cultivated farmland.

The Pazo de Oca garden, the oldest in Galicia, is a magnificent example of a garden in the wet part of Spain. What comes as a complete surprise is its perfect integration into its surroundings, where the damp climate has enabled vegetation to grow on rocks, creating an intimate relationship between its architectural and vegetal features. Water plays a vital role, appearing in basins, fountains or trickling through the garden. The most attractive part, with its two ponds, is hidden behind a parterre. A delightful bridge with benches enabling visitors to enjoy this enchanting spot separates the two sections, overcoming the difference in height between them. The lower pond contains the *pazo*'s most representative and famous feature: the stone boat, with its two petrified sailors, planted with hydrangeas.

The combination of both climate and vegetation gives the site an unquestionably romantic air.

A.de la Rosa

Jardín Botánico de Marimurtra (20C) -Blanes- Gerona

Carlos Faust, the German impresario who settled on the Costa Brava, created this botanical garden in 1921 for research purposes to enable scientists to carry out studies on flora, and to catalogue and preserve plants threatened with extinction. It is situated in a delightful spot between the sea and the mountains and offers visitors magnificent views of the coast.

Marimurtra is a fine example of a contemporary Mediterranean garden, although a number of exotic species from every continent have also adapted perfectly here. It contains an interesting cactus garden, an impressive aquatic garden, as well as a collection of medicinal, toxic and aromatic plants. The scientific aims of the garden have not interfered in any way with the aesthetic direction it has taken. The only architectural feature with a purely decorative function is the small temple built at the end of the steps running down to the sea.

At present, only a third of Marimurtra is open to the public.

F.Bouillot/MARCO POLO

Literature

Roman Spain produced great Latin authors such as **Seneca the Elder** or the Rhetorician, his son **Seneca the Younger** or the Philosopher, Quintilian, the satirist Martial and the epic poet **Lucan**. In the 8C, the monk Beatus wrote the Commentary on the Apocalypse which gave rise to a series of outstanding illuminated manuscripts known as **Beatus**. Arab writers won renown during the same period. Works written in Castilian began to emerge only in the Middle Ages.

Monasterio de El Escorial/H. Stierlin

A Beatus illuminated manuscript
(in the Monasterio de El Escorial)

The Middle Ages – The Reconquest provided material for epic poems, tales of adventure recited by wandering minstrels. In the 12C, the first milestone of Spanish literature appeared in the form of *El Cantar del Mío Cid*, an anonymous Castilian poem inspired by the adventures of **El Cid**. In the 13C, the monk **Gonzalo de Berceo**, drawing on religious themes, won renown through his works of *Mester de Clerecía*, the learned poetry of clerics and scholars. **Alfonso X, the Wise**, an erudite king who wrote poetry in Galician, decreed that in his kingdom, Latin should be replaced as the official language by Castilian, an act subsequently followed throughout Spain except in Catalunya where Catalan remained the written language. In the 14C, **Don Juan Manuel** introduced the use of narrative prose in his moral tales while Juan Ruiz, **Archpriest of Hita**, wrote a brilliant satirical verse work entitled *El Libro de Buen Amor*, which later influenced the picaresque novel.

The Renaissance – In the 15C, lyric poetry flourished under Italian influence with poets such as **Jorge Manrique** and the **Marquis of Santillana**. **Romanceros**, collections of ballads in an epic or popular vein, perpetuated the medieval style until the 16C when *Amadís de Gaula* (1508) set the model for a great many romances or tales of chivalry. In 1499, *La Celestina*, a novel of passion in dialogue form by Fernando de Rojas, anticipated modern drama in a subtle, well-observed tragicomic intrigue.

The Golden Age (Siglo de Oro) – Spain enjoyed its greatest literary flowering under the Habsburgs (1516-1700), with great lyric poets such as **Garcilaso de la Vega**, disciple of Italian verse forms, **Fray Luis de León** and above all **Luis de Góngora** (1561-1627) whose obscure, precious style won fame under the name Gongorism. Pastoral novels became popular with works by Cervantes and Lope de Vega. The **picaresque** novel, however, was the genre favoured by Spanish writers at the time. The first to appear in 1554 was *Lazarillo de Tormes*, an anonymous autobiographical work in which the hero, an astute rogue (*pícaro* in Castilian), casts a mischievous and impartial eye on society and its woes. There followed Mateo Alemán's *Guzmán de Alfarache* with its brisk style and colourful vocabulary, and *La Vida del Buscón*, an example of the varied talents of **Francisco de Quevedo** (1580-1645), essayist, poet and satirist. The genius of the Golden Age, however, was **Cervantes** (1547-1616), with his masterpiece, the universal **Don Quixote** (1605). Lope de Rueda paved the way for *comedia*, which emerged at the end of the 16C. Dramatists proliferated, among them the master **Lope de Vega** (1562-1635), who perfected and enriched the art form. This "phoenix of the mind" wrote more than 1 000 plays on the most diverse subjects. His successor, **Calderón de la Barca** (1600-81), wrote historical and philosophical plays (*La vida es sueño* or *Life's a Dream* and *El alcalde de Zalamea* or *The Mayor of Zalamea*) in which he brilliantly reflects the mood of Spain in the 17C. **Tirso de Molina** (1583-1648) left his interpretation of Don Juan for posterity while **Guillén de Castro** wrote *Las Mocedades del Cid* (youthful adventures of the Cid). Mention should also be made of works on the conquest of America by **Cortés** and **Bartolomé de las Casas** among others. Finally, the moralist **Fray Luis de Granada** and the mystics **Santa Teresa de Ávila** (1515-82) and **San Juan de la Cruz** (St John of the Cross) (1542-91) wrote theological works.

18C and 19C – The critical mode found expression in the works of essayists such as **Benito Jerónimo Feijóo** and **Jovellanos**, also a poet. Elegance dominated the plays of **Moratín**, while Ramón de la Cruz delighted audiences with his *sainetes*, or satiric comic interludes. The great romantic poet of the 19C was **Bécquer** (1836-70) from Sevilla, while **Larra** was a social satirist, **Menéndez Pelayo** a literary critic and **Ángel Ganivet** a political and moral analyst. Realism was introduced to the Spanish novel by **Alarcón** (*The Three-Cornered Hat*) and **Pereda** (*Peñas arriba*) who concentrated on regional themes. By the end of the 19C, the best realist was **Pérez Galdós** whose prolific, lively work (*National Episodes*) is stamped with a great sense of human sympathy.

20C – A group of intellectuals known as the Generation of '98' saddened by Spain's loss of colonies like Cuba, pondered over the future and character of their country and, more generally, the problems of human destiny. The atmosphere was reflected in the work of essayists such as **Miguel de Unamuno** (1864-1936) who wrote *El sentimiento trágico de la vida (The Tragic Sense of Life)*, and **Azorín**, as well as the philologist **Menéndez Pidal**, the novelist **Pío Baroja** and the aesthete **Valle Inclán**, who created an elegant poetic prose style. Among their contemporaries were **Jacinto Benavente** (winner of the 1922 Nobel Prize for literature), who developed a new dramatic style, and the novelist **Vicente Blasco Ibáñez**. Henceforth Spain opened up to literary contributions from abroad. Some great poets began to emerge, including **Juan Ramón Jiménez** (Nobel Prize 1956), who expressed his feelings through simple unadorned prose poems *(Platero y yo)*, **Antonio Machado** (1875-1939) the bard of Castilla, and **Rafael Alberti**. **Federico García Lorca** (1898-1936) equally great as both poet and dramatist *(Bodas de sangre)*, was Andalusian through and through. His work was, perhaps, the most fascinating reflection of a Spain whose mystery **Ortega y Gasset** (1883-1925), essayist and philosopher, spent his life trying to fathom.

Post-war writing – Several years after the Civil War, writing rose from its ashes with works by essayists (Américo Castro), playwrights (Alfonso Sastre) and above all, novelists such as **Miguel Delibes**, **Camilo José Cela** (*La familia de Pascual Duarte*) who won the Nobel Prize for Literature in 1989, **Juan Goytisolo**, **Ramón Sender** and Antonio Ferres, all preoccupied with social issues.

Among contemporary authors, mention should be made of novelists Juan Benet, Juan Marsé, **Manuel Vázquez Montalbán**, Terenci Moix, Javier Marías and **Eduardo Mendoza**, and playwrights Antonio Gala, Fernando Arrabal and Francisco Nieva.

In conclusion, the Spanish-speaking countries of Latin America are making enormous contributions to Spanish literature with works by Jorge Luis Borges, Gabriel García Márquez, Pablo Neruda and Miguel Ángel Asturias.

Music

Alongside its impressive wealth of folk music, Spain has developed an extraordinarily rich musical repertory since the Middle Ages, marked by a large number of influences including Visigothic, Arabic, Mozarabic and French. Polyphonic chants were studied in the 11C and the oldest known piece for three voices, the *Codex calixtinus*, was composed at Santiago de Compostela c 1140. During the Reconquest, bishops in towns recaptured by Christians encouraged great musical creativity in the form of liturgical chants, church plays *(autos)* like the *Elche Mystery* which is still performed today, and poetry like the 13C **Cantigas de Santa María** by Alfonso the Wise. As music was intimately linked with religion, it retained its sacred character for centuries. At the end of the 15C, the dramatist **Juan de la Encina** composed secular songs thus proving that he was also an excellent musician. Music, like the other arts, however, reached its climax in the second half of the 16C, under the protection of the early Habsburgs. **Victoria** (1548-1611) was one of the most famous composers of polyphonic devotional pieces, while among his contemporaries, **Francisco de Salinas** and **Fernando de las Infantas** were learned musicologists and **Cristóbal de Morales** and **Francisco Guerrero** were accomplished religious composers. As for instruments, the organ became the invariable accompaniment to sacred music, while a favourite for profane airs was the *vihuela*, a sort of guitar with six double strings which was soon replaced by the lute and eventually by the five-string Spanish guitar. In 1629, Lope de Vega wrote the text for the first Spanish opera. **Pedro Calderón de la Barca** is credited with creating the **zarzuela** (1648), a musical play with spoken passages, songs and dances, which, since the 19C, has based its plot and music on popular themes. The major composer of religious and secular music in the 18C was Padre **Antonio Soler**, a great harpsichord player.

In the 19C, the Catalan **Felipe Pedrell** brought Spanish music onto a higher plane and opened the way for a new generation of musicians. He was a prolific composer, the first to combine traditional tunes with classical genres. At the beginning of the century, while works by French composers (Ravel's *Bolero*, Bizet's *Carmen*, Lalo's *Symphonie Espagnole* and Chabrier's *España*) bore a pronounced Hispanic stamp, Spanish composers turned to national folklore and traditional themes: **Isaac Albéniz** (1860-1909) wrote *Iberia*, **Enrique Granados** (1867-1916) became famous for his *Goyescas* and **Joaquín Turina** (1888-1949) for his *Sevilla Symphony*. This popular vein culminated in works by **Manuel de Falla** (1876-1946) including *Nights in the Gardens of Spain*, *El amor brujo* and *The Three-Cornered Hat*.

Among the best-known classical guitar players of our day, **Andrés Segovia** (1894-1987), **Joaquín Rodrigo** (b 1902), famous for his *Concierto de Aranjuez*, and **Narciso Yepes** (b 1927), have shown that this most Spanish of instruments can interpret a wide variety of music. Another Spaniard, **Pablo Casals** (1876-1973), was possibly the greatest cellist of all time. Spain holds a leading position in the world of opera with singers such as Victoria de los Ángeles, Montserrat Caballé, Plácido Domingo, Alfredo Kraus, José Carreras and Teresa Berganza.

Cinema

Spanish cinema dates back to a short film in 1897 which shows people leaving the Basílica de Nuestra Señora del Pilar in Zaragoza after Mass. Studios for silent movies were later set up in Barcelona.

In the 1920s, several Surrealists tried their hand at the new art form. Among them were **Dalí** and above all **Buñuel**, the master of Spanish cinema, who made *Un chien Andalou* (*Un perro andaluz*) in 1928 and *L'Age d'Or* (*La edad de oro*) in 1930. When talking films appeared in the 1930s, Spain was in the throes of a political and economic crisis and so her studios lacked the means to procure the necessary equipment.

At the end of the 1930s, when films like *Sister Angelica* (*Sor Angélica*) by Gargallo tended to address religious themes, Juan Piqueras launched a magazine called *Nuestro Cinema* which was strongly influenced by Russian ideas and gave star billing to films which could almost have been qualified as propaganda. One of these, *Las Hurdes – Land without Bread* (*Las Hurdes – Tierra sin pan*, 1932) by Buñuel, showed poverty in a remote part of Spain.

During the Civil War and the ensuing Franco era, films were heavily censored and the cinema became one of the major vehicles for the ideology of the time, with historical and religious themes glorifying death and the spirit of sacrifice. One such success was *Marcelino, Bread and Wine* (*Marcelino, pan y vino*, 1955) by Ladislao Vajda. Change came with works by **Juan Antonio Bardem** like *Death of a Cyclist* (*Muerte de un ciclista*, 1955) and with **Berlanga**'s *Welcome Mr Marshall* (*Bienvenido, Mr Marshall*, 1953) and *The Executioner* (*El verdugo*, 1964).

The 1960s enjoyed a period of renewal with directors like **Carlos Saura**, whose first film, *The Scoundrels* (*Los golfos*), came out in 1959. More than ever before, the 1970s saw a new wave in Spanish cinema with outstanding directors and films. These were mainly concerned with the problems of childhood and youth marked by the Franco régime. Saura's *Ana and the Wolves* (*Ana y los lobos*, 1973) shows a young girl arriving as an outsider in a family in which three 50-year-old brothers personify the all-powerful hold of the army and religion during the Franco era. Mention should also be made of *Cría* (*Cría cuervos*, 1975) also by Saura, *The Spirit of the Beehive* (*El espíritu de la colmena*, 1973) and *The South* (*El sur*, 1983) by **Víctor Erice**, *The Beehive* (*La colmena*, 1982) by **Mario Camus**, and films by **Manuel Gutiérrez Aragón** such as *Demons in the Garden* (*Demonios en el jardín*, 1982) and *The Other Half of Heaven* (*La Otra mitad del cielo*, 1986) which illustrate the economic changes between Spain under Franco and Spain as a democracy. **Pedro Almodóvar** breaks with this serious, nostalgic type of cinema so critical of the Franco era. His films are of a completely different, modern Spain in which the *Movida* (a fashionable, progressive anti-establishment movement in the arts during the 1980s) in Madrid is shown in a comic light, as in *Women on the Edge of a Nervous Breakdown* (*Mujeres al borde de un ataque de nervios*, 1988).

Collection Cahiers du Cinéma, Paris

Death of a Cyclist by Juan Antonio Bardem

Two Spanish films have won an Oscar for Best Foreign Film: *Volver a empezar*, directed by **JL Garci** (1983), and **F Trueba**'s *Belle Epoque* (1993). The last five years have seen a resurgence in Spanish cinema with young directors such as **Alejandro Amenabar** (*Tesis*, 1996) and **Alex de la Iglesia** (*El día de la bestia*, 1995). This development has resulted in huge box office successes which were previously the exclusive territory of large-scale Hollywood productions. These include *El perro del hortelano* (1996) by the late **Pilar Miró**, and *Secretos del corazón* (1997) by **Montxo Armendáriz**. Other successful films of recent years include *La buena estrella* (1997) by **Ricardo Franco** and *Barrio* (1998) by **Fernando León de Aranoa**.

The chapter on art and architecture in this guide gives an outline of artistic creation in the region, providing the context of the buildings and works of art described in the Sights section.

This chapter may also provide ideas for touring.

It is advisable to read it at leisure/before setting out.

Handicrafts

Spain has always had a rich tradition of arts and crafts reflecting the character of each region as well as the influence of the various civilizations – Iberian, Roman, Visigothic, and Muslim – that have marked the country's history. Traditional wares such as pottery, ceramics, basketwork and woven goods are produced countrywide.

Ceramics and pottery – The variety and quality of these crafts give them pride of place in Spain. In Castilla, pottery is mainly made by women who use a primitive technique. Among their specialities are kitchen utensils, jars and water pitchers. The basic items of crockery used in farmhouses – dishes, soup tureens and bowls made of glazed earthenware *(barro cocido)* – appear in villages and on stalls in every market. The technique, patterns and colours of ceramics in many parts of Spain have been influenced by Islamic art. There are two large pottery centres in the Toledo region. The first, **Talavera de la Reina** is famous for its blue, green, yellow, orange and black ceramics while the second, **El Puente del Arzobispo**, mainly uses shades of green. Pottery from **La Bisbal d'Empordà** in Catalunya has a yellow background with green decorative motifs. The Mudéjar tradition is evident in Aragón and the Levante region where blue and white pottery is made in **Muel**, green and purple ceramics in **Teruel** and lustreware in **Manises** (Valencia). Most of the figurines used as decoration for cribs at Christmas are produced in **Murcia**. Spain's richest pottery region is Andalucía with workshops in **Granada** (glazed ceramics with thick green and blue strokes), **Guadix** (red crockery), **Triana** in Sevilla (polychrome animal figures, glazed and decorated), **Úbeda, Andújar** (jars with cobalt blue patterns) and in **Vera** (white pottery with undulating shapes). In Galicia, porcelain and earthenware goods with contemporary shapes and designs are factory-made at the **Sargadelos** centre in the province of La Coruña, but there is also a craft industry at **Niñodaguia** in Orense (where the yellow glaze only partially covers the pottery) and at **Bruño** (where yellow motifs set off a dark brown background). Mention should be made of the famous *Xiurels* whistles decorated in red and green in the Balearic Islands.

Lace, woven and embroidered goods – The textile industry was very prosperous under the Muslims and several workshops still thrive today. Brightly coloured blankets and carpets are woven in the Alpujarras region, la Rioja, the area around Cádiz (**Grazalema**) and at **Níjar** near Almería (where *tela de trapo* carpets are made from strips of cloth). Blankets from Zamora, Palencia and Salamanca are well known. In some villages in the province of Ciudad Real (particularly in **Almagro**) women lacemakers may still be seen at work in their doorways with bobbins and needles. Lacework from **Camariñas** in Galicia is also famous. The most popular craft, however, is embroidery, often done in the family. The most typical, geometrically patterned embroideries come from the Toledo region (**Lagartera** and **Oropesa**). Embroidery has been raised to the level of a veritable art in two thoroughly Spanish domains: firstly, in the ornaments used for *pasos* during Holy Week and secondly in bullfighters' costumes.

Gold, silver and ironwork – Iron forging, a very old practice in Spain, has produced some outstanding works of art like the wrought-iron grilles and screens that adorn many of the country's churches. Blacksmiths continue to make the grilles for doors and windows so popular in architecture in the south of Spain (La Mancha, Extremadura and Andalucía).
Copper smelting continues to this day at **Guadalupe** in Extremadura where pots, boilers, braziers and stills are made. Damascene weapons (steel inlaid with gold, silver and copper) are still being produced today, in **Eibar** (País Vasco) and in **Toledo** particularly, according to pure Islamic tradition. Traditional knife-making is centred around **Albacete**.

Ceramic tiles from Talavera de la Reina

B. Brillion/MICHELIN

Gold and silver smithing, of which outstanding treasures may be seen in Spain's archeological museums, was developed in Antiquity and throughout the Visigothic period and has retained some of its traditional methods. An example is filigree ornamentation (soldered, intertwined gold and silver threads) crafted in **Córdoba** and **Toledo**. Salamanca, Cáceres and Ciudad Rodrigo specialise in gold jewellery.

Leather goods – Leather-making has always been an important trade, especially in Andalucía, and has become industrialised in some areas. (Fine leather goods and shoes are made in Andalucía, in the Alicante area and in the Islas Baleares). The production of the famous **Córdoba** leather *(guadameciles)*, embossed polychrome leatherwork which was once highly prized throughout Europe, has retained its craft status.

Typically Spanish gourds and wineskin containers are made in the provinces of Bilbao, Pamplona and Burgos and in other wine-growing areas.

Basketwork – Basket-making remains one of the most representative of Spanish crafts. Although carried out countrywide, it is particularly rich on the Mediterranean coast and in the Balearic Islands.

The type of product and the material used vary from region to region. Baskets, hats and mats are made of reeds, willow, esparto grass, strips of olive-wood and birch and chestnut bark, while furniture may be rush or wickerwork. Willow is used in Andalucía and in the Levante, hazel and chestnut in Galicia and in the Asturias, and straw and esparto grass on the island of Ibiza.

Tradition and folklore

The main festivals in Spain are listed in the Calendar of events at the end of the guide.

A DEEPLY RELIGIOUS COUNTRY

The people's deeply-rooted Catholic faith and their ability to express their feelings freely, combined with their love of spectacle and devotion to traditional ceremonies make religious festivals in Spain incredibly splendid occasions. Festivities vary according to the region – bucolic in Galicia, exuberant in Andalucía, reserved in Castilla – and are generally mixed with local folklore and purely profane rejoicings. Epiphany, Corpus Christi and Holy Week are celebrated throughout the country while each town and region also has its own saint's day. The main festivals take the form of processions and *romerías*.

Romerías – These are pilgrimages made to an isolated shrine or hermitage by a procession of people grouped in brotherhoods or guilds or by town quarter or even whole villages. Most *romerías* are to chapels of the Virgin famous for their statues, which are usually held in deep veneration. The best-known are those of Pilar (Zaragoza), Guadalupe, Montserrat and Rocío.

Pilgrims may dress in local costume and sing folksongs along the way. A *romería* is a good opportunity to get together, picnic and dance. Some *romerías* in the northern *rías* take place at sea, on boats bedecked with flowers.

Processions – Every religious occasion, whether it is an important Christian festival or the feast day of a local saint, is accompanied by a procession. **Semana Santa** (Holy Week) is without doubt the festival which inspires the most fervent display of devotion throughout Spain. It begins on Palm Sunday with the blessing of palm fronds followed by demonstrations of mourning. Rich church ornaments are veiled in black while processions of **pasos** or floats bearing groups of lifesize wooden statues illustrate the different stages of the Passion. The most spectacular of these slow solemn processions is that of Sevilla with its hooded penitents. In Catalunya, the villagers themselves act out the scenes of the Passion. Among other major religious festivals are the processions of **Nuestra Señora de Monte Carmel**, patron saint of sailors, and of **Corpus Christi** when streets are carpeted with flower petals and the Holy Sacrament is carried inside a gold or silver monstrance.

Ferias – *Ferias* or agricultural fairs, often held in conjunction with religious festivals, are very popular events, especially in Andalucía. Those of Sevilla and Jerez de la Frontera attract large crowds in Andalusian costume.

REGIONAL TRADITIONS AND FOLKLORE

Andalucía – The **flamenco**, derived from gypsy and Arab sources, is a befitting expression of the Andalusian soul. It is based on the *cante jondo* or deep song which describes the performer's profound emotions in ancient poetic phrases. The rhythm is given by hand-claps, heel-clicks and castanets. The **sevillana**, from Sevilla, is a more popular type of dance. Sevilla and Málaga are the best places to see **tablaos** or performances of Andalusian music. Flamenco and Sevillana owe much of their grace to the Andalusian costume of brilliantly coloured flounced dresses for women and close-fitting short jacketed suits, wide flat hats and heeled boots for men.

The Castells forming a human pyramid in Valls

Aragón – No general rejoicing here goes without a *jota*, a bounding, leaping dance in which couples hop and whirl to the tunes of a *rondalla* (group of stringed instruments), stopping only for the occasional brief singing of a *copla* by a soloist.

Catalunya and the Comunidad valenciana – The **sardana** dance is still very popular in Catalunya where it is performed in a circle in main squares on Sundays. The **Castells**, who form daring human pyramids, may be seen in festivals at El Vendrell and Valls.

In the Levante, the rich local costume notable for its colour and intricate embroidery is worn during lively, colourful festivals. Valencia's **Fallas** in March are a veritable institution which Alicante's **Fogueres** try to rival. The citizens indulge their taste for decoration, parody and exuberance by making giant pasteboard figures, which are set alight amid noisy rejoicings and fireworks displays. Lastly, the *Moros y Cristianos* festivals – those of Alcoy are the best-known – give a colourful replay of the confrontations between Moors and Christians during the Reconquest.

The Cantabrian coast and Galicia – *Romerías* in Asturias and Galicia are always accompanied by the shrill tones of the **gaita**, a type of bagpipe, and sometimes by drums and castanets. The *gaita* is played during events in honour of cowherds, shepherds, sailors and others who work in the country's oldest occupations. The most typical festivals are those held in summer for *vaqueiros* or cowherds in Aristébano and others for shepherds near the Lago de Enol. Common dances in Galicia include the *muñeira* or dance of the miller's wife, the sword dance performed only by men, and the *redondela*.

Bowls (*bolos*) is a very popular game.

País Vasco and Navarra – These regions have preserved many of their unusual traditions. Men dressed in white with red belts and the famous red berets dance in a ring accompanied by **zortzicos** (songs), a **txistu** (flute) and a *tamboril*. The most solemn dance, the *aurresku*, is a chain dance performed by men after Mass on Sundays. The **espata-dantza** or sword dance recalls warrior times while others, like the spinners' dance or another in which brooms are used, represent daily tasks. The

Basques love contests, such as trunk cutting, stone lifting and pole throwing. But by far the most popular sport is *pelota*, played in different ways: with a **chistera** or wickerwork scoop, or with the very similar **cesta punta** in an enclosed three-walled court *(jai alai)*, or with a wooden bat or *pala* or, finally, simply with the hand, **a mano**. There is a famous Pelota university at Markina in Vizcaya.

The most important festival in Navarra is the **Sanfermines**, or bull-running, held in Pamplona.

Castilla – Few regions in Spain are as mystical or have as sober customs as Castilla. Traditional dances include the **seguidilla** and the **paloteo**, also known as the **danza de palos**, which is accompanied by flute, tambourine, and sometimes by a bass drum or the most typical of Castilian instruments, the local reed-pipe or **dulzaina**. Peasant costumes around Salamanca are richly embroidered with precious stones, silk thread and sequins.

Islas Baleares – Mallorca's traditional dances include the *copeo*, the *jota*, the *mateixes* and the *bolero*. Dances and festivals are accompanied by a *xeremía* (local bagpipes) and a tambourine. In Menorca, a festival dating back to medieval times and calling for about 100 horsemen in elegant costumes, is held at Ciutadella on Midsummer's Day. Popular dances in Ibiza have a poetical accompaniment to guide the performers' movements.

BULLFIGHTING

The bullfight was performed on horseback from the Middle Ages to the 18C. It subsequently became a popular form of entertainment and was carried out on foot. Present-day rules governing bullfighting were established during the 18C and 19C by the **Romero** family and the *toreros* **Costillares**, **Francisco Montes "Paquiro"** and **Juan Belmonte** (1892-1962). **Pepe Hillo** (1754-1801) created the spontaneous, graceful Sevillian style which contrasts with the solemnity and sobriety of that of Ronda. He was succeeded by the Córdobans **Lagartijo** (1841-1900), **Guerrita** (1862-1941), **Joselito** (1895-1920), **Manolete** (1917-47) and **El Cordobés**.

The stock – Bulls are reared in almost total freedom on properties in Andalucía and in Castilla between Salamanca and Ciudad Rodrigo. When they are about two years old, their fighting ability is judged during a **tienta**, or test of bravery. Each stock farm acquires its own qualities which are analysed by connoisseurs or **aficionados**.

The corrida – The programme starts at 5pm and is made up two kills each by three *matadores* (matadors). The six 4-year-old bulls each weigh around 450kg/992lb. The action begins, to the tune of a *paso doble*, with the **paseo** or grand entry led by two mounted *alguazils* (servants of the *corrida* president) in 17C costume. These are followed by the *toreros* or ring contestants: the three matadors, each in what is known as his costume of lights, leading his *cuadrilla* or team. The contests **(lidias)** are divided into three acts **(tercios)**, marked by trumpet calls. As the action unfolds, the matador should progressively gain domination over the bull.

1: Arrival and appraisal of the bull – The peones attract the bull's attention with the aid of a cape. The matador enters and plays his wide pink cape in front of the bull to make it turn swiftly so that he can judge its behaviour. This exercise comprises various formal figures including the famous *verónica* pass. Next the *picadores* on their padded, caparisoned horses, wait with pikes for the bull to charge and thrust their weapons into its withers.

Like a red rag to a bull...

This saying reflects the commonly held belief that it is the colour of the matador's cape which enrages the bull. However, since bulls are almost certainly colour-blind, it is the repeated, sudden movements as the matador plays his cape which disorientate the bull and work it into a rage. The brightly coloured capes used in the bullring are more likely to be for the benefit of the onlookers, particularly those without ringside seats!

2: The banderillas – To allow the bull to regain its wind and to rouse it further, the *banderilleros* thrust beribboned darts *(banderillas)* into the back of its neck.

3: The kill – Deft work with the *muleta*, a red serge cloth bound to a stick which is smaller and easier to handle than the cape, opens the last act. After saluting the president and dedicating the bull to a particular person or to the crowd, the *matador* with his sword in his right hand and the *muleta* in his left, attracts the attention of the bull. He controls it through a series of passes which, by their elegance and daring, may win him triumphant applause.

Playing the cape

At the final *estocada* stage, the bull stands still. The *matador* advances, his sword straight before him, and aiming between the shoulder blades thrusts to the bull's heart as his body brushes the right horn of the animal still fascinated by the *muleta*. If the *matador* has fought well, he may be awarded one or both of the bull's ears and sometimes also its tail.

Other types of fight – **Capeas** are popular festivals during which young amateurs match their skills against bulls in village squares, as at the well-known Ciudad Rodrigo contests. At **novilladas**, young 3-year-old bulls or *novillos* are fought by apprentice bullfighters known as *novilleros*. A **rejoneador** is a mounted bullfighter who takes part in the traditional three-act *corrida*.

Food and wine

Spanish food is distinctively Mediterranean: it is cooked with an olive oil base, seasoned with aromatic herbs and spiced with hot peppers. It nevertheless varies enormously from region to region. Among dishes served throughout the country are garlic soup, **cocido** or a type of stew accompanied by beans in the north and by chick-peas in the south, omelettes with potatoes, like the famous **tortilla**, typical pork meats like **chorizo** (a kind of spicy sausage) and delicious lean *serrano* hams. Fish and seafood are also used in a great many dishes.

No description of Spanish food should be complete without mentioning the ubiquitous **tapas**, the hors d'œuvres which appear on the counters of most bars and cafés just before lunch and dinner. This often vast array of colourful appetizers comes in two different forms, *tapas* (small saucer-size amounts) or *raciones*, more substantial portions. A selection of two or three *tapas* or one or two *raciones* makes for a very pleasant lunch accompanied by a glass of draught beer (*caña*).

Northern regions – **Galicia's** cuisine owes its delicacy to the quality of its seafood: octopus, hake, gilt-head, scallops (*vieiras*), mussels (*mejillones*), goose-barnacles (*percebes*), prawns (*gambas*), king prawns (*langostinos*) and mantis shrimps (*cigalas*). There is also **el caldo gallego**, a local stew, **lacón con grelos** (hand of pork with turnip tops) and another common traditional recipe, **pulpo gallego** (Galician-style octopus), often served as a *tapa* or *ración*. All these dishes may be accompanied by local wines such as red or white Ribeiro or white Albariño.

In **Asturias** fish and seafood are also important but the main speciality is a casserole dish called **fabada** made with white beans, pork, bacon and spicy sausages. As far as cakes and pastries are concerned, mention should be made of **sobaos**, delicious biscuits which originated in Cantabria and are cooked in oil. Cider is often drunk at meals.

Cooking in the **País Vasco** (Basque country) has been raised to the level of a fine art and requires laborious preparation. There are a good many meat dishes cooked in a sauce, and fish stews in which cod or hake are accompanied by a green parsley sauce *(salsa verde)* or by peppers. *Chipirones en su tinta* is a dish of baby squid in their own ink. *Marmitako*, a typical fishing village dish, is composed of tunny, potatoes and red peppers, and is often served with a good *txacolí*, a tart white wine.

The Ebro region – **Navarra** and **La Rioja** are the regions for game, excellent market-garden produce and the best Spanish wines, especially reds. The food is varied and refined, with partridge, quail and woodpigeon competing with trout for pride of place in local dishes. Navarra has noteworthy rosés and fruity white wines. Delicious Roncal cheese is made in the valleys from ewes' milk.

Aragón is the land of **chilindrón**, a savoury tomato and red pepper sauce served with meat and poultry, and also of **ternasco** or roast kid or lamb. These dishes may be washed down with heavy red Cariñena wines.

Meseta regions – Castilian specialities from local produce include roast lamb (**cordero asado**), suckling-pig (**cochinillo tostón** or **tostado**) and the ubiquitous **cocido**, all of which may be accompanied by a light fresh Valdepeñas red.

Rueda wines from the province of southern Valladolid are fresh fruity whites, while those from Ribera del Duero are generally acidic reds.

The Meseta is also a cheese-producing region with a ewes' milk speciality from Burgos and many varieties of *manchego*, Spain's best-known cheese. Among local sweets are the famous marzipans from Toledo.

Yemas de Santa Teresa (candied egg-yolk)

Mediterranean regions – Catalunya and the Levante have a typically Mediterranean cuisine. Look out in particular for Catalan *pan con tomate* (bread rubbed with a cut tomato and occasionally garlic and sprinkled with olive oil), red peppers cooked in oil, and wonderful fish dishes with a variety of sauces such as *alioli* (crushed garlic and olive oil) and *samfaina* (tomatoes, peppers and aubergines). Among pork meats are **butifarra** sausages, various kinds of slicing sausage and the *fuet* sausage from Vic. Dried fruit is used in a great many dishes or may be served at the end of a meal. The most widespread dessert is **crema catalana**, a kind of custard cream mould with a thin layer of caramel. Catalunya is home to *cava*, a sparkling wine. Excellent light wines are made in the Empordà region, fruity whites in Penedès and reds in Priorato.

The **Levante** is the kingdom of the famous **paella** which is cooked with a saffron rice base and chicken, pork, shellfish, squid, shrimps and king prawns. As for sweets, **turrón** (made of almonds and honey or castor sugar, rather like nougat) is a Levantine speciality.

Soups are specialities in the **Islas Baleares** (Balearic Islands); Mallorca's *mallorquina* has bread, leeks and garlic, while other soups are made with fish. **Tumbet** is a well-known casserole of potatoes, onions, tomatoes, courgettes and peppers. **Sobrasada**, a spicy sausage, flavours many local dishes. **Cocas**, pastries with sweet or savoury fillings, and **ensaimadas**, light spiral rolls, make delicious desserts.

Andalucía – The region's best-known dish is **gazpacho**, a cold cucumber and tomato soup made with oil and vinegar and flavoured with garlic. Andalusians love their food fried, especially fish and seafood. Pigs are reared in the Sierra Nevada and Sierra de Aracena for the exquisite *serrano* ham. Among local desserts, *tocino de cielo* is as sweet as an Oriental pastry.

The region is especially well-known for its dessert wines: the famous **Jerez** or sherries (*see JEREZ DE LA FRONTERA*), **Manzanilla** and **Málaga**.

Gazpacho

On a gastronomic level, Andalucía is renowned mainly for its fried fish dishes, and also its *gazpacho*, a cold soup which is particularly refreshing and tasty during the hot summer months.

Ingredients: Tomatoes, peppers (red or green), chillies, garlic, olive oil, vinegar, seasoning, breadcrumbs, stock.

Method: Grind the chillies, garlic and a little salt in a large pestle and mortar. The traditional method would be to add the diced peppers and tomatoes and the breadcrumbs and pound by hand until well mixed – but these days, most people liquidize everything with the help of a food processor! Slowly pour the oil onto the mixture stirring all the time. Leave to soak for a while, then add some cold stock and strain the mixture through a sieve. Add a little vinegar and seasoning. Serve well chilled, with croutons, diced cucumber, red peppers and raw onion sprinkled on top.

Paella valenciana

Ingredients (*serves 4*): small cup of olive oil, 2 cloves of garlic (crushed), 1 green pepper (finely sliced), half a cup of tomato purée, 100g chicken (diced into medium-sized pieces), 100g pork (diced into medium-sized pieces), 250g arborio rice, 1 tsp saffron, salt and pepper, 500ml fish stock, 500ml chicken stock, 100g clams, 100g mussels, 100g prawns, 50g squid (cut into thin slices), 50g sweet red peppers (cut into thin slices), 25g frozen peas.

Method: Heat the olive oil in a large frying pan or paella dish. Add the garlic and green peppers and fry for 2min. Add the chicken, pork and squid and cook, stirring, for a further 5min. Add the rice, saffron and tomato purée, followed immediately by the fish and chicken stock and salt and pepper. Cook for 10min, stirring occasionally. Once the rice is almost cooked, add the mussels, clams, prawns, sweet red peppers and green peas. Cook for a further 3-5min or until shellfish is cooked through. Garnish with slices of lemon.

¡Que aproveche!

D. Ball/DIAF

Paella

The Mezquita, Córdoba

D. Ball

Sights

AGUILAR DE CAMPÓO

Castilla y León (Palencia) – Population 7 594
Michelin map 442 D 17

The landscape in this region on the northern edge of the Meseta is broken b
limestone escarpments thrust up by the folding which formed the Cordiller
Cantábrica. From its position on one of these high outcrops Aguilar Castle ha
withstood time as it looks down on the old town which still possesses rampa
gateways with pointed arches, in some cases surmounted by a carved figure or cres
and mansions emblasoned with coats of arms.

The vast **Aguilar reservoir** 2km/1.5mi to the west is a water sports centre.

Monasterio de Santa María la Real ⊘ – *On the edge of town towards Cerver
de Pisuerga.*
This fine transitional Romanesque Gothic (12C-13C) monastery is known for it
historiated capitals inside the church, its cloister and chapter-house. It is presentl
undergoing extensive restoration.

Colegiata de San Miguel ⊘ – The church at the end of the long, porticoed Plaz
de España shelters within its vast Gothic aisles two fine mausoleums: the first
16C, of the Marquises of Aguilar praying, the second, in the north apsidiole
carved in a surprisingly realistic manner, of the archpriest García González.

Parque Nacional de AIGÜESTORTES i ESTANY DE SANT MAURICI★★

Catalunya (Lleida)
Michelin map 443 E 32-33 – Local map see PIRINEOS CATALANES

This national park in the Catalan Pyrenees covers an area of 10 230ha/25 279 acres a
an altitude between 1 500m/4 900ft and 3 000m/9 800ft. This particular range consists of granite and slate, a very different terrain from that of the limestone Pyrenees
in the Ordesa national park. The glacially eroded landscape in Aigüestortes nationa
park has a harsh type of beauty with U-shaped valleys and high mountain lakes.

It is a well-watered area abounding in waterfalls and rushing streams. The twisting
waterways or *aigües tortes* that have given the park its name wind gently through
valleys between moss-covered meadows and wooded slopes. The vegetation consists
of a variety of coniferous trees such as firs and Scots pines but there are also birch
and beech trees which change colour in autumn. Herds of light brown cows graze the
pastures while ibex roam the peaks and ridges and capercaillies still haunt the woods.

National parks

Areas are designated national parks with a view to protecting particularly beautiful or unusual, but often also fragile, natural environments, while contributing
to the local economy by encouraging tourism. Visitors are able to learn about
nature and also how to show their appreciation of it by treating it with respect.

Spain has 11 national parks, of which

– six are in mainland Spain:

Los Picos de Europa, founded in 1995, with an area of 64660ha/159 780 acres
(incorporating the old Montaña de Covadonga National Park in the west of the
Picos de Europa, founded in 1918, with an area of 17 000ha/42 000 acres);

Ordesa y Monte Perdido (Spanish central Pyrenees), founded in 1918, with an area
of 15 608ha/38 569 acres;

Aigüestortes y Estany Sant Maurici (Catalan Pyrenees), with an area of 10 230ha/
25 279 acres;

Cabañeros in the mountains southwest of Toledo, with an area of 40 000ha/
98 840 acres;

Tablas de Daimiel (La Mancha), with an area of 1 928ha/4 764 acres;

Doñana (Andalucía), with an area of 50 720ha/125 332 acres;

– four are in the Canary Islands

Teide (Tenerife);

Caldera de Taburiente (La Palma);

Timanfaya (Lanzarote);

Garajonay (Gomera);

– and one is in the Balearic Islands:

Cabrera (small island south of Mallorca).

B. Brillon/MICHELIN

EXCURSIONS

The **parque nacional** ⊘ may be reached from the east via Espot or from the west via Boí.

Estany de Sant Maurici – *Reached by road from Espot*. The lake is surrounded by forest and dominated by the peaks of the Sierra dels Encantats.

Portarró d'Espot – *3hr there and back on foot along a forest track leaving from Sant Maurici Lake*. The path gradually delves deeper into the Sant Nicolau Valley. When you draw level with the lago Redó, admire the splendid **panoramas**★★ of the Aigüestortes area.

Aigüestortes – *Reached by a branch off the Barruera-Caldes de Boí road*. The track (5km/3mi) is practicable for private vehicles although there are also organised jeep tours. The road leads into Aigüestortes where a stream winds its way through rich pastures. There is a path to Estany Llong lake (*3hr there and back on foot*).

Estany Negre – *5hr there and back on foot from Espot or 4hr on foot along a forest track leaving from Sant Maurici Lake*. The path takes you through the ravishing Peguera Valley. In its last stretch, the river throws itself into the Estany Negre (Black Lake), hemmed in by a circle of awesome summits. The lake owes its name to its dark, mysterious waters.

Estany Gran – *3hr there and back on foot along a path leaving from Sant Maurici Lake*. Beside the lake, the mountain streams and their gushing waterfalls form an impressive sight.
There are a number of signposted paths, including the one that crosses the park, and four mountain refuges where hikers may spend the night.

ALACANT/ALICANTE★

Comunidad valenciana – Population 275 111

Michelin map 445 Q 28

In this friendly, typically Mediterranean town, unhurried provincial calm mixe
pleasantly with the bustle of a major tourist centre.

Alicante has always been enjoyed for its remarkably luminous skies - the Greek
called it *Akra Leuka* (the white citadel), the Romans *Lucentum* (the city of light). Th
town came under Arab domination in 711 and was not reconquered until 1296 whe
James II incorporated it into the kingdom of Aragón.

The town stretches out below the castillo de Santa Bárbara, along an immense ba
between the capes of Huertas to the north and Santa Pola to the south.

Tourism and port activity - Its mild climate and proximity to vast beaches (Ɛ
Postiguet, La Albufereta and **San Juan**) have made Alicante the tourist capital of the Cost
Blanca. Seaside resorts such as **Santa Pola, Guardamar del Segura, Torrevieja** and **Campoamc**
have sprung up all along the southern part of this flat, sandy coast.

ALACANT
ALICANTE

Abad Enalva	AZ 5
Alfonso X el Sabio (Av. de)	AY
Ayuntamiento (Pl. del)	BZ 8
Capitán Meca	BZ 12
Cervantes	BZ 15
Chapi (Pl.)	AZ 18

Chapuli	AZ 21
Constitución (Av. de la)	AZ 24
Doctor Gadea (Av. del)	AZ 25
Duque de Zaragoza	AZ 27
Elche (Portal de)	AZ 30
Gabriel Miró (Pl. de)	AZ 33
Juan Bautista Lafora (Av. de)	BZ 41
López Torregrosa	AY 44
Major	AZ

Manero Mollá	AZ 4
Mendez Núñez (Rambla)	AZ
Rafael Altamira	AZ 5
Rafael Terol	AZ 5
Ramiro (Pas.)	BZ 5
San Fernando	AZ 6
San José	AZ 6
Santa María (Pl.)	BZ 6
Teatre Chapi	AZ 6
Vicente Inglada	AY 6

H Ayuntamiento   M Colección de Arte del s. XX. Museo de La Asegurada

Apart from its function as a tourist centre, Alicante plays an important role in the region's economy through its port which handles produce from the surrounding *huerta* (wine, almonds, dessert grapes) and from Murcia. Industry is also relatively important: metallurgy - particularly aluminium - and chemicals.

Hogueras - On 24 June, Midsummer's Day, Alicante gives itself over to the joys of the Hogueras festival. The creation of giant pasteboard figures which are set alight amid noisy rejoicings beneath sparkling fireworks, gives citizens the chance to indulge their taste for display, satire, caricature and exuberance.

OLD TOWN

Follow the route marked on the town plan

★ **Explanada de España** (ABZ) - This is the most pleasant promenade in the region with its multicoloured marble pavement adorned with geometric designs and its magnificent palms providing shade as you sit or walk beside the pleasure boat harbour. Concerts are held on the bandstand on Sundays.

Catedral de San Nicolás ⊙ (AZ) - The present building, which stands on the site of a former mosque, dates back to the beginning of the 17C. The nave, Herreran in style, is dominated by a well-proportioned cupola.

Ayuntamiento (town hall) (BZ H) - This 18C palace of golden stone has a beautiful Baroque façade flanked by two towers. Visit the Rococo **capilla** (chapel) ⊙ decorated with azulejos from Manises, and two Romantic reception rooms with blue silk hangings.

Iglesia de Santa María ⊙ (BZ) - The church stands in a picturesque square in the old town, just below Santa Bárbara Castle. The façade is characteristic of 18C Baroque with its wreathed columns, its pillars and the breaks in its cornices. Once a mosque, the church was rebuilt in the 14C and has since been altered several times inside, particularly in the 17C when the nave was enlarged and the sanctuary disfigured by heavy Churrigueresque decoration. Near the entrance are graceful Renaissance marble fonts and a painting on wood of John the Baptist and John the Apostle by Rodrigo de Osuna the Younger.

★ **Museo de la Asegurada** ⊙ (BZ M) - Housed in a 17C palace, the museum contains an interesting collection of 20C painting and sculpture donated by the sculptor Eugenio Sempere. There are works by Spanish artists (Miró, Picasso, Gargallo, Tàpies, Saura, Genovés, Chillida and Dalí) and also by foreigners (Vasarely, Bacon, Braque, Chagall and Kandinsky).

Castillo de Santa Bárbara ⊙ (BY) - *Go up by lift and walk back down the path, either all the way (good views) or to the halfway stop.*
The fortress originally built, it is said, by the Carthaginian Hamilcar Barca, stands in a remarkable strategic position on the Benacantil hill and has played a major role in every episode of the city's history. There are three different sections; the first, the Plaza de la Torreta (*at the lift terminus*), is surrounded by the oldest buildings, of which one houses the **Museu de Fogueras** with its exhibition of *ninots* or pasteboard figures burned on Midsummer's Day. A platform commands a fine **view** of the harbour, the town, castillo de San Fernando on another hill, and of San Juan beach. The second section is 16C (*halfway point for the lift*) and the lowest, third perimeter dates back to the 17C. The footpath leads down into the narrow streets and tiny squares of the working-class Santa Cruz quarter of town, medieval in origin.

EXCURSION

From Alicante to Alcoi (Alcoy) - *70km/43mi north. Leave Alicante on N 340* (BZ). *Take the Alcoi road at San Juan and then turn right.*

Cuevas de Canalobre ⊙ - *700m/2 300ft up Mount Cabezón de Oro, the caves form a maze of stalactites and stalagmites, some shaped like candelabra (canalobre).*
Return to N 340 and continue north.
The road crosses dry country dotted with fig and carob trees.

Xixona (Jijona) - The speciality of this small town is the manufacture of *turrón*, a sweet made of almonds and honey, exported worldwide. A small **museum** (El Lobo) and several factories are open to visitors.
Beyond Xixona the road threads its way through terraces of almond trees and up round a series of hairpin bends to a pass, the **Puerto de la Carrasqueta**★ (1 024m/3 360ft), which commands a view of the entire Torremanzanas Valley with Alicante and the sea in the far distance.

Alcoi (Alcoy) - Alcoi is an industrial town (textiles, paper, metallurgy and confectionery) set in incredible mountain scenery at the confluence of the Serpis, Molinar and Barchell rivers.
At the end of April, Alcoi holds the **Moors and Christians** (Moros y Cristianos) **festivals** to commemorate an attack by the Moors in 1276 which ended with a Christian victory thanks to the intervention of St George.

ALARCÓN ★

Castilla-La Mancha (Cuenca) – Population 245
Michelin map 444 N 23

Alarcón stands atop a mound of brown earth almost completely encircled by a meander of the Júcar river. The 13C-14C castle, now a parador, is one of Spain's best examples of medieval military architecture. This fortress, a square construction of gold-coloured stone, is guarded by two rows of fortifications and adds considerably to the melancholy beauty of the site★★.

Alarcón, meaning Alaric's town, was founded by the son of the Visigothic king of the same name. It was reconquered from the Muslims in 1184 by Alfonso VIII, then ceded to the Knights of Santiago and eventually came into the hands of the Infante **Don Juan Manuel** (1284-1348) who wrote many of his cautionary tales while living there. In the 15C, the castle became the object of bloody battles between its owner, the Marquis of Villena, and the Catholic monarchs who wished to put an end to feudal power. The Alarcón dam, 3km/2mi away, controls the Júcar's variable flow.

The village – Roughcast obscures many a fine stone house front in the modest country village.

Apart from its elegant Plateresque (16C) west door, the church of **Santa María** possesses a vast Gothic interior and a remarkable carved altarpiece dating from the same period.

The parish church of San Juan stands on the **Plaza de Don Juan Manuel** as does the porticoed town hall (Ayuntamiento).

ALBACETE

Castilla-La Mancha – Population 135 889
Michelin map 444 O 24, P 24

Albacete (*Al Basite* meant the Plain to the Arabs), the capital of the south of La Mancha, stands on a plateau which forms an arid Castilian promontory jutting into the fertile greenery of the huerta country between the Beatic chains and the Iberian Cordillera.

Albacete has specialised in the manufacture of knives and scissors since the Muslim era.

Museo de Albacete ⊙ – The museum, a modern building on the edge of Abelardo Sánchez park, was designed to display finds from excavations in the province. The archeological section houses a rich collection of Iberian and Roman artefacts. Examples of the former include a **sphinx from Haches** and sculptures from the sanctuary at Cerro de los Santos. Among Roman finds note the **dolls with movable joints** ★ – four dolls made of ivory and one of amber – and some of the funerary items discovered in a 4C burial-ground at Ontur in 1946.

EXCURSION

★ **Alcalá del Júcar** - *50km/31mi northeast. Take CM 332 and turn left onto the road through Villavaliente.*
The village spreads between its castle tower and church over a **site**★ equally magnificent by day or night. It has been built into the very face of the cliff which is circled below by the Júcar. A walk through the steep alleys is well worthwhile. Most of the dwellings hollowed out of the rock have long corridors leading to balconies overlooking the other side of the cliff. Some of these dwellings, like the Masagó, can be visited.

A visit to Alcalá could well be followed by a drive along the Jorquera road which snakes its way beside the Júcar through steep-sided **gorges**.

ALBARRACÍN ★

Aragón (Teruel). – Population 1 164
Michelin map 443 K 25

Hidden away in the Sierra de Albarracín, this medieval city tinged with pinkish hues stands in an exceptional **site**★, perched on a cliff above the Guadalaviar river. The ramparts extending up the hill behind the town were built by the Moors in the 10C then restored to a large extent by the Christians in the 14C. The Sierra de Albarracín has been inhabited since the Upper Paleolithic era, as can be seen from the many **rock engravings** in prehistoric sites at Callejón del Plou and Cueva del Navaza (*5km/3mi southeast towards Bezas and Valdecuenca*).

The spirit of independence – In the 11C the Almoravid Beni Razin dynasty, from which the town took its name, founded a small *taifa* kingdom on the spot. A defensive wall was built against Almohad incursions and help sought from Navarra. In the mid 12C the town was ceded to the Azagras, Christian nobles from Estella in Navarra. The lords of Albarracín refused submission to the powerful Kingdom of Aragón for 50 years until James II was able to bring the fief within the royal domain in 1300.

★THE VILLAGE 45min

A random wander through the narrow, steep and winding, cobbled streets will reveal a different aspect of the town at every corner. Starting out from the **Plaza Mayor**, you come to a quarter where the houses have ground floors built of limestone and overhanging upper storeys faced with rose-coloured roughcast. Fine woodwork balconies, wrought-iron grilles at the windows and the occasional coat of arms add character to the façades. The covered roof galleries are quite different from those to be found on houses elsewhere in Aragón.

Catedral ⊙ – The belfry, crowned by a smaller lantern, marks the position of the cathedral slightly south of the town centre. One of the chapels off the vast 16C nave contains a small wooden altarpiece (1566) carved with scenes from the life of St Peter. The chapter-house is well worth a visit for its **treasure** which includes gold and silverwork as well as some 16C **tapestries★**, of which seven were woven in Brussels and recount the life of Gideon.

The chapter on art and architecture in this guide gives an outline of artistic creation in the region, providing the context of the buildings and works of art described in the Sights section.

This chapter may also provide ideas for touring.

It is advisable to read it at leisure/before setting out.

La ALBERCA★★

Castilla y León (Salamanca) – Population 958
Michelin map 441 K 11

La Alberca lies at the heart of the Sierra de la Peña de Francia. The region is an isolated one, traversed by few roads, and consequently has kept its character.

The village – The village exudes charm with its winding streets and unusual old houses. These are built of stone up to first floor level and surmounted by overhanging half-timbered upper storeys. The main square, known here as the **Plaza Pública** in recognition of its active community life, has an irregular shape and is partly arcaded.

Traditionally religious, the community fervently celebrates the Feast of the Assumption on 15 August with the ancient mystery play or *Loa* relating the triumph of the Virgin Mary over the devil. Intricately embroidered costumes are worn for the occasion.

Plaza Pública, La Alberca

F. Gouverneur/MICHELIN

EXCURSIONS

★★ **Peña de Francia** – *15km/9mi west*. The Peña, a shale crag of 1 732m/5 682ft and the highest point in the range, can be distinguished from a considerable distance. The approach road is spectacular, affording wide **panoramas**★★ of the Hurdes mountains, the heights of Portugal, the Castilian plain and the Sierra de Gredos. There is a Dominican monastery with a dependent hostelry *(open in summer only)* at the top.

★ **Carretera de Las Batuecas** – This road climbs imperceptibly to the Portillo pass (1 240m/4 068ft) before plunging through 12km/7mi of sharp bends into a deep, green valley in which the Batuecas Monastery lies hidden. It continues beyond Las Mestas, to the desolate and long isolated **Las Hurdes** region of Extremadura, the setting in 1932 for Buñuel's film *Land without Bread*.

Miranda del Castañar – *15km/9mi east*. The narrow alleys of the village are lined with houses with widespread eaves and flower-filled balconies.

ALCALÁ DE HENARES

Madrid – Population 162 780

Michelin map 444 or 442 K 19

Under the Romans the city was an important centre known as *Complutum* but the history of Alcalá is mainly linked to that of its university, founded by Cardinal Cisneros in 1498. It became famous for its language teaching and in 1517, Europe's first Polyglot Bible was published with parallel texts in Latin, Greek, Hebrew and Chaldean. The university was moved to Madrid in 1836. Today, Alcalá once again has a university and benefits from extensive industrial development.

Alcalá was the birthplace of **Cervantes**, **Catherine of Aragon**, daughter of the Catholic monarchs and first wife of Henry VIII, and the Renaissance architect **Bustamante**.

Cervantes

Adventure and storytelling are the words that best sum up the life of **Miguel de Cervantes Saavedra** who was born in Alcalá in 1547. As a young man he spent four years in Italy after which he enlisted and fought at the Battle of Lepanto (1571) where he was wounded. In 1575 he was captured by the Turks, taken off to Algeria as a slave and rescued only after five years by Fathers of the Holy Trinity. In 1605 he published the first part of **Don Quixote** which was an immense and immediate success. In this tragicomic masterpiece an elderly gentleman sets out as a doughty knight errant in search of adventure, hoping to redress wrongs in the terms of the storybooks he loves; he is accompanied by his simple but astute squire, Sancho Panza. The interaction of the ideal and the real, the true and the illusory, reveals the meditations of a man of 58 deeply involved in philosophy, life and the Spain of his day. His writing continued with *Exemplary Novels* or humorous stories of adventure and intrigue, comedies, *entremeses* or one-act prose farces, novels and, in 1615, the second part of *Don Quixote*. He died a year later, on 23 April 1616 – the same day as Shakespeare.

Antigua Universidad or **Colegio de San Ildefonso** ⊘ – The old university building, now used to house the University education offices, stands on the Plaza de San Diego. Its beautiful **Plateresque façade**★ (1543) is by Rodrigo Gil de Hontañón. The **Patio Mayor**, known as the Santo Tomás de Villanueva *patio*, with its three-storey buildings, has a certain dignity; at the centre is a well-head with a swan motif, the emblem of Cardinal Cisneros. Across the Patio de los Filósofos stands the delightful **Patio Trilingüe** (1557) where Latin, Greek and Hebrew were taught. The **Paraninfo**, a small room formerly used for examinations and degree ceremonies, is now the setting for the solemn opening of Alcalá University terms. The decoration includes a gallery delicately ornamented in the Plateresque style, and an **artesonado** ceiling.

Capilla de San Ildefonso ⊘ – This 15C chapel houses the richly-carved **mausoleum**★ of Cardinal Cisneros by Fancelli and Bartolomeo Ordóñez. Note the fine Mudéjar **artesonado** ceiling.

ALCÁNTARA

Extremadura (Cáceres) – Population 1 948
Michelin map 444 M 9

Alcántara stands in a countryside of ancient shale rocks through which the Tajo river has cut its course, watching over the old Roman bridge which once brought it renown and from which it took its name (*Al Kantara* is the Arabic for bridge).

The Order of Alcántara – The Knights of San Juan de Pereiro changed the name of their order to Alcántara when they were entrusted with the defence of the town's fortress in 1218. Like the other great orders of chivalry in Spain – Calatrava, Santiago and Montesa – the Order of Alcántara was created to free the country from the Moors in the 12C. Each order, founded as a military unit under the command of a master, lived in a community bound by the Cistercian rule. These religious militias, always prepared for combat and capable of withstanding long sieges in their fortresses, played a major role in the Reconquest.

Puente romano, Alcántara

★ **Puente romano** – *2km/1mi northwest of Alcántara on the road to Portugal.* This magnificent construction was thrown across the Tajo, slightly below its junction with the río Alagón, by the Romans under Emperor Trajan in AD 106. The bridge is made of massive granite blocks held together without mortar. It is 194m/636ft long with a central arch 70m/230ft high, built to withstand the most formidable floodwaters. More damage, however, has been caused by man and it has had to be restored several times. The small temple at one end and the central triumphal arch are both Roman.

Convento de San Benito ⊙ – The old headquarters of the Military Order of Alcántara stands high above the Tajo. The 16C monastery buildings, now restored, include a richly decorated Plateresque church with star vaulting, a Gothic *patio* and outside, a graceful arcaded Renaissance gallery used as the backdrop for plays.

ALCAÑIZ

Aragón (Teruel) – Population 12 820

Michelin map 443 I 29

Alcañiz, set amid orchards and fertile olive groves, is the capital of Lower Aragón. The region is famous for its Holy Week ceremonies accompanied by incessant drum playing known as *tamborrada*.

The film director **Luis Buñuel** (1900-83) was born in Calanda, 17km/10.5mi southwest of Alcañiz.

Plaza de España – Two memorable façades meet at one corner of the square: the tall Catalan Gothic arcade of the **Lonja**, where a market was once held, and the Renaissance town hall (Ayuntamiento). Both buildings are crowned by the typical Aragón gallery with overhanging eaves.

Colegiata ⊘ – A rhythmic interplay of vertical lines and curves marks the upper part of the façade of the collegiate church, rebuilt in the 18C, while below is an exuberantly Baroque **portal★**. The spacious interior is divided by massive columns with composite capitals reaching up to a noticeably projecting cornice.

Castillo – The castle standing on the hilltop was the seat of the Aragón commandery of the Order of Calatrava in the 12C. Most of the buildings now used as a parador date from the 18C. At the far end of the courtyard are the Gothic chapel, with its single aisle of equilateral arches, and on the first floor of the keep, 14C wall paintings.

ALCARAZ

Castilla-La Mancha (Albacete) – Population 2 087

Michelin map 444 P 22

Alcaraz stands isolated upon a clay rise tinted with the wine colour typical of the region, in the middle of the sierra of the same name. The town, which grew rich manufacturing carpets, retains a Renaissance character marked by the style of the architect Andrés de Vandelvira who was born here in 1509.

Plaza mayor – Among several elegant, porticoed buildings overlooking the square are the 18C **Lonja** which abuts the **Torre del Tardón** (clock tower), the 16C **Pósito**, a former municipal granary, the 16C **Ayuntamiento** (town hall) with a coat of arms and the 15C church of **La Trinidad** with a Flamboyant Gothic portal.

The main street or Calle Mayor, off which run stepped alleys, is fronted by old houses, testaments to the past importance of the town. Note the façade with the two warriors and the **Casa Consistorial** with its Plateresque doorway (Puerta de la Aduana).

The path leading out of the village to the cemetery affords an attractive **view** of the brown rooftops and the surrounding countryside.

EXCURSION

Nacimiento del río Mundo – *62km/39mi south.*

The road passes through a wooded valley to emerge onto the Sierra de Alcaraz. 6km/4mi after Ríopar, take the turning left to cueva de los Chorros. At the cave a spring at the foot of the steep sierra del Calar marks the source of the río Mundo, a tributary of the Segura, which drops down a wall of rock in a series of waterfalls. The best time to visit is in the spring. *For further information contact the Albacete tourist office ☎ 967 58 05 22.*

ALICANTE★

See ALACANT

ALMAGRO★

Castilla-La Mancha (Ciudad Real) – Population 8 962

Michelin map 444 P 18

Standing in the middle of the vast La Mancha tableland, Almagro was the stronghold of the Military Order of the Knights of Calatrava from the 13C to the end of the 15C. The architectural wealth of the town's elegant, emblasoned façades may be explained by its distinguished past. The town had a university from 1574 to 1828 and many religious orders built convents and monasteries.

The explorer **Diego de Almagro** (1475-1538) was born here and later became Governor of Chile.

A 16C Franciscan monastery now houses the parador.

Almagro is known for its aubergines and lace.

SIGHTS

★★ **Plaza Mayor** – This elongated square is one of the
most unusual in Castile. It
has a continuous stone colonnade framing two sides,
supporting two storeys of
windows all with green surrounds. It was once the setting for bullfights and jousting tournaments.

★ **Corral de Comedias** ⊙ – This
small 16C theatre (no 17,
Plaza Mayor) with its wooden porticoes, oil lamps,
stone well and scenery wall
forms a charming composi-
tion in dark red and white.
The International Festival
of Classical Drama is held
here every year.

The old streets – The walk
described below takes you
through cobbled streets lined with whitewashed hou-
ses where several convents
and monasteries have fine
carved stone doorways and
grand coats of arms recalling the power of the Knights of Calatrava.

Suggested walk – Go to the
end of the Plaza Mayor
with the statue of Diego de
Almagro and take calle de

Plaza Mayor, Almagro

Nuestra Señora de las Nieves (which has some fine doorways) to the left. This
leads to the triangular plaza Santo Domingo, surrounded by mansions. Turn left
into calle de Bernardas and then take calle de Don Federico Relimpio. Continue to
the left along calle de Don Diego de Almagro which is dominated by the imposing
façade of the Dominican convent and its magnificent crest.

Convento de la Asunción ⊙ – The double-storey 16C cloisters have a fine
Renaissance staircase and Plateresque doorways.

ALMANSA

Castilla-La Mancha (Albacete) – Population 22 488
Michelin map 444 or 445 P 26

Almansa, once the Moorish Al-Manxa, spreads out around a steep limestone crag
crowned by a medieval castle.
It was here that the battle of 1707, won by the Duke of Berwick against the English
and their allies, secured the Spanish throne for the Bourbon king, Philip V (although
peace was not signed until 1713).

Iglesia de la Asunción – This church standing at the foot of the castle was
completely transformed in the neo-Classical period and retains a monumental
Renaissance portal which is thought to be by Vandelvira.
The nearby seignorial mansion, the **Casa Grande**, has a fine 16C doorway with
armorial bearings flanked by twin giants. Inside is a patio with superimposed
galleries.

Castillo – The 15C ramparts (restored), perched precariously along the rock
ridge, command a view of the plain and make a pleasant walk.

EXCURSION

Cueva de la Vieja – 22km/14mi northwest via Alpera.
This is one of the rare caves in the region that is easy to reach and still has clearly
visible paintings. The elongated figures of men hunting stags with bows and
arrows are typical of Levante cave painting. One of the figures has a plumed
headdress and the women are dressed in long robes.

ALMERÍA

Andalucía – Population 159 587
Michelin map 446 V 22

The white town of Almería spreads out between the sea and an arid hill upon which stands an impressive alcazaba. This Arab fortress is a reminder of the important role that *Al-Meriya* (meaning the Mirror of the Sea in Arabic) played in the 11C when it was the principal city of a *taifa* kingdom. Under the Almoravids, Almería became a den for pirates who raided as far abroad as Galicia. Determined to wipe them out, Alfonso VII captured the town in 1147 but on his death 10 years later, it fell to the Moors again until the Reconquest in 1489.

Its especially mild winter climate has made it the centre of a rich farming region and an ideal tourist resort. The port exports fruit, vegetables and flowers produced by means of advanced technology in irrigation and greenhouse cultivation methods.

Life in the town centres on **Paseo de Almería**, an elegant tree-lined avenue bordered with shops, banks and cafés. The **Parque de Nicolás Salmerón** stretches out along the harbour beneath shading palms. **La Chanca**, to the west, is the fishermen's quarter, where the houses, each with its own terrace, stand in uneven lines like so many coloured cubes set into the living rock.

★ **Alcazaba** ⊘ – On a privileged site – a little hill overlooking Almería and its bay – Abd ar-Rahman III ordered the construction of this fortress in the 10C to defend the city. It was subsequently enlarged by Almotacín, who built a splendid Moorish palace, and by the Catholic kings, who erected a Christian palace after they had regained control of the town. However, its high, crenellated, ochre-coloured walls still dominate the town's white houses. A long wall, vestige of the old ramparts, links the fort to a second hill, the Cerro de San Cristóbal, which was formerly crowned by a castle.

Attractive **public gardens**★ have been laid out within the first walled enclosure where rivulets spring from fountains and flow between a variety of flower-beds. Excavations in the second enclosure, on the site of the royal apartments, have revealed sculptures and specimens of Arabic calligraphy, now displayed in the small **museum**. Immediately alongside is the former mosque, surmounted by a watchtower (Torre de la Vela). The keep with its incredibly thick walls was built by the Christians in the 15C.

The **view** from the battlements takes in the town, the Chanca district, the surrounding hills and the sea.

★ **Catedral** ⊘ – The cathedral was built in 1524 to replace the former mosque. Raids by Barbary pirates, however, decreed the construction of a fortified building – a rare necessity at the time.

In spite of its military character, the cathedral has two well-designed portals and at the east end, a delicately carved sunburst. The spacious interior is homogeneous; the high altar and the pulpits of inlaid marble and jasper are 18C, the choir stalls date from 1560 and the jasper *trascoro* with three alabaster statues is again 18C. The axial chapel contains the recumbent statue of the bishop who built the cathedral.

Monsul beach

EXCURSIONS

The Almería countryside has a distinctive, desert-like appearance with cacti, aloes and prickly pears.

★ **Cabo de Gata** – *29km/18mi east. Take the road to the airport then a signposted road to the right.*
The road crosses the salt flats of Acosta before reaching this desolate cape. The lighthouse on the rocky spur faces Mermaid Reef, a popular haunt for underwater fishing enthusiasts.
On the other side of the mountain is the small, pleasant summer resort of **San José** with its two beautiful beaches; los **Genoveses** and **Monsul**★ *(about 2km/1mi from the centre of the town).*

Níjar – *34km/21mi northeast. Take the road to the airport, then N 344.*
The old village, a fine example of popular architecture set high up off the road, carries on the traditional craft of *jarapas* or the weaving of thick hangings and bedspreads in pale colours. The wefts in the process are made of strips of already woven material *(trapo).*

★ **The road northeast** – *55km/34mi along N 340.*
A tableland of sand dunes stretches for miles between Benahadux and Tabernas – it was used as the setting for *Lawrence of Arabia* and various westerns. Film sets are open to the public at **Mini-Hollywood**. Beyond Tabernas, the land is red and barren; pottery-making is the main occupation in the surrounding villages. **Sorbas** has an amazing **site**★ with its houses clinging to a cliff, circled below by a loop in the river course.

The road northwest – *71km/44mi along N 340 and N 324.*
The road climbs to Guadix through a grandiose but desolate landscape of hills cut by great gorges. The aridity is occasionally relieved by a small green valley growing lemon and orange trees, or vines famous for their large sweet grapes. On 31 December, it is the Spanish custom to eat a grape at each stroke of midnight.

Castillo de ALMODÓVAR DEL RÍO ★

Andalucía (Córdoba)
Michelin map 446 S 14

This imposing **castle** ⊙, its origins lost in history, is perched on an impressive hill dominating the wide expanses of the Cordoban countryside. The town sits at the foot of the hill on its southern side, by the Guadalquivir river. In the 8C, under Muslim domination, a large fortress already existed on this site, although its present construction dates mainly from the 14C. The castle was restored at the beginning of this century at which time a neo-Gothic mansion was added to the interior. The castle consists of two walled enclosures – one in the form of a barbican with eight different sized towers, while the larger of the two, known as the *torre del Homenaje* (keep), is in fact a turret. Once inside the castle, the narrow path behind the parapet, the parade ground and the towers are all well worth a pleasant stroll.

Las ALPUJARRAS ★

Andalucía (Granada)
Michelin map 446 V 20

This mountainous region offering a variety of landscapes stretches across the southern slopes of the Sierra Nevada between the Gádor and Controviesa massifs. Because of its isolation from the rest of Spain it has managed to keep a traditional character.

HISTORICAL NOTES

In 1499 the Arabs who did not wish to leave Spain were forced to renounce their religion and to convert to Christianity. They were known as **Moriscos**. In 1566 Philip II forbade them their language and traditional dress, which sparked off a serious uprising, especially in Las Alpujarras where the Moriscos proclaimed as king Fernando Válor under the name Aben Humeya. In 1571 Philip II sent in the army under Don Juan of Austria who crushed the rebellion. However, a tense feeling of unrest remained, and in 1609 Philip III ordered the expulsion of all the Moriscos (who numbered about 275 000) from Spain.

FROM LANJARÓN TO UGÍJAR *93km/58mi - half a day*

The High Alpujarras encompass the valley of the Guadalfeo river where the houses blend in perfectly with the landscape. The distinctive architecture of these dwellings recalls that of North Africa – white houses with a waterproof covering on their terraces made from *sierra* sand are built one against the other forming small rural settlements stepped neatly in rows up the mountainside.

From **Lanjarón**, a famous spa, the road climbs to the picturesque villages of **Pampaneira, Bubión** and **Capileira**. From here a track *(in poor condition and only open in summer)* goes up to Pico Veleta.

The route from Capileira to Pitres affords fine views of the deep valley and passes through woods of poplars, chestnuts and oaks to **Trevélez** which is famed for its hams. Beyond this point the valley begins to widen. **Yegen** is set high above the Eastern Alpujarras, while **Ugíjar**, a market town, is known for its cloth.

ALQUÉZAR★

Aragón (Huesca) – Population 215

Michelin map 443 F 30

Alquézar's **setting**★★ is striking; at a bend in the road, the village seems to cling to a cliff dominated by a collegiate church built on the edge of the río Vero canyon.

The village is a maze of uneven streets bordered by emblasoned house façades with rounded stone doorways. It has a charming little arcaded Plaza Mayor.

Alquézar

Colegiata ⊘ – The Moors built an *alcázar* on the site which later fell to Sancho Ramírez, King of Aragón. In the late 11C and early 12C, the still visible walls were constructed together with a church which was rebuilt in 1530. The north gallery of the Romanesque cloister has fine capitals carved in anecdotal archaic style illustrating the Sacrifice of Isaac, Balaam and his ass, Adam and Eve and the Last Supper. Inside the collegiate church is a beautiful Romanesque Christ dating from the 12C.

★ **Cañón del río Vero** – The ascent of the river is quite spectacular. It takes at least a day, mostly on foot although some parts have to be swum. On the other hand, a walk to the Roman bridge at Villacantal *(2hr there and back)* is enough to get a general impression of the canyon and its steep grey and ochre-coloured sides.

EXCURSION

Rodellar – *38km/24mi northwest. Take HU 340, then turn right after Adahuesca and take HU 343 and 341.*
This typically Aragonese village is set in the **Sierra de Guara**, a massif formed for the most part of limestone, consisting of barren plateaux through which rivers have cut impressive canyons. The best-known are the río Vero and the Mascún ravine *(barranco)* which may be reached from Rodellar. Both are popular with walkers and climbers.
Barranco de Mascún (Mascún ravine) – Natural relief features such as arches, monoliths and eroded cliff faces may be seen on a walk down into the gorges *(allow 3hr there and back).*

Cuevas de ALTAMIRA★★

ALTAMIRA CAVES – Cantabria
Michelin map 442 B 17

In 1879, the archeologist **Marcelino de Sautuola**, noticed rock paintings on a cave roof which he eventually dated as prehistoric. These were the first such paintings ever to be discovered and as they were in such good condition there was widespread disbelief and scepticism in their authenticity. Only after 20 years and the discovery of similar paintings in the Dordogne Valley in France was the amazing pictorial art of Paleolithic man fully recognised.

GUIDED TOUR ⊘

The Altamira caves consist of several galleries containing black outlines and very ancient engravings dating back to 25000 BC, the Aurignacian Age at the beginning of the Upper Paleolithic Period, but it is the chamber with the painted bison that has made the site famous. Known as the Sistine Chapel of Quarternary Art, this 18m/59ft long and 9m/30ft wide cave has an outstanding **ceiling**★★★ painted during the Magdalenian Period (15000-12000 BC) like the Lascaux cave paintings in the Dordogne (France). Polychrome bison are shown asleep, crouched, stretching and galloping with extraordinary realism. The natural bulges on the rock face have been used with great skill to bring out body shape and to give the impression of movement. Other beasts include a wild boar running at speed and a stocky, primitive horse with a doe inside. The drawings are huge – 2m/6.5ft doe at the far end of the cave, though the average is nearer 1.60m/5ft.
The artists – who must have been in a crouched position to paint (the floor level has been lowered recently) – used natural pigments, chiefly ochre, yellow, red and brown which they reduced to a powder and mixed with animal fat. They outlined their subjects in black (with the use of charcoal) to give a firm edge to their colourwork.

Museo ⊘ – The three sections of the museum, beside the caves, have exhibitions on the Paleolithic Period and the importance of the discovery of Altamira, as well as a video film of the paintings on the ceiling. There is an excellent copy of the bison ceiling at the Museo Arqueológico in Madrid.

Michelin Green Guides to European destinations:
Austria – Belgium and Luxembourg – Berlin – Brussels – Europe – France – Germany – Great Britain – Greece – Ireland – Italy – London – Netherlands – Portugal – Rome – Scandinavia and Finland – Scotland – Sicily – Spain – Switzerland – Tuscany – Venice – Vienna – Wales – The West Country of England... and the collection of regional guides to France

Principat d'ANDORRA★★

Principality of ANDORRA – Population 62 400

Michelin map 443 E 34-35

The seven parishes that make up the principality of Andorra occupy 454km²/175sq mi of high plateaux and valleys cut across by charming mountain roads.

Until 1993 Andorra was a co-principality subject to an unusual political regime dating back to the days of feudalism. The rulers of the bordering countries, which up to 1993 were the Bishop of Urgell and the President of the French Republic, enjoyed rights and exercised powers over this small territory, which was jointly governed by them. At present Andorra is a sovereign state in its own right – an official member of the United Nations Organization.

In recent years life in Andorra has undergone significant change on account of its large-scale town-planning schemes, the development of hydroelectric stations and the emergence of foreign tourism. However, tradition remains very much alive, both in the local economy (the terraced slopes of the Sant Julià de Lòria Valley are planted with tobacco) and in religious pilgrimages (the famous Catalan *aplec*).

VISITORS' TIPS TO ANDORRA

Customs and other formalities – Visitors need a valid passport and, for those driving a car, a green card and current driving licence. There are customs checkpoints on the borders.

Money matters – Both Spanish and French currencies are accepted. Pesetas and francs can be easily obtained from banks and post offices. Withdrawals can also be made from cash machines using credit and debit cards.

Postal service – Andorra has both Spanish and French postal services, with full-time post offices in Andorra la Vella and local offices elsewhere. There are plans to create an Andorran mail service at an as yet unspecified future date.

Shopping – Andorra has long held a reputation as a shopper's paradise, due to its duty-free status. A wide variety of products are on offer at very reasonable prices (food, luxury items, clothes, electronic goods etc). Shops are generally open from 9am to 1pm and 4pm to 8pm, although department stores tend to open all day.

Telephoning – The code for Andorra is 376 followed by the five-digit correspondent's number.

Tourist information – There is a tourist office at 1, Carrer Docteur-Vilanova in Andorra la Vella, ☎ (376) 82 02 14.

Web site – www.turisme.ad

Andorra la Vella – Here, in the capital of the Andorra valleys, the houses are clustered onto a terrace overlooking the Gran Valira. Away from the main traffic routes, the streets in the old quarter of Andorra la Vella have remained almost intact, as has the **Casa de les Valls** ⊙, which continues to welcome debates on major national issues. This ancient stone building houses the seat of the Consell General de les Valls, which acts as both Parliament and courthouse to the small nation.

To the east, Andorra la Vella is extended by the lively municipality of Les Escaldes, dominated by **Caldaea**, a thermal spa with futuristic lines featuring Turkish baths, jacuzzis, bubble beds, hot marble slabs etc.

Estany d'Engolasters – The Engolasters plateau, covered with pastures, is an extension of Andorra la Vella currently used for sporting and recreational activities. The fine Romanesque tower of the church of Sant Miquel stands out proudly against the rolling plains.

After reaching the end of the road, climb over the crest among the pine trees and then continue your descent on foot towards the dam. Prettily surrounded by trees, this impressive hydroelectric construction has raised the waters of the lake (alt 1 616m/5 301ft) by a total of 10m/33ft.

Santuari de Meritxell – After the pass of Los Bons lies a lovely **site**★ with a group of houses gathered under a ruined castle which once defended the area as well as the Capilla de Sant Romà. Nearby stands the church of Nuestra Señora de Meritxell, a national sanctuary of the principality since 1976.

Canillo – The bell-tower of the church backing onto the rocks is the highest one in Andorra. At its side, you can see the ossuary, painted in white – a characteristic feature of Iberian civilization.

Iglesia de Sant Joan de Caselles ⓥ – Beneath the openwork tower and its three rows of ornamental windows, this church is one of the best examples of Romanesque architecture in Andorra. Inside, behind the wrought-iron grid of the presbytery stands a painted altarpiece, executed by the master **Canillo** (1525), representing the life and visions of the Apostle St John. The Romanesque **Crucifixion**★ was restored when the church underwent renovation work in 1963: a Christ in stucco has been placed on top a fresco illustrating a scene from the Calvary.

★ **Port d'Envalira** – *The roads are often blocked by snow but they are usually reopened within 24hr.* Alt 2 407m/7 897ft. Of all the Pyrenean passes served by a reliable road, Envalira boasts the highest altitude. It lies on the dividing line between the Atlantic and the Mediterranean slopes and so commands a lovely panorama of the Andorra mountains.

★ **Pas de la Casa** – Alt 2 091m/6 861ft. Formerly no more than a small frontier-post, the highest village in the principality has now developed into the main ski resort of the region.

Ordino – *Leave your car on the church square, in the upper part of town.* Ordino is a quaint village with a maze of charming alleyways surrounding the church. Inside, admire the wrought-iron grilles, similar to those that can still be seen in many sanctuaries near old Catalan forges. Not far from the church, note another fine example of wrought-iron artistry: an 18m/60ft balcony adorning the casa de Don Guillem, executed in his day by a master blacksmith.

ANDÚJAR

Andalucía (Jaén) – Population 35 803
Michelin map 446 R 17

Many of Andújar's old houses and chapels date back to the 15C and 16C. The region, with Martos *(some 55km/34mi south)*, is Spain's major olive-producing area.

Santa María – Plaza de Santa María. El Greco's painting *Christ in the Garden of Olives*, hangs in a north chapel closed by a fine Bartolomé **grille**★. An *Assumption of the Virgin* by Pacheco can be seen in the north apsidal chapel.

EXCURSION

Santuario de la Virgen de la Cabeza – *32km/20mi north on J 501.*
There are good **views**★★ through pines from the corniche road after Las Viñas.
On an August night in 1227, the Virgin appeared to a shepherd on the rocky head – *cabeza* – where, not long afterwards, a commemorative chapel was built.
In the 16C this was replaced by a monastery. Four centuries later, when civil war broke out, guards, their families and 1 000 Nationalists sought refuge on the lonely rock. From September 1936 to May 1937, under their captain, Cortés, they held out against an enemy which outnumbered them tenfold. When they surrendered the sanctuary was in ruins. It has since been restored and is now a popular place of pilgrimage, particularly at the end of April.

ANTEQUERA ★

Andalucía (Málaga) – Population 38 827
Michelin map 446 U 16

The white-walled town, a small industrial centre in the heart of a fertile valley, successfully integrates old and new buildings. Its cobblestone alleyways, windows with wrought-iron grilles, unusual roofs with coloured tiles and the many churches help to preserve its individuality. The San Sebastián belfry has fine brick Mudéjar decoration.

Museo Municipal ⓥ – The museum is housed in the 18C **Palacio de Nájera** and exhibits sacred and archeological artefacts. The most outstanding item is the **Ephebus of Antequera**★, a bronze Roman sculpture dating from the 1C.

Santa María – Go through the 16C **Arco de los Gigantes** (Arch of the Giants) to the far end of plaza Alta, beside the castle. The church, dating from 1514, has a façade decorated with cleverly composed geometric motifs, one of the earliest examples of Renaissance architecture in Andalucía.

Castillo – This was the first fortress captured by the Christians during the reconquest of the Kingdom of Granada (1410). It could not be held, however, as the position was encircled by the Moors. Today, there is a pleasant garden within its walls and from the towers, a fine **view**★ over Antequera's roofs and church towers to the plain and the Torcal plateau beyond.

Iglesia del Carmen ⊙ – The central nave of the church boasts a Mudéjar *artesonado* ceiling and a magnificent Churrigueresque altarpiece.

EXCURSIONS

★ **Los Dólmenes** ⊙ – *On leaving town, turn left off the Granada road.*
The **Menga, Viera** and **El Romeral dolmens**, prehistoric constructions dating from 2500 to 1800 BC, take the form of funerary chambers beneath tumuli noteworthy for their Cyclopean size. Menga, the oldest and largest of the three, is an oblong chamber divided by a line of pillars supporting enormous stone slabs. The walls of Romerol, the most recent chamber, consist of small flat stones so laid as to produce a trapezoidal section in the corridor.

★ **El Torcal** – *16km/10mi south. Leave Antequera on the Málaga road. Bear right after 12km/7.5mi for El Torcal.*
Signposted paths lead to a monumental group of strangely shaped limestone rocks *(red arrows: 3hr; yellow: 1hr 30min). For further information apply at the Refugio de El Torcal.*

★ **From Antequera to Málaga** – *62km/39mi south along N 331, C 340 and C 345.*
These pleasant well-planned roads, always within sight of majestic hills, afford splendid **views**★★ beyond the Puerto del León (Lion Pass, 960m/3 150ft) of Málaga and the Mediterranean.

ARACENA

Andalucía (Huelva) – Population 6 739
Michelin map 446 S 10

Aracena is an attractive town set at a high enough altitude to soften the harshness of the Andalusian climate. It rises in tiers up a hillside crowned by the remains of a Templar's castle. The tower abutting the church is a former minaret and is decorated on the north side in the style of the Giralda of Sevilla.

★★ **Gruta de las Maravillas (Cave of Marvels)** ⊙ – Underground rivers below the castle have hollowed out vast caves covered in concretions which mirror their size in limpid pools. The series of high chambers and increasingly narrow passages follows the line of rock faults. The concretions consist of draperies, pipes and coral formations coloured by iron and copper oxide or brilliant white calcite crystal as in the first chamber discovered, which is known as El Pozo de la Nieve (Snow Well).

★ SIERRA DE ARACENA

The western part of the Sierra Morena is refreshingly green; drives along winding roads between cork and eucalyptus trees are especially pleasant. The road from Aracena passes through a dense pinewood to reach Minas de Riotinto *(35km/22mi south of Aracena),* near the Campofrío reservoir.
As you approach **Minas de Riotinto**, the oldest working opencast mines in the world come into view. Although copper production stopped in 1986, gold and silver are still mined here. The landscape becomes drier to the south.
Serrano ham, which comes from this area, is considered a delicacy in Spain, especially that from Jabugo.

Michelin Green Guides cover the world's
great cities:

New York, London, Paris, Rome, Brussels,
Barcelona, Berlin, Vienna, Washington DC,
San Francisco, Chicago, Venice

ARANJUEZ★★

Aranjuez appears like an oasis at the centre of the harsh Castilian plain (particularly if you approach it from the south), green with shrubs and leafy avenues around the royal palaces. The shaded walks described by writers, sung by composers (Joaquín Rodrigo's famous *Concierto de Aranjuez*) and painted by artists (the Catalan, Rusiñol) are now popular with Madrileños, especially for Sunday strolls. Specialities from Aranjuez include strawberries and asparagus.

The Aranjuez Revolt (El motín de Aranjuez)

In March 1808, Charles IV, his queen and prime minister, Godoy, were at Aranjuez. They were preparing to flee (on 18 March) first to Andalucía, then to America, as Godoy had allowed Napoleon's armies free passage to Portugal through Spain the year before. In Portugal, the French were fighting the Portuguese who were strongly supported by the British. The Spanish people, however, had objected to the passage of the French and Godoy had advised his king to follow the Portuguese royal house (which had fled from Lisbon to Brazil) into exile.

On the night of 17 March, Godoy's mansion was attacked by followers of the heir apparent, Prince Ferdinand; Charles IV dismissed his minister and was compelled to abdicate in favour of his son. This was not enough, however: Napoleon summoned both to Bayonne and made them abdicate in his own favour (5 May).

These intrigues and the presence of a French garrison in Madrid stirred the Spaniards to the revolt of May 1808 which marked the beginning of the War of Independence.

★ ROYAL PALACE AND GARDENS

The Catholic monarchs enjoyed staying in the original 14C palace, then Emperor Charles V enlarged the domain, but the present palace is mainly the result of an initiative by Philip II who called on the future architects of the Escorial to erect a new palace surrounded by gardens.

In the 18C, the town became one of the principal royal residences and was considerably embellished under the Bourbons. It was, however, ravaged by fire in 1727 and, no sooner was it rebuilt in 1728, it burned again. Most of the palace was then reconstructed, including the present frontage. Ferdinand VI built the town to a grid plan; Charles III added two wings to the palace and Charles IV erected the delightful Labourer's Cottage.

Tren de la Fresa (Strawberry Train)

Weekends and public holidays from April to October. ☎ *902 22 88 22.*

This small steam train is a charming alternative method for those travelling from Madrid to Aranjuez; it is a copy of the original train which first went into service in 1851. The journey includes a guided visit of the palace and museums.

★ **Palacio Real** ⊙ – This Classical style royal palace of brick and stone was built in the 16C and restored in the 18C. In spite of many modifications it retains considerable unity of style and symmetry. The court of honour, overlooking a vast outer square, is framed by the main building with wings at right angles on either side; domed pavilions mark the angles.

The apartments have been left as they were at the end of the 19C.

The grand staircase was designed by the Italian Giacomo Bonavia during the reign of Philip V. The bust of Louis XIV by Coysevox recalls Philip V's French ancestry. In María Luisa's apartments, in an antechamber, are paintings by the Neapolitan artist Luca Giordano, and in the music room, a piano presented by Eugenia de Montijo to Isabel II.

The **Salón del Trono** (Throne Room), with crimson velvet hangings and Rococo furnishings, has a ceiling painted with an allegory of monarchy – ironically it was in this room that Charles IV signed his abdication after the attack on 17 March 1808.

Palacio Real

The **Salón de Porcelana**★★ (Porcelain Room) is the palace's most appealing and gracefully appointed room. It is covered in white garlanded porcelain tiles, illustrating in coloured high relief scenes of Chinese life, exotica and children's games, all made in the Buen Retiro factory in Madrid in 1763. They are enhanced by carved and painted wood doors, a chandelier and a marble floor.

In the king's apartments a music room precedes the smoking or Arabian Room – a diverting reproduction of the Hall of the Two Sisters in the Alhambra in Granada. A fine Mengs Crucifixion hangs in the bedroom, and the walls of another room are decorated with **203 small pictures** painted on rice paper with Oriental style motifs. At the end of the guided tour you can also visit a museum of palace life at the time of Alfonso XIII, where you will see rooms and exhibits which include a gymnasium and a tricycle.

★ **Parterre and Jardín de la Isla (Parterre and Island Garden)** ⊘ – The **Parterre** extending along the palace's east front is a formal garden laid out by the Frenchman Boutelou in 1746. The fountain of Hercules brings a mythological touch to the balanced display of flower-beds and trees (cedars and magnolias).

The **Jardín de la Isla** was laid out on an artificial island in the Tajo tiver in the 16C. Cross the canal which once drove mill wheels to reach the park and its many fountains hidden among copses of chestnut, ash and poplar trees and banks and hedges of boxwood.

★★ **Jardín del Príncipe (The Prince's Garden)** ⊘ – *Entrance in Calle de la Reina.* The garden beside the Tajo is more a vast gracefully laid-out park (150ha/371 acres). It has a surrounding grille and four monumental gateways by Juan de Villanueva. In 1763, called upon by the future Charles IV, the Frenchman Boutelou landscaped the park according to the romantic vision of nature fashionable at the end of the 18C. Within its bounds were a model farm, greenhouses with tropical plants and stables for exotic animals.

★★ **Casa del Labrador (The Labourer's Cottage)** ⊘ – The so-called cottage, named after the peasant farm which originally stood on the site, stands at the eastern end of the Jardín del Príncipe and is a Versailles type Trianon built on the whim of Charles IV in a neo-Classical style similar to that of the Royal Palace but with more luxurious decoration. The wrought-iron grille and balustrade surrounding the courtyard entrance are surmounted by 20 Carrara marble busts of figures from Antiquity.

The interior, a reflection of Spanish Bourbon taste, is an excellent example of sumptuous 18C decoration: Pompeian style ceilings, embroidered silk hangings, mahogany doors, marble floors, furniture and lamps, canvases by Bambrilla, clocks and porcelain. The billiard room on the first floor has a ceiling by Maella illustrating the Four Elements and magnificent embroidered silk hangings showing views of Madrid.

The statue gallery is embellished with Greek busts and a marble floor covering inlaid with Roman mosaics from Mérida. The French clock in the middle of the gallery incorporates a reproduction of Trajan's column. The María Luisa room has remarkable embroidered hangings made up of 97 small pictures showing a variety of views. In the centre of the ballroom stand a magnificent malachite table and chair given to Charles IV by the Czar Alexander III. The Platinum Room or Gabinete de Platino is decorated with gold, platinum and bronze inlays while the figure of a bird in the anteroom is carved from a single piece of ivory.

Casa de Marinos (The Sailors' House) ⊙ – A museum beside the former landing-stage contains the **falúas reales**★★ *(royal vessels)* which once made up the Tajo fleet of launches that ferried the royal family and guests to the Labourer's Cottage. The vessels belonged to six sovereigns: Isabel II, Charles IV (whose ship has paintings by Maella), Alfonso XII (whose ship is made of mahogany), María Cristina (whose ship has paintings resembling woven hangings), Alfonso III and finally Philip V, whose vessel, a gift by a Venetian count, is remarkable for its ornate decoration in gilded, finely-carved wood.

EXCURSION

Tembleque - *47km/29mi south on the NIV.*
The picturesque 17C **Plaza Mayor**★ in this La Mancha

Plaza Mayor, Tembleque

village is a very large quadrilateral, which must have once been used as a bullring. It is framed by a graceful three-storey portico in which the lowest arches are of stone, the upper of wood. An unusual cobweb style roof crowns one of the entrances to the square.

ARCOS DE LA FRONTERA★

Andalucía (Cádiz) – Population 26 466
Michelin map 446 V 12
See PUEBLOS BLANCOS DE ANDALUCÍA

Arcos has a remarkable **site**★★ atop a crag enclosed by a loop in the Guadalete river. The best views are from the narrow El Bosque road that runs alongside the reservoir. The old town, right at the top of the rock, is huddled against the formidable crenellated castle walls and those of the two churches.
Holy Week processions are known for their fervour.

Park the car below the village in plaza de Andalucía and walk up through the narrow alleys to plaza del Cabildo (following the signs to the parador).

Plaza del Cabildo - One side of the large square overhangs the deep river precipice. The **view**★ extends to a wide meander of the Guadalete which encloses fields of cereals and fruit trees.

Iglesia de Santa María ⊙ – The **west face**★ of this church is a good example of Plateresque. The interior, with its mixture of Gothic, Mudéjar, Plateresque and Baroque, has some fine star-vaulting and a late Renaissance altarpiece. An alley, Callejón de las Monjas, runs along the north side beneath the church's flying buttresses.
A charming maze of narrow alleys leads to the other side of the cliff and the **Iglesia de San Pedro** with its Baroque bell-tower.

Michelin travel publications:
more than 220 maps, atlases and town plans;
12 Red Guides to hotels and restaurants in European countries;
more than 160 Green Guides in 8 languages to destinations around the world.

ASTORGA

Castilla y León (León) – Population 13 802
Michelin map 441 E 11

In Roman times, *Asturica Augusta* (as Astorga was then known) was a major roa
junction; in the Middle Ages it was famous for its fairs and as a halt for pilgrims o
their way to Santiago de Compostela.
Food lovers will relish Astorga's **mantecadas** or light bread rolls.

La Maragatería – Long ago an ethnic group of unknown origin, but possibly of mixe
Gothic-Moorish blood, settled in this part of the Astorga region. These Maragatos le
an isolated existence in the heart of an inhospitable region where they becan
muleteers. They may still be seen at religious festivals or weddings in their nation
costume of voluminous knee breeches, shirt front and wide embroidered belt. Jack
in full Maragato dress can be seen striking the hours on the clock of the **Ayuntamien**
on the **Plaza Mayor**.

SIGHTS

★ **Catedral** ⊙ – Building began with the east end of the church in a Flamboyar
Gothic style in the late 15C and was not completed until the 18C, which explair
the rich Renaissance and Baroque work on the façade and towers. The front **porch**
low reliefs illustrate specific events in the Life of Christ such as the Expulsion o
the Moneylenders from the Temple and the Pardoning of the Adulterous Woma
Above the door is a beautiful Deposition.

Interior – The nave is large, with an impressive upsweeping effect created by th
innumerable slender columns soaring from the pillars. Behind the high altar is
retable★ by three artists named Gaspar – Gaspar de Hoyos and Gaspar de Palenc
were responsible for the painted, gilt decoration, and **Gaspar Becerra** (1520-70), a
Andalusian, for the low reliefs. After studying in Renaissance Italy, Gaspa
Becerra developed a personal style of humanist sensitivity far removed from th
Baroque Expressionism of the Spanish sculptors.

Museo de la Catedral ⊙ – The cathedral museum contains a rich collection of gold an
silver plate, including a 13C gold filigree Holy Cross reliquary and a 10C reliquar
of Alfonso III, the Great. There is also a beautiful 13C Romanesque painted woo
chest.

Palacio Episcopal ⊙ – This fantastic pastiche of a medieval palace was dreame
up by **Gaudí** in 1889. The original, brilliant interior decoration, especially that i
the neo-Gothic chapel on the first floor, is a profusion of mosaics, stained glas
and intersecting ribbed vaults.
The palace houses the **Museo de los Caminos** ⊙ (Museum of the Way of St James)
a collection of medieval art reflecting the theme of pilgrimage.

*The scallop shell, the attribute of St James the Great, became the emblem o
pilgrims to Santiago de Compostela.*

ÁVILA★★

Castilla y León – Population 49 868
Michelin map 442 or 444 K 15

Ávila, *Ciudad de cantos, ciudad de santos* (city of stones, city of saints), stands within
magnificently preserved 12C walls. It is Spain's highest provincial capital, situatec
on one of the plateaux of the Meseta at 1 131m/3 710ft. The Castilian climate at
such an altitude is extreme – winters are long with bitingly cold winds. Ávila, the
birthplace of St Teresa, has long been marked by the saint's strong personality; her
spirit pervades the entire town. Even the local speciality **yemas de Santa Teresa**, or
candied egg yolk, bears her name.

The city of St Teresa – St Teresa of Jesus (1515-82), whose visions deeply affected
her contemporaries, is one of the greatest mystics of the Roman Catholic Church.
Living at a time when the Reformation was gaining adherents throughout Western
and Central Europe, and the monastic orders, grown rich in power and possessions,
were relaxing their discipline, she succeeded in widely re-establishing the strict
observance of the Carmelites, gaining converts and founding convents.
Her letters are famous, particularly those to her spiritual director, St John of the
Cross, as are her mystical writings and her autobiography, *Life*, published in 1588.
She was canonised in 1622 and made a Doctor of the Church in 1970.
Several buildings in Ávila preserve the memory of the saint, including two museums,
one in the **Convento de San José (Las Madres)** (B R), the other in the **Convento de La Encarnación**
(B). The **Convento de Santa Teresa (La Santa)** (A B) was built on the site of the house where
she was born. The remains of the saint, however, are not in Ávila but in Alba de
Tormes.

J.Hidalgo – C.Lopesino/MARCO POLO

The city walls

SIGHTS

★★ Murallas (City walls) – The ramparts are complete and form one of Europe's most striking examples of medieval fortifications. The best place for a general **view** of them is a spot known as **Cuatro Postes** or Four Posts on the Salamanca road. The crenellated walls punctuated by advanced bastions and towers (90 in all), nine gateways and various posterns, enclose a quadrilateral area of 900m/2 953ft by 450m/1 476ft). The greater part dates from the 11C and has managed to keep an overall impression of unity in spite of modifications in the 14C. The sentry path along the top is open to the public.

★★ Catedral ⊙ (B) – The fortified **east end** of the cathedral serves as an advanced bastion in the ramparts and is crowned with a double row of battlements. The use of granite and the church's defensive stance give the exterior an austere appearance despite the window tracery, portal carvings and a ball decoration along the upper outlines of the tower, buttresses and pinnacles. The 14C **north doorway** with French Gothic decoration, unfortunately in stone too friable to resist erosion, originally stood in the **west front** but was removed in the 15C by Juan Guas when he redesigned the main entrance there. This was remodelled in the 18C in an unusual style more suitable for a palace.

The **interior** is a total contrast to the exterior with its high Gothic nave, its chancel with sandstone patches of red and yellow and its many **works of art★★**. These include the **trascoro** (1531) which has many beautifully detailed Plateresque statues (from left to right: the Presentation of Jesus in the Temple, the Adoration of the Magi and the Massacre of the Innocents) which blend into a harmonious whole, the **choir stalls** from the same period, and two delicately worked wrought-iron **pulpits** – one Renaissance, the other Gothic.

At the end of the apse, in which the windows are still Romanesque – the cathedral's construction lasted from 1135 to the 14C – is a large painted **altarpiece** (c 1500) by Pedro Berruguete and Juan de Borgoña. It has a gilt wood surround with Isabelline features and Italian Renaissance style pilasters. Against the back and sides of the high altar which face onto the double ambulatory are five carved Renaissance panels: those on the sides show the four evangelists and the four holy knights (Hubert, George, Martin and James). The central panel is the sculptor Vasco de la Zarza's masterpiece: the alabaster **tomb★★** of Don Alonso de Madrigal, theologian and prolific writer, who was Bishop of Ávila in the 15C and nick-named El Tostado or The Swarthy. He is shown writing before a beautiful Epiphany. The embroidery on the chasuble has been rendered with particular delicacy.

Museo ⊙ – The way to the museum leads through a 13C ante-sacristy followed by a **sacristy★★** from the same period which has a remarkable eight-ribbed vault, a massive 16C alabaster altarpiece and, in place of windows, wood sculptures of the four scenes of the Passion in imitation alabaster.

In the museum are a head of Christ by Morales painted on a tabernacle door
portrait by El Greco, a monumental Isabelline grille, late-15C antiphonaries a
a colossal monstrance 1.70m/5ft 8in high made by Juan de Arfe in 1571. T
Gothic **cloisters** have recently been restored.

In the Plaza de la Catedral the former **Palacio de Valderrábanos (B F)**, now a hotel, h
a fine 15C doorway surmounted by the family crest.

★★ Basílica de San Vicente ⓥ (B) – This vast Romanesque basilica, which took fro
the 12C to the 14C to build, and, therefore, has ogive vaulting, stands on th
alleged site of the 4C martyrdom of St Vincent of Zaragoza and his sisters, Sabi
and Cristeta. The 14C south gallery with its slender columns clustered and ringe
the carved cornice extending the full length of the nave, the tall porch added
the west front and the two incomplete towers, all combine to form a harmonio
whole.

The **west portal★★** is outstanding for the statue columns beneath the rich
decorative cornice and covings which seem so lifelike that they might almost
gossiping at the church entrance. The style of their clinging robes recalls that
sculptures in Vézelay, France. Inside, beneath the 14C **lantern★** is the **marty**
tomb★★, a late 12C masterpiece under an unusual 15C Gothic canopy with
pagoda shaped top. The martyrdom of St Vincent and his sisters is depicted o
the tomb so masterfully, both technically and evocatively, that it has bee
attributed to the same unknown sculptor as the west portal. The scenes of th
martyrs' capture below the walls of Ávila, their stripping and torture, a
particularly powerful.

★ Monasterio de Santo Tomás ⓥ (B) – This Dominican monastery founded at th
end of the 15C and embellished with gifts from the Catholic monarchs, who o
occasion made it their summer residence, was also the university.

The **church** façade incorporates the principal decorative motifs to be found o
other buildings in the monastery: architectural details are emphasised with lor
lines of balls – a common feature throughout Ávila but here used profusely
and the yoke and fasces adopted by Ferdinand and Isabel as their emblem. Th
church, in accordance with Dominican custom of the time, has only a single aisle
its arches resting on clusters of slender columns. A rare feature are the tw
galleries, one on the west for the choir, the other on the east containing th
high altar. As they are accessible only from the cloisters, the monks alone ha
access.

ÁVILA

Alemania	B 2	Cardenal Pla y Deniel	B 10	Reyes Católicos ... B 2
Alférez Provisional		Esteban Domingo	B 12	San Segundo ... B 2
(Av. del)	B 4	General Mola (Plaza)	A 13	San Vicente ... B 2
Caballeros	B 6	Generalísimo Franco	B 14	Santa (Pl. la) ... A 2
Calvo Sotelo (Plaza de)	B 8	Jimena Blázquez	A 15	Sonsoles (Bajada de) ... B 2
		Lope Núñez	B 16	Telares ... A 2
		Marqués de Benavites	AB 18	Tomás Luis de Victoria ... B 3
		Ramón y Cajal	A 19	Tostado ... B 3

A Iglesia de San Pedro	F Palacio de Valderrábanos
B Convento	J Palacio de Núñez Vela
de Santa Teresa	(Palacio de Justicia)
D Torre de Guzmán	N Palacio de Polentinos
	P Palacio de los Verdugos
	R Convento de San José
	(Las Madres)
	V Palacio de los Dávila

The fine **mausoleum**★ (1512) in the transept crossing is that of Prince Juan, only son of the Catholic monarchs, who died at 19. Its alabaster table with delicate Renaissance carving is by the Florentine, Domenico Fancelli who also carved the Catholic monarchs' mausoleum in the Capilla Real (Royal Chapel) in Granada. In one of the north chapels another fine Renaissance tomb belongs to Juan Dávila and his wife, the prince's tutors.

Claustro (Cloisters) – Beyond the unadorned 15C **Claustro de los Novicios** is the **Claustro del Silencio**★, small enough to be intimate and generously carved on its upper gallery. Beyond is the **Claustro de los Reyes** (Catholic Monarchs' Cloister), larger and more solemn with spectacularly bare upper arching.

From the Claustro del Silencio, stairs lead to the gallery of the *coro* containing beautiful 15C Gothic **choir stalls** carved with pierced canopies and arabesques. From the same cloister's upper gallery, more stairs go to the high altar gallery where one can see in detail Berruguete's masterpiece in high relief, the **retable of St Thomas Aquinas**★★ (c 1495).

Iglesia de San Pedro ⓥ **(B A)** – Standing on the vast **plaza Santa Teresa**, this fine Romanesque church shows early Gothic influence in its pointed arches and especially in the delicate rose window in the façade. A lantern lights the transept.

Palacio de los Verdugos (B P) – The façade of this Gothic Renaissance palace, emblazoned above the entrance and window with the family crest, is flanked by two stout square towers.

Palacio de Polentinos (A N) – This palace, now a barracks, has a finely decorated Renaissance entrance and *patio*.

Torre de Guzmán (A D) – The Oñates' palace is distinguished by this massive square corner tower, complete with battlements, dating from the early 16C.

Palacio Núñez Vela (A J) – Now the Law Courts, the former residence of the viceroy of Peru is a Renaissance palace with windows framed by slender columns surmounted by coats of arms. There is a beautiful inner *patio*.

Palacio de los Dávila (B V) – The palace consists of several seignorial mansions: two 14C Gothic buildings embellished with coats of arms give onto Plaza Pedro Dávila and two others, belonging to the Episcopal Palace, give onto plaza de Rastro.

BADAJOZ

Extremadura – Population 130 247
Michelin map 444 P 9

possible, approach Badajoz from the north so as to be able to appreciate the majestic entrance afforded by the alignment of the **Puente de Palmas**, a Herreran style granite bridge, and the 16C crenellated gateway of the same name. The town rises tiers up a hill dominated by the walls of an Arab fortress.

Today, the modern quarters stretching beyond the old town are a reminder that Badajoz is the capital of Spain's largest province. It is emerging economically as a result of the Guadiana Valley development scheme.

An eventful history – Badajoz, in Roman times a modest town dependent on Mérida, became capital in the 11C, of a Moorish kingdom or *taifa*. In the 16C it held a key position in peninsular strategy and was caught up in the Wars of Succession between Spain and Portugal, which meant that it was often besieged and pillaged.

For centuries, the embattled town was shut away in narrow streets, protected by the Moorish fortress and medieval ramparts. Today, Badajoz has abandoned this frontier mentality and is projecting itself as a city with an open, modern character as shown by the **Puente Real** (Royal Bridge) and its new contemporary art museum, the **Museo Extremeño e Iberoamericano de Arte Contemporáneo**.

The fall from grace of Don Manuel

Manuel Godoy Álvarez de Faria (1767-1851), the son of a modest provincial *hidalgo*, left his family at 17 for the Court where he enlisted in the Guards. Favours from Queen María Luisa assisted him in a meteoric career in politics; by the age of 25 he had been appointed Prime Minister. His rapid success earned him little sympathy from the Court, or from the common people who, outraged, accused him of being in Napoleon's pay. They insisted on his leaving the country. After the Aranjuez uprising, he followed the royal family into exile at Bayonne where he drew up Charles IV's act of abdication which was to deliver Spain to Napoleon. He died, unknown, in Paris.

SIGHTS

Catedral ⊙ – The cathedral, built in the 13C in the Gothic style, was considerabl[y] remodelled at the Renaissance and is consequently full of contrasts: it has [a] fortress type tower as well as a delicate Plateresque decoration of friezes a[nd] window surrounds. Inside, in the middle of the nave and masking the general vie[w] is an impressive *coro* for which the stalls were carved in 1557.

In the sacristy to the right of the chancel hang six fine 17C Flemish tapestrie[s].

Museo Arqueológico Provincial ⊙ – The 16C Palacio de la Roca inside t[he] *alcazaba* now houses a modern museum with rich collections of local archeologic[al] finds. These include prehistoric and proto-historic stelae and figurines; Rom[an] mosaics and tools made of bronze; beautiful Visigothic **pilasters** carved with pla[nt] and geometric motifs; medieval artefacts and exhibits of work from the Islam[ic] civilization.

Museo Provincial de Bellas Artes ⊙ – This fine arts museum is housed in t[wo] elegant 19C mansion houses. It contains a fine collection of paintings, sculptu[re] and sketches, particularly from the 19C and 20C.

BAEZA ★★

Andalucía (Jaén) – Population 17 691
Michelin map 446 S 19

Baeza, once a prominent frontier town, stands peacefully surrounded by olive grov[es] on the Andalucía-La Mancha border. Its many seignorial mansions and other buildin[gs] of golden stone give an idea of its days as a *taifa* capital, of its importance as the fir[st] town to be reconquered in Andalucía (1227) and its position as a march in t[he] Kingdom of Castilla until the 15C. Peace allowed the city to develop and intellectu[al] interests to emerge: in 1551 a printing press was established and in 1595 [a] university was founded (disbanded in the 19C).

★★ ARCHITECTURAL CENTRE *1hr*

Route marked on town plan

★ **Plaza del Pópulo** (Z) – Standing in the centre of the small, irregular square is t[he] **Fuente de los Leones** (Fountain of the Lions), built with antique remains. The form[er] **carnicería** (abattoir) (**A**), on the left, is a building of noble appearance consideri[ng] its function (1550-1962); the blazon over the first floor portico represents t[he] imperial coat of arms.

The **Casa del Pópulo** (former court), at the end of the square, has decorati[ve] Plateresque windows and medallions. The six doors once opened on six notarie[s'] offices; court hearings were held on the first floor. An attractive quarter-cir[cle]

Plaza de Santa María

BAEZA

Aguayo . . . . Y 2
Alcalde Garzón
   Nebrera (Av. del) . . . . . . Y
Barbacana . . . . Z 3
Cardenal Benavides
   (Pasaje) . . . . Y 5
Carmen . . . . Z
Cipriano Tornero
  o del Rojo . . . . Y
Compañía . . . . Z 6
Concepción . . . . Y
Conde de Romanones . . . Z 7
Constitución (Plaza de la) . Z 8
Córdoba (Puerta de) . . . . . Z 9
Corvera . . . . Y
España (Pl. de) . . . . Y
Gaspar Becerra . . . . Y 12
General Cuadros . . . . Y 13
José M. Cortés . . . . Y 15
Julio Burel . . . . YZ
Los Molinos . . . . Y
Magdalena . . . . Y 16
Merced . . . . Z
Motilla . . . . Y
Obispo Mengibar . . . . . . Z 17
Obispo Narváez
  o Barreras . . . . YZ
Pintada Baja . . . . Y
Pópulo (Pl. del) . . . . Z
Real (Camino) . . . . Z 19
Sacramento . . . . Z 20
San Andrés . . . . Y 21
San Felipe Neri (Cuesta) . Z 23
San Francisco . . . . Y
San Gil (Cuesta de) . . . . . Z 25
San Juan Bautista . . . . . . Z
San Pablo . . . . Y
Santa María (Pl. de) . . . . . Z

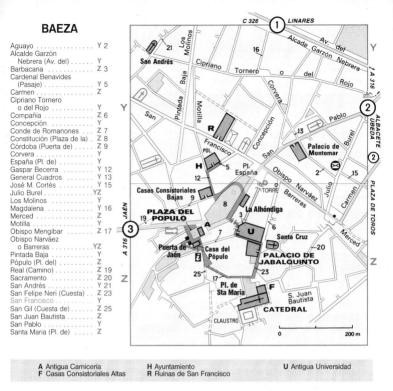

A Antigua Carnicería   H Ayuntamiento   U Antigua Universidad
F Casas Consistoriales Altas   R Ruinas de San Francisco

balcony projects onto the **Puerto de Jaén**, which, along with the Villalar arch, was dedicated to Charles V. The Jaén gate was erected to mark the emperor's visit on his way to Sevilla for his marriage to Isabel of Portugal on 12 March 1526. The **Arco de Villalar** was dedicated as a gesture of submission to the king after his victory, in 1521, over the Comuneros whom the town had supported.

Plaza de Santa María (Z) – On the left the walls of the 1660 Seminary are covered with inscriptions – the ancient custom having been to inscribe in bull's blood one's name and date on graduation. Behind the **Fuente de Santa María**, a triumphal arch adorned with atlantes, is the Gothic façade of the **Casas Consistoriales Altas** (F), emblasoned, between twin windows, with the arms of Juana the Mad and Philip the Fair.

Catedral ⊙ (Z) – The interior★ was almost entirely remodelled by Vandelvira and his followers between 1570 and 1593. Some of the chapels are outstanding: the Gold Chapel beside the fonts has a delicate Italianate relief; St James' has a fine antique setting and St Joseph's is flanked by caryatids. The graceful door to the sacristy is adorned with scrollwork and angels' heads. A monumental iron grille by Bartolomé closes the first bay in the nave while a pulpit of painted beaten metal (1580) stands in the transept crossing. In a chapel at the end of the north aisle is a gold and silver monstrance (1714) which is carried in procession on the feast of Corpus Christi. The arches in the cloisters were once part of the mosque.

★ **Palacio de Jabalquinto** (Z) – The palace's façade★, a perfect example of the Isabelline style, is best seen in the morning when the finials cast impressive shadows and the sun accentuates the Gothic decoration of the windows and pinnacles beneath slanting armorial bearings. The patio, built c 1600, is of more sober style, the only informal feature being the two lions guarding the great Baroque stairway.
Opposite the palace is the Romanesque church of **Santa Cruz**, the only one to remain of those built immediately after the town's reconquest.

Antigua Universidad (Z U) – The plain façade and elegant patio of this former university were built between 1568 and 1593. A fine Mudéjar ceiling can be seen in the large lecture hall.

La Alhóndiga (Z) – The old Corn Exchange features a frontage of arches and porticoes (1554).

Casas Consistoriales Bajas (Z) – This was built in 1703 as a gallery for officials attending celebrations held in the square.

★ **Ayuntamiento (town hall)** (Y H) – The façade of the former prison stands transformed by magnificent Plateresque windows, the armorial bearings of Philip II and of the town, and a wide cornice embellished with portraits of important persons carved on modillions.

ADDITIONAL SIGHTS

Iglesia de San Andrés ⓥ (Y) – Delicate Plateresque sculpture ornaments the sou
entrance of this church. The sacristy contains a group of nine Gothic **paintings**★.

Ruinas de San Francisco (Ruins) (Y R) – Only the vast transept and apse, wi
majestic carved stone altarpieces, remain to give an idea of the beautiful 16
church that once stood here.

Palacio de Montemar (or **Palace of the Counts of Garcíez**) (Y) – Beautiful Goth
windows and a Plateresque style *patio* adorn this early-16C nobleman's palac

BAIONA/BAYONA ★

Galicia (Pontevedra) – Population 9 690

Michelin map 441 F 3 – Local map see RÍAS BAJAS

The port of Baiona at the mouth of the Vigo inlet or *ría* faces out across its vast ba
and is protected from ocean storms to the north and south by the Monte Ferro an
Monterreal rock promontories. On 10 March 1493, the caravel *Pinta* – one of t
three vessels in Christopher Columbus's fleet – captained by **Martín Alonso Pinzó**
sailed into Baiona bringing news of the discovery of the New World. In the 16C a
17C, the town developed considerably through sea trade.

The old town – Baiona has grown into a lively summer resort with a harbour f
fishing boats and pleasure craft fronted by a promenade of terrace cafés. In t
old quarter houses may still be seen with coats of arms and glassed-in balconie
The **excolegiata** (former collegiate church) ⓥ at the top of the town was built in
transitional Romanesque-Gothic style between the 12C and 14C. Symbols on t
arches of chisels, axes and knives represent the various guilds that contribute
to the building of the church. Note also the stone pulpit dating from the 14C

Monterreal ⓥ – The Catholic monarchs had a defence wall built around Monte
real promontory at the beginning of the 16C. The fort within, which became t
governor's residence, has been converted into a parador, surrounded by a pleasa
pinewood. A **walk round the battlements**★ *(about 30min)*, rising sheer above t
rocks, is well worthwhile for the splendid **views**★★ of the bay, Monte Ferro, t
Estela islands and the coast with its sandy coves stretching south to the ca
Silleiro headland.

★ THE ROAD FROM BAIONA TO A GUARDA 30km/19mi – about 1

The coast between the two towns is a flat, semi-deserted area indented by the se

Oia – The houses in the fishing village are clustered around the former Cisterci
abbey of **Santa María la Real** with its Baroque façade. On the other side of the ro
are the outlying slopes of green hills where wild horses roam. Festivals known
curros, during which the wild foals are rounded up for branding, are held in t
hills on certain Sundays in May and June.

A Guarda – This small fishing village stands at the extreme southern end of t
Galician coastline. To the south, **monte Santa Tecla**★ (341m/1 119ft) rises above t
mouth of the Miño, affording fine **views**★★ from the top. On the slopes are t
extensive remains of a **Celtic city**, testimony to habitation by man from the Bron
Age to the 3C AD. Two round huts with stone walls and thatched roofs have be
reconstituted on the side of the road.

BARBASTRO

Aragón (Huesca) – Population 15 827

Michelin map 443 F 30

Barbastro lies at the centre of the Somontano, a fertile plain into which two lon
rugged Pyrenean valleys descend. The first leads down from the Parque de Ordes
the second incorporates a canyon, the Congosto de Ventamillo. The town was
substantial market centre at the time of the Moors and later became and still is
episcopal see, a mark of its regional importance. On 11 August 1137, Barbastro w
the setting for the marriage of Princess Petronila and Ramón Berenguer IV, a mat
sealing the union of Aragón and Catalunya.

★ **Catedral** ⓥ – The cathedral is a typical Spanish hall-church of the 16C but h
particularly slender columns. While the capitals are plain, the network vaulting
ornate with abundant relief work. The side chapel doors are decorated
Churrigueresque style with an incredible quantity of stucco. An **altarpiece** with
alabaster base by Damián Forment decorates the high altar. The first north cha
contains a fine early-16C painted altarpiece.

EXCURSION

Torreciudad ⊙ – *24km/15mi north on N 123 and A 2211.*
In 1804, an 11C Romanesque statue of Our Lady of Torreciudad was placed in a small shrine and venerated by the local people. In 1975 a church, now a place of pilgrimage, was built for the statue under the auspices of Monsignor José María Escrivá de Balaguer, founder of Opus Dei (1928). Preceding the brick buildings is a vast esplanade affording beautiful **views**★★ of the Pyrenees and, in the foreground, the El Grado dam. The church itself has a large nave and a modern alabaster altarpiece with relief work illustrating scenes from the Life of the Virgin. The statue of Our Lady of Torreciudad stands in the lower part of the altarpiece.

BARCELONA★★★

Catalunya – Population 1 681 132
Michelin map 443 H 36
Plan of the conurbation on Michelin map 443
Michelin Plan Barcelona 1 : 12 000 n° 41

Barcelona, the capital of Catalunya and the second largest city in Spain, stretches along the Mediterranean shore between the hills of Montjuïc, Vallvidrera and Tibidabo. It is a most attractive, stimulating city, especially from an architectural point of view.

Find your way around Barcelona with Michelin street map 41 at a scale of 1:12 000 which indicates one-way streets and includes an index of street names.

The growth of the city – The city was founded by the Phoceans. It grew in the Roman era and was known as **Barcino** in the 1C BC. The Romans settled on Mount Taber (the site of the present cathedral) and a fortified wall was built in the 3C. In the 12C, Barcelona took control of most of the former Catalan earldoms and became the capital of Catalunya and the seat of the joint kingdom of Aragón-Catalunya as well as a very important market centre. It conquered considerable territories on the Mediterranean. At the same time, the Catalan Gothic style of architecture blossomed, many new buildings were erected and the city spread beyond its walls.
During the War of the Spanish Succession (1701-14), Catalunya took sides with Charles, Archduke of Austria. After the victory of the Bourbons (on 11 September 1714) Barcelona lost its municipal government and its historical independence. Montjuïc hill was then fortified, a citadel, Ciutadella, was built and the district of Barceloneta was developed. The townspeople were not allowed to build beyond the walls within a radius of 2km/1.2mi, a distance corresponding to the range of cannon fire. The town then grew upwards inside the ramparts, with an extraordinarily high population density. The ban on building was not lifted until the middle of the 19C when a decision was taken to urbanise all the no-man's land around the old city. To this end the Cerdà plan was chosen. Over a period of 30 years, Barcelona grew quickly and substantially, rapidly incorporating small neighbouring villages such as Gracia, Sants, Horta, Sarrià and Pedralbes. Industrialisation made Barcelona one of the most active towns in Europe and two International Exhibitions were held here, one in 1888 on the site of the Ciutadella) and the other in 1929 on Montjuïc hill. There was an explosion of Modernist architecture during this period.

Barcelona present and future – More dynamic than ever, Barcelona is not only a large industrial centre with a very busy port, it is also a university town and the seat of the Generalitat de Catalunya. It is an important cultural centre with an opera-house and many museums, theatres and concert halls.
The Olympic Games, held in Barcelona in 1992, brought about the development of large-scale planning projects which have had an enormous impact on the city's appearance. These included the extension of the Diagonal, the building of a ring-road and the reconstruction of part of the seafront which was converted from a free port zone into a residential area.

Catalan identity – Barcelona is above all a Catalan town. This is evident in the use of Catalan which is considered the official language along with Castilian Spanish. The Catalan people are proud to speak their own language which was banned for many years under the Franco regime. A simple stroll around the city will reveal that all the street names and signs are in Catalan. The same goes for the literature, as a glance at a bookshop window will show.

A thriving centre for artists – Barcelona has been and still remains a thriving city and place of residence for great artists. Among the best-known modern artists are the painters Picasso, Miró, Dalí, Tàpies, the sculptor Subirachs and the architects Gaudí, Josep Lluís Sert, Bofill and Bohigas.

DISTRICTS

Barri Gòtic (**CDST**) – Following an intense restoration programme undertake during the 1920s, the area containing the city's major historical buildings wa renamed the Gothic quarter.

Ciutat Vella (**CST**) – The old city includes districts as diverse as Santa Ann La Mercè, Sant Pere and Raval. The latter, which used to be known as th Barrio Chino (Chinatown), now contains Barcelona's leading cultural centre and is a fine example of urban renovation.

Eixample (**CRS**) – Eixample (Ensanche) developed following the destruction c the city's medieval walls. The district personifies the bourgeois, elegar Barcelona of the end of the 19C, with its prestigious boutiques, smart avenue and some of the best examples of Modernist architecture.

Gràcia (**BR**) – This *barrio*, situated at the end of the Passeig de Gràcia, is one of the city's most characteristic areas. Gràcia developed from its early agricultural origins into an urban area as a result of the influx of shopkeepers, artisans and factory workers. During the 19C, Gràcia was renowned for its Republican sympathies. Today, it still hosts a number of popular fiestas.

Ribera (**DS**) – With its narrow alleyways and Gothic architecture, this former fisherman's quarter still retains an unquestionable charm. Its main attractions are the Calle Montcada and the Iglesia de Santa Maria del Mar.

Barceloneta (**DS**) – Barceloneta is famous for its outdoor stalls, restauran and nautical atmosphere.

Vila Olímpica (**DS**) – The Olympic Village was built to accommodate sportsme and sportswomen participating in the 1992 games. Nowadays, it is a mode district with wide avenues, landscaped areas and direct access to some Barcelona's restored beaches.

Les Corts (**AS**) – This district is located at the upper end of Diagonal a includes the **Ciudad Universitaria** (**AS**) and the **Camp Nou** (**AS**), the home Barcelona Football Club and its football-orientated **Museo del Barça** ⓥ.

Sarrià (**AR**) – Sarrià nestles at the foot of the Sierra de Collserola and h managed to retain its traditional, tranquil character. The neighbourir districts of **Pedralbes** (**AS**) and **Sant Gervasi de Cassoles** (**BR**), at the foot of Tibidab have become a favourite hangout for the city's well-heeled inhabitants.

Sants (**BS**) – One of the city's main working class districts close to the railwa station of the same name.

Horta-Guinardó (**CR**) – This *barrio* at the foot of Collserola was first populat by peasants and then by factory workers. It is home to the **Laberinto de Horta** *(to the north)*, an 18C property with attractive gardens, and the **Velódromo**, venue for sporting events and major music events.

Poble Sec (**CT**) – Poble Sec is spread over the slopes of Montjuïc Mountain a is one of Barcelona's oldest working class areas.

WHERE TO STAY

The **Michelin Red Guide España & Portugal** offers a wide selection of hotels listed district. Those specified below have been chosen for their surrounding character, excellent location or value for money.

The letters given after the name of the hotel correspond to its location on t Barcelona maps in this guide.

BUDGET HOTELS

Peninsular (**LY** ⓫) - *Sant Pau, 34 (Ciutat Vella).* ☏ *93 302 31 38. 60 rooms (many without air conditioning).*
The spartan rooms (those overlooking the street can be noisy) in this centrally located hotel are situated around a quaint inner courtyard where breakfasts and aperitifs can also be enjoyed. Popular with young people.

Abalón (**CR** ❸) - *Travessera de Gràcia, 380-384 (Gràcia).* ☏ *93 450 04 60, fax 93 435 81 23. 40 rooms.*
Located next to the Hospital de Sant Pau, near the Sagrada Familia. Clean rooms and efficient service.

Turín (**LX** ⓥ) - *Pintor Fortuny, 9-11 (Ciutat Vella).* ☏ *93 302 48 12. 60 rooms.*
Excellent location close to La Rambla, in the heart of the El Raval district. A building lacking charm but with spacious rooms, some with a balcony. The breakfast room is decorated with colourful *azulejos* and rustic wooden beams.

OUR SELECTION

Aragón (**DR** ❾) - *Aragón, 569 (Eixample).* ☏ *93 245 89 05, fax 93 247 09 23. 115 rooms.*
Centrally located, although somewhat noisy. Reservations recommended as it is often full. The rooms are modern in style and the service efficient.

Gaudí (**LY** ❶) - *Nou de la Rambla, 12 (Ciutat Vella).* ☏ *93 317 90 32, fax 93 412 26 36. 73 rooms.*
Situated opposite the Palacio Güell. The foyer is decorated in Modernist style. The rooms are spacious, with those on the upper floors facing the street enjoying superb views of the city and the Palacio Güell from their balconies.

Mesón Castilla (**CS** ❻) - *Valldonzella, 5 (Ciutat Vella).* ☏ *93 318 21 82, fax 93 412 40 20. 56 rooms.*
Located in an interesting building near the MACBA and CCCB. Attractively decorated with rustic, painted wooden furniture. A pleasant hotel with a friendly atmosphere and good service.

Metropol (**NY** ❼) - *Ample, 31 (Ribera).* ☏ *93 310 51 00, fax 93 319 12 76. 68 rooms.*
An attractively-decorated hotel near the Ribera district. Spacious, functional rooms.

Mercure Barcelona Rambla (**LX** ❷) - *La Rambla, 124 (Ciutat Vella).* ☏ *93 412 04 04, fax 93 318 73 23. 74 rooms.*
Impressive, tastefully-furnished hotel on La Rambla, near the Plaça de Catalunya. Bright rooms with delightful views of this famous street.

TREAT YOURSELF!

Arts (**DS**) - *Marina, 19-21 (Vila Olímpica).* ☏ *93 221 10 00, fax 93 221 10 70. 455 rooms.*
Barcelona's most modern and luxurious hotel. Located in the heart of the Vila Olímpica, with 42 floors offering impressive views of the city.

Palace (**CS** ❽) - *Gran Via de les Corts Catalanes, 668 (Eixample).* ☏ *93 318 52 00, fax 93 348 37. 161 rooms.*
The former Ritz continues to uphold the prestigious reputation it has maintained since opening its doors in 1919. The elegant, luxurious decoration and superb service are in keeping with its five-star rating. The hotel also has a restaurant, the Restaurante Diana.

Hotel Arts and Torre Mapfre

C. Sarramon/MARCO POLO

EATING OUT

The restaurants listed below have been chosen for their surrounding ambience or unusual character. For a wider selection and more detaile gastronomic information, consult the *Michelin Red Guide España & Portuga*

Ciutat Vella

BUDGET

Ca l'Estevet – *Valldonzella, 46.* ☎ *93 302 41 86.*
Small, family-run restaurant with a friendly atmosphere. Decorated wit attractive *azulejos* and photographs of famous people.

Agut – *Gignàs, 16.* ☎ *93 315 17 09.*
Located close to the Moll de la Fusta, in an area of narrow streets. A spaciou dining room with a certain decadent charm, with wood decoration covering th lower half of its walls, white tablecloths and old office chairs. Lunchtime men around 2 000 pts.

OUR SELECTION

Brasserie Flo – *Jonqueres, 10.* ☎ *93 319 31 02.*
French-style brasserie popular with musicians and artists.

Can Ramonet – *Maquinista, 17.* ☎ *93 319 30 64.*
One of La Barceloneta's most typical fish and seafood restaurants.

Los Caracoles – *Escudellers, 14.* ☎ *93 302 31 85.*
A traditional restaurant in an attractive setting. Popular with tourists.

Ca l'Isidre – *Flors, 12.* ☎ *93 441 11 39.*
A well-known restaurant once frequented by Barcelona's bohemia.

Casa Leopoldo – *Sant Rafel, 24.* ☎ *93 441 30 14.*
The famous detective Pepe Carvalho, created by Manuel Vázquez Montalbá is a regular customer at this classic Barcelona restaurant. Attractive dec including bullfighting mementoes, signed photos of famous customers and superb collection of bottles.

Eixample

BUDGET

La Llotja – *Aribau, 55.* ☎ *93 4 53 89 58.*
A modern, centrally-located restaurant decorated with photographs Barcelona F.C. footballers.

La Provença – *Provença, 242.* ☎ *93 23 23 67.*
Pleasant restaurant with cheerful, tasteful, decor.

OUR SELECTION

Folquer – *Torrent de l'Olla, 3.* ☎ *93 217 43 95.*
This small restaurant, decorated with works by Catalan artists (Tàpie Hernández Pijuan, Ràfols Casamada etc), is close to the Passeig de Gràcia. Th lunchtime menus (around 1 500 pts) are particularly good value.

El Tragaluz – *Passatge de la Concepció, 5.* ☎ *93 487 01 96.*
This elegant restaurant, which has been decorated like a greenhouse, has glass roof and contains a number of modern design features, as well as a tap bar and a fast-food dining area.

TREAT YOURSELF!

Casa Calvet – *Casp, 48.* ☎ *93 412 40 12.*
Located in a magnificent Modernist building designed by Gaudí inside th former offices of a textile company.

Gràcia

OUR SELECTION

Roig Robí – *Sèneca, 20.* ☎ *93 218 92 22.*
Elegant restaurant with a superb terrace for outdoor dining.

OT – *Torres, 25.* ☎ *93 284 77 52.*
This restaurant is located in the popular Gràcia district and contains a mixtu of traditional ornamental motifs and ultramodern designs. Modern, lig cuisine.

TREAT YOURSELF!

Jean Luc Figueres – *Santa Teresa, 10.* ☎ *93 415 28 77.*
This famous restaurant is one of the leading lights in Barcelona gastronom

Sarrià-Sant Gervasi

OUR SELECTION

El Asador de Aranda – *Avda. del Tibidabo, 31.* ☎ *93 417 01 15.*
This restaurant occupies Frare Blanc's former Modernist palace on the slopes of Tibidabo Mountain. Pleasant ambience with spacious dining rooms and terraces.

TREAT YOURSELF!

Via Véneto – *Ganduxer, 10-12.* ☎ *93 200 72 44.*
A Barcelona classic with 25 years' experience serving Catalan cuisine in Belle Epoque decor.

Neichel – *Beltran i Rozpide, 16 bis.* ☎ *93 203 84 08.*
A restaurant serving some of the city's most refined Catalan cuisine. Decor ranging from modern designs to traditional furniture.

Vila Olímpica

OUR SELECTION

Agua – *Passeig Marítim Barceloneta, 30.* ☎ *93 225 12 72.*
Spacious restaurant with designer furniture and African sculpture. Its terrace, always crowded in summer, is the perfect spot for a quiet dinner by the sea.

TREAT YOURSELF!

Talaia Mar – *Marina, 16.* ☎ *93 221 90 90.*
Ultramodern restaurant situated alongside the Olympic Port with superb views of the city and its waterfront.

TAPAS

Although Catalunya does not have a great tapas tradition, unlike other parts of Spain, visitors can still find some excellent tapas bars in the city.

Txacolín – *Pl. Montcada, 1-3 (Ciutat Vella).*
An ideal spot for a glass of *txacolí* (a Basque white wine) or some appetizing Basque delicacies.

Tapa Tapa – *Passeig de Gràcia, 44 (Eixample).*
A wide range of tapas and small sandwiches.

Casa Tejada – *Tenor Viñas, 3 (Sarrià-Sant Gervasi).*
Known for its *patatas bravas* (spicy potatoes) and cured hams.

El Xampanyet – *Montcada, 22 (Ciutat Vella).*
Famous for its anchovies and sparkling wine, which gives the bar its name.

NIGHT-LIFE

Barcelona nights can extend way into the small hours, particularly at weekends. The city offers visitors a huge choice of entertainment, ranging from cafés for a quiet get-together with friends to lively bars and clubs and discos with state-of-the-art technology.

Cafés

Café de la Opera – *Rambla dels Caputxins, 74 (Ciutat Vella).*
Situated along La Rambla, this famous landmark has one of the best reputations in the city. Not to be missed!

Quatre Gats – *Montsió, 3 bis (Ciutat Vella).*
The symbol of Modernist and bohemian Barcelona. This classic café was a meeting place for famous artists such as Picasso, Casas and Utrillo.

Café del Sol – *Plaça del Sol, s/n (Gràcia).*
A quiet old café with a very pleasant terrace for summer evenings.

El Paraigua – *Pas de l'Enseyança, 2.*
This delightful café, which is housed in a former umbrella shop, contains numerous mirrors and Modernist furniture.

Café de la Opera

Bars

The bars of the city tend to adopt the atmosphere of the area in which the
are located. The most crowded are to be found in the Vila Olímpica ar
Maremàgnum, while the upper part of the city and L'Eixample have attracte
a whole host of so-called designer bars. In Ciutat Vella, you are more likely
come across bars with a more bohemian atmosphere – particularly around th
Born district and in La Ribera – while the Plaça Reial is the traditional area fo
colourful bars with a more local clientèle. The Gràcia district, meanwhile, is th
place to be for live bands and shows. All bars tend to close one day a wee
(Mondays or Wednesdays).

CIUTAT VELLA

Pastís – *Santa Mònica, 4.*
Now past its 40th anniversary, this bar is the place to enjoy the famous Frenc
aperitif which gives the bar its name and to listen to the music of Jacques Bre
Georges Moustaki and Edith Piaf.

Marsella – *Sant Pau, 65.*
19C mirrors and marble tables decorate this bar which opened its doors
1820.

London – *Nou de la Rambla, 34.*
A favourite with circus performers when it first opened in 1909. Hemingwa
Miró and others also came here to enjoy its lively atmosphere.

Glaciar – *Plaça Reial, 3.*
This classic Barcelona bar, situated in the bustling Plaça Reial, was particular
popular earlier this century with writers, artists and socialites. Its ple
sant terrace is an ideal meeting place for those who enjoy a drink in the ope
air.

EIXAMPLE

Nick Havanna – *Rosselló, 208.*
A bar famous for its modern design.

Luz de Gas – *Muntaner, 246.*
This former Belle Epoque theatre is now home to a lively bar which attrac
the city's in-crowd. Hosts live bands once a week (country, jazz, soul ar
salsa).

Dry Martini – *Aribau, 162.*
Sophisticated cocktail bar. No prizes for guessing the house speciality.

Snooker – *Roger de Llúria, 42.*
A pleasant place for a drink and a game of snooker.

La Fira – *Provença, 171.*
Attractive bar decorated with robots and fairground amusements.

VILA OLÍMPICA – POBLE NOU

Ceferino – *Pamplona, 88 interior.*
One of the first places to open in the former factories of the Poble Nou distric
Rock music and the latest Spanish hits dominate the play-list.

SARRIÀ – SANT GERVASI

Merbeyé – *Plaça Dr. Andreu, s/n.*
On the slopes of Tibidabo. Lively outdoor terrace in summer.

Mirablau – Situated opposite the Merbeyé with a magnificent view of th
city.

Nightclubs

Barcelona has a huge number of discos and clubs. The following is a list of som
of the best known:

Zeleste – *Almogàvers, 122 (Vila Olímpica – Poble Nou).*
This former industrial building is now one of the city's most popular concer
halls.

Torres de Ávila – *Poble Espanyol, Avda. del Marqués de Comillas – Montjuïc.*
Decor by the designers Mariscal and Arribas. In summer it attracts a hug
number of Barcelona's night-owls.

Bikini – *Déu i Mata, 105 (Les Corts).*
A lively nightclub and concert venue in the Diagonal district.

Up & Down – *Numància, 179 (Les Corts).*
Upmarket nightclub with a strict dress code.

Otto Zutz – *Lincoln, 15 (Sarrià – Sant Gervasi).*
Doubles as a disco and concert venue.

LEISURE

Music

The **Palau de la Mùsica Catalana** *(see p 112)*, **Gran Teatre del Liceu** *(see p 105)* and the recently opened **Auditorio** *(see p 113)* are the city's biggest concert halls. Major pop and rock concerts are held in the **Palau Sant Jordi** *(see p 108)*, **Velódromo de Horta**, **Plaza de Toros Monumental** and **Sot del Migdia**.

The **Festival del Grec** (end of June to early August) is held at several venues, including the **Teatre Grec de Montjuïc**.

Art Galleries

Barcelona's most prestigious galleries can mainly be found in the calle Consell de Cent **(Carles Tatché, René Metras, Sala Gaudí)**, along the Rambla de Catalunya **(Joan Prats)**, on the periphery of the Born market and around the MACBA. The **Galeria Maeght** and the **Sala Montcada** are both located in the calle Montcada.

E. Simmons/DIAF

Antiques

Plaza de la Catedral – *(Ciutat Vella)*. A small market with stalls selling an eclectic range of antiques is held here on public holidays.

Plaza del Pi – *(Ciutat Vella)*. Craft products and reasonably priced antiques.

Plaza Sant Josep Oriol – *(Ciutat Vella)*. Mirrors, furniture, paintings and household goods are all on sale at this weekly market.

Calle de la Palla y calle Banys Nous – *(Ciutat Vella)*. Well-known for its reputable antique shops.

Bulevard Antiquaris – *Passeig de Gràcia, 55 (Eixample)*. An area containing over 70 shops selling a range of artwork and antiques.

TOURIST INFORMATION

Barcelona tourist office – *Passeig de Gràcia, 107 (Palau Robert). 08008 Barcelona. ☎ 93 238 40 00, fax 93 238 40 10.* **Internet:** www.gencat.es/probert

Publications – The *Guía del Ocio* is a weekly guide containing a list of every cultural event in the city. It can be purchased at newspaper stands. The city's airport and tourist offices are also able to provide visitors with a full range of booklets and leaflets produced by the Generalitat de Catalunya's Department of Industry, Commerce and Tourism.

Useful numbers

Emergency services: ☎ 061.

Duty chemist: ☎ 93 481 00 60.

State Police: ☎ 091.

Municipal Police: ☎ 062.

Train information – Renfe (international): ☎ 93 490 11 22; Renfe (domestic): ☎ 93 490 02 02.

Taxis – Radio Taxi Barcelona: ☎ 93 300 11 00; Tele-Taxi: ☎ 93 392 22 22.

Post Office: ☎ 93 318 38 31.

Airport: ☎ 93 298 38 38.

Barcelona Nord Bus Station: ☎ 93 265 65 08.

Ferry Port: ☎ 93 443 13 00/93 443 02 62.

TRANSPORT

Airport – 15km/9mi from the city centre. Can be reached by local train *(tre de cercanía)* at regular intervals throughout the day, or by the half-hourly bu service from the plaça de Catalunya and plaça de Espanya. By taxi, the far from the city centre will be approximately 2 000 pts.

Taxis – The city's black and yellow taxis are an efficient way of getting aroun the city.

Buses – Information (in Spanish) on ☎ 93 318 70 74. A good way of seein the city, although traffic jams are a major problem. Most of the city's bu network runs until 2am.

Bus Turístic – This excellent service offers visitors a variety of bus itinerarie throughout the city. Daily departures from plaça de Catalunya starting a 9am.

Metro – *Metro stations are shown on the maps in this guide.* For furthe information call ☎ 93 318 70 74. Many stations have access for the disabled For further details, call ☎ 93 412 44 44.
The network consists of five lines and is open from 5am to 11pm weekday (except Fridays and days preceeding public holidays); from 5am to 1am c Fridays, Saturdays and days preceeding public holidays; from 6am t midnight on Sundays and from 6am to 11pm on weekday public holidays. free metro guide is available.
Metro tickets and cards can also be used on train services operated b Ferrocarriles de la Generalitat de Catalunya. In addition to single tickets multi-journey cards *(tarjetas)* are also available. These include the T-2 (valid fc 10 trips), T-DIA (unlimited travel for one day), T50-30 (for 50 trips in 30 days and the T-MES (unlimited travel for one month).

Regional Railway Network – *"Ferrocarriles Catalanes"* train stations ar shown on the maps in this guide. For further information, ca ☎ 93 205 15 15. The following stations can be used for free connections t the metro system: Av. Carrilet/L'Hospitalet, Espanya, Catalunya an Diagonal/Provença.

Tramvia Blau – This tourist tram operates on public holidays through th upper part of the city (Diagonal, Pedralbes, Sarrià). ☎ 93 318 70 74.

★★ BARRI GÒTIC (THE GOTHIC QUARTER) (MX)

3hr including museum visits. See town plan.

The Gothic quarter, so named on account of its many buildings constructe between the 13C and 15C, is, in fact, far older. There are traces of the Roma settlement as well as of the massive 4C walls built after barbarian invasions.

Plaça Nova (128) – This is the heart of the Gothic quarter. The Romans bui a rectangular site with walls 9m/30ft high and attendant watchtowers of whic the two that guarded the West Gate remain to this day. In the Middle Age when the town expanded beyond the walls, the gateway was converted into house.
Opposite the cathedral, the **Collegi d'Arquitectes** (College of Architects) **(L)** stands ou as an architectural surprise among the old buildings. Its modern façade has decorative band of cement engraved by Picasso.

★ **Catedral** ⊘ – The cathedral adjoins the Pla de la Seu, fronted by the **Casa de Canonja** (16C), and the **Pia Almoina**, housing the **Museo Diocesano de Barcelona** ⊘ on on side and the **Casa de l'Ardiaca★** (12C-15C) on the other.
The present edifice, dedicated to St Eulàlia and the Holy Cross, was built on th former site of a Romanesque church. Construction began in the late 13C, endin only in 1450. The front façade and the spire are modern (19C) additions base on original designs by a builder from Rouen in France (hence the French influenc in the gables, pinnacles and crockets).
The Catalan Gothic **interior** has an outstanding elevation due partly to the del cate, slender pillars. The nave is clearly lit by a fine lantern-tower above th first bay but the perspective is unfortunately broken by the **coro★★**. Th features double rows of beautifully carved **stalls**. Note the fine workmanshi and the humorous scenes adorning the misericords. In the early 16C, th backs of these were painted with the coats of arms of the knights belo ging to the Order of the Golden Fleece during one of their many gathering presided over by Charles V. The artist was Juan de Borgoña, who signe here one of the most impressive achievements in the history of Europea heraldry.

The white marble **choir screen**★ was sculpted in the 16C after drawings by Bartolomé Ordóñez, one of Spain's greatest Renaissance artists, who may have also worked on the stalls. The statues illustrate the death of St Eulàlia, a 4C virgin and martyr born in Barcelona who became the patron of the town. Her relics lie in the **crypt**★ in a 14C alabaster sarcophagus carved in the style of Pisa.

The Capilla del Santísimo, to the right as you enter the main door, contains the 15C *Christ of Lepanto* which is thought to have been mounted on the prow of the galley belonging to Don Juan of Austria during the Battle of Lepanto (1571). The side chapels are rich in Gothic altarpieces and marble tombs: note the retable to St Gabriel in the central ambulatory chapel; the **retable of the Transfiguration**★ by Bernat Martorell, the one adorning the Capilla de San Benito (St Benedict's Chapel – *2nd on the right*) and finally the retable representing the Visitation in the adjoining chapel.

Outside, opposite the cathedral, stands the Casa del Archidiácono (**A**) with a charming *patio*.

★ **Claustro** – The cloisters, dating from 1448, open onto huge bays built according to Gothic tradition. They form a restful oasis of greenery with their palms and magnolias, and are home to a flock of geese. The chapter-house off the west gallery houses a **museum** ⊙ where you can admire a *Pietà* by Bermejo (1490), altarpiece panels by the 15C artist Jaime Huguet and the missal of St Eulàlia, enhanced by delicate miniatures.

When you leave the cloisters, take Carrer Montjuïc del Bisbe opposite.

Plaça Sant Felip Neri (163) – The Renaissance houses surrounding this small square were moved here when Via Laietana was being built, to make room for the new street. The square is home to the unusual **Museu del Calçat** ⊙ (**MX M**¹⁷), a shoe museum whose exhibits include Columbus' shoes.

Leave the square on carrer Sant Sever and turn right into carrer del Bisbe Irurita.

Carrer del Bisbe Irurita (15) – The right of the street is bordered by the side wall of the Palau de la Generalitat (Provincial Council). Above a doorway is a fine early-15C medallion of St George by Pere Johan.

The left of the street is bordered by the **Casa dels Canonges** (Canons' Residence) (**B**), now the residence of the President of the Generalitat. A neo-Gothic covered gallery (1929), over a star-vaulted arch, spans the street to link the two buildings.

Palau de la Generalitat (Provincial Council) – This vast 15C-17C edifice is the seat of the Autonomous Government of Catalunya. It has a Renaissance style façade on plaça Sant Jaume (c 1600).

Ajuntament (town hall) (H) – The town hall façade on plaça Sant Jaume is neo-Classical while that on carrer de la Ciutat is an outstanding 14C Gothic construction.

Carrer Paradis (133) – At no 10 stand four Roman **columns**★, remains of the Temple of Augustus.

Carrer Paradis leads into carrer de la Pietat which is bordered on the left by the Gothic façade of the Casa dels Canonges. The cathedral cloister doorway opposite is adorned with a wooden 16C sculpture of a *Pietà*.

★★ **Plaça del Rei (149)** – On this splendid square stand some of the important medieval buildings of the city: the Palau Reial Major (at the back), the Capilla de Santa Àgata (on the right) and the Palau del Lloctinent. In the right-hand corner is the Casa Clariana-Padellàs, which houses the Museu d'Història de la Ciutat.

★ **Museu d'Història de la Ciutat** ⊙ (**M**¹) – *Enter by calle Veguer.* The Museum of Local History is set up in a fine 15C Gothic mansion that was moved here stone by stone while the Via Laietana was being built in 1931.

The visit is divided into two parts: the remains of the old Roman city, lying underground beneath the main square, and the outbuildings attached to the Palau Reial Major, including the Salón Tinell and the Capilla de Santa Àgata.

★★ **The Roman City** – An interesting stroll underneath the museum and Plaça del Rei will allow you to discover the vestiges of the ancient Roman town, with the houses' foundations, canalizations, reservoirs etc. In the adjoining rooms, covered with barrel vaulting, are displayed sculptures dating from the 1C-4C (busts portraying Agrippina, Faustina and Antoninus Pius). In the mezzanine of the Casa Padellàs are exhibited Jewish and Arab vestiges of medieval Barcelona.

Palau Reial Major – *Cross the square.* Initially built in the 11C and 12C, the palace was gradually enlarged over the years until it acquired its present appearance in the 14C. It used to be the official residence of the counts of Barcelona and subsequently that of the kings of Aragón. The façade features huge buttresses linked together by arches. At the back of these arches lies the original Romanesque façade with its trilobate windows and Gothic rose windows.

BARCELONA

Amadeu Torner . . . . AT 2
Armes (Pl.) . . . . DS 3
Berlin . . . . BS 12
Brasil . . . . AS 25
Carles III (Gran Via de) . . . . AS 38

Corts Catalanes
  (Gran Via de les) . . . . . BCS
Creu Coberta . . . . BT 53
Enric Prat de la Riba . . . . . AT 66
Exposició (Pg. de) . . . . CT 75
Galileo . . . . AS 81
Ganduxer . . . . AR 82
Gràcia (Pg. de) . . . . CS

Guinardó (Ronda de) . . . . CR 9
Hospital Militar
  (Av. de l') . . . . BR 93
Joan Bordó Comte de
  Barcelona (Pg. de) . . . DST 99
Joseph V. Foix . . . . AR 10
Lluís Campanys
  (Pg. de) . . . . DS 10

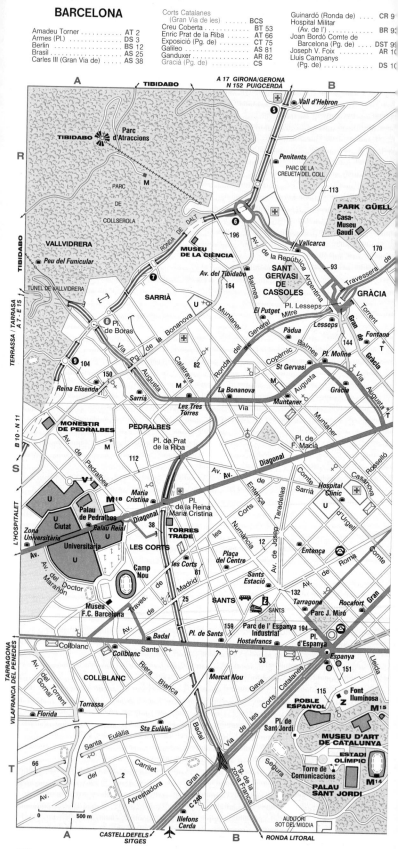

Manuel Girona (Pg. de) ... AS 112
Mare de Déu del Coll
  (Pg. de la) .... BR 113
Marquès de Comillas
  (Av.) .... BT 115
Montalegre .... CS 121
Olímpic (Passeig) .... CT 131
Països Catalans (Pl. dels) . BS 132

Princep d'Astúries
  (Av. del) .... BR 144
Pujades (Pg. de) .... DS 145
Reina Elisenda de
  Montcada (Pg. de la) .. AR 150
Reina Maria Cristina (Av.) . BT 151
Sant Antoni .... BT 159
Sant Antoni (Ronda de) .. CS 160

Sant Antoni Abat .... CS 161
Sant Gervasi (Pg. de) .... BR 164
Sant Josep de la Muntaya . CR 170
Sant Pau (Ronda de) .... CT 174
Tarragona .... BT 194
Tibidabo (Av. del) ...... BR 196
Universitat
  (Pl. de la) .... CS

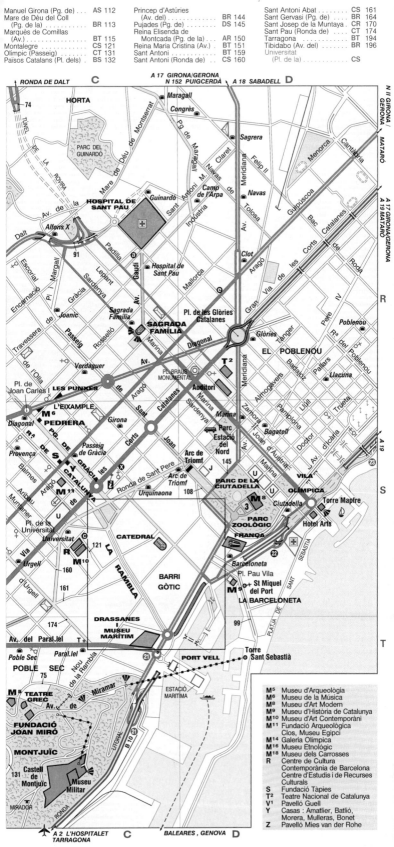

M5 Museu d'Arqueologia
M6 Museu de la Música
M8 Museu d'Art Modern
M9 Museu d'Història de Catalunya
M10 Museu d'Art Contemporàni
M11 Fundació Arqueològica
    Clos, Museu Egipci
M14 Galeria Olímpica
M16 Museu Etnològic
M18 Museu dels Carrosses
R   Centre de Cultura
    Contemporània de Barcelona
    Centre d'Estudis i de Recursos
    Culturals
S   Fundació Tàpies
T2 Teatre Nacional de Catalunya
V1 Pavelló Güell
Y   Casas : Amatller, Batlló,
    Morera, Mulleras, Bonet
Z   Pavelló Mies van der Rohe

BARCELONA

Bacardí (Pas.)	MY	4
Banys Nous	MX	7
Bergara	LV	10
Bisbe	MX	15
Bòria	MV	18
Born (Pas. del)	NX	20
Boters	MX	23
Canaletes (Rambla de)	LV	27
Canonge Colom (Pl.)	LY	28
Canvis Vells	NX	32
Caputxins (Rambla dels)	MY	35
Cardenal Casañas	LX	36
Catalunya (Pl. de)	LV	
Catedral (Av. de la)	MV	40
Ciutat	MX	43
Comercial (Pl.)	NV	45
Cucurulla	LX	55
Doctor Joaquim Pou	MV	61
Estudis (Rambla dels)	LX	
Francesc Gambó (Av.)	MV	79
Garriga i Bach (Pl.)	MX	81
Isabel II (Pas. d')	NX	98
Montcada	NV	122
Montjuic del Bisbe	MX	123
Nou de Sant Francesc	MY	126
Nova (Pl.)	MX	128
Paradis	MX	133
Pi (Pl. del)	LX	137
Pintor Fortuny	LX	140
Portal de Santa Madrona	MX	142
Ramon Berenguer et Gran (Pl. de)	MX	147
Rei (Plaça del)	MX	149
Sant Felip Neri (Pl.)	MX	163
Sant Josep Onol (Pl.)	LX	167
Sant Joseph (Rambla de)	LX	168
Sant Iu (Pl. de)	MX	170
Sant Miquel (Pl. de)	MX	173
Sant Sever	MX	181
Santa Anna	LV	182
Santa Maria (Pl.)	NX	189
Santa Mònica (Rambla de)	MY	
Seu (Pl. de la)	MX	192
Tapineria	MX	193
Universitat (Ronda de la)	LV	199

A	Casa de l'Ardiaca
B	Casa dels Canonges
C	Saló del Tinell
E	Palau del Lloctinent
F	Capella Sta-Agata
G	Duana Nova
H	Ajuntament
K	Mirador del Rey Martí
L	Col. legi d'Arquitectes
M¹	Museu d'Història de la ciutat
M²	Museu Frederic Marès
M³	Museu de Cera
M⁷	Castell dels tres Dragons' (Museu Zoologia)
M¹²	Museu Barbier-Mueller d'art precolombí
M¹³	Museu Geologia
M¹⁶	Palau del Marquès de Lió (Museu Textil i de la Indumentária)
M¹⁷	Museu del Calçat
M²⁰	Convento de Santa Mònica
N	Casa Pia Almoina
S	Palau Marc
V	Casa de la Canonja

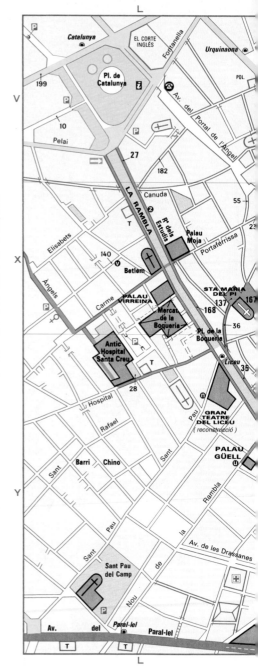

★ **Capilla de Santa Àgata** (**F**) – This 14C chapel with a single nave is covered by intricate polychrome woodwork panelling. It houses the **Altarpiece of the Constable**★★ executed by Jaime Huguet in 1465, depicting scenes from the life of Jesus and the Virgin Mary. In the centre, the *Adoration of the Three Wise Men* is a masterpiece of pictorial art from Catalunya.

A side staircase leads to the **Mirador del Rei Martí** (**K**), a five-storey tower commanding a lovely **view**★★ of the old city, with the cupola of the Basílica de la Mercè looming in the distance.

Salón del Tinell (**C**) – This lofty 14C room 17m/56ft high is covered with a two-sloped ceiling resting on six vast round arches.

According to tradition, it was here that the Catholic kings received Christopher Columbus in 1493 after he returned from his first voyage to America.

Palau del Lloctinent (**E**) – This 16C Late Gothic palace with Renaissance additions used to be the residence of the viceroys of Catalunya.

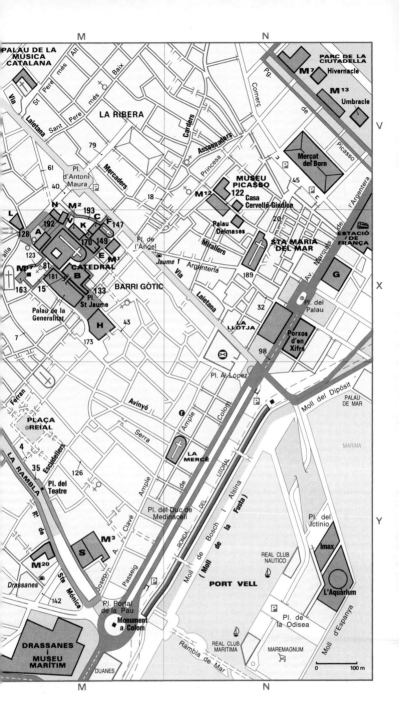

★ **Museu Frederic Marès** ⊘ (**M²**) – The collections displayed in this museum, set up in the Palau Reial Major *(enter through plaça de Sant Iu)*, were bequeathed to the city by the sculptor Frederic Marès. There are two parts to the museum:

Sculpture Section – This part occupies two floors of the palace and the crypt. The works are displayed in chronological order from the Iberian period up to the 19C. Note the imposing **collection of Christs and Calvaries★** carved in polychrome wood (12C-14C), a 16C **Holy Entombment★** and **The Vocation of St Peter★**, a highly expressive 12C relief attributed to the master Cabestany.

Museo Sentimental – This houses an extensive collection of small everyday objects. Particularly interesting are the various recreational rooms, the smoking parlour and the women's boudoir (spectacles, fans, clothes etc).

Plaça Ramón Berenguer el Gran (**147**) – A section of the Roman city wall has been incorporated into the palace precincts.

** LA RAMBLA *2hr*

The most famous street in Barcelona, La Rambla, made up of five differen
sections, follows the course of an old river-bed bordering on the Gothic quarter
La Rambla forms a long exuberant promenade between plaça de Catalunya
separating the Eixample district from the old quarter, and plaça Portal de la Pau
where the Columbus Memorial stands. At all times of the day and night a colourfu
crowd of locals, tourists and down and outs moves along the street beneath th
plane trees, passing the bird and flower sellers and the news-stands that se
papers and magazines in every language.

The upper section of La Rambla, level with plaça de Catalunya, is called Rambl
de Canaletes (**LV 27**), and the following stretch Rambla dels Estudis or Rambla del
Ocells (Avenue of the Birds).

Iglesia de Betlem (**LX**) – This church built in Baroque style – the interior was raze
by a fire in 1936 – has retained its imposing façade, which gives onto carrer de
Carme.

* **Palau de la Virreina** (**LX**) – This elegant palace dating back to 1778, originally buil
for the Vicereine of Peru, is charmingly decorated with both Baroque and Rococ
elements. It hosts major temporary exhibitions.

Turn back towards Betlem Church and take Carrer del Carme on the left.

* **Museu d'Art Contemporàni de Barcelona (MACBA)** ⓥ (**CS M¹⁰**) – Designed by th
American architect Richard Meyer, this museum is a huge **building**★★ that present
characteristics of the rationalist Mediterranean tradition while also introducin
modern elements of contemporary architecture. Two significant works can b
seen outside: *La Ola* by Jorge Oteiza and Eduardo Chillida's mural, *Barcelona*.
The **standing collections**★ housed in large, pristine white exhibition rooms cover th
major artistic movements to have emerged in the past 50 years. Exhibits includ
works influenced by Constructivism and Abstract art (Klee, Oteiza, Miró, Calder
Fontana), as well as creations by experimental artists (Kiefer, Boltanski, Solano
and names typically associated with the 1980s (Hernández, Pijuán, Barceló
Tàpies, Ràfols Casamada, Sicilia).

Centre de Cultura Contemporània de Barcelona (CCCB) ⓥ (**CS R**) – This busy art
centre (temporary exhibitions, lectures, courses etc) is set up on newly restore
premises whose unusual **patio**★ combines original decorative elements (mosaics o
silk-screen floral motifs) with modern characteristics, like the large central pan
of glass.

Antic Hospital de la Santa Creu (**LY**) – This complex of Gothic, Baroque an
neo-Classical buildings is a veritable haven of peace in the middle of a very livel
district. This old hospital building now houses the Library of Catalunya. Th
courtyard has been converted into a public garden. A charming **Gothic patio**★ ca
be reached through a hall decorated with *azulejos*.

La Rambla

As you leave the complex in carrer del Carme, you will be able to see the future Museo de Arte Contemporáneo (Museum of Contemporary Art) at the end of carrer dels Angels opposite. Part of the museum will be housed in the former Casa Caritat hospital.

Return to La Rambla, cross onto the other side and take carrer del Cardenal Casañas.

★ **Iglesia de Santa Maria del Pi** ⊘ (LX) – This 14C Catalan Gothic church is striking for its simplicity and the size of its single nave. It stands in an attractive square (that bears its name) in which a flea market is held on Thursdays.

Return to La Rambla.

Further down La Rambla, on the right, the 1845 opera-house or **Gran Teatre del Liceu** (LY) (its interior destroyed by fire in January 1994 – reopening scheduled for autumn 1999) is held by some to be one of Europe's most beautiful concert halls. Opposite the Liceu lies the **Pla de la Boqueria**, a charming little esplanade whose pavement was decorated by the artist Joan Miró.

Turn right into Carrer Nou de la Rambla.

★ **Palau Güell** ⊘ (LY) – The former residence of the Güell family is a curious building designed by Gaudí in 1889. Note the parabolic arches at the entrance and the extravagant bars so typical of the Modernist movement. The most striking features of the interior are the upper hall and the floor mosaics, artfully combining stone and ceramics.

Turn back to La Rambla and cross over.

★ **Plaça Reial** (MY) – This vast pedestrian square shaded by palm trees and lined with cafés is surrounded by neo-Classical buildings constructed between 1848 and 1859. With its shoe-shiners and other small tradespeople it has kept its picturesque air. The fountain in the middle is flanked by lampposts designed by Gaudí. A stamp and coin market is held here on Sunday mornings.

Return to La Rambla.

La Rambla de Santa Mònica (MY) marks the point where La Rambla meets up with the sea. Here stand the former **Convento de Santa Mònica** ⊘ (MY M²⁰), now a modern art centre that hosts temporary exhibitions, and the **Museo de Cera** ⊘ (MY M³), a wax museum.

Columbus Memorial (MY) – Erected in 1886, this monument commemorates the welcome that the Catholic kings gave the navigator when he returned from the Americas.

★ **THE SEA FRONT** *allow half a day*

It runs from the foot of the Montjuïc Mountain to the mouth of the Besòs river. The whole district was completely redesigned and upgraded for the 1992 Olympic Games. Ironically, Barcelona, which has always turned its back to the sea, is now regarded as a coastal town.

R. Campnabi/GC (DICT)

★★ **Drassanes (Shipyards) and Museum Marítim** ⊘ (MY) – The **ropeworks** here ar
among the best examples of non-religious Gothic architecture in Catalunya. Te
sections – seven from the 14C and three beside La Rambla from the 17C – remai
from the former shipyard: they are covered by a long timber roof supported b
a row of sturdy arches carved in stone. Such a place was the ideal setting for
Maritime Museum, in which Catalan naval history is recreated through interactiv
displays and priceless exhibits. Among the many models of sailing boats an
steamships is a lifesize replica of *El Real*, the galley in which Don Juan of Austr
sailed at the Battle of Lepanto. The area devoted to cartography contains th
Portulan of Gabriel de Vallseca (1439), which belonged to Amerigo Vespucci, while th
Pere IV building displays a fine collection of figureheads.
The rehabilitation of the area around the port began with the refurbishment o
the Moll de Bosch i Alsina (NY), commonly referred to as **Moll de la Fusta**,
promenade lined with palm trees, flanked by a raised terrace.

★ **Port Vell** (NY) – The old harbour has been converted into a lively leisure are
featuring a great many bars, the **Maremàgnum** shopping and leisure centre,
modern **aquarium** and the **Imax** ⊘, a spectacular cinema screen showing thre
dimensional films.

★ **Aquarium** ⊘ – This is one of Europe's most impressive sub-aquatic zoos displayir
a full range of Mediterranean species and exotic tropical specimens. A spectacul
tunnel, 80m/262ft long, crosses this magnificent aquarium.

★ **Basílica de la Mercè** ⊘ (NY) – The building such as it stands today dates fro
1760. Its main façade is the only existing example of curved Baroque architectu
in Barcelona. The façade giving onto Calle Ample is Renaissance and was take
from a different church. The late 19C cupola is crowned by a monument
sculpture portraying the Virgin de la Mercè, to whom a pretty Gothic statue
also dedicated in the interior, and the **Mare de Déu de la Mercè**★, attributed to Pe
Moragues (1361).

After crossing Via Laietana, whose construction in the first decade of the 20
involved razing or moving a great many buildings, continue along the Passe
d'Isabel II.

★ **La Llotja** (NX) – The building presently houses the headquarters of the Chamb
of Commerce and Industry. It was completely rebuilt in the neo-Classical style
the late 18C. Of the original medieval construction there remains only the lof
Gothic hall★★, a huge chamber with three naves separated by triple round arche

★ **Estació de França** (NVX) – Recently restored, supported by its huge iron structu
crowned by glass roofing, this is Barcelona's station for long-distance trains.
also stages important cultural events, like the Annual Comics Fair.

★ **Parc de la Ciutadella** ⊘ (DS) – Originally built by Philip V to keep watch over th
rebels of Barcelona, the citadel was destroyed in 1868 and replaced by garden
Its grounds were used to host the 1888 edition of the World Fair, whose symbo
entrance was the Triumphal Arch (DS).

★★ **Castell dels Tres Dragons** (NV M⁷) – Domènech i Montaner built this pavilion for th
World Fair in a functional, neo-Gothic style, using stark materials (brick and iro
without any form of covering.

★ **Museu Zoologia** ⊘ (NV M⁷) – All the zoological species are represented in th
extensive collections displayed here.

Waterfall – This impressive waterfall was designed by Gaudí when he was still
student. The small nearby lake is suitable for leisurely boat rides.

★ **Parc Zoològic** ⊘ (DS) – This zoo takes up a large part of the Parc de la Ciutadell
Animals from all over the world can be seen in their natural environment. Do n
miss the main attraction, Snowflake (Floquet de Neu), an albino gorilla, and th
dolphin show in the Aquarama.

Museu d'Art Modern ⊘ (DS M⁸) – Set up in a wing of the former citadel, the museu
presents the work of Catalan artists from the 19C and especially the 20
Fortuny, Ramón Casas, Nonell, Regoyos, Gargallo, Sert...

Return to Pla del Palau along Avenida Marquès d'Argentera and take the Passe
Nacional.

★ **La Barceloneta** (DS) – This district, known as the "Iberian Naples" and tradit
nally associated with fishermen, sailors and dockers, will delight visitors becau
of its quaint narrow streets and its typical fish restaurants and stalls, offeri
mouthwatering seafood dishes.

★ **Museu d'Història de Catalunya** ⊘ (DS M⁹) – This museum is housed in the form
general stores of the port of Barcelona, a group of buildings which date from t
beginning of the century. It provides an insight into the history of Catalunya fro
prehistory to the present day.

At the end of the Passeig Nacional, continue into the Passeig Marítim.

★ **Vila Olímpica** (DS) – Built to provide accommodation for the 15 000 athletes competing in the 1992 Olympic Games, this is one of the most modern areas of present-day Barcelona. The overall project was entrusted to the team of architects M.B.M. (Martorell, Bohigas & Mackay), but the plans for each individual building were conceived by local architects. The Olympic Village boasts many gardens and avenues dotted with modern sculptures.

The new **marina**★★ designed by engineer JR de Clascà has become one of the city's most popular leisure areas with numerous bars, restaurants and pavement cafés. The most striking buildings are the **twin towers** 153m/502ft high (Hotel Arts and the Torre Mapfre). The **view**★★★ from the top of these towers is truly breathtaking: on a clear day you can even glimpse the outlines of Mallorca.

★★ **CARRER DE MONTCADA** (NV 122)

1hr 30min including a visit to the Museu Picasso – see plan of old city

During the 13C and the 14C the Catalan fleet exercised unquestionable supremacy over the western basin of the Mediterranean. Important merchant families acquired considerable social status and the Carrer de Montcada became a showcase for their high expectations and new standards of living. This street, named after the Montcada, an influential family of noble descent, is a unique ensemble of merchants' palaces and aristocratic mansions, most of which date back to the late Middle Ages. Behind the austere façades are quaint little *patios* with galleries and porches typical of Catalan Gothic architecture.

The following is a selection of small palaces: the 15C Palau de Berenguer de Aguilar, now the Museu Picasso, the 14C Palau del Marqués de Llió (NV M¹⁶) which houses the **Museu Tèxtil i d'Indumentària** ⊘ (Textile and Costume Museum), the 17C Palau Dalmases at no 20 with Baroque frieze decorations on the staircase, and the 16C Palau Cervelló-Giudice at no 25, now the Maeght Gallery, with a fine flight of steps.

★ **Museu Picasso** ⊘ (NV) – The Gothic palaces of Berenguer de Aguilar and Baron de Castellet provide a wonderful setting for the museum. Many of Picasso's (Málaga 1881-Mougins 1973) works are displayed, dedicated, in most cases, to his friend Sabartès of whom there are several portraits (including an abstract painting of him wearing a ruff).

Picasso's advanced genius is evident in work from his youth: portraits of his family, *First Communion* and *Science and Charity* (1896). Among examples of his early work in Paris are *La Nana* and *La Espera*, while *Los Desemparados* (1903) is from his Blue Period and the portrait of *Señora Casals* from his Rose Period. His **Las Meninas series**★ consists of liberal variations on the famous picture by Velázquez.

Picasso's skill as an engraver may be seen in his outstanding etchings of bull-fighting and his talent as a ceramist in the many vases, dishes and plates (donated to the museum by Jacqueline Picasso) that he made in the 1950s.

Museu Barbier-Mueller d'art precolombí ⊘ (NVX M¹²) – The Palacio Nadal houses this collection of pre-Columbian art which includes votive figures from Amazonia.

★★ **Iglesia de Santa Maria del Mar** ⊘ (NX) – The recently restored church is one of the most beautiful examples of the Catalan Gothic style. It was built in the 14C by local sailors who in spite of their modest means, wanted to compete with the wealthy townspeople who were building the cathedral. The result is a gracefully proportioned church, outstanding in its simplicity. The walls are unadorned in the Catalan manner and the west front decorated only by a portal gable and the buttresses flanking the superb Flamboyant **rose window**★. The interior gives the impression of harmonious spaciousness due to the elevation of the nave and the side aisles divided only by slender octagonal pillars.

★ **MONTJUÏC** (CT) *1 day, including museum visits – see general plan*

The "mountain of the Jews" is a 173m/568ft hill overlooking the city. When the citizens of Barcelona rose in revolt against Philip IV in 1640 they built a fort (CT) on the hill (now home to a military museum). The castle terraces command extensive **views**★ of the city and the harbour to the south. Montjuïc hosted the International Exhibition in 1929 and since then **Plaça de Espanya** (BT), the gateway to the exhibition, has remained a major centre for World Fairs. Among the many remaining monuments and pavilions built for the event are the illuminated **fountain** (BT) or **Font Lluminosa** by Carles Buïgas, at the end of Avinguda de la Reina Maria Cristina, the recently reconstituted **reception pavilion**★★ (BT Z) by Mies van der Rohe, outstanding for its simplicity, modernity and the variety of materials used, and the Spanish Village (Poble Espanyol in Catalan, Pueblo Español in Castilian). A Frenchman, Forestier, designed the flower-filled gardens which descend the slope.

Esp. ang. 5

Romanesque altarfront,
Museu Nacional d'Art de Catalunya

H. Stierlin

*** Museu Nacional d'Art de Catalu ya (BT) – Set up in the Palacio Naci nal that was built for the 1929 Wor Fair, this museum features remark ble **Romanesque and Gothic collections** ** taken from many churches in Cat lunya and Aragón, and a selectic of exhibits from the **Francesc Caml** collection, with works from the 16 18C. In the near future, the museu will also include Renaissance ar Baroque sections, as well as a c(lection from the Museo de Ar Moderno.

Romanesque Art – In the 12C-13C t Pyrenean valleys saw the develo ment of a highly expressive and m ture art form.

The frescoes are displayed in ch pels and large rooms that evoke t atmosphere of contemporary chu ches. Clearly influenced by Byzantir mosaics, they are characterised t heavy black outlines, superimpose frieze compositions, lack of perspe tive and rigidity of stance. Howeve the addition of realistic or expressiv details lend a distinctive Catalan touc to these paintings. Note the 12C fre coes by Sant Joan de Boí (Room with *The Stoning of St Stephen, T*

Falconer and *Paradise and Hell*, the late 11C lateral apses by Sant Quirze de Pedr (Room III), the Santa María de Taüll ensemble (12C), presenting a host of image dominated by a fine *Epiphany* and the paintings from Sant Climent de Ta (Room V) with its remarkable *Christ in Majesty*: the apse is considered to be one the finest examples of Renaissance painting. Note the deliberate anti-naturalist approach and the subtle geometry of the drawing.

The **altar frontals** fall into two categories: those painted on a single panel (Igles de Sant Martí d'Ix, Catedral de Santa María at La Seu d'Urgell, known as th Apostles' altarfront) and those carved in relief (Esterrí de Cardós, Santa María c Taüll). The museum also presents superb **collections of capitals**★ (Room V silverware and enamels (Room XV).

Gothic Art – This section provides visitors with an overview of Catalan Goth art during the 13C and 14C. Exhibits include the *Annunciation* by th **Master of Anglesola** (Room III), clearly showing the influence of the Frenc linear Gothic style; the stone retables attributed to **Jaime Cascalls** (Rooms and V); the large collection of Catalan international Gothic art (Room IX), wi works by the city's most influential artists (**Guerau Gener, Juan Mates, Ramón Mur, Juan Antigó, Bernardo Despuig** and **Jaime Cirera**); the room dedicated **Bernardo Martorell** (Room XI), an artist for whom detail and pictorial matrix were of paramount importance; the famous **Virgin of the Councillors** by **Lu Dalmau** (Room XII); the set of works by the **Master of Seu d'Urgell** (Room XV) an lastly, the section dedicated to funerary sculpture in the 14C and 15C (Roo XVIII).

★ Poble Espanyol (Spanish Village) (BT) – The village was built for the 192 exhibition to illustrate regional styles in Spanish architecture. A walk through will reveal a picturesque variety of local features ranging from a small Castilia square, a street in an Andalusian village with white-walled houses set off t flowering geraniums, to a Mudéjar tower from Aragón. There are also resta rants, old shops (a chemist's and a perfume shop) and craftsmen at work makin traditional Spanish wares. The village is also home to the **Museo de Artes, Indústri y Tradiciones Populares** .

★ Anella Olímpica (BCT) – Built as a venue for the sporting events of the 199 Olympic Games, this huge complex occupies a wide esplanade situated high up c the mountain. Basically, it consists of the **Olympic Stadium**★ , with its 1929 façac and fully renovated interior, and the nearby **Palau Sant Jordi**★★ , a modern spor centre designed by the Japanese architect Arata Isozaki, housed under a larg metallic structure.

The **telecommunications tower** commissioned by Telefónica, the work of Santiag Calatrava, offers a pleasing combination of modernity and aesthetics.

Galería Olímpica ⊘ (BT M¹⁴) – This gallery commemorates the 1992 edition of the Olympic Games: it displays medals won by Spanish athletes, detailed photographs of sporting events which were particularly moving that year, and a host of miscellaneous objects associated with the history of the Olympic movement.

★★ **Fundació Joan Miró** ⊘ (CT) – **Joan Miró** (1893-1983) was unquestionably one of Europe's leading figures in the field of avant-garde art. His name is closely associated with Palma de Mallorca *(see p 418)* as well as Barcelona, his native town on which he has clearly left his mark. Examples of his work can be found in many different parts of the city: a ceramics mural at the airport, pavement mosaics on La Rambla, not to mention the famous logo he designed for the savings bank La Caixa, symbolising all its local branches.

Fundació Joan Miró, Barcelona – © ADAGP 1997

People, birds, star by Joan Miró

Born in Barcelona, Miró spent 1921 and 1922 living in Paris, where he painted **La Masía**, a canvas that prefigured his departure from figurative art. Between 1939 and 1941 he executed **Constellations**, his famous series of 23 panels expressing his horror of the Second World War. The themes illustrated in this series (the night, the sun, women etc) were to become recurring motifs in his later work. Miró's art consists in exploring the many possibilities offered by colours, shapes and symbols. His work is a skilful combination of joy and tragedy, enhanced by a strong touch of magic and poetry *(see video presentation of the artist)*.

Created by Miró in 1971, the Foundation was officially opened in 1976. It is housed in a modern building of harmonious proportions, designed by the architect Josep Lluís Sert, a close friend of the artist whose main concern was to conceive a building that blended in well with the surrounding landscape. The collections, totalling over 10 000 exhibits (paintings, sculptures, drawings, collages and other graphic works) bring together many of Miró's works, the majority of which were executed during the last 20 years of his life. You can also visit a small exhibition of contemporary art featuring Alexander Calder's **Fountain of Mercury**, along with works by artists such as Matisse, Tanguy, Max Ernst, Chillida, Saura, Rauschenberg etc.

Next to the Foundation lies a small **garden of sculptures**, presenting the work of young contemporary artists.

★ **Teatre Grec** (CT) – Based on the Epidaurus model from ancient Greece, this 1929 open-air theatre is set against a rocky backdrop belonging to an abandoned quarry. In summer it hosts dances, concerts and stage performances organised by the **Festival del Grec**.

★ **Museu Arqueològic** ⊘ (CT M⁵) – Catalan archeology has a great tradition and is responsible for some important discoveries. Through the exhibits on display (implements, ceramics, votive figures, household effects etc), visitors are able to follow distinct periods in history from Paleolithic times through to the Visigothic era, including the periods of Greek and Roman colonization.

★★ EIXAMPLE AND MODERNIST ARCHITECTURE
See general plan

The word *Eixample* (in Catalan) or *Ensanche* (in Castilian) means enlargemen Barcelona's Eixample district was added to the town as a result of the Cerdà Pla in the 19C.

The Cerdà Plan – 1859. The plan adopted for Eixample consists of a grid patter of streets, some parallel to the sea, others perpendicular to it. The stree circumscribe blocks of houses (called *mançanes* in Catalan or *manzanas* Castilian, also meaning apples) which are octagonal in shape because th right-angled corners have been trimmed off. This plan is crossed by two wic diagonal avenues, avinguda Diagonal and La Meridiana, which meet on plaça c les Glòries Catalanes. One of the great attractions of the Eixample district is i wealth of Modernist architecture.

Modernist architecture – This developed between 1890 and 1920 alongsic similar movements in other parts of Europe, such as Art Nouveau in both Franc and Great Britain and Jugendstil in Germany. Modernist architecture sprang fro artistic exploration that combined new industrial materials with modern techr ques, using decorative motifs like curve and counter-curve and asymmetric shapes in stained glass, ceramics and metal. It enjoyed great success in Cataluny at a time when large fortunes were being made as a result of industrialisation. Th most representative architects of the style were Antoni Gaudí, Domènech Montaner, Puig i Cadafalch and Jujol. A parallel movement in Catalan literatui known as Renaixença also flourished during this period.

Gaudí (1852-1926) – Antoni Gaudí, born in Reus, studied architecture in Barc lona. His style was influenced first by Catalan Gothic architecture with i emphasis on large areas of space (wide naves, the effect of airy spaciousness) ar subsequently by the Islamic and Mudejar styles. He also studied nature, observir plants and animals which inspired his shapes, colours and textures. He gave fu rein to these images – liana-like curves, the rising and breaking of waves, rugge rocks and the serrations on leaves and flowers – when designing his fabulou buildings. Part of his great originality lay in his use of parabolic arches and spira (as can be seen in the chimneys of Casa Milà). An intensely religious man, Gau drew upon a great many symbols for his buildings, especially for the Sagra Familia (Church of the Holy Family) on which he worked for over 40 years. H spent his last years here, hidden away in a small room in the middle of the sit until his tragic death when he was run over by a tram.

Gaudí worked a great deal for the banker **Eusebi Güell**, his patron and admirer, wh asked him to design his private houses.

Gaudí's main works: Sagrada Familia, Casa Batlló, La Pedrera, Casa Vicens, Pala Güell, Pavellons Güell and Parc Güell.

Lluís Domènech i Montaner (1850-1923) – He attained his highly decorative sty through extensive use of mosaics, stained glass and glazed tiles.

His main works: Palau de la Mùsica Catalana, Casa Lleó Morera, Castell dels Tr Dragons, Hospital de Sant Pau and Casa Montaner i Simó.

Josep Puig i Cadafalch (1867-1956) – The mixture of regional and foreign architect ral tradition in his work reflects the Plateresque and Flemish styles.

His main works: Casa de les Punxes, **Casa Macaya** (1901) and Casa Quadras (1904

★★★ **La Sagrada Familia (Church of the Holy Family)** ⊘ (CR) – The project begun by Fra cisco de P Villar in 1882 was taken over by Gaudí in 1883. He planned a chur shaped like a Latin Cross with five aisles and a transept with three aisles. On th outside, three façades were each to be dominated by four tall spires representir the Twelve Apostles and, above the transept crossing, a central spire flanked b four other spires were to represent Christ and the Evangelists. The nave wa planned to look like a forest of columns. In his lifetime, only the crypt, the apsid walls and the **Nativity façade**★★ were finished. The Nativity façade comprises thr

---

"Taxi!"

Since Spring 1997 and the Barcelona Motor Show, plans have been afoot to import traditional London cabs to Spain's crowded city streets, as one of the few purpose-built vehicles designed to survive and manœuvre in heavy traffic. As a concession to their new Mediterranean environment, the cabs are more likely to be yellow, white or some other colour than black, and they will be fitted with air-conditioning and, of course, left-hand drive. So British visitors to cities such as Barcelona, Madrid or Sevilla should not be surprised to see a vaguely familiar shape pulling up to the kerb to take their fare.

La Sagrada Familia

doorways, Faith, Hope and Charity, richly decorated with statues and groups of carved figures. Just one spire was completed. After Gaudí's death, work resumed in 1940 and today there are eight spires together with the Passion façade which was completed in 1981. The Sagrada Familia is still a vast building site which can be disappointing to visitors if they have not been warned. From the top of the east spire there is a good overall **view**★★ of the work on the church as well as of Barcelona beyond. One of Domènech i Montaner's main works, **Hospital Sant Pau**★ (CR), with its remarkable glazed tile roofs, may be seen at the end of avinguda de Gaudí.

★★ **Passeig de Gràcia** (CS) – This luxurious street, adorned with elegant wrought-iron street lamps by Pere Falqués (1900), contains the finest examples of Modernist architecture in Barcelona. The styles of the three most famous Modernist architects can be compared in the block of houses known as the **Manzana de la Discordia**★★ (Apple of Discord): no 35 **Casa Lleó Morera**★ (1905) (Y) by Domènech i Montaner, no 41 **Casa Amatller**★ (1900) (Y) by Puig i Cadafalch and lastly no 43 **Casa Batlló**★★ (1905) (Y) by Gaudí, with its extraordinary mosaic façade and its undulating roof covered in scales. From the street corner, in Carrer d'Aragó, you can see Domènech i Montaner's Casa Montaner i Simó which now houses the Tàpies Foundation *(see Fundació Antoni Tàpies below)*. A little further along Passeig de Gràcia on the right, Gaudí's **Casa Milà**★★★ ⓥ or quarry (1905) (CS), also known as **La Pedrera**, resembles an underwater cliff face. The rooms inside are used to house temporary exhibitions. A visit to the roof-top, with its chimneys and ventilation funnels arrayed like some weird, wild army, is an eerie experience. The **Espai Gaudí** has exhibits of drawings and models by the artist, as well as audio-visual presentations on his work.

Turn right from plaça de Joan Carles I into avinguda Diagonal.

Avinguda Diagonal – Casa Quadras (1904) (CS M⁶) on the right, by Josep Puig i Cadafalch, houses the **Museu de la Mùsica** ⓥ, which has a remarkable collection of instruments from all over the world. A little further along on the left, **Casa de les Punxes** or **Casa Terrades**★ (CR), by the same architect, bears the stamp of Flemish influence.

★★ Parc Güell ⊘ **(BCR)** – The park is the most famous of Gaudí's undertaking. commissioned by Güell. Gaudí's extraordinary imagination is particularly eviden. here.

Visitors have the impression that they are entering an enchanted forest peopled with mushroom-shaped pavilions, a flight of steps climbed by a mosaic dragon and avenues leading to an extravagant fantasy world: the artful combination o architecture and nature produces a curious effect, intermingling both rusti and fantastic elements. The **Chamber of the Columns**, in which an undulating mosai. roof covers a forest of sloping columns, and the remarkable **rolling bench★★** are telling examples of the artist's fertile imagination.

Your tour of the Park Güell ends with a visit to the **Casa-Museu Gaudí** ⊘ **(BR)**, located in the house where the famous architect once lived.

★★ Palau de la Mùsica Catalana ⊘ **(MV)** – *In Carrer de Sant Pere Mès Alt.* Thi. unusual concert hall, the seat of the Orfeó Català, is Domènech i Montaner': most famous work. It was built between 1905 and 1908. Its surroundings have recently been redeveloped, providing visitors with a better perspective of it. spectacular exterior, with its lavish mosaic decoration. The interior, dominate. by the large **inverted cupola★★** of polychrome glass, is profusely and artisti. cally decorated with sculpted groups and mosaic figurines. Today the Palau de la Mùsica Catalana is Barcelona's most important concert hall. Visitors who attend a concert in this strange venue find it to be a memorable experienc. indeed.

★★ Fundació Antoni Tàpies ⊘ **(CS S)** – The foundation was created by the artist himself – who was born in Barcelona in 1923 – and set up in a former publishing house in the Modernist Montaner i Simó building designed by Domènech Montaner. The brick building is crowned by a large aerial sculpture by Tàpies called *Núvol i Cadira* (cloud and chair), the emblem of the museum. It is a fitting example of the painter's symbolic universe.

The interior, a vast bare sober space where everything is painted in colours favoured by Tàpies (brown, beige, grey and ochre), is lit by skylights (a cupola and a pyramid) and sets off the artist's work remarkably well. The collection of over 300 paintings and sculptures tracing the development of Tàpies' work since 1948 is displayed on a rota basis. The foundation is also a research centre and the wooden bookshelves that once belonged to the publishing house have been kept for a library.

ADDITIONAL SIGHTS

★★ Monastir de Santa Maria de Pedralbes (Pedralbes Monastery) (AS) ⊘ – Although the village of Pedralbes has been incorporated into a residential quarter of Barcelona it still preserves its rustic charm.

Founded in the 14C by King James II of Aragón and his fourth wife, Doña Elisenda de Montcada, the monastery has a fine Catalan Gothic **church★** which houses the sepulchre of the foundress. The vast three-storey **cloisters★** surrounded by cells and oratories are sober and elegant. The Sant Miquel Chapel is adorned with beautifu **frescoes★★★** by Ferrer Bassá (1346), a Catalan artist strongly influenced by Italy whose works artfully combine the close attention to detail that characterised the Sienna School with the acute sense of volume and perspective associated with the great Tuscan masters.

The **Thyssen-Bornemisza collection★** *(access via the cloisters)* is on display in the former monk's dormitory and in the Sala de la Reina (Queen's Room). It contains 72 paintings and eight sculptures (from the Middle Ages to the 18C) which were part of the large collection (over 800 works) on show at the Museo Thyssen-Bornemisza in Madrid. Among the numerous works with a religious theme, **Fra Angelico**'s magnificent *Virgin of Humility* and **Zurbarán**'s *Santa Marina* stand out, as do several paintings of the *Virgin and Child* (B Daddi, 14C and L Monaco, 15C). Another room worthy of special mention is the **Sala de los Retratos** (Portrait Room) which contains some fine examples of various 15C and 18C schools.

Palau de Pedralbes (Pedralbes Palace) ⊘ **(AS)** – The palace is located in the university quarter.

Between 1919 and 1929 the city of Barcelona built a residence for King Alfonso XIII which was influenced by palaces of the Italian Renaissance. This particular palace houses the **Museu de les Artes Decoratives★** ⊘, with its displays of household items from the Middle Ages through to the industrial design era. It is also home to the **Museu de Ceràmica** ⊘, with exhibits showing evolutions in this art form from the 13C to the present day. Particularly worthy of note are the collections of Catalan and Alcora ceramics (18C-19C).

★ Pabellones Güell (AS V') – These former stables converted by Gaudí feature a lovely **wrought-iron grille** decorated with a dragon.

★ **Museu de la Ciència** ☉ (**AR**) – This science museum is housed in a building dating from the turn-of-the-century. Its many attractions include Foucault's pendulum, a planetarium and rooms dedicated to optics and meteorology.

Sant Pau del Camp (St Paul in the Fields) (LY) – The church was built as part of a Benedictine monastery at the end of the 10C and has preserved some of its original pavement and capitals on the portal. It has a charming little 11C-12C **cloister★** with trilobate arches.

★ **Teatre Nacional de Catalunya (DR T²)** – The architect, Ricardo Bofill, has skillfully combined both modern and classical designs in this delightful theatre. The foyer resembles a greenhouse with its profusion of plants. Opposite the theatre is the **Auditorio**, a work by Rafael Moneo.

BÉJAR

Castilla y León (Salamanca) – Population 17 027
Michelin map 444 or 441 K 12

Béjar's hill site is seen to best advantage when you approach the small town from the northwest. The town (known for its sheets and woollen fabrics) stretches out along a narrow rock platform at the foot of the Sierra de Béjar.

EXCURSIONS

★ **Candelario** – *4km/2.5mi south.*
The picturesque village of Candelario is a maze of very steep, unevenly paved alleys lined with whitewashed houses. These have exposed grey stone window surrounds and tie-beams as well as flower-filled upper galleries of wood beneath spread eaves. An unusual feature is the waterproofing by means of upturned tiles on whole sections of walls. Similarly, house entrances are protected by gates to combat the rushing torrents in the streets when the mountain snows melt.

F. Gouverneur/MICHELIN

Candelario

Baños de Montemayor – *17km/11mi southwest on N 630.* The thermal spa retains its old quarter with the wooden balconies typical of houses in the sierra.

Hervás – *23km/14mi southwest on N 630.* The bustling **judería** or old Jewish quarter with its winding alleyways has a lively atmosphere reminiscent of the Middle Ages.

The star ratings are allocated for various categories: regions of scenic beauty with dramatic natural features; cities with a cultural heritage; elegant resorts and charming villages; ancient monuments and fine architecture, museum and picture galleries.

BELMONTE★

Castilla-La Mancha (Cuenca) – Population 2 601
Michelin map 444 N 21

Belmonte, the native town of the 16C prose writer **Fray Luis de León**, retains som
monumental gateways and part of the perimeter which linked town and castle.

*Enter through one of the gateways and head towards Plaza Mayor where the
is a tourist information office.*

Antigua Colegiata – This 15C collegiate church contains an interesting collectio
of altarpieces made by local artists in the 15C, 16C and 17C. The 15C **choir stalls**★
from Cuenca Cathedral, illustrate, with stark realism, scenes from Genesis an
the Passion. The font in which Fray Luis de León was christened has bee
preserved.

Castillo ⊙ – This hexagonal fortress, flanked by circular towers, was built in th
15C by Juan Pacheco, Marqués de Villena, as part of the defences of his vas
domain. It was subsequently abandoned until the 19C when it was restored
although it had lost all its furnishings. In 1870 the triangular *patio* was disfigure
by a brick facing ordered by the new owner, Eugenia de Montijo. All that remain
in the empty rooms are beautiful Mudéjar **artesonado**★ ceilings – the audienc
chamber is outstanding – and delicately carved stone window surrounds. Follo
the curtain walls to the stepped merlons for a view of the village and the auster
La Mancha countryside beyond.

EXCURSION

Villaescusa de Haro – *6km/4mi northeast.*
The 1507 **Capilla de la Asunción**★ (Chapel of the Assumption) belonging to the parish
church is a magnificent late Gothic construction. It has crenels, a Gothic
Renaissance altarpiece and a wrought-iron screen with a flowery Gothic design o
three arches.

EUROPE on a single sheet:
Michelin Map 70, at a scale of 1: 3 000 000.
Tourism, roads, relief, index of names.

BETANZOS★

Galicia (La Coruña) – Population 11 871
Michelin map 441 C 5

Betanzos, a onetime port now silted up, stands at the end of its *ría*. It was once the
flourishing market for the rich Las Mariñas Valley which provided wheat for the
whole La Coruña province. At the centre of the town a substantial reminder of this
former prosperity may be seen, in the form of three Gothic churches remarkable for
their pure lines and rich ornamentation. The precincts with steep streets and old
houses with glassed-in balconies maintain the old-world atmosphere.

★ **Iglesia de Santa María del Azogue** ⊙ – The name of the 14C-15C church comes
from *suk* or market-place in Arabic. The gracefully asymmetrical façade is given
character by a projecting central bay pierced by a rose window and a portal
with sculptured covings. Niches on either side contain archaic statues of the
Virgin and the Archangel Gabriel, symbolising the Annunciation. Inside, three
aisles of equal height, beneath a single timber roof, create an effect of
spaciousness.

★ **Iglesia de San Francisco** ⊙ – This Franciscan monastery church, in the shape of
a Latin Cross embellished with a graceful Gothic east end, was built in 1387 by
the powerful Count Fernán Pérez de Andrade, Lord of Betanzos and Puente-
deume. It is chiefly remarkable for the many tombs aligned along its walls, the
carved decoration on its ogives and chancel arches and the wild boar sculpted in
the most unexpected places. Beneath the gallery to the left of the west door is
the **monumental sepulchre**★ of the founder, supported by a wild boar and a bear, his
heraldic beasts. Scenes of the hunt adorn the sides of the tomb; his hounds lie
couched at his feet, while at his head an angel greets his soul.

Santiago – The church, built in the 15C by the tailors' guild, stands on higher
ground than the two mentioned above. Its interior resembles that of Sta María.
Above the main door is a carving of St James *Matamoros* or Slayer of the Moors,
on horseback. The 16C **Ayuntamiento** (town hall) abutting the east end is embellished with an arcade and a fine sculpted coat of arms.

BILBO/BILBAO

País Vasco (Vizcaya) – Population 372 054
Michelin map 442 C21
Local map see COSTA VASCA

Bilbao, capital of Vizcaya province, 14km/9mi from the sea at the end of the Bilbao *ría* which forms the Nervión estuary, stands at the centre of a vast industrial area. Local industry began to develop in the middle of the 19C when iron mined from the surrounding hills was shipped to England in exchange for coal. Iron and steelworks were subsequently established.

The old city, founded in the early 14C, stands on the right bank of the Nervión river, up against the mountain on which stands the Santuario de Begoña (Begoña Sanctuary). It was originally named *las siete calles*, or seven streets, on account of its layout.

The modern *El Ensanche*, a business centre, stands on the left bank of the river on the other side of Puente del Arenal. Like other new areas that developed around large towns in the 19C, it was named *ensanche*, meaning enlargement. The town's rich residential area spreads around Doña Casilda Iturriza park.

Exciting architectural developments underway since the early 1990s have helped to embellish Bilbao and improve its image. The city boasts a sleek and stylish new Metro system with distinctive glazed station entrances designed by Norman Foster. A new airport terminal and footbridge have been commissioned from Santiago Calatrava (architect of Barcelona's Torre de Comunicaciones de Telefónica) and a riverside development and park from Cesar Pelli (architect of London's Canary Wharf tower). The jewel in modern Bilbao's crown, however, is its spectacular new museum of modern art, the Guggenheim Bilbao.

Bilbao's main annual festivity takes place during **Semana Grande** in August with bullfights and Basque *pelota* championships.

Bilbao was the birthplace of the great writer and humanist **Miguel de Unamuno** (1864-1936).

Greater Bilbao and the ría – Since 1945 Greater Bilbao has included all the towns along the *ría* to the sea, from Bilbao itself to Getxo. Industrial works (iron and steel, chemicals and shipbuilding) are concentrated along the left bank in **Baracaldo, Sestao, Portugalete** with its **transporter bridge** built in 1893, and in **Somorrostro** where there is a large oil refinery. **Santurtzi**, a fishing port, is well-known for its fresh sardines.

Algorta, a residential town on the right bank, provides an attractive contrast to the heavy industry, while **Deusto** is famous for its university.

The *ría* is a vast river port, the largest commercial port in Spain. Only ships of less than 4 000t can navigate it although the large quays at the *ría* mouth can accommodate ships of 500 000t.

SIGHTS

★★★ **Museo Guggenheim** ⊙ – *Avenida Abandoibarra 2.* This important new museum, funded primarily by the Basque government, is a European showcase for the renowned collection founded in New York by wealthy art patron Solomon R Guggenheim (1861-1949). The Bilbao institution is the youngest member of the prestigious family of museums managed by the Guggenheim Foundation that comprises two New York sites (Fifth Avenue and SoHo) and the Peggy Guggenheim in Venice. With this stunning museum complex, inaugurated in October 1997, acclaimed California-based architect **Frank Gehry** has created what is widely considered one of the great buildings of the late 20C, making it an appropriate counterpart to the famous spiral monument designed in the 1950s by Frank Lloyd Wright to house the Guggenheim's Fifth Avenue Museum. Previous European projects by Pritzker Prize winner Gehry include the Festival Disney entertainment complex at Disneyland Paris (1988-92) and the American Center at Bercy, Paris (1994).

Cafés

Café Iruña - *Jardines de Albia-Berástegui, 5*
This café, which was founded in 1903, has become something of an institution in Bilbao. It is situated in a pleasant square and contains some attractive Mudéjar-inspired ceilings and decoration. An enjoyable place for a drink, particularly at night.

Café La Granja - *Plaza Circular, 3.*
This famous café dates from 1926 although its style is more in keeping with the 19C with its marble tables, wooden chairs and decadent air. On evenings during the weekend the quiet, contemplative mood is replaced by a more lively atmosphere and loud music.

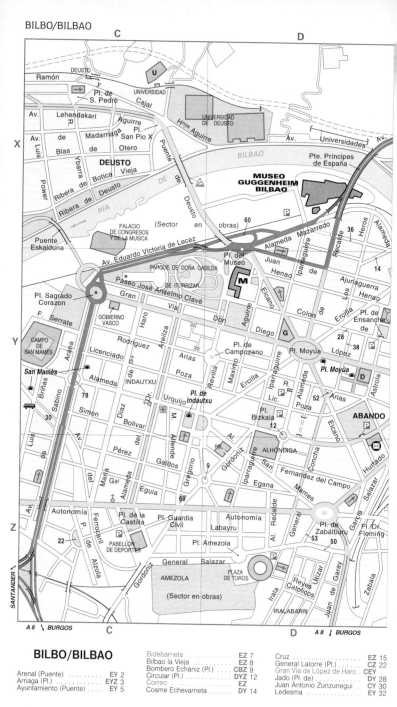

BILBO/BILBAO

Arenal (Puente)	EY 2	Bidebarrieta	EZ 7	Cruz	EZ 15
Arriaga (Pl.)	EYZ 3	Bilbao la Vieja	EZ 8	General Latorre (Pl.)	CZ 22
Ayuntamiento (Puente)	EY 5	Bombero Echániz (Pl.)	CBZ 9	Gran Via de López de Haro	CEY
		Circular (Pl.)	DYZ 12	Jado (Pl. de)	DY 28
		Correo	EZ	Juan Antonio Zunzunegui	CY 30
		Cosme Echevarrieta	DY 14	Ledesma	EY 32

Architectural panache – The museum rises from the banks of the Nervión like a vast and complex ship with billowing sails. Formal geometry and symmetry are abandoned as Gehry skilfully juxtaposes free forms, creating harmony and gracefully flowing lines out of potential chaos. The resulting eye-catching architectural composition, clad in shimmering titanium, demands to be seen from all angles and takes on a different aspect with every change of light. The south entrance is made of golden limestone, used for both walls and paving. It opens into a vast, soaring atrium (50m/165ft high) of glass, white walls and steel ribs, in which there are echoes of Wright's great spiral, transformed here into a whirl of smoothly moulded shapes and natural light. Access to the galleries fanning out from the central atrium on the three floors inside is by glass-fronted lifts or vertiginous suspended walkways and staircases. The galleries are spacious, ranging from 8m/25ft to 15m/50ft inheight. The largest gallery measures

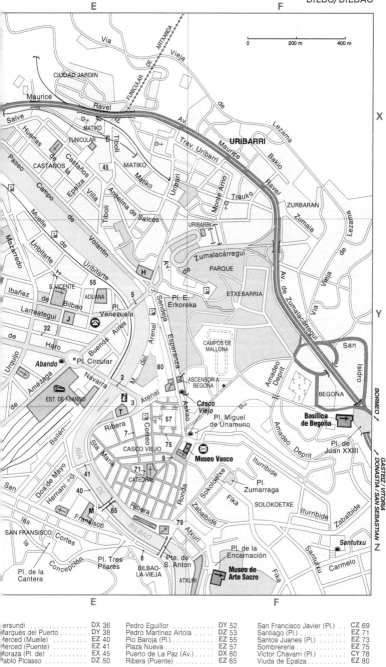

...ersundi	DX 36	Pedro Eguillor	DY 52	San Francisco Javier (Pl.)	CZ 69
...larqués del Puerto	DY 38	Pedro Martínez Artola	DZ 53	Santiago (Pl.)	EZ 71
...lerced (Muelle)	EZ 40	Pío Baroja (Pl.)	EZ 55	Santos Juanes (Pl.)	EZ 73
...lerced (Puente)	EZ 41	Plaza Nueva	EZ 57	Sombrerería	EZ 75
...loraza (Pl. de)	EX 45	Puerto de La Paz (Av.)	DX 60	Víctor Chavarri (Pl.)	CY 78
...ablo Picasso	DZ 50	Ribera (Puente)	EZ 65	Viuda de Epalza	EZ 80

130m/450ft long and 25m/80ft wide, running the length of the riverside site, passing beneath the road bridge and culminating in a V-shaped metal and stone tower.

Extensive collections – Drawing on the reserves of the vast and world-renowned Guggenheim collections in New York and Venice (more than 6 000 paintings, sculptures and works on paper), the latest Guggenheim Museum focuses on art from the 1950s to the present. Among the artists well represented in the collections are Modern masters (Picasso, Mondrian, Kandinsky) and proponents of the major movements such as Abstract Expressionism (Rothko, De Kooning, Pollock), Pop art (Oldenburg, Rosenquist, Warhol), and Conceptual and Minimalist art (Carl André, Donald Judd). More contemporary artists likely to be on view include Anselm Kiefer, Francesco Clemente and Damien Hirst. To complement the works on loan from the Guggenheim Foundation, the Basque government has

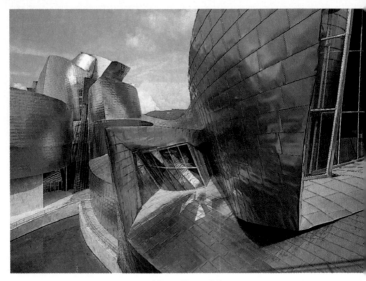

Museo Guggenheim

budgeted for the museum to invest in its own acquisitions and has commissione several site-specific works including a vast mural by Sol LeWitt and Richa Serra's *Snake*, three gigantic sheets of undulating steel standing upright ar parallel. Spanish talent is also present, with works by Antoni Tàpies, Eduarc Chillida, Francesc Torres, Cristina Iglesias and Susana Solano likely to be c display.

The opening of the museum has given a new lease of life to the Basque long-standing campaign to bring **Picasso**'s *Guernica* home to the Basque capital. special space has already been reserved for the mural in the Guggenheim Bilba However, to date concerns regarding the fragile condition of the work and th political issues that surround it prevail, with the result that it remains firmly the Reina Sofía museum in Madrid.

Facts and figures

- **Cost:** $100 million
- **Total area:** 24 290m²/29 050sq yd
- **Exhibition space:** 10 560m²/12 650sq yd
- **No of galleries:** 19
- **Estimated annual visitors:** 500 000
- **Visitor facilities:** boutique-bookshop, restaurant, cafeteria
- **Computer programme used for the design:** Catia

---

* **Museo de Bellas Artes** ⊘ (**DY M**) – The **fine arts museum** is housed in two buildin in Doña Casilda Iturriza park.
** **Ancient Art** – *Old building, ground floor*. Pride of place is given to the Spanish Scho from the 12C to the 17C. Noteworthy Romanesque works include a 12C Crucifixi from the Catalan School, while the section on 16C-17C Spanish classical painti has canvases by Morales, El Greco, Valdés Leal, Zurbarán, Ribera and Goya.
 Dutch and Flemish painting (15C-17C) is also well represented with *The Usure by Quentin Metsys, a *Pietà* by Ambrosius Benson and a *Holy Family* by Gossae
 Basque Art – *First floor*. This section contains a comprehensive collection of wor by the great Basque painters: Regoyos, Zuloaga, Iturrino etc.
 Contemporary Art – *New building*. This is a rich collection of works by artists bo Spanish – Solana, Vázquez Díaz, Sunyer, Gargallo, Blanchard, Luis Fernánd Otieza, Chillida and Tàpies – and foreign – Delaunay, Léger, Kokoschka, Vieira Silva and Bacon.

 Museo Vasco (Basque Museum) ⊘ (**EFZ**) – The museum, which is housed in the form **Colegio de San Andrés** in the heart of the old town, contains an extensive collection ethnographic exhibits providing visitors with a detailed insight into the tradition activities of the Basque people (linen weaving, arts and crafts, fishing and irc work). In the middle of the classicist cloisters the primitive, animal-like **idol of Mike** may be seen. The top floor contains an immense relief model of Vizcaya provinc

Museo Diocesano de Arte Sacro (Diocesan Museum of Sacred Art) ⊙ (FZ) – This interesting museum, housed in the former Convento de la Encarnación (16C), contains a collection of Basque silverware and a series of 12C-15C sculptures of the Virgin and Child.

Basílica de Begoña ⊙ (FZ) – *You can drive up along the San Sebastián road (Avenida de Zumalacárregui) but it is easier to take the lift from Calle Esperanza Ascai. There is an interesting view of Bilbao from the upper terminus footbridge. On leaving the public gardens, take the second street on the right.*
The church contains the venerated figure of Nuestra Señora de Begoña, patron of the province, in a silver *camarín* in the chancel.

El BURGO DE OSMA★

Castilla y León (Soria) – Population 5 054
Michelin map 442 H 20

Approaching from the west you can see the tall Baroque tower of El Burgo Cathedral. The town is 18C with porticoed streets and squares and elegant Baroque institutional buildings such as the San Agustín Hospital on the Plaza Mayor.

★ **Catedral** ⊙ – The Gothic sanctuary was built in 1232 as a result of a vow taken by a Cluniac monk, Don Pedro de Osma, to replace the former Romanesque cathedral which had stood on the site. The east end, transept and chapter-house were completed in the 13C; the Late Gothic cloisters and the chancel were embellished with Renaissance decoration in the 16C, while the large sacristy, royal chapel and 72m/236ft belfry were built in the 18C.
The Gothic decoration on the late-13C **south portal** includes on the splays, statues of (left to right) Moses, Gabriel, the Virgin, Judith, Solomon and Esther; on the lintel, a Dormition of the Virgin and on the pier, Christ displaying his wounds (late 15C).
The interior is remarkable for the elevation of the nave, the finely wrought-iron **screens** (16C) by Juan de Francés, the **high altar retable** by Juan de Juni with scenes from the Life of the Virgin and the 16C white marble **pulpit** and **trascoro altarpiece**. The 13C polychrome limestone **tomb of San Pedro de Osma**★ may be seen in the west arm of the transept. In the **museum** ⊙, among the **archives** and **illuminated manuscripts**★ are a richly illustrated 1086 **Beatus** and a 12C manuscript with the signs of the Zodiac.

EXCURSION

Berlanga del Duero – *28km/17mi southeast on C 116 and SO 104.*
Berlanga still appears protected in medieval fashion with stout ramparts below the massive walls of its 15C castle – the town was a strongpoint in the fortified line along the Duero. In the Gothic **Colegiata** ⊙, a monumental 16C hall-church, are two chapels containing altarpieces carved and painted in the Flamboyant style and two 16C recumbent alabaster statues.
Some 8km/5mi southeast in **Casillas de Berlanga** is the **Iglesia de San Baudelio de Berlanga** ⊙, an isolated 11C Mozarabic chapel with a highly original layout. At the centre of the square nave is a massive pillar on which descend the eight flat ribs supporting the roof. The gallery rests on a double line of horseshoe-shaped arches and like the rest of the building, was covered with frescoes in the 12C. Some hunting scenes and geometric patterns may still be made out.

Castillo de Gormaz – *15km/10mi south on SO 160.* 380m/1 245ft long, with 28 towers, this 10C castle is the largest fortress of its kind in Europe.

Calatañazor – *25km/15mi northeast on N 122 towards Soria.* Calatañazor is one of those places in which time appears to have stood still. A stroll along its steep, stone-paved streets is quite an experience. The plain on which Almanzor was defeated by Christian troops can be seen from the medieval castle.

Cañón del río Lobos ⊙ – *15km/10mi north on SO 920.* This 25km/15mi stretch of canyon has been formed by the erosive action of the Lobos river (from Ucero to Hontoria del Pinar). The landscape here is riddled with caves, depressions and chasms, and has an abundance of juniper bushes, pines and young oaks. *For further information, contact the Centro de Interpretación del Parque Natural on ☎ 975 36 35 64.*

BURGOS★★★

Castilla y León – Population 169 111
Michelin map 442 E 18-19

Burgos, known as the cradle of Castilla, stands on the banks of the río Arla‑
zón with the slender, openwork spires of its famous cathedral rising high into th‑
sky. It has an exposed position on a windswept plateau at an altitude ‑
900m/2 953ft.

HISTORICAL NOTES

Burgos was founded by Diego Rodríguez in 884 and selected capital of the unite‑
kingdom of Castilla and León in 1037, a title it relinquished in 1492, on the fall ‑
Granada, when the royal court moved to Valladolid. However, the loss of politic‑
involvement appears to have released energy for commercial and artistic enterprise‑
the town became a wool centre for the sheep farmers of the Mesta (see SORIA‑
architects and sculptors arrived, particularly from the north, and transforme‑
monuments into the currently fashionable Gothic style. Burgos became Spain‑
Gothic capital with outstanding works including the cathedral, the Monasterio de la‑
Huelgas Reales (Royal Convent of Las Huelgas) and the Cartuja de Miraflore‑
(Carthusian monastery). Yet, the end of the 16C brought the decline of the Mest‑
and a halt to the town's prosperity.
Burgos was chosen by Franco to be the seat of his government from 1936 to 1938‑

★★★ CATEDRAL ⊙ (A) 1hr 30min

The cathedral, the third largest in Spain after Sevilla and Toledo, is a remarkabl‑
example of the transformation of French and German Flamboyant Gothic into ‑
style that is typically Spanish through the natural exuberance of its decoration‑
The many works of art adorning the interior of the cathedral make it a‑
outstanding showcase of European Gothic sculpture.
Ferdinand III laid the first stone in 1221 and there followed two principal stage‑
of building which corresponded with distinct periods in the evolution of the Gothi‑
style.
At the beginning of the 13C, under the aegis of Maurice the Englishman, the‑
Bishop of Burgos, who had collected drawings during a journey through Franc‑
(at that time very much influenced by the Gothic style), the nave, aisles and portal‑
were built by local architects.
The second period in the 15C saw the building of the west front spires and th‑
Capilla del Condestable (Constable's Chapel) as well as the decoration of othe‑
chapels. These were directly influenced by foreigners from the north, through th‑
architects and sculptors from Flanders, the Rhineland and Burgundy, whom‑
another great Burgos prelate, Alonso de Cartagena, had brought back on hi‑
return from the Council of Basel.

The Land of El Cid (1026-99)

The exploits of Rodrigo Díaz, native of Vivar (9km/5.5mi north of Burgos)
light up the late-11C history of Castilla. The brilliant captain first supported
the ambitious King of Castilla, Sancho II, then Alfonso VI who succeeded
his brother in somewhat dubious circumstances. Alfonso, irritated at
Díaz's suspicions and jealous of the prestige he had won following an attack
on the Moors in 1081, banished the warrior hero although he was, by then,
married to the King's cousin, Ximena.
Díaz, as a soldier of fortune, entered service first with the Moorish king of
Zaragoza and subsequently fought Christian and Muslim armies with equal
fervour. His most famous enterprise came when at the head of 7 000 men,
chiefly Muslims, he captured Valencia after a nine-month siege in 1094. He
was finally defeated by the Moors in an exploit at Cuenca and died soon
afterwards (1099). His widow held Valencia against the Muslims until
1102 when she set fire to the city before fleeing to Castilla with El Cid's
body. The couple were buried in the San Pedro de Cardeña Monastery
(10km/6mi southeast of Burgos), but their ashes were moved and interred
in Burgos Cathedral in 1921.
Legend has transformed the stalwart but often ruthless 11C warrior, the
Campeador or Champion of Castilla, El Cid (Seid in Arabic), into a chivalrous
knight of exceptional valour. The first epic poem **El Cantar del Mío Cid**
appeared in 1180 and was followed by ballads. In 1618 Guillén de Castro
wrote a romanticised version of El Cid in his **Las Mocedades del Cid** (Youthful
Adventures of El Cid) upon which Corneille, in 1636, based his drama Le
Cid.

Catedral, Burgos

These artists, from a Europe in which the influence of Flamboyant Gothic was beginning to wane, found new inspiration in Mudéjar arabesques and other Hispano-Moorish elements in Spanish art. The most outstanding among them, the Burgundian **Felipe Bigarny**, the Fleming **Gil de Siloé** and the Rhinelander **Johan of Cologne**, integrated rapidly and with their sons and grandsons – Diego de Siloé, Simon and Francis of Cologne – created what was essentiatly a Burgos School of Sculpture.

The cloisters were built in the 14C, while the magnificent lantern over the transept crossing – the original of which collapsed after some particulary daring design work by Simon of Cologne – was rebuilt by Juan de Vallejo in the mid 16C.

Exterior

A walk round the cathedral will reveal how the architects took ingenious advantage of the sloping ground (the upper gallery of the cloisters is level with the cathedral pavement) to introduce delightful small precincts and closes cut by stairways.

West front – The ornate upper area, with its frieze of Spanish kings and its two openwork spires, pinnacled and crocketed, is the master-work of Johan of Cologne.

Portada de la Coronería (Coronería Doorway) (1) – The statues at the jambs have the grace of their French Flamboyant Gothic originals, although the folds of their robes show more movement. The Plateresque **Portada de la Pellejería** (2) or Skinner's Doorway in the adjoining transept wall was designed by Francis of Cologne early in the 16C.

As you continue round by the east end it becomes obvious that the Constable's Chapel, with its Isabelline decoration and lantern with pinnacles, is one of the cathedral's later additions.

Portada del Sarmental (Sarmental Doorway) **(3)** – The covings are filled with figures from the Celestial Court, while the tympanum is an incredible sculpture in which each of the four Evangelists sits in a different position as he writes.

Interior

The design of the interior is French inspired while the decoration bears an exuberant Spanish stamp.

★★ **Crucero, Coro and Capilla Mayor** (Transept crossing, choir stalls and chancel) – The splendid star ribbed lantern of the transept crossing rises on four massive pillars to a height of 54m/177ft above the funerary stones of El Cid and Ximena, inlaid in the crossing pavement.

The imposing unit of 103 walnut choir stalls, carved by Felipe Vigarny between 1507 and 1512, illustrates Biblical stories on the upper, back rows and mythological and burlesque scenes at the front. The handsome recumbent statue of wood plated with enamelled copper, on the tomb at the centre, dates from the 13C and is of Bishop Maurice.

The high altar **(4)** retable is a 16C Renaissance work in high relief against an intrinsically classical background of niches and pediments.

Claustro – The 14C Gothic cloisters present a panorama of Burgos sculpture with stone, terracotta and polychrome wood figures.

The **Capilla de Santiago** (St James' Chapel) **(5)** contains the cathedral treasure, a rich collection of church plate and liturgical objects.

In the **Capilla de Santa Catalina** (St Catherine's Chapel) are manuscripts and documents, including the marriage contract of El Cid. Note the 15C carved and painted consoles showing Moorish kings paying homage to the King of Castilla.

The **sacristía** (sacristy) **(6)** houses the *Christ at the Column* by Diego de Siloé, a supreme example of Spanish Expressionism in post-16C Iberian sculpture. The **sala capitular** (chapter-house) **(7)** displays, besides 15C and 16C Brussels tapestries symbolising the theological and cardinal virtues, a Hispano-Flemish diptych, a *Virgin and Child* by Memling and above, a painted wood Mudéjar *artesonado* ceiling (16C).

★★ **Capilla del Condestable** (Constable's Chapel) – A magnificent grille closes off the area. The Isabelline chapel founded by Hernández de Velasco, Constable of Castilla, in 1482 and designed by Simon of Cologne, is lit by a lantern surmounted by an elegant cupola with star-shaped vaulting. All the great early Renaissance sculptors of Burgos cooperated in the subsequent decoration of the walls and altarpiece. The heraldic displays in the chapel are striking. On either side of the altar, the constable's escutcheon, held by male figures, appears to be suspended over the balustrades of the tribune.

Statues of the constable and his wife lie on their tomb, carved in Carrara marble, and beside them is an immense garnet-coloured marble funerary stone for the names of their descendants. On the right side of the chapel is a Plateresque door to the sacristy **(1512)(8)** where there is a painting of *Mary Magdalene* by Pietro Ricci.

★ **Girola** (ambulatory) – The *trasaltar* (at the back of the high altar), carved partly by Felipe Vigarny, includes an expressive representation of the Ascent to Calvary.

Plaza de Santa Maria

0   30 m

BURGOS

Almirante Bonifaz	B 2	Eduardo Martínez del Campo	A 10	Monasterio de las Huelgas (Av. del)	A 21
Alonso Martínez (Pl. de)	B 3	España (Pl.)	B 12	Nuño Rasura	A 23
Aparicio y Ruiz	A 5	Gen. Sanjurjo (Av. del)	B 14	Paloma (La)	A 24
Cid Campeador (Av. del)	B 8	Gen. Santocildes (Pl. del)	B 15	Reyes Católicos (Av. de los)	B 26
Conde de Guadalhorce (Av. del)	A 9	Libertad (Pl.)	B 17	Rey San Fernando (Pl. del)	A 27
		Mayor (Plaza)	AB 18	Santo Domingo (Pl. de)	B 28
		Miguel Primo de Rivera (Pl.)	B 19	Vitoria	B
		Miranda	B 20		

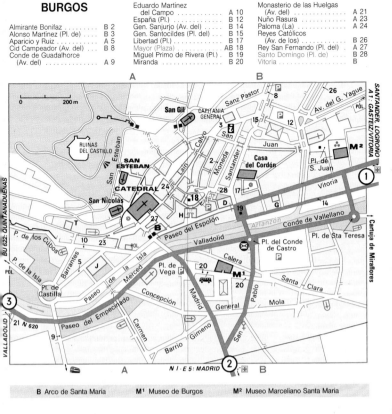

B Arco de Santa María   M¹ Museo de Burgos   M² Museo Marceliano Santa María

Escalera Dorada or **de la Coronería** (Golden or Coronation Staircase) **(9)** – The majestically proportioned staircase was designed in the pure Renaissance style by Diego de Siloé in the early 16C. The twin pairs of flights are outlined by an ornately elegant gilded banister by the French master ironsmith, Hilaire.

Capillas – Each of these side chapels is a museum of Gothic and Plateresque art: Gil de Siloé and Diego de la Cruz cooperated on the huge Gothic altarpiece in the **Capilla de Santa Ana**★ which illustrates the saint's life. In the centre is a Tree of Jesse with at its heart, the first meeting of Anne and Joachim and at the top, the Virgin and Child. At the beginning of the cathedral nave, high up near the roof, is the **Papamoscas** or **Flycatcher Clock (10)**, with a jack which opens its mouth on the striking of the hours. In the **Capilla del Santo Cristo** (Chapel of Holy Christ) is a Crucifixion with the particularly venerated figure complete with hair and covered with buffalo hide to resemble human flesh.

The **Capilla de la Presentación** (Chapel of the Presentation) **(11)** contains the tomb of the Bishop of Lerma, carved by Felipe Vigarny and the **Capilla de la Visitación** (Chapel of the Visitation) **(12)**, that of Alonso de Cartagena by Gil de Siloé.

★ **Arco de Santa María** ⊘ **(A B)** – The 14C gateway once defended the city walls. In the 16C it was modified to form a triumphal arch for Emperor Charles V and embellished with statues of the famous: below, Diego Porcelos Rodríguez is flanked by two semi-legendary judges said to have governed Castilla in the 10C, and above, Count Fernán González and El Cid (right) are shown with Charles V. In the interior can be seen the **Sala de Poridad**, with its magnificent Mudéjar cupola, and the apothecary from the former Hospital de San Juan.

Iglesia de San Nicolás ⊘ **(A)** The **altarpiece**★ of this Gothic church, carved by Simon of Cologne in 1505, is both large and ornate with more than 465 figures. The upper part shows the Virgin crowned at the centre of a circle of angels; St Nicholas in the central part is surrounded by scenes from his life - note the voyage by caravel to Alexandria - and below, there is a back view of the Last Supper.

Iglesia de San Esteban: Museo del Retablo ⊘ **(A)** – The city's Retable Museum is housed in this delightful **church**★, built in the 14C in Burgos Gothic style. The interior is a magnificent setting for the 18 retables which are exhibited according to their religious significance in the church's three naves. The *coro alto* contains a small collection of gold and silverwork.

Iglesia de San Gil ⊘ **(AB)** – One of the city's most beautiful churches. Hidden behind its sober façade is a temple from the end of the Gothic period. Particularly worthy of note are the Nativity Chapel and Buena Mañana chapels, the latter containing a retable by Gil de Siloé.

★★ REAL MONASTERIO DE LAS HUELGAS
(ROYAL CONVENT OF LAS HUELGAS) ⊙

1.5km/1mi west of Burgos; take avenida del Monasterio de las Huelgas

Las Huelgas Reales, originally a summer palace of the kings of Castilla, w
converted in 1180 into a convent by Alfonso VIII and his wife Eleanor, daugh
of Henry II of England. The religious were Cistercians of high lineage; the abbe
all-powerful; by the 13C the convent's influence, both spiritual and tempor
extended to more than 50 towns and it had become a common place of retre
for members of the house of Castilla and even the royal pantheon.

Rearrangement over the centuries has resulted in a heterogeneous and somewh
divided building in which, although the Cistercian style of the 12C and 1
predominates, there are Romanesque and even Mudéjar features (13C-15C)
well as Plateresque furnishings.

Iglesia – The clean lines of the exterior of this church are pure Cistercian. T
interior is divided into two by a screen: from the transept, open to all, you can s
the revolving pulpit (1560), in gilded ironwork, which enabled the preacher to
heard on either side of the screen. Royal and princely tombs, originally colour
rich in heraldic devices and historical legend, line the aisles, while in the mid
of the nave, the nuns' *coro*, is the double sepulchre of the founders, Alfonso V
and Eleanor of England. The rood screen retable, delicately carved and colour
in the Renaissance style, is surmounted by a fine 13C Deposition. The altar
flanked on each side by two handsome 13C and 14C tombs.

Gothic cloisters – 13C-15C. Enough fragments of Mudéjar vaulting stuc
remain in these Gothic cloisters to give an idea of the delicacy of the strapwc
inspired by Persian ivories and fabrics.

Sala Capitular – This chapter house contains the **pendón★**, a trophy from t
Battle of Las Navas de Tolosa, decorated with silk *appliqué*.

Romanesque cloisters – Late 12C. In these Romanesque cloisters, slender pair
columns, topped by highly stylised capitals, combine to create an effect
elegance. Several rooms in this part of the building, Alfonso VIII's former pala
were decorated by the Moors. The **Capilla de Santiago** (Chapel of St James) reta
an *artesonado* ceiling with its original colouring and stucco frieze. According
legend, the statue of the saint with articulated arms conferred knighthood up
princes of royal blood.

★★ **Museo de Telas Medievales (Museum of Medieval Materials)** – The fabrics, court dre
and finery displayed in the former loft provide a vivid review of royal wear in 1.
Castilla. Of the clothes, (mainly tunics, pelisses and capes) found in the tombs, t
most valuable items come from that of the Infante Fernando de la Cerda (who di
in 1275), son of Alfonso X,
the Wise. This tomb, one
that was not desecrated by
French troops in 1809, contained a long tunic, *pellote*
(voluminous trousers with
braces) and a very large
mantle, all made of the
same material embroidered
with silk and silver thread.
There is also a *birrete*, a silk
crown adorned with pearls
and precious stones.

CARTUJA DE MIRAFLORES
(MIRAFLORES CARTHUSIAN MONASTERY) ⊙ (B)

4km/2.5mi east of Burgos

This former royal founda-
tion, entrusted to the Carthu-
sians in 1442, was chosen by
Juan II as a pantheon for himself and his second wife, Isabel of Portugal. The church
was completed in full Isabelline Gothic style in 1498.

★ **Iglesia** – The sobriety of
the façade, relieved only by

Detail of the altarpiece
in the Cartuja de Miraflores, Burgos

the buttress finials and the founders' escutcheons, gives no indication of the richness inside. This appears in the church's single aisle with its elegant vaulting and gilded keystones and particularly in the magnificent apse.

★ **Sculptured unit in the Capilla Mayor** (apse) – This was designed by the Fleming, Gil de Siloé at the end of the 15C and comprises the high altarpiece, the royal mausoleum and a funerary recess.

The polychrome wood **altarpiece**, the work of Siloé and Diego de la Cruz, has a striking design: the usual rectangular compartments have been replaced by circles, each crowded with Biblical figures.

The white marble **mausoleo real** (royal mausoleum) is in the form of an eight-pointed star in which can be seen the recumbent statues of the founders, Juan II and Queen Isabel, parents of Isabel the Catholic. Dominating the exuberant Flamboyant Gothic decoration of scrolls, canopies, pinnacles, cherubim and armorial bearings, executed with rare virtuosity, are the four Evangelists. In an ornate **recess** in the north wall is the tomb of the Infante Alfonso, whose premature death gave the throne of Castilla to his sister Isabel the Catholic. The statue of the young prince at prayer is technically brilliant but impersonal (compare with that of Juan de Padilla, *see below*).

Also in the church are a 15C Hispano-Flemish triptych (to the right of the altar) and Gothic **choir stalls** carved with an infinite variety of arabesques.

ADDITIONAL SIGHTS

★ **Museo de Burgos** ⊙ (B M¹) – Two sections, housed in separate buildings:

Prehistoric and Archeological Department – Housed in the Casa de Miranda, a Renaissance mansion with an elegant *patio*, this section contains finds discovered in the province covering the Prehistoric to Visigothic periods.
Note the rooms devoted to Iron Age sites, to the Roman settlement of Clunia and the collection of Roman funerary steles.

Fine Arts Department – The Casa de Angulo houses works of art from the Burgos region covering the period from the 9C to the 20C. There are several precious items from the Santo Domingo Monastery at Silas: an 11C **Hispano-Moorish casket**★, delicately carved in ivory in Cuenca and highlighted with enamel plaques, the 12C **Frontal or Urn of Santo Domingo**★ in beaten and enamelled copper, and a 10C marble diptych.
In the section on 14C-15C funerary sculpture is the **tomb**★ of Juan de Padilla on which Gil de Siloé has beautifully rendered the countenance and robes of the dead man.
The collection of 15C painting contains a *Christ Weeping* by the Fleming, Jan Mostaert.

Casa del Cordón (B) – The recently restored palace of the Constables of Castilla was built in the 15C and presently houses the Caja de Ahorros savings bank). Still decorating its façade is the thick Franciscan cord motif which gave the palace its name. It is interesting historically as the place where Columbus was received by the Catholic monarchs on his return from his second voyage to America and also where Philip the Fair died suddenly of a chill after a game of *pelota*, reducing to despair his already much disturbed wife, Juana the Mad.

Plaza Mayor (AB 18) – This delightful circular main square, typically lined by a portico, is the setting for all public festivities.

Museo Marceliano Santa María ⊙ (B M²) – The museum, in the ruins of the former Benedictine monastery of San Juan, displays Impressionist type canvases by the Burgos painter Marceliano Santa María (1866-1952).

Hospital del Rey – Founded by Alfonso VIII as a hospital for pilgrims. It has preserved its entrance, known as the Patio de Romeros, with its fine 16C plateresque façade. Today, it is the headquarters of the University of Burgos

EXCURSIONS

Archeological finds in the Sierra de Atapuerca – *Take the N 120 towards Logroño. When you reach Ibeas de Juarros, head for the Emiliano Aguirre hall (on the side of the main road).*
The construction of a trench for a railway line at the end of the last century led to the discovery of the world's most important paleontological finds. Excavations at **La Dolina** have brought to light the remains of hominids who lived around 800 000 years ago. The fossil register at the **Sima de los Huesos** (literally the Chasm of Bones), is the largest in Europe dating from the Middle Pleistocene age between 400 000 and 200 000 years ago. Visitors are able to walk along the trench and visit a small archeological museum.

CÁCERES★★

Extremadura – Population 84 319

Michelin map 444 N 10

Cáceres, capital of an agricultural province (cereals and stock rearing), is a lively tow
with a remarkable historical centre dating back several centuries.

★★★ CÁCERES VIEJO (OLD CÁCERES) 1hr 30min

Within its defensive walls and towers built by the Moors, this old quarter include
a group of Gothic and Renaissance seignorial mansions beyond compare in Spai
The unadorned, ochre coloured façades of the residences belonging to th
noblemen of the 15C and 16C bear no ostentatious flourishes as they reflect th
nature of their owners, the Ulloas, the Ovandos and the Saavedras, proud warrio
all, who in their fight against the infidel – Moor or American Indian – won mo
in prestige than in wealth. Minimal decoration consists of a narrow fillet aroun
the windows, a sculptured cornice or a proud coat of arms. The fortified towe
which once stood guard over the mansions and proclaimed their owners' powe
were lopped on the command of Isabel the Catholic in 1477.

*Follow the route marked on the plan, setting off from plaza del General Mola, th
former Plaza Mayor. An evening visit is highly recommended.*

Pass beneath the **Arco de la Estrella** (Star Arch) which was built into the wall b
Manuel Churriguera in the 18C.

★ **Plaza de Santa María** – This irregularly shaped square forms the monument
heart of the old city; rising on all sides are attractive golden ochre façades. Th
front of the **Palacio Mayoralgo** (Mayoralgo Palace) (**B**), now restored, has elegan
paired windows while the **Palacio Episcopal** (Bishop's Palace) (**C**) has a 16C bosse
doorway with medallions of the Old and New Worlds on either side (left and righ
respectively).

Iglesia de Santa María ⊘ – This nobly styled church, completed in the 16C, serves a
the city cathedral. The three Gothic aisles of almost equal height, have lierne an
tierceron vaulting from which the ribs descend into slender columns engage
around the main pillars. The carved retable at the high altar (16C) is difficult t
see but with its high standard of workmanship is well worth the effort.

By continuing round to the left of Santa María to the top of calle de las Tiendas
you will see the **Palacio de Carvajal** (Carvajal Palace) ⊘ flanked by a 15C tower. Th
chambers, *patio* and chapel of this nobleman's residence are open to the public

★ **Palacio de los Golfines de Abajo** (Lower Golfines Palace) – This rich mansion, twic
honoured by visits by the Catholic monarchs, has a rough stone façade, Gothic i
style with the Plateresque traits characteristic of civil architecture of the late 15C
The paired window derives from the Moorish *ajimez*, while the fillet, delicatel
framing the two windows and the door, recalls the *alfiz*. To lighten the front, a
Plateresque frieze with winged griffons was added to the top of the central are
in the 16C, while medallions and the Golfines coat of arms – a fleur-de-lis and a
tower – complete the decoration.

Plaza San Jorge (31) – Note the austere 18C façade of the Jesuit church of Sa
Francisco Javier.

San Mateo – The church's high Gothic nave, begun in the 14C, was abutted in the
16C by a *coro alto* resting on an arcade with basket vaulting. The interior is bare
except for the Baroque altarpiece and the side chapels containing tombs with
decorative heraldic motifs.

Continuing round the church by the north wall you come, in succession, on two
15C towers both of which have lost their battlements but have retained unusual
parapets – they are respectively the **Torre de la Plata** (Silver Tower) (**P**) and the **Casa
del Sol** (Sun House) (**Q**) which owes its name to the elegant crest of the Solís family
boldly carved over the arch.

Casa de las Cigüeñas (The House of the Storks) – The house, now occupied by the
military, proudly sports a battlemented tower – the only one to escape the lopping
decreed in the late 15C.

Casa de las Veletas (Weather Vane House) – The mansion, its fine 18C façade
emblazoned with Baroque family crests, was built over a Moorish *alcázar* of which
the cistern still remains. It houses the **Museo de Cáceres** ⊘: collections of archeology
(engraved Bronze Age steles, Celtiberian statues of wild boar known as *verracos*,
Roman remains) and ethnology (local dress, arts and crafts).

The 11C *aljibe* (Arab cistern) is still fed by a trickle of water from the roof and
sloping square outside. It is covered by five rows of horseshoe-shaped arches
supported by granite capitals with carving which is unfortunately barely noticeable.

Casa del Comendador de Alcuéscar – The palace, now a parador, has a fine
Gothic tower, delicate window surrounds and an unusual corner balcony.

Palacio de los Golfines de Abajo

By taking the alley alongside the ramparts you reach the **Palacio de los Golfines de Arriba** (Upper Golfines Palace) with an austere, imposing façade and an attractive *patio*. The **Casa de la Generala (V)** a little further on, houses the law faculty.

Go through the door in the ramparts opposite.

The steps leading down to Plaza Mayor del General Mola afford an interesting view of the walls, particularly high at this point, and the Torre del Horno.

ADDITIONAL SIGHTS

Casa de los Toledo-Moctezuma – The mansion, its imposing façade surmounted by a gallery, was built by Juan Cano de Saavedra with the fabulous dowry brought him by his wife, none other than the Aztec princess, Montezuma's daughter (Moctezuma in Spanish).

Torre de los Espaderos (Tower of the Armourers) – This was truncated along with the other towers in the late 15C.

Iglesia de Santiago (St James' Church) ⊙ – The Romanesque church, rebuilt in the 16C, is traditionally held to be the birthplace of the Military Order of the Knights of Cáceres who in turn founded the Order of the Knights of St James. Inside, the altarpiece carved by Alonso Berruguete in 1557 bears scenes from the Life of Christ. These surround a vigorous, finely portrayed St James *Matamoros* or Slayer of the Moors.

The **Palacio de Godoy** opposite has an impressive coat of arms on the corner and a fine inner *patio* with decorative *azulejos*.

127

CÁCERES

Adarve del Padre Rosalio ... 2
Adarve de Sta Ana 3
Adarve la Estrella 5
Aldana (Cuesta de) 6
Amargura 7
Ancha 8
Camberos 9
Compañia (Cuesta de la) ... 12
Condes 13
Defensores del Alcázar 15
Fuente Concejo 18
General Ezponda 19
Marqués (Cuesta del) 24
Pereros 25
Pintores 26
Plaza Mayor
Rincón de la Monja 27
Sancti Espiritu 28
San Jorge (Pl.) 31
San Mateo (Pl. de) 33
Santa Ana (Arco de) 34
Santa Clara (Pl. de) 36
Tiendas 39
Veletas (Pl. de las) 40

B Palacio Mayoralgo
C Palacio episcopal
P Torre de los Plata
Q Casa del Sol
V Casa de la Generala

EXCURSIONS

Santuario de la Virgen de la Montaña (The Mountain Virgin) ⊙ - 3km/2mi eas
A 17C Baroque shrine, built on a hill cloaked in olive trees, shelters a famou
statuette of the Virgin. A picturesque *romería* to the shrine is held on the fir
Sunday in May. The esplanade affords an extensive **view**★ across the Extremadur
plateau.

Garrovillas - 36km/22mi northwest on N 630 and C 552.
In this typical Extremadura town, the Plaza Mayor is lined by arcades in whic
in a delightfully artless way, fantasy has run rife with every pillar askew!

Arroyo de la Luz - 20km/12mi west on N 521 and C 523. To find the Iglesia d
la Asunción, take the tower as a bearing and proceed along the widest street.
The church has a 15C-16C Gothic nave. The altarpiece is worth looking at for th
16 pictures★ and four medallions it comprises which were painted on the spot b
Morales the Divine between 1560 and 1563. As the artist's paintings are scattered
the collection here provides an opportunity to appreciate more fully than usual hi
delicate, elegant style.

Museo Vostell-Malpartida ⊙ - 10km/6mi on N 521 towards Malpartida d
Cáceres. The museum is located 3km/2mi beyond the town. Follow the signpost
In 1976 the Hispano-German artist Wolf Vostell created a private contemporar
art museum in this 18C-19C wool washing factory. Vostell was the leading ligh
in the Fluxus movement founded in 1962 by George Maciunas. The museu
contains seven rooms created by Vostell, a large collection of conceptual art
including works by Canogar, the Crónica team and Saura, and a donation from
the Fluxus collection by Gino di Maggio with works by Maciunas, Brecht, Higgin
and Vautier.

CÁDIZ★

Andalucía – Population 157 355
Michelin map 446 W 11

Cádiz, a bastion ringed by the sea, is attached to the mainland by a narrow san
isthmus. Its outstanding site and vast sheltered bay have attracted settlers since
earliest times. It was founded by the Phoenicians in 1100 BC and subsequently came
under Roman and Moorish rule. In the 18C, Cádiz became one of Europe's greates
ports once it had acquired trading rights with Spanish America, hitherto the
monopoly of Sevilla.

During the French occupation and siege of 1812, Spanish patriots convened the
Cortes which promulgated the famous liberal constitution of March 1812, known as
the **Constitution of Cádiz**.

Modern Cádiz - Cádiz is an industrial town and port with shipbuilding and nava
dockyards. It is also an important fishing centre and a strategic hub for tourism to
the Canary Islands and other parts of Spain.

The Battle of Trafalgar

On 21 October 1805, Admiral Villeneuve sailed out of Cádiz harbour with his Franco-Spanish fleet to confront the English under Nelson off the **Cabo de Trafalgar** headland. The ships were ill-equipped and poorly manned; after some heroic combat Villeneuve's fleet was destroyed and he was taken prisoner. Nelson had been mortally wounded during the course of the battle but England's supremacy at sea was established.

SIGHTS

★ **Seaside promenades** – The south and west promenades look out over the sea while those to the north and east with their public **gardens**★ (Parque Genovés, Alameda Marqués de Comillas and Alameda de Apodaca), some of the most attractive places in the city, look across to the far shore of the bay.

★ **Museo Provincial de Cádiz** ⊙ (**BY M**) – *Access by calle Antonio López.* The museum is housed in two buildings, one modern and the other a former Franciscan convent, and comprises three sections: archeology, fine arts and ethnology.

Archeological department – The wealth of the displays confirms the city's long history. One of the rooms is devoted to Roman necropolises and various funeral rites. There is a collection of vases, oil lamps and jewellery. The colossal statue of Trajan was found near Tarifa.

The most outstanding exhibits are the two 5C BC **Phoenician sarcophagi**★; that of the man was discovered in 1887 and that of the woman in 1980. They were copied by Greek artists after Egyptian models.

Fine Arts department – This presents a rich collection of 17C Spanish painting with works by Morales the Divine, Murillo, Ribera and in particular, **Zurbarán**★. His canvases, brought from La Cartuja (Carthusian monastery) in Jerez, were painted when he was at the height of his glory between 1630 and 1640.

Ethnological department – Cádiz folklore since the 18C is represented by the Tía Norica puppet theatre, with its props and characters, including the popular Tía and her nephew Batillo.

CÀDIZ

Ancha	BY 2	Mina (Pl. de)	BY 12	
Calderón de la Barca	BY 3	Montañés	BZ 13	
Candelarias (Pl.)	BZ 5	Novena	BY 15	
Columela	BYZ	Pelota	BZ 18	
Compañía	BZ 6	Ramón de Carranza	BZ 19	
Doctor Marañón	AY 7	San Antonio (Pl. de)	AY 21	
Fernando El Católico	BY 8	San Francisco	BY 22	
Mentidero (Pl. del)	AY 9	San Juan de Dios	BZ 24	
		San Juan de Dios (Pl. de)	BZ 25	
		San Roque	BZ 27	
		Santo Cristo	BZ 28	
		Topete (Pl.)	BZ 30	

A Iglesia de San Felipe Neri   **M** Museo provincial de Cádiz   **M¹** Museo Histórico Municipal

Museo Histórico Municipal ⊘ (AY M') – The museum contains an outstandin
ivory and mahogany **model**★ of the town in Charles III's reign (18C).

Iglesia de San Felipe Neri ⊘ (AY A) – It was in the oval-shaped interior of th
church with its vast cupola that the Cortes gathered in 1812 to proclaim th
constitution. Above the high altar is a Virgin by Murillo.

Catedral ⊘ (BZ) – The neo-Classical church, after plans by Vicente Acero, too
from 1720 to 1838 to build. The great composer **Manuel de Falla** (1876-1946)
buried in the crypt.

Museo ⊘ – The rich collection of **church plate**★ in this museum includes a proce
sional cross by Enrique de Arfe, a monumental silver tabernacle (5m/16ft hig
and the 1721 "million monstrance", so called since its decoration is said t
comprise nearly a million jewels.

EXCURSION

Medina Sidonia – *44km/27mi east on N IV, N 340 and C 346.*
The road from Cádiz follows an offshore bar with beaches on one side and the Sa
Fernando **salt-pans** on the other.
Medina Sidonia is a hilltop village with beautiful views of the surrounding plai
one may see as far as the coast on clear days.
The Gothic **Iglesia de Santa María** ⊘, at the top of the village, has an outstandin
Renaissance **altarpiece**★ by the sculptor Juan Bautista Vázquez the Elder.

Castillo-convento de CALATRAVA LA NUEVA★

CALATRAVA CASTLE-MONASTERY – Castilla-La Mancha (Ciudad Real)
Michelin map 444 P 18

The Castillo de Calatrava, a ruined citadel with its crumbling walls crowning a hig
hill, still inspires a feeling of awe. It conveys, as no other site, the lonely ordea
undergone by the Knights of the Reconquest.

Soldiering monks

In the mid 12C, the Campo de Calatrava plain was the scene of unceasing
warfare between Christians and Muslims. The old Fortaleza de Calatrava, a
fortress built originally by the Moors on the banks of the Guadiana, was
captured and subsequently abandoned by the Templars, before being taken
over by Raimundo, Abbot of Fitero. A soldier before he became an abbot, he
installed a garrison in the castle where in 1158 he founded the **Orden Militar de
Calatrava**, the first of Spain's military orders. Al-Mansur, however, captured the
castle, which remained in Muslim hands until the victory of Las Navas de Tolosa
(1212) when the knights regained control of the region. They determined to
build a new fortress in an impregnable position; it was completed by 1217.

Castillo-convento ⊘ – *7km/4mi southwest of Calzada de Calatrava, turn righ
onto a 2.5km/1.5mi long surfaced uphill road.*
There are three stout perimeter walls, the second actually built into the rock.
The **church**, restored and lit by an immense rose window, has fine brick vaulting
described as swallow's nest in design and probably the work of Moorish prisoners
The ruins of the **Castillo de Salvatierra** are visible from the fortress towers.

CANGAS DE NARCEA

Asturias – Population 19 083
Michelin map 441 C 10

Cangas, gateway to the upper Narcea Valley, is a meeting place for trout fishermen
excursionists and hunters.

EXCURSIONS

Corias – *3km/2mi north.*
The large **monastery** (monasterio) ⊘ re-erected in neo-Classical style after being
burned down in the 19C, was founded in the 11C and occupied for 800 years by
Benedictines. There are ornate Churrigueresque altars in the **church**.

Tineo – *30km/19mi northeast.*
The town perched 673m/2 208ft up the mountainside commands an im
mense **panorama**★★ of the surrounding sierras.

CARAVACA DE LA CRUZ

Murcia – Population 21 238
Michelin map 445 R 24

aravaca stretches around the foot of a hill crowned by castle ramparts. In May each
ear, the town celebrates the miracle which took place within its walls in 1231. Then,
is said, a priest named Chirinos was celebrating Mass before the Moorish king who
ad taken him prisoner, when the Cross, which had been missing from the altar,
uddenly reappeared; the Moor was moved to immediate conversion and the Cross,
elieved to be part of the True Cross, became an object of great popular veneration.
was stolen in 1934.

Castillo-Iglesia de la Santa Cruz ⊘ – The restored ramparts of the 15C castle
enclose the church which for so long sheltered the Holy Cross *(Santa Cruz)*. The
1722 doorway in local red marble has a surprisingly bold Baroque character.
Estípites or inverted balusters and delicately twisted pillars add to the vertical
effect of the entrance without detracting from the robustness and, in fact, give
it something of a Latin-American appearance. Inside there is a strictly Herreran
elegance. From the battlements at the top of the building there is an interesting
view of the surrounding town.

On all town plans north is at the top of the page.

CARDONA★

Catalunya (Barcelona) – Population 6 402
Michelin map 443 G 35

erched on top of a 589m/1 933ft hill with the appearance of a sturdy citadel, the
lded silhouette of the castle overlooks this charming village. It was rebuilt in the 18C
ad currently houses an inn. Of the original 11C buildings there remain only a trunca-
d tower, the Torre de la Minyona, and the collegiate church, a perfect example of
omanesque art in Lombardy. The top of the citadel commands a view of a **salt mine**,
orked since Roman times, with some galleries more than 1km/0.5mi deep.

★ **Colegiata de Sant Vincenç** ⊘ – The collegiate church was built in 1040 and has
several features from the Lombard style of architecture which flourished at the
time in Catalunya. The smooth, unadorned walls, the lantern over the transept
crossing, the different types of vaulting – barrel in the nave with its impressive
elevation and groined in the aisles – all testify to a skilful mastery of the art.
Below, the groined vaulting in the **crypt**★ rests on six graceful columns. The interior
was used as a backdrop by Orson Welles when he shot *Chimes at Midnight*.
Outside, the charming Gothic cloisters date from the 15C.

Castillo de Cardona and the Colegiata

CARMONA★

Andalucía (Sevilla) – Population 23 516
Michelin map 446 T 13

The ancient walls of Carmona rise up on the edge of the plateau overlooking the v
cereal-growing plain of the Guadalquivir.

CIUDAD VIEJA (OLD TOWN) *1hr*

Park the car near the Puerta de Sevilla in the lower part of town.

The Puerta de Sevilla, its double Moorish arch a striking contrast to the Baro
tower of the Iglesia de San Pedro opposite, opens onto the old town with
convents, white-walled alleys and stone gateways leading to the *patios* of for
noble residences.

Calle Prim leads to plaza San Fernando which is lined by 17C and 18C houses. 1
Ayuntamiento (town hall) *(in calle de San Salvador)* retains a large Roman mos
in its *patio*.

Continuing along calle Martín López, you come to the **Iglesia de Santa María** ⊙ wh
is preceded by the former mosque's ablutionary courtyard. A little further alo
in the church of **Convento de Santa Clara**, the walls of the nave are hung w
portraits of 17C women. The style of the paintings recalls that of Zurbarán. 1
street continues to the **Puerta de Córdoba** which was built into the Roman wal
the 17C.

Calle de Calatrava and calle G Freire lead uphill to the **Alcázar del Rey Don Pe**
(Alcázar of King Peter I, the Cruel), which is now a parador.

ADDITIONAL SIGHT

Necrópolis Romana ⊙ – *Access to the Roman necropolis is indicated on the r*
to Sevilla. More than 800 1C-4C tombs have been discovered. Most compris
vaulted funerary chamber with niches for the urns. The most interesting are 1
Tumba del Elefante (so called on account of the statue of an elephant) with th
dining rooms and a kitchen, and the Tumba de Servilia, which is the size o
patrician villa.

CARTAGENA

Murcia – Population 173 061
Michelin map 445 T 27

Cartagena, a major naval base, lies in a unique position in the curve of a deep t
sheltered by fortified promontories.

Cartago Nova – In 223 BC the settlement was captured by the Carthaginians w
named it *Cartago Nova*. Subsequently, it developed into a prosperous colony un
the Romans (traces of the *forum* have been discovered beneath Plaza de los T
Reyes); it was neglected in preference for Almería by the Arabs and Murcia by 1
Christians who also removed its bishopric. It returned to favour, however, in the re
of Philip II who fortified the surrounding hilltops and that of Charles III who built 1
Arsenal.

The construction of an oil refinery at Escombreras, 9km/6mi away, together w
the export of lead, iron and zinc, have brought the town renewed prosperity.
Dramatic processions take place in the city during Semana Santa (Holy Week).

SIGHTS

City life centres around calle Mayor, the main street. Near plaza del Ayuntamie
is the early **submarine** invented by a native of the city, Lieutenant Isaac Peral,
1888.

From the top of the **Castillo de la Concepción**, a former fort which is now a pu
garden (Parque Torres), there is a good general **view** of the harbour and the ru
of the former Romanesque **Catedral de Santa María la Vieja**.

Museo Nacional de Arqueología Marítima ⊙ – *Navidad dike, in the harbc*
Take the Algameca road and when you reach the Empresa Nacional Bazán, tu
onto the road on the right and follow it to the end.
This museum of maritime archeology displays finds from various underwa
excavations, notably a rich collection of Phoenician, Punic and Roman amphor
Seafaring activity during Antiquity is illustrated by maps, small-scale models
vessels (galleys, biremes and triremes) as well as a model of the Mediterrane
sea bed.

EXCURSION

Mar Menor – *35km/22mi east on N 332.*
Mar Menor, or Little Sea, is a lagoon separated from the open Mediterranean by the **Manga**, a sand bar 500m/1 640ft wide which extends northwards for 20km/12mi from the eastern end of the rocky Cabo de Palos headland. Gilt-head, mullet and king prawns are fished from its shallow saltwater. The low-lying hinterland is cloaked in almond trees with here and there a palm or a windmill. **La Manga del Mar Menor** is a large, elongated seaside resort with surrealistic tower blocks stretching for miles along the sand bar. Its sandy beaches and calm water are ideal for sailing, windsurfing and water-skiing.
In **Santiago de la Ribera**, where there is no natural beach, pontoons with changing cabins line the seafront. **San Javier**, nearby, is the seat of the Academia General del Aire (General Air Academy).

Sierra de CAZORLA★★

Andalucía (Jaén)
Michelin map 446 R 21-S 21

The Sierra de Cazorla is part of the **Parque Nacional de las Sierras de Cazorla, Segura y Las Villas**, a national park covering 214 336ha/529 646 acres which was created in 1986 to protect the natural resources of the region.
The Baetic ranges in this sierra reach an altitude of more than 2 000m/6 562ft. Springs rise in abundance, one of which eventually becomes Andalucía's greatest river, the Guadalquivir. At first the stream flows northeastwards before, at length, finding a passage west and finally south to the Atlantic. Altitude and rainfall produce an upland Mediterranean type vegetation, with thyme, lavender and other aromatic shrubs. The forest, the most extensive woodland area in Andalucía, is open to the public along marked paths. There is a good variety of wildlife – deer, moufflons or wild mountain sheep, golden eagles, ospreys and vultures. The Sierra de Cazorla is a hunting reserve.

B. Brillion/MICHELIN

Cazorla

NORTH TO SOUTH ACROSS THE SIERRA

110km/68mi including the ascent to the parador; allow 4hr along winding road

9km/6mi north of Villacarrillo the road enters the Guadalquivir **gorges** (garganta which lead to the Tranco dam, one of Andalucía's biggest reservoirs which, in tur provides water for the irrigation of the Úbeda region. When you come with sight of the picturesque **setting**★ of the perched village of **Hornos**, turn rig onto a road which skirts the lake and from which you will get good **views**★★ of th mountains and, at certain times of the day, of deer drinking at the water's edg The Sierra del Pozo can be seen on the horizon.

Parque Cinegético (Game Reserve) – *Beyond Bujaraiza*. You may observe some the typical wildlife in the sierra from lookout points. The call of stags echo throughout the reserve in late summer.

A little further on you come to the **Centro de Interpretación Torre del Vinagre** which h a hunting museum.

★ **Road up to the parador** – The steep road through the pines leads to the parad set in a splendidly isolated position. It is popular with hunters.

Return to the Cazorla road.

From a lookout a little further on there is a good **view**★★ of the upper valley of th Guadalquivir. An impressive mountain crest section precedes the puerto de La Palomas (1 290m/4 232ft), a pass marking the dividing line between ferti green mountainsides and ochre-coloured hills. There are magnificent **views**★★ ov an immense sweep of olive groves.

La Iruela – Turn right in the village square for the **carretera de los miradores** (a *unsurfaced but car-worthy forest track*) where three successive lookouts com mand steep **views**★★ of the town and the Castillo de Cazorla. A little further o there are fine **views** of the mountain circus.

Cazorla – The town is dominated by its castle. Cazorla's steep and sometim stepped alleys are full of character as are its two large squares, framed by o houses.

Michelin on-line gives motorists the freedom to create their own itineraries, to stop an discover tourist attractions. At any time, you can print out your complete route map, a well as the information from the Red Guides and the cost of tolls on the selected itinerar

Log in at www.michelin-travel.com

CELANOVA

Galicia (Orense) – Population 5 902
Michelin map 441 F 6

During the Middle Ages Celanova was an important halt on the pilgrim route fro Portugal to Santiago de Compostela.

Monasterio ⊙ – The large, imposing monastery on Plaza Mayor was founded i 936 by San Rosendo, Bishop of San Martín de Mondoñedo.

Church – The **façade** of this monumental late-17C edifice displays hints o Classicism. The coffered vaulting is decorated with geometrical designs, th cupola with volutes. An immense altarpiece (1697) occupies the back of the apse Note also the choir stalls, Baroque in the lower part and Gothic in the upper, a well as the fine organ.

★★ **Claustro** – The construction of these cloisters began in 1550 to plans by a mon from Celanova and took until the 18C to complete. The cloisters are among th most beautiful in Galicia: light and shade contrast brilliantly in the interplay o lines and ornamental relief.

Capilla de San Miguel (St Michael's Chapel) – This is one of the monastery's earlies buildings (937) and one of the rare Mozarabic monuments still in good condition

EXCURSION

Santa Comba de Bande – *26km/16mi south on N 540.*
The small 7C Visigothic **iglesia**★ ⊙ overlooks the lake. Inside the church, the pla is that of a Greek cross, lit by a lantern turret. The apse is square and is precede by a horseshoe-shaped triumphal arch resting on four pillars with Corinthia capitals. Pure lines and perfect wall masonry add a rich quality to this uniqu building.

CEUTA ★

North Africa – Population 73 208

Michelin map 959 folds 5 and 10

euta, the closest African port to the Iberian Peninsula, occupies a strategic
osition dominating the Straits of Gibraltar. The city, with its typically Euro-
ean style architecture, is situated on the isthmus linking Monte Hacho with
e African continent. Conquered by the Portuguese in 1415, the port passed
to the hands of the Spanish in 1580, when Philip II annexed the Kingdom of
ortugal.

MONTE HACHO

*10km/6mi – about half an
hour. Best seen in the morning.*

Calle Independencia and
calle Recintor Sur, running
parallel to the seafront,
lead to the foot of monte

> ### Getting to Ceuta
>
> **By ferry** – **Trasmediterránea** operates ser-
> vices between Algeciras and Ceuta. Jour-
> ney time: 40min. For information and
> bookings, call ☎ 902 45 46 45.

Hacho which has a citadel at its summit. The corniche road encircling the
peninsula offers beautiful **views** of the Western Rif coastline to the south and
the Spanish coast and the Rock of Gibraltar to the north.

Before reaching the lighthouse (no entry), bear left.

Ermita de San Antonio – *Leave your car in the car park.* At the end of a charming
square is the 16C Capilla de San Antonio (Chapel of St Anthony). From the
platform of the monument commemorating the passing through of General
Franco's troops in 1936, there is a magnificent **view★★** of, to the left, the town
spread out on its slightly curved isthmus around the port, and to the right, far off
views of the peninsula coastline.

ADDITIONAL SIGHTS

Museo Municipal ⊘ – This municipal museum houses a white marble Roman
sarcophagus, Punic and Roman amphorae, a collection of coins and old weapons
as well as various items of ceramic ware.
Other places worthy of interest are the **Iglesia de Nuestra Señora de África** (Church of
Our Lady of Africa), housing the statue of the patron saint of the town, the 18C
Catedral and the **Foso de San Felipe**, an old Portuguese fort where San Juan de Dios,
the founder of the Orden de los Hospitalarios (Order of the Hospitallers of St
John), worked in 1530.

Parque marítimo del Mediterráneo ⊘ – Palm trees, exotic plants, swimming
pools, lakes, waterfalls and sculptures have all been perfectly integrated by César
Manrique to create this spectacular park.

CHINCHÓN ★

Madrid – Population 3 994

Michelin map 444 or 442 L 19

he name Chinchón has been made famous by its aniseed spirit and more importantly
 the Countess of Chinchón to whom the west owes quinine. The countess, wife of
17C viceroy of Peru, was cured of tropical fever by an Indian medicament prepared
om tree bark; having proved the remedy she brought it back to Europe. In the 18C,
nnaeus, the Swedish botanist, named the bark-bearing tree chinchona, in the
cereine's honour.

Plaza Mayor – The uneven but picturesque arcaded square, dominated by its
church, is surrounded by three-storey houses with wooden balconies. Bullfights
are held here in summer.
The brick buildings of the former Augustinian monastery beside the square now
house a parador.
Aniseed, gin and other spirits are distilled in the old castle at the top of the
town.

CIUDAD RODRIGO★

Castilla y León (Salamanca) – Population 14 973
Michelin map 441 K 10

Ciudad Rodrigo appears high on a hilltop, guarded by the square tower of its 1▮
Alcázar (now a parador) and medieval ramparts and, if you are coming from Portug▮
on the far side of the río Águeda spanned by a Roman bridge. After the Moori▮
invasion it was re-established in the 12C by Count Rodrigo González from whom▮
takes its name; later it became a stronghold on the Spanish-Portuguese border a▮
was involved in all the conflicts between Castilla and Portugal. Wellington's succe▮
in the bloody battle against the French in 1812 won him the title of Duke of Ciud▮
Rodrigo and Grandee of Spain.
The surrounding region is given over to large estates of ilex trees beneath which gra▮
black pigs and fighting bulls.

★ **Plaza Mayor** – Two Renaissance palaces stand on the city's lively main squa▮
the first, now the **Ayuntamiento** (town hall), has a façade with two storeys of bask▮
arcading forming a gallery and a loggia, while the second, the **Casa de los Cueto**, h▮
a decorative frieze separating its first and second storeys.

★ **Catedral** ⊘ – The cathedral was built in two main stages, first from 1170 ▮
1230 and then in the 14C; in the 16C Rodrigo Gil de Hontañón added the centr▮
apse. The stiffness of the figures of the Disciples in a gallery in the upper pa▮
of the south transept façade contrasts with the delicate ornamentation of t▮
surrounding blind arcades. The 13C **Portada de la Virgen**★ (Doorway of the Virgi▮
masked outside by a classical belfry which forms the cathedral narthex, has ▮
line of Apostles carved between the columns beneath the splayings and t▮
covings.
In the interior, the Isabelline choir stalls in the *coro* were carved by Rodri▮
Alemán. The fine Renaissance **altar**★ in the north aisle is adorned with an alabast▮
Deposition, beautifully composed and carved in low relief, a masterpiece by Luc▮
Mitata.
The **cloisters**★ are made up of diverse architectural styles. In the west gallery, t▮
oldest part, Romanesque capitals illustrate man's original sin, while grotesqu▮
on the column bases symbolise greed and vanity. Opening off the east gallery ▮
a Plateresque door in the pure Salamanca style decorated with medallio▮
including one (on the right) of the architect Pedro Güemes.

Capilla de Cerralbo – *South of the cathedral.* The chapel, built between 1588 a▮
1685, is pure and austere but harmonious in the Herreran style. Adjoining t▮
south side is the Plaza del Buen Alcalde, a quiet arcaded square.

Palacio de los Castros (or **Palacio del Conde de Montarco**) – *Access via the easte▮
arcade of plaza del Buen Alcalde.* This late 15C palace, on plaza del Conde (Squa▮
of the Count), has a long façade and an interesting off-centre doorway surround▮
by an *alfiz* and flanked by twisted columns.

Murallas (Ramparts) – The walls built on the remains of Roman foundations in t▮
12C, were converted to a full defensive system on the north and west flanks ▮
1710. There are several stairways up to the 2km/1mi long sentry path.

Castillo de COCA★★

Castilla y León (Segovia)
Michelin map 444 or 442 I 16

This fortress, **castillo** ⊘, (on the outskirts of Coca village) is the most outstandi▮
example of Mudéjar military architecture in Spain. It was built in the late 15C ▮
Moorish craftsmen for the archbishop of Sevilla, Fonseca, and consists of thr▮
concentric perimeters, flanked by polygonal corner towers and turrets with, at t▮
centre, a massive keep. It is the epitome of all fortresses, but with the sun mellowi▮
the pink brick and the interplay of shadows on battlements and watchtowers, it c▮
be attractive as well as awesome.
The *Torre del Homenaje* (keep) and *Capilla* (chapel), which contains Romanesq▮
wood carvings, are open to the public.

Ch. Sappa/CEDRI

Castillo de Coca

EXCURSION

Arévalo – *26km/16mi southwest.*
Isabel the Catholic spent her childhood in the 14C **castle** with its massive crenellated keep that dominates the town. Of note also in the town are the Romanesque-Mudéjar churches built of brick and several old mansions.

★ **Plaza de la Villa**, the former Plaza Mayor, is one of the best preserved town squares in Castilla with its half-timbered brick houses resting on pillared porticoes. They blend in perfectly with the Mudéjar east end of the Iglesia de Santa María and its blind arcading.

CÓRDOBA★★★

Andalucía – Population 310 488

Michelin map 446 S 15

Córdoba stands at the halfway point on the right bank of the Guadalquivir where the ranches and farmlands of the Sierra de Córdoba plateau to the north meet the wheatlands and olive groves of the southerly Campiña plains. The city owes its fame to the brilliance of the civilizations which it has twice fostered and which each time raised it to the position of capital.

It could live on its past but has chosen to develop modern industries on its outskirts and maintain its longstanding crafts of silver filigree and tooled leatherwork in their traditional setting in the heart of the city. Mid May is festival time, with competitions in decking crosses, *patios*, windows and balconies, streets and squares with flowers until the end of the month when the *feria* brings celebrations in Andalusian costume and flamenco dancing. Between Montilla and Lucena, approximately 50km/30mi south of Córdoba lies a wine region known as **Montilla-Moriles** which produces excellent wines and spirits comparable to those of Jerez.

The Roman town – Córdoba, capital of Baetica, was the birthplace of **Seneca the Rhetorician** (55 BC-AD 39), his son **Seneca the Philosopher** (4 BC-AD 65), who became tutor to Nero, and Lucan (39-65), Seneca the Philosopher's nephew and companion to Nero in his student days. His writing, particularly the poem *Pharsalia* which recounts the war between Caesar and Pompey, won him great acclaim.

The early Christian period was marked by the episcopacy of **Ossius** (257-359), counsellor to Emperor Constantine, protagonist of orthodoxy against Arianism and reorganiser of the Church in Spain.

The Córdoba Caliphate – Emirs from the Damascus Caliphate established themselves in Córdoba as early as 719. In 756 **Abd ar-Rahman I**, sole survivor of the **Umayyads** of Damascus who had been annihilated by the Abbasids, arrived to found the dynasty which was to rule over Muslim Spain for three centuries and bring untold prosperity and fame to Córdoba. In 929 **Abd ar-Rahman III** proclaimed himself Caliph, and Spain independent. In the 10C a university was founded which won high renown. The open-mindedness and tolerance alive at the time allowed the three communities – Christian, Jewish and Muslim – not only to live side by side but to enrich one another intellectually and culturally. On the accession, in 976, of the feeble **Hisham II**, power fell into the hands of the ruthless but remarkable **Al-Mansur** (the Victorious); his descendants, however, failed to prevent Al-Andalus from fragmenting into small warring kingdoms, the **reinos de taifas**.

WHERE TO STAY

BUDGET HOTELS

Marisa (BZ ❾) – *Cardenal Herrero, 6.* ☎ *957 47 31 42, fax 957 47 41 4*
28 rooms. Garage.
A simple hotel splendidly located opposite the Mezquita. Typical Spani
decor. 10 rooms looking out onto the Mezquita. Small bathrooms.

Albucasis (AZ ❌) – *Buen Pastor, 11.* ☎ *957 47 86 25, fax 957 47 86 2*
15 rooms. Garage.
A small, basic hotel in a typical Cordoban house in the Judería. Access via
patio. Spacious, comfortable rooms.

OUR SELECTION

NH Amistad Córdoba (AZ ❷) – *Plaza de Maimónides, 3.* ☎ *957 42 03 5*
fax 957 42 03 65. 69 rooms. Garage. Special weekend rates.
This attractive hotel situated in the heart of the Judería, opposite part of t
city's walls, has a large Mudéjar patio and spacious public areas. Ve
comfortable, well-appointed rooms which have been tastefully decorated.

Maimónides (ABZ ❾) – *Torrijos, 4.* ☎ *957 47 15 00, fax 957 48 38 0*
82 rooms. Garage.
This hotel enjoys a superb location opposite the Mezquita, the city's mo
famous attraction. Twenty of its rooms have views of this magnifice
building. Cordoban-style patio.

EATING OUT

Tapas

Córdoba does full justice to Andalucía's great tapas tradition with a wide rang
of bars offering a huge selection of tapas, providing visitors with the perfe
opportunity to try the local specialities such as *salmorejo* (a type of loc
gazpacho), *rabo de toro* (braised oxtail), *embutidos* (local sausage) ar
sherries (finos, amontillados, olorosos).

LA JUDERÍA

Casa Salinas – *Puerta de Almodóvar, 2 (near to the Puerta de Almodóvar).*
Typical, traditional *taberna* with a bar by the entrance, a small room and patio
Friendly atmosphere, with *azulejo* decoration and numerous photos of the ric
and famous adorning the walls.

Taberna Guzmán – *Judíos, 9 (opposite the Sinagoga).*
Traditional *taberna* with lots of character, decorated with *azulejos*, bullfigh
ing mementoes and posters advertising the local *feria*. Local sausage ar
cheeses served.

Pepe "de la Judería" – *Romero, 1 (between the Zoco and the Mezquita).*
A tavern opened in 1928 with a bar dating from this period. Several rooms fc
tapas around a patio. Restaurant on upper floor.

La Bacalá – *Medina y Corrella (near the Mezquita).*
A bar with whitewashed walls and arches. Cod tapas specialities. In a sma
square with pleasant tables outside.

AROUND THE PLAZA DE LA CORREDERA – PLAZA DEL POTRO

Taberna Salinas – *Tundidores, 3 (close to the Plaza de la Corredera).*
Attractive bar founded in 1924 with several rooms radiating off a centra
covered patio.

Sociedad de Plateros – *San Francisco, 6 (close to the Plaza del Potro).*
The Sociedad de Plateros owns several bars and taverns. This one, dating back
over a century (1872), has particular character.

Bodegas Campos – *Lineros, 32 (near to the Plaza del Potro).*
Occupies some old wine storehouses founded in 1908. Restaurant designe
around several patios. At the entrance *(to the right)*, there is a bar decoratec
with photos of famous visitors.

GRAN CAPITÁN – CRUZ CONDE

La Canoa – *Ronda de Tejares, pasaje CAJASUR (near Cruz Conde).*
Very pleasant tavern with round arches and barrel tables. *Canoa* is the name
of a funnel used to refill the barrels.

Gaudí – *Av. Gran Capitán, 22.*
A bar with modernist decor. A pleasant location for lunch, a snack or ar
aperitif. Wide selection of tapas.

Taberna San Miguel "El Pisto" – *Plaza de San Miguel, 1 (next to the Iglesia de Sar
Miguel).*
Typical tavern dating back more than a century. Frequented in the past by
famous bullfighters such as Manolete and Guerrita. Attractive wooden bar.

Restaurants

UR SELECTION

Churrasco – *Romero, 16.* ☎ *957 29 08 19.*
ypical tavern-style restaurant with an attractive small patio. Tapas served at
he bar downstairs.

a Almudaina – *Jardines de los Santos Mártires, 1.* ☎ *957 47 43 42.*
legant restaurant with a delightful covered wooden patio.

l Caballo Rojo – *Cardenal Herrera, 28.* ☎ *957 47 53 75.*
ne of the city's institutions. Classic decor. Tapas available at the bar by the
ntrance.

órdoba itself became part of the Kingdom of Sevilla in 1070. Political decline in
o way diminished intellectual life, however. There lived in the city from 1126
o 1198 the Moor **Averroës**, a universal scholar – physicist, astrologer, mathema-
ician, doctor and philosopher – who, although he was prevented from teaching
y the doctrinaire Almohad leader, Yacoub al-Mansur, who opposed his theories,
id much to bring the learning of Aristotle to the west. A contemporary of
verroës, the Jew **Maimónides** (1135-1204) was famed for his learning in medicine,
heology and philosophy, but had to flee to Morocco and later Egypt to escape
ersecution.
ventually reconquered by the Christians in 1236, the city's prosperity waned until
he 16C and 17C, when Córdoba leatherwork, embossed, tooled and coloured,
ecame the fashion for wall and seat coverings.

ome famous Córdobans – Among the city's sons are Gonzalo Fernández de
órdoba, the **Gran Capitán** (1453-1515) born in the nearby town of Montilla, who
onquered the Kingdom of Naples in 1504, and **Luis de Góngora** (1561-1627), the great
Baroque poet and major exponent of *culteranismo*, a school of poetry characterised
y its cultured verse. His main works include the *Fábula de Polifemo y Galatea*, and
Soledades.

★ THE MEZQUITA AND THE JUDERÍA *3hr*

Córdoba's three faiths are represented in this quarter of the city: Islamic with its
outstanding *mezquita* (mosque), Christian with its cathedral strangely incorporated into the mosque, and Jewish with its synagogue.

★ **Mezquita-Catedral (Mosque-Cathedral)** ⊘ **(BZ)** – Each part of the heterogeneous
edifice must be admired separately.

Mezquita – The overall plan is the traditional Muslim one of a crenellated square
perimeter enclosing the Patio de los Naranjos (Orange Tree Court) with a basin
for ritual ablution – in this case that of Al-Mansur **(1)** – a hall for prayer and a
minaret.
The mosque was built in several stages. The first Muslims to arrive in Córdoba
were content to share the Visigothic church of St Vincent with the Christians.
Soon, however, this proved insufficient and Abd ar-Rahman I (758-788) purchased their part of the site from the Christians. He razed the church and around the
year 780 began the construction of a splendid mosque with 11 aisles each opening
onto the Patio de los Naranjos. Marble pillars and stone from former Roman and
Visigothic buildings were reused in the mosque which became famous for an
architectural innovation: the superimposition of two tiers of arches to give added
height and spaciousness.
The mosque was enlarged over the years: in 848 Abd ar-Rahman II had it extended
to the present-day Capilla de Villaviciosa (Villaviciosa Chapel), in 961 El Hakam II
built the *mihrab*, and lastly, in 987, Al-Mansur gave it its present size by adding
eight more aisles (recognisable by their red brick pavement).
The interior is a forest of columns (about 850) and the horseshoe-shaped arches
consist of alternating white (stone) and red (brick) voussoirs.

Make your way to the Puerta de las Palmas.

The aisle off the doorway, wider than the others and which served as the main
aisle of the original mosque, has a beautiful *artesonado* ceiling. It leads to the
mihrab★★★ before which the faithful, led by the imam, would pray. What is
normally a simple niche is in this case a sumptuously decorated room preceded
by a triple **maksourah (2)** or enclosure reserved for the caliph. The enclosure is
roofed by three ribbed domes which rest on a most unusual series of apparently
interweaving multifoil arches, as striking as the cupolas themselves which are
faced with mosaics against a background of gold. Decoration throughout
adds to the richness of the architecture: on the mosaics, alabaster plaques and
stucco are ornate arabesques and palm-leaf motifs sometimes framed by Cufic
script.

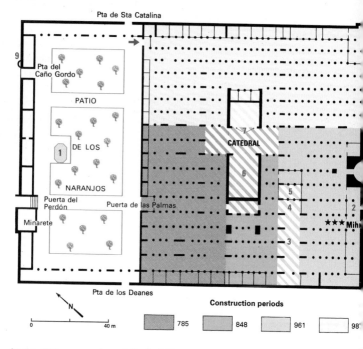

Pta de Sta Catalina

Pta del Caño Gordo

PATIO

DE LOS

NARANJOS

Puerta del Perdón

Puerta de las Palmas

Minarete

CATEDRAL

★★★ Mih

Pta de los Deanes

N

0   40 m

Construction periods

785   848   961   98

In the 13C, conversion of the building to Christian use brought certain physi
alterations: the aisles (except that off the Puerta de las Palmas) were wall
off from the court; a few columns were removed and pointed arches substitut
for the Moorish ones when the first cathedral was built (3) – fortunately nothi
was done which destroyed the perspectives in the mosque. Alfonso X w
responsible for the chancel in the **Capilla de Villaviciosa** or **Lucernario** (4) and bu
the **Capilla Real**★ (5) decorated in the 13C with Mudéjar stucco which harmonis
with the whole.

Catedral – In the 16C the cathedral canons desired more sumptuous surroundin
They began by cutting away the centre of the mosque to erect loftier vaulting.
spite of the talent of the architect Hernán Ruiz and his followers, Emper
Charles V was far from pleased with the result: "You have destroyed somethi
unique", he said, "to build something commonplace". The search for grandeur l
to a Gothic style transept and apse (1523-1547); Renaissance style decorati
figures in medallions in the apsidal vaulting (1560); and dense Italian style stuc
crowded with cherubim decorating the nave vaulting (1598) and in the coffer
dome over the transept (1600). Additional enrichments are the Baroque ch
stalls★★ (6) by Pedro Duque Cornejo (c 1750) and two **pulpits**★★ (7) of marb
jasper and mahogany.

Tesoro – The treasury, built by the Baroque architect Francisco Hurtado Izquierd
can be found in the **Capilla del Cardenal** (Cardinal's Chapel) (8). A monumental 1€
monstrance by E Arfe and an exceptional Baroque figure of Christ in ivory stand o
in this collection of liturgical objects.

Exterior features of the complex include the **minaret** (267 steps, fine **views**), fro
the top of which the muezzin called the prayer. In the 17C the minaret w
enveloped in a Baroque tower. At its foot, giving onto the street, is the 14
Mudéjar **Puerta del Perdón** (Pardon Doorway) which is faced with bronze. A litt
further on is a small chapel to the deeply venerated **Virgen de los Faroles** (Virgin
the Lanterns) (9).

★★ **Judería (Old Jewish Quarter)** (ABZ) – Narrow streets, white walls spilled over wit
brilliant flowers, doors half open onto cool *patios*, delicate window grilles, ba
where a group of Córdobans may burst into song to the accompaniment of
guitar, snapping fingers or sharp handclaps – such are the features of the ol
Jewish quarter, a colourful maze northwest of the cathedral.

Sinagoga ⓥ (AZ) – The Córdoba and Toledo synagogues are the only maje
synagogues which remain in Spain today. Built in the early 14C, this one consist
of a small square room with a balcony on one side for the women. The upper part
of the walls are covered in Mudéjar stucco.

Not far away is the **Museo Municipal Taurino** or Bullfighting Museum (see below) an
the **Zoco** or suk, where craftsmen work around a large *patio* which in summer
the setting for *flamenco* dancing.

ADDITIONAL SIGHTS

Palacio de Viana ⊘ (BY) – Viana Palace, a fine example of 15C Cordoban civil architecture, has 12 *patios* and an attractive garden. The city is famous for the beauty of its *patios* and those in this palace, with their charm and sensitivity are, without doubt, worthy of their renown.

The interior is lent a sense of harmony by its rich furnishings. On the ground floor are precious collections of porcelain, 17C-19C side-arms and tapestries. The staircase to the first floor has a beautiful Mudéjar *artesonado* ceiling made of cedar. Of the many rooms open the most interesting are the gallery of Córdoban leather with magnificent 15C-18C work, the room hung with tapestries made in the royal workshops after cartoons by Goya, the library and the main room adorned with a rich *artesonado* ceiling and tapestries illustrating the Trojan War and various Spanish tales.

The old stables are also open.

Museo Arqueológico Provincial ⊘ (BZ M²) – The archeological museum is in the Palacio de los Páez, a 16C Renaissance palace designed by Hernán Ruiz. Displayed in rooms around the cool *patios* are prehistoric Iberian and particularly Roman collections of low reliefs, capitals, sarcophagi and mosaics, testifying to the importance of Córdoba at the time, as well as remains from the Visigothic period. The first floor galleries house examples of Córdoba's Muslim decorative arts: ceramics, a model of the mosque, capitals and bronze sculptures including the outstanding 10C work from Medina Azahara of a **stag**★ or *cervatillo* decorated with plant motifs. Note also the Abad Samson bell and a large collection of well copings.

Alcázar ⊘ (AZ) – The Alcázar of the Umayyads stood at the centre of magnificent gardens facing the mosque on the site of what is now the Palacio Episcopal (Bishop's Palace). The present edifices were built under Alfonso XI in the early 14C. Of the palace there remain attractively cool Moorish *patios* with ornamental basins and pools, baths, a few rooms with Roman **mosaics**★ and a fine 3C **sarcophagus**★. From the towers there is a **view** of the gardens, the Guadalquivir, the Roman bridge and the Torre de la Calahorra. The **gardens**★, in Arabic style, are terraced and refreshed with pools and fountains, and cypresses.

The Moorish Garden

The Patio de los Naranjos inside the Mezquita is Spain's oldest Moorish garden. Its charm lies in the simplicity of its rows of orange trees, the water supplied to its narrow irrigation ditches and the scent of its fruit.

The importance of the garden in the Islamic world stems from its associations with Koranic paradise. Water, symmetry and the idea of privacy are just a few of its main features. The garden creates a world of subtlety in which the overriding element is the harmony of the setting.

As oases of peace and beauty, Moorish gardens always attempt to heighten the pleasure of the senses through scent and colour. Water is not just a purifying element; it is also a source of pleasure. The gentle murmuring acts as background music, and the water provides welcome cool on a hot summer's day. The idea of privacy, another vital ingredient in an Arab garden, combines with Greco-Roman tradition in the construction of the high walls which offer protection against prying eyes.

Ideas for the development of these gardens were passed on from *mezquitas* and palaces to private dwellings, even resulting in changes to the characteristic features of the typical Andalusian *patio*.

Iglesias Fernandinas – On 29 June 1236, Ferdinand III reconquered Córdoba. The arrival of the Christians had a large impact on the city's architecture with the construction of 14 parish churches under Ferdinand (Fernando). The beauty of these churches can still be seen today, particularly in **Santa Marina de Aguas Santas** (St Marina of the Holy Waters) (BY), **San Miguel** (St Michael) (BY) and **San Lorenzo** (St Lawrence) (BY). These late-13C and early-14C temples of stone, built in primitive Gothic style, are endowed with a sober yet rounded beauty by the purely structural elements. The addition of single trumpet-shaped doorways introduces the only lighter aspect to these edifices.

Torre de La Calahorra ⊘ (BZ) – The Moorish fortress was built in the 14C to defend the Roman bridge. It now houses a museum which, through audio-control techniques, traces the history of the Cordoban Caliphate, a period of great cultural, artistic, philosophic and scientific prosperity. Major trends in 12C

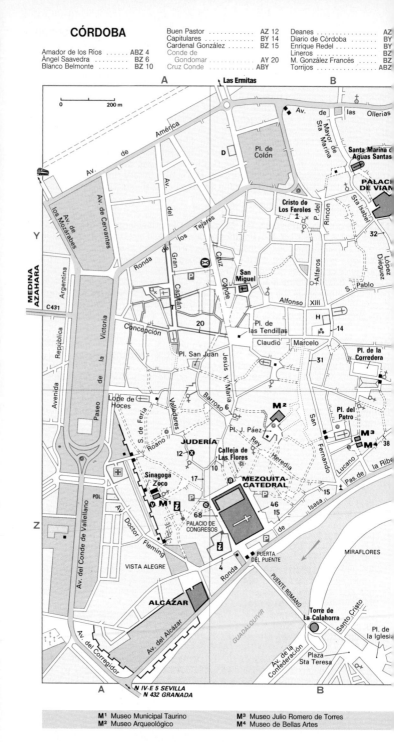

CÓRDOBA

Buen Pastor	AZ 12	Deanes	AZ	
Capitulares	BY 14	Diario de Córdoba	BY	
Cardenal González	BZ 15	Enrique Redel	BY	
Amador de los Ríos	ABZ 4	Conde de		Lineros	BZ	
Ángel Saavedra	BZ 6	Gondomar	AY 20	M. González Francés	BZ	
Blanco Belmonte	BZ 10	Cruz Conde	ABY	Torrijos	ABZ	

M¹ Museo Municipal Taurino
M² Museo Arqueológico
M³ Museo Julio Romero de Torres
M⁴ Museo de Bellas Artes

Christian, Jewish and Muslim thought are illustrated through information
Alfonso X, Maimónides, Averroës and Ibn-Arabi respectively. There is also a f
model★ of the mosque as it was in the 13C.

Museo Municipal Taurino (Municipal Bullfighting Museum) ⊙ **(AZ M¹)** – The museu
housed in a 16C mansion, has collections of items related to tauromachy includi
engravings, posters, bullfighters' costumes and documents on Córdoba's mc
famous matadors: Lagartijo, Guerrita, Manolete and Machaquito.

Plazuela del Potro (Square of the Colt) (BZ) – On this square, named after its fount
statue, stands the charming inn, **Posada del Potro** ⊙, described by Cervantes in D
Quixote. It now houses an interesting exhibition on Córdoban leatherwork.

The Sephardic Jews

No history of Spain is complete without a mention of the Jews whose presence may still be felt in *juderías* (old Jewish quarters) and synagogues. The main Jewish towns in the past were Córdoba, Toledo, Sevilla, Palma de Mallorca and Girona.

The Sephardim or Sephardic Jews (Sefarad is the Hebrew word for Spain) came to the Iberian Peninsula in Antiquity at the same time as the Greeks and Phoenicians. In the 8C during the Arab occupation, they welcomed the Muslims who regarded them as sympathetic allies. The Muslims put them in charge of negotiating with the Christian community. As merchants, bankers, craftsmen, doctors and scholars. Jews played an important economic role and influenced the domains of culture and science. Some became famous, like Maimónides of Córdoba.

The Jews were particularly prosperous under the Caliphate of Córdoba (10C-11C). However, at the end of the 11C, Jews from Andalucía moved to Toledo and Catalunya, especially Girona, as a result of intolerance and persecution under the Almohads. They were often persecuted by Christians during the Reconquest (a royal decree forced them to wear a piece of red or yellow cloth). In the end they were expelled by the Catholic monarchs in 1492. Some chose to convert, others (known as Marranos), in spite of having publicly converted, continued practising their Jewish faith in hiding, while most emigrated to other parts of the Mediterranean, to the Netherlands, to England and America.

Today the Sephardic Jews represent 60% of the Diaspora. Some of them have kept their language, Ladino, which is pure 15C Castilian.

O.Torres/MARCO POLO

On the far side of the square are the **Museo Julio Romero de Torres** ⊘ (**BZ M³**), a museum housing works by the early 20C Córdoban who painted beautiful women, and the **Museo de Bellas Artes** (Fine Arts Museum) ⊘ (**BZ M⁴**) with paintings by Spanish artists.

Cristo de Los Faroles (Christ of the Lanterns) (**BY**) – The Calvary surrounded by wrought-iron lanterns in a silent, austere square, is well known throughout Spain.

Plaza de la Corredera (**BY**) – The square, lined with 17C arcades, was formerly used for bullfighting.

EXCURSIONS

★ **Medina Azahara** ⊘ (**AY**) – *Leave Córdoba on C 431. After 8km/5mi bear right onto a road (3km/2mi) which ends on an esplanade.*
Excavations have revealed the remains of a sumptuous city built by Abd ar-Rahman III. Construction began in 936, however, hardly had the caliphs had time to complete the undertaking when it was sacked in 1013 by the Berbers, grown angry after aiding Al-Mansur's descendants who had not granted them power as expected. The city extended upwards in three tiers – a mosque below, gardens at the centre, and an *alcázar* at the top, of which two wings have been restored. In one of them the Abd ar-Rahman III room has gradually been reconstituted with the incredible floral decorations which once covered the walls, arches and capitals; whereas displayed on the floor are admirably carved stucco and marble pieces.

Las Ermitas (**BY**) – *13km/8mi west of Córdoba on the El Brillante road.*
Hermitages have stood on this site since as far back as the 6C.
There are lovely **views**★ of Córdoba and the Guadalquivir Valley from the lookout.

In Spain, use Michelin map 990 or Michelin regional maps 441-446.
For the Canary Islands, use Michelin detailed maps 220-222.

143

CORIA

Extremadura (Cáceres) – Population 11 260
Michelin map 444 M 10

Coria stands at the centre of a tobacco growing region overlooking the Alagón Valley. The city, once the Roman township of *Caurium*, still contains walls and gateways rebuilt on the ancient foundations in the Middle Ages. Coria has been the seat of bishopric since the Reconquest.

★ **Catedral** ⊙ – The cathedral, a Gothic edifice embellished with elegant Plateresque decoration in the 16C, is crowned with a Baroque tower and has a sculptured frieze on the top of its walls. Inside, the tall, single aisle has vaulting adorned with lierne and tierceron ribs which are typical of the region. Note the 18C altarpiece and, in the *coro*, the wrought-iron grilles and the Gothic choir stalls.

A CORUÑA/La CORUÑA★

Galicia – Population 252 694
Michelin map 441 B 4

The site of this pleasant Galician city is a rocky islet, linked to the mainland by narrow strip of sand. The lighthouse stands to the north, the curved harbour to the south, with the impressive glass tower of the pleasure port, and along the west side of the isthmus, the sandy Riazor and Orzán beaches. Three distinct quarters testify to La Coruña's growth: the **City** (Ciudad), at the northern end of the harbour, charming old quarter with its small peaceful squares and Romanesque churches, the business and commercial centre on the isthmus with wide avenues and shopping streets (**avenida de Los Cantones** (AZ 7 and 8), **calles Real** and **San Andrés**), and the **Ensanche** to the south, built up with warehouses and industrial premises, a reminder that La Coruña is the sixth largest commercial port in Spain as well as an important industrial and fishing centre.

HISTORICAL NOTES

The town was already well developed in Roman times as can be seen from the old lighthouse, the **Torre de Hércules** (BY). The city walls date back to the 13C although they were constantly being rebuilt until, by the 18C, they formed a complete defence system to which was then added a castle, the **Castillo de San Antón** (BZ). General Sir John Moore, born in 1761 in Glasgow and mortally wounded in the Battle of Elviña in 1809, lies buried at the centre of the old city, in the **Jardín de San Carlos** (St Charles Gardens) (BZ).
It was from La Coruña (A Coruña in Galician) that Philip II's **Invincible Armada** set sail in 1588. The fleet of 130 men-of-war, manned by 10 000 sailors and transporting 19 000 soldiers, set out for England ostensibly to punish Elizabeth for the execution of Mary, Queen of Scots. The ill-fated expedition, however, dogged by bad weather and harassed by the smaller, more easily manœuvred English ships, was a failure. 63 ships and more than 15 000 men were lost. The defeat marked the end of Spanish sea power. A year later, in 1589, Elizabeth sent Drake to attack the Iberian coast. The invaders fired La Coruña but the town was saved by **María Pita** who seized the English standard from the beacon where it had been planted and gave the alarm. Over two centuries later, during the Peninsular War, Marshal Soult led Napoleon's forces to a decisive victory over the English in the Battle of Elviña in 1809. Throughout the latter years of the 19C, during the period of frequent liberal uprisings, La Coruña consistently supported the insurgents and in consequence suffered severe reprisals.
The town is proud of being the birthplace of the novelist **Emilia Pardo Bazán** (1852-1921) and to have been a home to the poet **Rosalía de Castro** (1837-85).

SIGHTS

La Ciudad Vieja (The Old City) (BYZ) – La Ciudad Vieja is the original town with narrow cobbled streets and peaceful squares at the northern end of the harbour.

Colegiata de Santa María del Campo ⊙ (BY M¹) – A Romanesque church with three barrel-vaulted naves strengthened by arches with plaster borders. Worthy of note on the exterior are the fine 13C-14C portal, the Gothic rose window and the tower. A **Museum of Sacred Art** (Museo de Arte Sacro) is housed on one side of the church. In the square, between Santa María and a fine Baroque house, stands a 15C calvary.

Plazuela de Santa Bárbara (BY) – This peaceful square, which hosts concerts of chamber music during August (fiestas de María Pita), lies in the protective shadow of Santa Bárbara convent's high, sombre walls. Above the doorway of the convent is a Romanesque lintel depicting the weighing of souls in the presence of Christ.

Iglesia de Santiago (Church of St James) ⊘ **(BZ)** – The church's three apses, which overlook plaza de Azcárraga, and the north door are Romanesque. The west door is Gothic; Santiago *Matamoros* or St James Slayer of the Moors is shown on horseback below the tympanum while the figures of St John and St Mark are carved against the piers. The massive arches supporting the timber roof above the nave are also Gothic. The church contains a beautifully carved stone pulpit.

Castillo de San Antón: Museo Arqueológico e Histórico ⊘ **(BZ)** – This fortress, which dates from the period of Philip II, formed part of La Coruña's system of defence in former times. Its casemates served as a prison for several famous inmates such as Malaspina. It now houses an archeological museum, which includes a room dedicated to prehistoric gold and silverware.

Centro (BAY) – The city's central district acts as a natural extension to the old quarter. Nowadays it is a lively commercial area.

* **Avenida de la Marina (ABY)** – The avenue, facing the harbour, is lined by tall houses with glassed-in balconies typical of La Coruña. Extending it on one side is the paseo de la Dársena and on the other the attractively landscaped **Jardines de Méndez Núñez (AZ)**, gardens with a variety of flowering trees.

M.Raurich/STOCK PHOTOS

Plaza de María Pita (BY 28) – The vast pedestrian square just behind Avenida de la Marina is named after the town's 16C heroine. It has a great many terrace cafés and is lined on three sides by arcades upon which rest houses with glassed-in galleries.

Museo de Bellas Artes ⊘ **(AY M²)** – The main feature of this modern fine arts museum is the light and spacious feel of its exhibition rooms, dedicated to art from the 16C to the 20C. Of particular note are the sketches by Goya.

Domus-Casa del Hombre ⊘ **(AY)** – This unusual **building**★, designed by the Japanese architect **Arata Isozaki**, is located on the Riazor bay, and has become one of the architectural symbols of the city. The façade, facing the bay, is composed of a double curve which adopts the shape of a large sail, and is covered with pieces of slate to give a scaly appearance. The building's other wall has made use of the city's old quarry to create an area of large stone blocks which act as a screen. The museum itself is dedicated to Man, and deals with various aspects of human life such as genetics, reproduction and the senses through texts, photographs, interactive displays, holographs etc.

Torre de Hércules (Hercules Tower or Lighthouse) ⊘ **(BY)** – This was built in the 2C AD and is the oldest lighthouse still functioning. In 1790 when Charles III modified the tower to its present square shape, the original outer ramp was enclosed to form an inner staircase. From the top (104m/341ft), there is a **view** of the town and the coast.

Cantón Grande . . . . AZ 7
Cantón Pequeño . . . . AZ 8
Compostela . . . . AZ 13
Damas . . . . BY 14
Ferrol . . . . AZ 18
Finisterre (Av. de) . . . . . . AZ 19
Gómez Zamalloa . . . . AZ 20
Herrerías . . . . BY 23

Juan Canalejo . . . . AY 24
Juana de Vega (Av.) . . . . . AZ 26
Maestranza . . . . BY 27
María Pita (Pl. de) . . . . . . BY 28
Padre Feijóo . . . . AZ 32
Payo Gómez . . . . AZ 36
Picavia . . . . AZ 37
Pontevedra (Pl. de) . . . . . AZ 40
Real . . . . AY
Riego del Agua . . . . BY 42
Rubine (Av. de) . . . . BY 45
San Agustín . . . . BY 46

San Agustín (Cuesta de) . . BY
San Andrés . . . . AYZ
Sánchez Bregua . . . . AZ
Santa María . . . . BY
Santa Catalina . . . . AZ
Teresa Herrera . . . . AZ

M¹ Colegiata de Santa María del Campo,
Museo de Arte Sacro
M² Museo de Bellas Artes

EXCURSION

Cambre ⊙ - *11km/7mi south.*
The 12C Romanesque **Iglesia de Santa María**★ ⊙ has a lovely façade, divided in
three sections corresponding with the nave and two aisles inside. Multifoil arche
emphasizing the windows on either side, reflect Moorish influence as do t
buttress capitals. The tympanum is carved with the Holy Lamb in a medalli
supported by angels. The interior, with its great purity of style, has a feature oft
found in churches on the Santiago pilgrim route, an apse circled by an ambulato
with five radiating chapels.

COSTA BLANCA★

Comunidad valenciana (Alicante), Murcia
Michelin map 445 P 29-30, Q 29-30

The Costa Blanca or White Coast stretches south from the shores of the Valenci
province of Alicante to those of Murcia. It is mainly flat and sandy with the occasion
area of high land where the *sierras* drop to the sea. The hot climate, low rainf
(350mm/14in a year), dazzling white light after which the coast is named, lo
beaches and turquoise water attract a vast number of Spanish and foreign touris
throughout the year.

FROM DENIA TO GUADALEST *165km/103mi - allow 1 day*

Dènia (Denia) - The former Greek colony was taken over by the Romans w
named it *Dianium*. Dènia today is a commercial port, fishing harbour, industri
centre specialising in the manufacture of toys, and a popular seaside resort. T
fortress overlooking the town houses an archeological museum.
The coast south of Dènia becomes steep and rocky with pine forests.

★ **Cap de Sant Antoni** – From near the lighthouse on this headland, a last foothill of the Sierra del Mongó, there is a good **view**★ towards Xàbia and the Cabo de la Nao headland.

Xàbia (Jàvea) – The old quarter stands on high ground, its houses closely grouped around a fortified 14C Gothic church. The resort's modern quarter has grown up near its harbour, around the sandy beach where there is a parador.

★ **Cabo de la Nao** – The climb affords views over Xàbia at the foot of the Sierra del Mongó, before you enter thick pinewoods relieved only by villas standing in individual clearings. Cabo de la Nao is considered to be the eastern outpost of the Sierras Béticas (Baetic Cordillera) chain although in fact the formation continues under the sea to reappear as the island of Ibiza. There is a beautiful **view**★ south from the point along the indented coastline to the Penyal d'Ifac. Sea caves (approached by boat) and charming creeks such as **La Granadella** (south) and **Cala Blanca** (north) are excellent for underwater swimming.

Calp (Calpe) – The **Penyal d'Ifac**★, an impressive rocky outcrop 332m/1 089ft high, provides Calp with a distinctive setting. A path leads to the top of the Penyal (*about 1hr walk*) from which, as you climb, you will get interesting views along the coast of Calp and its salt pans, of the darkish mountain chains, and northwards of the precipitous coast as far as cabo de la Nao.
The sierra de Bernia road twists and turns before crossing the spectacular barranco de Mascarat (Mascarat Ravine) in the mountain hinterland to cabo de la Nao.

Altea – Altea, white walls, rose coloured roofs and glazed blue tile domes, rises in tiers up a hillside overlooking the sea – a symphony of colour and reflected light below the Sierra de Bernia. A walk through the alleys to the church and then the view from the square over the village and beyond to the Penyal d'Ifac will reveal the attraction of so many painters towards Altea.

Benidorm – The excellent climate and two immense beaches (the Levante and the Poniente), curving away on either side of a small rock promontory, have provided the basic elements for Benidorm's incredible success as a tourist resort. It has grown from a modest fishing village in the 1950s to a kind of Mediterranean Manhattan with modern tower blocks overlooking the sea, all manner of entertainment and a very lively nightlife.
From the lookout on **El Castillo** point, there are **views**★ of the beaches and the Island of Plumbaria. The old quarter stands behind the point, close to the blue domed church.

An excursion inland from Benidorm to Guadalest is a must.

Take the road to Callosa d'En Sarrià and from there head for Alcoi.

On the drive inland, you pass through small valleys cloaked in all sorts of fruit trees, including citrus and medlars. The village of **Polop** stretches up a hillside in a picturesque mountain setting. Beyond, the landscape becomes more arid but the views more extensive, the mountains more magnificent.

★ **Guadalest** – Guadalest stands out from the terraced valleys of olive and almond trees to face the harsh limestone escarpments of the Sierra de Aitana. The **site**★ is impressive with the village, in self-defence, forced halfway up a ridge of rock, a natural stronghold accessible only through an archway cut into the stone. Walk round the **Castillo de San José** (now the site of a cemetery) of which only ruins remain of the castle fortifications wrecked by an earthquake in 1744, to see the view over the green Guadalest reservoir with its reflections of the surrounding mountain crests, the amazing site of the old village, and beyond, the sea.

Michelin on the Net: www.michelin-travel.com

Our route planning service covers all of Europe – twenty-one countries and one million kilometres of highways and byways – enabling you to plot many different itineraries from wherever you are. The itinerary options allow you to choose a preferred route – for example, quickest, shortest, or Michelin recommended.

The network is updated three times weekly, integrating ongoing road works, detours, new motorways, and snowbound mountain passes.

The description of the itinerary includes the distances and travelling times between towns, selected hotels and restaurants.

COSTA BRAVA★★★

Catalunya (Girona)

Michelin map 443 E39, F39, G38-39

The Costa Brava or Wild Coast, comprising the entire coastline of the province
Girona, derives its name from its twisted, rocky shoreline. The Catalan mounta
ranges form a line of cliffs which fall away into the sea. The beautiful inlets alor
the whole of the coast, its clear waters, quiet, picturesque harbours and fishir
villages have earned it an international reputation, attracting a great many forei
tourists in recent years.

★★ THE ALBERES COASTLINE

① From Portbou to Roses

65km/40mi - allow half a day

The last foothills of the Sierra de l'Albera extend right up to the sea and form hug
enclosed bays, like those of Porthou and El Port de la Selva. The route continue
to wind its way upwards along the cliff tops, especially on the **road section**★★ fro
Portbou to Colera, offering fine views of one of the most craggy coastlines
Catalunya.

★ **El Port de Llançà** – A pleasant tourist resort located around a bay facing the se
that shelters it from offshore winds like the *tramontana* as well as sudde
Mediterranean storms. The charming beach and its shallow waters are ideal fo
bathing.

★ **El Port de la Selva** – This tourist locality lies in a natural bay that basks in golde
sunlight at dusk. Besides its traditional white houses, in which the fishermen onc
lived, the village features newly-constructed buildings with many flats and hotel:
Fishing continues to be one of the main activities of the port.

★★ **Monasterio de Sant Pere de Rodes** ⓥ –
7km/4mi from El Port de la Selva. Leave your car in the car park and proceed on foot for 15min.

The ruins of this impo-
sing Benedictine mona-
stery stand on the slo-
pes of the Monte de
Sant Salvador in a beau-
tiful **setting**★★ that dominates the Gulf of
Lion and the Cabo de
Creus peninsula. Its
construction began in
the 10C but it was
subsequently pillaged
and eventually abando-
ned in the 18C. The
church★★, a truly remarkable building showing
pre-Romanesque influ-
ence, is a fine, if some-
what unusual, exam-
ple of architectural
harmony. The three
naves are crowned with
vaulting: the central
nave with barrel vaul-
ting the two lateral
ones with surbased
vaulting. They are sepa-
rated by huge pillars,
reinforced with col-
umns leaning on raised
bases. The splendid
capitals★ are delicately
carved with intricate
tracery and acanthus
leaves, evoking the tra-
dition of Córdoba and

Byzantium. The transept has a central chapel and two radiating chapels with a narrow ambulatory and a crypt. The left arm of the transept leads to an upper ambulatory offering a sweeping view of the central nave.

The coast running between El Port de la Selva and Cadaqués features many small irregular creeks with crystal-clear waters, accessible only by sea. The road continues inland, offering lovely views of the surrounding region.

★ **Cadaqués** – Tucked away behind the very last Pyrenean foothills, Cadaqués lies south of the Cabo de Creus in a delightful **setting**★ enclosed by mountains, with the sea as its only natural outlet. It used to be a humble fishing village until a bunch of contemporary artists (Dalí, Picasso, García Lorca, Buñuel, André Breton, Paul Éluard etc) took to coming here, turning it into a fashionable resort.

Built along steep, narrow streets, the white houses and their picturesque porticoes are clustered around the **Iglesia de Santa María** ⊙, whose sober exterior contrasts sharply with its interior: note the lovely **Baroque altarpiece**★★ carved in gilded wood. The **Museu Perrot-Moore** ⊙ displays an interesting collection of graphic art (15C-20C).

★ **Portlligat** – *(2km/1mi north)*. This small bay is home to the **Casa-Museo Salvador Dalí**★ ⊙, housed in a cluster of fishermen's houses. Dalí's workshop, library, rooms and garden are all open to the public.

★ **Parque Natural Cap de Creus** – *4 km/2.5mi north*. Steep roads and paths wind their way along sheer cliffs and around hidden bays through this attractive park. A spectacular **view**★★★ can be enjoyed from the **lighthouse** perched on the park's highest point.

★ **Roses** – It was here that the sailors of Rhodes founded a colony bearing that name. Located in a splendid natural harbour overlooked by the Golfo de Roses, the town has an important fishing fleet but is also a popular seaside resort. Its 16C Renaissance **citadel**★ was commissioned by Charles V, who feared an invasion of the Turkish army. It was designed after a pentagonal plan and features a great many bastions. Its interior houses the vestiges of a Benedictine monastery destroyed by the French during the War of Independence.

★THE EMPORDÀ PLAIN

② **From Roses to Begur**

75km/46.5mi – allow one day

This stretch of the Costa Brava, at the foot of the cordillera, is taken up by the fertile Empordà plain.

★ **Empuriabrava** – A pleasant luxury marina built on top of an intricate network of canals in 1973, where boats can take people right up to their own door.

★ **Castelló d'Empúries** – The former capital of the country of Empúries (between the 11C and the 14C) proudly stands on a small promontory at a short distance from the coast. The **Iglesia de Santa María**★ ⊙, built in the 14C-15C, is flanked by a typical Catalan belfry. The imposing **portal**★★ is a unique example of Gothic art in Catalunya: the tympanum illustrates the Adoration of the Magi while the Apostles are represented on the jambs. The large central nave, separated from its lateral naves by fine cylindrical pillars, is supported by ribbed vaulting. The alabaster **retable**★ in the high altar (15C), crowned by conical pinnacles, depicts scenes taken from the Passion. The village has kept some of the administrative buildings dating from its golden age: the **Ajuntament** (former Maritime Commodities Exchange), combining Romanesque and Gothic elements, and the **Casa Gran**, of Gothic inspiration.

★ **Empúries** – *See EMPÚRIES.*

★ **L'Escala** – This tourist resort has a long-established fishing tradition and nice sandy beaches. Two inlets protect its harbour. Its speciality is the salting of anchovies.

★ **Torroella del Montgrì** – This village is still arranged in the manner of a Roman encampment, with two main streets joining up on an arcaded square. Despite its Baroque front, the 14C **Iglesia de Sant Genís** is a fine example of Gothic Catalan art. The **castle** which stands on the heights of the Montaña de Montgrí *(1hr on foot along a signposted path among the rocks)* is an extraordinary **belvedere**★★ from which you can admire the sea and the Gavarres mountain range.

★ **Islas Medes** ⊙ – Boat trips around the islands are available, leaving from l'Estartit. This small archipelago, consisting of seven islets and some coral reefs, is the marine extension of the calcareous massif of Montgrí. The site is particularly interesting for ecologists on account of the many different marine species and ecosystems that can be observed. The islets are extremely popular among amateurs of diving and underwater exploration.

★ **Pals** – Dominating the mouth of the Ter river, this village features an attractive old quarter, **El Pedró**, where the vestiges of fortified ramparts enclose ancient houses and winding alleyways, some of which have covered flights of steps.

★★THE COAST ROAD

▣ From Begur to Blanes

98km/61mi – allow one day

The coastline along this part of the Costa Brava features alternately plains an
mountains that extend down to the sea, giving way to a series of long beaches an
coves of astounding beauty: **Aigiiafreda, Aigiiablava, Tamariu**, forming a haven of pea
sheltered by pine trees and dotted with luxury villas and exclusive hotels.

Aigiiablava

★ **Begur** – The town overlooks a pretty series of creeks from an altitude
200m/656ft above the sea. The castle ruins (16C-17C), the highest point of th
locality, offer a nice view of Begur and its haphazard network of streets.

★ **Far de Sant Sebastià** – *2km/1mi from Llafranc.* Built in 1857, the lighthous
stands on a tiny isthumus surrounded by steep cliffs. The nearby hermitac
commands a lovely **view**★ of the sea.

★ **Calella de Palafrugell** – This attractive fishing port is also a popular summe
resort known for its **Festival de Habaneras**, which takes places on the popular Carr
dels Voltes, facing the sea front, on the first Saturday in July. The public can enjc
Afro-Cuban songs and dances while sipping the local *cremat*, coffee laced wit
flambé rum.
A road leaving Calella by the south leads to a pretty farm which houses the Jard
Botánic del Cap Roig★ ⊙. An attractively-terraced park carved out of the roc
overlooking the Mediterranean Sea, presents more than 1 200 plant species la
out along shaded avenues. These gardens offer some wonderful **views**★★ of th
coast.
After Palamòs the road follows the coastline, consisting alternately of rocky inle
and beaches.

★ **S'Agaró** – An elegant resort with chalets and luxury villas surrounded by tic
gardens and pine forests. The camino de Ronda offers pretty **views**★ of the she
cliffs.

★ **Sant Feliu de Guíxols** – Nestling in the curve of a bay, sheltered from the la
spurs of the Sierra de les Gavarres, this is one of the most popular locations
the Costa Brava. Its famous seaside boulevard Passeig de la Mar is lined wit
pavement cafés and their bustling terraces. The **Iglesia-Monasterio de Sant Feliu**★ ⊙
is part of a former Benedictine monastery whose vestiges tower over the sm;
municipality. It has retained its Romanesque façade, known as the **Porta Ferrada**★
with horseshoe arches dating back to pre-Romanesque times. The interior (14(
is Gothic in style.
The lookout point by the chapel of Sant Elm commands beautiful **views**★★ of th
coastal road.

* **Tossa de Mar** – Situated in a splendid natural setting, this sandy beach curves around to Punta del Faro, the promontory on which stand the lighthouse and the 13C walls of the **Vila Vella**★, the old town and its cobbled streets. The **Museu Municipal**★ ⊘ contains archaeological artefacts unearthed in an ancient Roman villa nearby and an **exhibition of contemporary art** displaying the work of artists who visited the town in the 1930s (Chagall, Masson, Benet etc).

  Between Tossa and **Lloret de Mar** (the most important and popular tourist resort of the Costa Brava), the road follows a spectacular **clifftop route**★★ overlooking wide sandy beaches.

* **Blanes** – The magnificent **Passeig Marítim**★ offers a lovely panorama of Blanes and its sun-drenched beach. On a hill to the east stand the remains of the Castillo de Sant Joan: at its foot lies the 14C Gothic Iglesia de Santa Maria. To the southeast is located the **Jardín Botánic de Marimurtra**★ ⊘. This botanical park presents around 5 000 plant species from countries all over the world, including many rare exotic varieties. At each new bend the twisting paths reveal wonderful **views**★ of Cala Forcadera and the coast.

COSTA DE CANTABRIA★

CANTABRIAN COAST – Cantabria

Michelin map 442 B 16-20

The Cantabrian coast stretches in a succession of gulfs, capes, peninsulas, splendid bays like those of Santander and Santoña, *rías* and long sandy beaches from Castro Urdiales to San Vicente de la Barquera. The resorts of Santander and Comillas are special favourites with Spanish holidaymakers while Laredo, San Vicente de la Barquera and Noja tend to attract foreigners. The hinterland, a very green wooded area, is given over to stock raising. In some places in the province summer haymaking is carried out according to age-old methods. Village houses often bear coats of arms, of which the finest examples are in Santillana del Mar.

Cantabria is rich in prehistoric caves with more than 20 bearing traces of human habitation in the Paleolithic Age.

SIGHTS

Castro Urdiales – The village, clustered round a Gothic church, a ruined castle and a lighthouse, stands on a promontory overlooking a vast bay. The annual Coso Blanco festival is held on the first Friday in July.

Laredo – The **old town** huddled around its church adjoins a long beach lined by modern buildings. It is a maze of narrow alleyways climbing up a hillside which shelters the fishing boat harbour below.

Fishermen in Santoña

Limpias – The small fishing village on the banks of the ría Asón is known for miracle which occurred here in 1919. The local church contains the deep venerated Crucifix said to have shed tears of blood, a wonderfully carved Baroqu figure attributed to Juan de Mena.

La Bien Aparecida – A winding uphill road leads to the Baroque shrine of Nuestr Señora de la Bien Aparecida. Veneration for the patron of Cantabria provinc dates back to 1605. Splendid **panorama**★ of the Asón Valley.

Santoña – The fishing port facing Laredo was selected as a military headquarter by the French in the Peninsular War. The **Iglesia de Nuestra Señora del Puerto** ⊘, whic was remodelled in the 18C, has, in addition to Gothic aisles, Romanesque feature including carved capitals and an old font.

Bareyo – The small **Iglesia de Santa María** ⊘ stands on a slope overlooking the r de Ajo. It retains interesting features from its original Romanesque desig including slender, moulded arches and historiated capitals in the apse. The **font** probably Visigothic.

★★ **Peña Cabarga** – A road with a 16% gradient (1 in 6) leads to the summ (568m/1 863ft) on which stands a monument to the Conquistadores and th Seamen Adventurers of Castilla. From the top there is a splendid **panorama**★★ c Santander bay and town.

★ **Santander** – *See SANTANDER.*

★★ **Santillana del Mar and Cuevas de Altamira**★★ **(Caves)** – *See SANTILLANA DE MAR and ALTAMIRA.*

★ **Comillas** – Comillas is a pleasant seaside resort with a delightful Plaza Mayor, local beach and easy access to the extensive sands at Oyambre – 5km/3mi west The town was a royal residence at the time of Alfonso XII. Buildings which catc the eye include, in the vast park surrounding the neo-Gothic **Palacio de los Marquese de Comillas**, a freakish pavilion by Gaudí, **El Capricho** (now a restaurant) and overlooking the sea from the crown of the hill, the Universidad Pontíficia (Papa University).

★ **San Vicente de la Barquera** – This resort has an unusual **site**★, a vast beach or the other side of the *ría* and interesting old houses. The **Iglesia de Nuestra Señora d los Ángeles** (Our Lady of the Angels) at the top of the partially fortified hill, has tw Romanesque portals, Gothic aisles and several tombs dating from the 15C an 16C.
If you are continuing to Unquera, look back after a few minutes for a pleasin **view**★ of San Vicente.

COSTA DE LA LUZ

Andalucía (Huelva, Cádiz)

Michelin map 446 U7-X13

The Spanish coast from the Portuguese frontier to Tarifa on the Straits of Gibralta is edged with beaches of fine sand interrupted by the Guadiana, Tinto, Guadalquivi and other river mouths. Although this Atlantic coast has attracted less tourism in th past than the Mediterranean coast of southern Spain, several resorts are bein developed. Because of its dazzling white sand and translucent skies it is known as the Coast of Light.

THE HUELVA COAST

From Ayamonte to the Parque Nacional de Doñana

135km/84mi – about half a day

Ayamonte – Ayamonte, bustling with cars crossing into Portugal, stands at the mouth of the Guadiana river which forms the Portuguese-Spanish border. It is a fishing port with picturesque alleyways.
The parador on the hill commands a beautiful **view**★ of the village, the Guadiana estuary and Portugal beyond.
Sand dunes, anchored by pines and eucalyptus trees, fringe the coast between Ayamonte and Huelva.
Secondary roads perpendicular to the coast lead to the resorts of **Isla Canela**, **Isla Cristina**, **La Antilla** and **Punta Umbría**.
Take N 431 and H 414 (right) to Huelva.

Huelva – Huelva, a large port and capital of its province, has developed through the export of copper mined in the hinterland, oil refineries, canneries and chemical industry.

In the 16C, the Tinto estuary was one of the principal anchorages of the Conquistadores, and in particular of Christopher Columbus. A large **monument** to the navigator straddles the Tinto river, near the harbour at Punta del Sebo.

Leave Huelva south on N 442; after crossing the Tinto river, turn left onto H 624.

La Rábida – In 1484, the Prior of the Convento de la Rábida, Juan Pérez, believed the theory put to him by Christopher Columbus, that the world was round and that it was therefore possible to sail to the Indies by a westerly route. The prior's support finally won Columbus the necessary commission from the Catholic monarchs to set up his expedition.

Among the present buildings of the **Monasterio de la Rábida** ⊘ are vestiges of a 15C church and its frescoes. A small, interesting museum contains models of the three ships used in the first voyage Columbus made, as well as navigation charts and old books.

Head north on H 624.

Palos de la Frontera – It was from this port, now silted up, that Christopher Columbus sailed on 3 August 1492 and to which he returned on 15 March 1493 after having discovered the island of San Salvador (Bahamas) on 12 October, a day still celebrated annually throughout Spain as the Day of the Hispanidad.

It was also at this port that Hernán Cortés, conqueror of Mexico, disembarked in 1528. The 14C **Iglesia de San Jorge** (Church of St George) has a Mudéjar portal.

Moguer – Moguer was another port from which expeditions ventured to the unknown. Alabaster **tombs★** of the navigators who founded the **Convento de Santa Clara** ⊘ can be seen before the altar and underneath the Isabelline and Renaissance style niches in the church.

In the main street, now named after him, a plaque marks the birthplace of the poet and 1956 Nobel prizewinner, Juan Ramón Jiménez (1881-1958).

Turn back to N 442 which continues southeast along the coast.

Pine-covered sand dunes give way to endless beaches of fine sand dominated occasionally by cliffs as at **Mazagón** where there is a parador. Matalascañas is the main resort on this stretch of the coast.

★ **Parque Nacional de Doñana** – *See Parque Nacional de DOÑANA.*

THE CÁDIZ COAST

From Sanlúcar de Barrameda to Tarifa

168km/104mi – allow 1 day

The landscape is hillier south of the Guadalquivir and there are vineyards north of Cádiz.

Sanlúcar de Barrameda – The fishing port of Sanlúcar, at the mouth of the Guadalquivir, is the home town of Manzanilla, a sherry matured like Jerez Fino but which has a special flavour thanks to the sea air. The *bodegas* (cellars) are in the old quarter on the hill around the massive castle. The **Iglesia de Nuestra Señora de la O** close by has a fine Mudéjar **doorway★**.

The **Iglesia de Santo Domingo★** ⊘, a church in the lower *barrio*, has the noble propor-tions of a Renaissance building and inside, beautiful coffered **vaulting★** and cupolas.

Take C 441 to Chipione and then CA 604.

Rota – The old town inside its ramparts has an almost medieval atmosphere, particularly in the streets leading to the castle and the church. Rota is an important American naval base.

Take CA 603 east.

El Puerto de Santa María – The harbour, in the bahía de Cádiz, played an active role in trade with the New World. Today, fishing, the export of sherry (there are Terry *bodegas* in the town) and tourism (beaches and golf courses) make up the town's principal activities.

A palm-shaded promenade overlooking the quays along the north bank leads to the 12C **Castillo de San Marcos**, a castle which was once the seat of the dukes of Medinaceli.

★ **Cádiz** – *See CÁDIZ.*

Take NIV and N 340.

South of Cádiz, past San Fernando salt pans, there are good beaches at La Barrosa and Conil de la Frontera.

Vejer de la Frontera – Vejer, perched on a rocky crag, is one of the prettiest white villages of Andalucía. The best way to approach is along the road cut into the hillside from the south. There is a **view★** from the car park at the north end of the town, down into the winding Barbate Valley.

The road runs through the foothills of the Baetic ranges between Vejer and Tarifa.

Tarifa – *See Straits of GIBRALTAR.*

COSTA DEL SOL★

Andalucía (Málaga, Granada, Almería)

Michelin map 446 W14-V22

The Sunshine Coast stretches along Andalucía's Mediterranean shore from Tarifa the Straits of Gibraltar to the Cabo de Gata, a headland east of Almería. Protecte from the extremes of the inland climate by the Serranía de Ronda and the Sier Nevada, it enjoys mild winters (12°C/54°F), hot summers (26°C/79°F) and sufficie rain in winter and spring to allow subtropical crops to grow in the small alluvial plain

★THE WESTERN COASTLINE

From Estepona to Málaga 139km/86mi – allow half a day

This highly developed strip of land between the mountains and the sea is a succes sion of beach resorts, hotels and large blocks of flats with all manner of touris amenities including pleasure boat harbours, golf courses and tennis courts.

Estepona – Fishing port and pleasure boat harbour.

Casares, 24km/15mi inland to the west on MA 539, is a remarkable white-walle village clinging to its hilltop **site**★.

Casares

San Pedro de Alcántara – Fine beach.

★ **Marbella** – See MARBELLA.

Fuengirola – A large resort bristling with modern tower blocks.

Take the road left out of Fuengirola for Mijas.

★ **Mijas** – This village of appealing white houses decorated with iron grilles, which often turn out to be restaurants or cafés, is a market centre for Andalusian crafts (pottery, basketwork, woven goods). There are lovely **views** of the coast from the upper terraces.

Torremolinos – This has grown from a quiet fishing village in the 1950s into an enormous tourist complex where high rise blocks have run wild. It is famous for its shopping arcades and entertainment facilities. There's a good sandy beach.

★ **Málaga** – See MÁLAGA.

★THE EASTERN COASTLINE

From Málaga to Almería 209km/130 mi – allow half a day

This, at times, beautiful coast is punctuated along its entire length by the ruins of Moorish towers – defences built after the Reconquest by local inhabitants against attacks by Barbary pirates.
Market gardening, largely in greenhouses around Almería, sugar refining and the export of iron ore are the area's main economic activities.

Nerja – Its palm shaded terrace-promenade, washed on either side by small sea inlets has rather curiously become known as the *balcón de Europa*.

Cueva de Nerja

★★ Cueva de Nerja ⓥ – *4.5km/3mi east along the Motril road.* This natural cave is remarkable for its size and the numerous concretions which skilful illumination highlights to full advantage. Traces of paintings, the discovery of weapons and tools, jewels and bones, indicate that the cave was inhabited in the Paleolithic era. An annual festival of music and dance is held in the Sala de la Cascada (Cascade Chamber).

★ Road from Nerja to La Herradura – The road follows a russet and purple coloured mountainside while the old scenic route commands delightful **views★★** of the coastline.

Almuñécar – The amenities of this cosmopolitan resort include a palm-shaded promenade which skirts its pebble beach. Bananas, medlars, pomegranates and mangoes are grown on the small alluvial plain *(hoya)* behind the town.

Motril – This is a large market centre for sugar cane. Motril port is kept busy handling products from the local sugar refineries and produce from the Genil Valley.

★ Road from Calahonda to Castell de Ferro – The road hugs the rocky coastline, offering views of the mountain and the sea.
After Balanegra the N 340 leaves the coast and turns inland through an immense sweep of greenhouses, a veritable sea of plastic around El Ejido, where flowers, vegetables and tropical fruit are grown.

Road from Aguadulce to Almería – Aguadulce was the pioneer beach for Almería's tourist industry. The sweeping view from the coast road takes in the town of Almería, with its bay, sheltered harbour and fortress.

Almería – *See ALMERÍA.*

COSTA VASCA★★

BASQUE COAST – País Vasco (Guipúzcoa, Vizcaya)
Michelin map 442 B21-C24

The Basque Coast (Costa Vasca) stretches from the golfo de Vizcaya (Bay of Biscay) to the pointed headland of the cabo de Machichaco. The steep shoreline, lined by cliffs and indented by estuaries, is an almost uninterrupted line of small fishing villages nestling in inlets below green hills.

FROM SAN SEBASTIÁN TO BILBAO

184km/114mi – allow 1 day – see local map

★★ San Sebastián – *See DONOSTIA.*
7km/4mi south of San Sebastián bear right into the Bilbao road (N 634).

Zarautz – The resort has been fashionable since Queen Isabel II made it her summer residence in the 19C. The town is pleasantly situated in the centre of an amphitheatre of hills around a vast beach. Two **palaces** stand in the old quarter: the

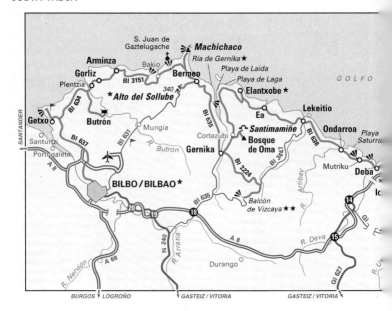

16C property of the Marqués de Narros from which corner watchtowers look ou
over the beach, and the Luzea tower, on Plaza Mayor, with its mullioned window
and a machicolated corner balcony. The tower of the church of Santa María ca
be seen to one side.

Beyond Zarautz, the road rises to a picturesque **corniche section**★★ overlooking th
sea as far as Zumula. Getaria rock (monte de San Antón), also known as *el rató.
(the mouse), soon comes into sight.

Getaria – Getaria is a small fishing village known locally for its *chipirones* or squi
and its rock – *el ratón*, or San Antón Island – to which it is linked by an ancient
narrow road *(at present closed to traffic)*. From the rock you can see the harbour
the beach and Zarautz. Long ago fishermen sailed from Getaria harbour to hun
whales, and navigators like **Juan Sebastián Elcano** set out for the Indies. A native o
Getaria, Elcano sailed with Magellan and after the navigator died in th
Philippines, brought his only surviving ship home, the first sailor to actuall
circumnavigate the world (1522). A narrow street, lined with picturesque houses
leads to the 13C-15C **Iglesia de San Salvador** (Church of our Saviour). The chance
rests on an arch beneath which an underground alley passes, from which one car
see into the crypt. Inside is a Flamboyant Gothic gallery.

Zumaia – Zumaia is a large seaside resort situated at the mouth of the Urola wit
two fine beaches: Itzurun, a delightful beach nestled between cliffs, and Santiago
at the entrance to the town. Close to the latter is the house of the painter **Ignacio
Zuloaga** (1870-1945), which has been converted into a **casa-museo** ⊘ showing his own
works – realistic and popular themes illustrated by brilliant colours and strong lines
– and his personal collection of paintings by El Greco, Goya, Zurbarán and Morales.
The 15C **Iglesia de San Pedro** (Church of San Peter) contains a 16C altarpiece by Juan
de Anchieto.

The journey by road to Deba is one of the most beautiful in the Basque country.

Icíar – The fortress-like church contains a Plateresque altarpiece in dark wood with
at the centre, a smiling 12C Romanesque Virgin, attired in a sumptuous mantle.

Deba – Deba is a small fishing port at the mouth of the Deba. The **Iglesia de Santa
María la Real** conceals beneath the porch in its fortified front, a superb Gothic porta
decorated with extremely lifelike statues. The cloister galleries with their intricate
tracery are particularly worthy of note.

From Deba, take GI 638.

There is a splendid **view**★ of the coast from the **cliff road**★ as it circles the
promontory enclosing the Deva estuary.

The road then passes through **Mutriku**, which has one of the region's most
delightful beaches, the **playa de Saturraran**.

Ondarroa – Ondarroa spreads over a spit of land between a hillside and a loop of
the río Artibay.

The church, upstanding like a ship's prow at one end, the tall Basque houses with
washing at the windows and the encircling river, make an attractive **picture**★.
Canning and fish salting are the two main local livelihoods.

The road between Ondarroa and Lekeitio is pleasant; on rounding a point you have a good view★ of Lekeitio, its beach and the island of San Nicolás, joined to the mainland at low tide.

Lekeitio – A deeply indented bay at the foot of monte Calvario, divided by the island of San Nicolás, serves as the harbour for Lekeitio's long-standing fishing industry. The town is a resort with good sand beaches. The 15C **iglesia** guarding the harbour has three tiers of flying buttresses and a tall Baroque belfry.

3km/1.5mi after Lekeitio, turn right.

Ea – Miniature harbour between two hills at the end of a quiet creek.

★**Elantxobe** – An attractive, peaceful village off the main road. Fishermen have long used the bay as a natural harbour and built their houses overlooking the water, against the steep side of cabo Ogoño (300m/1 000ft).

Once beyond **Playa de Laga**, a vast expanse of rose-coloured sand circling the foot of cabo Ogoño, you can see along the coastline, the peaceful waters of the **Gernika ría**★ (Estuary), the island of Izaro, the white outline of the town of Sukarrieta on the far bank and the island of Chacharramendi.

The resort of Playa de Laida, on the *ría*, is popular with Gernika residents.

Bear left at Cortézubi for the Cuevas de Santimamiñe.

Cuevas de Santimamiñe Ⓥ – Wall paintings and engravings from the Magdalenian Period and interesting archeological deposits were discovered in these **caves** in 1917. For conservation reasons, the caves containing the paintings are currently closed to visitors.

Nearby, a small road leads to the Bosque de Oma (3km/2mi).

Bosque de Oma – Fanciful geometric shapes, human silhouettes hiding behind tree trunks, and huge colourful canvases demonstrate the union between art and nature that Agustín Ibarrola wanted to create in this wood.

Return to the Gernika road.

Gernika – Picasso's famous painting, *Guernica (see MADRID p 248 and Introduction p 38)*, has immortalised the tragic event that took place in this little town during the Civil War: on 26 April 1937, on Franco's orders, a Nazi German air squadron bombed the town and local inhabitants who had come to the market, killing more than 2 000.

In the Middle Ages, the Gernika oak was one of the four places where newly created Lords of Biscay came to swear that they would respect the local *fueros* or privileges. Gernika was, on this account, visited by Queen Isabel in 1483. Today, the remains of the 1 000-year-old tree are in the small temple behind the **Casa de Juntas** where representatives of the Biscay Provincial General Assembly meet.

Return to Gernika and take the Bermeo road north (BI 635).

Some 18km/11mi south on BI 2224 and 3231, is the **Balcón de Vizcaya**★★ (Balcony of Biscay), a remarkable viewpoint overlooking the mountainous Biscay landscape, a chequerboard of meadows and forests.

Two viewpoints built beside the road at the mouth of the inlet before you reach Mundaka, enable you to take a last look back along its still waters. As the road drops downhill, you get a magnificent **view**★ of Bermeo.

Bermeo – Bermeo is an important inshore fishing port. The fishermen's quarter, still crowded onto the Atalaya promontory overlooking the old harbour, the Puerto Menor, was protected by the ramparts (traces remain), and the grim granite Torre de los Ercilla (now the Museo del Pescador, a fishermen's museum). In the Iglesia de Santa Eufemia, kings and overlords used to swear to uphold Biscay privileges.

Take BI 631 southwest towards Mungia.

★ **Alto del Sollube (Sollube Pass)** – From the road up to the low pass (340m/1 115ft) there is a good view of Bermeo's semicircular site.

Return to Bermeo, follow the coast road left for 3km/1.8mi then turn right.

Euskadi

Euskadi, or Euskal Herria, land of the Basques, corresponds more or less to the 11C Kingdom of Navarre. Historically, it consists of seven provinces, three of which make up the autonomous Spanish region of the Basque Country (Álava, Guipúzcoa and Vizcaya/Bizkaia), one of which has its own autonomous government (Navarra) and the three most northerly of which (Labourd, Basse-Navarre and Soule) form part of the French Pyrénées-Atlantiques *département*. These separate states nonetheless share a common race and language on both sides of the Pyrenees; their motto in Basque is *Zaspiak-bat* (the seven that make one).

The origins of the Basque people and their tongue, which bears some resemblance to Finnish, remain something of a mystery. They are known to have been driven out of the Ebro Valley in Spain by the Visigoths and subsequently to have founded their own kingdom of Vasconia in the western Pyrenees. Those who settled in the plain intermarried with the people of Aquitaine and became known as the Gascons. But those who settled in the mountains fiercely defended their traditions and in particular their language from outside influences. It is above all the common language, **Euskara**, which binds the Basques together, although fewer than 20% of Spanish Basques – and fewer still of French – actually now speak it. Their distinctive culture sets them apart from the other peoples of Europe and nationalist feeling runs strong.

The Spanish Basque provinces traditionally enjoyed a large degree of autonomy, with their own Parliaments and special tax status. For centuries Spanish kings swore to respect the rights of Vizcaya beneath an ancient oak tree in Gernika (Guernica), the symbolic heart of the Basque country, which was decimated on Franco's orders in 1937, crushing the fledgling Basque Republic declared in 1936 and bringing the Basque cause to worldwide attention. Basque nationalism in its modern form dates back to the founding of the now moderate Basque Nationalist Party by Sabino Arana in 1895, when Spanish unification threatened to undermine Basque autonomy. After Franco's victory, the Basque country was absorbed into Spain and efforts were made by the Spanish government to suppress Basque cultural identity. The separatist movement has been growing in strength since the 1960s, which is when the militant ETA (Euzkadi Ta Askatasuna) began its terrorist activities. Since the death of Franco, some of the separatists' demands, such as a degree of regional autonomy, a Basque-language television station and language teaching in schools, have been granted, but full independence remains the aspiration of a solid core, with some 13% of the Basque population voting for Herri Batasuna, the Basque equivalent of Sinn Fein in Northern Ireland. The split between moderates and extremists was widened by the increased violence surrounding the issue of a Basque nation during the 1980s. The song *Gernikako Arbola* (The Tree of Guernica), in which the tree symbolizes local freedom, has been adopted as the national anthem of the Spanish Basques.

Faro de Machichaco – From slightly left of this lighthouse there is a good view west along the indented coastline.

The road rises in a corniche to a **viewpoint**★ overlooking the **San Juan de Gaztelugache** headland on which stands a hermitage *(pathway)*, the goal of a local *romería* (pilgrimage) each Midsummer's Day. Below, waves have eroded the rocks into flying buttresses.

After Bakio, take BI 3151 on the right.

There are extensive views from the **corniche road**★ between Bakio and Arminza. A belvedere commands an interesting **view**★ of the coast, Bakio, the valley farmlands and wooded hinterland.

Arminza – The only harbour along a wild section of high, inhospitable coast.

Gorliz – Attractive beach resort at the mouth of the río Butrón. **Plentzia** nearby *(2km/1mi)*, once a fishing harbour and commercial port, is now an oyster farming centre and a resort.

Castillo de Butrón ⊘ – This fantasy 19C castle is a good example of eclectic, picturesque architecture from the last century. It has been built on the remains of a 14C-15C construction, and provides visitors with an insight into life inside a medieval castle.

Getxo – A **Paseo marítimo** or sea promenade overlooks the coast. From the road up to Getxo's well-known golf course there is an interesting view of the Bilbao inlet and on the far bank, Santurtzi and Portugalete.

★ **Bilbao** – See BILBO/BILBAO.

COSTA VERDE★★★

Asturias

Michelin map 441 B 8-15

he Green Coast of Asturias, one of Spain's most beautiful, is so called on account
f the colour of the sea, the pine and eucalyptus trees along the shoreline and the
ooded pastures inland. On a clear day the Picos de Europa mountains, not far from
e coast itself, lend a backdrop to the scene.
he coast from Unquera to Ribadeo is very rocky but follows an almost straight line
ue west except for where the cabo de Peñas headland, west of Gijón, juts out to sea.
he shore is lined by low cliffs interrupted by frequent sandy inlets; the estuaries are
arrow and deep and although they are known locally as *rías*, they bear little
esemblance to those in nearby Galicia.
hree ports in this area handle Asturian coal and ore: San Esteban de Pravia, Gijón
nd Avilés. Other local ports are mostly small and go in for catching and canning fish.
plateau, never more than 20km/12mi wide, follows the line of the shore, its far
de bordered by high mountain ranges.
he coast from Cudillero westwards is steeper and more jagged; the coastal plain
nds in a sheer line of cliffs overlooking small beaches tucked away in river mouths.
here are fishing villages in the creeks.

EAST TO WEST ALONG THE COAST

Llanes – A small peaceful fishing port (crayfish) and holiday resort. The clifftop
promenade, paseo de San Pedro, affords a good view of the old, once fortified
town, the rampart ruins and castle and the squat Iglesia de Santa María. If you
can, be there for the St Roch festival in August to see the dances (the *Pericote* and
in particular the children's *Prima* dance) in brilliant local costume.
The shoreline between Llanes and Ribadesella is a succession of sandy beaches
sheltered by rock promontories: **Celorio, Barro** and **Cuevas del Mar**.

Llanes beach

Ribadesella – The town and port of Ribadesella are on the right side of the estuary
while opposite, a holiday resort has grown along the beach.
Crowds of spectators come on the first Saturday in August every year to see the
international kayak races down the río Sella.

★ **Cuevas de Tito Bustillo** ⊙ – These caves are famous for their **wall of paintings★**
decorated by the Paleolithic inhabitants of 20000 BC (between the Solutrean and
the middle of the Magdalenian periods). A few animals – a horse, two stags, a doe,
another stag and a horse – precede the smoothest area of rock, a sort of low
ceiling where, in the hollows of the stone, there are animal shapes 2m/6.5ft long,
painted red or ochre and outlined in black.

La Isla – Squat drying sheds or *hórreos*, typical of Asturias, stand beside the
houses in the small, attractive village built on a rock headland close to the road.
The vast bay is lined with beaches separated by rocks, one of which, lying
offshore, gave the village its name.

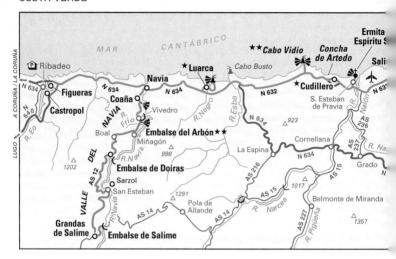

★★ **Mirador del Fito** – *12km/7mi southeast of La Isla on AS 260.* This viewpoir commands a **panorama** of the Picos de Europa and the coast.

Lastres – Lastres is a typical fishing village built against the side of a steep cli between the beach and the harbour. It is known for its clams.

Priesca – The **Iglesia de San Salvador** has been restored. The chancel in this churc contains capitals resembling those at Valdediós *(see below).*

Villaviciosa – It was in Villaviciosa that the future **Emperor Charles V**, aged 17 an accompanied by a full escort of Flemish courtiers, landed in 1517 to take possessic of his newly inherited kingdom. The ships' intended destination was Santander bu by an error of navigation they sailed up the long *ría* to Villaviciosa harbour.
Modern visitors are greeted by a town with narrow streets, emblasoned house and the **Iglesia de Santa María**, its west front decorated with a Gothic rose windov and its Romanesque portal flanked by statue columns.
A short distance inland are Amandi and Valdediós with interesting churches.

Amandi – *3km/2mi south of Villaviciosa.* The bell gable of the **Iglesia de San Juan** ca easily be picked out as it stands perched on high ground at the centre of the village Though remodelled in the 18C the church still has its 13C portal and apse of whic the **decoration**★ shows a high degree of sophistication. Inside the **apse**★, the friez from the façade reappears to form a winding ribbon that follows the curves of th intercolumniation. The capitals have been beautifully and imaginatively carved

★ **Valdediós** – *7km/4mi south of Villaviciosa.* In the same valley are a small Asturia church, full of character and ancient charm, and a monastery.
The **Iglesia de San Salvador** ⊙, which was consecrated in 893 and is known locally a *El conventín* or the little monastery, dates from the end of the Asturian period o architecture (8C-10C). The raised nave is abutted by narrow aisles; the capitals o the triumphal arch are decorated with the Asturian cord motif. The side portico was intended to serve as a covered walk or cloister; the strapwork capitals arcaded windows and artistically sculpted *claustra* all show Mozarabic influence The **monasterio** (monastery) ⊙ consists of a 13C Cistercian church and cloister dating from the 15C, 17C and 18C.

Tazones – *12km/7mi north of Villaviciosa.* This is a delightful little fishing villag hidden away in a cove.

Gijón – Gijón is a lively modern city with a population of over 250 000. It wa originally built on the narrow Santa Catalina headland between two inlets which today serve as harbour (west) and beach, the vast Playa de San Lorenzo (east) **Plaza del Marqués**, near the port, is surrounded by well-proportioned buildings among them the late-17C **Palacio de Revillagigedo**, with an elegant façade. The palace stands on the high Santa Catalina side of the square adjoining the fishermen's quarter known as Cimadevilla.
Gijón was the birthplace of **Gaspar Melchor de Jovellanos** (1744-1811), one of Spain's most eminent 18C men of letters. He was a poet, reformer, liberal economist, author and politician.

Luanco – Luanco harbour lies in a bay sheltered by the Punta de Vaca. It has a smal beach and a sea promenade.

★ **Cabo de Peñas** – The road runs through moorland to this cape, the northernmost point in Asturias. From the cliff and its large rock extension, all dominated by a lighthouse, there are fine **views** of the coast on either side of the cape.

Salinas – This is a rapidly expanding resort bordered to the east by a pine forest. The rock islet of La Peñona (footbridge) affords an overall **view**★ of the beach, one of the longest on the Costa Verde. Waves crash against the jagged rocks below.

Ermita del Espíritu Santo (Hermitage of the Holy Spirit) – As the road climbs there are glimpses through the eucalyptus trees of the Nalón estuary also known as Pravia ría and of waves lapping the immense San Juan de la Arena beach. The hermitage commands an extensive **view**★ west along the coastal cliffs.

★ **Cudillero** – The fishing village surrounded by steep hills makes an attractive **scene**★ from the end of the jetty: tall houses on the hillsides, white cottages with brown tiled roofs leading down to the small harbour nestling between two rock points and a foreground of fishing boats, masts and nets drying in the sun.

Concha de Artedo – Superb beach.

★★ **Cabo Vidio** – From near the lighthouse, the **views**★★ from this headland along the inhospitable coastline extend east to the Cabo de Peñas and west to Cabo Busto.

★ **Luarca** – Luarca has a remarkable **site**★ at the mouth of the winding río Negro. The town, a distinctively attractive centre with its white houses and slate roofs, has seven bridges spanning the river, a sheltered fishing harbour and three beaches. At the end of the estuary, a lighthouse, church and cemetery stand on the headland once occupied by a fort. A narrow street leads to the top. For an interesting **view**★ of Luarca, take the lighthouse road left, then circle the church to the right and return to the harbour. On 15 August, the harbour fills with boats decked with flags.

Navia – See Valle del NAVIA.

Figueras – From the port of Figueras on the ría Ribadeo you have a good view of Castropol, which from across the water, resembles an Austrian village casting its reflection in a lake.

Castropol – Castropol, the most westerly port in Asturias, lies along a promontory at the centre of a ría which marks the boundary with Galicia. The quiet village with an all-white square faces Ribadeo, its Galician counterpart (see RÍAS ALTAS).

COVADONGA

Asturias

Michelin map 441 C 14

Local map see PICOS DE EUROPA

Covadonga, a famous shrine and landmark in Spanish history, is nestled in a magnificent **setting**★★ at the bottom of a narrow valley surrounded by the impressive summits of the Parque Nacional de los Picos de Europa. It was from here that the Christian Reconquest began.

The cradle of the Spanish monarchy – The Muslims followed up the defeat of the Visigoths at the Battle of Guadalete in AD 711 by occupying the entire peninsula. **Pelayo**, a Visigothic nobleman, took refuge in Covadonga with his men to organise a revolt. When in 722, the Emir Alçama sent a military company from Córdoba to wipe

out the rebellious force, Pelayo and his supporters won a resounding victory again[st]
the Muslims at Covadonga. Christians everywhere gained new heart and determin[ed]
to re-establish a national monarchy: the Asturians elected Pelayo who set up his cou[rt]
at Cangas de Onís, thereby making Asturias the cradle of the Spanish monarchy a[nd]
forever after a symbol of resistance.

SIGHTS

La Santa Cueva ⊙ – The cave is dedicated to the Virgin of the Battlefield a[nd]
contains the deeply venerated 18C wooden statue of the Virgin, patron [of]
Asturias. It is known as **La Santina** and is the centrepiece of a major procession [on]
8 September.

Basílica ⊙ – In front of the neo-Romanesque basilica built between 1886 a[nd]
1901 stands a statue of Pelayo beneath the Cruz de la Victoria (Cross of Victor[y])
which Pelayo brandished during the battle (the original is on display in the Cáma[ra]
Santa in Oviedo).

Museo de la Virgen ⊙ – This museum contains the gifts to the Virgin of Covadong[a]
including the magnificent **crown★** with more than 1 000 diamonds.

EXCURSION

★ **Lagos de Enol and Ercina** – See PICOS DE EUROPA ⑤ : the road to Covadong[a]
and the lakes.

Every year,
the Michelin Red Guides
are updated for those who appreciate fine dining, selected restaurants, local wines a[nd]
specialities.
The guide lists a range of establishments from the simplest to the most elegant, tho[se]
with local flavour and the best value for the cost.
Plan better and save money by investing in this year's guide.

COVARRUBIAS★

Castilla y León (Burgos) – Population 629
Michelin map 442 F 19

Covarrubias, on the banks of the Arlanza, is partly surrounded by medieval rampart[s]
guarded by the Doña Urraca tower, strangely shaped like a truncated pyramid. [A]
Renaissance palace straddles the street to the picturesque old quarter wher[e]
half-timbered houses supported by stone columns have been restored.

The town is the burial place of one of Castilla's great historic figures, **Fernán González**
who united several fiefs into a vast County of Castilla to fight relentlessly against th[e]
Moors and sweep them south. This gave the region a leading role in the Reconques[t]
and so ultimately in the unification of Christian Spain.

★ **Colegiata** ⊙ – This collegiate church, with a nave and two aisles and cloisters wit[h]
ornamental vaulting, makes an impressive Gothic unit. It is also a pantheon
worthy of some 20 medieval tombs including those of Fernán González and th[e]
Norwegian Princess Cristina who married the Infante Philip of Castilla in 1258.
There is a very fine church organ.

Museo-Tesoro (Museum and Treasury) ⊙ – A painting by Pedro Berruguete an[d]
another by Van Eyck stand out from the collection of Primitives; note especiall[y]
the 15C Flemish **triptych★** in which the central high relief of the Adoration of th[e]
Magi has been attributed to Gil de Siloé. There is also a splendid processional cross
made by the goldsmiths of Calahorra in the 16C.

EXCURSIONS

Quintanilla de las Viñas – 24km/15mi northeast. Take C 110 and N 234 toward[s]
Burgos, then a small signposted road right.
The road follows the Arlanza Valley out of Covarrubias into pleasant wooded
gorges. You will see, below and to the right, the ruins of the **Monasterio de San Pedro**
de Arlanza with beautiful Romanesque apses.

★ **Iglesia de Quintanilla de las Viñas** ⊙ – The church's great age – it is generally reputed
to be 7C Visigothic – makes it of great archeological interest. All that remains are
the apse and transept, built of skilfully bonded blocks of stone. The outside walls
are decorated with a frieze of bunches of grapes, leaves and birds as well as
medallions and highly stylised motifs. The same foliated scrollwork is repeated
inside on the keystones of the triumphal arch of which the imposts, on either side,
are adorned with symbolic figures of the sun and moon.

Iglesia de Quintanilla de Las Viñas – detail of frieze

Lerma – *23km/14mi west on C 110.*

Lerma owes its splendour to the **Duke of Lerma**, Philip III's ambitious favourite who ruled the country from 1598 until he was usurped by his son, the Duke of Uceda, in 1618. The period was one of untold extravagance and corruption; the court, dizzied by celebrations and balls, divided its time between Madrid and Valladolid; the duke, once having feathered his own nest, turned his attention to his home town which as a result became one of Spain's rare examples of Classical town planning.

The quarter built by the duke in the 17C, in the upper part of the town, retains its steep narrow cobbled streets and its houses, some of which are very old, with their wood or stone porticoes. The ducal palace, with its austere façade, stands on the spacious **Plaza Mayor**★. The **Colegiata** ⊘ church has a 17C gilded bronze statue by Juan de Arfe of the Duke's nephew, the Archbishop Cristóbal de Rojas, shown at prayer.

CUENCA★★

Castilla-La Mancha – Population 46 047

Michelin map 444 L 23

uenca stands in a spectacular **setting**★★ at the heart of the Serranía de Cuenca in the estern part of the Montes Universales range. Here, on the eastern edge of the panish Meseta, the limestone massif has been eroded into a rugged terrain dotted ith fantastic rock formations.

oly Week processions are considerably enhanced by the site; at dawn on Good ⁻iday the slow ascent to Calvary is enacted along the steep alleys to the accompa- ment of drums. A festival of sacred music is also held throughout Holy Week.

★ CIUDAD ANTIGUA **(OLD TOWN)** *2hr 30min*

The old town clings to a rock platform high above the precipices of the Júcar and Huécar ravines. The winding streets are narrow and the houses tall for lack of ground space.

Go through the 18C Arco del Ayuntamiento (Town Hall Arch) and park in the Plaza Mayor de Pío XII.

Catedral ⊘ – The cathedral façade, rebuilt at the beginning of the century, fronts a 13C Gothic edifice, French and Norman in architectural style and Renaissance in decoration. Among the building's most outstanding features are the wrought-iron chapel **grilles**, a twin ambulatory, a triforium and an elegant Plateresque **door**★ into the chapter-house with carved walnut panels by Alonso Berruguete.

Walk along the cathedral south wall.

★ **Museo Diocesano** (Diocesan Museum) ⊘ (**M¹**) – The museum is housed in the Palacio Episcopal or Bishops' Palace. Among its key pieces are eight panels of an altarpiece by Juan de Borgoña (c 1510), two El Greco paintings, a Calvary by Gérard David and an exceptional collection of gold and silver plate. One of the most outstanding works is a 13C **Byzantine diptych**★ painted in a monastery on Mount Athos and covered in silver, pearls and precious stones. There is also the gilded bronze **Báculo de San Julián** (Crozier of St Julian) from Limoges (c 1200) decorated with enamel. Tapestries and carpets are displayed on the first floor.

The Casas Colgadas (Hanging Houses) of Cuenca

★ **Casas Colgadas (Hanging Houses)** – These famous 14C houses, now thorough restored, are home to a museum of abstract art and a restaurant. Go through arched passageway beside the *mesón* to the Puente de San Pablo. From this brid there is a **view**★ of the most spectacular houses hanging over the Huécar ravin an enchanting sight when the scene is illuminated in the evening.
On the far side of the bridge is the **Monasterio de los Paúles**. Part of this form monastery now houses a parador.

★★ **Museo de Arte Abstracto Español** (Museum of Spanish Abstract Art) ⊘ – The museu was inaugurated in 1966. Its setting and the views it commands are such th some of the windows are veritable works of art in themselves. The collection, p together by Fernando Zóbel and enriched since its foundation, is a fine selecti of Spanish abstract art including works by Chillida, Tàpies, Saura, Zóbel, Cuixa Sempere, Rivera and Millares.

★ **Museo de Cuenca** ⊘ (**M²**) – The first floor of this museum displays prehisto objects. The second floor has the most interesting exhibits: sculpture, numisma items and ceramics found in the Roman excavations at Segóbriga, Valeria a Ercávica. Note the top of a Roman altar found at Ercávica illustrating items us in sacred rites.

Turn back to the cathedral and along calle San Pedro; bear first left for plaza S Nicolás from which steps lead down to plaza de los Descalzos.

★ **Plaza de las Angustias** (**15**) – A Franciscan monastery and hermitage, known the Virgin in Anguish, stands in the quiet, tree-lined square between the town a the Júcar ravine.

CUENCA

Alfonso VIII	2
Alonso de Ojeda	5
Andrés de Cabrera	8
Angustias (Bajada a las)	12
Angustias (Pl. de las)	15
Carmen (Pl. del)	20
Colegio San José	25
Fray Luis de León	30
Júcar (Ronda del)	40
Julián Romero (Ronda)	43
Mayor (Pl.)	44
Obispo Valero	45
Pósito	55
Puerta de Valencia	58
San Nicólas (Pl.)	65
San Pablo (Puente de)	68
Trabuco	71

M¹ Museo Diocesano
M² Museo de Cuenca

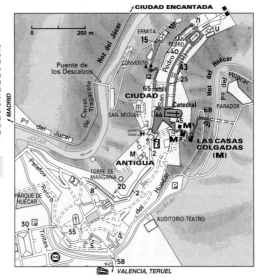

Return to the calle San Pedro and continue to the church of the same name. Bear left into an alley which ends at the edge of the Júcar ravine (good view). Return to the church and walk down ronda Julián Romero.

Ronda Julián Romero (43) – This delightful stepped alley with its small squares runs above the Huécar gorge and brings you back to the cathedral.

EXCURSIONS

Las Hoces (Ravines) – Roads which parallel the river on either side as it circles the bottom of the precipitous rock spur, afford amazing views of the hanging houses.

Hoz del Júcar – The Júcar is the shorter and more enclosed ravine. Poplars stand reflected in the green river waters below the ochre-coloured cliff.

Hoz del Huécar – *Round tour of 15km/9mi.* The Huécar course swings from side to side between less steep slopes as it drains a small valley given over to market-gardening. The Cuenca houses, seen from below, appear to defy gravity.

Turn left at the end of the ravine for Buenache de la Sierra and then left again for the Convento de San Jerónimo (monastery).

Shortly afterwards, in a right bend, there's a remarkable **view**★ of the valley's tall grey rock columns, and, in the distance, of Cuenca. Enter the town through a gateway set in the ramparts of the old quarter.

★ **Las Torcas** – *Take N 420 then bear left after 11km/6.5mi.* The road passes through an attractive wood of conifers where the *torcas*, strange, circular depressions of earth which occasionally reach spectacular proportions, can be seen. The Torca del Lobo (Wolf's Hollow) is particularly interesting.

Serranía de CUENCA★

Castilla-La Mancha (Cuenca)
Michelin map 444 K23-L24

The unusual landscapes of this limestone area have been formed over the centuries by the infiltration of river water and wind erosion. The whimsical rock formations, the pine groves and the numerous streams all combine to form a sierra of unquestionable beauty.

TOUR OF THE SIERRA *270km/168mi – allow 1 day*

Ventano del Diablo – *25.5km/16mi from Cuenca on CM 2105.* The Devil's Window, an opening carved out of the rock, overlooks the depths of the **Garganta del Júcar**★ (Júcar Gorges).

★ **Ciudad Encantada** – *Follow the road signposted to the right of the CM 2105.* The Enchanted City is a strange rock formation created by the shaping of limestone by the natural elements. An arrowed circuit directs visitors through this dreamlike forest of rocks, the most interesting of which are the Tobogán (Toboggan Slope) and the Mar de Piedras (Sea of Stones).

To reach the **Mirador de Uña** *(2km/1mi)*, continue along the road which leaves t
car park. Enjoy the extensive **view** of the Júcar Valley which is dominated alo
its entire course by towering cliffs, with, in the distance, Uña and its small lak

*Return to CM 2105 and continue until you reach Villalba de la Sierra. Turn rig
into a road heading north towards Las Majadas.*

Los Callejones - *3km/2mi from Las Majadas, on the Uña road. Leave your c
on the esplanade.* Although less spectacular than the Ciudad Encantada, th
isolated geological spot is a strange natural sight with unusual shapes in a ma
of eroded blocks, arches and the narrow alleyways which lend their name to t
area: The Alleyways.

*At Las Majadas, resume your route towards the north, then the west, heading f
Priego.*

★ **Hoz de Beteta (Beteta Ravine)** - Before reaching Priego *(3km/2mi)*, a road off
the right leads to the **Convento de San Miguel de las Victorias**. From its privileged sit
it dominates the entrance to the **Valley of the River Escabas**. *(Return to CM 2023*
Continue along the valley for a few kilometres, the road then leaves the river an
having passed Vadillos, comes into the impressive gorge of the **Hoz de Beteta**
through which the Guadiela river flows between towering vertical cliffs and lu
vegetation.

★ **Nacimiento del río Cuervo (Source of the Cuervo)** - *30km/19mi southeast of Betet
Leave the car just after the bridge and walk up 500m.* A footpath leads to th
waterfalls★ where water rushing through grottoes and out of moss-covere
hollowed out rocks forms the beginnings of the Cuervo river.

As you continue back towards Cuenca on CM 2106, then CM 2105, there are love
views of the embalse de la Toba (Toba Reservoir).

Now on the Web! Visit our site at **www.michelin-travel.com**

Route planning service complete with tourist information and maps which you can pri

Have a good trip !

DAROCA★

Aragón (Zaragoza) – Population 2 630
Michelin map 443 I 25

Daroca is lodged between two ridges over which runs its 4km/2mi long perimeter
battlemented **walls**★. These were originally defended by more than 100 towers ar
fortified gateways like the impressive **Puerta Baja** (Lower Gate) flanked by squa
towers.
The town was founded by Muslims, but fell from the Moors' control in 1120 and w
granted civic independence in 1142.

El Milagro de los Sagrados Corporales - The miracle of the holy altar cloths too
place in 1239, after the conquest of Valencia, when Christian troops in Daroca, Teru
and Calatayud were setting out to recover territory occupied by the Moors. Just
mass was being celebrated, the Moors attacked and the priest had to hide th
consecrated hosts between two altar cloths. Shortly afterwards, it was seen that th
hosts had left bloodstained imprints on the linen. The three towns of Daroca, Teru
and Calatayud claimed the precious relic. To settle the dispute the holy cloths we
placed upon a mule which was then set free. It made straight for Daroca, dyin
however, as it entered the Puerta Baja.

SIGHTS

Colegiata de Santa María ⊙ - This collegiate church, built in the Romanesq
period as a repository for the holy cloths, was modified in the 15C and 16C.
the north wall beside the belfry is a Flamboyant Gothic portal.

Interior - The late Gothic nave includes several Renaissance features like the cupo
above the transept crossing.
The **south chapels**, partly faced with locally manufactured 16C *azulejos*, contain
series of interesting altarpieces. To the right of the entrance is a 15C **altarpiece**
in multicoloured alabaster which is believed to have been carved in England – no
the anecdotal detail. Gothic tombs stand on either side of the nave. The 15C **Capi
de los Corporales**★ (Chapel of the Holy Relics) is on the site of the origin
Romanesque apse. The altar, behind a kind of Flamboyant rood screen and fram
by scenes of the miracle on the walls, includes a shrine enclosing the holy alt
cloths. All around stand statues in delightful poses carved out of multicolour
alabaster. The painted Gothic **retable**★ is dedicated to St Michael.

Museo Parroquial (Parish Museum) ⊙ – Among the paintings on wood are two rare though badly damaged 13C panels and **altarpieces** to St Peter (14C) and St Martin (15C). All the gold and silver plate was made in Daroca except for the **reliquary** which once held the holy altar cloths, which was made by the 14C Catalan, Moragues. The figures are gold, the foundation silver. Most of the **chasubles**, many of them very old, were woven in the town, while others, dating from the 17C, are Mexican.

Iglesia de San Miguel ⊙ – This church, equally outstanding in its fine appearance for the purity of its Romanesque east end and its 12C portal, has recovered its original design. The 13C wall paintings in the apse have, unfortunately, faded. Outside, a short distance below, you can see the restored Mudéjar style belfry of the **Iglesia de Santo Domingo** ⊙.

DONOSTIA/SAN SEBASTIÁN★★

País Vasco (Guipúzcoa)
Population 176 019
Michelin map 442 C 23
Local map see COSTA VASCA

The resort and its setting – San Sebastián – Donostia in Basque – long known as the Pearl of Cantabria, stretches between Monte Urgull and Monte Igueldo alongside its scallop shaped bay, the bahía de la **Concha**. The islet of Santa Clara partly closes off the bay.

Two vast sand beaches follow the curve of the bay: La Concha, and beyond the promontory, the fashionable **Ondarreta** (A). Behind are gardens, promenades and luxury apartment blocks and beyond the playa de Ondarreta, at the foot of monte Igueldo, can be found the **Peine de los Vientos**, a sculpture by Eduardo Chillida.

Historically, San Sebastián's recognition as a resort began in 1889 with the construction of the **Palacio de Miramar** (A), a palace built to designs by an English architect, Selden Warnum. It was patronised by the Regent, María Cristina of Habsburg-Lorraine and thereafter by the Spanish aristocracy.

The summer calendar includes international jazz and film festivals, a Semana Grande (in August) and Basque folklore festivals, golf and tennis tournaments, racing and regattas.

A gastronomic capital – A feature of the city where one eats well and copiously, are the 30 or so gourmet clubs. The all-male members prepare excellent meals which they then consume, accompanied by cider or the local *chacolí* wine. Basque specialities include fish dishes (gilt-head, hake, sardines) and the wonderful squid or *chipirones*.

La Concha

Andía . . . . B 2
Arbol de Gernika (Paseo del) . . B 5
Bizkaia (Paseo de) . . . . B 6
Boulevard (Alameda del) . . . . . B 8
Constitución (Pl. de la) . . . . . . B 12
Fueros (Paseo de los) . . . . B 14
Garibai . . . . B 9

Hernani . . . . B 18
Kursaal (Puente del) . . . . B 15
Libertad (Av. de la) . . . . B 21
Mayor . . . . B 27
Miramar . . . . B 30
Prim . . . . B 33
República Argentina (Paseo) . . B 36
Salamanca (Paseo) . . . . B 39
San Juan . . . . B 42
Sancho el Sabio (Av. de) . . . . B 43
Santa Catalina (Puente de) . . . B 44

Satrustegi (Av. de) . . . . A
Urbieta . . . . B
Urdaneta . . . . B
Zubieta . . . . B
Zumalakarregi (Av.) . . . . A
Zurriola (Paseo de) . . . . B

B Santa María
M¹ Museo de San Telmo
M² Museo Naval

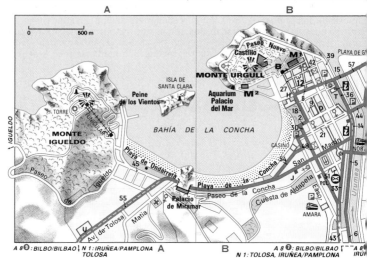

PANORAMIC VIEWS

★★★ **Monte Igueldo** ⊘ (A) – *Access by funicular; or by car, follow the Concha a* Ondarreta beaches and then bear left. At the top are an amusement park, ho and restaurant. There is also a splendid **panorama** of the sea, the harbour with Sar Clara island and San Sebastián itself, set within a mountain cirque. The view beautiful in the evening when the town lights up.

★★ **Monte Urgull** (B) – Monte Urgull, now a public park, is crowned by a fortres **Castillo de Santa Cruz de la Mota**. From the summit there is a good **panorama** of t monuments of the old town directly below and the Bahía de la Concha.

OLD TOWN 2hr

San Sebastián was founded at the foot of monte Urgull and there, between t harbour and the mouth of the Urumea, you can still see the old city. Although, fact, it all dates only from the last century – the original town was devastated fire in 1813 – the narrow streets have considerable character. The area com alive at the evening aperitif hour when locals and tourists (especially the Frenc many of whom cross the border for a meal) crowd the bars and small restaurar in the *calles* Portu, Muñoa and Fermín Calbetón to pick at the tapas (reputed be the best in Spain), shellfish, crustaceans and *chipirones*.

Plaza de la Constitución (B 12) – The square is lined with houses with tall arcad and numbered balconies – a reminder of the days when they served as ringsi seats when bullfights were held in the square.

Iglesia de Santa María ⊘ (B B) – The church has a strikingly exuberant late-1 portal. Baroque altars adorn the vast sober interior.

Museo de San Telmo ⊘ (B M¹) – The museum is in an old 16C monastery. T Renaissance cloisters contain Basque stone funerary crosses carved in t traditional Iberian style and dating for the most part from between the 15C a the 17C. The cloisters' upper gallery is dedicated to the ethnographic section, wi a reconstruction of a Basque interior. This gallery opens onto the rooms housi the museum's paintings, which include a Ribera, an El Greco, and a 19C a section.

Paseo Nuevo (B) – The wide corniche promenade almost circles Monte Urgull a affords good **views** of the open sea and the bay. At the end is a bustling a colourful port with numerous fishing boats and pleasure craft.

★ **Aquarium-Palacio del Mar (Sea Palace)** ⊘ (B) – This complex houses an ocean graphic museum and an aquarium. Although the museum contains an interesti collection of models, it is the newly-designed aquarium, now one of the best Europe, which is particularly impressive. A new **tactile aquarium**, in which visito are actually able to touch harmless species of fish, two **microworld aquariums**, whe cameras observe the underwater life of the very smallest fish, and, in particular, the **Oceanarium**★, an aquarium with a large 360° tunnel which is totally surrounded by water, are just some of the centre's new facilities which provide a valuable insight into the diversity of the world's oceans.

Museo Naval ⏲ (**B M²**) – The ground floor of this plain 18C consular building, which now houses the city's naval museum, exhibits traditional construction tools and materials, while the first floor is dedicated to models and navigational instruments, all of which highlight the importance of the sea in Basque history.

EXCURSION

★ **Monte Ulía (view from)** – *7km/4mi east.*
Follow the N 1 towards Irún and before reaching the summit and descending to San Sebastián, take the first road on the right. While driving to the top via a series of hairpin bends there are good **views** of the town and its setting. A path at the top leads off to the right across a park to Monte Ulía restaurant.

Parque Nacional de DOÑANA★

Andalucía (Huelva, Sevilla)
Michelin map 446 U 10, V 10-11

Doñana National Park, created for the protection of its flora and fauna, stretches across the provinces of Huelva and Sevilla between the Atlantic Ocean and the mouth of the Guadalquivir river. Given its geographical position – the fact that it is close to Africa and is affected climatically by both the Atlantic and the Mediterranean – it is a rest stop for a great many African and European migratory birds. Doñana is Spain's largest wildlife reserve with a total protected area (inner and outer park) of 73 000ha/180 390 acres. It is home to several animal species including lynx, wild boar, deer and a wide variety of birds: Spanish imperial eagle, flamingo, heron, wild duck and coot.

El Acebuche Information Centre, 2km/1.2mi north of Torre de la Higuera

Guided tours ⏲ in four-wheel-drive vehicles are organised by the Information Centre in El Acebuche. The park has a variety of ecosystems depending on the habitat; on the **moorland** *(marisma)* there are cork oak and pine forests (you may see branch covered hides still used by pine-kernel gatherers); the **lagoons** which form the largest part of the reserve, are home to numerous waterfowl in winter, while the **moveable sand dunes** advance inland from the beach an average 6m/20ft every year.

El Rocío – El Rocío village, north of the Doñana reserve, has a shrine to Nuestra Señora del Rocío (Our Lady of the Dew) to which crowds of pilgrims from all over Andalucía flock annually at Whitsun. They arrive in flower decorated carts or riding horses saddled and bridled in rich Andalusian style; pilgrims from Cádiz take boats across the Guadalquivir and then cross Doñana National Park. During the week of pilgrimage El Rocío is host to about a million people but the rest of the year it is a ghost town.

ÉCIJA

Andalucía (Sevilla) – Population 35 727
Michelin map 446 T 14

Écija, which was founded by the Romans, has a mild climate except in summer when it becomes so hot that it is known as the "Frying-pan of Andalucía". The town lies in the Guadalquivir depression, its Baroque belfries decorated with ceramic tiles visible at some distance across the plains. The most interesting tower, that of **San Juan**★, together with the belfries of San Gil and Santa Cruz, belong to churches now in ruins; Santa María *(to the left of the Ayuntamiento)* stands on a square of the same name lined by old houses.

SIGHTS

Park the car on plaza de España.
The streets on either side of avenida Miguel Cervantes still feature old palaces with beautiful façades: Baroque for the 18C **Palacio de Benamejí** and Plateresque for the **Palacio de Valdehermosa**. The **Palacio de Peñaflor** front is concave and adorned with frescoes.

★ **Iglesia de Santiago (St James' Church)** ⏲ – In front of the church is a pleasant 17C *patio.* Inside, the Mudéjar windows of an earlier building were retained when the nave and side aisles were rebuilt after caving in, in 1628. The **retable**★ at the high altar illustrates the Passion and the Resurrection.

ELX/ELCHE★

Comunidad Valenciana (Alicante) – Population 187 596

Michelin map 445 R 27

Elche (Elx in Valencian), standing on the banks of the Vinalopó river, is famed for
Dama, its palm grove and its mystery play.

La Dama de Elche (The Lady of Elche) – Elche has been the site of several civilizatic
including that of the Romans when the town was known as *Illicis*. It was amo
Iberian and Roman ruins in **La Alcudia** *(2km/1.2mi south)* in 1897, that archeologi:
discovered the great sculpture known as the Lady of Elche (4C BC), a masterpic
of Iberian art now exhibited in the Museo Arqueológico de Madrid.

★★ **El Palmeral (Palm Grove)** – The grove, believed to have been planted by 1
Phoenicians, is the largest in Europe with more than 100 000 trees. The pali
flourish in the mild climate, with the aid of a remarkable irrigation system. Dates a
cut in winter from the female trees and the fronds, after blanching, from the m
trees for Palm Sunday processions and various handicrafts. Cereals and vegetab
are grown beneath the trees outside the city limits.

El Misteri (Mystery Play) – The Elche Mystery, a medieval verse drama performed
an all-male cast, recounts the Dormition, Assumption and Coronation of the Virg
It is played in the Basílica de Santa María on 14 and 15 August.

SIGHTS

★★ **Huerta del Cura** ⊘ (Z) – The *huerta* is a garden of bright flowers planted benea
particularly magnificent palm trees, including the Imperial Palm, with sev
trunks, said to be 150 years old. There is also an interesting cactus section.

ELX
ELCHE

Alfonso XII	Z 3	
Almórida	Z 4	
Antonio Machado (Av. d')	Z 6	
Baix (Pl. de)	Z 7	
Balsa dels Moros (Camí)	Y 8	
Camino del Gato	Z 12	
Camino de la Almazara	Z 13	
Canalejas (Puente de)	Z 15	

Conrado del Campo	Z 16	
Corredora	Z	
Diagonal del Palau	Y 17	
Eres de Santa Llucia	Y 19	
Escultor Capuz	Z 20	
Estació (Pas. de l')	Y 21	
Federico García Lorca	Z 23	
Fernanda Santamaría	Z 24	
Jiménez Díaz (Doctor)	Y 28	
Jorge Juan	YZ 29	
José María Pemán	Z 31	
Juan Ramón Jiménez	Z 32	
Luis Gonzaga Llorente	Y 33	
Maestro Albéniz	Y 35	

Major de la Vila	Y	
Marqués de Asprella	Y	
Ntra Sra de la Cabeza	Y	
Pont dels Ortissos	Y	
Porta d'Alacant	Y	
Rector	Z	
Reina Victoria	Z	
Sant Joan (Pl. de)	Z	
Santa Anna	Z	
Santa Teresa (Puente)	Z	
Santa Pola (Av. de)	Z	
Vicente Amorós Candela	Y	
Vicente Blasco Ibáñez	Z	
Xop II. Licità	Z	

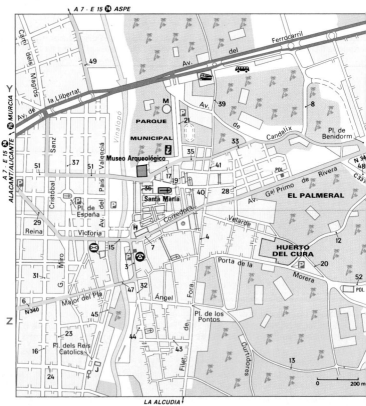

★ **Parque Municipal** ⊘ (Y) – A leafy, well-tended garden covered with palm trees with a 50 000m²/59 800sq yd extension divided into four separate *huertas*, the most impressive of which is the **Hort de Baix**.

Museo Arqueológico ⊘ (Y) – The archeological museum, housed in the Palacio de Altamira, displays finds taken mostly from excavations at La Alcudia. Among the most noteworthy items are sculpture and ceramics from the Iberian period and the *Venus of Illicis*, a delicately carved white marble Roman sculpture.

Basílica de Santa María (Y) – The monumental 18C Baroque basilica, designed from the first as a setting for the mystery play, has an interesting portal by Nicolás de Bari.

EMPÚRIES/AMPURIAS★★

Catalunya (Girona)
Michelin map 443 F 39
Local map see COSTA BRAVA

The Graeco-Roman town of Ampurias (or *Emporion* as it was known to the Greeks, meaning market or trading station) was built on a striking **site★★** beside the sea. Nowadays, it is still possible to make out three centres: the old town, or **Paliápolis**, the new town or **Neápolis**, and the Roman town.

In the mid 6C BC, the Phoenicians (who had already settled in Marseille), founded Palaiápolis, a commercial port on the then offshore island now joined to the mainland and occupied by the village of Sant Marti d'Empúries. Some years later, a town began to develop on the shore facing the island, and so Neápolis came into being. As a Roman ally during the Punic Wars, it saw the arrival of an expeditionary corps led by Scipio Africanus Major in 218 BC. However, it wasn't until 100 BC that the Roman town was established to the west of Neápolis. The two centres coexisted independently until Augustus bestowed Roman citizenship upon the Greeks. The colony continued to grow but suffered severely from Barbarian invasions in the 3C AD. At one time, however, it was a bishopric as the basilica ruins discovered in Neápolis prove. It finally succumbed to the Moors in the 8C.

Neápolis ⊘ – The piling up of different edifices over a period of 1 000 years has made an analysis of the ruins difficult. Near the gate was the **Templo de Asclepio** (Aesculapius – god of healing) and a sacred precinct which contained altars and statues of the gods. Nearby stood the **watch tower** and, at its foot, drinking water cisterns (a filter has been reconstructed). Another point of interest, the **Templo de Zeus Serapis** (a god associated with the weather and with healing), was surrounded by a colonnade. At the other end of the main street was the **Agora**, general meeting place and heart of the town, where the bases of three statues remain. A street ran from the agora to the sea, bordered on its left by the **stoa** or covered market formed of alleyways and shops. Behind the stoa are the clearly distinguishable ruins of a 6C **paleo-Christian basilica** with a rounded apse.

Museo Arqueológico de Ampurias – A section of Neápolis is displayed together with models of temples and finds from the excavations including a mosaic of the sacrifice of Iphigenia, a Hellenistic work from the 2C or 1C BC, a mosaic of a partridge and yet another of a mask.

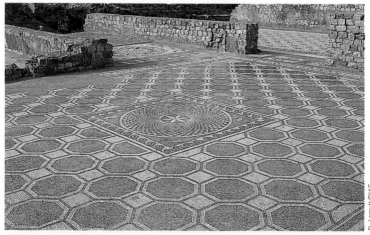

Roman mosaic floor

D. Lerauty/DIAF

The Roman town – This stands on a hill behind the museum and unlike Neápolis, is a vast, geometrically laid out town. It has been but partially excavated, with restorations to some of the walls. **House no 1** (entrance at the back) has an atrium or inner courtyard with six columns. Around this are the residential apartments, the peristyle or colonnaded court, and the impluvium or basin for catching rainwater. The reception rooms are paved in geometric black and white mosaic. At the house's northern end are the private baths.

Next door, **house no 2B** has rooms paved with their original mosaic. One of these, near the atrium, has been reconstituted in clay (by the rammed earth method in use at the time) with its walls resting on stone foundations.

The **forum**, a large square lined by porticoes and to north and south respectively by temples and shops, was the centre of civic life in the town. A porticoed street led to the city gate and beyond the walls to the oval **amphitheatre** which is still visible.

Monasterio de El ESCORIAL★★★

EL ESCORIAL MONASTERY – Madrid

Michelin map 444 or 442 K 17

The impressive monastery of San Lorenzo el Real, or El Escorial, stands at the foot of monte Abantos on the southern slopes of the sierra de Guadarrama at an altitude of 1 065m/3 494ft. The massive building is a monument to King Philip II who commissioned it, the architect, Juan de Herrera, and 16C Spain.

There is a good **view**★ of the monastery and the surrounding countryside from **Silla de Felipe II** (Philip II's Seat).

Turn left beyond the monastery into the road marked Entrada Herrería-Golf and follow the signs to Silla de Felipe II.

The feast day of San Lorenzo (St Lawrence), patron of the village and monastery, is celebrated annually on 10 August.

DIAF

The building of the monastery – On 10 August 1557, St Lawrence's Day, Philip II's forces defeated the French at the memorable battle of St Quentin. In commemoration the king decided to build a monastery and dedicate it to the saint. It was consigned to the Hieronymites and served as the royal palace and pantheon.

The project was stupendous – there are nearly 1 200 doors and 2 600 windows; it required 1 500 workmen and was completed in a mere 21 years (1563-84) which is why the building has an exceptional unity of style.

The general designs of the first architect, Juan de Toledo, were followed, after his death in 1567 by his assistant **Juan de Herrera**, who, however, is responsible for the final overall elegance. Reaction to the sumptuous ornamentation fashionable in Charles V's reign spurred the architects to produce a sober monument with cleancut, majestic lines.

It is said that the monastery recalls St Lawrence's martyrdom with its gridiron ground plan. It measures 206m × 161m (676ft × 528ft) and is built of grey granite – the austerity of the stone serving to emphasise, if anything, the severity of the architecture. When the king commanded an increase in height to accommodate a larger religious community, Herrera took the opportunity to position the rows of windows asymmetrically to lessen the monotony of horizontal lines which, otherwise, are only relieved by the pointed corner towers. The edifice finally has the grandeur of a great palace and the austerity of a committed monastery.

TOUR ⊘ *half a day*

★ Palacios (Royal Apartments) – While Philip II and the Spanish Habsburgs remained on the throne, El Escorial was a place of regal splendour: the king resided in apartments encircling the church apse, other royal apartments extended around the Patio de los Mascarones (Mask Courtyard). The Bourbons, who in fact preferred the palaces of La Granja, El Pardo and Aranjuez to El Escorial, when nevertheless in residence, occupied suites on the north side of the church. The palace took on renewed glory in the 18C in the reigns of Charles III and IV but lost its position as a centre of court life again later. A staircase built in the time of Charles IV goes up *(3rd floor)* to the **Palacio de los Borbones** (Bourbon Apartments). These are sumptuous with Pompeian ceilings and fine **tapestries★**. The hangings include many made in the Real Fábrica (Royal Tapestry Works) in Madrid after cartoons by Spanish artists, notably Goya, as in the series on popular subjects and pastimes. In later rooms are Flemish tapestries – a *Neptune* (from the Telemachus series) and several *(in the last room)* in realistic style by Teniers.

The style of decoration changes, introducing the austerity of the Habsburgs. The large **Sala de las Batallas** (Battle Gallery) contains frescoes (1587): on the south wall, of the Victory at Higueruela in the 15C against the Moors and on the north wall, the Victory at St-Quentin against the French.

The restraint of the **Habitaciones de Felipe II** (Philip II's apartments) *(2nd floor)* is all the more striking after the luxury of the Bourbon rooms. Those of the Infanta Isabel Clara Eugenia, like those of her father, comprise a suite of relatively small rooms in which the principal decoration derives from dados of Talavera ceramic tiles. The king's bedroom, where he died in 1598, aged 71, is directly off the church. A communicating door allowed him to walk in at any time in the early years and at the end, when he was dying of gangrene caused by advanced gout, to be present during services and contemplate the high altar from his bed. The paintings in the apartments include a *St Christopher* by Patinir and a portrait of the king in his old age by Pantoja de la Cruz. Facing the gardens and the plain, the Salón del Trono (Throne Room) is hung with 16C Brussels tapestries, the Sala de los Retratos (Portrait Gallery), which follows, with royal portraits. Finally, visitors are shown Philip's sedan chair in which he was carried when no longer able to walk.

★★ Panteones (Pantheons) – Access is through the Patio de los Evangelistas (Evangelists' Courtyard) in which the walls are painted with frescoes by Tibaldi (east wall) and his followers.

A marble and jasper staircase leads down to the **Panteón de los Reyes★★★** (Royal Pantheon) which lies beneath the chancel. It contains the mortal remains of all the Spanish monarchs from the time of Emperor Charles V, with the exception of Philip V, Ferdinand VI and Amadeus of Savoy who are buried respectively in La Granja, Madrid and in Italy.

The chapel, which is octagonal in shape, was begun in 1617 in the reign of Philip II and completed in 1654. The main architect was Juan Bautista Crescenci. Facing the door is the jasper altar; on either side stand the 26 marble and bronze sarcophagi in wall niches. The kings are on the left and the queens whose sons succeeded to the throne, on the right. The sumptuous decoration is completed by an ornate chandelier, the work of an Italian artist.

The 19C **Panteón de los Infantes★** (Infantes' Pantheon) includes not only children but also queens whose children did not succeed to the throne. The decoration includes delicately carved sculptures. Climatic conditions are such that the room has been well preserved.

★ Salas Capitulares (Chapter-houses) – Two fine rooms, with ceilings painted by Italian artists with grotesques and frescoes, form a museum of Spanish (16C and 17C) and Italian (16C) religious painting.

The first room contains canvases by El Greco and Ribera, a St Jerome by Titian and Joseph's Tunic painted by Velázquez in Rome. The second room has works from the 16C Venetian School, including paintings by Tintoretto, Veronese and Titian (Ecce Homo). A room at the back contains works by Bosch and his followers: the Haywain, an example of his unbounded imagination, and the Crown of Thorns (Los Improperios), his satirical verve.

★★ Basílica – Herrera based his final plan for the basilica on Italian drawings, introducing an architectural novelty, a flat vault, in the atrium. The church's interior owes much to St Peter's in Rome with a Greek cross plan, a 92m/302ft high cupola above the transept crossing supported by four colossal pillars and barrel vaulting in the transept. The frescoes in the nave vaulting were painted by Luca Giordano in Charles II's reign. Wide, red marble steps lead to the sanctuary which has paintings on the vaulting of the Lives of Christ and the Virgin by Cambiasso.

The massive **retable**, designed by Herrera, is 30m/100ft tall and is composed of four registers of jasper, onyx and red marble columns between which stand 15 bronze sculptures by Leone and Pompeo Leoni. The tabernacle is also by Herrera. On either side of the chancel are the royal mausoleums with funerary figures at prayer by Pompeo Leoni. Charles V is shown with his Queen, Isabel of Portugal, their daughter María and her two sisters, while Philip II is portrayed in company of three of his wives, and his son, Don Carlos. The door at the end on the right is the one communicating with Philip II's room.

In the first chapel off the north aisle is the Martyrdom of St Maurice by Rómulo Cincinato, which Philip II preferred to that of El Greco (see below). In the adjoining chapel is a magnificent sculpture of Christ carved by Benvenuto Cellini in 1562.

Patio de los Reyes (Kings' Courtyard) – One of the three Classical gateways in the palace's principal façade opens onto this courtyard. The court is named after the statues of the kings of Judea which adorn the majestic west front of the church.

★★ Biblioteca (Library) – 2nd floor. The gallery is 54m/177ft long and richly decorated; the shelving, designed by Herrera, is of exotic woods; the ceiling, sumptuously painted by Tibaldi, represents the liberal arts with Philosophy and Theology at each end. There are also magnificent portraits of Charles V, Philip II and Philip III by Pantoja de la Cruz and one of Charles II by Carreño.

Philip II furnished the library with over 10 000 books of which many suffered in the 1671 fire and the ravages of Napoleon's army. It is now a public library with over 40 000 books and some 2 700 manuscripts dating from the 5C to the 18C. The unusual presentation of the books on the shelves, with the spine facing inwards, is for preservation purposes.

In the cases, on the marble tables, are precious manuscripts including some in Arabic, autographs of St Teresa, the finely illuminated Cantigas de Santa María, a poem by King Alfonso the Wise, and an 11C Beatus.

★★ Nuevos Museos (New Museos) – The **Museo de Pintura** (Picture Museum) contains an interesting collection of works illustrating religious themes.

First room: canvases by Italian artists mainly from the 16C Venetian School (Titian, Veronese and Tintoretto). Second room: among others, two works by Van Dyck and a small painting by Rubens. Third room: works by Miguel de Coxcie, Philip II's Court Painter. Fourth room: Rogier Van der Weyden's outstanding Calvary, a sober and expressive painting, is flanked by an Annunciation by Veronese and a Nativity by Tintoretto. Fifth room: canvases by Ribera including

St Jerome Penitent, the philosopher *Chrysippus* and *Aesop*, all with the artist's characteristic style of portraying especially vivid faces, together with two paintings by Zurbarán – *St Peter of Alcántara* and the *Presentation of the Virgin* – examples of his marvellous approach to light and subject matter. Last room: two paintings by Alonso Cano and various works by Luca Giordano.

The **Museo de Arquitectura** (Architectural Museum) in the vaulted basement outlines the construction of the monastery with biographies of the principal men involved, including craftsmen, as well as account books, Herrera's designs and so on.

On the ground floor, a continuation of the painting section, El Greco's **Martyrdom of St Maurice and the Theban Legionary**★ is given pride of place. The work, commissioned by Philip II but too original in composition, too acid in colouring to suit his taste, was rejected by the king. Nevertheless, this picture of the martyrdom of the legionary who refused to sacrifice to the gods, and of St Maurice trying to convince his companions that he should be executed in the other's place, is now considered one of El Greco's greater works.

ADDITIONAL SIGHTS

★ **Casita del Príncipe (Prince's Pavilion)** ⊙ – *Southeast along the road to the station.* Charles III commissioned Juan de Villanueva to build a leisure lodge for the future Charles IV in the Prince's Gardens, which stretch out below Philip II's apartments. Its exquisite decoration makes it a jewel of a palace, in miniature. There are painted **Pompeian**★ style ceilings by Maella and Vicente Gómez, silk hangings, canvases by Luca Giordano, chandeliers, porcelain and a beautiful mahogany and marble dining room.

Casita de Arriba (Upper Pavilion) ⊙ – *3km/2mi southwest beyond the golf-course.* Like the Prince's Pavilion, this lodge, also known as the Casita del Infante (Infante's Pavilion), was designed by Villanueva. It was built for the Infante Gabriel, Charles IV's younger brother. The interior is furnished in the style of the period; the first floor was arranged as apartments for Prince Juan Carlos before his accession to the throne.

The chapter on art and architecture in this guide gives an outline of artistic creation in the region, providing the context of the buildings and works of art described in the Sights section.

This chapter may also provide ideas for touring.

It is advisable to read it at leisure/before setting out.

ESTELLA★★

See LIZARRA

FIGUERES/FIGUERAS★

Catalunya (Girona) – Population 35 301
Michelin map 443 F 38

Figueres, capital of Alt Empordà, is a commercial centre and strategic road link between French and Spanish Catalunya. It is the birthplace of Salvador Dalí (1904-89), the famous Surrealist artist.

SIGHTS

★★ **Teatre-Museu Dalí** ⊙ – The Dalí theatre-museum, a world of folly and caprice which may charm or exasperate but never fails to impress, is a good reflection of the artist himself who said this of his creation: "The museum cannot be considered as such; it is a gigantic surrealist object, where everything is coherent, where nothing has eluded my design." It is housed in the former local theatre (1850) which was burnt down during the Civil War and restored in 1966. Dalí added an immense glass dome (beneath which he is now buried) and a vast *patio*, and decorated everything with fantasy objects: giant eggs, bread rolls – which cover the façade like the shells all over the Casa de las Conchas in Salamanca – basins and gilt dummies. He gave his eccentricity full rein in the squares around the museum where there are figures perched on columns of tyres, and inside, for instance in the Mae West sitting room where there is a lip-shaped sofa, a nose-chimney and eye-frames. Some of his canvases are exhibited in the museum (including a series showing him painting his wife Gala) as well as works by other artists such as Pitxot, Duchamp and Fortuny.

Teatre-Museu Dalí

★ **Torre Galatea** – The decoration of this tower was the work of Dalí, wh
introduced ornamental motifs of his choice (vivid colours and fantastic objects

Iglesia de Sant Pere ⊘ – Built in the late 14C, this church has a single nave tha
reflects the influence of Gothic art in Catalan architecture. The apse, the transep
and the belfry are all modern.

★ **Museu de Joguets** ⊘ – The museum displays toys from many different countrie
and periods. Note the interesting collections of automata, puppets and teddy bear:

Museu de l'Empordà ⊘ – This building houses various collections devoted to th
art, history and archeology of the region. Of particular note is the exhibition c
works by 19C and 20C painters (Nonell, Sorolla, Dalí and Tàpies).

Iglesia de FRÓMISTA★★

FRÓMISTA CHURCH – Castilla y León (Palencia)

Michelin map 441 or 442 F 16

Many pilgrims on the way to Santiago de Compostela halted at Frómista with its fou
hospices and the opportunity of making a pious offering at the Monasterio benedictin
de San Martín. Of this, only the church remains at the centre of a large square.

★★ **Iglesia de San Martín** ⊘ – The church, built in 1066 with beautifully matche
rough hewn stone blocks of considerable size, marks a climax in the developmen
of Romanesque architecture in Castilla: after earlier essays in Palencia, Jaca an
León (San Isidoro), it demonstrates the achievement of perfect ordinance in th
particular style. Outside, the eye travels over the classic east end, rising from th
apses up over the transept walls, almost imperceptibly to the **cupola** squinches an
finally to the lantern. The decorative features are all there – billets outlining th
windows, engaged columns and cornices with ornately carved modillions. Th
interior has a perfect basilica design with a nave, two aisles and a transept whic
does not project outside. The pure Romanesque lines of the exterior are apparen
inside, in the barrel vaulting, apsidal oven vaults, the dome on squinches an
double ribbed arches. The richly carved **capitals** with human figures or plant moti
provide indispensable decorative relief.
The church suffered a somewhat over-zealous restoration in 1904.

FUENTERRABÍA★

See HONDARRIBIA

GANDÍA

Comunidad valenciana – Population 52 000

Michelin map 445 P 29

Gandía lies on the Costa Blanca south of Valencia at the centre of a *huerta* which produces large quantities of oranges. These are exported from nearby **El Grao de Gandía**. A seaside resort has developed near the harbour along an immense sand **beach**.

The Borja fief – Gandía became the fief of the Borja family, better known under its Italian name, Borgia, when in 1485, the Duchy of Gandía was given by Ferdinand the Catholic to Rodrigo Borgia, future Pope Alexander VI. The Pope is chiefly remembered for his scandalous private life and for his children – Lucrezia, renowned for her beauty and culture and victim of political intrigue between her father and brother, and Cesare who for political ends had his brother murdered and served as a model for Machiavelli's *The Prince*. However, the fourth duke and great-grandson of Alexander VI, who became **St Francis Borja** (1510-72), was to redeem the family name. He served as equerry to Queen Isabel at the court of Emperor Charles V; and on her death, after having opened her coffin and seen her decomposed body, he resolved that if his own wife should die, he would devote himself to God. His wife did indeed die; he joined the Society of Jesus and became vicar-general.

Palacio Ducal (Former Palace of the Dukes of Borja) ⓥ – The mansion in which St Francis was born, now a Jesuit college, underwent considerable modification between the 16 and 18C. Only the *patio* remains Gothic in appearance and typical of those along the east coast of Spain. The tour includes richly decorated apartments with painted or coffered ceilings, *azulejos* and marble floors. Several rooms have been converted into chapels. The last room off the golden gallery has a beautiful floor, a Manises mosaic representing the four elements.

GASTEIZ/VITORIA★

País Vasco (Álava) – Population 209 704

Michelin map 442 D 21-22

Vitoria (Gasteiz in Basque), capital of the largest of the Basque provinces, is the seat of the Autonomous Basque (Euskadi) Community government. It lies at the centre of the *Llanada alavesa*, a vast cereal covered plateau far closer in appearance to the plains of Castilla than the green hills of the Cantabrian coast. The town has developed rapidly this century around the hill on which in 1181, Sancho the Wise, King of Navarra, founded a walled city.

Today it is a city of business, trade and industry – food processing, chemicals, engineering and farm machinery. It is also the capital of the manufacturing of playing cards (the Fournier factory was founded in 1868) and has been famous since the 18C for its chocolate truffles. The modern quarters around Calle Dato provide a lively contrast to the quiet, serene atmosphere of the old town.

Among the local amenities are water sports at two vast reservoirs, Urrunaga and Ullívarri, north of the town.

The August Virgen Blanca festival is colourful and perpetuates a strange tradition: everyone lights a cigar as the angel descends from the Torre de San Miguel (St Michael's Belfry).

CIUDAD VIEJA (OLD TOWN) *1hr 30min*

Seignorial houses with balconies and fronts bearing family coats of arms stand in concentric streets – each named after a trade – around the cathedral. The liveliest streets, full of charming shops and bars, are those to the left of the plaza de la Virgen Blanca. The **Iglesia de San Pedro (ABY)**, with its interesting Gothic façade, can also be found in this part of the old town.

Plaza de la Virgen Blanca (BZ 55) – The square is the most characteristic feature of Vitoria and its historic centre. It is dominated by the Iglesia de San Miguel (St Michael's Church) and is surrounded by house fronts with glassed-in balconies or *miradores*, framing the massive monument at the square's centre which commemorates Wellington's decisive victory at the Battle of Vitoria on 21 June 1813, after which King Joseph and 55 000 of his men fled north of the Pyrenees. It acts as a link between the old and new towns and communicates with the nobly ordered 18C **Plaza de España** also known as **Plaza Nueva (BZ 18)**.

The square's attractive 18C and 19C buildings are fronted by several attractive cafés (Café Marañón, Café Vitoria).

Iglesia de San Miguel (BZ) – A jasper niche in the church porch exterior contains the polychrome statue in Late Gothic style of the Virgen Blanca, patron of the city. The church is entered through a late-14C portal. Its tympanum illustrates the Life of St Michael. Also worthy of note inside are the chancel altarpiece by Gregorio Fernández and, to its right, a Plateresque sepulchral arch.

Plaza del Machete (BZ 30) – This small, elongated square lies at the back of th
Arquillos, a tall arcade which links the upper and lower towns. A niche in the eas
end of San Miguel church formerly contained the *machete* or cutlass, on which th
procurator general had to swear to uphold the town's privileges *(fueros)*. The 16
Palacio de Villa Suso, on its right-hand side, has been converted into a cultural centre

Climb the steps adjoining the palace.

A stroll along the **calle Fray Zacarías Martínez** (BY), with its old wood-framed house
and former palaces is particularly pleasant. The Renaissance north doorway of th
Palacio de los Escoriaza-Esquivel, built on a section of the former town walls,
worthy of special note.

Catedral de Santa María ⊘ (BY) – 14C. The north wall of the cathedral still ha
a fortified appearance. The west door is covered by Gothic vaulting in which th
ribs radiate with a sunburst effect from behind large statues. A polychrome *Virg
and Child* stands at the central pier. The tympana over the 14C Gothic doorway
illustrate the lives of the saints most venerated in Spain, namely Lawrence
Ildefonso, James (right portal) and Nicholas and Peter (left portal).
Inside, in a chapel off the south aisle, there is a striking portrayal of th
Martyrdom of St Bartholomew. One of the pillar capitals between the nave an
the south aisle shows a bullfighting scene – a carving unique in a church even
Spain! In the south transept are a Plateresque altarpiece in polychrome wood an
a painting by the 17C artist, Carreño, the *Immaculate Conception;* in the nort
arm are an interesting *Descent from the Cross* by Gaspar de Crayer (17C) and
polychrome stone tympanum from the original church. A decorative Plateresqu
funerary stone can be seen inlaid into the wall of a chapel near the entrance.

Museo de Arqueología (Archeological Museum) ⊘ (BY M¹) – This small museum
housed in the Casa Godeo-Guevara-San Juan in a half-timbered and brick hous
rebuilt in the 16C, displays finds from excavations in Álava province, covering th
period from the Paleolithic to the Middle Ages. Note the dolmen collections an
Roman steles and sculptures, including the *Estela del Jinete* (Knight's stele).
The **Casa de Portalón** (BY L) facing the museum is a typical 15C shop which is no
occupied by a well-known local restaurant. The **Torre de los Anda**, the lower part o
which was built as part of the town's medieval defences, forms a triangle with th
two houses.

* **Museo "Fournier" de Naipes**
(Playing Cards Museum) ⊘ (BY M⁴) –
The Palacio de Bendaña, a building
noted for its corner turret and plain
doorway with *alfiz* surround, is
home to this unusual museum.
Inside, a part of the delightful
Renaissance patio has been preserved. Félix Alfaro Fournier, grandson of
the founder of the playing cards
factory, has assembled a valuable
collection of playing cards which
was acquired by the City Council of
Álava in 1986. The present collection, from all over the world,
numbers over 15 000 packs,
dating from the late 14C to the
present day illustrating history
(wars, battles, revolutions), geography, politics (caricatures of personalities) and local customs (traditional dress and pastimes). There
is also a display of a variety of
materials (paper, parchment,
cloth, metal etc) demonstrating
printing and engraving techniques.
The **Casa del** Cordón, a 16C house at
no 24 in the same street, is used for
temporary exhibitions.

Spanish playing card (1570)

CIUDAD NUEVA (MODERN TOWN)

As Vitoria grew in the 18C, neo-Classical constructions began to appear such
the **Arquillos** arcade *(see above)* and **Plaza Nueva**. In the 19C, the town expande
southwards with the **Parque de la Florida** (Florida Park) (AZ) – near to which th
Catedral Nueva (New Cathedral) (AZ N) was built in 1907 in neo-Gothic style – a
two wide avenues: the Paseo de la Senda and the Paseo de Fray Francisco. Th

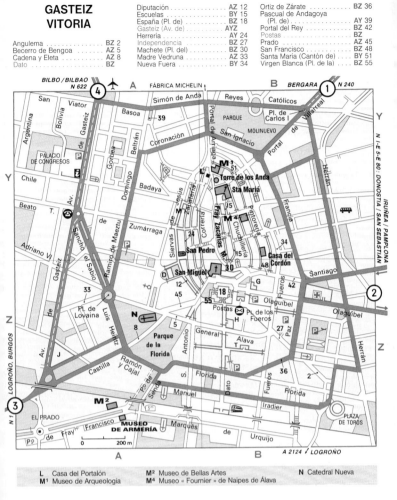

GASTEIZ VITORIA

Angulema	BZ 2	Diputación	AZ 12	Ortiz de Zárate	BZ 36
Becerro de Bengoa	AZ 5	Escuelas	BY 15	Pascual de Andagoya	
Cadena y Eleta	AZ 8	España (Pl. de)	BZ 18	(Pl. de)	AY 39
Dato	BZ	Gasteiz (Av. de)	AYZ	Portal del Rey	BZ 42
		Herrería	AY 24	Postas	BZ
		Independencia	BZ 27	Prado	AZ 45
		Machete (Pl. del)	BZ 30	San Francisco	BZ 48
		Madre Vedruna	AZ 33	Santa María (Cantón de)	BY 51
		Nueva Fuera	BY 34	Virgen Blanca (Pl. de la)	BZ 55

L	Casa del Portalón	M²	Museo de Bellas Artes	N	Catedral Nueva
M¹	Museo de Arqueologia	M⁴	Museo « Fournier » de Naipes de Álava		

latter was built up in the late 19C-early 20C with mansions and large town houses, one of which, the Palacio de Ajuria Enea, is now the seat of the Lehendakari or Basque government.

Museo de Bellas Artes (Fine Arts Museum) ⊙ **(AZ M²)** – The museum, housed in the neo-Renaissance Palacio de Agustí, displays painting and sculpture from the 14C to the present day.

On the first floor landing are interesting wood reliefs from Erenchun and Gauna and a 16C collection of Flemish triptychs. In the galleries to the left are a *Descent from the Cross* by a painter of the Flemish School, a series of five 16C reliquary busts influenced by the Rhenish School and, in rooms devoted to the Baroque period, canvases by Ribera and Alonso Cano.

The museum also has a comprehensive section on **Basque painting** with works by Iturrino, Regoyos and Zuloaga and a rich collection of **contemporary Spanish art** since 1960 (Miró, Tàpies, Millares, Serrano etc).

★ **Museo de Armería (Museum of Arms and Armour)** ⊙ **(AZ)** – The well presented collection housed in a modern building traces the tradition and evolution of weaponry in the Basque country from prehistoric axes to early-20C pistols. Note the 15C-17C **armour**, including suits of 17C Japanese armour, and a model reproducing the Battle of Vitoria.

EXCURSIONS

Tour east of Vitoria – 25km/16mi. Leave Vitoria by ② on the town plan and take N 1 as far as junction 375.

Gaceo – Superb 14C **Gothic frescoes**★★ decorate the chancel of the church (**iglesia**) ⊙. The south wall shows hell in the form of a whale's gullet, the north, the Life of the Virgin with the Crucifixion and Last Judgement at the centre and a Trinity above. On the roof are scenes from the Life of Christ.

Alaiza – *Follow A 411 for 3km/2mi, turn right, then left after a few yards.* In 198
obscure **paintings**★ were discovered on the walls and roof of the church **(iglesia)** (
apse. The paintings, which probably date from the late 14C, consist of a serie
of strange rough red outlines representing castles, churches, soldiers and man
other personages. They remain an enigma.

Santuario de Estíbaliz – *10km/6mi east. Leave Vitoria by ② on the town pla
and then take A 132. Bear left after 4km/2.5mi.*
The shrine, a popular pilgrimage with the Basques, comprises a Late Romanesqu
sanctuary **(santuario)** ⊘. The south front has an attractive wall belfry. Inside, th
12C Romanesque statue of the Virgin has been restored.

Tour west of Vitoria – *105km/65mi. Leave Vitoria by Calle Beato Tomás c
Zumárraga* **(AY)** *then bear left onto A 3302.*

Mendoza – In the heart of the village stands the Castillo de Mendoza, a fortress wit
embrasures, a stout outer wall lacking battlements but flanked by four tower:
This former residence of the Duke of Infantado is now the **Museo de Heráldica Alaves**
(Álava Heraldry Museum) ⊘ with a collection of the coats of arms of all th
nobility of the region. The castle commands a view of the plateau.
Head south back towards N 1 and bear right onto A 2622 towards Pobes.

Salinas de Añana – The salt pans rising in tiers up the hillside in the form of a
amphitheatre next to the village produce a most unusual effect – water fror
several local springs is channelled between the ridges. The **church** contains
Flemish picture of the *Annunciation* with sensitively painted faces. At Easter a
the salt makers walk in a procession known traditionally as the *Quema de Juda:*
Continue west on A 2622.

Tuesta – The **Romanesque church**, dating from the 13C and later modified, has a
interesting portal with a pointed arch and a decoration of archivolts an
historiated capitals, one of which shows a man hunting a boar *(left)*. Above is th
Epiphany. Inside, note the naive wood sculpture of St Sebastian *(north wall of th
nave)* and a 14C figure of the Virgin.
Take A 2625 north towards Orduña.

Once over the **Puerto de Orduña** (Orduña Pass) (900m/2 953ft), a beautif
panorama★ opens up of the lush hollow in which Orduña town nestles; in th
distance are Amurrio and the Basque mountains *(viewpoint)*. The descent t
the plain is down a series of hairpin bends.
In Orduña, take A 2621 and return to Vitoria via Murguía.

GIBRALTAR

Population 30 000
Michelin map 446 X 13

Gibraltar, one of the last remaining outposts of the British Empire and
self-governing Crown Colony, lies at the southwest tip of Spain and the northea:
of the Straits of Gibraltar, only 24km/15mi away from the north African coas
The towering bulk of the rock on which it stands is an impressive and distinctiv
sight, clearly visible from the foothills of neighbouring Andalucía some miles of
For many visitors, the first contact with Gibraltar is likely to be the incredib
landing strip, which the main road into town actually crosses, physically linking th
territory with mainland Spain.

★ **The Rock of Gibraltar** – This gigantic monolith of Jurassic limestone forms
craggy promontory connected with mainland Spain in the north and stretchin
south into the straits. It covers an area of about 6.5km²/2.5sq mi (4.5km/3mi lor
and 1.4km/0.9mi at its widest), rising to 423m/1 388ft at its highest point, Moun
Misery. The east face of the Rock drops sheer into the sea, while the less stee
west face has been augmented by fill at the water's edge and forms the site c
the town.

Key to the Mediterranea
– Archeological discoverie
on Gibraltar, for example
Gorham's Cave *(not open t*
the public) on the east fac
of the Rock, testify t
100 000 years of h
man occupation, with per
ods of use by the Carthagir
ans, Phoenicians and eve
Neanderthal Man.

Eight years before the discovery in 1856 of
a 60 000-year-old skeleton in the Neander
Valley, east of Düsseldorf, Germany, a skull
of the same age, thought to be that of a
woman, was discovered on Gibraltar.
However, delays in publicizing the Gibraltar
findings meant that Gibraltar Woman is
known as Neanderthal Man.

The Rock of Gibraltar, considered by the Ancient Greeks to be one of the Pillars of Hercules marking the western boundary of the Classical world, was transformed into an Islamic citadel after the Moors invaded it under **Tarik-ibn-Zeyad** in AD 711. The Moorish general named the rock Jebel Tarik (Tarik's Mountain), from which Gibraltar takes its name, and built a castle on it, now in ruins but still known as the Moorish Castle.

Gibraltar was recaptured by Spain on 20 August 1462, the feast of St Bernard, who was duly elected patron saint of the town. It was not until Columbus made his great voyage of discovery in 1492, heading west through the legendary Pillars, that Gibraltar ceased to be regarded as marker of the edge of the world. During the War of Spanish Succession, Anglo-Dutch naval forces, under **Admiral Rooke**, captured the Rock in 1704. Gibraltar was officially ceded to Britain in the Treaty of Utrecht in 1713. The citadel guarding the Straits of Gibraltar has remained in British hands ever since, despite a number of attempts by the Spanish and the French to seize it. The most notable of these was the **Great Siege of 1779-83**, during which the garrison under General Elliot heroically resisted all efforts to starve or bomb them into submission. Most of the old city of Gibraltar was destroyed during this epic struggle, but the Rock lived up to its reputation of being impregnable. Gibraltar became a British Crown Colony in 1830 and served as a naval base during both World Wars a century later.

In 1967, Gibraltar's inhabitants voted resoundingly in favour of retaining their connection with Britain – by 12 138 votes to 44 – in a referendum proposing Spanish sovereignty. In 1969, Spain closed the border, cutting telephone lines and postal communications, a blockade it maintained until 1985. Gibraltar became a member of the European Economic Community in 1973 along with Britain. Despite the reopening of the border, it is not unusual for Spanish customs officials to undertake thorough searches of vehicles which can cause lengthy delays. Most of the inhabitants of Gibraltar are united in their opposition to Spanish rule and they continue with their aspirations for self-determination with an overwhelming desire to become

VISITORS' TIPS TO GIBRALTAR

Customs and other formalities – Gibraltar is a British Crown Colony. The border is open 24hr a day and there are no restrictions on the number of crossings made. Visitors must be in possession of a valid passport. Holders of UK passports and citizens of other EU countries do not need a visa. Other nationalities should check visa requirements with the appropriate authorities. Gibraltar is a duty (VAT) free shopping area.

Travel and accommodation – There are daily scheduled flights from London Heathrow, Gatwick and Manchester and a daily ferry service between Gibraltar and Morocco. Regular flights also operate to and from North Africa. Hotel and Bed and Breakfast accommodation is available, but there are no camp sites.

Money matters – The official currency is Gibraltar Government notes and coinage. Spanish pesetas are accepted in most establishments. The territory offers a full range of UK and international banks, and credit cards and traveller's cheques are widely accepted.

Language – The official language spoken on the Rock is English, but most people speak Spanish as a second language.

Time – Gibraltar has the same time as in the rest of Europe (one hour ahead of GMT).

Motoring – Driving is on the right and the wearing of seatbelts is recommended but not compulsory. Drivers must have a current driver's licence, vehicle registration documents, evidence of insurance and nationality plates.

Telephoning – The international telephone code for Gibraltar is 350 (to call Gibraltar from Spain, however, dial 9567 before the five-digit correspondent's number).

Tourist information – Further tourist information is available from the Gibraltar Information Bureau, Arundel Great Court, 179 Strand, London WC2R 1EH; ☎ (0044) (0)171 836 0777; fax (0044) (0)171 240 6612; Email: giblondon@aol.com

Web site – www.gibraltar.gi

Modern Gibraltar – Gibraltar's economy is based on a growing financial services sector and tourism, although the boom in these areas in the 1980s was slowed once recession hit Europe. The territory has retained its status as a free port and trade is based on transit and refuelling activities.
The naval and commercial ports, as well as the town with its mixture of English and Spanish style houses, pubs and shops, lie at the foot of the west face of the Rock. Numerous examples of Moorish architecture are still to be found, notably in the cathedral which has the ground plan of a mosque.

a British Crown dependency. With its people descended from a variety of races, religions and cultures, their identity shaped by years of resisting sieges, modern Gibraltar is an excellent example of a thriving, harmonious, multicultural society.

Tour of the Rock – The top of the Rock can be reached on foot, by cable-car and in official tour vehicles (*private cars are not allowed on the Upper Rock*). Go down Queensway and follow the signs to Upper Rock, designated a **nature reserve** ⊘ and home to some remarkable flora and fauna and a number of Gibraltar's most interesting historical sites. The road leads first to **St Michael's Cave**, a natural cavern once inhabited by Neolithic man which features some spectacular stalactites and stalagmites. From here, it is possible to walk to the top of the Rock (*1hr there and back*), from where there are excellent **views**★★ of both sides of the rock and of the Spanish and north African coasts.

The road continues to the **Apes' Den**, home of the famous Barbary Apes.

Barbary Apes

The origin of the apes, one of Gibraltar's best-known attractions, is unknown. Legend has it that British rule will last as long as the apes remain in residence on the Rock. When it looked as if they might become extinct in 1944, Churchill sent a signal ordering reinforcements. The ape colony has since flourished – there are currently just under 200 of them. They are renowned for their charm and highly inquisitive natures. The apes, in reality tailless monkeys, are the protégés of the Gibraltar Regiment.

Visitors interested in military history should not miss the **Great Siege Tunnels**, excavated in 1779 to make it possible to mount guns on the north face of the Rock creating a defence system still impressive for its ingenuity. A military heritage centre is housed in Princess Caroline's Battery. Finally there are the ancient ruins of the **Moorish Castle** and the northern defences dominating the hillside.

Back down in town, the **Gibraltar Museum** ⊘ contains extensive collections on local military and natural history. It also houses the well-preserved **Moorish Baths**. The **Alameda Gardens** ⊘, recently restored and one of the most beautiful botanic gardens in the Mediterranean, are home to many interesting and exotic plants including Canary Islands dragon trees, cacti, succulents and a variety of Mediterranean vegetation. Gibraltar is home to some 600 species of flowering plants which flourish in the sub-tropical climate, including a few unique to the Rock, such as its national flower, the Gibraltar Candytuft.

For those interested in seeing more examples of Gibraltar's plant and bird-life, the **Mediterranean Steps**, leading from Jew's Gate (good view of the other Pillar of Hercules, Jebel Musa in Morocco) round the south of the Rock and up the east face of the Rock to the summit (*3hr walk from Jew's Gate to summit; wear good boots as some sections are quite steep*), makes a fascinating walk.

Straits of GIBRALTAR

Andalucía (Cádiz)

Michelin map 446 X 13

The straits, gateway to the Mediterranean and a mere 14km/9mi wide at the narrowest point, have always played an important strategic role in the history of the local towns.

Algeciras – Population 86 042. The Arabs arrived in Algeciras from Africa in 711 and remained until 1344, naming the town Al Djezirah, the island, after the Isla Verde, the Green Island, now joined to the mainland. The Bahía de Algeciras has always served the dual purpose of safe anchorage and vantage point overlooking the Straits of Gibraltar. Algeciras is Spain's busiest passenger port with crossings to Tangier and Ceuta several times a day (3.5 million passengers annually).

It is from across the bay that you get the world famous **views**★★ of the Rock of Gibraltar.

Tarifa – Population 15 220. Tarifa stands on the most southerly point of the Iberian Peninsula. Atlantic and Mediterranean air masses converge over the area giving Tarifa the sea breezes ideal for windsurfing. It has become one of Europe's major centres for the sport.

Castillo – In 1292 this fortress, which had been taken by the Christians, was under the command of Guzmán el Bueno whose son was captured by the Moors. When Guzmán had to choose between the death of his child and the surrender of his town, he replied by throwing his dagger to the enemy for the execution.

The Muralla Sur (south wall) commands a fine **view**★ of the Straits of Gibraltar and the coast of Morocco only 13.5km/8mi away.

GIRONA/GERONA★★

Catalunya (Girona) – Population 70 409

Michelin map 443 G 38

rona stands on a promontory at the confluence of the Ter and Onyar rivers. Its
rategic site has been so coveted and its history so eventful that it has become
own as the city of a thousand sieges. Its ramparts were built and rebuilt by the
erians, the Romans and throughout the Middle Ages. Charlemagne's troops are
scribed, in the *Song of Roland (Canción de Rolando)*, as assaulting the city; in
309, under General Álvarez de Castro's command, Girona resisted attacks from
apoleon's troops for more than seven months.

rona and Judaism – Girona's Jewish community, in the old quarter around **Calle
la Força** (BY), became famous in the Middle Ages for its prestigious Cabalistic School.
is past can be felt in atmospheric narrow alleyways like those of Cúndaro and Sant
orenç. In this latter is the Centre Bonastruc ça Porta (**BY A**) which is given over to
e town's Jewish history (exhibitions, lectures etc).

GIRONA/GERONA

Álvarez de Castro	AZ 2	Devesa (Pg. de la)	AY 14	Rei Ferran el Católic	BY 33
Argenteria	BY 3	Eduard Marquína (Pl. de)	AZ 15	Rei Martí (Pujada del)	BY 34
Ballesteries	BY 4	General Fournàs	BY 16	Reina Isabel la Católica	BZ 36
Bellaire	BY 6	General Peralta (Pg. del)	BZ 17	Reina Joana (Pg. de la)	BY 37
Berenguer Carnicer	AY 7	Joaquim Vayreda	AY 18	Sant Cristófol	BY 39
Bonastruc de Porta	AY 9	Juli Garreta	AZ 19	Sant Daniel	BY 40
Carme	BZ 10	Llibertat (Rambla de la)	BZ 23	Sant Doménec (Pl. de)	BY 42
Ciutadans	BZ 12	Nou	AZ	Sant Feliu (Pujada de)	BY 44
Cundaro	BY 13	Nou del Teatre	BZ 27	Sant Francesc (Av. de)	AZ 45
		Olivai i Prat	BY 26	Sant Pere (Pl. de)	BY 48
		Palafrugell	BY 28	Santa Clara	ABYZ
		Pedreres (Pujada de les)	BZ 29	Santa Eugénia	AZ 49
		Ramon Folch (Av.)	AY 31	Ultónia	AZ 53

A Centre Bonastruc ça Porta
E Fontana d'Or
F Convent de Sant Doménec
K Farinera Teixidor
L Hospici
M¹ Museu d'Art
M² Museu del Cinema
N Pia Almonia
R Collegiata de Sant Feliu
S Banys Àrabs
U Edifici de les Àligues

FORÇA VELLA (OLD TOWN) *3hr*

From footbridges over the Onyar (**BY**), there are views of the picturesque oran and ochre-coloured buildings along the river banks, the cathedral tower and spire of Sant Feliu.

Narrow alleys lead up to the cathedral which is preceded by a vast flight 90 steps, known as the **Escaleras de la Pera**. The 14C **Pia Almoina** building (**BY N**) the right is an elegant example of Gothic architecture.

* **Catedral** ⊙ (**BY**) – The Baroque façade has been designed like a sto altarpiece with a single huge oculus above. The rest of the building is Goth the chancel (1312) is surrounded by an ambulatory and radiating chape early in the 15C the decision was taken to add only a single **aisle★★** but to ma it outstandingly spacious (it is the largest Gothic nave in the world) and lig The two parts of the building have a similar, powerful, unadorned sty decoration having been restricted to the chapel arches, triforium niches a windows.

In the chancel, beneath a silver canopy symbolising the sky, is a silv gilt embossed 14C **altarpiece★**, highlighted with enamelwork, which tra the Life of Christ. Among the chapels, many of which contain works of a that of Sant Honorat (First north chapel), is outstanding for the tomb, in Gothic niche, with three superimposed registers, of Bishop Bernard de F (d 1457).

★★ **Tesoro** ⊙ – The treasury houses an extraordinarily rich collection of religious a including one of the most beautiful copies of the **Beatus★★**, St Joh Commentary on the Apocalypse, written in the 8C. These miniatures, dated 97 by the monk Emeteri and the nun Eude, are notable for the bright colours a lively expressions used to illustrate the series of fantastic beasts. They Caliphate influenced and show traces of Visigothic decoration. There is a 1 Virgin of the Cathedral (Virgen de la Seu) in the same room. Some splen church plate is displayed in the rooms that follow, including a 14C enamel cr and, of particular interest, the 10C embossed silver **Hixem Casket**, a fine exam of Caliphate art.

The end room contains the famous **Tapiz de la Creación★★★** (Tapestry of Creation), a unique work dating from about 1100. It is a marvellously delica embroidery with well preserved colours which shows Christ in Majesty in a circu area at the centre, surrounded by the different stages of creation. The four win fill the corners.

Tapestry of the creation

Claustro – The 12C-13C Romanesque cloisters, irregular in shape, with a double line of columns, date, like the 11C Torre de Carlomagno (Charlemagne Tower) which dominates them, from the former Romanesque cathedral. The beautiful friezes on the pillars at the gallery corners and centres, illustrate, in most cases, scenes from Genesis. Note the finely-drawn outlines, the delicate draperies and the serenity of the faces.

Museu d'Art de Girona ⊘ (BY **M¹**) – The museum is housed in the Palacio Episcopal and contains a comprehensive collection of art covering periods from the Romanesque to the 20C. The Romanesque section includes a 10C-11C altar from Sant Pere de Rodes of wood and stone faced with silver, and a 12C-13C **beam from Cruïlles★**. The Gothic section has a lovely alabaster Virgin of Besalù dating from the 15C. Among the richly decorated altarpieces displayed in the Throne Room is that of **Sant Miquel de Cruïlles★★** by Luis Borrassá (15C), one of the most beautiful works of Catalan Gothic art. Note the splendid Púbol **altarpiece★**, executed in the Gothic style by Bernat Martorell in 1437. The Sant Feliu altarpiece by Juan de Borgoña marks the transition between the Gothic and Renaissance styles.

Colegiata de Sant Feliu (BY **R**) – This former collegiate church outside the town walls must originally have been a martyry built over the tombs of St Narcissus, Bishop of Girona, and St Felix, both patrons of the city.
A Gothic church with a tall east end was later built on the Romanesque foundations. In the apse are eight **early Christian sarcophagi★** let into the walls. Two have outstanding carvings – on the right, the abduction of Proserpine, opposite, a spirited **lion hunt★**.

Baños árabes (Arab Baths) ⊘ (BY **S**) – These late 12C-baths were built in accordance with Muslim tradition. They consist of a central corridor giving onto four rooms: the **apoditerium**, a relaxation area with a central pool surrounded by columns supporting a lantern; the **frigidarium**, designed for cold baths; the **tepidarium**, a warm room where one could stay away from the intense heat or cold; finally, the **caldarium**, an area for hot baths.

Passeig Arqueològic (Archeological Promenade) (BY) – Steps opposite the baths lead to gardens at the foot of the ramparts from which you can look along the Ter Valley.

Monasterio de Sant Pere de Galligants ⊘ (BY) – Not far from Sant Nicolau, with its clover leaf apse, stands the Romanesque church of Sant Pere. It has been repeatedly fortified; its east end appears embedded in the town walls and the belfry once served as a watchtower.
The church and cloisters house the **Museu Arqueològic de Girona** ⊘ which has a collection of finds from excavations in the province. 13C-14C Hebrew memorial plaques are displayed in the cloisters while in the former sacristy there is Roman art from Empúries and the magnificent 4C **tomb of Las Estaciones★** (the seasons; autumn in particular).

ADDITIONAL SIGHTS

Museu del Cinema ⊘ (AZ **M²**) – Tomás Mallol's collection forms the nucleus of this original museum dedicated to the history of cinema. Visitors are taken on a journey to the world of illusion where they are able to admire the very first moving silhouettes, delicate light boxes and the inventions which have led to the extraordinary developments in the film industry.

EXCURSIONS

Casa-Museu Castell Gala Dalí ⊘ – *16km/10mi east. Leave Girona along C 255, proceed towards La Bisbal d'Empordà, then turn right in the direction of Púbol. Leave your car in the public car park (free) and take one of the narrow streets leading to the castle.*
In 1970, Salvador Dalí bought the 14C castle that had once belonged to the barons of Púbol and gave it to his wife Gala as a present. The visit is full of surprises. In a Surrealist ambiance, you will discover a host of unusual objects, all testifying to the strong devotion the painter felt for his wife. In the Heraldic Gallery on the first floor, note the huge fresco adorning the ceiling, painted by Dalí himself. Gala's bedroom *(Room 3)* features a strange chess game, in which the pawns are replicas of human fingers. On the second floor *(Room 7)* you can admire some of the clothes specially made for Dalí's favourite muse, along with designs by famous names from the fashion world: Chanel, Pierre Cardin, Christian Dior and even Dalí. Shrouded in a solemn atmosphere, the basement *(Room 11)* houses the mortal remains of Gala, together with various sculptures and a stuffed giraffe.

From Girona to Olot *55km/34mi – about 2hr*

Leave Girona by ① on plan.

* **Banyoles** – This delightful town stands beside a **lake**★ carrying the same nam used as an important venue for nautical events. Among its many archeologi artefacts, the **Museu Arqueològic Comarcal**★ ⓥ, set up in a Gothic building, displa the famous Jaw of Banyoles, dating back to the Lower Paleolithic era. On arcaded main square (13C) a lively, popular market is held every Wednesday A road 8km/5mi long circles the lake and, on the left bank, passes in front of 13C **Iglesia de Santa Maria de Porqueres**★ ⓥ. The interior consists of a single na separated from the apse by a huge central arch: the capitals and tops of columns are carved with curious-looking characters.

Besalù bridge

* **Besalù** – From the 11C to the 12C, Besalù was the capital of a county t stretched from Figueres to the Ter Valley. At the town entrance, spanning Fluvià river, is an old Roman **fortified bridge**★, rebuilt during the medieval peri Of its past, Besalù has retained the **ancient city**★★ of Romanesque origin, w vestiges of ramparts and many medieval buildings with pretty paired windo The Romanesque **Iglesia de Sant Pere**★ ⓥ presents a fine window flanked by lions an ambulatory – an unusual feature for the area. Arab baths, referred to **Mikwa** ⓥ can be found in the old Jewish quarter, cut across by narrow, wind streets.

* **Castellfollit de la Roca** – The village is perched on a basalt pile 60m/197ft hi in the midst of a spectacular volcanic setting that is part of the **Parc Natural d Garrotxa**★. Following the orogenic movements triggered off by the subsidence the Empordà (Ampurdán), the Olot plain became subject to volcanic eruption. park features 30 volcanic cones of the Stromboli type and more than 20 ba piles, which make for a somewhat surprising landscape.

* **Olot** – Surrounded by mountains, many of which are volcanic craters, Olo situated at the junction of three valleys formed by the Fluvià river. An import centre for both farming and crafts, it is well known for its cattle fairs, as wel for its production of religious imagery and miniature figurines for Christm cribs.
Two sights deserve a visit. First, the 18C neo-Classical **Iglesia de Sant Esteve**★ ⓥ w its Baroque front and porch: it houses a fine canopy, a Baroque retable a an unusual painting by El Greco – **Christ Bearing the Cross**★. Second, the Mu **Comarcal de la Garrotxa**★ ⓥ, set up in a former hospice, that displays a fine coi tion of paintings and drawings by 19C and 20C Catalan artists. Note the splen **Modernist façade**★★ of the Casa Solà-Morales, which we owe to Domènec Montaner.

GRANADA ★★★

Andalucía – Population 287 864
Michelin map 446 U 19

ranada has everything: prestigious and exceedingly beautiful Moorish buildings,
minous skies and a luxuriantly green **setting**★★ over which the city, built on three
lls at the centre of a wide plain or *vega*, looks out to the snow-capped Sierra
evada on the horizon. From the Albaicín, Sacromonte and Alhambra hills, there
e also infinitely varied views, particularly from the first, of the red-walled
hambra.
eligious festivals are lively, colourful events, especially those held in Holy Week and
Corpus Christi. The city also holds an annual Music and Dance Festival in June and
ly.

WHERE TO STAY

UDGET HOTELS

otel Maciá (**BY** ❻) – *Plaza Nueva, 4.* ☎ *958 22 75 36, fax 958 22 75 33.*
4 *rooms.*
his recently-renovated hotel has a whitewashed façade and small balconies.
he rooms are carpeted and simply furnished with wicker furniture, although
e bathrooms are rather antiquated.

otel Universal (**AZ** ❸) – *Recogidas, 16.* ☎ *958 26 00 16, fax 958 26 32 29.*
6 *rooms.*
ypical building from the "expansion" period with a somewhat charmless
çade. Functional rooms and lounge area. Its main advantages are its price
d central location.

UR SELECTION

mérica (**DY** ❻) – *Real de la Alhambra, 53.* ☎ *958 22 74 71, fax 958 22 74 71.*
2 *rooms.*
lthough more modest than the neighbouring parador, this small, secluded
tel has an enviable position between the gardens of the Alhambra. It has a
ne terrace, well-appointed rooms and an attractive staircase in the reception
ea. Peace and quiet guaranteed.

lacio de Santa Inés (**CX** ❶) – *Cueta de Santa Inés, 9.* ☎ *958 22 23 62,*
x *958 22 24 65. 6 rooms and 5 suites.*
mall hotel in a 16C Mudéjar-style building in the Albaicín quarter, at the foot
f the Alhambra. Its sombre, yet attractive, inner patio still displays the
emains of some Renaissance frescoes (16C). Spacious, comfortable
edrooms.

REAT YOURSELF!

arador de San Francisco (**DY**) – *Real de la Alhambra.* ☎ *958 22 14 40,*
x *958 22 22 64. 34 rooms.*
his magnificent parador is housed in the former Convento de San Francisco
6C). Its position within the grounds of the Alhambra, the views of the
eneralife gardens and the Sierra Nevada have made it a retreat worthy of the
nousand and One Nights.

EATING OUT

UR SELECTION

ariquilla – *Lope de Vega, 2.* ☎ *958 52 16 32.*
simple restaurant which is excellent value for money.

alatino – *Gran Vía de Colón, 29.* ☎ *958 80 08 03.*
he decor in the Galatino is very 1970s. Lots of artificial light and a chess-
ard design floor with many curves. Something different near the city
entre.

TAPAS

lar del Toro – *Hospital de Santa Ana, 12.*
good address for evening tapas on a pleasant patio.

Trastienda – *Placeta de Cuchilleros, 11.*
nis old shop is the perfect place to enjoy some delicious *jamón ibérico*.

odega Castañeda – *Almireceros, 1-3.*
timeless bar with good tapas and superb *finos* and *manzanillas*.

hikito – *Plaza del Campillo, 9.*
ne of Granada's great institutions with tapas galore.

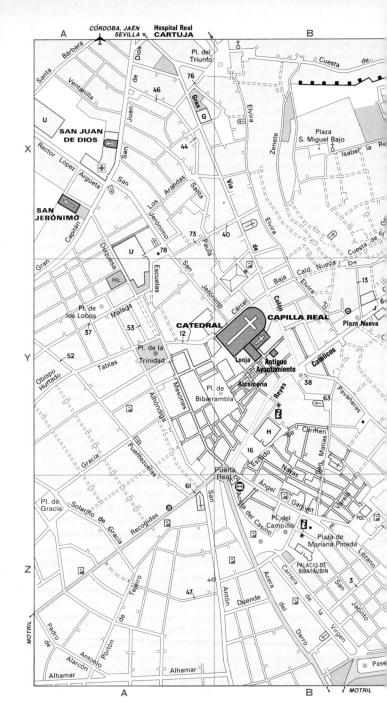

HISTORICAL NOTES

Granada began to gain importance in the 11C when the caliphate of Córdoba declined became the capital of a kingdom founded by the Almoravids who were ousted a cent later by the Almohads. It was in the 13C, however, that Granada reached the height of glory when Muslims from Córdoba, which fell to the Christians in 1236, sought refu here. In 1238, a new dynasty, that of the **Nasrids**, was founded by Mohammed I el-Ahmar who acknowledged allegiance to Ferdinand III. For the next two and a h centuries (1238 to 1492) the kingdom of Granada flourished, becoming a symbol economic, cultural and artistic prosperity, with magnificent buildings like the Alhamb

The fall of Granada – In the 15C, as more of the Muslim-controlled territory Spain was being lost to the Christians, the Catholic monarchs were looking conquer Granada, one of its last bastions. A quarrel in the royal harem inadverten

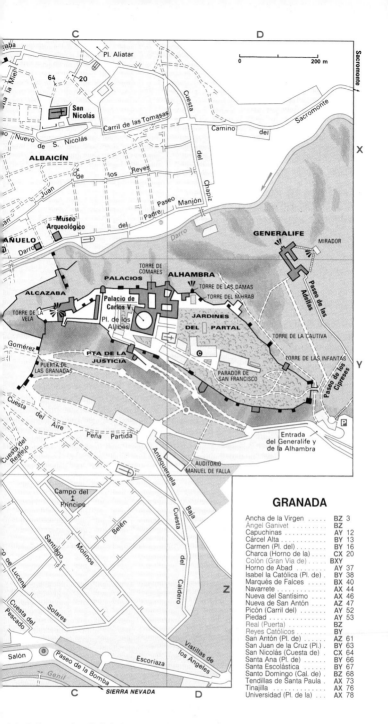

GRANADA

Ancha de la Virgen	BZ	3
Ángel Ganivet	BZ	
Capuchinas	AY	12
Cárcel Alta	BY	13
Carmen (Pl. del)	BY	16
Charca (Horno de la)	CX	20
Colón (Gran Vía de)	BXY	
Horno de Abad	AY	37
Isabel la Católica (Pl. de)	BY	38
Marqués de Falces	BX	40
Navarrete	AX	44
Nueva del Santísimo	AX	46
Nueva de San Antón	AZ	47
Picón (Carril del)	AY	52
Piedad	AY	53
Real (Puerta)	BZ	
Reyes Católicos	BY	
San Antón (Pl. de)	AZ	61
San Juan de la Cruz (Pl.)	BY	63
San Nicolás (Cuesta de)	CX	64
Santa Ana (Pl. de)	BY	66
Santa Escolástica	BY	67
Santo Domingo (Cal. de)	BZ	68
Tendillas de Santa Paula	AX	73
Tinajilla	AX	76
Universidad (Pl. de la)	AX	78

sisted them: the Caliph became enamoured of a Christian girl, Zoraya, for hom he considered repudiating his queen, Aisha, by whom he already had a son, **abdil**. Aisha fled with her son but soon returned, to depose the infatuated monarch d set the Boy King – El Rey Chico – upon the throne. As the great Moorish milies divided in allegiance, Ferdinand of Aragón seized the opportunity to pture the young king and force his submission. Intrigue and sieges followed for veral months; the powerful **Abencerrajes**, accused of desiring the downfall of abdil and of having sold themselves to the Christians, were one of several families see some of their leading members (36 in this case) massacred at a palace ception.

2 January 1492, after a six-month siege, the Catholic Monarchs had entered anada; Boabdil gave them the keys of the city and went into exile. As he looked ck on Granada from the Motril road his mother is said to have rounded on him:

189

"You weep like a woman for what you could not hold as a man"; the spot rema
known as the Moor's Sigh – **Suspiro del Moro**. After 781 years the Moorish dominat
of Spain was ended.
Granada continued to flourish in the Renaissance which followed the Reconqu
although the city's fortunes suffered an eclipse during the ruthless suppression
the Las Alpujarras revolt in 1570.

Great Granadines – **Alonso Cano** (1601-67), architect, sculptor and painter, was
moving spirit behind the blossoming of art in 17C Granada. His art, eschew
Renaissance tradition, turned towards Classicism; he banished pathos from
sculpture and was in favour of restrained emotion. **Pedro de Mena** (1628-1688),
follower, carved realistic sculptures on religious themes.

Eugenia de Montijo, future wife of Napoleon III (Empress Eugénie: 1853) was borr
Granada in 1826, daughter of a grandee and, on her mother's side, granddaugh
of William Kirkpatrick, Scots by birth, American by nationality and consul at Mála

Federico García Lorca, poet and dramatist, talented musician, friend of Dalí and Buñ
was born 20km/12mi from Granada in Fuentevaqueros in 1899 (he died in 19.
shot by Franco's soldiers at the outbreak of the Spanish Civil War).

Modern Granada – Granada is the capital of an agricultural province (cereals, be
fruit and beef) as well as an archbishopric and university town. Its main resourc
tourism.
There is a striking contrast between the old quarters of the town east of **Plaza Nu**
(**BY**), a haven of peace and greenery on the Alhambra and Albaicín hills, and the no
bustling lower town with its network of shopping streets and the pedestrian quar
around the cathedral set between the city's two main avenues, **Gran Vía de Colón** (**AB**
and **calle de los Reyes Católicos** (**BY**). Restaurants in the town centre serve Granad
speciality – a dish of ham and beans called *habas con jamón*.

★★★ **THE ALHAMBRA AND THE GENERALIFE** ⊘ *half a day*

The architecture of Granada – Muslim architecture in Spain reached its clim
in Granada where it becomes the ultimate expression of aesthetic refinement
a sophisticated civilization at its moment of decline. The Nasrid princes built
the moment, with no thought of posterity: beneath the fabulous decoration
ill-assorted bricks, plaster and rubble; each sovereign razed the monuments of
predecessor to provide a site for his own new palace which would retain only
architectural principle of grouping all rooms round a central *patio*.

Decoration was the main concern. Although wall hangings and carpets h
disappeared and little furniture remains, the sculpture covering walls and ceili
everywhere reveals an art without equal since. This sculptural decoration is
fact, stuccowork, both outside and in. The finely modelled plaster, sometim
pierced, is worked in patterns in a low relief of flat planes to catch the lig
another type of decoration was made by building up layers of plaster which w
then cut away to form stalactites *(mocárabes)*. This type of ornament, pain
in bright colours and even gilded in places, covered capitals, cornice mouldin
arches, pendentives and entire cupolas.

Ceramic tiles were used to provide a geometric decoration for most of the walls: *alicatados* formed a colourful marquetry, with lines of arabesque motifs making star designs; *azulejos* gave colour, different hues being separated by a thin raised fillet or a black line *(cuerda seca)*. Calligraphic decoration employed the so-called Andalusian cursive which was particularly elegant; the more decoratively complicated Cufic was reserved for religious aphorisms which appear framed in scrollwork.

The Alhambra (CDY)

The beautiful Calat Alhambra (Red Castle) must be one of the most remarkable fortresses ever built. It stands at the top of a wooded hill commanding views of the town, the bleak Sacromonte heights, nearby hillsides and gardens.

The Alhambra's outer perimeter is entered through the Puerta de Las Granadas or the Pomegranate Gateway built by Emperor Charles V. A paved footpath leads through the **shrubbery**★ to the massive **Puerta de la Justicia**★ (Justice Gateway), built so that its tower forms part of the inner ramparts defending the castle terrace.

Palacios Nazaríes (Nasrid Palace) – The Nasrid Palace was built around two courtyards, the Patio de los Arrayanes and the Patio de los Leones, in the 14C. Its richness and variety and the originality of its decoration defy description. The tour begins in the **Mexuar**, part of the first palace, which was used for government and judicial administration. After the Reconquest, it was converted into a chapel and lengthened by the addition of an oratory from which there is a good **view**★ of the Albaicín. Cross the **Patio del Cuarto Dorado** (1), in which the south wall, protected by a remarkable carved wood cornice, exemplifies the essentials of Granada art: windows are surrounded by panels covered with every variety of stucco and tile decoration. Opposite is the **Cuarto Dorado** (Golden Room), a wide room with tiled panelling, fine stucco work and a beautiful wooden ceiling.

Adjoining this is the beautiful oblong **Patio de los Arrayanes** (Myrtle Courtyard). A narrow central pool banked by myrtles runs the length of the court and reflects the massive bulk of the **Torre de Comares** (Comares Tower) which contrasts sharply with the light, slender porticoes that give onto the **Sala de la Barca** (a name arising from the Arabic word *barakha* meaning benediction) and the **Salón de Embajadores** (Hall of Ambassadors). This, the jewel of the Alhambra, was the audience chamber of the emirs. It has a magnificent domed cedarwood ceiling and is lit by bay windows offering remarkable **views**★★ of the surrounding countryside. *Azulejos* and stucco bearing inscriptions, some from the Koran, others in honour of various princes, complete the decoration.

Another opening off the Patio de los Arrayanes leads to the second palace, the residence of the royal family, at the heart of which stands the justly famous **Patio de los Leones** (Lion Courtyard) built by Mohammed V. Twelve rough stone lions support an ancient low-lying fountain while delicate arcades of slender columns around the court lead to the main State apartments.

The **Sala de los Abencerrajes**, so called after Boabdil had ordered the family massacre and piled the heads into the room's central basin, has a stalactite ceiling and a splendid star-shaped lantern cupola. Adorning the end of the **Sala de los Reyes** (Kings'

E. Graney/STOCK PHOTOS

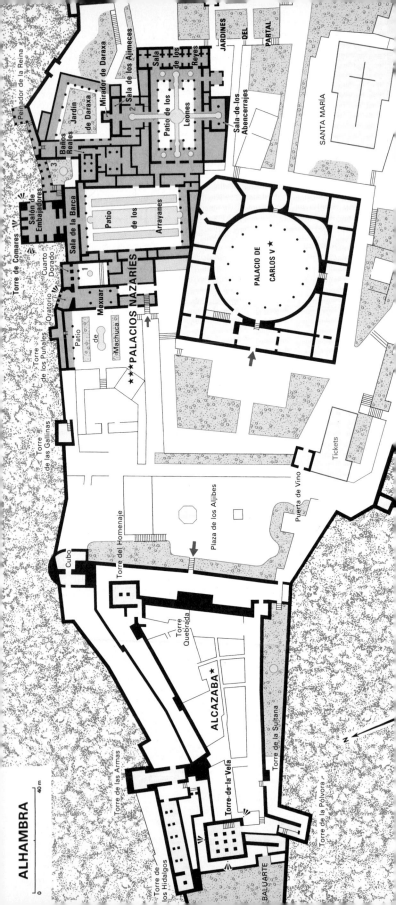

ALHAMBRA

0   40 m

★★★PALACIOS NAZARÍES

Peinador de la Reina

Mirador de Daraxa

Sala de los Ajimeces

Sala de los Reyes

Jardín de Daraxa

2 Sala de los Ajimeces

Baños Reales

Patio de los Leones

Sala-de-los-Abencerrajes

JARDINES DEL PARTAL

SANTA MARÍA

Salón de Embajadores

Torre de Comares

Sala de la Barca

Patio de los Arrayanes

Cuarto Dorado

Oratorio

Mexuar

Torre de los Puñales

Torre de las Gallinas

Patio de Machuca

PALACIOS NAZARÍES

PALACIO DE CARLOS V ★

Cubo

Torre del Homenaje

Tickets

Plaza de los Aljibes

Puerta de Vino

Torre de las Armas

Torre Quebrada

Torre de los Hidalgos

ALCAZABA ★

Torre de-la-Vela

Torre de la Sultana

Torre de la Pólvora

BALUARTE

N

Patio de los Leones

Chamber) are alcoves containing vaulting painted to illustrate the pastimes of Moorish and Christian princes – the style is so atypical that it is not known whether the artist was a Christian working for the sultan before the Reconquest or later. The **Sala de las Dos Hermanas** (Hall of the Two Sisters) **(2)**, named after the two large white identical marble slabs in the pavement, is renowned for its honeycomb cupola vaulting. Beyond are the **Sala de los Ajmeres** and the **Mirador de Daraxa** (Daraxa Mirador), both equally resplendent. Leave the palace building and enter the Partal gardens through which you reach the green and silent Daraxa garden. A gallery leads to the **Patio de la Reja** (Window Grille Court) **(3)**. Steps go down to the **Baños Reales** (Royal Baths) with their sumptuous multicoloured decoration where the light enters through small star-shaped apertures.

Cross the Daraxa garden to the Partal gardens.

Gardens and perimeter towers – Spreading to the east of the royal palaces are the terraced Jardines de Partal which descend to the gracefully *artesonado* porticoed **Torre de las Damas** (Lady Tower). From this early 14C building, which is as ornately decorated inside as the royal palaces, there are views of the Darro directly below, of Albaicín and Sacromonte.

The Torre de Mihrab on the right, is a former Nasrid oratory – a rarity since the princes were not notably pious. The Torre de la Cautiva and Torre de las Infantas (Captive's and Infantas' towers) are sumptuously decorated inside.

Enter the Palacio de Carlos V from the Partal gardens.

Palacio de Carlos V (Emperor Charles V's Palace) – The Nasrid palaces were not considered sufficiently majestic to serve as the imperial residence. In 1526, Pedro Machuca, who studied under Michelangelo, was commissioned with the design of a suitable palace to be financed from a tax levied on the Moors. Their uprising in 1568 interrupted the building and the palace was completed at a much later date. This purely Classical style building, always thought one of the most successful creations of the Renaissance period in Spain, is the only construction of Machuca's

to remain. Although in comparison with the Nasrid palaces the palace may at fi
appear somewhat lacking, its grandeur soon becomes apparent, so perfect are
lines, so dignified its appearance, so simple its plan of a circle within a square. T
palace contains two museums:

Museo Hispano-musulmán (Hispano-Moorish Museum) – The museum is in roo
overlooking the Patio de los Arrayanes and the Patio del Cuarto Dorado a
displays objects from the Alcázar: fragments of sculpture, perfume burne
braziers and vases. Outstanding objects include the famous **blue amphora**
1.32m/52in high, the Nasrid masterpiece which stood for years in the Sala de
Dos Hermanas, and a 10C ablutions basin adorned with lions chasing stags a
ibex.

Museo de Bellas Artes (Fine Arts Museum) – Religious sculpture and paintings of 1
16C to the 18C predominate, with works by Diego de Siloé, Pedro de Me
Vicente Carducho, Alonso Cano as well as a magnificent still life, **Thistle and Carrots**
by Brother Juan Sánchez Cotán.

★ **Alcazaba** – The Alcazaba has existed since the 9C and is by far the oldest part
the Alhambra. The two towers overlooking the Plaza de los Aljibes (Cistern Cou
date back to the 13C. The lofty Torre de la Vela (Watchtower) command
magnificent **panorama**★★ of the palace, the Generalife, Sacromonte, Granada a
the Sierra Nevada.

★★ The Generalife (DX)

One of the most enjoyable aspects of the 14C Generalife, the summer pal
of the kings of Granada, is its cool, green, terraced water gardens. Both 1
Patio de los Cipreses (Cypress Alley) and the Patio de las Adelfas (Oleande
which are at their best in July and August, lead to the palace, a building
modest dimensions surrounding an elongated court, its axis marked by a narr
channel of water. This **Patio de la Acequia** (Canal Court), bordered by roses, h
a graceful pavilion at either end. Linking these pavilions are, on the left, a gall
and on the right, the palace apartments. The *mirador* commands a fine **view**
Albaicín.

CATHEDRAL QUARTER 45min

★★ **Capilla Real (Chapel Royal)** ⏱ (BY) – The Catholic monarchs wanted to be buried
the site of their definitive victory against the Moors and ordered the construct
of this chapel by Enrique Egas. It was begun in 1506 and completed un
Emperor Charles V in 1521. Its unity of style, richness of decoration and the
objects it contains, lend the chapel a unique interest. To enter (*by the south do*
cross the courtyard of the old **Lonja** (Exchange) (BY), also designed by Egas. T
chapel's south front has an elegant Renaissance façade of two superimpos
arcades with turned columns; opposite is the early 18C **Ayuntamiento** (town h
(BY) in Granada Baroque, built on the former 14C Muslim *madraza* or univers
of Yusuf I.

Every conceivable decoration of the Isabelline style is to be seen inside the chap
ribbed vaulting, walls emblazoned with the arms of the Catholic monarchs, 1
yoke and fasces (revived in 1934 by the Falange), a monogram of the initials
their first names, and the eagle of St John. Beautiful wrought-iron grilles clo
two chapels. The chancel, closed by a **screen**★ by Master Bartolomé, contains 1
mausoleums★★★ of the Catholic monarchs, on the right, and of Philip 1
Handsome and Juana the Mad, the parents of Charles V, on the left. The first v
carved by Fancelli in Genoa in 1517, the second, which is magnificent
proportion and workmanship, by Bartolomé Ordóñez between 1519 and 15
(the sarcophagi are in the crypt). The high altar **retable**★ (1520) is one of the fi
to be free of all Gothic influence; the lower register of the predella depicts the si
of Granada.

Museo – *Access by the north arm of the transept.* Numerous objects of incalcula
historical value can be seen in this museum which is situated in the sacris
Among exhibits on display are **Queen Isabel's sceptre and crown, King Ferdinand's swo**
plus an outstanding **collection of paintings**★★ by Flemish (Rogier Van der Weyd
Memling), Italian (Perugino, Botticelli) and Spanish (Bartolomé Bermejo, Pe
Berruguete) artists. In the rear of the museum can be found the famous **Tript**
of the Passion by the Fleming Dirk Bouts and two sculptures of the Cathe
monarchs at prayer by Felipe Vigarny.

★ **Catedral** ⏱ (BY) – *Enter from Gran Vía de Colón.* The cathedral illustrates 1
development of architecture in Granada between the 16C and the 17C. C
struction, in this case, was entrusted to Diego de Siloé in 1528 and continued af
his death in 1563 according to his plans, apart from the façade (1667), over
by three tall arcades, which is by Alonso Cano.

The **Capilla Mayor**★ is the first thing you notice inside, for its plan and decoration are surprising. Siloé designed a rotunda circled by an ambulatory, the whole cleverly linked to the nave and four àisles of the basilica. The rotunda combines two superimposed orders, the uppermost with paintings by Alonso Cano of the Life of the Virgin and beautiful 16C stained glass in paired windows. Marking the rotunda entrance on twin facing panels, are the figures at prayer of the Catholic monarchs by Pedro de Mena and, in a medallion by Alonso Cano, those of Adam and Eve.

The impressive **organ** in the nave dates from about 1750 and was made by Leonardo of Ávila.

The finely carved Isabelline doorway in the south transept is the original **north portal**★ of the older Capilla Real.

Alcaicería (BY) – The area, which has been reconstructed and is now a kind of *souk* or oriental bazaar with craft and souvenir shops, was a silk market in Moorish times.

ADDITIONAL SIGHTS

★ **Cartuja** ⊘ – The Carthusian monastery is northwest of town, near the university. Leave the centre of town on the Gran Vía de Colón or the calle San Juan de Dios (AX). Go through the cloisters into the church, exuberantly decorated with Baroque stucco in 1662. At the back of the apse is the early 18C Holy of Holies (Sancta Sanctorum), a *camarín* decorated with multicoloured marble; beneath the cupola, painted in false relief, is a marble Sagrario which contains the Tabernacle. The **sacristy**★★ (1727-64) is an outstanding example of Late Baroque. Some call it the Christian Alhambra on account of the intricate white stuccowork on the walls and vaulting, where straight lines and curves form never-ending patterns on mouldings and cornices. This stucco ornamentation contrasts sharply with the cupola paintings and the strong colours of the marble ogee moulding. The magnificent door and cedarwood furnishings inlaid with tortoiseshell, mother-of-pearl and silver, are by a Carthusian monk, Brother José Manuel Vásquez.

★ **Iglesia de San Juan de Dios** ⊘ **(AX)** – The Church of St John of God is one of Granada's most important churches. The interior, access to which is through a beautiful carved mahogany doorway, is magnificent in both its richness and its stylistic uniformity. Behind the massive Churrigueresque altarpiece of gilded wood, is a lavishly decorated *camarín* which contains the funerary urn of **San Juan de Dios**. He founded the Order of Knights Hospitallers and died in Granada in 1550.

★ **Monasterio de San Jerónimo** ⊘ **(AX)** – This 16C monastery was principally designed by Diego de Siloé. Fine Plateresque and Renaissance doorways lead onto its harmonious cloisters, characterised by their sturdy pillars. The church contains the tomb of Gonzalo Fernández de Córdoba, the Gran Capitán. The richness of its Renaissance style apse, magnificently illuminated by the transept windows, and the roof with its superb coffers and vaulting adorned with saints, angels and animals, stands out. The **retable**★, worked on by a number of artists, is a jewel of the Granadine School. The paintings on the walls are from the 18C.

★ **Albaicín (CX)** – The quarter, on the right bank of the Darro, covers a slope facing the Alhambra. It was here that the Moors built their first fortress, the refuge to which they retreated when the Christians reconquered the city. The alleys are lined by white-walled houses or the long walls that enclose luxuriant gardens of prosperous town houses called *cármenes*. Go to the **Iglesia de San Nicolás** (Church of St Nicholas) **(CX)** (*access by the Cuesta del Chapiz*, **DX**), if possible at sunset, for a really beautiful **view**★★★ of the Alhambra and the Generalife. The Sierra Nevada beyond is particularly spectacular in winter when covered in snow.

★ **El Bañuelo (Moorish Baths)** ⊘ **(CX)** – The 11C baths are the best preserved in Spain. Star-pierced vaulting decorates a room surrounded by columns.

Hospital Real (Royal Hospital) ⊘ **(AX)** – *Follow same route as for Carthusian monastery.* The hospital, now the university rectorate, was founded by the Catholic monarchs. The ground plan, similar to those in Toledo and Santiago de Compostela, is of a cross within a square and provides four spacious courtyards. Four Plateresque windows adorn the façade, while a Virgin and Child flanked by statues of the Catholic monarchs at prayer, by Alonso de Mena, dominates the main doorway. Of interest in the interior are the two harmonious *patios* in the left wing, decorated with heraldic motifs.

Sacromonte (DX) – The hillside opposite the Generalife is covered by a network of paths which lead past clumps of Barbary figs to the gypsies' caves. Folk dances are performed in these troglodyte dwellings in the evenings.

Museo Arqueológico ⊘ **(CX)** – The archeological museum is housed in C
Castril, a Renaissance palace with a fine **Plateresque doorway**★. It contains
outstanding collection of Egyptian alabaster vases found in a necropolis
Almuñecar, a bull figure from Arjona and a selection of decorative Roman a
Moorish art.

EXCURSIONS

Sierra Nevada – The Sierra Nevada lines Granada's horizon to the south: oft
snow-capped, massive, beautiful, and in season preceded by a wave of pi
almond blossom. There is skiing in winter around Solynieve.
A road *(46km/29mi)*, which winds through an arid mountain landscape before
climbs to an altitude of 3 398m/11 148ft, a feat which has earned it the nan
of the highest road in Europe – brings you to the **Pico de Veleta**★★ *(the road fro
the ski resort is usually impassable due to snow from November to June).*
The panorama is wonderful, extending north to the Cordilleras Béticas, northea
to the sierra de la Sagra, east to the wall of lofty summits dominated by t
Mulhacén and Alcazaba, and south to the Mediterranean. Finally, in the west
the jagged outlines of the sierra de Tejeda and the sierra de Almijara.

Alhama de Granada – *53km/33mi southeast on C 340.*
Alhama is scarcely more than an overgrown village in a gently rolling, cere
covered plain. The twisting streets and alleys leading to the well-proportion
church of golden stone are lined with white houses roofed with brown tiles.
Alhama's outstanding feature, which can best be seen from the esplanade belo
the public gardens, is its cliff face **site**★★. The houses are built into the steep ro
below which the Río Alhama pours through a cleft, driving a series of waterwhee
Outside the village, a path *(3km/2mi)* follows the ravine to a spa set in the hea
of a mass of greenery beside a gurgling stream.

Palacio de La GRANJA DE SAN ILDEFONSO★

Castilla y León (Segovia)
Michelin map 444 or 442 J 17
Local map see Sierra de GUADARRAMA

The palace of La Granja is a little Versailles at an altitude of 1 192m/3 911ft at the fo
of the Sierra de Guadarrama in the centre of Spain. It was built in 1731 by Philip '
grandson of Louis XIV, in pure
nostalgia for the palace of his
childhood.

Palacio ⊘ – Galleries and
chambers, faced with mar-
ble or hung with crimson
velvet, are lit, beneath painted ceilings and gilded
stucco mouldings, by or-
nate chandeliers, made by
the local royal workshops
which became renowned
in the 18C. A **Museo de
Tapices**★★ (Tapestry Museum)
on the first floor contains
principally 16C Flemish
hangings, notably *(3rd gallery)* nine of the *Honours
and Virtues* series and a
15C Gothic tapestry of
St Jerome after a cartoon
by Raphael.
Philip V and his second
wife, Isabel Farnese, are
buried in a chapel in the
collegiate church.

★★**Jardines (Gardens)** ⊘ –
Rocks were blown up and
the ground levelled before
the French landscape gar-
deners (Carlier, Boutelou)
and sculptors (Dumandré,
Thierry) could start work in

The Andromeda Fountain in the palace garden

the 145ha/358 acre park which is to a great extent inspired by the gardens and parkland of Versailles. The woodland vistas are more natural, however, the rides more rural, the intersections marked by less formal cascades. The chestnut trees, brought from France at great expense, are magnificent. The **fountains**★★ begin at the Neptune Basin, go on to the New Cascade (Nueva Cascada), a multicoloured marble staircase in front of the palace, and end at the Fuente de la Fama or Fame Fountain which jets up a full 40m/131ft.

Real Fábrica de Cristales de La Granja (Royal Glass Factory) ⊘ – Although the glass-works dates back to the reign of Philip V, the present building was built in 1770, under Charles III. It is one of the few examples of industrial architecture in Spain and is now the headquarters of the National Glass Centre. A glass museum (Museo del Vidrio) with exhibits and machinery from the royal factory is now housed inside the building.

Sierra de GREDOS★★

Castilla y León (Ávila)

Michelin map 442 or 444 K 14, L 14

he granite massif of the sierra de Gredos, which includes the pico de Almanzor 2 592m/8 504ft), the highest peak in the Cordillera Central, is bordered by four ivers: Tormes and Alberche to the north, Tiétar to the south and Alagón to the west. he contours of the sierra are dissimilar, the north face being marked by the remains f glacial features such as mountain cirques and lakes, the south, a steep granite wall, y eroded gullies. The valleys are fertile; those in the north produce fruit (mainly pples) and French beans (the speciality of Barco de Ávila); those in the south, heltered by the sierra, grapes, olives and tobacco.

n order to preserve the trout in the Alberche and Tormes rivers, the deer and the *apra hispánica*, a type of mountain goat, which haunt the upper heights, the Reserva Nacional de Gredos was created.

SIGHTS

★ **Cuevas del Águila (Águila Caves)** ⊘ – *9km/6mi south of Arenas de San Pedro. Bear right immediately beyond the village of Ramacastañas and continue for 4km/2.5mi along the unsurfaced road.*
A single vast chamber is open to the public. Among the many concretions are lovely frozen streams of calcite, ochre crystals coloured by iron oxide and massive pillars still in process of formation.

★ **Puerto del Pico Road** – *29km/18mi northeast of Arenas de San Pedro.* The road cuts through the centre of the sierra. After crossing **Mombeltrán** (15C castle with well preserved exterior), the road rises to a corniche, paralleling the old Roman road, used for years as a stock route, which one can see below. From the pass (1 352m/4 436ft) there is a good **view**★ of the mountains and, in the foreground (south), of the Tiétar Valley and, beyond, the Tajo. Beyond the pass the landscape becomes austere with granite boulders crowning the hilltops.
The **Parador de Gredos**, the first in Spain (1928), stands in a magnificent **setting**★★ commanding far-reaching views.

★ **Laguna Grande** – *12km/7mi south of Hoyos del Espino. Park the car at the end of the road.*
A well-defined path leads up to Laguna Grande *(2hr)*, a glacial basin fed by mountain torrents. Halfway along the walk, there is an unforgettable **panorama**★ of the Gredos cirque.

GUADALAJARA

Castilla-La Mancha – Population 67 847

Michelin map 444 K 20

Guadalajara, which takes its name from the Arabic meaning river of stones, has developed into a satellite town on account of its proximity to Madrid.
The town became the fief of the **Mendozas** in the 14C, a name famous in Spanish history. It includes among its members Íñigo López de Mendoza, first **Marquis of Santillana** (1398-1458), poet and author of the pastoral *Serranillas*; his son, **Cardinal Pedro González de Mendoza** (1428-95), adviser to the Catholic monarchs; and the second Duke of Infantado, who built the palace at the north entrance to the town in the 15C.

★ **Palacio del Infantado (Palace of the Duke of Infantado)** ⊘ – The palace, built at the end of the 15C by Juan Guas, is a masterpiece of civil Isabelline architecture in which the Gothic and Mudéjar styles combine. The magnificent **façade**★ is adorned with diamond stonework and a large crest, the Mendoza family coat of arms, abc the doorway. The upper gallery consists of a series of paired ogee windo interposed between corbelled loggias. The effect of the whole is splendid in sp of the later windows, which were added in the 17C. The two-storey **patio**★ is ju as remarkable with its multifoil arches resting on turned columns and extremely delicate Mudéjar ornamentation. The decoration of the palace interi equally sumptuous at the outset, was damaged during the Spanish Civil War When Francis I of France, captured at Pavia in 1525, was on his way imprisonment in Madrid, he was received at the palace with the pomp due to I station.

EXCURSION

Pastrana - *42km/26mi southeast on N 320*. This delightful town, once a du city, retains memories of the **Princess of Eboli**, favourite of Philip II. The **Palacio Duc** with its plain rough hewn stone façade, stands on Hour Square or Plaza de la Ho so named because the duke, the princess's husband, confined her to the pala for the last five years of her life, allowing her to appear at the window for o an hour a day. The **Colegiata** ⊘, a collegiate church built by the dukes in the 1€ contains, in the sacristy, four Gothic **tapestries**★ woven in Tournai after cartoo by Nuno Gonçalves which illustrate the capture of Arzila and Tangier by Alfons of Portugal in 1471. They reveal the Portuguese painter's mastery of compo tion, love of detail (armour and costume) and talent for portraiture.

GUADALUPE★★

Extremadura (Cáceres) – Population 2 447
Michelin map 444 N 14

Suddenly before you as the road climbs, there is Guadalupe, set in a perfect **picture** The monastery, bristling with battlements and turrets, stands above the villa which clusters around the foot of its austere ramparts. The road above the villa commands a good **view**★ of the monastery.
The **old village**★ with its steeply pitched brown tile roofs is attractively picturesqu particularly in spring when flowers bring colour to the balconies. The traditional cra of copper smelting (jugs and pots) is still very much alive.

Patron of Todas las Españas (All the Spains) – The first shrine is believed to have be built following the discovery of a miraculous Virgin by a cowherd in 1300. Alfonso) having invoked the Virgin of Guadalupe, as she was known, shortly before his victc over the Moors at the **Battle of Salado** (24 October 1340) had a grandiose monaste built in gratitude and entrusted it to the Hieronymites. The pilgrimage centre, ric endowed by rulers and deeply venerated by the people, exercised a great influer in the 16C and 17C when it became famous for craftsmanship - embroidery, g and silversmithing, illumination - and more importantly, situated as it was at t heart of the Kingdom of the Conquistadors, the symbol of the **Hispanidad** - t community of language and civilization which links the Spanish of the Old and N Worlds. Christopher Columbus named a West Indian island after the shrine; the fi American Indians converted to Christianity were brought to the church for baptis and Christians freed from slavery came in pilgrimage to leave their chains as vot offerings.
Solemn processions on 12 October celebrate the day of the Hispanidad.

★★ MONASTERIO ⊘ 1hr 15min

The monastery, abandoned in 1835, was taken over by Franciscans in 1908 a restored. The heart of the building dates from the Gothic period, late 14C-ea 15C, but with rich donations, numerous additions were made in the 16C, 17C a 18C. The resulting plan appears confused because the monks had to crowd ev more buildings within the fortified perimeter. The monastery contains some ve valuable artistic treasures.

Façade - 15C. The façade, golden in colour, exuberant in its Flamboyant Got decoration, overlooks a picturesque square. It is set between tall crenellat towers of rough stone like the sombre defensive walls on either side. Moori influence, characteristic of Mudéjar Gothic, can be seen in the exaggerate sinuous decoration in imitation of Moorish stuccowork. Bronze reliefs on the 1 doors illustrate the Lives of the Virgin and Christ.

Iglesia (Church) - 14C. The church was one of the first monastery buildings to erected but in the 18C additions were made such as the gilt Baroque decoration the vaulting and the pierced balustrade above the nave to take votive lamps honour of the Virgin. An intricate iron grille, wrought at the beginning of the 1 by two famous Valladolid ironsmiths, closes the sanctuary which is ornamented with a large classically ordered retable carved by two 17C sculptors, Giraldo de Merlo and Jorge Manuel Theotocopuli, son of El Greco. The Virgin of Guadalupe stands in the middle of the altarpiece (1) but can be seen more clearly from the *Camarín*.

Sala Capitular (Chapterhouse) – The chapterhouse contains a remarkable collection of 87 **antiphonaries**★ by the monks of Guadalupe. The richly illuminated works cover a period from the 14C to the 18C, most of them dating from the 16C.

Claustro Mudéjar – 14C-15C. The cloisters are remarkable for their great size and the two storeys of horseshoe-shaped arches. There is a small Mudéjar Gothic temple in the middle and in a corner, a lavabo faced with multicoloured tiles.

Museo de Bordados (Embroidery Museum) – The museum, in the former refectory, displays a fine collection of richly decorated **copes and altarfronts**★★, skilfully embroidered by the monks between the 15C and the 19C.

Museo de Pinturas y Esculturas (Painting and Sculpture Museum) – The works include a 16C triptych of the *Adoration of the Magi* by Isembrandt, an ivory Christ attributed to Michelangelo, an *Ecce Homo* by Pedro de Mena, eight small canvases of the monks by Zurbarán, and another small painting by Goya, *Prison Confession*.

Monasterio, Guadalupe

★★ **Sacristía (Sacristy)** – 17C. Canvases by Carreño de Miranda hang in the antecha
ber. The sacristy is a magnificently successful combination of Classical st
architecture and highly ornate Baroque decoration. The unexpected harmony a
rich colouring set off the well-known series of **paintings by Zurbarán**★★ to perfecti
The 11 canvases, painted in a serene yet forceful style between 1638 and 164
are of the Hieronymite monks and scenes from the Life of St Jerome includ
The Temptation in which he is shown resisting beautiful lady musicians.

Relicario (Reliquary Cabinet) – This contains a collection of the Virgin of Guadalup
mantles and the crown, which is worn only in solemn processions.

★ **Camarín** – 18C. A chapel-like room where the Virgin of Guadalupe rests. Ric
of every description abound: jasper, gilded stucco and marble and precious wo
marquetry frames for nine canvases by Luca Giordano. The Virgin herself sits
an enamelwork throne (1953), a small 12C figure carved in now darkened o
almost obscured beneath a richly embroidered veil and mantle.

Claustro Gótico (Gothic Cloisters) – In the *hospedería* (hostelry). The cloisters w
built in the 16C in an elegant Flamboyant Gothic style to serve as a dispens
for the four hospitals then in the monastery's care.

EXCURSION

Puerto de San Vicente (San Vicente Pass) – *40km/25mi east on C 401.*
The **road**★ to the pass crosses the Las Villuercas mountain ranges. During the cli
(8km/5mi) beyond the Guadarranque Valley, there are wonderful **views**★ of gr
mountain ranges, their jagged crests aligned like the waves of the sea in the w
moorland landscape.

Sierra de GUADARRAMA★

Castilla y León (Segovia), Madrid
Michelin map 444 or 442 J 17-18

The Sierra de Guadarrama stretches for 100km/62mi from the puerto de Malac
(Malagón Pass) to that of Somosierra, providing a northwest barrier for the provi
of Madrid. It is lower than the sierra de Gredos of which it is a continuation, and
highest point, Peñalara, has an altitude of 2 429m/7 970ft.
The range is part of the Hercynian massif uplifted by Tertiary earth movements. T
countryside comprises granite and gneiss outcrops, steep slopes covered up
halfway in evergreen oaks and pinewoods but above, near the crests, are traces
glaciation, such as the Laguna de Peñalara, its waters covering the bottom of a gla
basin. Abundant rainfall in the upper heights gives rise to streams (Lozo
Guadarrama, Manzanares and Jarama) which feed the province's many reservo
(Pinilla, Navacerrada, Santillana and El Atazar).
The sierra de Guadarrama is a green oasis in the desert of Castilla, so close to Áv
Segovia and Madrid that you can see the range's snow-capped peaks from th
towns in winter. Mountain and rural resorts have developed in the sierra to wh
Castilians flee in summer to escape the torrid heat of the Meseta: Navacerra
Cercedilla, Guadarrama and El Escorial. Madrid's three ski resorts centre around
puerto de Navacerrada and the puerto de los Cotos.

FROM MANZANARES EL REAL TO SEGOVIA

*106km/66mi – allow half a day excluding visits to Segovia, La Granja and Riof
See local map.*

Manzanares el Real – The **castillo**★ standing at the foot of the sierra de la Pedr
was built by the Duke of Infantado in the 15C. This gem of civil architecture
well-proportioned fortress, the austerity of its lines relieved by bead mouldir
on the turrets and the Plateresque decoration applied to the south front, wh
could be the work of Juan Guas.

Sierra de la Pedriza – This granite massif, foothill to the sierra de Guadarrar
which presents by turns a chaos of rose-coloured rock and eroded screes w
mountain streams, is popular with rock climbers, particularly in the peña
Diezmo area (1 714m/5 623ft).

Miraflores de la Sierra – Summer resort. Attractive view from a lookout on
village outskirts.

Puerto de la Morcuera – As you reach the pass (1 796m/5 892ft), an extens
view which includes the El Vellón reservoir, opens to the south.
A descent through bare moorland brings you to the wooded Lozoya depressi
In the distance by Lozoya town, is the Pinilla dam, supplied by the río Lozoya
well-known trout stream.

★ Real Monasterio de Santa María de El Paular ⊙ – Castilla's earliest Carthusian monastery stands in the cool Lozoya Valley. It was founded in 1390 and was subsequently enriched by the kings of Castilla and those of unified Spain in the 15C and 16C. In 1954, the Benedictines began reconstruction of the complex, which comprises a monastery, church and a hotel (a former palace). The **church** has a Flamboyant doorway by Juan Guas. Inside is a finely wrought Gothic

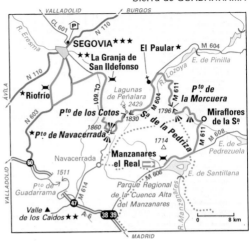

screen and a magnificent 15C alabaster **altarpiece★★**, illustrating the Lives of the Virgin and Christ and which from its emphasis on the picturesque and detail in costume and bourgeois interiors, is certainly Flemish. In contrast, the Tabernáculo (Tabernacle), behind the high altar, is decorated in exuberant Baroque.
The road continues through dense pinewoods.

Puerto de los Cotos – 1 830m/6 004ft. The pass is the departure point for ski-lifts to the slopes. From the upper chair-lift terminus at Zabala, excursions may be made in summer to the laguna de Peñalara *(15min)*, the picos de Dos Hermanas (Summit of the Two Sisters) *(30min)* and Peñalara, the highest point *(45min)*.

★ Puerto de Navacerrada – 1 860m/6 102ft. The pass, on the borders of the two Castillas, commands a beautiful **view★** of the Segovian plateau and the line of the valley, hidden beneath dense pines, through which the road to Madrid runs.
The pass is a popular ski resort and is linked by train to Cercedilla.

★★ La Granja de San Ildefonso – *See Palacio de La GRANJA DE SAN ILDEFONSO.*

★ Riofrío – *See SEGOVIA: Excursions.*

★★ Segovia – *See SEGOVIA.*

GUADIX

Andalucía (Granada) – Population 19 634
Michelin map 446 U 20

Guadix, a farming centre, stands where the irrigated plain meets the dry plateau. The plateau's soft stone has been deeply ravined into fantastic shapes by erosion.
The town's origins go back to prehistoric times; it became important under the Romans and the Visigoths. Under the Moors, it was allowed to remain Christian. The town's peaceful, modest air belies its eventful past which is nevertheless recalled by the cathedral, the 15C Moorish fortress and the Plaza Mayor, which dates from the reign of Philip II.

SIGHTS

★ Catedral ⊙ – The cathedral's Baroque **façade★** (1713) with its undulating lines draws the eye even more than does the fine Renaissance belfry. The interior has intricate star vaulting in the nave and aisles. The east end is by Diego de Siloé.

★ Barrio Troglodita (Troglodyte Quarter) – *Walk up the street which leads to the Iglesia de Santiago.* Beyond the church is an area of dwellings which have been hollowed out of the soft tufa hillside. The rocks round the entrances are whitewashed and the homes have conical chimneys built to emerge on a level with the paths.

Iglesia de Santiago (St James' Church) – The church stands on a pleasant square. Fine Plateresque decoration adorns its façade.

Alcazaba ⊙ – *In the street near the Iglesia de Santiago. Access through the Saminario.* From the 15C crenellated walls there is a good **view★** of Guadix, particularly of the troglodyte quarter and the Sierra Nevada beyond.

Castillo de la Calahorra

EXCURSIONS

Purullena - *6km/4mi northwest.* The **road**★★ winds through tufa rocks to rea
the **troglodyte village**★ of Purullena. Pottery-making is a well-developed cotta
industry as the many stalls along the roadside testify.
Beyond Purullena, the Granada road rises in a corniche, affording extensive **view**
over the plateau, cut deep by canyons. It then enters a wild landscape to reach t
puerto de Mora (Mora Pass) at 1 390m/4 560ft.

La Calahorra - *18km/11mi southeast.* La Calahorra stands in a vast plain whi
lies between the Sierra Nevada and the Sierra de Los Filabres. It is dominated
a **castillo** ⊘ imprisoned by four round towers with such an austere appearance th
the graceful interior is completely unexpected. Park the car in the village and wa
up to the castle. A heavy door opens onto a delightful Renaissance **patio**★★
masterpiece of refinement. The design of the arcades and balustrade, the Itali
style carving surrounding the windows and the skilful proportions of the stairca
convey a highly sophisticated artistic style.

HONDARRIBIA/FUENTERRABÍA★

País Vasco (Guipúzcoa) – Population 13 974
Michelin map 442 B 24

Fuenterrabía (Hondarribia in Basque), now a popular seaside resort and large fishi
port, was for centuries the target of attack by the French on account of its strate
position on the frontier. The old stronghold with its steep streets built on high grou
above the Bidasoa river is still encircled by ramparts. As a reminder of its histor
annually on 8 September, Fuenterrabía celebrates with a military parade (*alarde*
festival to the Virgen de Guadalupe who is said to have delivered the town from
two-month siege by the French in 1638.
On the outskirts of the town near the harbour, the **Marina**, a bustling fishermen
quarter with characteristic wood balconies, is popular for its pavement cafés.

OLD TOWN *1hr*

Puerta de Santa María - The gateway through the 15C ramparts is surmount
by the town's arms and twin angels venerating the Virgen de Guadalupe.

Calle Mayor - The narrow main street is picturesquely lined with old houses wi
wrought-iron balconies and carved wooden cornices.

Iglesia de Santa María - The impressive Gothic church, remodelled in the 1
when it was given a Baroque tower, is supported round the apse by massi
buttresses. It was in this church, on 3 June 1660, that the proxy wedding to

place between the Spanish minister, Don Luis de Haro, on behalf of Louis XIV, and the Infanta María Teresa, six days before the solemnisation of the marriage in France.

Castillo de Carlos V – According to legend, the 10C founder of this austere fortress was Sancho Abarca, King of Navarra. The fortress served a key role as strongpoint throughout the history of the Kingdom of Navarra. Charles V restored it in the 16C; it has now been transformed again – this time into a parador.

EXCURSIONS

★ **Cabo Higuer** – *4km/2.5mi north. To reach this headland, leave Fuenterrabía on the road to the harbour and beach.* Turn left and as the road climbs, you will get a good **view**★ of the beach, the town and the quayside and from the end of the headland, the French coast and the town of Hendaye.

★ **Ermita de San Marcial** (Hermitage) – *9km/6mi east. Leave Fuenterrabía on the Behobia road and take the first right after the Palmera factory; bear left at the first crossroads.*
A narrow road leads up to the wooded hilltop (225m/738ft). The **panorama** from the hermitage terrace includes Fuenterrabía, **Irún** and the **Isla de los Faisanes** (Pheasant Island) in the mouth of the River Bidasoa which marks the frontier and has been the setting for several historic events including, in 1659, the signing of the Treaty of the Pyrenees which stipulated the marriage between Louis XIV and the Infanta María Teresa. In the distance you can see San Sebastián and Hendaye beach.

★ **Jaizkibel Road** – *West of Fuenterrabía.*
The **drive**★★ is glorious at sunset. After 5km/3mi you reach the Capilla de Nuestra Señora de Guadalupe (Chapel of our Lady of Guadalupe) where there is a lovely **view**★ of the mouth of the Bidasoa and the French Basque coast. The road overlooks the sea as it rises through pines and gorse to reach the Hostal de Jaizkibel at the foot of a 584m/1 916ft peak and a lookout with a superb **view**★★ *(viewpoint indicator).* The road down to Pasai Doni-bane affords **glimpses**★ of the indented coastline, the Cordillera Cantábrica range and the three mountains which dominate San Sebastián – Ulía, Urgull and Igueldo.

Pasaia/Pasajes – *17km/11mi west along the Jaizkibel road.*
Pasaia, in fact, comprises three villages around a sheltered bay connected with the open sea only by a narrow channel: **Pasai Antxo** is a trading port, **Pasai Donibane**★ and **Pasai San Pedro** are both deep-sea fishing ports, processing cod in the town. They hold the highest catch value along the Cantabrian coast. To get to **Pasai Donibane**, either park the car at the entrance to the village or take a motorboat from San Pedro. The **view** from the water is picturesque – tall houses with brightly painted wooden balconies. The one and only village street winds between the houses and beneath arches offering glimpses of boats and landing-stages. A path runs alongside the harbour to the lighthouse *(45min).*

HUESCA★

Aragón – Population 50 085
Michelin map 443 F 28 – Local map see JACA

Huesca, the capital of Alto Aragón (Upper Aragón), has a tranquil, provincial appearance which belies its turbulent historical past. In Roman times, the town was made capital of an independent state by praetor Sertorius, then became an important Moorish stronghold and was finally reconquered by **Pedro I of Aragón** in 1096. It was capital of Aragón until 1118 when Zaragoza was awarded the privilege.

"Resounding like the bell of Huesca" is a Spanish expression for describing a dire event with far-reaching effects. The saying goes back to the 12C, when the King, Ramiro II, angry at the insolence of his nobles, summoned them to his palace ostensibly to watch the casting of a bell *(compana)* which he promised would be heard throughout Aragón. When the lords assembled, the king had the most rebellious beheaded – thereby making the fame of the bell indeed resound throughout his kingdom.

During the Civil War, Huesca was besieged by the Republicans from September 1936 to March 1938. The devastation suffered by the upper part of the city was considerable.

OLD QUARTER *1hr 30min*

The old hilltop city is ringed by a belt of streets, among them the **Calle del Cos** which run over the site of the former ramparts.

★ **Catedral** ⊘ – The cathedral's façade is elegant, ornate Gothic and is divide unusually by a gallery and a typically Aragonese carved wood overhang. A narro gable encloses a small rose window and the portal covings where the statues carve out of friable limestone are weatherworn. On the tympanum are the Magi a Christ appearing before Mary Magdalene. The late-Gothic (15C-16C) church, or square plan, is divided into a nave and two aisles covered by star vaulting. The hig altar alabaster **retable**★★ dates from 1533. In this masterpiece by Damián Forme (one of Donatello's followers), three scenes of the Crucifixion appear in high reli in the middle of Flamboyant canopy and frieze decoration. Facing the cathedral the Palacio Municipal (town hall), a tastefully decorated Renaissance town hous

★ **Museo Arqueológico Provincial** ⊘ – The museum is in the old university on attractive old square. The university itself was built in 1690 as a series of eight ha round a fine octagonal *patio*. Parts of the former royal palace were incorporated the building, including the gallery in which the Campana de Huesca massacre too place. The museum contains archaeological items (mainly from the prehistor period) and paintings, in particular a **collection**★ of Aragonese Primitives. Among t most interesting works are several by the Maestro de Sigena (16C).

★ **Iglesia de San Pedro el Viejo** ⊘ – Although restored, the 11C monastery **cloisters**★, with their historiated capitals, remain a major example of Romanesq sculpture in Aragón. On the side facing the church, the tympanum of the cloist doorway has an unusual Adoration of the Magi with all the emphasis on the givi of gifts. The capitals in the east gallery are the least restored. A Romanesq chapel contains the tombs of Kings Ramiro II (Roman sarcophagus) and Alfonso the Battler, the only Aragonese kings not to be buried in the royal pantheon in S Juan de la Peña.

EXCURSION

Monasterio de Monte Aragón – *5km/3mi east along N 240.*
The monastery ruins are visible from the road. It was originally built as a fortre by Sancho I Ramírez when investing the Moorish stronghold of Huesca.

IRUÑEA/PAMPLONA★

Navarra – Population 191 197
Michelin map 442 D 25

Pamplona is the main town of the Spanish Pyrenees. From the period when it w capital of the kingdom of Navarra and a fortified city, there remain, around t cathedral, a quarter of old houses lining narrow streets and ramparts to the nor and east overlooking the Río Arga.
Modern quarters – wide, straight avenues, lined by luxurious buildings **(Paseo Sarasate) (AY 72)**, arcaded squares decorated with fountains and flowers **(Plaza Castillo) (BY)** – have been developed, extending the southern periphery. Finally, a wi green belt of parks and gardens **(La Taconera) (AY)**, rings this now prosperous lookir city and its large private university.
On a lighter note, Pamplona is renowned for its coffee-flavoured caramels and famous *feria*.

The "Sanfermines" – The *feria* of San Fermín is celebrated with joyous ardour fro 6 to 14 July each year. Visitors pour in, doubling the town's population, to see t great evening bullfights and enjoy the carefree atmosphere (described by Hemir way in *Fiesta, The Sun Also Rises*). The most spectacular event, and the one mo prized by "Pamplonés", however, is the **encierro** or early morning *(around 8a* running of the bulls. The beasts selected to fight in the evening are let loose to ru through the streets along a set route, 800m/875yd long, which leads to the bullri in a matter of minutes. Youths costumed in white with red berets, scarves ai sashes, and brandishing rolled-up newspapers, run with them. The festival broadcast live on Spanish television and eagerly watched by the entire country. T following ditty is sung in accompaniment:

"Uno de enero, dos de febrero   "1 January, 2 February
Tres de marzo, cuatro de abril   3 March, 4 April
Cinco de mayo, seis de junio   5 May, 6 June
Y siete de julio, San Fermín"   and 7 July, San Fermín"

On occasion tourists have failed to keep a safe distance between themselves ai the action, with fatal results in some cases. This is a sport which is definite best left to the experts.

ISTORICAL NOTES

mplona dates back to Roman times and is said to have been founded by Pompey
no, tradition has it, gave the town his name. In the 8C, the Moors occupied the town
iefly before being expelled with the help of Charlemagne, who, however, took
lvantage of the weakness of the native forces to dismantle the city walls. In revenge
e people of Navarra took part in the historic massacre of Charlemagne's rearguard
the Roncesvalles pass.
the 10C Pamplona became the capital of Navarra. Throughout the Middle Ages,
e city was troubled by disputes between the citizens of the old quarter – the
avarrería – who supported an alliance with Castilla, and the freemen who lived on
e city outskirts in the districts of San Cernin and San Nicolás and favoured the
tention of the Navarra crown by a French line.
e disputes were settled in 1423 when Charles III, the Noble, promulgated the Union
etween the three municipalities. They joined to become a single city and Pamplona
ached the peak of its power. Building of the citadel began during the reign of
ilip II in 1571.

SIGHTS

★ **Catedral** ⊙ **(BY)** – The present Gothic cathedral was built in the 14C and 15C over
an earlier Romanesque edifice whose only remains (doorway and cloister capitals)
are now in the Museo de Navarra. At the end of the 18C, Ventura Rodríguez rebuilt
the west front in the Baroque and neo-Classical style then fashionable. The nave,
only two tiers high, has wide arches and windows and, with plain ribbing and great
bare walls, the unadorned appearance typical of Navarra Gothic. In front of the
finely wrought grille closing the sanctuary, stands the alabaster **tomb**★, commissioned in 1416 by Charles III the Noble, founder of the cathedral, for himself and

IRUÑEA
PAMPLONA

Amaya	BYZ 4
Ansoleaga	AY 5
Bayona (Av. de)	AY 13
Carlos III (Av. de)	BYZ
Castillo de Maya	BY 17
Chapitela	BY
Conde Oliveto (Av. del)	AZ 19
Cortes de Navarra	BY 20

Cruz (Pl. de la)	BZ 22
Esquiroz	AZ 25
Estafeta	BY 26
Garcia Castañón	ABY 30
Juan de Labrit	BY 33
Leyre	BYZ 36
Mayor	AY 40
Mercaderes	BY 43
Navarrería	BY 48
Navas de Tolosa	AY 50
Paulino Caballero	BZ 51
Principe de Viana (Pl. del)	BZ 54
Reina (Cuesta de la)	AY 56
Roncesvalles (Av. de)	AY 59

Sancho el Mayor	ABZ 60
San Fermín	BZ 63
San Francisco (Pl. de)	AY 65
San Ignacio (Av. de)	BYZ 66
Sangüesa	BZ 69
Santo Domingo	AY 70
Sarasate (Paseo de)	AY 72
Taconera (Recta de)	AY 73
Vinculo (Pl. del)	AYZ 78
Zapateria	AY 89

H Ayuntamiento
M Museo de Navarra

his queen. The expressive reclining figures and mourners were carved by t Frenchman, Janin Lomme. Note the late-15C Hispano-Flemish altarpiece (sou ambulatory chapel).

★ **Claustro** – 14C-15C. The cloisters have a delicate appearance, with elegant Got' arches surmounted, in some cases, by gables. Sculptured tombs and doors a interest; note the Dormition of the Virgin on the tympanum of the cloister dc which is almost Baroque in expression.

Off the east gallery is the Capilla Barbazán – a chapel named after the bishop w had it built to house his tomb – which has beautiful 14C star vaulting. On the sou side the doorway of the Sala Preciosa is a key piece in the sculpture of the perio with tympanum and lintel beautifully carved with scenes from the Life of t Virgin and, on either side of the door, two statues together forming a fi Annunciation.

Museo Diocesano ⊘ – The Diocesan Museum is in the old refectory and adjoini kitchen, which date from 1330. The refectory, a lofty hall with six pointed arch contains a reader's rostrum decorated with an enchanting scene of a unicorn hu The square kitchen, with a fireplace in each corner, has a central lantern rising a height of 24m/79ft. The museum displays religious objects including a 1. *Reliquary of the Holy Sepulchre* donated by St Louis (Louis IX of France) a polychrome wood statues of the Virgin and Christ from all parts of the provin *On leaving the cathedral follow the narrow, picturesque Calle del Redín to t ramparts.*

Murallas (Ramparts) – A small bastion, now a garden, commands a view of t fortified Puerta de Zumalacárregui (a gate which is visible below and to the le and a stretch of the old walls and, further away, a bend in the Río Arga and mor Cristóbal.

★ **Museo de Navarra** ⊘ (AY M) – The Navarra museum was built on the site of a 1 hospital of which the Renaissance gateway has been preserved. The Roman peri is represented by lapidary exhibits such as funerary steles, inscriptions a **mosaic★** pavements from 2C and 4C villas. The mosaics are principally geomet and often in black and white – gallery 3 contains an illustration of Theseus a the Minotaur.

Pride of place is given to the Romanesque period with **capitals★** from the form 12C cathedral of Pamplona on which an unknown artist carved three Bibli scenes – the Passion, the Resurrection and the Story of Job – with a care for det only equalled by his mastery of composition and brilliance of imagination.

Gothic and Renaissance paintings are also on display. The first three galleri reconstituted as the interior of the Palacio de Oriz, are decorated with monochrome painted panels depicting the story of Adam and Eve and the wa of Emperor Charles V. The galleries that follow contain fragments of v **paintings★** from different periods and all areas of the province: Artaíz (13 Artajona and Pamplona (13C-14C), Gallipienzo (14C-15C) and Olleta (15C). T apparently diverse collection has common characteristics – the unobtrus emphasis on face and feature, the crowds, the sideways stance – passed do from French miniaturists and well exemplified in Juan Olivier's refectory mur painted in 1330 *(gallery 24)*. Among the major works exhibited in the muse are the early-11C Hispano-Arab ivory **arqueta★** (casket) from Córdoba and t portrait of the *Marqués de San Adrián* by Goya.

Before leaving, look at the large mosaic from the Roman villa of Liédena (2C) the courtyard.

Iglesia de San Saturnino ⊘ (AY) – This composite church at the centre of a tan of narrow streets in the old quarter has a mingled architecture of Romanesq brick towers, 13C Gothic porch and vaulting and numerous later additions.

Ayuntamiento (Town Hall) (AY H) – This has a reconstructed Baroque faça originally dating from the late 17C with statues, balustrades and pediments

EXCURSION

★ **Santuario de San Miguel de Aralar** ⊘ – *36km/22mi west on A15 motorwa then N240ᴬ as far as the Irañeta turnoff, which you take.* There are good vie from the road as it runs for 10km/6mi through attractive rocky countryside a oak forests.

The **santuario**, which dates from different periods – the apse and part of the wa are Visigothic (9C), while the rest is pre-Romanesque (10C) – encloses a sm 11C-12C Romanesque chapel which replaced a church built in the 8C. It was he that a magnificent gilt and enamel **altar front★★**, now considered one of the ma works of European Romanesque goldsmithery, was discovered in the 18C. It m be late-12C Limousin.

★ **Valle del Bidasoa** – *Leave town to the east by the Avenida de la Baja Navarra* (B *100km/62mi north on N 121ᴬ, NA 254 and N 121ᴮ.*

The Bidasoa has cut a course through the lower foothills of the western Pyrenees. Villages of typical Basque houses lie surrounded by lush meadows and fields of maize.

The N 121^A winds through hilly country over the Velate pass. The NA 254 then leads through Berroeta, Irurita and onto **Elizondo**, capital of the **Valle del Baztán** which is home to the many *Indianos* or *Americanos*, as Basques who go to Latin America to make their fortune and then return, are known. Many of the house façades are decorated with armorial bearings.

By returning to the N 121^A and heading north, you enter the ancient confederation of the **Cinco Villas** or five delightful towns (off minor roads on either side of the N 121^A): **Etxalar, Arantza, Igantzi, Lesaka** and **Bera**. The house façades, typical of Basque architecture, have deep eaves which shelter wooden balconies with delicate balustrades. The Bidasoa enters a narrow gorge the Garganta de Endarlaza, and continues through the Basque country to the sea, marking the frontier between Spain and France.

JACA★

Aragón (Huesca) – Population 14 426

Michelin map 443 E 28

Jaca stands on a terrace site in the Valley of the River Aragón, overlooked by the Peña de Oroel. Its strategic position is marked by a well-preserved 16C **ciudadela** (citadel). Jaca won renown early in its history by repelling the Moorish invasion (8C) and then by becoming the kingdom of Aragón's first capital city.

Jaca today, at the end of the road to the Puerto de Somport, serves as a busy gateway north to the Pyrenees, south to the rest of Spain and as a stopping place for hikers in summer and skiers in winter.

Many festivals are held in the town: in May, a pilgrimage of historic figures and local dancing commemorates the battle against the Moors and every other year, at the end of July or the beginning of August, there is an international folk festival.

★ **Catedral** ⊘ – This, Spain's oldest Romanesque cathedral, dates back to the 11C. Its carved decoration was to influence the Romanesque craftsmen who worked on the churches along the pilgrim route to Santiago de Compostela. Outside, note the **historiated capitals**★ of the south porch and behind it the south doorway where great attention has been given to the draperies on the figures in the Sacrifice of Isaac and in King David and his musicians.

Gothic vaulting, regrettably embellished with ornate keystones in the 16C, covers the aisles which are unusually wide for the period. The apse and side chapels are profusely decorated with Renaissance sculpture but the cupola on squinches over the transept crossing has retained its original simplicity.

Museo Diocesano (Diocesan Museum) ⊘ – The cloisters and adjoining halls contain Romanesque and Gothic **wall paintings**★ from village churches in the area: Urríes, Sorripas, de Ruesta, Navasa, Bagüés and a reconstitution of the Osia church apse. There is also a collection of Romanesque paintings of the Virgin and Christ.

EXCURSIONS

★ **Round tour of 220km/136mi via Huesca, Castillo de Loarre and San Juan de la Peña** – *Allow 1 day. See local map. Leave Jaca on the southbound N 330 towards Huesca.*

★ **Embalse de Arguis** – The Arguis reservoir, deep green in colour against its mountain background, is the highlight of the Sabiñánigo-Huesca road.

★ **Huesca** – *See HUESCA.*

Continue northwest on A 132 to Ayerbe, then take A 1602 to Loarre.

★ **Castillo de Loarre** ⊘ – As you approach the castle, the sheer beauty and tranquillity of the site, a veritable eyrie, become ever more compelling. In the 11C, Sancho Ramírez, King of Aragón and Navarra, had this impenetrable fortress built at an altitude of 1 100m/3 609ft and then installed a religious community within it. The walls, flanked by round towers, command a vast **panorama**★★ of the Ebro depression. After the massive keep and fine covered stairway, turn to the church which was completed only in the 12C. Standing over a crypt are a tall nave, a cupola and an apse adorned with blind arcades, all in the purest Romanesque style. The capitals with stylised motifs are very beautiful.

Return to Ayerbe and continue northwest on A132 towards Puente la Reina de Jaca. After 9km/5.6mi take the Agüero road to the left.

Agüero – The setting of the village with its tiled roofs is made spectacular by a background of upstanding *Mallos (see below)*. Half a mile before Agüero, a road leads off, right, to the Romanesque **Iglesia de Santiago** where the three aisles of the church are covered by three separate stone roofs. Note the carvings on the tympanum (Epiphany, Joseph Asleep) and the covings (Salome's Dance, left).

Return to A 132 and continue north.

The road becomes more enclosed. The río Gállego soon comes into view, banked by tall crumbling cliffs, red ochre in colour. The **Mallos**★, as they are called, are a formation of rose pudding-stone, highly vulnerable to erosion which has here created sugar loaf forms – the most dramatic group stands to the right of the road, its flamboyant mass completely dominating the small village of **Riglos**. Further up the valley is the Peña reservoir.

Bear right, before Puente la Reina de Jaca, onto N 240, then, after 10km/6mi, right again onto A 1603 for Santa Cruz de la Serós.

★ **Santa Cruz de la Serós** –
See Monasterio de SAN JUAN DE LA PEÑA: Excursion.
Beyond Santa Cruz de la Serós, the road rises through woodland into the Sier de la Peña where the Monasterio de San Juan suddenly comes into view, nestl beneath an immense overhanging rock.

★★ **Monasterio de San Juan de la Peña** – *See Monasterio de SAN JUAN DE LA PEÑA.*
The road continues past the upper monastery of San Juan de la Peña and th leads back to Jaca, commanding fine **views**★ of the Pyrenees along the way.

★ **Roncal and Ansó Valleys** – *Round tour of 144km/89mi – about 4hr. See loc map.*
These two high valleys played an important part in the Reconquest. They have f a long time lived self-sufficiently, preserving an ancient economy based on she rearing with common pastureland for grazing. Religious festivals are st celebrated in traditional costume.
Leave Jaca on N 240, heading west.
The road runs along the Valley of the River Aragón between arid marl hills f 47km/29mi.
Turn right onto A 137 to the Roncal Valley.
The road goes up the green **Roncal Valley**★ watered by the río Esca. It crosses narrow humpbacked bridge just before its arrival in **Burgui**.
1km/0.6mi south of Roncal, bear right onto NA 176 heading towards Garde a Ansó.
When it drops down towards **Ansó**, this spectacular **road**★ with vertiginous cli sections affords a good bird's-eye view of the town and church rising from cluster of brown tile roofs. There is an interesting **Museo Etnológico** ⊙ wi ethnological exhibits inside the church.
To return south, take A 1602, a road that follows the winding Río Veral Valle
The river flows for 3km/2mi through the Veral's narrow gorge known as the H de Biniés.

Somport Road – *95km/59mi north along N 330. See local map.*
The road leads north of **Canfranc-Estación**, an international rail link and summ mountain resort, to **Candanchú**, the most well-known ski resort in Aragó 1km/0.6mi from the Puerto de Somport.
The **Puerto de Somport**★★ (alt 1 632m/5 354ft) is the only pass in the Centr Pyrenees which generally remains snow-free all the year round. Its history as thoroughfare goes back to the Romans who built a road over it which was trodd by Pompey's legions, Saracen hordes and later cohorts of pilgrims on their wa to Santiago de Compostela. Climb the mound to the right of the monumen commemorating the building of the road for an extensive **panorama**★★ of t Spanish Pyrenees.

Siresa – *49km/30mi northwest. Leave Jaca on N 240, west, to Puenta de la Reina de Jaca; there, take A 176 north to Siresa. See local map.*
The road runs along the Valley of the River Aragón Subordán. The village of Siresa lies clustered at the end of a narrow valley, its stone houses with windows outlined in white, slate roofs and mountain-type chimneys, a total contrast to the majesty of Iglesia de San Pedro. The Monasterio de San Pedro existed before the 9C since we are told that it was visited by **St Eulogus of Córdoba** who was martyred by the Infidels in 859. It was reformed at the end of the 11C and admitted Augustinian monks. The church, **Iglesia de San Pedro**★ ⊙, which dates from the same period, has a fine elevation and walls decorated by the ornamental use of blind arcades and buttresses. The interesting **altarpieces**★ are principally 15C.

The Michelin on-line route planning service is available on a pay-per-route basis, or you may opt for a subscription package. This option affords you multiple route plans at considerable savings. Plan your next trip in minutes with Michelin on Internet: **www.michelin-travel.com**
Bon voyage !

JAÉN

Andalucía – Population 107 413
Michelin map 446 S 18

Jaén came under the domination of the Carthaginians, grew to importance under the Romans and, in the 11C, became a *taifa* capital.
The town stands open on one side to a plain covered with olive trees while the Sierra de Jabalcuz rises behind it and Cerro de Santa Catalina (St Catherine Hill) actually overlooks it. The **view** from the Alameda de Calvo Sotelo gardens embraces the town, the never-ending sweeps of **olive groves**★★ and the surrounding mountains.

★ **Museo Provincial** ⊙ – Of the museum's collections of fine arts *(first floor)*, and **archeology**★ *(ground floor)*, the latter is particularly interesting since there are such rare items as a fine Roman **mosaic** of Thetis, Iberian carvings from Porcuna and a 4C paleo-Christian sarcophagus from Martos.

Catedral ⊙ – The architect most typical of the Renaissance in Andalucía, **Andrés de Vandelvira**, designed the cathedral in 1525, giving it a grandeur of Classical proportions. The immense façade with its Baroque decoration of statues, balconies and pilasters resembles that of a palace. Behind the high altar is a chapel containing the Santo Rostro relic, one of the veils used by St Veronica to wipe Christ's face.
The **choir stalls**★ are richly carved in the Berruguete manner.

★ **Museo de la Catedral** ⊙ – The cathedral treasure, displayed in three under-ground chambers, includes antiphonaries, paintings by Ribera, a delightful Flemish Virgin and Child and some large bronze candelabra modelled by Master Bartolomé.

Capilla de San Andrés (St Andrew's Chapel) – The **Capilla de la Immacula**★★ (Chapel of the Immaculate Conception), with a minutely-decorated drum supporting its star vaulting, is a masterpiece of Plateresque art. The gilded wrought-iron screen which stands before the chapel, worked as delicately as a curtain of gold lace, is by **Maestro Bartolomé** (16C), a native son of Jaén.

Iglesia de San Ildefonso – Each of the portals of this church has a different style: Gothic, Renaissance and the third, neo-Classical, by Ventura Rodríguez.

Baños àrabes (Moorish Baths) ⊙ – The baths, the largest in Spain (470m²/5 059sq ft), are beneath the 16C palace of the Count of Villardompardo. They have been restored to their 11C appearance. The palace houses a **Museo de Artes y Tradiciones Populares** (Museum of Popular Art and Traditions).

Castillo de Santa Catalina (St Catherine's Castle) – *4.5km/3mi west.* The approach **road**★ affords views of the blue-tinged Sierra de Jabalcuz. The castle, now a parador, commands a vast **panorama**★ of olive groves.

JÁTIVA
See XÀTIVA

JEREZ DE LA FRONTERA⭐

Andalucía (Cádiz) – Population 184 364
Michelin map 446 V 11

Jerez produces Spain's sherries and brandies. The town's proximity to the sea w
one of the factors which brought about its rapid development in the 18C wh
English shippers were searching for alternatives to French wines. The name sher
from the former English spelling of the town's name, Xeres, was first used
England in 1608.

Sherry

History would appear to show that the vine was first brought to this part of
Spain by the Phoenicians, and that the Romans later exported large quantities
of wine from the region during their long period of occupation. Following the
Reconquest of 1264 by the troops of Alfonso X, and then once again at the
end of the 16C, two varieties of grape were introduced here; namely Palomino
and Pedro Jiménez, both of which provide sherry with its particular character.
Sherry is a blended white wine which is divided into five main types: **Fino**
(15-17º), or extra dry, the lightest in body and strawlike in colour; **Amontillado**
(18-24º), an older fino; **Oloroso** (18-24º), a medium, fragrant, full bodied and
golden wine; **Dulce**, an oloroso with a higher concentration of sugar, and
Manzanilla, a dry, light sherry from the coastal town of Sanlúcar de Barrameda.
Their quality is the result of two principal factors: the region's special climate,
and a careful maturing process which involves gradual blending and the use of
solera or mother wines, with three or four American oak barrels placed one on
top of the other. Each year a specific quantity of new wine is transferred to the
top barrel; the same amount is then transferred from this barrel to the one
immediately below it. This process continues until the very last barrel, which
contains the desired wine. A visit to a **bodega**⭐ (a wine storehouse) is an
interesting experience: **Sandeman** (**AY B**), **Williams** (**BY C**), **Harvey's** (**BZ F**) and
González Byass (**AZ A**).

Ferias and festivals – Horses are no less important than sherry in Jerez and, in t
region, locally bred mounts are equally famous. In the 16C, the Carthusi
monastery (Cartuja) crossed Andalusian, Neapolitan and German breeds, giving r
to the famous **Cartujana** horse. Annually in April or May there is the **Feria del Caballo**
Horse Show with racing as well as dressage and carriage competitions.
In September there is a **Fiesta de la Vendimia** (Wine Harvest Festival) which include
cavalcade and a flamenco festival; the *cante jondo* is particularly alive and popular in Je
(which is home to such famous singers as **Antonio Chacón** (1870-1929) and **Manuel Torre**

Women in traditional costume at a *feria*

JEREZ DE LA FRONTERA

Algarve .... BZ 2
Angustias (Pl. de las) ... BZ 5
Arenal (Pl. del) .... BZ 8
Armas .... ABZ 10
Arroyo (Calzada del) .... AZ 12
Asunción (Pl.) .... BZ 13
Beato Juan Grande ..... BY 15
Cabezas .... AYZ 18
Conde de Bayona ...... BZ 21

Consistorio .... BZ 23
Cordobeses .... AY 26
Cristina (Alameda) ..... BY 28
Cruces .... AZ 30
Doña Blanca .... BZ 31
Duque de Abrantes (Av.) . BY 32
Eguilaz .... BYZ 33
Encarnación (Pl. de la) .. AZ 35
Gaspar Fernández ..... BYZ 40
José Luis Díez .... AZ 42
Lancería .... BZ 45
Larga .... BZ 47
Letrados .... ABZ 50
Luis de Isasy .... AYZ 52

Manuel María
  González .... AZ 55
Monti (Pl.) .... BZ 57
Nuño de Cañas .... BY 60
Pedro Alonso .... BZ 62
Peones (Pl.) .... AZ 65
Plateros .... BZ 67
Pozuelo .... ABZ 70
Rafael Rivero (Pl.) ..... BY 72
San Agustín .... BZ 75
San Fernando .... AZ 77
San Lucas (Pl.) ...... AYZ 80
Torneria .... BY 82
Vieja (Alameda) ...... AZ 84

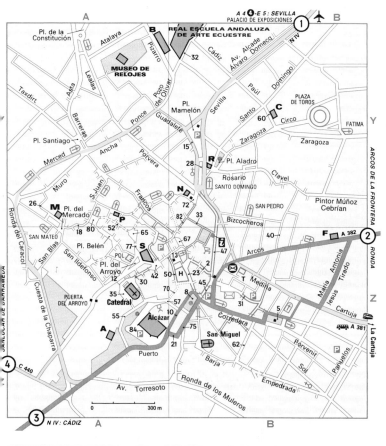

A	Bodega González Byass	F	Bodega Harvey	P	Casa de los Ponce de Léon
B	Bodega Sandeman	M	Casa del Cabildo	R	Casa de los Domecq
C	Bodega Williams	N	Palacio de los Pérez Luna	S	Palacio del Marqués de Bertematí

SIGHTS

Museo de los Relojes (Atalaya Clock Museum) ⊘ **(AY)** – The Palacio de Atalaya, set in a park, contains an outstanding collection of 300 English and French timepieces dating from the 17C to the 19C. They present a great variety of shape and decoration and are all in perfect working order. Everyday, at midday, there is a positive chorus of chiming clocks.

Real Escuela Andaluza de Arte Ecuestre (Royal Andalusian School of Equestrian Art) ⊘ **(BY)** – The school, set in the Recreo de las Cardenas (park), was founded in 1973 by Álvaro Domecq Romero. Apart from training riders for dressage, it specialises in the famous Cartujana horses.

Visitors may tour the buildings and watch training sessions but the main attraction is the remarkable **show**★★ by the Dancing Horses of Andalucía, an equestrian ballet performed by horse and rider in embroidered 17C costume.

Colegiata ⊘ **(AZ)** – The monumental 16C and 17C church, with five aisles, has well balanced Renaissance and Baroque decoration, and is given added dignity by being placed at the top of wide Baroque flights of steps. The transept crossing is covered by a dome.

Casa del Cabildo (Former chapter) **(AY M)** – The chapter's Renaissance front is the principal ornament of the attractive Plaza de la Asunción. Inside there is now a modest **Museo Arqueológico** ⊘ which includes a 7C BC Greek helmet.

Alcázar ⊘ **(AZ)** – Gardens now surround the walls of the old Moorish fortre:

Iglesia de San Miguel ⊘ **(BZ)** – The church has beautiful Isabelline portals in t side walls. The high altar retable was made by Martínez Montañés and José de Ar

Casas Señoriales (Seignorial mansions) – Interesting examples include the **Palacio Marqués de Bertemati (AZ S)** with its Baroque façade, the **Palacio de los Pérez Luna (BY** the **Casa de los Ponce de León (AY P)** with a Plateresque corner window and the **C: Domecq (BY R)**.

EXCURSION

La Cartuja (Carthusian monastery) – *5km/3mi southeast.* The monastery, found in 1477, has a Greco-Roman style portal attributed to Andrés de Ribera. T Flamboyant Gothic church has a richly decorated Baroque façade. Inside, the h: altar was originally adorned with the famous canvases by Zurbarán which are n: exhibited in museums in Cádiz and Grenoble (France).

JEREZ DE LOS CABALLEROS

Extremadura (Badajoz) – Population 10 295

Michelin map 444 and 446 R 9

Jerez stands in a fortified position on a hillside, its exuberantly Baroque decorat belfries and towers pointing to the sky. On the summit is the even more ornate S Bartolomé with its façade and belfry faced with painted stucco, molten glass mosa and *azulejos*. With its steep narrow streets lined by white-walled houses, Jerez gi: a foretaste of Andalusian architecture.

The town's name, tradition and atmosphere stem from the Knights Temp – Caballeros del Temple – to whom the town was given by Alfonso IX of León on recapture from the Moors in 1230. It is also the birthplace of the conquistador, Va Núñez de Balboa (1475-1517) who crossed the Darien Isthmus (now Panama) and 1513 discovered the Southern Sea (the Pacific Ocean).

LEÓN★★

Castilla y León – Population 147 625

Michelin map 441 E 13

León, one-time capital of the Kingdom of León, stretches along the banks of t Bernesga and is surrounded on all sides by the Meseta. The city was an importa halt along the Way of St James and has preserved many fine monuments from prestigious past, including masterpieces of Romanesque (San Isidoro), Got (cathedral) and Renaissance architecture (San Marcos).

The medieval town – In the 10C, as their territory expanded, the kings of Astur moved their capital from Oviedo to León. They built a walled city on the site of earl Roman fortifications and peopled it with Mozarabs, Christian refugees from Córdo and Toledo; by the 11C and 12C León had become virtually the centre of Christi Spain.

The east part of the city recalls the early medieval period clearly in the still evide remains of the ramparts and the houses fronting alleys where peeling roughca reveals brickwork façades. The most evocative quarter, known as the Barrio Húme (wet quarter or watering-hole) on account of its many small bars and restaurants, l between the arcaded **Plaza Mayor** and **Plaza de Santa María del Camino (B)**, a particula attractive square with wooden porticoes, a fountain and church belfry.

The modern city – As León flourishes thanks to its industry, the city limits a extending westwards along the river banks. Its development has depended hydroelectric power from the basin of the Esla river, local mineral resources (iron a coal) and livestock farming.

León's artistic tradition has also been maintained, as can be seen in Gaud neo-Gothic palace, **Casa de Botines (B)** on plaza de San Marcelo.

SIGHTS

★★★ **Catedral** ⊘ **(B)** – The cathedral, built mainly between the mid 13C and late 14C true Gothic in style even to the very high French-inspired nave with vast window

West front – The façade is pierced by three deeply recessed and richly carved port: separated by unusual, sharply pointed arches. The gently smiling Santa Ma Blanca *(a copy: original in the apsidal chapel)* stands at the pier of the cent: doorway in which the lintel carries a carving of the Last Judgement with grap:

LEÓN

Alcalde Miguel Castaño	B 2	Generalísimo Franco ...... B 16

Alcalde Miguel Castaño .... B 2
Almirante Martin-Granizo
  (Av. del) .... A 3
Arquitecto Ramón
  Cañas del Rio .... B 4
Calvo Sotelo
  (Pl. de) .... A 5
Caño Badillo .... B 8
Espolon (Pl. de) .... B 12
Facultad (Paseo de la) ..... A 15

Generalísimo Franco ...... B 16
General Sanjurjo
  (Av.) .... A 17
Guzmán el Bueno
  (Glorieta de) .... A 23
Independencia .... B 25
Jorge de Montemayor ...... B 26
Mariano Andrés
  (Av. de) .... A 28
Murias de Paredes ...... B 30
Ordoño II .... A
Padre Isla (Av. del) ...... AB
Palomera .... B 31

Papalaguinda (Paseo de) ... A 33
Puerta Obispo .... B 38
Quevedo (Av. de) .... A 40
Ramiro Valbuena .... A 45
Rúa .... B
Saez de Miera
  (Paseo de) .... A 47
San Francisco (Paseo) ..... B 48
San Isidoro (Pl. de) ..... B 50
San Marcelo (Pl.) .... B 52
San Marcos (Pl. de) ...... A 55
Santo Domingo (Pl. de) .... B 58
Santo Martino (Pl. de) .... B 61

portraits of the blessed and the damned. The left portal tympanum illustrates scenes from the Life of Christ, while the right portal, the Puerta de San Francisco, includes the Dormition and the Coronation of the Virgin.

South face – The statues decorating the jambs of the central doorway are extremely fine.

Interior – The outstanding **stained glass windows**★★★ – 125 windows and 57 oculi with an area of 1 200m²/12 917sq ft – are unique in Spain but by their sheer mass are endangering the resistance of the walls (the last restoration was at the end of the last century). The west front rose and the three central apsidal chapels contain the oldest, 13-15C glass; the Capilla de Santiago (St James's Chapel) has glass in which the Renaissance influence is already apparent while the nave windows, which were made much later, some are even considered modern, illustrate three major themes: the vegetable and mineral kingdom (below), historic personages and heraldic crests (behind the triforium) and, high up, the blessed.

The Renaissance **trascoro**★ by Juan de Badajoz, includes four magnificent alabaster high reliefs framing Esteban Jordán's triumphal arch through which there is an attractive view down the length of the nave.

The high altar **retable**, painted by Nicolás Francés, is a good example of the 15C international style. To the left is a remarkable **Entombment**★, which shows a Flemish School influence and is attributed to the Master of Palanquinos. At the foot of the altar, a silver reliquary contains the relics of San Froilán, the city patron.

Several Gothic tombs can be seen in the ambulatory and transept, in particular that of Bishop Don Rodrigo – in the Virgen del Carmen Chapel to the right of the high altar – which is surmounted by a multifoil arch.

★ **Claustro** – Before entering the cloisters, note the well-preserved, sheltered north transept doorway dedicated to the figure of the Virgin with the Offering, at the pier.

The galleries are contemporary with the 13C-14C nave but the vaulting, with its ornately carved keystones, was added at the beginning of the 16C. The galleries are interesting for the frescoes by Nicolás Francés and the tombs dating from the Romanesque and Gothic periods.

Museo Catedralicio ⊘ – This museum collection includes a French-inspired 1
statue of St Catherine, a Christ carved by Juan de Juni in 1576 (proportioned
such a way as to be viewed from below), a Mozarabic Bible, with miniatures, frc
920, an antiphonary dating from the same period, a 13C codex illustrated wi
engravings and the Plateresque staircase which used to lead up to the chapt
house.

★ **San Isidoro** (B) – The basilica, built into the Roman ramparts, its belfry like
watchtower overlooking the walls, was dedicated in 1063 to Isidore, Archbish
of Sevilla and Doctor of the Visigothic church, whose ashes had been broug
north for burial in Christian territory since Sevilla was then under Moorish ru
Of the 11C church there remains only the pantheon. Construction of the prese
basilica began at the very end of the 11C and it underwent modifications at a la
date: the apse and transept are Gothic while the balustrade and the pediment
the south front were added during the Renaissance. The sculptures on t
Romanesque portals, depicting Abraham's Sacrifice and the Descent from t
Cross, are contemporary with those of the church at Frómista.

★★ **Panteón Real** ⊘ – The Royal Pantheon is one of the earliest examples of Ron
nesque architecture in Castilla. The **capitals**★ crowning the short, thick colum
bear traces of the Visigothic tradition yet at the same time introduce great nove
into Romanesque carving in Spain. Some, with plant motifs, show influenc
from Asturian art, while others are fully historiated.

Panteón Real de San Isidoro, León

The beautifully preserved 12C **frescoes**★★ are outstanding. They illustrate not o
classic themes from the New Testament but also scenes from country life; no
on the inside of an arch, a calendar of seasonal tasks.
The pantheon is the resting place of 23 kings and queens and many children

★★ **Tesoro** ⊘ – The treasury contains works of great artistic value. The 11C reliqua
containing the relics of San Isidoro is made of wood, faced with embossed silv
and covered in a Mozarabic embroidery. Other items include the famous **Cáliz**
Doña Urraca★ or Doña Urraca's chalice comprising two Roman agate cups mount
in the 11C in a gold setting inlaid with precious stones, the 11C **Arqueta de**
Marfiles★ (Ivory Reliquary) in which each finely carved plaque represents
Apostle, and another reliquary decorated with Limoges enamelwork (13C). T
library contains over 300 incunabula and a large number of manuscripts adorn
with miniatures, including a Mozarabic Bible dating from 960.

★ **Antiguo Convento de San Marcos** (**Former Monastery of St Mark**) (A) – Part of t
monastery has been converted into a parador. The site has been connected wi
the Knights of the Order of Santiago or St James since the 12C: first as that
the mother house of the soldier friars, protectors of pilgrims on the way
Santiago de Compostela and, three centuries later, when the Catholic monarc
did away with the privileges of the Military Orders and became the Grand Maste
themselves, as that of the monastery planned by Ferdinand as being worthy
the dignity and riches acquired by the Knights during the Reconquest. Th
resulted in the present sumptuous edifice, built finally at the height of t
Renaissance. The church was completed in 1541 but work continued right up
the 18C.

The 100m/328ft long **façade**★★ has a remarkable unity of style in spite of the addition of a Baroque pediment in the 18C. It consists of two storeys of windows and niches set within a regular layout of friezes and cornices, engaged columns and pilasters. Medallions in high relief, of people from the Bible, Rome, or Spain, provide additional decoration: Lucretia and Judith flank Isabel the Catholic, Trajan and Augustus and Charles V. Carving above the main entrance traces St James' life from his slaying of the Moors to his apotheosis (at the apex of the pediment). The **church** front (on the extreme right), emblazoned with scallop shells, symbols of the pilgrimage to Santiago de Compostela, remains incomplete. The shell theme is repeated inside, on the wall behind the high altar.

Museo de León ⊘ – The first gallery of the museum, with its star vaulting, displays among its works of art from the Mozarabic to the Late Gothic period, the 10C Votive Cross of Santiago de Peñalba and an outstanding 11C ivory crucifix, the **Cristo de Carrizo**★★★. A Byzantine influence is apparent in the small figure's great presence and penetrating gaze, the formally dressed hair and beard and the arrangement of the loincloth. Through a window can be seen the *artesonado* Renaissance ceiling of the old chapter-house (now part of the *parador*). The **cloister** galleries, built between the 16C and 18C, now serve as a lapidary museum (note the fine medallions on the keystones). The northeast corner contains a low relief of the Nativity with an interesting architectonic perspective by Juan de Juni.
The **sacristy**★, a sumptuous creation by Juan de Badajoz (1549), has ribbed vaulting decorated with scallop shells, ribands, cherubim and bosses carved as masks. Several works by Juan de Juni are displayed.

EXCURSIONS

San Miguel de Escalada – *28km/17mi via ② on the town plan.*
In the 11C, Alfonso III made a gift of an abandoned monastery to a group of monks who were expelled from Córdoba, enjoining them to rebuild. Of their work only the church remains (at the centre of a terrace) but even so, it is one of the few Mozarabic edifices in Spain and the best preserved. The **exterior gallery**★, built in 1050, has horseshoe-shaped arches resting on carved capitals at the top of smoothly polished columns. The monastery church (**iglesia**★ ⊘) building is considerably earlier, dating from 913. The nave and two aisles, covered with wooden vaulting, are divided from the apses by a triple-arched portico and a balustrade of panels carved with Visigothic (birds pecking seeds, bunches of grapes) and Moorish motifs (stylised foliage).

Cuevas de Valporquero (Valporquero Caves) ⊘ – *47km/29mi north on LE 311* (B). The caves hollowed out by underground streams are still in the process of formation *(be careful not to slip)*. The temperature is constant at 7°C/45°F. Neutral lighting sets off the extraordinary shapes of the concretions – there is a stalactite "star" hanging from the roof of the large chamber – and the variety of tones (35 have been counted) of red, grey and black of the mineral oxide-stained stone. The tour ends with a walk along a narrow passage 1 500m/1 640yd long cut obliquely by subterranean waters through a 40m/131ft thick layer of soft rock.

Monasterio de LEYRE★

Navarra
Michelin map 442 or 443 E 26

splendid **panorama**★★ opens out at the end of a steeply winding approach road to e monastery, over the man-made embalse de Yesa (lake); on all sides are marl hills, eir limestone crests forming majestic ramparts while in the Sierra de Leyre itself, reat walls of mixed ochre-coloured stone and local rock hang suspended, halfway o the the ridge face.

y the early 11C, the Abbey of San Salvador de Leyre had established itself as the ncontested spiritual centre of Navarra; Sancho III, the Great, and his successors ade it their pantheon and gave their blessing to the building of a church which, with s crypt, was to be one of the earliest examples of Romanesque art in Spain onsecrated 1057). Bishops of Pamplona were, by tradition, former abbots of Leyre hich held dominion over some 60 villages and 70 churches and monasteries.

the 12C, however, when Navarra was joined to Aragón, the royal house neglected eyre in favour of San Juan de la Peña; in the same period the Pamplona bishops ought greater authority and instituted a lawsuit which considerably reduced both e finances and the prestige of the old monastery. In the 13C, the monastery was ome to the Cistercian order but by the 19C it had been abandoned. In 1954, owever, a Benedictine community from Silos took it over. They restored the 17C nd 18C conventual buildings which have now been converted into a hostelry.

Hoz de Lumbier (Lumbier Gorge)

★★ IGLESIA (CHURCH) ⊘ 30min

East end - 11C. Three apses of equal height, together with the nave w surmounted by a turret and a further square tower with treble window make a delightful group. The beautiful smoothness of the walls and t absence of decoration, apart from several modillions, indicate the building great age.

★★ **Crypt** - The crypt, built in the 11C to support the Romanesque church abo (with which it shares the same ground plan), looks even older, so rough robust and archaic is its appearance. The vaulting is relatively high but divid by arches with enormous voussoirs and, in some cases, double ribs, curvi down onto massive capitals, incised only with the most rudimentary line Unusually these capitals stand on short shafts of unequal height, practically ground level.

★ **Interior** - In the 13C when the Cistercians rebuilt the church's central aisle include a bold Gothic vault, they nevertheless retained the first bays of the earl Romanesque church as well as the chancel and semicircular apses. The three aisl which have come down to us intact have barrel vaulting with double ribs springi throughout from the same height. The decorative elegance arises from engag pillars, finely designed capitals and beautifully assembled blocks of rough hev stone. In the north bay a wooden chest contains the remains of the first kings Navarra.

★ **West portal** - 12C. The portal's rich decoration has won it the name Porta Speciosa. Carvings cover every available space. On the tympanum a archaic statues - Christ *(centre)*, the Virgin Mary and St Peter *(on His rig* and St John *(on His left)*; the covings are alive with monsters and fantas beasts. Above, the spandrels show *(on the right)* the Annunciation and t Visitation.

EXCURSIONS

* **Hoz de Lumbier** – *14km/9mi west.* The gorge cut by the Irati through the Sierra de Leyre foothills between Lumbier and Liédana is barely 5km/3mi long and so narrow that it appears at either end as a mere crack in the cliff face. There is a good **view** of the gorge from a lookout point on the road (N 240).

* **Hoz de Arbayún** – *31km/19mi north on N 240 and NA 211.* The río Salazar is so steeply enclosed within the limestone walls of the Sierra de Navascués that the road has to diverge from the river course and the only way to see it is by going to the viewpoint north of Iso. From there a splendid **view**★★ opens onto the end of the canyon where the cliff walls are clad, at their base, in lush vegetation through which flows the sparkling stream.

LIZARRA/ESTELLA★★

Navarra – Population 13 569
Michelin map 442 D 23

stella spreads on hilly ground on either side of the río Ega and is divided into arishes which have grown in size without losing their local character. The nobility f the brick and rough stone façades recalls the destiny intended for the city selected the 12C by the kings of Navarra as their centre and in the 19C by the Carlists. On he first Sunday in May, the Carlists gather in remembrance.

stella la Bella – Such was the name pilgrims gave the town in the Middle Ages on heir way to Santiago. As Estella was a major halt on the pilgrim road, it was endowed vith several artistic buildings which date mainly from the Romanesque period. Moreover, in 1076, King Sancho Ramírez granted the town certain privileges which ttracted tradesmen and innkeepers most of whom were freemen who settled on the ight bank of the Ega.

Pilgrims stopped to venerate Our Lady on the Hill whose shrine, now a modern hurch, stands on the site on which, according to tradition, on 25 May 1085, hepherds, guided by a shower of stars, found a statue of the Virgin. Of the town's nany medieval hospices, the leper hospital of St Lazarus became the most famous.

SIGHTS

Plaza de San Martín – The small square was originally at the heart of the freemen's parish, bustling with the comings and goings around its shops and inns; today nothing, apart from the splashing fountain, disturbs the peace. On one side stands the **former Ayuntamiento** (town hall) with an emblazoned front dating from the 16C.

★ **Palacio de los Reyes de Navarra (Palace of the kings of Navarra)** – The building is a rare example of 12C Romanesque civil architecture. Its long front is punctuated by arcades and twin bays with remarkable capitals.

Iglesia de San Pedro de la Rúa ⊘ – The church stands facing the royal palace on a cliff spur formerly crowned by the city castle. It retains outstanding 12C and 13C features.
There is an unusual **doorway**★ at the top of a monumental flight of steps, in the north wall. The door's originality, with richly sculpted capitals and covings, lies in its equilateral scalloped arch, Caliphate influenced. Similar portals can be seen in Navarra at Puente la Reina and Cirauqui and in the Saintonge and Poitou regions of France.
Inside are three Romanesque apses, with, at the centre, a column of intertwined serpents.
The Romanesque **cloisters**★ lost two galleries when the nearby castle was blown up in the 16C. The loss becomes all the more regrettable as one discovers the skill and invention of the masons who carved the remaining capitals; the north gallery series illustrates scenes from the lives of Christ and Sts Lawrence, Andrew and Peter, while plant and animal themes enliven the west gallery where the architect unexpectedly included a group of four slanting columns.

Calle de la Rúa – The pilgrim road. Note the **Palacio de Fray Diego de Estella**, at no 7, a palace with an emblazoned Plateresque façade.

Iglesia del Santo Sepulcro (Church of the Holy Sepulchre) – The church is remarkable for its portal which is purely Gothic. Superimposed above the door are the Last Supper, the three Marys at the Holy Sepulchre and Hell, and Calvary. The niches framing the doorway contain somewhat mannered figures of saints.
Take the Puente de la Cárcel (rebuilt in 1973) across the river.

Iglesia de San Miguel – The church stands in a quarter that was lived in by nati
of Navarra at the end of the 12C and which still has a medieval atmosphere abc
its narrow streets. The **north portal**★ seems almost to have been designed a
challenge to the foreigners on the opposite bank of the river. On the tympanun
a figure of Christ surrounded by the Evangelists and other mysterious personag
Sculptures in the covings show censer-bearing angels, the Old Men of the A
calypse, prophets and patriarchs, martyrs and saints, and scenes from the Gospe
The capitals illustrate the childhood of Christ and some hunting scenes. On t
upper register of the walls are eight statue columns of the Apostles while on t
lower register, two **high reliefs**★★, the most accomplished and expressive of t
doorway show, on the left, St Michael slaying the dragon, and on the right, the th
Marys coming from the Sepulchre. The noble bearing, the elegance of the draper
and the facial expressions, make the carving a masterpiece of Romanesque ar

EXCURSIONS

★ **Monasterio de Irache** ⊙ – *3km/2mi southwest.*
A Benedictine abbey was founded on the site as far back as the 10C. Later, Irache
major halt on the Santiago pilgrim road, was a Cistercian community before be
ming a university under the Benedictines, in the 16C, which was to close in 183

★ **Iglesia** – This church's pure Romanesque style apse lies directly in line with t
original intersecting ribs of the nave vaulting. During the Renaissance the do
on squinches was rebuilt and the *coro alto* added to the original structure. T
main façade and most of the conventual buildings were rebuilt in the 17C.

Claustro – The Renaissance cloisters are decorated with brackets and capit
illustrating the lives of Christ and St Benedict.

★ **Sierras de Andía and Urbasa** – *Round tour of 94km/58mi – about 3hr.*
The pleasure of this tour lies in driving through beechwoods and, as you rise
the top of a pass, getting an extensive view over the countryside.

Leave Estella on NA 120 north towards the puerto de Lizarraga (Lizarraga Pas

Monasterio de Iranzu ⊙ – *9km/6mi north of Estella. Signposted from NA 120.*
The Cistercian monastery, built in lonely isolation in a wild **gorge**★ at the end
the 12C, is now a college. It is a good example of the Cistercian transitional st
from Romanesque to Gothic in which robustness and elegance combine.
The cloister bays, where they have not been given a later florid Gothic fenest
tion, are typical, with Romanesque blind arcades, oculi and wide relieving arch
The church, with somewhat primitive vaulting, has a flat east end decorated w
a triplet, or three windows, symbolising the Trinity, a feature found in ma
Cistercian churches.

★★ **Puerto de Lizarraga Road** – On emerging from the tunnel (alt 1 090m/3 576ft) pa
briefly at the **viewpoint**★ overlooking the green Ergoyena Valley before beginn
the descent through woods and pastures.

*Continue to Etxarri-Arantaz where you take N 240ᴬ west to Olatzi and then t
left towards Estella.*

★★ **Puerto de Urbasa Road** – The fairly steep climb between great free-standing bould
and clumps of trees has a beautiful wildness in total contrast to the wide and lus
wooded valley which follows. Beyond the pass (alt 927m/3 041ft) tall limesto
cliffs add character to the landscape before the road enters the series of gorg
through which the sparkling río Urenderra flows.

LLEIDA/LÉRIDA★

Catalunya – Population 119 380
Michelin map 443 H 31

Lleida was once a citadel, built on high ground to command a point where commu
cations crossed. Caesar's and Pompey's legions stormed it savagely; the Mo
occupied it from the 8C to the 12C. The ancient fortress, the Zuda or Azuda, sited I
an acropolis, and occupied in the 13C by the counts of Catalunya, was destroyed
artillery fire in 1812 and 1936 but the fortifications which surround it remain. T
glacis has been converted into gardens. From the terraces there is an extensive view
the town, the green Segre plain and, to the southeast, the sierra la Llena.

★★ **Seu Vella (Old Cathedral)** ⊙ – The cathedral stands on a remarkable **sit**
dominating the city from inside the walls. It was built between 1203 and 12
on the site of a mosque; the tall, octagonal belfry was added in the 14C. Phili
converted it into a garrison fortress in 1707. Recent work, however, has resto
the edifice to its original appearance.

★★ **Iglesia** – The outstanding decoration in this transitional style church occurs
its great variety of **capitals**★, many of which are historiated. Those in the apses a
transept illustrate themes from the Old Testament, those in the nave and aisl

scenes from the New. Moorish influences can be seen in the exterior decoration, particularly in the carvings of the Puerta de Els Fillols (Godchildren's Doorway) off the south aisle and in the Puerta de la Anunciata (Annunciation Doorway), in the corresponding transept. Above is a lovely rose window. The extremely delicate style of carving, reminiscent of Moorish stuccowork, on the capitals of the church doorways, has come to be known as the Romanesque School of Lleida and may be seen throughout the region, in particular on the superb portal from the Iglesia de **Agramunt** *(52km/32mi northeast)*.

★ **Claustro** – The cloisters' unusual position in front of the church recalls that of a mosque forecourt or a Romanesque church narthex. The galleries, completed during the 14C, are remarkable for the size of the bays and the beautiful stone tracery, different in each case. The delicately carved decoration of plant motifs on the **capitals**★ and friezes is Moorish influenced. There is a fine view from the south gallery extending over the town and surrounding countryside.

In the southwest corner stands the **church tower**★★, an interesting Gothic construction 60m/197ft high.

★ **Iglesia de Sant Llorenç** ⊘ – The late Romanesque church (13C) shows heavy Gothic influence, illustrated by its belfry and the pointed arches separating the central nave from the side aisles. Note the fine collection of Gothic retables.

LORCA

Murcia – Population 67 024

Michelin map 445 S 24

Lorca lies at the foot of a low mountain range crowned by a fortress, **Castillo**, in the fertile valley of the Guadalentín. It serves as agricultural market and main centre for the particularly arid southwest corner of the province of Murcia.

"Blancos" and "Azules" – Lorca is one of the cities of Spain where Holy Week is celebrated with full traditional panoply. Sumptuous embroideries, the pride of a local craftsmanship that is old and famous, adorn the *pasos*. Biblical and Imperial Roman characters in full costume join penitents in long processions, the brilliant colours of the former contrasting with the sombre robes of the latter. Finally, there is friendly competition between the White and Blue Brotherhoods who rival for solemnity and magnificence.

Plaza de España – The square is surrounded by the fine Baroque façades of the **Ayuntamiento** (town hall), the palace, now the **Juzgado** (Law Courts) embellished with a corner sculpture, and the **Colegiata de San Patricio** (collegiate church).

Casa de los Guevara – The doorway, unfortunately in not very good condition, is, nevertheless, an outstanding example of Baroque sculpture (1694).

LUGO★

Galicia – Population 87 605

Michelin map 441 C 7

Under the Romans Lugo was a provincial capital and a major road junction. The **walls**, **old bridge** and **thermal baths** all date from this period.

Now at the heart of an agricultural region specialising in cheese production, the town has taken on new life, building wide shopping streets such as the **rúa da Raiña** and **Plaza de Santo Domingo** while also preserving a distinguished old quarter around the cathedral.

SIGHTS

★★ **Murallas (town walls)** – The walls were built by the Romans in the 3C, although they have undergone siginificant modifications since that time, particularly during the Middle Ages. They are made of schist slabs levelled off at a uniform 10m/33ft to form a continuous perimeter over 2km/1.2mi long with 10 gateways into the old quarter.

Not to be missed

A stroll along the sentry path on the walls. Any of the flights of steps leading from the town's gateways, as well as the ramp at the **Puerta de Santiago**, opposite the cathedral, will take you up to the path, from where there are some fine **views** of Lugo and its surrounding countryside.

LUGO

Anxel López Pérez (Av.) .	Z 2
Bispo Aguirre	Z 3
Bolaño Rivadeneira	Y 5
Campo (Pr. del)	Z 8
Comandante Manso (Pr.)	Z 12
Conde Pallarès	Z 15
Coruña (Av. de la)	Y 21
Cruz	Z 23
Dezaoito de Xullo	
(Av. del)	Y 24
Doctor Castro	Z 27
Montero Ríos (Av.)	Z 37
Paxariños	Z 39
Pío XII (Pr. de)	Z 43
Praza Maior	Z 45
Progreso	Y 47
Quiroga Ballesteros	Y 50
Raiña	Y 53
Ramón Ferreiro	Z 56
Rodríguez Mourelo (Av.) .	Z 62
San Fernando	Y 65
San Marcos	Y 68
San Pedro	Z 71
Santa María (Pr. de)	Z 74
Santo Domingo (Pr. de) . .	YZ 77
Teniente Coronel Teijeiro	YZ 78
Tinería	Z 80
Vilalba	Z 83
Xeneral Franco	Y 85

A   Catedral
B   Palacio episcopal
H   Ayuntamiento
M   Museo Provincial

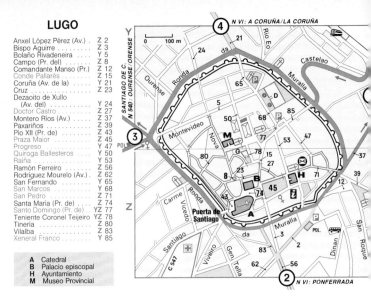

★ Catedral (Z A) – The Romanesque church (1129) was modified in later years b
Gothic and Baroque additions. The Chapel of the Wide-Eyed Virgin at the east end
by Fernando Casas y Novoa who built the Obradoiro façade in Santiago d
Compostela, has a Baroque rotunda enhanced by a stone balustrade. The nort
doorway, sheltered by a 15C porch, has a fine Romanesque **Christ in Majesty★**. Th
figure is above a capital curiously suspended in mid-air and carved with the Las
Supper.

Inside, the Romanesque nave is roofed with barrel vaulting and lined wit
galleries, a feature common in pilgrimage churches. There are two immens
wooden Renaissance altarpieces at the ends of the transept – the south one i
signed by the sculptor Cornelis de Holanda (1531). A door in the west wall of th
south transept leads to the small but elegant **cloisters**.

City squares – The 18C **Palacio Episcopal** (Z B), facing the north door of the cathedr
on **Praza de Santa María** (Z 74), is a typical *pazo*, one storey high with smooth ston
walls, advanced square wings framing the central façade and decoration confine
to the Gil Taboada coat of arms on the main doorway. Plays and concerts are give
in the square in summer. **Praza del Campo** (Z 8), behind the palace, is lined by ol
houses and has a fountain at its centre. Calle de la Cruz with its bars an
restaurants, and **Praza Maior** (Z 45), dominated by the 18C **town hall** (Z H), with it
gardens and esplanade, are popular with the townspeople as places to meet an
stroll. The Rúa do Raiña is home to the Alejo Madarro sweet shop, which firs
opened its doors in the middle of the last century.

Museo Provincial ⊙ (Y M) – This museum, which is dedicated to various aspect
of Lugo art, is housed in the 18C kitchens of the former Monasterio de Sa
Francisco. It has managed to recreate the atmosphere of a traditional countr
kitchen similar to those found in some of the more remote villages in the area (se
Santa Eulalia de Bóveda). The museum is on two floors and includes one roo
devoted to ceramics from Sargadelos, in addition to coins and numerous exhibit
from the Roman period. The former cloister of San Francisco contains a
interesting collection of sundials, as well as several altars and sarcophagi. Sever
entrances connect with the **Museo Nelson Zúmel**, dedicated to Spanish painting
from the 19C and 20C.

EXCURSION

Santa Eulalia de Bóveda – *14km/8mi southwest.* This attractive Galician villag
still has granite farm buildings with tile-stone roofs and drying sheds or *hórreo.
The **paleo-Christian monument** ⊙ discovered at the beginning of the 20C an
excavated in 1924, consists of a vestibule (now open to the sky), a rectangula
chamber with a basin and round-arched niche and frescoes of birds and leave
doubtless of Christian origin, on the walls. The dating and purpose of th
monument continue to intrigue archeologists.

*Use the Index to find more information about a subject mentioned in the guide;
people, towns, places of interest, isolated sites,
historical events or natural features...*

MADRID★★★

Population 3 084 673

Michelin map 442 or 444 K 18-19

Plan of the conurbation on Michelin maps 442and 444

Michelin Plan Madrid 1/12.000 n° 42

Madrid, Europe's highest-lying capital (alt 646m/2 120ft), stands in the foothills of the Sierra de Guadarrama in the middle of the Meseta, right in the centre of the Iberian Peninsula. It is a hospitable city, known for the quality of its light, with a dry continental climate that is very hot in summer, and cold, yet sunny, in winter.

It became the capital in the 16C at a time when Spain ruled over a vast empire. The city's main monuments, Classical and Baroque in style, were built during the 17C, 18C and 19C. Thanks to collections left by the Habsburgs and Bourbons, Madrid has an exceptional wealth of paintings which may be seen in the Prado, the Academia de San Fernando and the Museo Lázaro Galdiano, while the outstanding collections of the recently opened Museo Thyssen-Bornemisza have undoubtedly added to this wealth.

Madrid has undergone extraordinary development over the past few decades and now, renowned for its vitality, is a cosmopolitan centre with wide, busy thoroughfares.

Madrid in the past – Madrid, an unimportant village until the Moorish invasion, owes its name to the fortress (alcázar) of Majerit built under Mohammed I on the banks of the Manzanares in the 9C. In 1083 it was captured by Alfonso VI, who, it is said, discovered a statue of the Virgin by a granary (almudín) as he entered the town. He then converted the town mosque into a church, dedicating it to the Virgin of the Almudena who was declared the city patron. From the 14C the kings of Castilla came regularly to Madrid; Emperor Charles V rebuilt the Muslim alcázar and in 1561 Philip II moved the court from Toledo to Madrid. The medieval town expanded rapidly and the population tripled. Its layout of winding streets can still be seen today around Plaza Mayor.

The town really began to develop under the last of the Habsburgs, in the middle of Spain's Golden Age (16C). During the reign of Philip III, Juan Gómez de Mora undertook a series of reforms and from then on Plaza Mayor was to be the heart of the city. The town plan drawn up in 1656 by Pedro Texeira, gives a good impression of Madrid under Philip IV, when it had a large number of convents and churches. The king was an art lover who gave his patronage to many artists including Velázquez and Murillo, as well as men of letters such as Lope de Vega, Quevedo, Calderón and Tirso de Molina.

However, it was in the 18C under the Bourbons that the town underwent its greatest transformations. Philip V decided to build a royal palace, and Charles III, inspired by ideas from European courts, provided Madrid with a splendour hitherto unknown. This was the Prado and the Puerta de Alcalá, magnificent examples of neo-Classical town planning. In turn, the nobility began building **palaces**, such as Liria (KV) and **Buenavista** (MX), which they surrounded with gardens.

The 19C began with occupation by the French and the Madrid rebellion of May 1808 and the brutal reprisals it provoked (see p 244 and ARANJUEZ). In the second half of the 19C, Madrid underwent great alteration: in 1857 the remaining ramparts were demolished and a vast expansion plan (ensanche) gave rise to the districts of Chamberí (DU), Salamanca (HV) and Argüelles (DV), and, at the end of the century, **Arturo Soria's** Ciudad Lineal (JT), a revolutionary town planning project, provided for a residential quarter for 30 000 inhabitants around today's Avenida de Arturo Soria.

At the beginning of the 20C, architecture was French-inspired, as can be seen in the Ritz (NY) and Palace (MY) hotels; the neo-Mudéjar style was also popular and brick façades so characteristic of Madrid went up all over the city (Plaza de Toros de las Ventas) (JV). The Gran Vía, a fast thoroughfare which crosses the centre of town to link Madrid's new districts, was inaugurated in 1910 and has since been popularised in an operetta (zarzuela).

Madrid today – As capital, Madrid is Spain's leading city as far as banks, insurance companies, universities, administrative bodies and political institutions are concerned. It is also an important industrial and technological centre with most of these activities developing on the outskirts of the city.

The business district, centred around the Puerta de Alcalá and Paseo de la Castellana, was modified extensively between 1950 and 1960 when traditional mansions were demolished to make room for new buildings. The city's most modern edifices may be seen in the **Azca** (FT) area, the result of one of Madrid's most revolutionary projects, designed to fulfil various administrative, residential and commercial functions. Among its most noteworthy buildings are the avant-garde Banco de Bilbao-Vizcaya and the Torre Picasso.

DISTRICTS

Madrid is not as monumental as Paris, as romantic as Venice, nor is it a decadent as Lisbon; it is however full of charm and mystery, with its ow magnificent parks and impressive buildings. It is a city which is best explore by strolling through its streets and squares, discovering the delights of it many districts and getting to know its inhabitants.

Centro (XYZKL) – This district is made up of several areas, each with their ow individual character. It has a reputation for being noisy, chaotic and full of people although visitors are often surprised by its narrow alleyways and small squares

Sol-Callao (LXY) – The shopping area par excellence, packed with locals and visitor out for a stroll, heading for the main pedestrianised precinct (Preciados) or fo a drink or dinner in one of the many local cafés and restaurants. A number c cinemas are also located in this area. Visitors should take particular care in th evening, especially in streets such as Valverde and Barco.

Barrio de los Austrias (YZK) – Madrid's oldest district is wedged between calle Mayor, Bailén, Las Cavas and the Plaza de la Cebada. Its origins are mediev and it still retains its evocatively-named streets and Mudéjar towers. A excellent area for tapas, dinner or a drink. On Sundays, the famous El **Rastr** flea market *(see p 233)* is held nearby.

El Rastro flea market

Lavapiés (ZL) – This district is located around the square of the same name wit many houses dating from the 17C. It is considered to be Madrid's most colou ful district with a mix of locals, students and a large immigrant population.

Huertas (YLM) – Huertas was home to the literary community in the 17C an the Movida movement in the 1980s. Nowadays, it is packed with bars an restaurants and is particularly lively at night, attracting an interesting mixtur of late-night revellers.

Malasaña (LV) – This part of Madrid, which used to be known as Maravillas is situated between Las glorietas de Bilbao y Ruiz Jiménez and around plaz del Dos de Mayo. In the mornings, this 19C *barrio* is quiet and provincial, bu it is transformed at night by the legions of young people heading toward Malasaña's many bars. For those in search of a quieter night out, the distric also has a number of more tranquil cafés.

Alonso Martínez (MV) – The average age and financial standing of th district's inhabitants is somewhat higher than in neighbouring Bilbao an Malasaña, as shown by the myriad upmarket bars and restaurants frequente by the city's rich and famous.

Chueca (MVX) – This district covers an area around the plaza de Chueca; it approximate outer limits are the paseo de Recoletos, calle Hortaleza, Gran Vi and Calle Fernando VI. At the end of the last century it was one of Madrid' most elegant districts. Today it is the city's gay area with a multitude of sma and sophisticated boutiques.

Salamanca (GHUV) – In the 19C, Salamanca was Madrid's principal bourgeois district designed by the Marquis of Salamanca in the shape of a draughts board with large perpendicular streets. Nowadays, the district is one of the capital's most expensive areas and is home to some of Spain's leading designer boutiques (Serrano and Ortega y Gasset) and an impressive collection of stores selling luxury goods.

WHERE TO STAY

The *Michelin Red Guide España & Portugal* offers a wide selection of hotels listed by district. Those specified below have been chosen for their surroundings, character, excellent location or value for money.
The letters given after the name of the hotel allow the reader to locate the hotel on the Madrid maps in this guide.

BUDGET HOTELS

Centro Sol (LY ⑥) – *Carrera de San Jerónimo, 5 2º-4º.* ☎ *91 522 15 82, fax 91 522 57 78. 35 rooms.*
A hotel very close to the Puerta del Sol occupying the second and fourth floors of a building somewhat lacking in charm. However, its rooms are very reasonably priced and have been recently refurbished.

Mora (MZ ❷) – *Paseo del Prado, 32.* ☎ *91 420 15 69, fax 91 420 05 64. 61 rooms.*
The Mora is located just opposite the Jardín Botánico, a stone's throw from the Prado. Because of its superb position, this recently renovated hotel is a good choice for a stay in the city.

París (LY ❸) – *Alcalá, 2.* ☎ *91 521 64 96, fax 91 531 01 88. 120 rooms. Some without air conditioning.*
The París was built in 1863 and is one of Madrid's oldest hotels. Its public lounges have preserved the decadent charm of its former splendour, and although its rooms are somewhat old-fashioned, they are spacious and well-appointed.

OUR SELECTION

Galiano (NV ❺) – *Alcalá Galiano, 6.* ☎ *91 319 20 00, fax 91 319 99 14. 29 rooms.*
Hidden behind the sober façade of this small neo-Classical-inspired 19C palace is a charming hotel with an English air, antique furniture and spacious guest rooms. Because of its superb position and moderate price, this hotel is highly recommended.

Casón del Tormes (KV ❼) – *Río, 7.* ☎ *91 541 97 46, fax 91 541 18 52. 63 rooms.*
Located in a small, quiet street in the centre of the city, just behind the Senate building. Built in the middle of the 1960s, the hotel has large, comfortable rooms which have been recently renovated.

Carlos V (LX ❽) – *Maestro Victoria, 5.* ☎ *91 531 41 00, fax 91 531 37 61. 67 rooms.*
A good central option in a pedestrianised street. Although small and rather noisy, the English-style rooms are well-appointed. An eclectic cafeteria on the first floor.

NH Sur (NZ ❸) – *Infanta Isabel, 9.* ☎ *91 539 94 00, fax 91 467 09 96. 68 rooms. Special weekend rates.*
A 19C building opposite Atocha station and close to the Prado Museum and Retiro Park. The hotel, which is part of the NH chain, has been tastefully decorated in a modern, functional style with all necessary amenities. The rooms are slightly on the small side.

NH Embajada (MV ❼) – *Santa Engracia, 5.* ☎ *91 594 02 13, fax 91 447 33 12. 101 rooms. Special weekend rates.*
The attractive turn-of-the-century building is in the middle of an exclusive part of the city. Very comfortable, tastefully decorated rooms with large, modern bathrooms.

TREAT YOURSELF

Santo Mauro (FV ❻) – *Zurbano, 36.* ☎ *91 319 69 00, fax 91 308 54 77. 33 rooms.*
A luxury hotel occupying the delightful palace built as a private residence by the Duke and Duchess of Santo Mauro in 1894. The hall, main lounge and former library, which has been converted into the hotel's restaurant, all retain the full splendour of a 19C mansion. The avant-garde furniture and bright colours in the luxurious bedrooms come as something of a surprise. Pretty garden.

Ritz (NY ●) – *Pl. de la Lealtad, 5.* ☎ *91 521 28 57, fax 91 532 87 7*
164 rooms.
Famous five-star hotel with a great tradition, built at the beginning of the 20
by the same French architect who designed its namesakes in Paris and London
Elegant decor, spacious lounges and reception areas. Delightful terrac
garden.

Palace (MY ●) – *Pl. de las Cortes, 7.* ☎ *91 360 80 00, fax 91 360 81 0*
440 rooms.
Dating from the same period as the Ritz and opened by Alfonso XIII, this
Madrid's other traditional-style luxury hotel with a particularly charmir
rotunda with an attractive glass cupola. Although recently renovated, the hot
has managed to retain its timeless elegance.

EATING OUT

The restaurants listed below have been chosen for their surrounding
ambience or unusual character. For a wider selection and more detaile
gastronomic information, consult the *Michelin Red Guide España & Portuga*

Centro

BUDGET

Casa Marta – *Santa Clara, 10.*
☎ *91 548 28 25.*
Cosy, long-established restaurant decorated with
azulejos. Home cooking.

El Ingenio – *Leganitos, 10.*
☎ *91 541 91 33.*
Dedicated to Don Quijote,
this restaurant is decorated
with motifs alluding to this
famous character and to its
author, Cervantes. Friendly
atmosphere.

OUR SELECTION

La Bola – *Bola, 5.*
☎ *91 547 69 30*
Attractive, traditional restaurant renowned for its
excellent cuisine. Very popular with foreign visitors and
well-known personalities.

Casa Lucio – *Cava Baja, 35.*
☎ *91 365 32 52.*
One of Madrid's best-known
addresses frequented by po-
liticians, actors and visitors
alike. Typical Castilian decor. Famous for its *huevos
estrellados* (fried eggs).

A typical meal at La Bola

Botín – *Cuchilleros, 17.* ☎ *91 366 42 17.*
The city's oldest restaurant renowned for its roast meats, particular
suckling pig. Very popular with tourists.

Huertas

BUDGET

Champanería Gala – *Moratín, 22.* ☎ *91 429 25 62.*
A restaurant specializing in rice dishes. Pleasant covered patio with wrough
iron garden furniture.

La Vaca Verónica – *Moratín, 38.* ☎ *91 429 78 27.*
A small restaurant with exuberant Baroque decor. Bright yellow and bubb
gum pink for the walls, chandeliers, rustic cupboards, wooden chairs (
different) and sofas. Reasonably priced menus.

OUR SELECTION

Zeraín – *Quevedo, 3.* ☎ *91 429 79 09.*
Basque cider house decorated with barrels from which customers he
themselves to the house speciality. Excellent chops *(chuletón).*

Salamanca

BUDGET

Romarzo – *Jorge Juan, 16.* ☎ *91 431 58 40.*
Fashionable restaurant with finely detailed Baroque decor. Warm, friendly atmosphere. Fixed menu.

Beatriz – *Hermosilla, 15.* ☎ *91 577 53 79.*
Avant-garde design in this former theatre. Italian and international cuisine.

OUR SELECTION

La Giralda IV – *Claudio Coello, 24.* ☎ *91 576 40 69.*
Fish is the order of the day in this Andalusian-style restaurant. Popular tapas bar.

TREAT YOURSELF!

La Trainera – *Lagasca, 60.* ☎ *91 576 05 75.*
One of Madrid's best tables for fish and seafood with a nautical ambience. Upmarket clientele.

El Amparo – *Puigcerdà, 8.* ☎ *91 431 64 56.*
Top-class restaurant with an original design including split-level dining-rooms and roof skylights. Very pleasant atmosphere. Fine cuisine and polished service with prices to match.

Recoletos – Castellana

OUR SELECTION

Paradis Casa América – *Paseo de Recoletos, 2.* ☎ *91 575 45 40.*
The magnificent Palacio de Linares is home to this elegant restaurant specialising in Catalan cuisine. In summer, dinner on its delightful terrace is a must.

TREAT YOURSELF!

Zalacaín – *Álvarez de Baena, 4.* ☎ *91 561 48 40.*
The city's most famous top-class restaurant. Superb dining and service in elegant surroundings for a very upmarket clientele. Popular with the business community.

Zona Alonso Martínez

BUDGET

Ciao Madrid – *Apodaca, 20.* ☎ *91 308 25 19.*
One of Madrid's best Italian eateries with a young and relaxed atmosphere.

OUR SELECTION

Assai – *Genóva, 19.* ☎ *91 319 40 29.*
Fashionable restaurant frequented by the city's young jet-set and famous personalities. Situated in an attractive mansion with stylish decor with the occasional modern touch.

Foreign cuisine

Thai Gardens – *Jorge Juan, 5 (Salamanca).* ☎ *91 577 88 84. (Expensive).*
The city's most popular Thai restaurant. Superb decor.

Al Mounia – *Recoletos, 5 (Salamanca).* ☎ *91 435 08 28. (Expensive).*
This Moroccan restaurant has been delighting customers with its excellent cuisine in attractive Arabic-style surroundings for the past 30 years.

Zara – *Infantas, 5 (Centro).* ☎ *91 532 20 74. (Inexpensive).*
Small Cuban eatery always packed with a young crowd. The restaurant does not take reservations.

Kobata – *Reina, 31 (Centro).* ☎ *91 521 85 28. (Expensive).*
Good Japanese restaurant with a typical layout around its sushi bars. Popular with Japanese residents and visitors alike.

Annapurna – *Zurbano, 5 (Chamberí).* ☎ *91 308 32 49. (Moderate).*
A pleasant restaurant in which to enjoy traditional Indian dishes.

TAPAS

Centro

Casa Labra – *Tetuán, 12.* This old tavern dating back to the middle of the 19C is a Madrid institution. It was here that Pablo Iglesias founded the Spanish Socialist Party (PSOE) in 1879. Its house speciality is fried cod *(bacalao frito)*.

El Almendro – *Almendro, 13.* A new tavern with an old atmosphere which is always packed. Its tapas include cheese and sausage pastries *(roscas de queso y embutido)*, fried eggs *(huevos estrellados)* and its potato-based *patatas emporradas*.

Taberna de los cien vinos – *Nuncio, 17.* A large tavern with wooden beams an plenty of tables. A good selection of wines, many of which are served by th glass, and a wide choice of tapas and *raciones.*

Matritum – *Cava Alta, 17.* A small, tastefully decorated tapas bar. Friendl service and excellent hot tapas: croquettes, potatoes with four cheeses *(patata a los cuatro quesos)* and aubergines stuffed with meat *(berenjenas rellenas carne),* all of which can be accompanied by a carefully selected choice of wine

Casa Antonio – *Latoneros, 10.* A typical tapas bar decorated with bullfightin and football memorabilia. Vermouth on tap to accompany scrambled egg *(huevos revueltos),* patés, tripe etc.

Huertas

La Venencia – *Echegaray, 7.* If your taste is for sherry, this is the place. L Venencia is a small, narrow bar which more than makes up in atmosphere ar cuisine what it lacks in size. You won't be disappointed.

Los Gabrieles – *Echegaray, 17.* Tapas by day and a bar by night. A favourite haur for foreign students in Madrid, attracted, no doubt, by the historical chronicle on its *azulejo*-decorated panelling.

La Dolores – *Plaza de Jesús, 4. Azulejos* on the façade and a large, crowded b on the inside are the distinctive features of this popular bar. Excellent draugh beer, anchovies *(boquerones)* in vinegar, canapés etc.

Cervecería Cervantes – *Plaza de Jesús, 7.* Another recommended bar in this pa of the city which is lively at night. A good choice of sausages *(embutidos),* well as hot and fried tapas.

La Platería – *Moratín, 49.* Small, pleasant tavern with a good choice of wine by the glass. Tasty sausages and savoury pastries *(empanadas).*

Salamanca

Taberna La Daniela – *General Pardiñas, 21.* A new bar with traditional-sty decoration. *Azulejos* on the outside with vermouth on tap and a wide selectic of canapés and *raciones* inside.

Hevia – *Serrano, 118.* This long-established tapas bar has developed a fir choice of expensive snacks and *raciones.* Its specialities include smoked meat which in summer can be enjoyed on the pavement terrace.

José Luis – *Serrano, 89.* A Salamanca institution. In two parts, each with the distinct style, but sharing the same bar. A wide choice of superb tapas; i Spanish omelette is the most famous in the city. Tables outside in summe

El Cantábrico – *Padilla, 39.* One of the best places to enjoy seafood, washed dow with beer from the barrel. Very popular for aperitifs, particularly at the weeken

CAFÉS

Madrid has a multitude of pleasant cafés. Many of them have a great traditic and attract a wide cross-section of customers for a quiet coffee or a live discussion with friends.

The following is a list of some of the city's most popular meeting places:

Café Gijón – *Paseo de Recoletos, 31.* This café, which has long been famous as a meeting point for writers and artists, continues the tradition to this day. Outdoor terrace in summer.

El Espejo – *Paseo de Recoletos, 21.* An attractive, Modernist-style café close to the Café Gijón with a charming wrought-iron and glass canopy.

Café de Oriente – *Plaza de Oriente, 2.* This classic institution, located in the Plaza de Oriente opposite the Royal Palace, is a delightful place for a drink at any time of day. Pleasant terrace.

Café del Nuncio – *Segovia, 9.* Typical 19C-style café with its velvet seats and marble tables. Terrace during the summer months.

Café Gijón

Café del Círculo de Bellas Artes – *Marqués de Riera, 2. (Non-members must pay an entrance fee of 100 pts)*. The marked 19C atmosphere of this great café with its enormous columns and large windows is in sharp contrast to its young, intellectual clientele. Outdoor terrace in summer. Highly recommended.

Salón del Prado – *Prado, 4*. This café, which is in the heart of the Santa Ana district, occasionally hosts exhibitions and classical music concerts.

Café Central – *Plaza del Ángel, 10*. One of the city's main haunts for jazz-lovers since the early 1980s.

Café Comercial – *Glorieta de Bilbao, 7*. A café dating back over a century with a permanent flow of customers passing through its swing doors. Popular as a meeting place for young people, intellectuals and locals alike.

Café Ruiz – *Ruiz, 11*. A famous address in the Malasaña district. This quiet, typical café is decorated with wood, mirrors, photos and red velvet. A 19C fabric, but with a modern feel.

NIGHT-LIFE

Madrid has a huge variety of night-life catering to every taste and style. The city comes to life at the weekend until the small hours of the morning.

Music and live performances

Moby Dick – *Av. de Brasil, 5*. One of the best concert venues in the city. Some of the famous names in the Spanish rock and pop industry, such as Gabinete Caligari, Los Lunes and Jam Session, have performed here.

Irish Rover – *Av. de Brasil, 7*. A pub within a pub. A section which looks as though it has come straight out of one of Joyce's novels and a tiny lounge are just two of the features of this Irish home-from-home. Daily performances and a small market on Sundays. Young clientele.

Berlín Cabaret – *Costanilla de San Pedro, 11*. In just 12 years this venue has become an important centre for Madrid night-life. Its strengths are its live acts (magicians, drag queens etc). Fun atmosphere.

Libertad, 8 – *Libertad, 8*. A building over a century old is the setting for this atmospheric café, renowned for its poetry readings and storytellers, attracting young, bohemian audiences.

El Sol – *Jardines, 3*. A style which is in complete contrast to Libertad, 8. This venue, which was hugely influential during the 1980s, now organises an excellent programme of live music.

La Coquette – *Hileras, 14*. Small, dark and smoky – one of Madrid's authentic blues bars.

Galileo Galilei – *Galileo, 100*. This venue has carved a niche for itself in the pop-rock music world.

Cocktail bars

Rastatoo – *Lagasca, 120*. Along with the famous **Big Bam Boo** (*Barquillo, 42*), this is *the* place for reggae music-lovers with a decor in keeping with the music.

Paramond – *Claudio Coello, 10*. A journey back to the Salamanca district of the 16C along with Villamayor stone and blood-red inscriptions. Theme nights on Wednesdays and Thursdays. Popular with executives and the occasional famous name.

Villa Rosa – *Plaza de Santa Ana, 15*. One of the city's most popular dance venues is hidden behind this attractive *azulejo* façade.

Sala Maravillas – *San Vicente Ferrer, 33*. Indie and grunge in the Malasaña district.

El Cock – *La Reina, 16*. Yet another Madrid institution. A vast, decadently decorated bar for the over-30s. Quiet atmosphere.

Del Diego – *La Reina, 12*. A pleasant bar with some of the city's best cocktails.

Barnon – *Santa Engracia, 17*. Popular with Madrid's basketball players. A lively bar with a young following.

Torero – *Calle de la Cruz, 26*.

El Escueto – *Barco, 34*

Fortuny – *Fortuny, 34*. A bar and restaurant frequented by Madrid's thirty-something crowd. Worth having a drink on its superb terrace in summer.

Nightclubs

Joy Eslava – *Arenal, 11*. This well-known club, occupying a former 19C theatr
has been attracting a colourful crowd of club-goers and famous faces fe
several decades. On your way home, why not pay a visit to the famou
Chocolatería de San Ginés, in the street of the same name.

Palacio de Gaviria – *Arenal, 9*. A fascinating club which has been converted fro
one of Madrid's old palaces. Also famous for its ballroom dancing. I
Thursday-night *fiesta internacional* is very popular with foreigners.

Gabana 1800 – *Velázquez, 6*. A trendy club where famous names come to b
seen. One of Madrid's in clubs, with restricted entry. Expensive.

Kapital – *Atocha, 125*. A huge disco on seven floors in the centre of the cit
With its different areas (disco, cafeteria and restaurant) and versati
facilities, Kapital has something for everyone.

Flamenco

Madrid has developed into one of Spain's leading centres for flamenco with
huge number of venues in which to enjoy this magnificent art.

Café de Chinitas – *Torrija, 7*. ☎ *91 547 15 02*. Very popular with tourist
Dinner shows also available.

Casa Patas – *Cañizares, 10*. ☎ *91 369 04 96*. One of the best venues in whi
to enjoy a night of flamenco.

Suristán – *Cruz, 7*. ☎ *91 532 39 09*. Its varied programme covers every ty
of music, but at least one night a week is devoted to flamenco. Good Africa
and Cuban music.

Parks

Madrid has a large number of parks. The **Retiro** (GHXY), the origins of whi
date back to the time of Philip IV, is the city's most popular park, and
particularly lively on Sunday mornings when the path alongside the lake
home to artists, acrobats, puppets and musicians and its lake is taken over
hordes of rowers. On Sundays in summer Madrid's municipal band entertai
strollers with music from the park's bandstand.

The **Parque del Oeste** (DV) is a quiet, English-style park which was created at tl
end of the 19C. One of its most attractive areas is the rose garden.

The **Casa de Campo** (DX), originally a hunting reserve created by Philip II, is tl
city's largest park and has a countrified, forested appearance. Madrid
Zoo-Aquarium and fairground are both located in this park. The **Campo del Mc**
(DX), next to the Royal Palace, owes its name to the Moorish troops who ma
an encampment here during their assault on the city in the Middle Ages. Tl
Jardín Botánico (NZ) ⊘, is without doubt the city's most attractive and intima
garden. Created at the behest of Charles III and designed by Juan
Villanueva, it is now a haven of tranquility in the heart of the city. The **Parq
de la Fuente del Berro** (JVX) is also an oasis of peace and romance alongside tl
busy M30 motorway.

The lake in the Parque del Retiro

Cinemas and Art Galleries

Madrid has over 100 cinemas, 20 or so theatres, numerous concert halls and one casino. The **Auditorio Nacional (HT)** (opened in 1988) has a varied programme of classical music, the **Teatro de la Zarzuela (MY)** hosts a wide range of shows including zarzuelas and ballets, while the **Teatro Real (KX)** offers a season of opera. The **Veranos de la Villa** and the **Festival de Otoño** are two events held in the summer and autumn respectively with an interesting mix of cultural performances. The **Festival Internacional de Jazz** is another event also held during November.

Art Galleries – A number of galleries can be found in and around Atocha, close to the Centro de Arte Reina Sofía, in the Salamanca district (near the Puerta de Alcalá) and on the left side of the paseo de la Castellana, close to the calle Génova.

PRACTICAL INFORMATION

Tourist Offices – Barajas Airport, ☎ 91 305 86 56. Mon-Fri 8am to 8pm, Sat 9am to 1pm; Duque de Medinaceli, 2, ☎ 91 429 49 51, Mon-Fri 8am to 8pm, Sat 9am to 1pm; Plaza Mayor, 3, ☎ 91 588 16 36/ 91 366 54 77, Mon-Fri 10am to 8pm, Sat 10am to 2pm.
Internet: http://www.munimadrid.es

Publications – The *Guía del Ocio*, is a weekly guide containing a list of every cultural event and show in the city. It can be purchased at newspaper stands. *In Madrid* is a free monthly publication published by Madrid City Hall listing cultural events for the coming month.

Useful numbers

Emergency services – ☎ 112.

State Police – ☎ 091.

SAMUR (ambulance) and Municipal Police – ☎ 092.

Duty chemist – ☎ 010.

Tourist information – ☎ 901 300 600.

Consumer information – ☎ 010.

Lost property – ☎ 91 588 43 46.

Lost/stolen credit cards – **Servired y Visa** ☎ 91 519 21 00; **American Express** ☎ 91 572 03 03; **Mastercard** ☎ 91 402 26 00.

Transport

Airport – Madrid-Barajas airport is located 13km/8mi east of the city. A shuttle bus operates to the airport from Plaza de Colón, with six pick-up points along its route. It runs from 4.45am until 1.30am with a departure every 10min between 7am and 10pm. For further information, call ☎ 91 431 61 92.
A new metro line connecting the airport with the city centre is scheduled to open in 1999.
Airport information ☎ 91 393 60 00, 91 305 83 43/44/45/46.
Info-Iberia ☎ 902 400 500.

RENFE (Spanish State Railways) – The city's main railway stations are Atocha and Chamartín. For information and reservations, call ☎ 91 328 90 20. The AVE high-speed train departs from Atocha, taking just 2hr 30min to reach Seville via Córdoba. For information, call ☎ 91 534 05 05. Madrid also has a comprehensive local train network which can be used to get to El Escorial, the Sierra de Guadarrama, Alcalá de Henares and Aranjuez.

Inter-city buses – Most buses to other cities depart from the Estación Sur, calle Méndez Álvaro. ☎ 91 468 42 00.

Taxis – Madrid has a huge number of registered taxis with their distinctive white paintwork with a red diagonal stripe on the rear doors. At night, the green light indicates that the taxi is for hire.

Local buses – For information, call ☏ 91 406 88 00. A good way of getti
to know the city, although traffic jams are a major problem. Passenge
should also beware of pickpockets. Times vary from line to line, but genera
buses operate between 6am and 11.30pm. Night buses operate fro
11.30pm onwards, with most departing from Plaza de Cibeles. In addition
single tickets, passengers can also purchase a 10-trip Metro-bus ticket (
bono de 10 viajes) valid on both the bus and metro network, as well as
zone-based monthly ticket *(bono mensual)* which is valid for an unlimit
number of bus and metro journeys for one month.

Metro – *Metro stations are shown on the maps in this guide.* For informatic
call ☏ 91 552 59 09. The metro system is the fastest way to get around t
city and consists of 11 lines. It operates from 6am to 1.30am. Passenge
should beware of pickpockets.

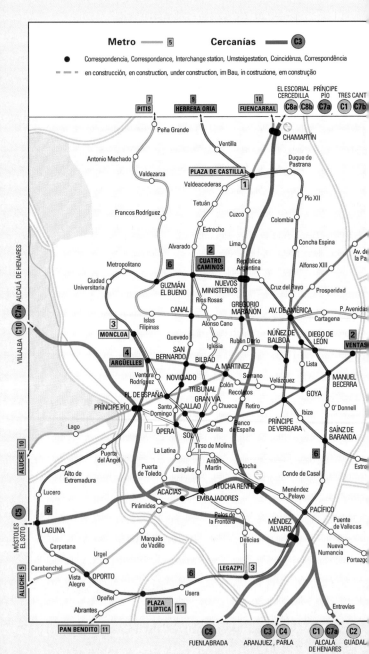

★VIEJO MADRID **(OLD MADRID)** *2hr 30min – see town plan pp 232-3.*

Steep, narrow streets, small squares, 17C palaces and mansions, houses with wrought-iron balconies dating from the 19C and early 20C provide the backdrop to this walk through Old Madrid, the very heart of the city, which first developed around Plaza Mayor and Plaza de la Villa. The old town is best visited early in the morning or late in the afternoon when the churches are open.

★Plaza Mayor – This was built by Juan Gómez de Mora during the reign of Philip III (1619) and forms the architectural centre of **Habsburg Madrid**. On the north side, flanked by pinnacled towers, stands the **Casa de la Panadería** (a former bakery) which was reconstructed by Donoso in 1672. Its mural decoration, the third since it was built, is the work of the artist Carlos Franco. The 17C equestrian statue of Philip III in the middle of the square is by Giambologna and Pietro Tacca.

The vast square was the setting for *autos-da-fé*, mounted bullfights, and the proclamations of kings Philip V, Ferdinand VI and Charles IV. Its present appearance is a result of the work carried out by Juan de Villanueva at the end of the 18C.

A stamp and coin market is held under the arches on Sunday mornings while at Christmas, stalls are set up selling

Plaza Mayor, Madrid

F. Bouillot/MARLO POLO

religious and festive decorations. The shops around the square, hatters in particular, have retained their look of yesteryear.

Pass through the **Arco de Cuchilleros** into the street of the same name, fronted by tall, aged houses with convex façades. The **Cava de San Miguel (45)** provides a rear view of the houses which look onto the square and gives an indication of the steep slopes around Plaza Mayor. The name *cava* derives from the ditches or moats that once stood here. This area is crowded with small restaurants (*mesones*) and bars (*tavernas*). The **Mercado de San Miguel**, an indoor market built early this century, has preserved its elegant iron structure.

Head down the calle Conde de Miranda, cross the pleasant plaza del Conde de Barajas and the calle de Gómez de Mora to get to plaza de San Justo or Puerta Cerrada, an old city gate. Continue right along the calle de San Justo.

★Pontificia de San Miguel ⊙ – The basilica by Bonavia is one of the rare Spanish churches to have been inspired by 18C Italian Baroque. Its convex façade, designed as an interplay of inward and outward curves, is adorned with fine statues. Above the doorway is a low relief of saints Justus and Pastor to whom the basilica was previously dedicated. The interior is graceful and elegant with an oval cupola, intersecting ribbed vaulting, flowing cornices and abundant stuccowork.

Follow calle Puñonrostro – to the left of the church – and calle del Codo, in former times one of Madrid's most dangerous streets because of its reputation for drink, to Plaza de la Villa.

★Plaza de la Villa – The quiet pedestrian square is presided over by a statue of Álvaro de Bazán, hero of Lepanto, by Benlliure (1888). Several famous buildings are arranged around the square including the **Ayuntamiento** (town hall) **(H)**, built by Gómez de Mora in 1617, the **Torre de los Lujanes** (Lujan Tower), one of the rare examples of 15C civil architecture preserved in Madrid and in which Francis I was imprisoned after the battle of Pavia, and the **Casa de Cisneros**, built several years after the death of the cardinal of the same name, which is connected to the Ayuntamiento by an arch. Of the original 16C edifice only an attractive window giving onto Plazuela del Cordón remains.

Calle Mayor – The name of this street, literally Main Street, gives us an indication of its historical importance. It has preserved several interesting buildings such as no 61, the narrow house in which the 17C playright, **Pedro Calderón de la Barca (D)**, lived. The Antigua Farmacia de la Reina Madre (Queen Mother's Pharmacy) close by, has preserved a collection of old chemist jars and pots. The **Instituto Italiano de Cultura** (no 86) occupies a palace dating from the 17C which has undergone more recent restoration. The Palacio Uceda opposite, a palace dating from the same period, is now the military headquarters of the **Capitanía General** (Captaincy General). This brick and granite palace is a fine example of civil architecture of the time. In front of the **Iglesia Arzobispal Castrense (F)** (17C-18C) is a monument commemorating the attack on Alfonso XIII and Victoria Eugenia on their wedding day in 1906. In the nearby Calle de San Nicolás, the Mudéjar tower of San Nicolás de los Servitas can still be seen.

Follow calle del Sacramento, which passes behind Plaza de la Villa, to Plazuela del Cordón.

Plazuela del Cordón (54) – Just before you reach the square, stop to admire the back of the Casa de Cisneros. From the centre of the *plazuela* there is an unusual view of the façade of the Iglesia de San Miguel. Isidro, future patron saint of Madrid, lived as a servant in the **Casa de Ju** **de Vargas**.

| D | Casa de Pedro Calderón de la Barca | H | Ayuntamiento |

Return to calle del Cordón and continue to calle de Segovia.

Across the street rises the 14C **Mudéjar tower** of the **Iglesia de San Pedro** (Church St Peter), which, apart from the Torre de San Nicolás, is the only example of t Mudéjar style in Madrid.

Go along calle del Príncipe Anglona to Plaza de la Paja.

Plaza de la Paja – This calm, irregularly built square was, along with the Pla de los Carros, the commercial centre of Madrid in the Middle Ages. The Palac Vargas, on one side of the square, obscures from view the Gothic **Capilla del Obis** a chapel built in the 16C by Gutiérrez Carvajal, Bishop of Palencia. Close to it, Plaza de los Carros, is a chapel, the Capilla de San Isidro, part of the Iglesia de S Andrés, built in the middle of the 17C in honour of Madrid's patron saint. T **Museo de San Isidro** ⊘, a museum containing a miracle well and a fine Renaissar patio, is situated next to this complex group of religious buildings.

Go along calle Redonilla and cross calle de Bailén. The first street on the right lea to the Jardines de los Vistillas.

Jardines de las Vistillas (Vistillas Gardens) – From the part of the gardens close to the calle Bailén there is a splendid **panorama★**, especially at sundown, of t Sierra de Guadarrama, Casa de Campo, the Catedral de la Almudena and t viaduct.

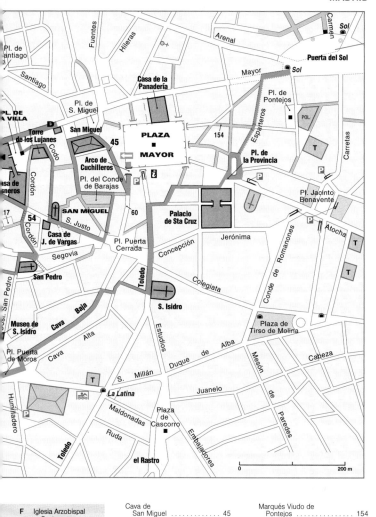

F Iglesia Arzobispal Castrense	Cava de San Miguel 45	Marqués Viudo de Pontejos 154
	Cordón (Pl. del) 54	Príncipe Anglona 188
	Cuchilleros 60	San Javier (Pl. de) 217

Iglesia de San Francisco El Grande ⓥ – The church's vast neo-Classical façade is by Sabatini but the building itself, a circular edifice with six radial chapels and a large dome 33m/108ft wide, is by Francisco Cabezas. The walls and ceilings of the church are decorated with 19C frescoes and paintings except those in the chapels of Sts Anthony and Bernardino which date from the 18C. The Capilla de San Bernardino, the first chapel on the north side, contains in the centre of the wall, a St Bernardino of Siena preaching before the King of Aragón (1781), painted by Goya as a young man. Some of the Plateresque **stalls**★ from the Monasterio de El Parral outside Segovia may be seen in the chancel. The 16C **stalls**★ in the sacristy and chapter-house come from the Cartuja de El Paular, the Carthusian monastery near Segovia.

Walk along Carrera de San Francisco and Cava Alta to calle de Toledo.

Calle de Toledo – This is one of the old town's liveliest streets. The popular **El Rastro** flea market sets up in neighbouring streets and along Ribera de Curtidores every Sunday morning and on public holidays.

Iglesia de San Isidro ⓥ – The church with its austere façade and twin towers is by the Jesuits Pedro Sánchez and Francisco Bautista. Formerly the church of the Imperial College of the Company of Jesus (1622), it was the cathedral of Madrid from 1885 until 1993. It contains the relics of Madrid's patron saint, Isidro, and those of his wife, Santa María de la Cabeza.

Plaza de la Provincia – Note the well-proportioned façade of the 17C **Palacio de Santa Cruz**, former court prison (Lope de Vega was incarcerated here) and present Ministry for Foreign Affairs. It was from here that prisoners were taken to be executed in the nearby Plaza Mayor.

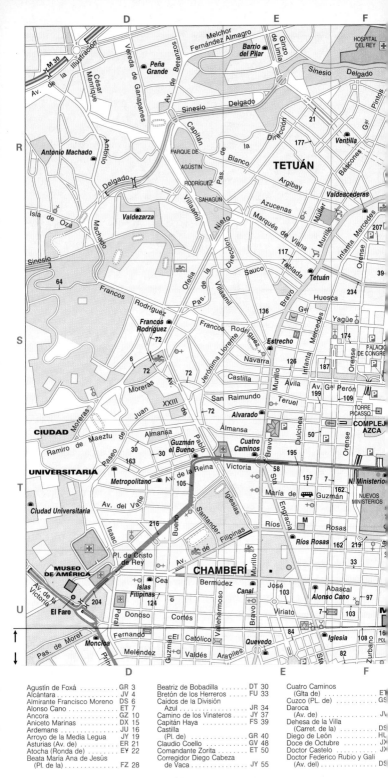

Agustín de Foxá	GR 3	Beatriz de Bobadilla	DT 30	Cuatro Caminos	
Alcántara	JV 4	Bretón de los Herreros	FU 33	(Glta de)	ET
Almirante Francisco Moreno	DS 6	Caídos de la División		Cuzco (PL. de)	GS
Alonso Cano	ET 7	Azul	JR 34	Daroca	
Ancora	GZ 10	Camino de los Vinateros	JY 37	(Av. de)	JV
Aniceto Marinas	DX 15	Capitán Haya	FS 39	Dehesa de la Villa	
Ardemans	JU 16	Castilla		(Carret. de la)	DS
Arroyo de la Media Legua	JY 19	(Pl. de)	GR 40	Diego de León	HL
Asturias (Av. de)	ER 21	Claudio Coello	GV 48	Doce de Octubre	JX
Atocha (Ronda de)	EY 22	Comandante Zorita	ET 50	Doctor Castelo	JX
Beata María Ana de Jesús		Corregidor Diego Cabeza		Doctor Federico Rubio y Galí	
(Pl. de la)	FZ 28	de Vaca	JY 55	(Av. del)	DS

Puerta del Sol – The itinerary ends at the Puerta del Sol, the liveliest a
best-known square in Madrid. It has been a crossroads for historical events in
city over the ages although its present layout only dates back to the 19C. A sr
monument illustrating Madrid's coat of arms – a bear and an arbutus (strawberr
tree – stands on the point at which Calle del Carmen joins the square. In fron
this monument is an equestrian statue of Charles III. At its base, the major wo
for which the king was responsible in the city have been highlighted. The clock

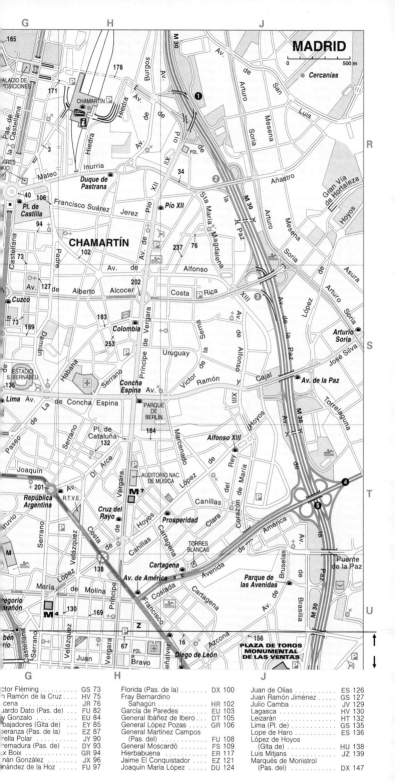

	G		H		J
ctor Fléming	GS 73	Florida (Pas. de la)	DX 100	Juan de Olías	ES 126
n Ramón de la Cruz	HV 75	Fray Bernardino		Juan Ramón Jiménez	GS 127
cena	JR 76	Sahagún	HR 102	Julio Camba	JV 129
uardo Dato (Pas. de)	FU 82	García de Paredes	EU 103	Lagasca	HV 130
y Gonzalo	EU 84	General Ibáñez de Ibero	DT 105	Leizarán	HT 132
bajadores (Glta de)	EY 85	General López Pozas	GR 106	Lima (Pl. de)	GS 135
peranza (Pas. de la)	EZ 87	General Martínez Campos		Lope de Haro	ES 136
rella Polar	JY 90	(Pas. del)	FU 108	López de Hoyos	
remadura (Pas. de)	DY 93	General Moscardó	FS 109	(Glta de)	HU 138
x Boix	GR 94	Hierbabuena	ER 117	Luis Mitjans	JZ 139
nán González	JX 96	Jaime El Conquistador	EZ 121	Marqués de Monistrol	
nández de la Hoz	FU 97	Joaquín María López	DU 124	(Pas. del)	DX 147

the former post office (now the headquarters of the Presidencia de la Comunidad de Madrid) chimes the traditional 12 strokes at midnight on New Year's Eve. Kilometre Zero, on the ground in front of the building, marks the point from which all the main roads of Spain radiate and distances are measured.

The many streets leading into Puerta del Sol are crowded with small traditional shops with their colourful wood fronts where customers can just as easily find fans and mantillas as cooked delicacies.

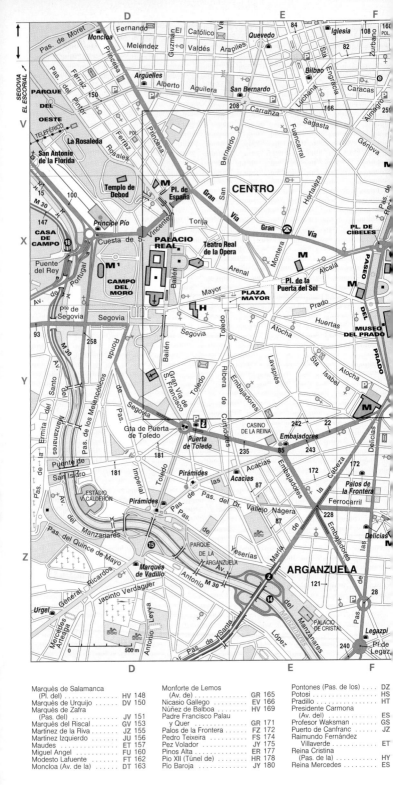

Marquès de Salamanca (Pl. del)		HV 148
Marquès de Urquijo		DV 150
Marquès de Zafra (Pas. del)		JV 151
Marquès del Riscal		GV 153
Martinez de la Riva		JZ 155
Martinez Izquierdo		JU 156
Maudes		ET 157
Miguel Angel		FU 160
Modesto Lafuente		FT 162
Moncloa (Av. de la)		DT 163

Monforte de Lemos (Av. de)		GR 165
Nicasio Gallego		EV 166
Núñez de Balboa		HV 169
Padre Francisco Palau y Quer		GR 171
Palos de la Frontera		FZ 172
Pedro Teixeira		FS 174
Pez Volador		JY 175
Pinos Alta		ER 177
Pio XII (Túnel de)		HR 178
Pío Baroja		JY 180

Pontones (Pas. de los)		DZ
Potosi		HS
Pradillo		HT
Presidente Carmona (Av. del)		ES
Profesor Waksman		GS
Puerto de Canfranc		JZ
Raimundo Fernández Villaverde		ET
Reina Cristina (Pas. de la)		HY
Reina Mercedes		ES

★★ BARRIO DE ORIENTE (EASTERN QUARTER) *1 day*

The walk combines monumental buildings with panoramic views.

★★ **Palacio Real (Royal Palace)** ⊘ **(KXY)** – The best view of the palace, which overlooks the Manzanares river, is from paseo de Extremadura and from the gardens of **Campo del Moro★** ⊘ **(DX)**.

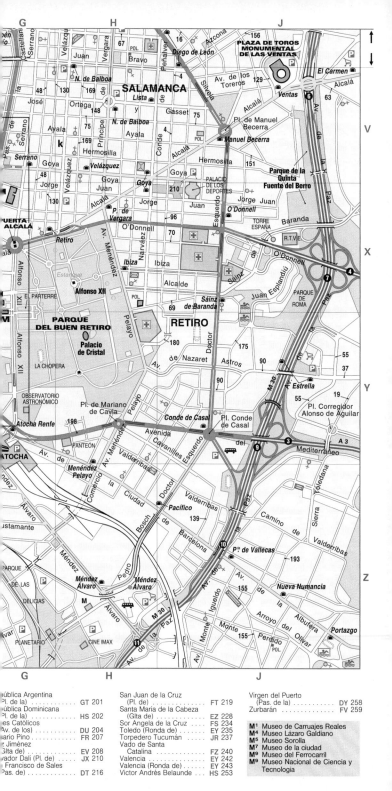

ública Argentina (Pl. de la)		GT 201
ública Dominicana (Pl. de la)		HS 202
es Católicos (Av. de los)		DU 204
sario Pino		FR 207
z Jiménez (Glta de)		EV 208
vador Dalí (Pl. de)		JX 210
Francisco de Sales (Pas. de)		DT 216

San Juan de la Cruz (Pl. de)		FT 219
Santa María de la Cabeza (Glta de)		EZ 228
Sor Angela de la Cruz		FS 234
Toledo (Ronda de)		EY 235
Torpedero Tucumán		JR 237
Vado de Santa Catalina		FZ 240
Valencia		EY 242
Valencia (Ronda de)		EY 243
Victor Andrés Belaunde		HS 253

Virgen del Puerto (Pas. de la)		DY 258
Zurbarán		FV 259

M¹	Museo de Carruajes Reales
M⁴	Museo Lázaro Galdiano
M⁵	Museo Sorolla
M⁷	Museo de la ciudad
M⁸	Museo del Ferrocarril
M⁹	Museo Nacional de Ciencia y Tecnología

The palace, an imposing edifice built by the Bourbons, was the royal family's official residence until 1931. Today, it is run by the Patrimonio Nacional (Spain's National Trust) and used by the king for state receptions.

On Christmas Day in 1734, while the royal family was staying at the Parque del Buen Retiro, a fire burnt the old Habsburg Alcázar to the ground. Philip V replaced it with a new palace, the present edifice, designed originally by the Italian

237

Palacio Real

architect, Felipe Juvarra. When Juvarra died, work continued under Sacche who modified his plans, and then under Ventura Rodríguez until completion in reign of Charles III. It forms a quadrilateral made of Guadarrama granite white stone, measuring some 140m/459ft on the sides, on a high bossaged ba The upper register, in which Ionic columns and Doric pilasters alternate crowned by a white limestone balustrade. Colossal statues of the kings of Sp from Ataulf to Ferdinand VI were originally intended to be placed above this, under Charles III they were put in Plaza de Oriente and the Retiro gardens. The north front gives onto the **Jardines de Sabatini**, the west the **Campo del Moro. P de la Armería** stands to the south between the west and east wings of the pala The east façade gives onto **Plaza de Oriente**.

Plaza de la Armería – The vast arcaded square is bounded to the south by incomplete façade of the **Catedral de la Almudena**. This cathedral, which has ta over a century to complete (the first construction project began in 1879), ha neo-Baroque façade which is in complete harmony with the palace and excessively cold neo-Gothic interior. It was consecrated by Pope John Paul I 1993.

The view from the west side of the square extends over the Casa de Campo the Campo del Moro gardens which slope down to the Manzanares river.

★ **Palacio** (Palace) – A monumental staircase with a ceiling painted by Giaquinto le to the Salón de Alabarderos (Halberdier Room), the ceiling of which was pain by Tiépolo. This leads to the **Salón de Columnas** (Column Room) in which the tre for Spain's membership of the European Community was signed on 12 J 1985, and where royal celebrations and banquets are held. The next room is **Salón del Trono**★ (Throne Room), which was known as the Salón de Reinos (Kingd Room) in the 18C. It has totally preserved its decoration from the period Charles III and is resplendent with crimson velvet hangings and a magnific ceiling painted by Tiépolo in 1764 symbolizing *The Greatness of the Spanish Monarchy*. The consoles, mirrors and gilded bronze lions are of Italian design. The following three rooms were the king's quarters, occupied by Charles III in 1764. The Saleta Gasparini was the king's dining room; only the ceiling painted by Mengs remains from its original, primitive decoration. The Gasparini antechamber, with a ceiling also painted by Mengs, and Goya portraits of Charles IV and Queen María Luisa of Parma, is followed by the **Cámara Gasparini**, covered from floor to ceiling in pure Rococo decoration.

The Salón de Carlos III was the king's bedroom. It was here that he died in 1788. The decor is from the period of Ferdinand VII. The **Sala de Porcelana** is, along with its namesake in Aranjuez Palace, the masterpiece of the Buen Retiro Porcelain Factory. Official banquets are held in the Alfonso XII **Comedor de Gala** or Banqueting Hall (for 145 guests), which is adorned with 16C Brussels tapestries. Subsequent rooms display various silver objects, table and crystalware used by the monarchs. The two music rooms contain a collection of instruments including several **Stradivarius**★. In the chapel are frescoes by Corrado Giaquinto and paintings by Mengs, *Annunciation*, and Bayeu, *St Michael the Archangel*.

The Queen María Cristina rooms display an unusual mix of styles ranging from the Pompeian decor in the Salón de Estucos (Stucco Room) to the neo-Gothic appearance of the Salón de Billar (Billiard Room).

Real Farmacia (Royal Pharmacy) – Several rooms have been redesigned to display a number of 18C-20C jars, including a fine 18C Talavera glass jar. The inside of a distillation room has also been recreated with retorts, glass flasks, scales and distillation equipment.

★ **Real Armería** (Royal Armoury) – The collection of arms and armour put together by the Catholic monarchs, Emperor Charles V and Philip II, is outstanding. The key pieces of the display include Charles V's suit of armour and the weapons and armour belonging to Philip II and Philip III. A vaulted hall in the basement contains an excellent collection of Bourbon shotguns, ranging from those made by Philip V's armourer to the Winchester given to King Alfonso XII by the President of the United States.

★ **Museo de Carruajes Reales** (Royal Carriage Museum) ⊘ (**DX M¹**) – A pavilion built in 1967 in the middle of the **Campo del Moro** winter garden, which commands a good view of the palace, houses the old royal horse-drawn carriages, most of which date from the reign of Charles IV, in the late 18C. Among the exhibits are the late-17C Carroza Negra or Black Coach made of stained beech and ash, and some 18C berlins, including that used by the Marquis of the House of Alcántara. The coronation coach (drawn by eight horses with accompanying footmen), was built in the 19C for Ferdinand VII and still bears marks of the assassination attempt made on Alfonso XIII and his bride, Victoria Eugenia, in May 1906.

Plaza de Oriente (KX) – This attractively landscaped square lies between the east façade of the Palacio Real and the main façade of the Teatro Real. It has recently been redesigned and is now a pleasant place for a stroll as it is closed to traffic. At the heart of the gardens, decorated with statues of Gothic kings, stands the magnificent equestrian statue of Philip IV, the work of Pietro Tacca (17C).

Teatro Real (KX) – This hexagonal neo-Classical building by architect López de Aguacio was inaugurated as an opera house in 1850 for Isabel II. It has two façades each overlooking a square, one the Plaza de Oriente and the other the Plaza de Isabel II. After almost 10 years closure for refurbishment it has finally been restored to its former glory. In October 1997 it reopened its doors to host the Madrid opera season.

★ **Monasterio de las Descalzas Reales** ⊘ (KLX) – Although the convent stands in one of the liveliest parts of Madrid, the moment one steps inside, one is taken right back to the 16C. It was Joanna of Austria, daughter of Emperor Charles V, who founded the convent of Poor Clares here in the palace in which she was born. For two centuries it served as a retreat for nobles who wished to live retired from the world. The nobility heaped gifts upon the order and its rich collection of religious art is now on display in buildings abutting the conventual cloisters.

The magnificent grand **staircase**★, decorated with frescoes, leads to the upper cloister gallery where each of the **chapels** is more sumptuous than its predecessor. Note the Recumbent Figure of Christ by the 16C sculptor Gaspar Becerra.

In the former nuns' dormitory are ten 17C **tapestries**★★ after cartoons by Rubens. Other convent treasures include, on the entresol, various portraits of the royal family and a *St Francis* by Zurbarán; in the chapter house, sculptures, a *Dolorosa* and an *Ecce Homo* by Pedro de Mena and a *Magdalene* by Gregorio Hernández; in the **Relicario** (Reliquary Chamber), a great many finely engraved chalices and caskets and, in the picture galleries, works by Titian, Bruegel the Elder and Rubens.

★ **Real Monasterio de la Encarnación (Royal Convent of the Incarnation)** ⊘ (KX) – The convent stands on a delightful square of the same name near the former Alcázar with which it was once connected by a passageway.

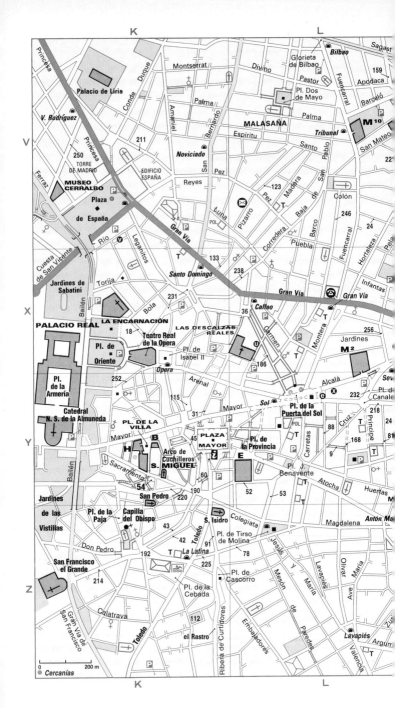

It was founded in 1611 by Margaret of Austria, wife of Philip III, and occupied▉
Augustines. The generosity of each successive Spanish monarch may be s▉
today in its impressive display of art works.

The collection of paintings from the 17C Madrid School is particularly rich a▉
includes the historically interesting *Exchange of Princesses on Pheasant Islan*▉
1615 by Van der Meulen and a *St John the Baptist* by Ribera. There i▉
noteworthy polychrome sculpture of *Christ at the Column* by Gregorio Hernán▉
on the first floor.

The **Relicario★**, with a ceiling painted by Vicencio Carducci, contains so▉
1 500 relics. Among the most notable are the Lignum Crucis and the p▉
containing the blood of St Pantaleon which is said to liquify each year on 27 J▉
The church with its sober quasi-Herreran style portal was originally by Gómez▉
Mora (1611) but was reconstructed by Ventura Rodríguez in the 18C after the ▉
in the Alcázar.

MADRID

Alcalá	MX	
Álvarez Gato	LY	9
Arenal	KY	
Arrieta	KX	18
Augusto Figueroa	MV	24
Ayala	NV	25
Bárbara de Braganza	NV	27
Bordadores	KY	31
Callao (Pl. del)	LX	36
Carmen	LX	
Cava Alta	KZ	42
Cava Baja	KZ	43
Cava de San Miguel	KY	45
Ciudad de Barcelona (Av. de la)	NZ	46
Colón (Pl. de)	NV	49
Concepción Jerónima	LY	52
Conde de Romanones	LY	53
Cordón (Pl. de)	KY	54
Cortes (Pl. de las)	MY	57
Cuchilleros	KY	60
Duque de Alba	LZ	78
Duque de Medinaceli	MY	79
Echegaray	LY	81
Espoz y Mina	LY	88
Estudios	KZ	91
Felipe IV	NY	
Fernando el Santo	NV	99
Fuencarral	LV	
General Vara del Rey (Pl. del)	KZ	112
Goya	NV	114
Gran Vía	LX	
Herradores (Pl. de los)	KY	115
Hortaleza	LX	
Independencia (Pl. de la)	NX	118
Infanta Isabel (Pas. de la)	NZ	119
Jesús del Valle	LV	123
Libreros	KX	133
Madrazo	MY	141
Marqués de Cubas	MY	145
Mayor	KY	
Mayor (Pl.)	KY	
Mejía Lequerica	LMV	159
Montera	LX	
Núñez de Arce	LY	168
Preciados	LX	186
Puerta Cerrada (Pl. de)	KY	190
Puerta de Moros (Pl. de)	KZ	192
Puerta del Sol (Pl. de la)	LY	
Recoletos	NX	196
San Bernardino	LV	211
San Francisco (Carrera de)	KZ	214
San Jerónimo (Carrera de)	LMY	218
San Justo	KY	220
San Lorenzo	LV	222
San Millán	KZ	225
Santa Engracia	MV	226
Santo Domingo (Cuesta, Pl. de)	KX	231
Sevilla	LX	232
Tudescos	LX	238
Valverde	LV	246
Ventura de la Vega	LY	249
Ventura Rodríguez	KV	250
Vergara	KY	252
Villa de París (Pl. de la)	NV	255
Virgen de los Peligros	LX	256

B	Torre de los Lujanes
E	Palacio de Sta-Cruz
H	Ayuntamiento
M²	Real Academia de Bellas Artes de San Fernando
M³	Museo Naval
M⁶	Museo Thyssen-Bornemisza
M⁸	Museo Nacional de Artes Decorativas
M¹⁰	Museo Municipal
M¹¹	Museo Romántico

Plaza de España (KV) – Every visitor to Madrid is bound to spend some time on the large esplanade during a tour of the city centre. The monument to Cervantes in the middle of the square, and the figures of Don Quixote and Sancho Panza, appear overwhelmed by the size of the skyscrapers built in the 1950s, in particular the Torre de Madrid and the Edificio España.
Starting from the square is the Gran Vía, a wide avenue lined by shops, cinemas and hotels, and Calle Princesa, popular with the young and with students, which leads towards the **Ciudad Universitaria**★ (University City) (DT).

Faro de la Moncloa (Moncloa Beacon) ⊙ (DU) – Completed in 1992. From its 76m/250ft high **balcony**★★, there is a wonderful view of Madrid and its surrounding area. To the northeast, the outline of the sierra madrileña can be seen.

★ **Parque del Oeste (West Park)** (DV) – This delightful landscaped garden, extending across slopes overlooking the Manzanares, was designed at the beginning of the century. In the southern part, on Príncipe Pío hill, stands the small 4C BC **Egyptian**

Temple of Debod (DX). It once stood beside the Nile in Nubia and was rescued fr
the waters when the Aswan Dam was being built. Note the hieroglyphs on t
interior walls.

The **Paseo del Pintor Rosales** nearby, stretching northwestwards, acts as a balco
overlooking the park. Its pavilions and pavement cafés command wonderful vie
of Velázquez-like sunsets. **La Rosaleda**, a rose garden, holds flower shows in Ju
A **teleférico** (cableway) ⊘ links the Parque del Oeste to the **Casa de Campo★** (DX), a va
natural expanse on the other side of the Manzanares. The park was reafforest
under Philip II in 1559 and today is very popular with Madrileños who come to stro
row on the lake, swim in the pools or visit the **amusement park** ⊘ and the z
aquarium★★ ⊘: the latter is one of the best in Europe with a wide variety of anim
and features an aquarium, a dolphinarium and exhibitions of birds of prey.

★★★ THE MUSEO DEL PRADO ⊘ (NY) 3hr

The museum is in the heart of Bourbon Madrid (see below).

The Prado is probably the greatest gallery of Classical paintings in the world. T
neo-Classical building was designed by Juan de Villanueva under Charles III
house the Natural Science Museum. After the War of Independence (the Pen
sular War), Ferdinand VII altered the project and instead installed the collectio
of Spanish painting made by the Habsburg and Bourbon kings which reflect t
development of royal artistic taste over the centuries. The Prado also conta
precious collections of work by Flemish painters, acquired by the Catho
monarchs, as well as a great many paintings from the Italian School favoured
Emperor Charles V and Philip II.

*Given the large number of works in stock, some paintings are only displayed
temporary exhibitions. As the museum is currently being modernised, sor
rooms are closed and their contents shown elsewhere in the museum.*

The Spanish School holds pride of place for the quality and quantity of its work

The Prado's Major Works

SCHOOL	ARTIST	PAINTING
Spanish 16C-18C	Juan de Juanes El Greco Zurbarán Velázquez Murillo Goya	*Ecce Homo* *Gentleman with his Hand on his Breas* *Adoration of the Shepherds* *Still Life* *St Isabel of Portugal* *The Surrender of Breda* *The Spinners* *The Maids of Honour (Las Meninas)* *Prince Baltasar* *Carlos on Horseback* *Infanta Doña Margarita of Austria* *The Forges of Vulcan* *Christ on the Cross* *Holy Family with a Little Bird* *Immaculate Conception of Soult* *The Good Shepherd* *Family of Charles IV* *Maja Naked, Maja Clothed* *Executions at Moncloa* *The Second of May* *The Witches' Coven*
Flemish 15C-17C	Robert Campin Van der Weyden Hans Memling Bruegel the Elder Hieronymus Bosch Rubens	*St Barbara* *Deposition* *Adoration of the Magi* *Triumph of Death* *Garden of Earthly Delights* *The Three Graces*
Italian 15C-17C	Fra Angelico Andrea Mantegna Botticelli Titian Tintoretto Veronese	*Annunciation* *Dormition of the Virgin* *Story of Nastagio degli Onesti* *Venus with the Organist* *Washing of the Feet* *Venus and Adonis*
German and Dutch 16C-17C	Albrecht Dürer Rembrandt	*Self-portrait* *Artemisa*

Spanish School (15C-18C) – **Bartolomé Bermejo** (*Santo Domingo de Silos* – with his costume rich in gold) and **Yáñez de la Almedina**, who developed the style and technique of Leonardo (*Santa Catalina*), stand out as two painters who cultivated an international style. Masip and his son **Juan de Juanes** (*The Last Supper*) are more associated with the style of Raphael, while Morales' favourite subject, a *Virgin and Child*, is also outstanding.

In those rooms devoted to the **Golden Age**, two painters stand out: **Sánchez Coello**, a disciple of the portrait painter Antonio Moro, and his pupil **Pantoja de la Cruz**, who was another portraitist at the court of Philip II. The personality of **El Greco**, who followed strong Byzantine traditions during his studies in Venice, stands apart within the Spanish School. Here, works dating from his early Spanish period (*Trinity*) through to his maturity (*Adoration of the Shepherds*) can be seen and the evolution of his style studied. Other works are proof that he was a great portraitist; pay particular note to the **Gentleman with his Hand on his Breast**.

Ribalta is the Spanish Baroque artist who first introduced tenebrism to Spain with its chiaroscuro technique already seen in Caravaggio's work. **José (Jusepe) de Ribera**, also known as **Lo Spagnoletto**, is represented by his major work, the *Martyrdom of St Felipe* – which was originally thought to be of St Bartholomew – in which the artist's vigorous use of chiaroscuro emphasizes the dramatic, horrifying nature of the scene.

Both the portraits and still-life paintings of **Zurbarán** are peaceful compositions in which the use of chiaroscuro and Realism are triumphant. In the Prado we discover the lesser known aspect of the style of this Painter of Monks, both in the series of *The Labours of Hercules* which he painted for the Casón del Buen Retiro and in the portrait of *St Isabel of Portugal*. **Murillo**, who mainly painted Marian religious scenes, also cultivates popular subjects with delightful Realism; note his enchanting child portraits (the *Good Shepherd* and *St John the Baptist Child*).

Velázquez (1599-1660) – The Prado possesses the greatest paintings of Velázquez. This artist of genius, born in Sevilla, was apprenticed first to Herrera the Elder and then to Francisco Pancheco whose daughter he married in 1618.

The Maids of Honour, by Velázquez

He later moved to Madrid where he was called to the court by Philip IV in 1[
and subsequently painted a great many portraits. On the suggestion of Rub[
he spent some time in Italy (1629-31) where he painted **The Forges of Vul**[
Influenced by Titian and Tintoretto he began to use richer, more subtle colo[
and developed his figure compositions as can be seen in his magnificent **C**[
on the Cross. On his return he painted **The Surrender of Breda** in which his origina[
emerges and where, as is borne out by the composition, the emphasis rests[
the psychological relationship between the protagonists. The use of light in[
pictures is crucial, setting off figures and objects yet also giving life to the sp[
between them; on the strength of this Velázquez developed his famous ae[
perspectives in which parts of the picture are left hazy in order to furt[
highlight the central figures. He strove towards naturalism, as is shown in[
royal hunting portraits of **Philip IV** and **Prince Baltasar Carlos, the Hunter** (163[
wonderful rendering of a child) and his equestrian portraits of the royal fan[
in particular that of **Prince Baltasar Carlos on Horseback** with the *sierra* in[
background. His predilection for realism is evident in his pictures of Aesop[
well as of buffoons and dwarfs, his favourite themes. In 1650 he returne[
Italy where he painted two light, modern landscapes, the **Gardens of the Villa Me**[
During the last years of his life, when he was laden with honours and all man[
of official functions, he portrayed the young princes and princesses very fre[
as in the picture of the **Infanta Margarita of Austria** (1659) in tones of pink[
grey. In his masterpiece, **The Maids of Honour (Las Meninas)** (1656), a magnific[
display of light and colour, the Infanta Margarita is shown in the arti[
studio accompanied by her maids and dwarves while the king and queen[
portrayed in a mirror in the background. In **The Spinners** (1657), Velázq[
has combined myth and reality in a wonderful interplay of oblique lines[
curves.

Among the disciples of Velázquez was the court painter **Carreño de Mira**[
(*Monstrua Naked* and *Clothed*). Mention should also be made of **Alonso Cano** v[
painted scenes of the *Immaculate Conception*.

Goya (1746-1828) – Spanish painting maintained its supremacy in the 18C[
19C with Goya (born in Fuendetodos in 1746) who is magnificently represen[
in several rooms. His many portraits of the royal and famous, his war scen[
his depiction of everyday life which served as a model for tapestries, and fin[
his **Majas**, all widely illustrate his extraordinary Realism and his enthusiasm[
colour. The museum contains some 40 cartoons painted in oil between 1[
and 1791 for weaving at the Real Fábrica (Royal Tapestry Works). The colou[
naturalness of the scenes gives a delightful picture of life in 18C Madrid. A li[
further on are the canvases of the **2 May** and the **Execution of the Rioters on 3**[
1808 painted by Goya in 1818. Here he was inspired by the rebellion in Ma[
in 1808 against the French occupying forces when the people wished to prev[
the departure of the queen and princes for Bayonne (*see ARANJUEZ*).[
reprisal by Murat that ensued was terrible. Goya condemned the horror of t[
night and the execution that took place on Príncipe Pío hill. The two pa[
ings bring out the violence and cruelty of war as do Goya's brutal etchi[
of the *Disasters Of War* (1808) and *La Tauromaquia*. The so-called B[
Paintings (1820-22) on the ground floor, which Goya made for his hou[
the Quinta del Sordo, are the anguished reactions of a visionary to the rea[
of life in Spain at the time (*The Witches' Coven*, *Cronus Swallowing*[
Son).

★★★ **Flemish School (15C-17C)** – The Prado has an exceptional collection of Flem[
painting due to the close relations Spain developed with the Low Countries in[
past. The new layout of this extraordinary collection is organised accordin[
theme.

Among the Flemish Primitives is the noticeable interest in interiors (*St Bart*[
by Robert Campin known as the Master of Flemalle) to which **Van der Weyden** ad[
great richness of colour, a sense of composition and the pathetic (*Descent fr*[
the Cross, Pietà). The dramatic aspect is interpreted differently, thro[
melancholy, by his successor, **Memling** (*Adoration of the Magi*).

There follow the weird imaginings of **Hieronymus Bosch**, known as El Bosco ([
Garden of Earthly Delights) which influenced his disciple Patinir (*Crossing*[
Stygian Lake), and a painting by **Bruegel the Elder**, the *Triumph of Death*.

Notable in the collection of Flemish paintings from the 16C and 17C are **Ambro**[
Benson's religious pictures, the portraits of personalities at the court of Phil[
by the Dutchman, **Antonio Moro** (16C), the series of the *Five Senses* by Brueghel[
Younger (17C) and his and **David Teniers the Younger**'s colourful scenes of every[
life.

The most Baroque of painters, **Rubens** (who was born in Germany), breathed[
life into Flemish painting (*The Three Graces*). There is a rich collection of his w[
in the museum completed by that of his disciples: **Van Dyck**, excellent portra[
Jordaens, everyday-life scenes, and animal paintings by their contemporar[
Snyders and Paul de Vos.

Dutch School (17C) – There are two interesting works by **Rembrandt**: a *Self-portrait* and *Artemesia*.

★ **Italian School (15C-17C)** – The Italian School is particularly well represented from the 15C and is especially rich in works by Venetian painters.
The Italian Renaissance brought with it elegance and ideal beauty as in paintings by **Raphael** (*The Holy Family*, *Portrait of a Cardinal*), Roman nobility and monumental bearing in the work of **Mantegna** (*Dormition of the Virgin*) and melancholic dreaminess in **Botticelli** (*Story of Nastagio degli Onesti*). On the other hand, the spirituality of the magnificent *Annunciation* by **Fra Angelico** belongs to the Gothic tradition. The collection also includes soft-coloured works by Andrea del Sarto, and others by Correggio, an artist from the Parma School who used chiaroscuro.
The triumph of colour and sumptuousness comes with the Venetian school: **Titian** with his exceptional mythological scenes (*Danae and the Golden Shower*, *Venus with the Organist*) and his admirable portrait of *Emperor Charles V*; **Veronese** with his fine compositions set off by silver tones; **Tintoretto**'s golden fleshed figures springing from shadow (*Washing of the Feet*) and finally **Tiepolo**'s paintings intended for Charles III's royal palace.

French School (17C-18C) – The French are represented by **Poussin** landscapes and canvases by **Lorrain** (17C).

German School – This is represented by a selection of **Dürer's** figure and portrait paintings (*Self-portrait*, *Adam and Eve*) and two hunting scenes and a religious canvas by Cranach.

★ **Casón del Buen Retiro** ⊙ (NY) – *Entrance in calle Alfonso XII, no 28*. This annexe to the Prado has an exceptional collection of the most innovative artistic trends in 19C Spain on exhibition (neo-Classicism, Romanticism, Realism, Impressionism, etc). The central **Gran Salón** (former Salón de Baile or Ballroom of the old Palacio del Buen Retiro) has preserved the beautiful roof decoration painted by Lucas Jordán. Exemplary works from Spanish historical painting hang from its walls, including *The Last Will and Testament of Isabel the Catholic* by Rosales, *Juana the Mad* by F Pradilla and *The Execution of Torrijos and his Companions on the Beaches of Málaga* by A Gisbert. Other artists represented elsewhere in the museum include José de Madrazo (*The Death of Viriato*), V López (*Portrait of Goya*), E Lucas, Alenza, Esquivel (*Contemporary Poets*), Federico de Madrazo, M Fortuny (*The artist's children in the Japanese Hall*), Rosales, I Pinazo (*Self-portrait*), Sorolla (*Children at the beach*), Regoyos, Rusiñol, Chicharro (*Pain*), Zuloaga etc.

★★ BOURBON MADRID *3hr*

This is the smart, residential part of Madrid with wide tree-lined avenues bordered by opulent-looking buildings, luxurious palaces and former mansions which now house museums. It is a pleasant area to stroll around in between a visit to the Prado and a walk in the Retiro.

★ **Plaza de Cibeles** (MNX) – Standing in the centre of the square is one of the emblems of the city and Madrid's most famous fountain, the 18C Cybele, goddess of fertility who rides a lion-drawn chariot.
The square, the nerve centre of the city, stands at the junction of Calle de Alcalá, Gran Vía, paseo del Prado and paseo de Recoletos with its continuation, paseo de la Castellana. Many an artist has been inspired to paint the perspectives opening from the square and the impressive buildings surrounding it such as the **Banco de**

Paseo del Prado

With the 18C drawing to a close, Charles III wanted to develop a public area which would be worthy of Madrid's position as capital of Spain and called upon the court's best architects for his project. In an area outside of the city at the time, Hermosilla, Ventura Rodríguez, Sabatini and Villanueva designed, drained, embellished and built a curved avenue with two large fountains, Cybele and Neptune, at each end, and a third, Apollo, in the centre. To complete the project, the **Botanical Gardens, Natural History Museum** (now the Museo del Prado) and the **Observatory**, were also built. The result was a perfect combination of the functional and the ornate dedicated to science and the arts. Since the 16C, the Paseo del Prado has been a favourite place for Madrileños to meet and to relax. Today, the avenue retains its dignified air, and provides locals and visitors alike with an opportunity to pass judgement on the vision and imagination of Charles III.

España (1891), the 18C **Palacio de Buenavista**, now the Ministry for Defence, late-19C **Palacio de Linares**, now the home of the Casa de América and the **Palacio Communicaciones** or Post and Telegraph Office (1919).

★★★ **Museo Thyssen-Bornemisza** ⏱ (**MY M⁴**) – The late-18C to early-19C neo-Classi Palacio de Villahermosa has been magnificently restored by the architect Raf Moneo to house an outstanding collection acquired by the Spanish State from **Ba Hans Heinrich Thyssen-Bornemisza**. The collection was assembled in the 1920s by father, Baron Heinrich, and bears witness to what is considered to be one of t largest and most inspired collections ever brought together in the private art wor Its proximity to the Prado creates a magnificent focal point in the city for art-love The museum contains approximately 800 works (mainly paintings) from the la 13C to the present day. They are exhibited in chronological order on three floc (the visit should start on the second (top) floor where the collection's olde exhibits are displayed), and provide an overview of the main schools of Europe art (Italian, Flemish, German, Dutch, Spanish, French) including examples Primitive, Renaissance, Baroque, Rococo and neo-Classical works. The gallery al devotes space to 19C American painting, the 20C European Romanticism a Realism movements and presents a representative selection from the Impr sionist, Post-Impressionist and Expressionist periods. The visit concludes w paintings from both the European and American avant-garde movements.

Second floor – The visit begins with the Italian Primitives *(Gallery 1)*: Duccio Buonisegna's *Christ and the Samaritan Woman*, in which concern for scenic realis – one of the predominant themes of the Renaissance – can be seen, stands o **Gallery 3** displays some splendid examples of 15C Dutch religious painting such **Jan van Eyck**'s *The Annunciation Diptych*, in which the artist parades his prodigio technique by giving the finely-proportioned Angel and the Virgin the appearan of high reliefs carved in stone; next to it is the small *Our Lady of the Dry Tree* **Petrus Christus** in which the Virgin and Child symbolize the flowering of the dry tr The museum possesses a magnificent **portrait collection**. It is worth spending sor time in **Gallery 5** which contains some superb examples of the Early Renaissan which encompass its values of identity and autonomy. These come to the fore in t beautiful and well-known *Portrait of Giovanna Tornuaboni* by the Italian paint **D Ghirlandaio**. The room also houses a further dozen portraits of exceptional quality which emanate from various schools from the period, notably *A Young Man at Prayer* by **Hans Memling**, *A Stout Man* by **Robert Campin**, *Henry VIII* by **Hans Holbein the Younger** and **Juan of Flanders**' extremely delicate *Portrait of an Infanta (Catherine of Aragón?)*.

Raphael's *Portrait of an Adolescent* can be seen in the Villahermosa Gal-lery *(Gallery 6)* while Gallery 7 (16C) reveals Vittore Carpaccio's *Young Knight in a Landscape* in which the protagonist's elegance stands out from a background heavy with sym-bolism. The *Portrait of Doge Fran-cesco Vernier* by Titian should not be missed, with its sober, yet diverse tones. After admiring Dürer's *Jesus Among the Doctors (Gallery 8)*, where the characters are portrayed in a surprising way given the period (1506), move on to Gallery 9, which contains an excellent selection of portraits from the 16C German School including *The Nymph from the Fountain*, one of several pain-tings by Lucas Cranach the Elder, and the *Portrait of a Woman* by

Henry VIII of England,
by Holbein the Younger, Madrid

Hans Baldung Grien, in which the original expression and the delicacy of contras give the portrait an attractive air. The display of 16C Dutch paintings in Gallery 1 includes Patinir's *Landscape with the Rest on the Flight into Egypt* whi Gallery 11 exhibits several works by El Greco as well as Titian's *Saint Jerome the Wilderness* (1575), with its characteristic use of flowing brush-stroke painted the year before his death. One of the splendid early works of **Caravagg** – the creator of tenebrism – *Saint Catherine of Alexandria*, can be admired **Gallery 12**. In the same gallery is the splendid sculpture *(Saint Sebastian)* b Baroque artist **Bernini**, executed at the tender age of 17. Also displayed here is th

Lamentation over the Body of Christ (1633) by **Ribera** – one of Caravaggio's followers – which captures the Virgin's suffering with great subtlety. After passing through several rooms dedicated to 17C Baroque art (including **Claude Lorrain**'s *Pastoral Landscape with a Flight into Egypt* and **Zurbarán**'s superb *Santa Casilda*), you reach the 18C Italian Painting section *(Galleries 16-18)* with its typical Venetian scenes by **Canaletto** and **Guardi**. The remaining galleries on this floor *(19-21)* are consecrated to Dutch and Flemish works from the 17C. **Van Dyck**'s magnificent *Portrait of Jacques le Roy*, **De Vos**' *Antonia Canis*, and two memorable **Rubens**: *The Toilet of Venus* and *Portrait of a Young Woman with a Rosary* all hang from the walls of **Gallery 19** while **Gallery 21** possesses the fine *Portrait of a young Man Reading a Coranto* by **Gerard ter Borch**, skilfully representing the model pictured in his daily environment.

First floor – The first few galleries *(22-26)* represent Dutch paintings from the 17C with scenes of daily life and landscapes. Pay particular note to **Frans Hals**' *Family Group in a Landscape*, a fine example of a collective portrait. The century is completed by the still-life paintings in **Gallery 27**. Several interesting portraits stand out from the 18C French and British schools, such as **Gainsborough**'s *Portrait of Miss Sarah Buxton* in **Gallery 28**. 19C North-American painting, virtually unknown in Europe, takes pride of place in the next two rooms *(29 and 30)* with works by the Romantic landscape artists Cole, Church, Bierstadt and the Realist Homer. The European Romanticism and Realism of the 19C is best expressed by **Constable**'s *The Lock*, **Courbet**'s *The Water Stream* and **Friedrich**'s *Easter Morning*, together with the three works in the collection by **Goya** *(Gallery 31)*

Galleries 32 and 33 are dedicated to Impressionism and Post-Impressionism. Here, admire the magnificent works by the principal masters of these movements: Monet, Manet, Renoir, Sisley, Degas, Pissarro, Gauguin, Van Gogh, Toulouse-Lautrec and Cézanne. *At the Milliner* by **Degas** is considered to be one of his major canvases. Other works which equally stand out include **Van Gogh**'s *"Les Vessenots" in Auvers*, a landscape painted in the last year of his life and which displays the explosion of brushstrokes synonymous with some of his later works, *Mata Mua* by **Gauguin**, from his Polynesian period, and **Cézanne**'s *Portrait of a Farmer*, in which his particular use of colour is used to build volumes, a style which opened the way to Cubism. Expressionism is represented in **Galleries 35-40**, following a small display of paintings from the Fauve movement in **Gallery 34**. The Expressionist movement, the best represented in the entire museum, supposes the supremacy of the artist's interior vision and the predominance of colour over draughtsmanship. The works exhibited illustrate the different focal points of German Expressionism. Two highly emblematic paintings by **Grosz**, *Metropolis* and *Street Scene*, hang in **Gallery 40**.

Ground floor – The first few galleries *(41-44)* contain exceptional Experimental avant-garde works (1907-24) from the diverse European movements: Futurism, Orphism, Suprematism, Constructivism, Cubism and Dadaism. **Room 41** displays Cubist works by **Picasso** *(Man with A Clarinet)*, **Braque** *(Woman with a Mandolin)* and **Juan Gris** *(Woman Sitting)*, while *Proun 1C* by **Lissitzky** and *New York City, New York* by **Mondrian** merit special mention in **Room 43**.

Gallery 45 shows post-First World War European works by **Picasso** *(Harlequin with a Mirror)* and **Joan Miró** *(Catalan Peasant with a Guitar)*, as well as a 1914 abstract composition by **Kandinsky** *(Picture with Three Spots)*. In the next gallery, mainly dedicated to North-American painting, can be seen *Brown and Silver I* by **Jackson Pollock** and *Green on Maroon* by **Mark Rothko**, two different examples of abstract American Expressionism. The last two galleries *(47 and 48)* are given over to Surrealism, Figurative Tradition and Pop Art. The following are worthy of particular note: *The Key to the Fields* by the Surrealist artist **Réne Magritte**, *Hotel Room* by the Realist Edward Hopper, *Portrait of George Dyer in a Mirror* by **Francis Bacon**, *Express* by **Robert Rauschenberg** and *A Woman in a Bath* by **Roy Lichtenstein**.

The **Jardín Botánico** (Botanical Gardens) ⓥ stretch alongside Paseo del Prado between the fountain of Neptune and the fine architecture of the Atocha Railway Station (note the curious tropical garden inside). They were designed by the architect Juan de Villanueva and the botanist Gómez Ortega in 1781.

★ **Museo Nacional Centro de Arte Reina Sofía** (Queen Sofia Art Centre) (MZ) ⓥ – Opposite the station, on Glorieta de Atocha, also known as Plaza Emperador Carlos V, stands the former Hospital de San Carlos founded by Charles III, which now houses the Centro de Arte Reina Sofía. The austere, grandiose granite building has recently been modified and now has modern glass lifts running up the façade. The vast arched halls inside form an impressive setting for the programme of temporary cultural exhibitions organised by the centre.

The **standing collections**★ are laid out on the second floor and the fourth floor.

Second floor – The 17 rooms exhibit canvases illustrating leading avant-gar
movements in Spanish painting and the international events that prompt
them, running from the late 19C to the years following the Second World Wa
Some of the rooms cover the work of a single artist. In Room 4, which displa
Cubist works by the great artist **Juan Gris**, note the remarkable *Portrait*
Josette. In the gallery devoted to **Picasso** *(Room 6)*, one is strongly impress
by **Guernica**★★★, commissioned for the Spanish Pavilion at the 1937 World Fa
Inspired by the terrible bombing of Guernica and much commented on becau
of its expressiveness and powerful symbolism, this monumental black and wh
picture is a stark denunciation of the atrocities of war. Room 7 shows
retrospective of the work of **Joan Miró**, with *Snail, Woman, Flower, Star* (193
and *Woman, Bird and Star (Tribute to Picasso)* (1970); his sculptures can
seen in Room 16. There are lovely sculptures by **Julio González** (1920-40s)
Room 8. **Dalí** is represented in Room 10, where you can admire some of his ea
works (*Little Girl at the Window* – 1925), together with later examples tak
from his Surrealist period (*The Great Masturbator*).

Fourth floor – *(Rooms 18 to 45)*. Here you can see works reflecting major artis
movements from the late 1940s to the early 1980s. Room 19 displays works
artists belonging to **Dau al Set** and **Pórtico**, the two main trends to have emerged
Spain in the wake of the Civil War. Rooms 20 to 23 cover the Abstract moveme
spanning the 1950s and the early 1960s, illustrated by Guerrero, Ràfe
Casamada, Hernández Mompó, Oteiza, Sempere, Palazuelo and members of t
Equipo Crónica. Informalism is extremely well represented in Rooms 27 to 29 wi
a fine collection of paintings, divided into those associated with **El Paso** (Millare
Saura, Rivera, Canogar, Feito and Viola) or with the **Cuenca Group** (Zóbel a
Torner). An interesting selection of works by **Tàpies** can be seen in Rooms 34 a
35. Figurative art is shown in Room 31 with canvases by Antonio López Garc
Julio López Hernández and Xavier Valls. In the next room, collages taken from t
series *Gravitations* of **Eduardo Chillida** accompany his sculpture *Omar Khayyan I*
Table (1983). The works of Alfaro, Arroyo, Luis Gordillo and the Equipo Crón
(Rooms 36 to 39) demonstrate the similarities and differences between Pop A
and figurative, narrative works.

Rooms 24, 25, 26, 30, 33, 40 and 41 exhibit the work of several foreign artis
providing an interesting perspective on this comprehensive panorama of Span
art: Bacon, Moore, Alechinsky, Fontana, Dubuffet, Tobey, Kounellis, Pistole
Flavin, Newman, Judd, Nauman etc).

Outside, the street bordering the Jardín Botánico to the south, the **Cuesta de Clau**
Moyano, is famous for its book stalls. Calle Alfonso XII leads off left towards t
Museo del Ejército.

★ **Museo del Ejército (Army Museum)** ⊙ **(NY)** – A wide range of weapons a
equipment (some 27 000 objects) are displayed in the vast rooms of the Palac
del Buen Retiro which was built in 1631. Arms and armour (16C), flags, banne
trophies, paintings and sculptures trace Spain's military history.

Museo Nacional de Artes Decorativas ⊙ **(NX M⁸)** – This museum is housed i
small 19C palace. It contains a splendid collection of objects ranging from Mudéj
rugs (15C) and Castilian carved desks to modernist furniture. Several rooms ha
also been recreated such as a chapel with a Mudéjar ceiling and walls covered wi
embossed leather★ and an 18C Valencian kitchen.

Museo Naval ⊙ **(NXY M³)** – The rooms display **ship models**★, books, nautic
instruments, weapons, portraits, navigation charts and paintings of naval battle
Of particular interest is the **map of Juan de la Cosa**★★, an invaluable document drav
in 1500, on which the American continent appears for the very first time.

★ **Puerta de Alcalá (Alcalá Arch)** **(NX)** – *Plaza de la Independencia*. The arch was bu
by Sabatini between 1769 and 1778 to celebrate the triumphant entrance
Charles III into Madrid.

★★ **Parque del Buen Retiro (Retiro Park)** ⊙ **(NXYZ** and **GHY)** – El Retiro is popular wi
Madrileños as a place to meet and go for a walk. The park originally formed t
grounds of a palace built in the 17C by Philip IV of which only the buildi
containing the Museo del Ejército (Army Museum) and the Casón del Buen Reti
remain, in the same way that the nearby church is all that is still standing of
Hieronymite monastery built by the Catholic monarchs in the 15C. The Duke
Olivares had the palace grounds developed into a park.

El Retiro (130ha/321 acres) is a beautiful island of greenery in the middle of t
city with dense clumps of trees (La Chopera at the south end), elegant, form
flower-beds (El Parterre at the north end) and a sprinkling of fountains, temple
colonnades and statues.

Beside the lake (Estanque) where boats may be hired, is the imposing **Monumer**
a Alfonso II. Near the graceful **Palacio de Cristal**★, in which exhibitions are held, are
pool and a grotto.

Puerta de Alcalá

ADDITIONAL SIGHTS

★ **Museo Arqueológico Nacional** (National Archeological Museum) ⊘ (NV) – *Entrance in calle de Serrano*. Founded in 1867 by Queen Isabel II. Since 1895 it has occupied the same building as the **Biblioteca Nacional** (National Library). The archeological museum is one of the city's most impressive museums and is without doubt the best museum of its type in Spain.

★ **Prehistoric Art and Archeology** – *Galleries 1-18*. The art of the Upper Paleolithic period is represented by the reproduction, in the garden, of the **Cuevas de Altamira** (Altamira Caves) and their paintings of bison. The arrival of metal in the Iberian Peninsula (around the middle of the 3rd millennium BC) coincided with the development of the Los Millares culture. The galleries that follow are devoted to the Bronze Age (2nd millennium BC); the so-called Bell Beaker and El Argar cultures and the Megalithic culture (Talayots) of the Balearic Islands – note the splendid bronze Costix **bulls**★. Several galleries exhibit numerous finds discovered outside of the Iberian peninsula. Gallery 13, dedicated to Ancient Egypt, displays various objects of a mainly funerary nature, including the sarcophagus of Amenemhat from the 21st Tebas dynasty. Classical Athens (gallery 15) is also represented by the magnificent collection of **Greek vases**★, which originate mainly from the collection acquired by the Marquis of Salamanca in Italy.

★ **Iberian and Classical Antiquities** – *Galleries 19-26*. Exhibits in two Iberian galleries illustrate the origin of local techniques and the artistic influence of the Phoenicians, the Greeks and the Carthaginians. The works displayed at the beginning of the section show an Eastern tendency: note the *Lady of Galera*, a 7C BC alabaster figurine flanked by sphinxes, and the terracottas from Ibiza, including the Dama de Ibiza, which perhaps represents the goddess Tanit. The second gallery, where the influence of Carthage is obvious, shows sculpture at a high peak of artistic expression: standing out from the greatest Iberian sculptures is the Lady of Elche, the **Dama de Elche**★★★, a stone bust, with a sumptuous head-dress and corsage, mysterious and imposing in expression *(see photograph, p 30)*. In the same gallery are the **Dama de Baza**★★, a realistic goddess figure of the 4C BC which has preserved much of its colour, and the woman bearing an offering discovered at Cerro de los Santos. Other galleries illustrate Spain's adoption, when under Roman domination, of the invader's techniques – bronze law tablets, sculptures, mosaics (including the 3C Labours of Hercules), sarcophagi, ceramics and, in particular, a hydraulic pump made of bronze – and later how she developed a Hispanic paleo-Christian art which incorporated ideas from Byzantium.

★ **Medieval and Renaissance Decorative Art** – *Galleries 27-35*. In this section are the magnificent **votive crowns of Guarrazar**★★ dating from the Visigothic period. Most of them were offered by the 7C Visigothic King Recceswinth and are made of embossed gold plaques decorated with pearls, revealing a mixture of Germanic and Byzantine techniques.

This section is also devoted to the incomparable art of Muslim Spain. Among oth
objects, ivory caskets are displayed. Gallery 31 shows the Romanesque por
from the Monasterio de San Pedro de Arlanza (12C) and contains some of t
treasures from San Isidoro de León, in particular the magnificent 11C iv
processional cross★★ of Don Fernando and Doña Sancha. Rooms 32 and 33 disp
various exhibits of Romanesque and Gothic art, including engravings, grilles a
capitals. The 14C polychrome wooden chairs from the Monasterio de las Claris
de Astudillo (Palencia) are particularly worthy of note. Romanesque tombs a
capitals, together with Gothic sculpture in subsequent galleries, continue to sh
deep Moorish influence. Gallery 35 is a reconstruction of a Mudéjar interi
complete with carved desks and a magnificent **artesonado**★★ ceiling.
Finally, the Renaissance brought with it influences from Italy, as can be seen
the bronzes and furniture.

16-19C Art – *Galleries 36-40 (temporarily closed)*. The building and furnishing
royal palaces under the Bourbons in the 17C, 18C and 19C encouraged t
decorative arts, particularly porcelain (Buen Retiro), ceramics (Talavera) a
crystal work (La Granja).

North of the Museo Arqueológico are the Jardines del Descubrimiento (Discove
Gardens), an extension to **Plaza de Colón (NV 49)** with massive carved stone block
monuments to the discovery of the New World. Madrid's Centro Cultural is belo
street level, beneath Plaza de Colón.

Museo de Cera (Waxworks Museum) ⊘ **(NV)** – This museum contains wax figur
from Spanish history and contemporary celebrities in a realistic setting.

★★ **Museo Lázaro Galdiano** ⊘ **(GU M¹)** – The museum in the neo-Classical mansi
is a bequest to the nation by a great art lover, José Lázaro Galdiano. The collecti
of **enamels and ivories**★★★ *(ground floor)* traces the evolution of enamelling fro
Byzantium to 19C Limoges; equally outstanding are the medieval gold and silv
work and the Italian Renaissance jewellery and other art objects.
The first floor galleries, full of precious furniture, contain paintings by Flemi
Primitives and Spanish masters (Morales, Murillo, Carreño and Sánchez Coello
The second floor is entirely devoted to painting, starting with Spanish (Ber
guete, the Master of Astorga) and Flemish Primitives (Hieronymus Bosch, a fi
Crucifixion by Quentin Metsys) and Spain's Golden Age which includes works k
El Greco, Zurbarán, Murillo and Carreño.
The English School is well represented with pictures by several artists includi
Gainsborough, Reynolds, Romney, Constable and Bonington. There are canvas
by the Italians, Francesco Guardi and Tiepolo, and also paintings from Goya
Black Period.
The collections on the third floor include embroideries, fabrics, fans and weapon

★ **Real Academia de Bellas Artes de San Fernando (San Fernando Royal Fine A**
Academy) ⊘ **(LX M²)** – Founded in 1752, during the reign of Ferdinand VI. T
picture gallery has a valuable collection of 16C-20C European paintings.
particular interest are the Spanish paintings from the Golden Age, superb
represented with works by José Ribera, Zurbarán, Murillo, Alonso Cano *(Chr.
Crucified)* and Velázquez. The 18C is also present with works by artists w
Bourbon connections (Van Loo, Mengs, Giaquinto, Tiépolo and Bayeu). The worl
in the room devoted to Goya, the most important in the museum, with h
Self-portrait and a series of studio paintings *(The Asylum, Inquisition Scene)* a
from the same century. Worthy of note in the collection of European paintin
are the enigmatic *Spring* by Arcimboldo and the *Descent* by Martín de Vos. T
museum also has a small room devoted to Picasso which contains a selection
his etchings.

★ **Museo de América (Museum of the Americas)** ⊘ **(DU)** – This archeological a
ethnological museum, which provides a general overview of European ties wi
the American continent, has brought together historical, geographical, cultura
artistic and religious aspects of the Americas, at the same time retaining t
vision of the New World held by Europe since its discovery. Over 2 500 objects a
on display on two floors and are accompanied by explanations, maps, model
reconstructions of dwellings etc. Among the exhibits of great historical valu
on display, the following stand out: the 17C *Conquest of Mexico*, the *Stele*
Madrid (Mayan), the powerful **Treasure of Los Quimbayas**★ (Colombian) and tw
manuscripts, the *Tudela Manuscript* (1553) and the 13C-16C **Cortesai**
Manuscript★★★, one of four remaining Mayan manuscripts in existence and th
museum's prized historical work.

San Antonio de la Florida ⊘ **(DV)** – The chapel, built in 1798 under Charles I
and painted by Goya, contains the remains of the famous artist. The **frescoes**★
on the cupola illustrate a religious theme, the miracle of St Anthony of Padua
but the crowd witnessing the miracle is of a far more worldly nature as Goya use
the beautiful women of 18C Madrid as models. The result is a marvellous portra
of Madrid society at the time.

★ **Museo Cerralbo** ⊘ (KV) – The museum, installed in a late 19C mansion, displays the collection left to the Spanish State by the Marquis of Cerralbo, a man of letters and patron of the Arts, on his death in 1922. A wide range of exhibits can be seen in the mansion's rooms and galleries, including an extensive collection of mainly Spanish paintings, furniture, fans, clocks, armour and weaponry, porcelain, archeological finds, photographs and personal mementoes belonging to the Marquis.

★ **Museo Sorolla** ⊘ (FU **M⁵**) – This eclectic 19C museum is housed in the Madrid home of the Valencian Joaquín Sorolla (1863-1923). It contains numerous works which include sketches drawn for the Hispanic Society of New York (1911) and *The Horse Bath* (1909). The residence is also a museum on the life of this Luminista artist.

★ **Plaza Monumental de las Ventas (Bullring)** (JU) – The bullring (1931), known as the cathedral of bullfighting, is Spain's largest, with a seating capacity of 22 300. Adjoining it is a **Museo Taurino** (Bullfighting Museum) ⊘ in honour of the great toreadors.

Museo de la Ciudad (City Museum) ⊘ (HT **M⁷**) – A stroll through the museum's rooms *(third and fourth floors)* provides the visitor with a journey through the history of Madrid, from prehistory through to the present day. Special mention should be made of the superb **models★** of various parts of the city and of some of the city's most emblematic buildings.

Zarzuela

This peculiarly Spanish form of operetta dates from the end of the 17C when playwright **Pedro Calderón de la Barca** and composer **Juan de Hidalgo** created a new, highly theatrical, musical genre, performing their works at the Palacio de La Zarzuela, residence of the King of Spain, northwest of Madrid *(11km/7mi)*. Zarzuela has continued to draw much of its inspiration from the traditions and folklore of Madrid, the city where it was born. Zarzuela flourished in particular in the late 19C and early 20C, after a period of works adapted from Italian comic opera. The secret of its popular appeal lies in the scores and lyrics which reflect everyday Spanish life and customs and the tastes of the day. It is enjoying renewed popularity nowadays with new recordings being made of the most important works by great Spanish opera singers such as Plácido Domingo and Alfredo Kraus. There are two types of zarzuela: single-act works, known as *chico*, on popular characters of Madrid; and works in several acts; known as *grande* or *gran Zarzuela*. Works can also be categorised according to plot: the most typical are those on the life and customs of Madrid, written in local slang or *castizo*; others are based on the theme of Spanish country life; and there are operettas generally set in a European context.

Some popular examples of the genre include *El Barberillo de Lavapiés* by Francisco Asenjo Barbieri (1823-94), *La Verbena de la Paloma* by Tomás Bretón (1850-1925), *Doña Francisquita* and *Bohemios* by Amadeo Vives (1871-1932), *Luisa Fernanda* by Federico Moreno Torroba (1891-1982) and *La Tabernera del Puerto* by Pablo Sorozábal (1897-1988).

Museo Municipal ⊘ (LV **M¹⁰**) – This interesting museum is housed in the former city hospice, an 18C building with a superb **portal★★** built by Pedro de Ribera in Churrigueresque style. The different sections of the museum retrace the history of the city from its origins to the present day, with particular emphasis on the periods under the Hapsburgs and Bourbons. Its wide-ranging collections (paintings, ceramics, furniture, coins etc) included porcelain from the Buen Retiro factory and an **1830 model of Madrid★**, by Gil de Palacio.

Museo Romántico ⊘ (LV **M¹¹**) – This museum paints an accurate picture of life in the 19th century. Its exhibits include a somewhat disorganised collection of paintings, miscellaneous objects and furniture.

Museo del Ferrocarril (Railway Museum) ⊘ (FZ **M⁹**) – Installed in the Delicias station, the oldest in Madrid. This wrought-iron and glass station, built in 1880, has a collection of steam engines, a restaurant car in which visitors can still enjoy a cup of coffee, electric locomotives etc. It is an ideal museum for children, who will have an opportunity to climb inside some of the exhibits.

Museo Nacional de Ciencia y Tecnología (National Science and Technology Museum) ⊘ (FZ **M⁹**) – The museum has put on show just a small percentage of its extraordinary collection of scientific objects. In one room, where a view of the sky has been reproduced, the museum has set out instruments used for navigation and astronomy. These include a **cross-staff★★** and a 16C astrolabe by the Flemish astronomer Arsenius.

MÁLAGA★

Andalucía – Population 534 683

Michelin map 446 V 16

Málaga, a vast white, sprawling city at the mouth of the Guadalmedina, is dominatby **Gibralfaro** (**DY**) or Lighthouse Hill. This is crowned by 14C ramparts which comman
a fine **view★★** of the town, the harbour and surroundings.
After its founding by the Phoenicians, the town became an important Roman colo
and under the Moors, the main port for the Kingdom of Granada.
Today, Málaga is the lively capital of the Costa del Sol and enjoys a particular
pleasant climate. There are ferry links with Melilla in Africa. Some of the distric
have retained a distinctive character, such as **Caleta** in the east with its old houses a
gardens, and **El Palo** (*7km/4mi east*), a former fishermen's quarter known for i
seafood restaurants.

Málaga wine – The town produces the sweet, full-bodied wine known as Málag
made from grapes from local hillside vineyards and which can be served either as
aperitif or dessert wine. Since its popularity has fluctuated grapes are now also dri
for sale as currants.

SIGHTS

★ **Alcazaba** ⊙ (**DY**) – The winding approach is lined with the ruins (fortifi
gateways, columns and capitals) of the Roman theatre unearthed at the foot
the fortress. Inside the final gateway, Puerta del Cristo (Christ's Door) (**DY C**
where the first Mass was celebrated on the town's reconquest (1487), a
Moorish gardens. There is a view of the harbour from the ramparts.
The former palace, located inside the inner perimeter, currently houses the **Mus**
Arqueológico★, displaying artefacts running from the Prehistoric era to the Mid
Ages. The galleries devoted to Roman art and Arabic art (exhibits dating ba

MÁLAGA

Aduana (Pl. de la)	**DY** 2	Compañía	**CY** 37	Nueva .... **CYZ**
Arriola (Pl. de la)	**CZ** 5	Constitución	**CY** 40	Postigo de
Atocha (Pasillo)	**CZ** 8	Cortina del Muelle	**CZ** 42	los Abades ...... **CDZ** 1
Caldereria	**CY** 13	Especerias	**CY** 56	Reding (Paseo de) .. **DY** 1
Cánovas del Castillo (Pas.)	**DZ** 18	Frailes	**CDY** 61	Santa Isabel
Cárcer	**CY** 27	Granada	**CDY**	(Pasillo de) ..... **CYZ** 1
Casapalma	**CY** 30	Huerto del Conde	**DY** 67	Santa Lucia .... **CY** 1
Colón (Alameda de)	**CZ** 32	Mariblanca	**CY** 77	Santa María ...... **CY** 1
Comandante Benítez		Marina		Sebastián Souvirón .. **CZ** 1
(Av. del)	**CZ** 35	(Pl. de la)	**CZ** 80	Strachan .... **CY** 1
		Margés de Larios	**CYZ** 84	Teatro (Pl. del) .... **CY** 1
		Martínez	**CZ** 86	Tejón y Rodríguez ... **CY** 1
		Molina Larios	**CYZ** 95	Tetuán (Puente de) .. **CZ** 1

A Palacio Arzobispal	**C** Arco del Cristo	**M²** Museo de Artes y Costumbres populares
B El Sagrario	**M¹** Museo de Bellas Artes	**M³** Museo-Casa Natal Picasso

from the 10C to the 15C) deserve special mention. One of the rooms *(enter through the garden)* features a superb *artesonado* ceiling and presents models of the Alcazaba as well as part of the cathedral.

★ Catedral ⊘ **(CZ)** – Construction of the cathedral spanned three centuries (16C-18C) but is still incomplete to this day as the south tower lacks its full elevation. Because of this, it is locally nicknamed La Manquita (the Missing One).
The three aisles of the vast hall-church are covered inside with cupolas studded with palm fronds, shells and other motifs but are supported on classically ordered Corinthian columns, entablatures and cornices. The decoration includes 17C choir stalls with figures by Pedro de Mena, pulpits of rose stone and two 18C organs.

The 18C **Palacio Arzobispal** (Archbishop's Palace) **(CYZ A)** on the cathedral square is built in Baroque style and has a lovely façade behind which are two beautiful *patios*.

El Sagrario ⊘ **(CY B)** – This curiously oblong church dating from the 16C features a fine north portal built in Isabelline Gothic style. The 18C interior is Baroque; at its end it presents a beautiful **Mannerist altarpiece**★, crowned by a well-preserved Calvary.

Museo de Bellas Artes (Fine Arts Museum) ⊘ **(CDY M¹)** – The former Moorish palace serves as a setting for interesting collections by local artists. A gallery contains works by Picasso, who was born in Málaga in 1881, and another one is dedicated to his very first master, Muñoz Degrain. In another *patio* are paintings by Murillo and Morales together with a great many 19C works.

Museo-Casa Natal Picasso (Picasso's Birthplace) ⊘ **(DY M³)** – The house is located in a mid-15C building on the Plaza de la Merced. The first floor is devoted to the museum with works by Picasso and other modern artists. The rest of the building houses the offices of the Pablo Ruiz Picasso Foundation, as well as a room used for temporary exhibitions.

Museo de Artes y Costumbres Populares (Museum of Popular Art and Costume) ⊘ **(CZ M²)** – The museum is housed in a restored 17C inn, the Mesón de la Victoria. The ground floor displays objects used in the past for work on the land or sea, such as ploughing implements, a sardine fishing boat and tools used for wine-making.
On the first floor is a collection of statuettes in 18C and 19C costumes.

EXCURSION

★ Finca de la Concepción ⊘ – *7km/4mi north.*
These lovely gardens were designed on the occasion of a wedding for an upper-class Málaga family. Visitors will enjoy strolling through this delightful jungle, planted with more than 300 tropical and subtropical species and charmingly dotted with streams, ponds, waterfalls and Roman ruins.

MARBELLA★

Andalucía (Málaga) – Population 84 410
Michelin map 446 W 15

Marbella stretches out alongside a bay sheltered by the Sierra Blanca mountains. It was the Costa del Sol's pioneer town and has since become one of the most famous resorts on the Andalusian coast, a holiday home to the international jet-set. Luxury hotels, elegant residential areas and golf-courses landscaped among pinewoods and gardens welcome celebrities from all over the world.

Village – The village has an attractive **casco antiguo** (old quarter) of white-walled houses and narrow streets which converge on a small lively square shaded by orange trees. There are several beaches and a pleasure boat harbour.

EXCURSIONS

★ Puerto Banús – Puerto Banús, west of Marbella in the Nueva Andalucía district, is an elegant white-walled complex of cafés, restaurants and fashion boutiques. The superb sailing boats and yachts of the very wealthy are moored in its marina.

Monda – *18km/11mi north on the Coín road.*
The road passes through the picturesque mountain village of **Ojén** set in the Sierra Blanca. Monda village is typical of the Andalusian hinterland with its whitewashed houses.

MEDINA DE RIOSECO

Castilla y León (Valladolid) – Population 5 037

Michelin map 441 G 14

Medina de Rioseco is the agricultural centre of the Tierra de Campos, the granary Castilla. The picturesque narrow main street, **Calle de la Rúa**, is lined by portico supported by wooden pillars.

In the 16C, the town benefited from the work of Castilian sculptors, mainly from 1 Valladolid School, such as Juni, Del Corral and Jordán, who have left their mark its churches.

Iglesia de Santa María ⊘ – 15C-16C. The church's central altarpiece was carv by Esteban Jordán. The **Capilla de Benavente★** (Benavente Chapel) (16C), to the l of the high altar, contains a 16C retable by Juan de Juni. The decoration on walls and cupola by Jerónimo del Corral illustrates scenes from the La Judgement and the Garden of Eden. The treasury contains ivories and gold a silverwork including a 16C monstrance by Antonio Arfe.

Iglesia de Santiago ⊘ – 16C-17C. The altarpieces in the church's three apsi chapels form a spectacular Churrigueresque group.

MELILLA

North Africa – Population 63 670

Michelin map 959 folds 6 and 11

In 1497, under the reign of Catholic monarchs, the Duke of Medinaceli's troo seized this town which then became Spanish territory. In the past, like many tow along the North African coast, Melilla fell prey to the waves of navigators a conquerors in the Mediterranean (Carthaginians, Phoenicians, Romans).

The enclave is situated at the entrance to a peninsula, its rugged landscape jutti into the Mediterranean for a length of 20km/12mi culminating in the Cabo de Tr Forcas (Three Forks headland). This almost exclusively European city is calm y lively and exudes an opulent air with its wide avenues and large buildings. T market-gardening area which surrounds the town to the south and west, the tw parks in the centre of the city and the sailing and fishing vessels all hold great interest for the visitor than the port area.

Getting to Melilla

By ferry – **Trasmediterránea** operates services to and from Almería (7hr) and Málaga (8hr). For information and bookings, call ☎ 902 45 46 45.

By plane – Iberia has daily flights to Melilla from Málaga. For information and bookings, call ☎ 902 400 500.

★OLD TOWN

At the end of avenida del General Macía, climb the steps which go through t ramparts.

The old town, built on a rocky peninsula and encircled by 16C and 1 fortifications, dominates the port area. The tiny **Capilla de Santiago** can be seen (*the end of a covered passageway*), recognisable by its Gothic vault.

Museo Municipal ⊘ – *In the Baluarte de la Concepción (bastion).* Exhibits display in this museum include pottery, vases, coins and jewels from t Carthaginian, Phoenician and Roman periods which have been discovered in th area. 17C-19C Spanish weaponry hangs from the walls.

Views – From the museum's terrace there are panoramics **views★** of the old a new towns, the port and, to the north, the Cabo de Tres Forcas.

A new concept in travel planning.

When you want to calculate a trip distance or visualise a detailed itinerary; when you need information on hotels, restaurants or campsites, consult Michelin on t Internet.

Visit our Web site to discover our full range of services for travellers:

www.michelin-travel.com

MÉRIDA★

25 BC, the Roman governor of Augustus founded the township of *Emerita Augusta*
this hitherto uncolonised region. It was well situated on the Guadiana river and at
e junction of major Roman roads between Salamanca and Sevilla, Toledo and
sbon. It soon became capital of Lusitania. The Romans lavished upon it temples,
theatre, an amphitheatre and even a 400m/437yd racecourse, now overgrown.
wo Roman bridges still span the Albarregas and Guadiana rivers (where an adjoining
uay was also built). Water for the colony was brought by means of two aqueducts,
an Lázaro and Los Milagros, of which a few elegant polychrome brick and stone
·ches remain. The water was fed from two reservoirs, the Cornalvo and Proserpina,
orth of the town.

★ROMAN MONUMENTS *3hr*

★ **Museo Nacional de Arte Romano (National Museum of Roman Art)** ⊘ – This museum
is housed in an imposing **building**★ designed by the architect Rafael Moneo Vallés
to display Mérida's rich Roman archeological collections. The vast construction,
its sober, majestic lines reminiscent of edifices built under the Roman Empire, is
made entirely of brick, an ideal material as its warm colour sets off the marble
statues inside. A ramp leads up to the main hall which is separated into bays by
nine semicircular arches. Its structure is similar to the main entrance of the
amphitheatre. The skilfully designed complex also includes two upper floors of
galleries and light passageways, suspended, as it were, above the hall. The
museum is organized according to theme in a clear, didactic manner.

Among the sculptures in the hall are statues from the Roman theatre including
the strong-featured head of Augustus *(at the end of the second bay)* and in the
last bay, parts from the portico of Mérida's *forum:* statues of important people,
caryatids and giant medallions (Medusa and Jupiter) which made up the frieze.
The upper floors display jewellery, coins and pottery. Wonderful **mosaics**★ may be
admired at close range from the passageways.

The basement, the excavation site around which the museum was built, contains
the remains of Roman villas and tombs.

Museo Nacional de Arte Romano

★ **Teatro Romano (Roman Theatre)** ⊘ – The theatre was built by Agrippa, Augustus's
son-in-law, in the Classical style of the great theatres in Rome, in 24 BC. A semicircle
of stone tiers afforded seating for 6 000, the front row being reserved for high
dignitaries; a pit held the orchestra or crowd players; a high stage wall was
decorated during Hadrian's reign (2C AD) with a covered colonnade and statues.
Behind the stage, overlooking the gardens, is a portico where the audience could
walk during intervals. The great blocks of granite in the vaulting of the passageways which lead to the tiers are secured by drystone construction alone.

★ **Anfiteatro (Amphitheatre)** ⊙ – The arena dates from the 1C BC and held, it
estimated, 14 000 spectators. It staged chariot races and the *naumachiae*
mimic sea battles performed when the amphitheatre had been especially floode
The steps to the audience seats and the *vomitoria*, the great covered passagewa
through which the crowd left, can still be seen. The tiers have disappeared apa
from those reconstituted on either side of the east *vomitorium* (right comi
from the theatre). Round the chariot course is a wall crowned by a cornice wh
protected the front row of spectators – usually notables – from wild beasts wh
there were gladiatorial combats. The open ditch in the centre presumab
contained arena machinery and workshops.

Casa Romana del Anfiteatro (Roman Villa) ⊙ – The remains of various co
structions, including water channels, pavements and bases of walls which form
part of a patrician villa built around a peristyle and dependent rooms can be se
here. The pavements and mosaics are in remarkably good condition. Some sho
intricate geometrical motifs while others illustrate scenes from everyday life. O
in particular, called *Autumn*, depicts grape-treading.

Casa del Mitreo ⊙ – *Next to the bullring*. This patrician villa was built outside t
town at the end of the 1C. It is laid out around three open patios with a du
purpose: the distribution of light to the internal rooms and the collection
rainwater. Some of the rooms have preserved the remains of paintings a
mosaics, which include the **Cosmological Mosaic**★.

Templo de Diana – *Calle Romero Leal*. The remains of a Roman temple dedicat
to imperial worship built under Augustus. A large part of the peristyle
Corinthian columns and fluted shafts is still visible. In the 16C its materials we
used to build the palace of the Count of Corbos.

ADDITIONAL SIGHTS

Alcazaba ⊙ – The Moors built the fortress in the 9C to defend the 792m/866y
Puente Romano★ (Roman Bridge) across the islet-strewn Guadiana river. Inside t
walls is an interesting **cistern** dug to the same depth as the bed of the river.
decorate the fortress, the Moors took Corinthian capitals and Visigothic marb
friezes from former buildings or ruins.

★ **Iglesia de Santa Eulalia** ⊙ – The excavations carried out in the basement of th
church have brought to light the interesting history of this particular site whic
has been occupied by a succession of Roman houses, a paleo-Christian necropoli
a 5C basilica and, from the 13C, this Romanesque church.

MOJÁCAR★

Andalucía (Almería) – Population 4 305
Michelin map 446 U 24

The white-walled village of Mojácar stands in a splendid **site**★ on an outcro
overlooking fine **views** of the coast (2km/1mi away) and, further inland, a plai
broken up by strange rock formations.
The heart of the village, spread out over the hill, shows unquestionable Arabi
influence with its steep, narrow streets and secluded corners enhanced by colourf
shrubs.

Mojácar to Carboneras road – *22km/14mi south*. The road first skirts the shor
before turning inland to climb up the pyramid-shaped mountains in a series o
twists and bends. There are beautiful viewpoints before it drops to Carbonera
beach.

MONDOÑEDO

Galicia (Lugo) – Population 5 774
Michelin map 441 B 7

The low slate-covered houses and wide golden stone cathedral façade of Mondoñed
rise out of the hollow of a lush, well cultivated valley as you drive along the Villalb
road.
The streets of the old town are lined with stylish white-walled houses ornamente
with armorial bearings and wrought-iron balconies. The cathedral square is particu
larly delightful with its arcades and *solanas* (glassed-in galleries).

★ **Catedral** ⊙ – The cathedral's immense façade combines the Gothic grace of the
three large portal arches and the rose window, all dating from the 13C, with the
grandiose Baroque style of the towers added in the 18C.

The **interior**, lit by a beautiful rose window, is transitional Romanesque with the plain walls setting off the works of art. These include a series of late-14C frescoes one above the other (below the extraordinary 1710 organ) illustrating the Massacre of the Innocents and the Life of St Peter. The retable at the high altar is Rococo. A polychrome wood statue of the Virgin in the south ambulatory is known as the English Virgin since the statue was brought from St Paul's, London, to Mondoñedo in the 16C. Off the south aisle is the burial niche of Bishop Juan Muñoz who gave the church its present façade.

The classical **cloisters** were added in the 17C.

MONTBLANC★★

Catalunya (Tarragona) – Population 5 612
Michelin map 443 H 33

ontblanc is located in a privileged **site**★★ on top of a small hill that commands sweeping view of the area: a stretch of fertile land consisting of huge plains anted with vines and almond trees and bordered with pines. During the Middle es, Montblanc was a thriving city with a prosperous Jewish community. Its lden age was the 14C: economic supremacy was soon reflected in the political ena when several Estates General were held in the town at the instigation of yalty.

e stone ramparts defending the old city provide a perfect setting for the dieval Week, when the local population re-enacts the legend of St George 3 April).

THE RAMPARTS

The fortified perimeter of Montblanc encloses a stone labyrinth characterised by winding streets, steep flights of steps, picturesque little corners and fine buildings. The ramparts were originally commissioned by Peter the Ceremonious in the 14C. Nowadays two thirds of the original walls (1 500m/5 000ft) are still extant, along with 32 square towers and two of the four doors: that of Sant Jordi *(south)* and that of Bover *(northeast)*.

Iglesia de Sant Miquel ⊘ – Fronted by a Romanesque façade, this small 13C church is built in the Gothic style with pure, sober lines. It was chosen by the Court of Catalunya to host the Estates General in 1307, 1333, 1370 and 1414.

Next to the church on the same square stands the **Palau del Castlà**, formerly the residence of the King's representative, which houses the 15C prison on its ground floor.

Another interesting building is the 14C **Casa Alenyà**, a Gothic house of slender proportions.

The Town walls

MONTBLANC

Castell	3
Corts	4
Dalt	7
Elionor d'Urgell	9
Espluga de Francoli	10
Font de la Vila	12
Font Major	13
Foradot	15
Guimrós	18
Joc de la Pilota	19
Jueus	21
Major	
Pere Berenguer V	22
Portalet	24
Raval de Santa Anna	25
River	
Sant Josep	27
Sant Marçal	28
Sant Miquel (Pl.)	
Santa Colomade Queralt	
Santa Maria (Pl.)	
Santa Tecla	
Serra (Pl. de la)	
Solans	
Xolladors	

M¹ Museu Comarcal de la Conca de Barberà

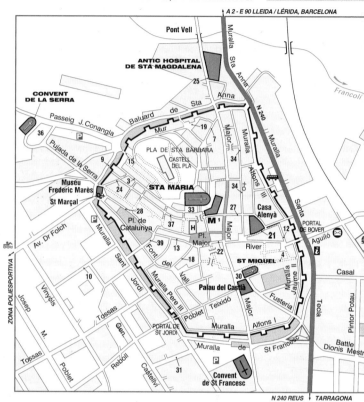

★★ **Iglesia de Santa Maria** ⊙ – Poised on a promontory overlooking the old city, the beautiful Gothic church has a single nave and radiating chapels that come right up to the foothills. The unfinished façade is Baroque. The interior features a sumptuous 17C **organ**★★, a Gothic altarpiece in polychrome stone (14C) and an elegant silver monstrance.

★ **Museu Comarcal de la Conca de Barberà** ⊙ (**M¹**) – Set up in a 17C house, the museum displays archeological and ethnographical artefacts discovered in the area as well as a fine collection of 18C ceramic flasks belonging to an apothecary.

Museu Frederic Marès ⊙ – Situated beside the Iglesia de Sant Marçal (14C), the museum contains interesting religious paintings and sculptures from the 13C to the 19C, in particular fine 14C wooden statues.

ADDITIONAL SIGHTS

★ **Convento de la Serra** ⊙ – This old convent, formerly occupied by nuns belonging to the Order of St Clare, stands on a small hill offering lovely views of the surrounding countryside. The convent once enjoyed the protection of several kings and Popes. It houses the much-venerated **Mare de Déu de la Serra**, an alabaster statue made in the 14C.

★ **Hospital de Santa Magdalena** – Despite their smallness, the 15C cloisters, illustrating the transitional period between Gothic and Renaissance, are truly remarkable. The vertical perspective on the ground floor, featuring fluted columns and pointed arches, is broken in the upper section.

*Admission times and charges for the sights described are listed
at the end of the guide. Every sight for which there are times
and charges is identified by the symbol ⊙ in the Sights section
of the guide.*

Sierra de MONTSENY*

Catalunya (Barcelona, Girona)

Michelin map 443 G 36-37

e Sierra de Montseny, a mighty range of Pyrenean foothills in the heart
Catalunya, is a vast granite dome covered in beeches and cork oaks. To the
utheast lies the Parque Natural de Montseny, covering a total area of
372ha/42 600 acres; its highest peaks are Matagalls (1 695m/5 560ft) and Turó
l'Home (1 707m/5 601ft). Many rivers rise in the area on account of the wet
mate and the impermeability of the rock face.

From Sant Celoni to Santa Fè del Montseny – *22km/14mi – about 45min*. This
drive into the heart of the mountains is the most interesting. Beyond Campins,
the road rises in hairpin bends, affording **views** of the coastal plain; it continues
in a magnificent **corniche** *(2km/1mi)* to the lake *(embalse)* of Santa Fè (alt
1 130m/3 707ft). The road then climbs up *(7km/4mi)* to the Ermita de Sant
Marçal (alt 1 260m/4 134ft), a hermitage perched on the side of the lofty
Matagalls ridge.

From Sant Celoni to Tona via Montseny – *43km/27mi – about 1hr*. There are
good views of the sierra from the **route** across the plain irrigated by the Tordera.
Beyond Montseny, the road rises, reaching a wild area, before descending to Tona
past the Romanesque church in **El Brull** and the tower of **Santa Maria de Seva**.

From Tona to Sant Celoni by the northern road – *60km/37mi – about
1hr 30min*. The road goes through pine and beechwoods and the delightful village
of **Viladrau** before beginning a gradual descent with mountain views off to the
right. The view opens out onto the steep Montseny slopes as the road continues
its hillside descent. After the attractively sited **Arbùcies**, it runs beside the river for
a distance before turning off for **Breda**, dominated by a beautiful Romanesque
tower, and Sant Celoni.

Sierra de MONTSERRAT**

Catalunya (Barcelona)

Michelin map 443 H 35

e Macizo de Montserrat (Montserrat Massif) has a grandiose **site**★★★ and was, in
ct, used by Wagner as the setting for his opera, *Parsifal*. The range is composed
hard Eocene conglomerates, which stand solidly above the more eroded surroun-
ng rock formations. The piling up of the boulders into steep cliffs, crowned by weird
nnacles, has produced a serrated outline which has given Montserrat the nickname
wtooth Mountain. It is the principal religious and cultural centre of Catalunya, its
arian shrine attracting thousands of pilgrims.

Access – The best approach, by far, is from the west. There are excellent **views**★★
all the way along the monastery road. Access to the Montserrat cableway is best
from near Monistrol de Montserrat on the Barcelona-Manresa road.

Monasterio – The history of Montserrat, one of the five main hermitages on the
mountain, begins in the 9C with the arrival of Benedictines from Ripoll. In 1025
Abbot Oliva founded a priory on the site which grew rapidly in importance, until
by the 13C the Romanesque buildings had to be greatly enlarged. It continued to

Monasterio de Montserrat

Ch. Sappa/CEDRI

flourish and, as an abbey, declared its independence from Ripoll in 1409. It ►
become powerful; its monks were learned – one of the abbots, Giuliano d
Rovere, the future Pope Julius II, was a scholar, artist and patron of the Ita
Renaissance – the community was rich; its pilgrims were fervent and numero
Every century saw additions to the monastery making it an anthology
masterpieces of every architectural style.

In 1812, however, disaster struck; the monastery was sacked by the French. ˈ
present buildings, therefore, are 19C and 20C (the church façade was comple
in 1968). At the end of the dark, overly ornate **basílica** ⊘ (15C), stands the shr
of the Black Madonna.

★★ **La Moreneta** – La Moreneta is the Catalan name for the Black Madonna. ˈ
polychrome wood statue is said to date from the 12C; the seated figure of
Infant Jesus was restored in the 19C. According to legend, the figure, now ►
niche *(camarín)* above the high altar, and venerated annually by thousands
pilgrims as the patron saint of Catalunya, was found by shepherds in a cave
the mountainside.

Access to the *camarín* for a closer view of the statue, is through the chapels in ˈ
south aisle. The church services by the monks (the Montserrat commur
consists of 80 members) are known for the high standard of their singi
concelebratory Mass is at 11am; Vespers at 6.45pm; there are special services
Christmas and in Holy Week.

The **Escolanía**, one of Europe's oldest boys' choirs – its foundation dates back
the 13C – may be heard every day at 1pm (Virolai) and 7.10pm (Salve).

Hermitages and viewpoints – Access is by mountain road, cableway and **funic
railway** ⊘.

Before the arrival of Napoleon's troops, there were 13 hermitages, ea
occupied by a hermit. Today, they are all deserted but some make interest
walks.

Ermita de la Trinitat – *45min on foot.* Charmingly nestled in a bucolic pla
this hermitage is sheltered by three unusually-named mountains:
Elefante (The Elephant), La Preñada (the Pregnant Woman) and La Momia (ˈ
Mummy).

★ **Sant Jeroni** – *Access on foot (1hr 30min) or by car along a forest track (1hr 30m.*
From the viewpoint (1 238m/4 062ft) there is a **panorama**, on a clear d
stretching from the Pyrenees to the Balearic islands.

Ermita de Santa Cecilia – Until the 16C Santa Cecilia was a Benedictine monast
like Santa María of Ripoll, but lacked its influence. The 11C **Romanesque church** ★ ►
a most attractive exterior with its east end circled by Lombard bands, its roof a
its asymmetric, free standing belfry.

Santa Cova – *1hr walk.* According to legend, it was in this cave that the statue
the Virgin was found. Views of the Llobregat Valley.

★ **Sant Miquel** – *30min walk from the monastery; 1hr from the upper terminal of ˈ
Sant Miquel funicular.* General view of the monastery.

Sant Joan – *30min from upper terminal of Sant Joan funicular.* Beaut
panorama; the Ermita de San Onofre may be seen clinging to the rock face.

MORELLA

Morella has an amazing **site**★: 14C ramparts, punctuated by towers, form a mile-lo
girdle round a 1 004m/3 294ft high hill on which the town has been built in tie
Crowning the rock summit are the ruins of a medieval castle.

El Maestrazgo – Morella lies at the heart of the mountain region wh
was the fief *(maestrazgo)* of the Knights of Montesa, a military order found
by James II of Aragón. The order, which had its seat at San Mateo *(40km/25
southeast of Morella)* as of 1317, fortified all villages in the region so as
better fight the Moors. Each community at the foot of its castle had a m
porticoed square and narrow streets lined by balconied houses. Most occu
attractive sites in isolated, strongpoint positions and have retained considera
character.

★ **Basílica de Santa María la Mayor** ⊘ – The basilica is one of the most interest
Gothic churches in the Levante. It has two fine portals surmounted by gables: ►
14C Apostle Doorway, and the later Virgins' Doorway with an openwo
tympanum. The unusual raised Renaissance *coro* at the nave centre has a spi
staircase magnificently carved by a local artist (Biblical scenes) and a delic

balustrade with a frieze illustrating the Last Judgement. The sanctuary was sumptuously decorated in Baroque style in the 17C and an elegant organ loft introduced in the 18C. There is a small museum with a beautiful Valencian *Descent from the Cross* and a 14C *Madonna* by Sassoferrato.

Castillo – *Access through the Convento de San Francisco. 15min climb.* On the way up there are good **views**★ of the town, the 13C-14C monastery ruins, the 14C-15C aqueduct and the reddish heights of the surrounding sierras.

EXCURSION

Mirambel – *30km/19mi west on CS 840. Bear left after 11km/7mi.*
The small *maestrazgo* village, its houses adorned with coats of arms, has retained its medieval character.

MURCIA★

Murcia – Population 338 250
Michelin map 445 S 26

urcia lies on either side of the Segura, at the centre of a fertile market-gardening ea *(huerta)*. The city, founded in the reign of Abd ar-Rahman II in 831 as Mursiya, s finally captured during the Reconquest in 1266 and was soon sufficiently secure r the Pope to transfer the episcopal seat to it from Cartagena, a city always nerable to pirate attack. Up to the 18C, Murcia prospered from agriculture and k weaving.

day it is a university town and a commercial and industrial centre (fruit canning), panding by wide avenues and walks (Paseo del Malecón) from the original kernel medieval streets.

vo famous 18C sons of Murcia – **Francisco Salzillo** (1707-83), the son of an Italian ulptor and a Spanish mother, is the last famous name in Spanish polychrome wood ulpture. *Pasos*, or processional groups, were his speciality (although he did do other pes of carving); 1 800 works are attributed to the artist.

e other notable 18C Murcian was the statesman, Don José Moñino, **Count of ridablanca** (1728-1808), minister to Charles III and IV. If Murcia owes him much, ain owes him more, for it was by his counsel that the country's economy was put its feet.

e Murcia Festivals – Murcia Holy Week processions are particularly solemn: on e morning of Good Friday, penitents in mauve robes bear eight Salzillo *pasos (see low)* in procession through the town. The week after the Spring Festival is the casion for general rejoicing with processions of floats and finally the Entierro de Sardina, or Burial of the Sardine, which symbolises the end of Lent.

J.-P. Garcin/DIAF

Murcia penitents

Alfonso X el Sabio
(Gran Vía) . . . . DY 2
Cardenal Belluga (Pl.) . . . . DY 5
Colón (Alameda de) . . . . . . DZ
España (Glorieta de) . . . . . DZ 15

Floridablanca . . . . DZ 18
Garay (Paseo de) . . . . DZ 20
Gómez Cortina . . . . CY 28
Infante Juan Manuel
(Avenida) . . . . DZ 33
Isidoro de la Cierva . . . . DY 40
José Antonio Ponzoa . . . . . . DY 44
Licenciado Cascales . . . . . . DY 56

Marcos Redondo C
Martínez Tornel (Pl.) . . . . . . D
Platería . . . . D
Proclamación . . . . D
San Francisco (Plano de) . . . CY
Sociedad . . . . D
Teniente Flomesta (Av.) . . . D
Traperia . . . . D

SIGHTS

★ **Catedral** ⊙ (DY) – The original cathedral, built in the 14C, is camouflaged outs
by Renaissance and Baroque additions.

The **façade**★, with an arrangement of columns and curves as successful architec
rally as decoratively, is a brilliant example of Baroque. The impressive belfry w
completed in the 18C.

The interior, however, beyond the entrance covered by a cupola matching t
façade, is preponderantly Gothic, apart from the 16C **Capilla de los Junterones** (fou
south chapel) which has rich Renaissance decoration. The **Capilla de los Vélez**★ (
the ambulatory) is sumptuous Late Gothic with splendid star vaulting and w
decoration which clearly includes Renaissance and Mudéjar motifs.

The sacristy, approached through two successive Plateresque doors (note t
beautiful panels of the first), is covered by an unusual radiating dome. The wa
are richly panelled with Plateresque carving below and Baroque above.

The interesting carved **stalls** (1567) in the coro are from an old Castilian monaste

Museo – At the entrance to the museum there is part of a Roman sarcophag
showing Apollo and the Muses, while the silver monstrance (1678) is the th
largest in Spain. The side rooms contain Salzillo's **St Jerome**★ and a 14C altarpie
by Barnaba da Modena of St Lucy and the Virgin. The **treasure**, in the chapter-hous
includes monstrances and chalices as well as the crowns of Murcia's venerat
Virgen de la Fuensanta.

Torre (Belfry) – A ramp leads up to the top which commands an interesti
panorama★ of Murcia and its huerta.

In the cathedral square is the Italianate **Palacio Episcopal** (DYZ), with elega
cloisters.

★ **Calle de la Traperia** (DY) – In the main street (pedestrian) through the old quar
is one of the most sumptuous **Casinos** in Spain, a late-19C building with an inn
Moorish patio and elaborate decoration.

★ **Museo Salzillo** ⊙ (CY) – The museum possesses many of Salzillo's mast
pieces including the eight polychrome wood sculptures of **pasos** carried in t
Good Friday procession during Holy Week. They stand in the side chapels

the rounded nave of the Church of Jesus. The deep emotion on the faces in the groups of the Last Supper and Christ's Arrest and the majesty of St John and the Angel in the Agony in the Garden are truly impressive. The museum also contains 565 of Salzillo's vivid terracotta pieces, used to create scenes from the life of Jesus.

EXCURSIONS

Alcantarilla – *9km/6mi west on N 340.* There is the **Museo de la Huerta** ⊙ on the outskirts of the village beside the road on the approach from Murcia. In this museum, which is dedicated to local farming and irrigation, there is an ethnographic pavilion providing background information, while outside, dispersed among the orange trees, are white *barracas* or rustic dwellings of another age and a **noria**, the giant waterwheel devised for irrigation by the Moors.

Santuario de la Fuensanta (La Fuensanta Shrine) – *7km/4mi south. Follow the signs from Puente Viejo* (DZ).
From the shrine of the Virgen de la Fuensanta, patron saint of Murcia, are fine **views** of the town and the *huerta*.

Orihuela – *24km/15mi northeast on N 340.*
The peaceful town of Orihuela, with its many churches, lies along the banks of the Segura at the foot of a deeply scored hill. The river provides water for the fertile *huerta* and for the local **palm grove**.
In the 16C Orihuela was made an episcopal see and for two centuries was a university town. The poet and dramatist Miguel Hernández was born in the town in 1910.
At the north end of the town is the former university, the **Colegio de Santo Domingo** ⊙. The Renaissance façade of the college conceals two cloisters: one Renaissance style and the other Herreran. The 18C church has coloured frescoes and rich Rococo stucco mouldings.
The Gothic **catedral** ⊙ (14C-15C) has a Renaissance style north doorway illustrating the Annunciation.
Inside, part of the vaulting is highly original as it has spiral ribs. The **Museo de la Catedral** ⊙ houses a *Temptation of St Thomas Aquinas* by Velázquez, a *Christ* by Morales and a *Mary Magdalene* by Ribera.
The **Iglesia de Santiago** ⊙ (near the Ayuntamiento) was founded by the Catholic monarchs whose emblems, together with a statue of St James, may be seen on the Gothic portal. In the interior, note the statues attributed to Salzillo in the side chapels.

Valle del NAVIA

Asturias

Michelin map 441 BC 9

e Navia, which rises in Galicia in the sierra de Cebreros, crosses several ep volcanic ridges before flowing into the Cantabrian Sea. The wild, enclosed ley is punctuated by three dams, in which the high mountains stand lected.

FROM NAVIA TO GRANDAS DE SALIME

82km/51mi – allow 2hr 30min

Navia – A new town and fishing port on the right bank of the *ría*. A road follows the bank to a point overlooking the inlet where a **belvedere dedicated to the Great Seafaring Discoverers** gives a pleasant view.
In Navia, take the Grandas de Salime road which runs alongside the *ría*.

Coaña – The circular foundations of a few houses and some paved streets remain from a Celtic village built on a mound.
For a striking **panorama**★★ of the **Arbón dam**, built just above a giant bend in the river, pause at the viewpoint.
Shortly after Vivedro, there is a **panoramic view**★★ extending from a loop in the river in the foreground, to the Navia Ría mouth in the far distance.
The **confluence**★★ of the Navia and the río Frío is impressive as you look down on it from a giddy height. Beyond the bridge across the Frío, the road returns to the Navia which it follows to Miñagón. The squat drying sheds or *hórreos* you see from the road are the same rectangular shape as those in nearby Galicia.

The road descends beyond Boal to the level of the Navia, where 3km/2mi furt
on, the valley is blocked by the high **Doiras dam**.
The small village of **Sarzol**, perched on a hillside on the far bank from San Estek
is surrounded by very steep slopes, all of which are cultivated.

Grandas de Salime – This is a large agricultural town. The **Museo Etnográfic**
housed in a former presbytery, traces aspects of traditional life in Astu
through reconstructed rooms, displays of objects found in a small agricult
holding or *casería* and tools used for various crafts. One of the functions of
living museum is to preserve local cottage industries (craftsmen give demons
tions) as well as ancestral farming methods.
4km/2.5mi away is the **embalse de Salime**. There are viewpoints overlooking
dam wall and the power station.

OLITE★

Navarra – Population 3 049
Michelin map 442 E 25

Olite, the best-loved residence of the kings of Navarra in the 15C, is known
the Gothic town. It still lives in the shadow of its castle which has all the appeara
and size of a medieval city. The San Martín de Unx road affords a good gen
view.

SIGHTS

★ **Castillo de los Reyes de Navarra (Fortress of the kings of Navarra)** ⊘ – Charles
the Noble, gave orders for the castle to be built in 1406. The French orig
of the prince – he was a Count of Evreux and native of Mantes – explain
foreign style fortifications, a transition between the massive stone
structures of the 13C and the royal Gothic residences of the late 15C v
galleries and small courtyards. The building was carried out by architects fr
north of the Pyrenees assisted by Moorish craftsmen. Behind the 15 or
towers marking the perimeter were hanging gardens; within were inner h
and chambers decorated with *azulejos*, painted stuccowork and colou
marquetry ceilings. The plan is now confused as a result of a great m
alterations and devastations. Restored areas have been converted for use
a parador.

Iglesia de Santa María la Real ⊘ – The church is the former chapel ro
An atrium of slender multifoil arches precedes the 14C **façade**★, a beaut
example of Navarra Gothic sculpture. The only figurative carving on
portal is on the tympanum which illustrates the lives of the Virgin
Christ. A painted 16C retable above the high altar frames a Gothic statu
Our Lady.

Iglesia de San Pedro – The church façade below the tapering octagonal spire
a somewhat disparate appearance. The portal covings are set off by tori (la
convex mouldings). Eagles on either side symbolise, right and left respectiv
Gentleness and Violence. Inside the church, at the beginning of the north aisl
a stone, carved to represent the Trinity (15C).

EXCURSION

★ **Monasterio de La Oliva** ⊘ – *28km/17mi southeast on NA 533*
NA 124.
La Oliva was one of the first Cistercian monasteries to be built by Fre
monks outside France during the lifetime of St Bernard (1090-1153).
monastery's influence was considerable in the Middle Ages. The buildings, r
stripped of treasure and trappings, retain the beauty of the pure Cister
style.

★★ **Iglesia** – Late 12C church. Apart from a triangular coping and the turret (1
the church front is unadorned – a perfect setting for the interplay of line
the portal and two rose windows. The interior is surprisingly deep v
pillars and pointed arches lined with thick polygonal ribs in austere Cister
style.

★ **Claustro** – Late 15C. The cloister bays appear exceptionally light. Gothic addit
were simply grafted onto an older construction, as can be seen by the a
springs which, in part, obscure the entrance to the 13C **Sala Capit**
(chapter-house).

OLIVENZA

Extremadura (Badajoz) – Population 10 004
Michelin map 444 P 8

Five centuries of Portuguese history have left their mark on the appearance and architecture of this quiet white-walled town set in the middle of olive groves. Olivenza is one of the few places in Spain where the Manueline style can be seen – that specifically Portuguese architecture of the early 16C, contemporary with the reign of King Manuel (1495-1521). This style brought to Late Gothic architecture Renaissance, Moorish and maritime features (sailors' knots, ropes and armillary spheres).

The War of the Oranges

At the end of the 13C, Olivenza was given in dowry to King Denis of Portugal. In 1801, it was ceded to Spain to prevent the Alentejo invasion – begun by Godoy's troops – becoming a major conflict between the two nations. The skirmish, however, left no other souvenir than the story of Godoy's futile gesture of sending oranges to Queen María Luisa from trees at the foot of the Elvas ramparts *(see Michelin Green Guide Portugal).*

★ Iglesia de Santa María Magdalena – The brothers Diego and Francisco de Arruda, architects of the Mosteiro dos Jerónimos and the Torre de Belém in Lisbon, are believed to have designed the church's Manueline nave. The sober elegance of the lierne and tierceron vaulting supported on cabled pillars contrasts with the sumptuous altarpieces and *azulejos* which decorate the Baroque sanctuary.

Museo Etnográfico González Santana ⊙ – This ethnographic museum is housed in an 18C building known as the Panadería del Rey (King's Bakery) inside the walls of a medieval castle. A keep built by João III in 1488 dominates the fortress and offers fine views of the town. In the museum, the workshops of several craftsmen have been recreated, including a tailor's and a blacksmith's, in addition to the inside of a 19C house.

Ayuntamiento (town hall) – The doorway, a delightfully graceful example of Manueline style decoration, is adorned with two armillary spheres, symbols of the discoveries by the great Portuguese navigators of the 15C and 16C.

OÑATI/OÑATE

País Vasco (Guipúzcoa) – Population 10 264
Michelin map 442 C22

Oñati with its seignorial residences, monastery and old university, is content now to sit back in its fertile valley. Twice during the First Carlist War the town served as Don Carlos' headquarters. Finally it fell to General Espartero, obliging the Carlists to sign the Convention of Vergara *(see Introduction: Historical table and notes)* and putting an end to the war.

The road 6km/4mi east affords a beautiful **panorama** of Oñati nestling in the valley at the foot of Monte Aloña (1 321m/4 334ft) and the distant Udala and Amboto peaks.

Antigua Universidad (Old University) ⊙ – The university, now administrative headquarters of the Guipúzcoa province, was founded in 1542 by a native prelate of Oñati and closed early this century; it was the only university in the Basque country and enjoyed considerable cultural prestige. The gateway by the Frenchman, Pierre Picart, is surmounted by pinnacles and crowded with statues. Among the figures is the founding bishop (at the centre) and Sts Gregory and Jerome (right and left respectively). The exuberant decoration reappears at the corner of each tower and again in the exceedingly elegant *patio*.

Ayuntamiento (town hall) – The fine 18C Baroque building was designed by the architect Martín de Carrera. At Corpus Christi, unusual traditional dances and processions which date back to the 15C are held in the square.

Iglesia de San Miguel ⊙ – The Gothic church facing the university was modified in the Baroque period. A Renaissance chapel off the north aisle, closed by beautiful iron grilles, contains an interesting gilded wood altarpiece and the marble tomb of the founder of the university. The golden stone cloister exterior with gallery tracery, ogee arches, and statue niches is Isabelline Plateresque in style.

EXCURSIONS

★ Santuario de Arantzazu ⊙ – *9m/6mi south.*
The **scenic cliff road★** follows the course of the río Arantzazu which flows through a narrow gorge. The **shrine** is perched at an altitude of 800m/2 625ft in a mountain **setting★** facing the highest peak in the province, Mount Aitzgorri (1 549m/5 082ft).

Dominating the church is an immense bell-tower 40m/131ft high, built, like t
towers framing the façade, with diamond-faceted stone symbolising the hawtho
bush (*arantzazu* in Basque) in which the Virgin appeared to a local shepherd in 146
A hermitage was then built on the spot and occupied by Franciscans in the 16C b
the present building only dates from 1955. Inside, a statue of the Virgin, patron
the province, stands at the centre of a huge wooden altarpiece painted by Luc
Muñoz.

Elorrio – *18km/11mi northwest on the Durango road.*
This small, ancient town in which many houses are emblasoned with coats
arms, possesses a collection of 15C and 16C crucifixes unique in the Basq
country. The one at the town's west entrance is decorated with a frieze of peopl
the one at the east with a cabled column. The **Iglesia de la Concepción** (Church of O
Lady of Holy Conception), which is a typically Basque church with its thick rou
pillars and star vaulting, contains an exuberant Churrigueresque altarpiece.

Parque Nacional de
ORDESA Y MONTE PERDIDO★★★

Aragón (Huesca)
Michelin map 443 E 29-30
Local map see PIRINEOS ARAGONESES

The Valle de Ordesa was declared a national park in 1918 and was expanded in 198
to cover an area of 15 608ha/38 569 acres, including the Monte Perdido massif an
the Ordesa, Añisclo, Escuain and Pineta valleys. The purpose of the park is t
safeguard its outstanding natural beauty – the massif's limestone relief of canyon
cliffs and chasms – as well as the variety and richness of its flora and fauna (Pyrenea
ibex, golden eagle and izard, a goatlike antelope of the Pyrenees).

*The park must be visited between May and September as the snow makes
inaccessible by car in winter.*

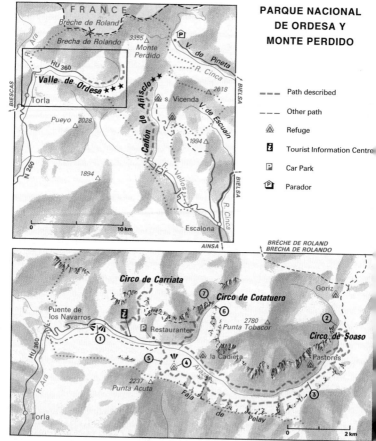

**PARQUE NACIONAL
DE ORDESA Y
MONTE PERDIDO**

- - - Path described

- - - Other path

⛺ Refuge

ℹ Tourist Information Centre

🅿 Car Park

🅿 Parador

★VALLE DE ORDESA

The Ordesa Valley is a grandiose canyon cutting through vast, layered limestone folds. The escarpments which rise nearly 1 000m/3 280ft from the valley floor, are divided into steel grey or red ochre strata. In spring, cascades of melted snow streak the vertical rock face. Along the valley bottom, the río Arazas, a turbulent trout stream, rushes beneath flourishing beech and maple trees. Growing up the lower slopes are pines, larches, firs – some 25m/82ft tall – and a carpet of box, hawthorn and service trees.

WALKING TOURS

A viewpoint on the road into the park offers a general panorama of the reserve and a little further on, a second point looks over the 60m/197ft high **cascada de Tamborrotera** ①. As the road soon comes to an end, the rest of the park may only be visited on foot.

The best route for inexperienced walkers or families with young children is along the path that runs through the bottom of the canyon beside the Arazas river itself, which makes for a pleasant, shady walk.

Allow a day for a round tour from the car park to the end of the canyon and back.
The three walks below are feasible for experienced, well-equipped hikers.

Parque Nacional de Ordesa

B. Brillon/MICHELIN

Circuito del Circo de Soaso (Tour of the Soaso Cirque) – *Start from the Cadiera refuge beyond the car park; 7hr.*
The first part of the walk as far as the valley floor is easy and can be attempted by anyone. The second part, via the Cola de Caballo (Horse's Tail) is more difficult, however, and is only recommended to those who are well equipped and in good physical condition (steep climbs).

This walk provides the best and most complete tour of the Ordesa Valley. Fro the Circo de Soaso path several waterfalls can be seen including the **Gradas Soaso** ③, or Soaso Steps, followed by the impressive, 70m/230ft high **Cola Caballo** ②. The path continues along the **Faja de Pelay** overlooking the canyon to depth of 2 000m/6 562ft at the foot of the Sierra de Cutas. Continue along t **Senda de los Cazadores** (Huntsman's Path) ⑤, from where there is a wonderful vie of the canyon. The best panorama can be had from the **Mirador de Calcilarruego** The path back to the refuge drops sharply (almost 1 000m/3 300ft).

Circo de Cotatuero (Cotatuero Cirque) – *Start from the restaurant; 4hr.*
On the park's northern border are the **Cotatuero** ⑥ and the **Copos de Lana** (Tufts Wool) *cascadas* (waterfalls) ⑦ with a drop of 250m/820ft.

Circo de Carriata – *Start from the Centro de Información; 4hr.*
The walk is worth doing although the *clavijas* or mountaineering peg track difficult and not recommended for those who suffer from vertigo.
A long hike is possible to Monte Perdido via the Goriz refuge, and beyond, alo paths leading to the Cirque de Gavarnie in France via the Brecha de Rolan (Roland Gap) *(ask at the Centro de Información).*

★★ CAÑÓN DE AÑISCLO

Access from Escalona village on the Bielsa-Ainsa road – a 13km/8mi drive.

The Añisclo canyon, narrower than that of Ordesa, is a cool, attractive valley wi pine trees clinging to the limestone walls.

Walk to Ripareta – *Start from San Urbez bridge. 5hr there and back.* The wi well-defined path follows the course of the enclosed río Vellos which cascad down the valley to its confluence with the Pardina.

ORENSE
See OURENSE

ORREAGA/RONCESVALLES ★
Navarra
Michelin map 442 C 26

Roncesvalles has come down to us rather as a heroic epic than as the geographi pass, known to countless medieval pilgrims on their way to Santiago de Composte It is the site where, in 778, the Basques of Navarra massacred the rearguard Charlemagne's army as Roland was leading it back through the Pyrenees to Fran The late-12C early-13C **Poem of Bernardo del Carpio** describes Bernardo as a national he who sought only with his Basque, Navarra and Asturian companions in arms avenge the Frankish invasion of Spain; the early-12C **Song of Roland**, the first Frer epic poem, on the other hand, glorifies the heroic but ultimately despairing resistan of a handful of valiant Christian knights – Roland and the 12 peers of the Empir against hordes of Saracen fanatics brought to the field by the traitor Ganelon.

Ecclesiastical buildings – This vast, grey walled mass of buildings with blu zinc roofs, dating back to the 12C, appears hidden by dense vegetation. T buildings served formerly as an important pilgrims' hostelry with a funer chapel, square in plan, now the Capilla del Sancti Spiritus (Chapel of the H Spirit), and a collegiate church rich in relics.

Iglesia de la Real Colegiata ⊘ – This Gothic collegiate church, inspired by those of t Paris region, was consecrated in 1219, since when it has been repeatedly, a unfortunately, restored. Beneath the high altar canopy is the centre-piece o pilgrimage, a **Virgin and Child** in wood, plated in silver and made in France in the 1 or 14C.

Sala Capitular (Chapter-house) ⊘ – The beautiful Gothic chamber, off the cloiste contains the tombs of the founder, Sancho VII, the Strong (1154-1234), King Navarra and his queen.

★ **Museo** ⊘ – Housed in the old stables, the museum contains fine pieces of ancie plate: a Mudéjar casket, a Romanesque book of the Gospel, a 14C enamel reliquary which, doubtless on account of its chequered design, is known *Charlemagne's chessboard*, a 16C Flemish triptych, an emerald, said to have be worn by Sultan Miramamolín el Verde in his turban on the day of the Battle of N Navas de Tolosa in 1212, and a lovely *Holy Family* by Morales.

Monasterio Santa María la Real de OSEIRA ★

Galicia (Orense)

Michelin map 441 E 6

The grandiose Cistercian monastery, commonly known as the Escorial of Galicia, was founded by Alfonso VII in the middle of the 12C. It stands in an isolated position in the Arenteiro Valley, a region that once abounded in bears *(osos)* as the monastery's name suggests.

Monasterio ⊙ – The façade (1708) consists of three sections. In a niche below the statue of Hope which crowns the doorway is the figure of a Nursing Madonna with St Bernard at her feet. Of note inside the monastery are an **escalera de honor** (grand staircase) and the **Claustro de los Medallones** (Medallion Cloisters) decorated with 40 busts of famous historic personages.

Iglesia – Behind the Baroque façade of 1637, the 12C-13C church has retained the customary Cistercian simplicity modified only by the frescoes in the transept which were painted in 1694.

★ **Sala Capitular** – This chapter-house dates from the late 15C and early 16C and is outstanding for its beautiful vaulting of crossed ribs descending like the fronds of a palm tree onto four spiral columns.

OSUNA ★

Andalucía (Sevilla) – Population 16 240

Michelin map 446 U 14

Osuna is an elegant Andalusian town with a beautiful **monumental centre** ★ *(follow the Zona Monumental signs)*, inherited from its former status as a ducal seat. The dukedom was created in 1562 and the house of Osuna has remained one of the greatest in Spain.

Colegiata ⊙ – This 16C Renaissance style collegiate church houses five **paintings** ★ by **José (Jusepe) de Ribera "Lo Spagnoletto"** (1591-1652), including **The Crucifixion**, in the side chapel off the Nave del Evangelio. The remainder are exhibited in the sacristy.

★ **Sepulcro Ducal** (Ducal Sepulchre) ⊙ – The first crypt is approached through a delightful *patio* with marble arcades decorated in the Plateresque style; it is a church in miniature. The ceiling roses, once blue and gold, are now black with candle smoke. Below, a second crypt (1901) contains the coffins of the major grandees.

Walk in the town – *Mainly around plaza del Duque and plaza España*. The straight lines of the streets are punctuated by the occasional noble Baroque façade; massive wooden doors, darkly shining and copper nailed, reveal, when opened, fine wrought-iron grilles and cool green *patios*. Of particular note are the **calle San Pedro** ★ (Cilla del Cabildo, Palacio de los Marqueses de la Gomera), the Antigua Audencia (former Law Courts), the Palacio de los Cepeda, the former Palacio de Puente Hermoso, several fine churches (Santo Domingo, San Agustín) and, near to the Colegiata, the Monasterio de la Encarnación and the former university, both 16C.

OURENSE/ORENSE

Galicia – Population 108 382

Michelin map 441 E, F 6

Since Antiquity, Orense (Ourense in Galician) – the name is said to come from the legendary gold believed to exist in the Miño Valley – has been famous for its waters which pour out from three springs, **Las Burgas**, at a temperature of 65°C/150°F. The town has preserved an old bridge, **Puente Romano**, which dates from the 13C when it was rebuilt on Roman foundations to provide a crossing for pilgrims on their way to Santiago de Compostela.
The town today is a busy commercial centre with modern buildings although there is still an old quarter around the cathedral.

SIGHTS

★ **Catedral** ⊙ – The cathedral, which took from the 12C to the 13C to build, has been constantly modified over the ages. The **Portada Sur** (South Door), in the Compostelan style, lacks a tympanum, but is profusely decorated with carvings on covings and capitals. The **Portada Norte** (North Door) has two statue columns and, beneath a great ornamental arch, a 15C Deposition framed by a Flight into Egypt and statues of the Holy Women.

OURENSE/ORENSE

Barreira	2
Bedoya	
Cabeza de Manzaneda	8
Capitán Eloy	
Cardenal Quiroga	
Palacios	12
Coronel Ceano Vivas	15
Cruz Vermella	18
Doctor Marañón	21
Ervedelo	24
Ferro (Pr. do)	30
Lamas Carvajal	37
Magdalena (Pr. de)	42
Parada Justel	45
Paseo	
Paz	46
Pena Corneira	48
Pontevedra (Av. de)	51
Praza Major	
Progreso	
San Miguel	54
Santo Domingo	57
Trigo (Pr. do)	60

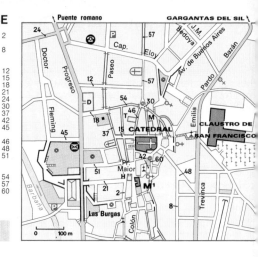

M¹ Museo Arqueológico y de Bellas Artes

The **interior** is noteworthy for its pure lines. At the end of the 15C, a Gothic Renaissance transitional style **lantern** was built above the transept. The high altar has an ornate Gothic retable by Cornelius de Holanda. The 16C and 17C **Capilla de Santísimo Cristo** (Chapel of the Holy Sacrament), decorated with exuberant sculpture in the Galician Baroque style, opens off the north transept. The triple-arched **Pórtico del Paraíso★★** (Paradise Door) at the west end, with its beautiful carvings and bright medieval colouring, illustrates the same theme as the Pórtico de la Gloria in Santiago Cathedral. The central arch shows the 24 Old Men of the Apocalypse; to the right is the Last Judgement. The pierced tympanum above, like the narthex vaulting, is 16C.

A door in the south aisle opens onto the 13C chapter-house, now a **museum**. Among the items displayed are church plate, statues, chasubles and a 12C travelling altar.

Museo Arqueológico y de Bellas Artes (Archeological and Fine Arts Museum) ⊘ (**M¹**) – The finely emblazoned façade overlooking plaza Mayor belongs to the former episcopal palace, now a museum. The collections inside include prehistoric specimens, *castro* cultural objects (mainly statues of warriors) and a section of fine arts with, in particular, an early-18C wood carving of the **Camino del Calvario** (Stations of the Cross).

★ **Claustro de San Francisco** ⊘ – The elegant 14C cloisters consist of slightly horseshoe-shaped Gothic arches resting on slender, paired columns to which diamond and leaf decoration adds simple sophistication. Some of the capitals illustrate scenes of the hunt or historic personages.

EXCURSION

★ **Round tour of 65km/40mi** – *2hr 30min plus 30min for a tour of the monastery. Leave Orense on C536 east; turn left after 6km/4mi onto a road going north to Luintra; continue for 18km/11mi.*

Monasterio de San Estevo de Ribas de Sil – The monastery appears suddenly in a majestic **setting★**, spread over a great spur, against a background of granite mountains deeply cut by the Sil. The church's Romanesque east end remains, as do the three cloisters, built to grandiose proportions largely in the 16C, although one still has Romanesque galleries surmounted by elegant low arches.

★ **Gargantas del Sil** (Gorges of the Sil river) – *Return on the downhill road on the left towards the Sil (do not take the signposted turning to the embalse de San Esteban).* Two dams, one vaulted, the other a buttressed type, control the waters of the Sil which flow through deep gorges.

At the second dam, without leaving the left bank of the river, turn onto the road marked embalse de San Pedro which joins N 120. Bear left for Orense.

OVIEDO ★

Asturias – Population 204 276
Michelin map 441 B 12

Oviedo, the economic and cultural capital of Asturias, is a modern town built on a rise in the middle of a fertile, green basin, with the added attraction of a large park at its centre. It developed in the 18C with the establishment of an arsenal and expanded rapidly in the 19C as the coal basin began to be exploited. It is a university town with a College of Mining Engineering.

The old town round the cathedral with its many ancient broad-fronted seignorial mansions contrasts sharply with the modern city.

The capital of the Kingdom of Asturias (9C-10C) – All that the Muslims left of the small city built by Fruela I (722-768) around a Benedictine monastery on a hill named Ovetum, was a pile of ruins. Fruela's son, Alfonso II, the Chaste (791-842), transferred the court from Cangas de Onís and Pravia where it had been previously to Oviedo. He rebuilt the town, encircling it with ramparts and embellishing it with religious buildings of which only traces remain – the Cámara Santa, the east end of San Tirso Church and Santullano Church. His successor Ramiro I (842-850) continued the royal patronage and built a splendid summer palace which remains, in part, on the slopes of nearby Monte Naranco *(see Excursions p 274)*.

But in 914, with the extension of the kingdom's boundaries southwards, the king, Don García, transferred the court to León. The Asturias-León Kingdom existed briefly from 1037 to 1157 and then in 1230 was finally incorporated into Castilla. Recognition of a sort returned to the old kingdom in 1388 when the heir apparent to the Castilian throne took the title, Prince of Asturias. The heir to the Spanish throne still carries the same title today.

The Battles of Oviedo – In 1934, following the insurrection in the Asturian mining area, the town was heavily damaged during fighting between insurgent miners and right-wing government forces: the Cámara Santa was destroyed, the university set on fire and the cathedral damaged. In 1937, Oviedo was once more the scene of heavy fighting, this time during the Civil War.

OLD TOWN *1hr 30min*

★ **Catedral** ⊘ – The cathedral, a characteristically Flamboyant Gothic edifice, was begun in the 14C with the construction of the cloisters, and completed in the 16C with that of the porch and the massive 80m/262ft south tower, which tapers into a delicate openwork spire (restored after the Civil War). Three Gothic portals pierce the asymmetrical façade. The doors, which are considerably later, are panelled in 18C walnut; the centre door bears a figure of Christ *(on the left)* and St Eulalia in a maize field *(on the right)*.

Interior – The triforium surmounted by tall windows, together with the façade and transept rose windows, have the wavy lines typical of Flamboyant Gothic. The open vista down the nave enhances the 16C high **altarpiece★** of wood, carved with scenes from the Life of Christ.

The side chapels were profusely ornamented during the Baroque period. On the left on entering, is the overly ornate 17C Capilla de Santa Eulalia, containing the relics of the patron saint of Asturias in a massive Baroque shrine.

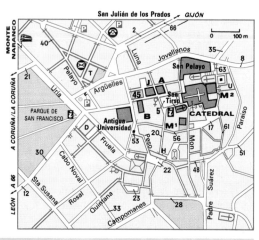

OVIEDO

Alcalde G. Conde 2
Alfonso II (Pl. de) 5
Azcárraga 8
Calvo Sotelo 12
Canóniga 17
Cimadevilla 20
Conde de Toreno 21
Constitución
  (Plaza de la) 22
Daoiz y Velarde
  (Pl. de) 23
Marqués de Gastañaga . . . 28
Marqués de Santa Cruz . . . 30
Martínez Marina 33
Martínez Vigil 35
Palacio Valdés 40
Pelayo
Porlier (Pl. de) 45
Postigo Alto 48
Postigo Bajo 51
Riego (Pl.) 53
San Antonio 56
San Francisco 58
San José 61
San Vicente 63
Uría
Víctor Chávarri 66

A Palacio de Valdecarzana
B Palacio de Toreno
J Palacio de Camposagrado

M¹ Museo de Bellas Artes
  de Asturias
M² Museo Arqueológico

The **Capilla de Alfonso II el Casto** – Alfonso II was known as The Chaste – off the nort transept, stands on the site of the original church and is the pantheon of th Asturian kings. The decoration inside the gate is Late Gothic. In the embrasure are the figures of the Pilgrim St James, Sts Peter, Paul and Andrew and, in th covings, the 12 old musicians. In the chapel lie the illustrious Asturian kings.

Cámara Santa ⊘ – The Cámara Santa was built by Alfonso II early in the 9C as shrine for a coffer containing holy relics brought from Toledo on the fall of th Visigothic Kingdom. It was remodelled in Romanesque times and destroyed in a explosion in 1934; the rebuilt chapel contains many of the original works of art Six groups of Apostles in the vestibule form a series of stylised **statue columns**★ which are among the most masterly sculptures of 12C Spain. The head of th Christ figure over the entrance is also remarkable – the artist was obviousl influenced by the Pórtico de la Gloria (Doorway of Glory) in Santiago Cathedra which is not surprising as the Cámara Santa was often a stop for pilgrims goin to Santiago de Compostela. Column capitals illustrate the marriage of Joseph an Mary, the Holy Women at the Tomb and lion and wild boar hunts.

The **tesoro**★★ (treasury) in the apse includes an outstanding collection of ancien gold and silver plate: the **Cruz de los Ángeles** (Cross of the Angels), a gift fror Alfonso II in 808, made of cedar wood and studded with precious gems, Roma cabochons and cameos, the **Cruz de Victoria** (908), faced with chased gold an precious stones, which was carried by Pelayo at the victory of Covadonga, th **Arqueta de las Ágatas** or Agate Reliquary, a gift by Fruela II in 910 and the 11C **Arc Santa**, a silver plated reliquary casket.

Claustro – The cloisters have intersecting pointed arches and delicate tracery in th bays. The **Capilla de Santa Leocadia** *(to the left on entering)* is in fact the Cámara Sant crypt. It is decorated outside *(garden)* with blind arcades and covered inside wit barrel vaulting and contains an altar, tombs from the time of Alfonso II and a unusually small stone cubicle. The **sala capitular** (chapter-house) contains fine stall dating from the late 15C.

Plaza de la Catedral (Plaza de Alfonso II) (5) – To the left of the cathedral is a garde with low reliefs and busts carved in homage to the Asturian kings. On the nort side of the cathedral square is the 17C **Palacio de Valdecarzana (A)**. *Walk south roun the cathedral*. Note the east window of the **Iglesia de San Tirso** – all that remains c the 9C church. The existence of the Moorish *alfiz* in a building of that date remain a mystery.

Museo de Bellas Artes de Asturias (Fine Arts Museum of Asturias) ⊘ **(M¹)** – Th elegant 18C Palacio de Velarde houses a large collection of paintings in whic Asturian artists are particularly well represented. Note the Flemish triptych of th **Adoration of the Magi**, painted during the reign of Emperor Charles V by the maste of the *Legend of Mary Magdalene*, and the portrait of Charles II by Carreño d Miranda.

Museo Arqueológico (Archeological Museum) ⊘ **(M²)** – The museum is housed in former convent.

Two galleries opening off the 15C Plateresque cloisters at ground level contai pre-Romanesque art. Humble fragments and reproductions provide strikin evidence of the delicate sophistication of monumental decoration in the Asturia period. Among the exhibits are altars such as that of Naranco surmounted by it original stone, reconstructions of chancel screens, low reliefs often showin Byzantine influence, column bases from San Miguel de Lillo and pierced bays inlai in walls.

Local prehistoric finds, coins and carved wood objects, including old music instruments, are on view in the upper cloister.

The façade next to the museum fronts the 17C and 18C **Monasterio de San Pelay**

Plaza de Porlier (45) – Among the fine palaces on the square are the **Toreno (B** dating from 1673 (now a library) and the **Camposagrado (J)**, a harmonious 18 edifice now the Law Courts (note the spread eaves).

Antiguo Universidad (Former University) – The austerely-fronted building wa completed in the 17C. The classical court, although restored, retains much of it former style.

ADDITIONAL SIGHTS

Antiguo Hospital del Principado (Former Hospital of the Principality) – *Leave Oviec on Calle Conde de Toreno (marked on the plan)*. The façade of the hospital, whic is now a hotel, is emblazoned with a fine Baroque **coat of arms**★.

Iglesia de Santullano or San Julián de los Prados ⊘ – The church is a outstanding example of Asturian art in the first half of the 9C with its porch, nav and twin aisles, wide transept and at the east end, three chapels vaulted in bric The walls are covered in frescoes which, from their composition, suggest a Roma influence. There is a fine Romanesque Crucifix in the central apse. Outside, th east end is typical with a window with a triple arcade and claustra.

ENVIRONS

★ **Santuarios del Monte Naranco (Mount Naranco Church and Chapel)** – *4km/2.5mi northwest.*

Of the summer palace built by Ramiro I on the south side of the mountain in the 9C, there remain the former audience chamber, now the Iglesia de Santa María, and the royal chapel, San Miguel. The **panorama** from the site includes Oviedo.

★ **Iglesia de Santa María del Naranco** ⊘ – The building is attractive, with harmonious lines: it is square, two-storeyed, supported by grooved buttresses and lit by vast bays. On the upper floor two loggias open off the great chamber covered by barrel vaulting. Exterior and interior decoration have been cleverly adapted to architectural necessity and are often similar in style: clusters of slender cabled colonnettes adorn the pillars; the loggia capitals are Corinthian, those abutting the walls polygonal; the arch ribs descend to the squinches on fluted pilasters and medallions minutely decorated in Byzantine style.

★ **Iglesia de San Miguel de Lillo** ⊘ – The chapel was truncated when the east end was remodelled in the 17C. The narrowness of the aisles accentuates the height of the walls in which several claustra type windows remain. The delicacy of the interior carving is a delight: on the door **jambs**★★ are identical scenes in relief of a consul, surrounded by dignitaries, presiding over contests in an arena. A cord motif is repeated on the capitals and on the vaulting in the nave and gallery.

San Miguel de Lillo

J.Hidalgo – C.Lopesino/MARCO POLO

EXCURSIONS

★ **Iglesia de Santa Cristina de Lena** ⊙ – *34km/21mi south on A 66, leaving
junction 92. At Pola de Lena, head for Vega del Rey and there take the signpost
road. Park the car before the viaduct and walk up the steep path (15min).*
Santa Cristina de Lena is a well-proportioned church built of golden stone.
stands on a rocky crag from which there is a **panoramic view**★ of the green Cauc
Valley.
The little building, which is later than those on Monte Naranco, has a Greek cro
plan unusual in Asturias, but the traditional stone vaulting remains, with bli
arcades, in which the columns have pyramid-shaped capitals emphasised by a co
motif, sculpted medallions extending the arch ribs and cabled columns in t
choir. The nave is separated from the raised choir by an iconostasis in which t
superimposed arches increase the impression of balance. The low reliefs in t
chancel are Visigothic sculptures, recognizable by their geometric figures a
plant motifs, which have been placed in a new setting.

Teverga – *43km/27mi southwest on N 634, then AS 228.*
The road follows the río Trubia which, after Proaza, enters a narrow gorge. As y
emerge, glance back for a **view**★ of the Peñas Juntas cliff face which marks t
end of the gorge. Beyond the Teverga fork the road penetrates the enclos
desfiladero de Teverga★ (Teverga Defile).
The **Colegiata de San Pedro de Teverga** ⊙ is just outside La Plaza village. This collegia
church, which is late 12C, has had a porch and tower added. The architecture
an obvious continuation of the pre-Romanesque Asturian style. The buildi
includes a narthex, a tall narrow nave and a flat east end, originally three chape
The narthex capitals are carved with stylised animal and plant motifs.

Puerto de PAJARES★★

PAJARES PASS – Castilla y León, Asturias
Michelin map 441 D 12

For many years the puerto de Pajares, between the provinces of León and Asturia
provided the least arduous route across the western part of the Cordillera Cantábric
The **road**★★ (N 630) approaching the pass from the south follows the course of t
Bernesga to La Robla from where it continues directly upwards across several gullie
In the village of **Arbás**, half a mile south of the pass, is the Romanesque **Colegiata**
Santa María. Although this collegiate church was modified during the Renaissance,
still retains interesting capitals decorated with plant motifs which show a Byzanti
influence.

★★ **The Pass** – At 1 379m/4 524ft above sea-level, the pass makes an excellent po
from which to scan the sharply pointed Cordillera Cantábrica mountain rang
Several ski-lifts provide easy access to the heights for winter sports. The hairp
road cutting down the north side of the mountains is steep in places (15% – 1:
There are opencast coalmines on the mountainsides and rocky escarpmer
overlooking the ravine.

PALENCIA

Castilla y León – Population 81 988
Michelin map 441 F 16

Palencia, in the fertile Tierra de Campos region, is a long narrow town built alon
north-south axis hemmed in to the west by the río Carríon and to the east by t
railway. Immediately surrounding the town is a green swathe of market garde
irrigated by the Canal de Castilla and its tributaries.
Palencia was the seat of Spain's first university, founded by Alfonso VIII in the ea
13C.

★★ **Catedral** ⊙ – Palencia's beautiful, unknown cathedral – the townspeople belie
the monument is not given sufficient recognition – is a 14C-16C Gothic edif
with a good many Renaissance features. In the 7C a chapel was built on the s
to enshrine the relics of a Visigotic saint, Antolín. The chapel lay forgotten duri
the Moorish occupation and for long after, until, according to tradition, Sancho
de Navarra came upon it while hunting wild boar. The king erected a Romanesq
chapel (1034) over the ruins which survives today as the crypt to the cathedr

★★ **Interior** – The centre of the cathedral contains an incredible concentration of wor
of art in all the different styles of the early 16C: Flamboyant Gothic, Isabellin
Plateresque and Renaissance. This wealth is due to Bishop Fonseca who gather
round him in the early 16C a group of highly skilled artists. The monumental hi

altar **retable** (early 16C), with its many compartments, was carved by Felipe Vigarny, painted by Juan of Flanders and is surmounted by a Crucifix by Juan de Valmaseda. The 16C tapestries on the sides were commissioned by Bishop Fonseca. The *coro* grille, with a delicately wrought upper section, is by Gaspar Rodríguez (1563); the choir stalls are Gothic, the organ gallery, above, is dated 1716. The **Capilla del Sagrario** (Chapel of the Holy Sacrament) behind the high altar and closed by a fine Romanesque grille, is exuberantly Gothic with a rich altarpiece by Valmaseda (1529). To the left, and slightly higher up, is the sarcophagus of Queen Urraca of Navarra (d 1189). The sculptures in the *trascoro* are the work of Gil de Siloé and Simon of Cologne; the central **triptych**★ is a masterpiece, painted in Flanders by Jan Joest de Calcar in 1505 – the donor, Bishop Fonseca, is depicted at its centre.

A Plateresque staircase beside the *trascoro* leads to the Romanesque **crypt** which retains several vestiges (arches and capitals) of the 7C Visigothic chapel.

★ **Museo** ⊘ – The museum is to the right of the west door. The collection includes a *St Sebastian* by El Greco and four 15C Flemish **tapestries**★ of the Adoration, the Ascension, Original Sin and the Resurrection of Lazarus. They were commissioned by Bishop Fonseca who had his crest woven into the corners.

EXCURSIONS

Baños de Cerrato – *14km/9mi southeast; cross the railway at Venta de Baños before turning right towards Cevico de la Torre. Bear left at the first crossroads.*

The Visigothic **Basílica de San Juan Bautista**★ ⊘ is the oldest church in Spain in a good state of preservation. It was built by the Visigothic King, Recceswinth, while he was taking the waters in Baños de Cerrato, in 661. The date is shown beneath the apsidal arch. The church consists of three aisles covered in timber vaulting, a transept and three apses. The horseshoe arches separating the aisles are supported on marble columns. The capitals are carved with a stylised foliage motif which includes the long, ribbed leaf which later appeared widely in Asturian art. Note the decorative frieze in the central apse.

PAMPLONA★

See IRUÑEA

El PARDO

Madrid

Michelin map 444 or 442 K 18

ne town, now on the outskirts of Madrid, has grown around one of the royal sidences. Its surrounding forests of holm oak, often painted by Velázquez, were e traditional hunting preserve of Spanish monarchs.

ing Juan Carlos I lives 5km/3mi to the southwest in the **Palacio de la Zarzuela**.

★ **Palacio Real** ⊘ – The royal palace was built by Philip III (1598-1621) on the site of Philip II's palace (1556-98) which had been destroyed in a fire in 1604, and remodelled by Sabatini in 1772. For a long time the palace was the residence of the Head of State; Franco lived here for 35 years. Today, it is used by foreign Heads of State on official visits. As you walk through the reception rooms and private apartments you will see elegant ensembles from Charles IV's collections including furniture, chandeliers and clocks. More than 200 **tapestries**★ illustrating hunting scenes and country life, hang on the walls; the majority are 18C from the Real Fábrica de Tápices (Royal Tapestry Factory) in Madrid after cartoons by Goya, Bayeu, González Ruiz and Van Loo.

Casita del Príncipe (The Prince's Pavilion) ⊘ – The pavilion, built in 1772 for the children of the future Charles IV and his wife María Luisa, was completely remodelled by Juan de Villanueva in 1784. It is a single-storey building of brick and stone decorated in the extremely ornate, refined taste fashionable in the late 18C with silk hangings and Pompeian style ceilings.

La Quinta ⊘ – The former residence of the Duke of Arcos became crown property in 1745. Inside, elegant early-19C wallpaper embellishes the walls.

Convento de Capuchinos (Capuchin Monastery) ⊘ – A chapel contains one of the major works of Spanish sculpture, a polychrome wood figure of **Christ Recumbent**★ by Gregorio Fernández. It was commissioned by Philip III in 1605.

PEDRAZA DE LA SIERRA★★

Castilla y León (Segovia) – Population 448
Michelin map 442 or 444 I 18

Pedraza, perched on a knoll, has kept much of the atmosphere of a seignorial tow
as it stands encircled by medieval walls and surveyed by a powerful castle on the cra
A fortified gateway opens into a maze of steep, narrow alleys, bordered with count
style houses, many with family crests. **Plaza Mayor**, one of the most delightful ma
squares in Castilla, is framed by ancient porticoes superimposed by wide balconie
and a slender Romanesque bell-tower.

Plaza Mayor

EXCURSIONS

Sepúlveda – *25km/16mi north.*
By approaching Sepúlveda from Pedraza you will get a good view of its terrac
site★ on the slopes of a deep gorge. Leave the car in the town hall squar
overlooked by the old castle ruins, and walk up to the **Iglesia de San Salvador** fro
which there is a fine view of the town and surrounding countryside. The chur
itself is typical Segovia Romanesque with a multiple-storey belfry with paired ba
and an east end decorated with a carved cornice. It has one of the oldest side doo
in Spain, dating from 1093.
The restaurants are renowned for their roast lamb *(cordero asado).*

Hoces del Duratón (Duratón Gorges) – *16km/10mi west of Sepúlveda. Head towar
Villar de Sobrepeña, continue 10km/6mi to Villaseca, from where a dirt track lea
to the hermitage.* The simple Romanesque hermitage of San Frutos is situat
above the gorge of the Duratón river. The view from here is particularly impressiv

PEÑAFIEL★

Castilla y León (Valladolid) – Population 5 003
Michelin map 442 H 17

Peñafiel was one of the strong points in the fortified line *(see SORIA)* built along t
Duero during the Reconquest.

★ **Castillo** – The village of Peñafiel is dominated by its redoubtable 14C castle, bu
to massive proportions at the meeting point of three valleys. The fortress consis
of two concentric oblong perimeters built along the ridge. Crowning it, within t
second, fairly well preserved perimeter, is a characteristically Castilian squa
keep, reinforced at its summit by machicolated turrets.

Iglesia de San Pablo – The church (1324) has a Mudéjar east end, and insi
Renaissance vaulting over the 16C Capilla del Infante (Infante Chapel).

Plaza del Coso – The vast, typically Castilian square is almost completely ringed
houses with wide balconies which serve as galleries for viewing bullfights held belo

PEÑARANDA DE DUERO★

Castilla y León (Burgos) – Population 609
Michelin map 442 G 19

he small Castilian town is dominated by the ruins of its **castle**.

★ **Plaza Mayor** – The square forms an interesting architectural unit of half-timbered houses resting on robust stone pillars; at its centre is a 15C pillory.

★ **Palacio de Avellaneda** ⊘ – The palace with its noble façade and fully ornamented Renaissance entrance fronts Plaza Mayor. The interior, designed by Francisco de Colonia, makes it one of the finest Renaissance residences in Spain. There is a *patio* surrounded by a two tier gallery, an inner *patio* arch, a grand staircase and chambers with **artesonado ceilings**★.

PEÑÍSCOLA★★

Comunidad valenciana (Castellón) – Population 3 677
Michelin map 443 or 445 K 31

eñíscola, a rocky peninsula (from which the name derives) closely built up now with hite-walled cottages to the foot of the stone castle at the summit, was the final fuge of the medieval antipope, **Benedict XIII**.

modern resort is developing on either side of the neck of the promontory, beside e vast sand beaches. The fishing harbour below the old town comes to life in the te afternoon when the boats bring home their catch.

ope Luna – On the death of the antipope Clement VII in 1394, the Aragonese ardinal Pedro de Luna was elected successor by the French cardinals in conclave at vignon. It was a dubious heritage, however, as his predecessor had never succeeded establishing his claim. The withdrawal of the support of King Charles VI of France nd of St Vincent Ferrer, the accusation of heresy by the Councils of Pisa (1409) and onstance (1416), in no way diminished the self-styled Benedict XIII's conviction of s right. He considered the proposal that he should abdicate and help to seal the chism inadmissible and, in the face of general hostility, sought refuge in the fortress n Peñíscola. There he remained until he died in 1422, a nonagenarian, tenacious as ver, who even named his own successor! (This prelate, however, soon abdicated in vour of the Rome elected Martin V.)

★ **OLD TOWN** *closed to cars – allow 1hr*

The old town huddled within the ramparts, which date from the reign of Philip II, makes for a pleasant stroll. It has narrow winding streets lined with souvenir shops.

Castillo ⊘ – The castle, built by the Templars in the 14C, was modified by Pope Luna whose coat of arms, which features a crescent moon in allusion to his name, can be seen on one of the gates. Grouped round the parade ground are the church, a vast hall with pointed vaulting and a free standing tower containing the conclave room and the study of the learned antipope who, among his many acts, confirmed in six bulls the foundation in 1411 of St Andrew's University in Scotland *(see Michelin Green Guide Scotland)* and promulgated the Statutes of Salamanca University.
There is a **panorama**★ of the village and coastline from the castle terrace.

Peñíscola

277

PICUS DE EUROPA★★★

Castilla y León, Asturias, Cantabria

Michelin map 441 C 14-16

The Picos de Europa, the highest range in the Cordillera Cantábrica (Torre Cerre
2 648m/8 688ft), stand massed between Oviedo and Santander, some 30km/2C
from the sea.

In 1995 the **Parque Nacional de los Picos de Europa** was created with a view to protect
and preserving the precious plant and animal species of the region. Covering a tc
area of 64 660ha/159 630 acres, it incorporates the former Parque de la Monta
de Covadonga.

Gorges, cut by torrents teeming with fish, circumscribe the Primary limesto
formation and have divided it into three blocks: the western or Covadonga mass
the central or Naranjo de Bulnes massif and the eastern or Andara massif. T
impressive landscape is one of deep clefts as well as high peaks, jagged with eros
and always snow-capped. The south face is less steep and looks out over a less abr
but harsher terrain.

Besides the traditional occupations of *cabrales* making – a blue cheese made of ew
milk – and stock raising, there is mining in the area. The Liébana region, arou
Potes, has a mild climate sheltered from the northwest winds and grows walnu
cherries and medlars and even grapes halfway up the slopes.

The Picos de Europa form a restricted hunting reserve (Reserva Nacional de Los Pi
de Europa) and the Parque Nacional de Covadonga which covers 17 000I
42 000 acres of the western massif. Since 1995, the park has been enlarged and
now part of the **Parque Nacional de los Picos de Europa** (64 660ha/159 780 acres).

★★ DESFILADERO DE LA HERMIDA (LA HERMIDA RAVINE)

① From Panes to Potes

27km/17mi - about 1hr

The outstanding feature of the drive
is the **ravine**★★, some 20km/12mi
long in all, which extends either side
of a basin containing the hamlet of
La Hermida. The gorge is narrow
and so lacking in sunlight as to be
bare of vegetation; the Deva has
sought out weaknesses in the rock
wall to carve out a sawtooth course.

**Iglesia de Nuestra Señora de Le-
beña** ⊘ – The small 10C Mozarabic
church stands surrounded by poplars
at the foot of tall cliffs. The belfry
and porch are later additions. The
semicircular vaulting over the three
aisles rests on horseshoe-shaped
arches decorated with beautifully
carved Corinthian style capitals.

Potes – Potes is a delightful village
in a pleasing **site**★ set in the hollow
of a fertile basin against a background of jagged crests, the peaks
of the central massif. From the
bridge there is a view, reflected in
the Deva, of old stone houses and
the austere 15C **Torre del Infantado**,
a restored tower which now serves as
the town hall (*Ayuntamiento*).

★★ THE CLIMB TO FUENTE DÉ

② 30km/19mi - about 3hr

The road follows the Deva through a
mixed landscape of mountain woods
and meadows dotted here and there
with the pink tile roofs of villages.
Finally it reaches the wild rock cirque
of Fuente Dé where the river rises.

**Monasterio de Santo Toribio de
Liébana** ⊘ – Approach along a signposted road on the left (*heading
back towards Potes from Fuente
Dé*). The monastery now occupied

by Franciscans, was founded in the 7C and grew to considerable importance in the following century when a fragment said to be of the True Cross, brought from Jerusalem by Turibius, Bishop of Astorga, was placed in its safekeeping. A *camarín* *(access through the north aisle of the church)* now contains the fragment (the largest known piece of the True Cross) in the *lignum crucis* reliquary, a silver gilt Crucifix. The church, transitional Romanesque in style, has been restored to its original harmonious proportions. The monastery was also the house of **Beatus**, the 8C monk famous for his **Commentary on the Apocalypse** which was copied in the form of illuminated manuscripts.

There is a **view**★ of Potes and the central range from the lookout point at the end of the road.

★ **Fuente Dé** – The parador is at 1 000m/3 300ft. Nearby is the starting point of the **teleférico** (cableway) ⊘ which rises a further 800m/2 625ft to the terminal at the top of the sheer rock face. During the **ascent** you may see wild chamois. The **Mirador del Cable**★★ at the terminal commands a splendid panorama of the upper valley of the Deva and Potes, and the peaks of the central range.

A path leads to the Aliva refuge. The effect of erosion on the upper heights of karst limestone are spectacular, producing long stony plateaus and huge sink-holes known as **hoyos**.

★ PUERTO DE SAN GLORIO (SAN GLORIO PASS)

③ From Potes to Oseja de Sajambre

83km/52mi - about 3hr

The road crosses the green Quiviesa Valley with its poplar woods, then begins to climb through mountain pastures. 10km/6mi beyond Bores, a series of bends affords a changing panorama on the left. The drive up to the San Glorio pass is through silent, lonely countryside.

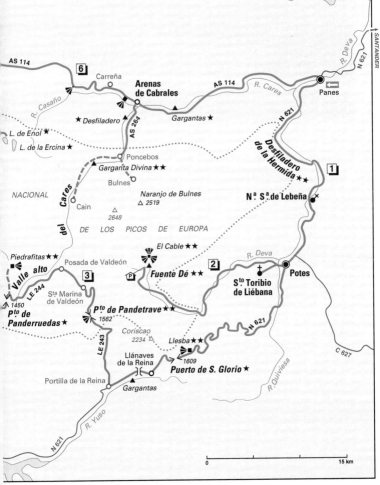

View from Santo Toribio de Liébana

★ **Puerto de San Glorio** – Alt 1 609m/5 279ft. A track leads north (1hr there an back) to near the Peña de Llesba, where the **Mirador de Llesba** forms a magnifice natural **viewpoint**★★ for the highest crests: to the right is the east range and to th left the central massif with its steep south face dominating the Fuente Dé. Th peak in the left foreground is the Coriscao (2 234m/7 330ft).
The scenery remains austere until you come to the village of **Llánaves de la Rein** tucked into the opening of the **Gargantas de Yuso** (Yuso Gorge) which is spectacul for its rock colouring.
At Portilla de la Reina, bear right onto LE 243.

★★ **Puerto de Pandetrave** – An ascent through the high mountains brings you to th pass (1 562m/5 125ft) and a **panorama** of the three ranges with, in the righ foreground, the Cabén de Remoña and Torre de Salinas, both part of the centr massif, and in the distance, lying in a hollow, the village of Santa Marina (Valdeón.
The road between Santa Marina de Valdeón and Posada de Valdeón is narrow b passable.

★ **Puerto de Panderruedas** – The road climbs to mountain pastures at an altitud of 1 450m/4 757ft. Walk up the path to the left (15min there and back) t the **Mirador de Piedrafitas**★★ *(viewing table)* from where there is an impressiv view of the immense cirque which closes off the Valdeón Valley. To th northeast can be seen the Torre Cerredo (2 648m/8 688ft), the highest pea in the range.

★ **Puerto del Pontón** – Alt 1 280m/4 200ft. From the pass you will get picturesque **view**★★ of the Sajambre Valley.
The descent to Oseja de Sajambre *(see below)* begins with tight hairpin bends full view of the western range; it continues as a spectacular road cut into th mountain side (tunnels) during which you can see the formidable rock wa through which the Sella has hollowed its course.

DESFILADERO DE LOS BEYOS (LOS BEYOS RAVINE)

④ From Oseja de Sajambre to Cangas de Onís

38km/24mi - about 1hr

Mirador de Oseja de Sajambre - There is an awe-inspiring **view**★★ of the Oseja de Sajambre basin with the sharp Niaja peak at its centre rising to 1 732m/5 682ft, and of the Los Beyos defile opening between walls of broken rock strata.

Desfiladero de Los Beyos - The defile, one of the most beautiful in Europe, is 10km/6mi long, cut by the Sella through an exceptionally thick layer of limestone. Though wide enough to allow sunlight to penetrate, it is too precipitous for anything other than an occasional tree to have gained a hold on its sides.

Cangas de Onís - An elegant humpbacked **Roman bridge** *(puente romano)* across the Sella lies west of the town.
The Capilla de Santa Cruz, also west of the town, was built in Contranquil, to celebrate the victory of Covadonga and was rebuilt after the Civil War. The chapel houses the region's only dolmen of which one stone is engraved.

Villanueva - The 17C **Monasterio benedictino de San Pedro** stands at the end of the village. The monastery was built around an already existing Romanesque church of which there remain the apse and an elegantly decorated side portal - note on the left the capitals illustrating the farewell of King Favila and his sad end, apparently being devoured by a bear. Inside there are further capitals to be seen in the apse and at the triumphal arch. Imaginatively ornamented stone modillions decorate the apse exterior.

THE ROAD TO COVA-DONGA AND THE LAKES

⑤ From Cangas de Onís to Covadonga

35km/22mi - about 3hr

Cueva del Buxu ⊘ - The cave in the cliff face contains charcoal drawings and rock engravings dating back to the Magdalenian period. There are a stag, horse and bison scarcely larger than the size of a hand.
The approach to Covadonga *(from a road to the right)* gradually reveals the town's impressive mountain setting.

Covadonga - *See COVADONGA.*

Take road CO 4 to the lakes.

The road is steep; on looking back you have an extensive panorama. After 8km/5mi, you reach the **Mirador de la Reina**★★ from where there is a picturesque view of the succession of rock pyramids which make up the Sierra de Covalierda. Beyond the pass, two rock cirques formed by *hoyos (see above)*, provide beautiful settings to the **Lago de Enol**★ and the **Lago de Ercina**★ (alt 1 232m/4 042ft). On 25 July, the Lago de Enol Shepherd's Festival draws large crowds for the dances and kayak races.

GARGANTAS DEL CARES (CARES GORGES)

⑥ From Covadonga to Panes 90km/56mi

As you come out of Las Estazadas village there is a splendid **panorama**★★ of the rock wall which closes off the Río Casaño Valley. From a viewpoint on the right, shortly after Carreña de Cabrales, there is a glimpse of the fang-like crest of **Naranjo de Bulnes** (2 519m/8 264ft).

Arenas de Cabrales - Arenas, as its name suggests, is the main production centre for *cabrales*, a blue ewes' milk cheese. The road now, for a while, skirts the Río Cares.

Bear right onto AS 264 which runs through the upper Cares Valley.

Upper Cares Valley - The Poncebos road leads south, through a pleasant **ravine**★. After the embalse de Poncebos (Poncebos Reservoir) a track *(3hr there and back on foot)* leads to the mountain village of Bulnes. From Poncebos to Caín *(3hr 30min walk one way)* a path follows the Cares and plunges down into the **defile**★★ before reaching the foot of the central massif *(here you can hire a car with a driver to take you back to Poncebos)*.

Return to Arenas de Cabrales.

Beyond Arenas the **gorges**★ are green with moss and even the occasional tree. Narrow humpbacked road bridges and fragile looking footbridges span the emerald waters of the river.

Monasterio de PIEDRA★★

PIEDRA MONASTERY – Aragón (Zaragoza)

Michelin map 442 or 443 I 24

On the approach to the monastery by way of Ateca or the spa, Alhama de Arag
the roads cross the arid, red earth countryside above the Tranquera reservoir.
village of **Nuévalos** comes into view, high up against a clay hillside.

The site – Hidden in a fold of the dried out plateau is a green oasis fed by the
Piedra. It was discovered and settled by Cistercian monks, who generally ch
pleasant surroundings for their retreats. The monks in this case came from the Ab
of Poblet in Tarragona and established a monastery on the spot in 1194. This v
rebuilt several times and suffered damage in the 19C. The conventual buildings h
been reconstructed as a hotel.

★★ **Parque y cascadas (Park and waterfalls)** ⊘ – Waterfalls and cascades are to be s
along the marked footpath through the heart of the forest (follow the
signposts to go and the blue ones to return). The paths, steps and tunnels laid
last century by **Juan Federico Muntadas** have transformed an impenetrable forest i
a popular park. The first fall is the **Cola de Caballo** (Horse's Tail), a cascade
53m/174ft. This you first look down on from a viewpoint and come on agai
the end of your walk if you descend the steep and slippery steps into the beaut
Cueva Iris (Iris Grotto), when you will see it from the back. **Baño de Diana** (Dian
Bath) and the romantic **Lago del Espejo** (Mirror Lake), cupped between tall cliffs,
both worth a halt.

The signposted route ends outside the park at the monastery ruins. Of the Got
building there remain the kitchen, refectory and cloisters.

PIRINEOS ARAGONESES★★

THE PYRENEES IN ARAGÓN – Aragón (Huesca)

Michelin map 443 D 28-32, E 29-32, F 30-31

The central Spanish Pyrenees, in the northern part of the province of Huesca, incl
the highest peaks in the Pyrenean chain: Aneto (3 404m/11 168ft), Pos
(3 371m/11 060ft) and Monte Perdido (3 355m/11 007ft). The foothills are of
ravined and covered only with sparse vegetation; the landscape at the heart of
massif, accessible up the river courses, is on a different scale altogether. The valle
whether wide and lush or narrow and gullied, lead to mountain cirques well wo
exploring.

Structure and relief – The geological division of the Pyrenees into vast longitudi
bands can be clearly seen in this region. The **axis of Primary terrain** and granite ro
comprises the Maladeta, Posets, Vignemale and Balaïtous massifs, where there
still remains of the Quaternary glaciers. There follows the Pre-Pyrenees or Mo
Perdido region where the deep **Secondary limestone** layer has been deeply eroded to fo
an area of sharp relief: the canyons, gorges and cirques of the upper valleys.
limestone area, which extends in broken mountain chains as far as the Ebro Ba
(Sierras de Guara and de la Peña) is divided at Jaca by a long depression through wh
the río Aragón flows. Tertiary sediment has accumulated into hills, some of wh
remain bare of vegetation, affording an unusual blue marl landscape like that aro
the Yesa artificial lake.

Life in the valleys – The upper valleys of the Kingdom of Aragón developed
independent political and pastoral way of life based on self-contained communi
very early in their history. In spite of improved roads, local individuality rema
folklore is still followed and native costume worn in certain valleys like the Ansó. H
no farm stands isolated from its neighbour; hamlets and villages are numerous
the inhabitants leave their slate covered cottages to work in Zaragoza, Pamplona
Barcelona. The raising of mountain sheep is declining while that of cattle
increasing.

There is some industry, such as the chemical and aluminium works at **Sabiñánig**
Major hydroelectric undertakings are bringing life to certain areas; artificial la
now lie in previously barren valleys: **Yesa** in the Aragón, **La Peña** in the Gállego, **El G**
in the Cinca, **Canelles** and **Escales** in the Noguera Ribagorçana.

Tourism is becoming one of the major economic activities in the region with
development of winter sports resorts such as Candanchú, Astún, Canfranc, Pa
cosa, El Formigal and Benasque.

① FROM VIELHA TO BENASQUE

122km/76mi - about 3hr

Vielha – See PIRINEOS CATALANES: Vall d'Arán.

The road cuts through the Maladeta massif by way of the Vielha tunnel which e
in the lonely upper valley of the Noguera Ribagorçana where the attractive han
of **Vilaller** stands huddled around a hillock. A little further south the valley op
onto the **Embalse de Escales★** (Escales Dam).

★ **Valle de Benasque** – **Benasque** (1 138m/3 734ft) lies in an open valley, lush and green in spite of its altitude, overshadowed by the Maladeta massif. The town serves as a base for walkers, climbers (ascending the Aneto) and skiers (Cerler 5km/3mi away). Benasque's narrow streets are lined with old seignorial mansions.

② FROM BENASQUE TO AINSA

180km/112mi – about half a day

As the road heads south through the Esero Valley, it follows the **Congosto de Ventamillo**★, a defile of 3km/2mi with sheer limestone rock walls.

Graus – The village huddles around its irregular shaped square, plaza de España, lined with old houses decorated with frescoes, carved beams and brick arcades. Some 25km/16mi northeast on A 1605 is the picturesque village of **Roda de Isábena** in a beautiful mountain **setting**★. The **catedral** ⊙ has an 11C east end with Lombard bands and contains, in the crypt, the **tomb of San Ramón**★ with polychrome low reliefs. A chapel off the cloisters is adorned with 13C frescoes. The cathedral square is overlooked by the façades of ancient buildings.

The road beyond Graus runs westwards past **Torreciudad**, then heads north skirting the turquoise El Grado and Mediano dams set in a weird black marl landscape.

★ **Ainsa** – Ainsa stands on a promontory still girded by a wall, commanding the juncture of the Cinca and Ara rivers. In the 11C the town was the capital of a small kingdom. Today, its arcaded **Plaza Mayor**★ in the upper part of town, dominated by the tower of a Romanesque church, is a gem of Aragonese architecture.

③ FROM AINSA TO BIESCAS

81km/50mi – about 3hr

Between Boltaña and Fiscal, the river course has uncovered uneven earth strata which now rise out of the water curiously like dorsal fins. From Broto the great mass of the Mondarruego (alt 2 848m/9 341ft), closing the Ordesa Valley to the north, provides a backdrop for the spectacular **landscape**★★ in which the small village of **Torla** can be seen massed against the western slope of the Ara Valley.

★★ **Parque Nacional de Ordesa y Monte Perdido** – *See Parque Nacional de ORDESA Y MONTE PERDIDO.*
Beyond **Torla** you get **views**★ down the entire length of the Ara Valley as the mountain road climbs to the pretty village of Linás de Broto.

4 THE PORTALET ROAD

52km/32mi – about 2hr

The **Tena** Valley beyond Biescas is at first narrow and boulder strewn but wide out majestically to be filled by the vast Búbal reservoir.

A short distance before Escarilla, bear right onto HU 610 for Panticosa.

★★ **Garganta del Escalar (Escalar Gorge)** – The gorge is so narrow that the sun seldo penetrates its depths; the stream below hollowed out a bed first throu limestone and later through lamellar schists and granite. The road cuts down t west slope by long ramps and tight hairpin bends to an austere mountain cirqu

★ **Balneario de Panticosa** – The spa (alt 1 639m/5 377ft), dominated by t Vignemale peak, is known for the curative properties of its six sulphur a radioactive springs.

Return to Escarilla and continue northwest to Portalet.

The mountain town of **Sallent de Gállego**, a little east of A 136 at a height 1 305m/4 281ft, is a centre for trout fishing and mountaineering while **El Formi** (alt 1 480m/4 856ft) further on is a well-equipped ski resort.

Carretera del Portalet – Alt 1 794m/5 886ft. The pass lies between the Porta peak and the sharply pointed Aneu summit to the west. The view northwe extends towards the Aneu cirque and the Pic du Midi d'Ossau in Fran (alt 2 884m/9 462ft).

PIRINEOS CATALANES★★★

THE CATALAN PYRENEES – Catalunya (Girona, Lleida)

Michelin map 443 D 32, E 32-37, F 32-37

This mountain chain forms a wide, almost unbroken barrier 230km/143mi lo extending from the Mediterranean Sea to the Arán Valley, which, due to its proximi to the Maladeta massif, is situated at quite a high altitude exceeding 2 500m/8 202 (Pica d'Estats: 3 145m/10 318ft; Puigmal: 2 910m/9 547ft). The last range, th Montes Alberes, reaches the Cabo de Creus, plunging into the water from a heig of around 700m/2 297ft. South of this granite axial ridge are the Cadí, Boumort a Montsec, forming a calcareous pre-Pyrenean chain.

The mountains are deeply cut across by side valleys – Arán, Ribagorça, Pallars, A Urgell, Cerdanya, Ripollès, Garrotxa and Empordà (Ampurdán) – which mak communication extremely difficult. As a result, these regions have develope separately from each other, acquiring their own individuality, personality a traditions. This applies more particularly to local art, especially during the Rom nesque period. All however offer delicious regional cuisine and provide countle opportunities for leisure and sporting activities: skiing, hunting, fishing, mounta climbing, adventure sports etc.

★ UPPER VALLEY OF THE TER

1 From the Collado de Ares to Vall de Núria

106km/66mi – allow one day

The Ripollès area features a large mountainous ensemble towering at arou 3 000m/9 843ft and dominated by Puigmal. Sheltered by this rocky amph theatre, the upper valley of the Ter is split into two large valleys: Camprodon a Ribes. The countryside surrounding the Collado de Ares (1 610m/5 283f features pleasant, rolling hills with green pastures.

Vall de Camprodon

Molló – The 12C Romanesque church has a lovely Catalan belfry.

Take the narrow, winding road which goes through Rocabruna and leads to Bege

★★ **Beget** – This attractive mountain village, with its stone houses and woode balconies, enjoys an extremely pleasant setting, in the deep recesses of a peacef valley, where the silence is broken only by the burbling of a stream.
The **Romanesque church**★★ ⊙ (10C-12C), presenting an apse adorned with Lombar arcatures and a slender lantern-tower, houses the **Majestad de Beget**★, a magnificer figure of Christ carved in the 12C.

Return to C 151 and proceed in the direction of Camprodon.

★ **Camprodon** – Camprodon stands at the confluence of the Ritort and Ter rive and is crossed by a fine 12C humpbacked bridge, **Pont Nou**★, renovated in the 14C The community developed around the **Monestir Sant Pere** ⊙, of which there remain only the 12C **Romanesque church**★, with its five apses and graceful belfry above th transept crossing.

★ **Sant Joan de les Abadesses** – *See SANT JOAN DE LES ABADESSES.*

Vall de Ribes

Ripoll – *See RIPOLL.*

Proceed along N 152 towards the north.

Ribes de Freser – This famous spa stands at the confluence of three rivers – the Freser, the Rigard and the Segadell – and is well known for its abundant waters and their healing properties. A rack railway takes you from Ribes to the Vall de Núria.

Vall de Núria – The valley is surrounded by a rocky amphitheatre stretching from Puigmal to the Sierra de Torreneules. The only access to the valley is by **rack railway** ⊘. Opened in 1931, this train service covers a 12km/8mi route and spans a height of 1 000m/3 281ft, offering wonderful **views**★★ of the mountain range, the streams and the ravines. The Virgin of Núria the patron saint of Pyrenean shepherds, is venerated in a sanctuary located in the upper part of the valley.

LA CERDANYA

② From Vall de Núria to La Seu d'Urgell

72km/45mi – about 2hr 30min

The Cerdanya Basin, located between the Andorran massifs and the Sierra de Cadí, was formed by subsidence. It owes its fertility to the fact that it is watered by the río Segre, a tributary of the Ebro. Since 1659 Cerdanya has been divided: the northern part, known in French as La Cerdagne, was ceded to France under the Treaty of the Pyrenees. In 1984 the opening of the Túnel del Cadí, which cuts across the mountainous barrier formed by the Sierra del Cadí and the Sierra de Moixeró, has facilitated access to Cerdanya from Manresa.

From Ribes de Freser to Puigcerdà, the road is cut into the cliff face for almost its entire length up to the Collado de Tosses, commanding impressive **views**★ of the Segre and its luxuriant slopes.

La Molina – This is one of Catalunya's most important ski resorts. The nearby village of **Alp** is a popular place for tourists, both in winter and in summer.

Leaving La Molina, N 152 joins up with E 09, which follows an upward course, offering a sweeping view of the vast Cerdanya plain.

Puigcerdà – The capital of Cerdanya, which developed on a terrace overlooking the River Segre, is one of the most popular holiday resorts of the Pyrenees. Its old-fashioned shops, ancient streets and balconied buildings have retained all of their picturesque charm. The lofty, turn-of-the-century mansions are hidden in the park beside the lake. The **bell-tower**★, serving as the town's symbol and landmark, is all that remains of the Gothic Iglesia de Santa María.

Llívia – The existence of this small 12km²/5sq mi Spanish enclave 6km/4mi from Puigcerdà can be ascribed to an administrative subtlety. Under the Treaty of the Pyrenees, France was to be granted the Roussillon area as well as 33 villages from Cerdanya. Since Llívia was considered to be a town, it did therefore not qualify and was to remain part of Spanish territory.

Llívia features charming narrow streets, the ruins of a medieval castle, perched on a mound overlooking the town, and several old towers. Among its many interesting exhibits, the **Museu Municipal** ⊘ contains a famous chemist's shop known as the **Farmacia de Llívia**★, said to be one of the oldest in Europe, with ceramic pots and old-fashioned utensils for apothecaries.

Return to Puigcerdà and take N 260 towards La Seu d'Urgell.

Bellver de Cerdanya – Poised on a rocky crag dominating the Vall del Segre, Bellver de Cerdanya has a fine main square with beautiful balconied stone houses and wooden porches.

La Seu d'Urgell – *See La SEU d'URGELL.*

VALL DEL SEGRE

③ From La Seu d'Urgell to Tremp

73km/45mi – allow 3hr

At the point where it flows into the Valira, the River Segre forms a huge basin sheltered by mountains. The massif is cut across by many side valleys, all quite different from each other.

Take N 260 towards Organyà.

Garganta de Tresponts – As it flows past, the Segre winds its way through dark-coloured rocks *(puzolana)* and green pastures. Further downstream the topography changes: the limestone rocks of Ares and Montsec de Tost offer a typically Pyrenean landscape extending down to a small cultivated basin, where the river disappears.

Embalse de Oliana – The dam, which looks more like a wide river, is surrounded by grey rocks with lively waterfalls in spring. From the road the sight is quite spectacular.

Coll de Nargó – This typical Pyrenean hamlet has one of the most spler
Romanesque churches in Catalunya, dating back to the 11C: **Sant Climent★★** ha
single nave and a pretty apse adorned with Lombard bands. Its sober bell-tor
is pre-Romanesque.

★★ **Collado de Bòixols Road** – Between the Coll de Nargó and Tremp, L 511 follo
a series of canyons which it overlooks for the whole stretch, either from slo
clad in pine and holm oak, or barren hillsides. Further on, the road proceeds
the slope, halfway between the river and the yellow and pink crests, offer
lovely views and **landscapes**, especially from the Collado de Bòixols.

Then the road leads into a wide U-shaped valley, where terraced cultivat
extends to the foot of the glacial ridge of Bòixols, onto which cling the church
a few nearby houses. The road continues to descend the valley until it eventu
merges into the Conca de Tremp.

VALL DEL NOGUERA PALLARESA

④ From Tremp to Llavorsí

143km/89mi – allow one day

Pallars is situated in the uppermost region of the Catalan Pyrenees, wh
the highest summit is Pica d'Estats (3 145m/10 318ft). It is divided into
different areas: to the north, **Pallars Sobirà**, lying at the heart of the Pyrene
to the south, **Pallars Jussà**, incorporating the vast pre-Pyrenean zone formed
Conca de Tremp. The road follows the bed of the Noguera Pallaresa. After
Pobla de Segur, it cuts across a limestone landscape of remarkable uniform

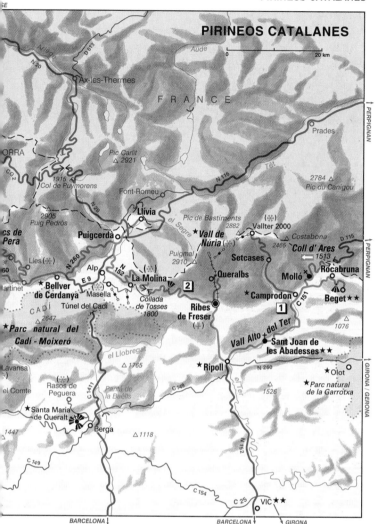

Tremp – Located in the centre of the Conca de Tremp – a huge basin with lush Mediterranean vegetation and crops – Tremp has retained its old quarter. The **Iglesia de Santa Maria** ⊙ houses an astonishing 2m/6.5ft high Gothic statue in polychrome wood: **Santa Maria de Valldeflors★** (14C). The municipality of Tremp has its own reservoir, the **pantano de Sant Antoni★**.

C 147 follows the river course and spans the pantano de Sant Antoni.

La Pobla de Segur – This popular tourist resort has been dubbed the gateway of the Pyrenees as it is the only means of access to the Valle de Arán, Alta Ribagorça and Pallars Sobirà.

Vall Fosca – Hemmed in by high peaks, this valley is dotted with delightful hamlets, each with their Romanesque church: **Torre de Cabdella**, **Espui** and **Cabdella**. In the upper part of the valley, you can tour a large lake area, whose main attraction is the **lago Gento**.

Return to La Pobla de Segur and proceed upwards along N 260.

Desfiladero de Collegats – Eroded by the torrent waters, the red, grey and ochre limestone rocks have taken on the appearance of spectacularly steep cliffs. Note the **Roca de l'Argenteria★**, a stalactite-shaped rock formation near the Gerri de la Sal.

Sort – The resort has become famous throughout Europe because of its stormy waters and the canoeing events that are held on this stretch of the Noguera Pallaresa.

When you reach Rialp, turn left towards Llessui.

Vall de Llessui – The road winds its way up to the northwest, taking you through a steep granite landscape featuring a great many ravines.

Skiing in the Pyrenees

★UPPER VALLEY OF THE NOGUERA PALLARESA

⑤ From Llavorsí to Puerto de la Bonaigua

105km/65mi - allow half a day

The mountain summits dominate a wild, secluded landscape.

Llavorsí - It lies at the confluence of the three main basins of the upper valle
the Noguera Pallaresa: Aneu, Cardós and Ferrera.

Take L 504 and proceed north.

★ **Vall de Cardós** - The Noguera de Cardós constitutes the central axis of this va
The capital Ribera de Cardós presents a 12C Romanesque church with a b
similar to those found in the Valle de Boí.

Return to Llavorsí and take C 147 in the direction of Baqueira.

★★ **Vall d'Aneu** - The Noguera Pallaresa crosses the valley with, on its left,
underlying valley of **Espot**, a picturesque village which has developed near
banks of a mountain stream. It is also the gateway to the Pallars sectio
the **Parque Nacional de Aigüestortes i Estany de Sant Maurici**★★ *(see AIGÜESTORT*
Beyond Esterri d'Aneu the road cuts across a breathtaking landscape, dotted
Romanesque churches such as the **Iglesia de Sant Joan d'Isil**★, glimpsed between
summits, and follows a corniche up to **Puerto de la Bonaiga** (2 072m/6 799ft), ci
by many peaks. On the left lies a magnificent glacial cirque.

★★LA VALL D'ARÁN

⑥ From Puerto de la Bonaiga de Bòssost

45km/28mi - about 2hr

The Arán Valley, situated in the northwest tip of the Pyrenees, occupies the u
valley of the Garonne river. Because of its Atlantic climate, it is more humid
less sunny than the southfacing valleys of the Pyrenean range.

Although the area has been subject to Spanish rule since the Middle Ages (1
its isolated location has helped it to preserve its local traditions and lang
(*aranes* is a variation of the *langue d'Oc*, or old southern French). Surrounde
mountains reaching an altitude of 3 000m/9 850ft, communications betwee
Arán Valley and neighbouring localities were difficult and for a long time pa
like the puerto de la Bonaigua or the Bòssost Portilhon were their only link
the outside world. The opening of the Vielha Tunnel in 1948 put an end to
state of seclusion.

Today, pastures have been replaced by cultivated fields and much time and money has been devoted to the exploitation of local forests, rivers and mines. However, such developments have in no way jeopardised the beauty of this natural site: the green meadows of the valley are dotted with the grey slate roofs of its 39 villages, often clustered around a Romanesque church. In recent years the region has seen the creation of several ski resorts.

Baqueira Beret – This alpine ski resort, sloping from 1 500m/4 922ft up to 2 510m/8 235ft, offers excellent sporting facilities.

Salardú – A charming village with granite and slate houses gathered around the **Iglesia de Sant Andreu** ⊘ (12C-13C). The interior features a fine 12C **Christ in Majesty**: carved in wood, this statue 65cm/25in high is stylised in the extreme and displays remarkable anatomical precision. Note the slender belfry, of octagonal design (15C).

Arties – It lies at the confluence of the Garonne and Valarties rivers. The Romanesque church has an apse decorated with painted scenes illustrating the Last Judgement, Heaven and Hell.

Vielha – 971m/3 186ft. The capital of the Arán Valley is a large holiday resort laid out along the banks of the Garonne. The old part of town still features many pretty houses dating from the 16C and 17C. Note the **Iglesia Parroquial de Sant Miquèu** ⊘, a parish church with a fine octagonal bell-tower and a 13C doorway. The interior contains the splendid **Cristo de Mijaran**★, a famous fragment belonging to a 12C *Descent of the Cross*, the features of which are carved with painstaking precision.

The Parador del Valle de Arán is a belvedere above Vielha commanding a superb **view**: in the distance lies the cirque closing off the Arán Valley to the south and, on the right, looms the formidable barrier of the Maladeta massif.

Bossòst – *16km/10mi north of Vielha.*

The **Iglesia de la Assumpció de Maria**★★ ⊘ is probably the area's most typical example of Romanesque architecture (12C). Its three naves are separated by sturdy columns which support the barrel vaulting for the massive roof. The three apses are adorned with Lombard bands and the pretty, colourful north **doorway** features archaic relief work in its tympanum, depicting the Creator surrounded by the Sun, the Moon and symbols of the Evangelists.

VALL DEL NOGUERA RIBAGORÇANA

⁊ From El Pont de Suert to Caldes de Boí

54km/34mi – about 3hr

The Upper Ribagorça region has a very abrupt landscape, with summits exceeding 3 000m/9 843ft, vast glacial cirques, pretty lake areas and steep valleys with small villages nestling below.

El Pont de Suert – The locality is dotted all over with attractive hamlets – **Castelló de Tor, Casòs, Malpàs** – located in a secluded setting that has kept its rustic appearance and charm.

Vilaller – Poised on a rocky outcrop, the village is dominated by the octagonal belfry of its 18C Baroque church, the Iglesia de Sant Climent.

Take the road that climbs up towards Caldes de Boí.

Vall de Boí – Watered by the Noguera de Tor and the Sant Nicolau, this valley is renowned for its cluster of Lombard **Romanesque churches** (11C-12C), the finest in the Pyrenees. Characterised by slate roofing and irregular masonry, they stand out for their pure, sober lines and for the wall frescoes which once decorated them *(several reproductions can be admired in the churches)* and which are now displayed in the Museu d'Art de Catalunya *(see BARCELONA)*. Note the highly distinctive silhouette of the belfries, separate but nonetheless resting against the nave, and their ornamentation with Lombard bands. Of particular interest are Santa Eulàlia at Erill la Vall, La Nativitat at Durro and Sant Joan at Boí.

Beyond Erill la Vall turn right onto a narrow road leading to Boí.

Taüll – This typical mountain village is famous for the frescoes adorning its two churches. Considered to be unique masterpieces of Romanesque art, they are currently exhibited in Barcelona's Museu d'Art de Catalunya. The **Iglesia de Sant Climent**★★ ⊘, just outside Taüll, was consecrated on 10 December 1123, only one day before Santa María was. In the southeast corner of the sanctuary stands the slender six-storey belfry, built in Lombard Romanesque style. The interior used to be entirely decorated with frescoes dating from the same period. A replica of the famous Pantocrator of Taüll can be seen in the apse.

Iglesia de Sant Climent, Taüll

With its labyrinthine streets, stone houses and wooden balconies, the village clustered around the **Iglesia de Santa Maria**★ ⊘, a Romanesque church with three naves separated by cylindrical pillars.

Return to the road leading to Caldes de Boí.

★★ **Parque Nacional de Aigüestortes i Estany de Sant Maurici** – Access by the road linking Boí to Caldes de Boí *(see AIGÜESTORTES).*

★ **Caldes de Boí** – Situated at an altitude of 1 550m/5 084ft, Caldes de Boí is an important thermal spa with 37 springs spurting out water at temperatures between 24ºC and 56ºC (75ºF to 133ºF). In the close vicinity lies **Boí-Taüll** satellite resort designed for downhill skiing.

*The current edition of the annual **Michelin Red Guide España & Portugal** offers a selection of pleasant and quiet hotels in convenient locations. Their amenities are included (swimming pools, tennis courts, private beaches and gardens, etc.) as well as their dates of annual closure. The selection also includes establishments which offer excellent cuisine: carefully prepared meals at reasonable prices, **Michelin stars** for good cooking.*

PLASENCIA★

Extremadura (Cáceres) – Population 36 826
Michelin map 444 L 11

The regional town of Plasencia stands on a hill at the meeting point of central limestone sierras and the Extremaduran plateau. Below flows the Jerte river, circling the jagged mountains with their massive granite boulders. Storks come to nest in the town from February to July.

★ **Catedral** – The cathedral is in fact two buildings from different periods. A Romanesque-Gothic edifice was built in the 13C and 14C. At the end of the 15C its east end was demolished and a new cathedral with a bolder architectural design was begun. Only the chancel and transept were completed. Enter the cathedral by the north door which has a rich Plateresque decoration. A door left of the corner opens into the old cathedral (now the parish church of Santa María). The cloister have pointed arches and Romanesque capitals while the chapter-house is covered by a fine dome on squinches which is disguised outside by a pyramid shaped belfry covered in tiles. The shortened nave houses a museum of religious art.

Inside the **Catedral Nueva** (New Cathedral), the tall pillars and slender ribs extending into network vaulting, illustrate the mastery of the famous architects responsible for the design: Juan de Java, Diego de Siloé and Alonso de Covarrubias.
The **altarpiece**★ is decorated with statues by the 17C sculptor Gregorio Fernández; the **choir stalls**★ were carved in 1520 by Rodrigo Alemán – look on the backs and misericords of the lower row for scenes, on the right, from the Old Testament, and on the left, of everyday life.

Barrio Viejo (Old Quarter) – The streets around the cathedral and plaza Mayor, well worth a walk, are lined by noble façades and houses with wrought-iron balconies.
Start from plaza de la Catedral and leaving on your right the **Casa del Deán** (Deanery) with its unusual corner window, and the **Casa del Dr Trujillo**, now the Law Courts (Palacio de Justicia), make for the Gothic **Iglesia de San Nicolás**, a church which faces the beautiful façade of the **Casa de las Dos Torres** (House with Two Towers).
Continue straight ahead to the **Palacio Mirabel**. This palace, flanked by a massive tower, contains a fine two-tiered *patio* and the Museo de Caza (Hunting Museum). A passage beneath the palace *(door on right-hand side)* leads to the **calle Sancho Polo** and the more popular quarter near the ramparts where there are stepped alleys, white-walled houses and washing hanging from the windows – a scene typical of villages further south. Turn right for **Plaza Mayor**, an asymmetrical square surrounded by porticoes, which is the bustling town centre.

EXCURSIONS

Parque Natural de Monfragüe – *25km/16mi to the south by C 524. Centro de Información (Information Centre) in Villareal de San Carlos. Various itineraries on foot or by car.* Some parts of the hills flanking the Tajo river at its confluence with the Tiétar are situated within the park (17 842ha/44 089 acres). The ecological importance of these areas is determined by their typically Mediterranean flora (rockrose, cork oak, gall oak, lavender, arbutus etc); and their rich and varied fauna, with, in this park, a large number of protected species (black and tawny vultures, Imperial eagles, Iberian lynx, mongooses etc).

La Vera – *Take C 501 to the east of Plasencia.* This fertile valley is given over to tobacco growing and market-gardening. Villages like that of **Cuacos de Yuste** where Don Juan of Austria grew up, have managed to preserve their picturesque character. The 15C castle in **Jarandilla de la Vera** has been converted into a parador.

Monasterio de Yuste ⊘ – *1.8km/1mi from Cuacos de Yuste.* In 1556, when Emperor **Charles V** had grown weary of power, he abdicated and retired to this modest Hieronymite monastery. He died on 21 September 1558. Even today, the serene atmosphere, particularly of the beautiful surrounding countryside, makes one understand why the great emperor chose this retreat in which to pass his last years.
The monastery which was devastated during the War of Independence and during the period following the passing of Mendizábal's decrees, has been partially restored. Of Charles V's small palace one sees the dining hall, the royal bedroom built to adjoin the chapel so that the emperor could hear Mass without having to rise, the Gothic church and, lastly, the two fine cloisters, one Gothic, the other Plateresque.

Monasterio de POBLET★★★

Catalunya (Tarragona)
Michelin map 443 H 33

ated in a splendid **site**★ sheltered by the Prades mountains, Poblet is one of the gest and best preserved Cistercian monasteries. A charming brook flows nearby, ttily set among the slender, white poplar trees that have given their name to the nastery: in Latin the word *populetum* means poplar grove. It was the Reconquest ich brought Poblet into existence, for after Ramón Berenguer IV had recaptured talunya from the Moors he gave thanks to God by founding the monastery. By 50 twelve Cistercians, sent from Fontfroide Abbey near Narbonne in France, had jun to construct the buildings and till the soil for the future community.
e kings of Aragón maintained a patronage of the monastery which with Santes eus, became a favourite halt on kingly progresses between the two capitals of ragoza and Barcelona. It also became a place of royal religious retreat – the abbot s the royal almoner. Finally the monastery was given the supreme honour of ng selected as the royal pantheon. It began to decline at the end of the 16C,

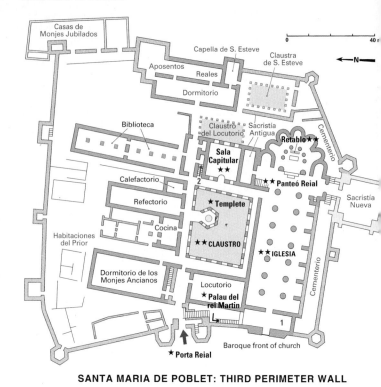

SANTA MARIA DE POBLET: THIRD PERIMETER WALL

Periods of construction: ▓ 12C-13C ▒ 14C ░ 16C ☐ 17C-18C

suffered particularly during the Napoleonic Wars and in the so-called Constitutic
Period (1820-23), when religious orders were suppressed, and in 1835 when ric
were sold and the monastery was left to ruin and pillage. A century later
buildings were restored and in 1940 a community was re-established. In spite
all its vicissitudes, the monastery remains a rare example of medieval mona
architecture.

TOUR ⊘ 2hr

An outer perimeter 2km/1mi long was built to protect the land and vegeta
gardens belonging to the monastery.

★★ **Capilla de Sant Jordi** – To the right of some sheds set aside for agricultural
industrial purposes, stands the precious 15C chapel. The Late Gothic interio
this tiny building features splendid broken barrel vaulting.

A second, inner wall fortified by polygonal towers enclosed the conven
annexes where visitors from the outside world were received. It is pierced
the 15C **Porta Daurada** (Golden Door), named after the gilded bronze sheets t
form its covering, commissioned by Philip II when he visited the monaster
1564.

★ **Plaça Major** – On this main square, of irregular design, stands the 12C **Capill
Santa Caterina**, flanked by various shops, a hospital for pilgrims and a carper
workshop. On the right are the ruins of the 16C Abbatial Palace and the large s
cross erected by Abbey Guimerà, dating from the same century.

A third wall, built by Peter the Ceremonious, surrounds the monastery prop
These crenellated walls, fortified by 13 towers, are an imposing si
(608m/1 995ft long, 11m/36ft high and 2m/6.5ft thick). On the right stands
Baroque front of the church, built around 1670 and flanked, 50 years later, by hea
ornate windows. Although this façade presents pleasing proportions, it bre
with the overall austerity of the monastery.

★ **Puerto Real** – This doorway opens onto the conventual buildings. Because of
somewhat forbidding appearance, squeezed in between two massive towers
looks more like the entrance to a fortress than to a monastery.

★ **Palacio del rey Martín** – Beyond the door, to the right, a narrow staircase le
up to this 14C Gothic palace built above the west wing of the cloisters. Its spler
rooms are wonderfully light thanks to the pointed bay windows.

Locutorio (Parlatory) – Originally used as a dormitory for Catholic converts, this room later became a press. The 14C vaulting rests directly onto the walls, without any other form of support.

Claustro – The size of these cloisters (40 × 35m/131 × 115ft) and their sober lines give some indication of the monastery's importance. The south gallery (c 1200) and huge lavabo or **templete**★ with its marble fountain and 30 taps are in pure Romanesque style; the other galleries, built a century later, have a floral motif tracery; beautiful scrollwork adorns the **capitals**★ throughout.

Cocina and Refectorio – The kitchen and refectory are 12C. The reader's lectern can be seen strategically placed overlooking the long refectory tables (in use to this day).

Biblioteca – Columns in the middle of the 13C library support the magnificent palm fan vaulting with its clearly defined design.

Sala Capitular – Access is through a Romanesque doorway. The 13C chapter room is fascinating on account of its harmonious proportions and sheer simplicity. Four slender octagonal columns support the nine palm-shaped brackets of the vaulting. Eleven tombstones celebrating the memory of 11 Abbots of Poblet have been sunk into the floor.

Iglesia – The light, spacious church, imbued with serenity, is typically Cistercian. It has pure architectural lines, broken barrel vaulting over the nave, two storeys in elevation, and unadorned capitals. The only decorative note lies in the windows and wide arches joined beneath an arch which dissolves into the piers of the engaged columns. In contrast to the lack of ornament, the church had to incorporate numerous altars because of the growing community; the apse was therefore ringed by an ambulatory and radiating chapels, a feature more commonly found in Benedictine churches.

The church's construction dates from the late 12C, and modifications in the 14C gave rise to the octagonal lantern-tower. In the narthex, an opening to the outside world added in 1275, is the Renaissance **altar of the Holy Sepulchre** (1).

Panteón Real (Royal Pantheon) – The church's major ornament and its most original feature, are the immense shallow arches spanning the transepts on either side of the crossing, surmounted by the alabaster, royal tombs. These were constructed in about 1350 to provide a repository for the kings of Aragón, buried at Poblet between 1196 and 1479. The sepulchres were desecrated in 1835 but were restored by the sculptor Frederic Marès.

Retablo del Altar Mayor – Damián Forment was commissioned in 1527 to carve the monumental marble Renaissance altarpiece. Figures in shell-shaped niches in four superimposed registers can be seen glorifying Christ and the Virgin.

A wide flight of stairs leads from the north transept to the monks' dormitory.

Dormitorio (2) – Massive central arches support the ridge roof above the vast, 87m/285ft long gallery. Part of the dormitory has been converted into monks' cells.

EXCURSION

★ **Monasterio de Vallbona de les Monges** ☉ – *27km/17mi north of Poblet.*
The Cistercian **Monasterio de Santa Maria**, in the heart of the village, completes the Cistercian Trinity along with the abbeys of Poblet and Santes Creus. The convent was founded in 1157 by the hermit Ramón de Vallbona and became a Cistercian community for women. In 1563, when, as a result of the Council of Trent, a decree was passed stipulating that convents could not remain isolated, the nuns of Vallbona encouraged inhabitants from the neighbouring village to settle around the abbey.

★ **Iglesia** – Built chiefly in the 13C and the 14C, this church is a fine example of transitional Gothic architecture. The interior is simple and surprisingly light thanks to two octagonal lantern-towers: one (13C) lies above the transept crossing while the other, dating from the 14C, overlooks the centre of the nave. The church contains the beautiful grave of Queen Violante of Hungary, wife of James I, and that of her daughter. A huge polychrome Virgin from the 15C dominates the *coro* and the abbesses' tombstones are inlaid in the floor.

★ **Cloisters** – The east and west galleries are Romanesque (12C-13C). The 14C Gothic north wing features pretty capitals with plant motifs. In the south gallery (15C but built in Romanesque style) note the 12C statue of Nuestra Señora del Claustro (Our Lady of the Cloisters), which was restored in the 14C.

In Spain, use Michelin map 990 or Michelin regional maps 441-446.
For the Canary Islands, use Michelin detailed maps 220-222.

PONFERRADA

Castilla y León (León) – Population 59 702

Michelin map 441 E 10

Ponferrada, centre of a mining area and capital of the fertile Bierzo, a subsided ba
owes its name to an iron bridge built at the end of the 11C across the Sil to
pilgrims on their way to Santiago de Compostela. The town is dominated by the r
of the **Castillo de los Templarios** (Templars' Castle).

EXCURSIONS

★ **Peñalba de Santiago** – *21km/13mi southeast.*
Peñalba stands isolated in the heart of the so-called Valle del Silencio (Valle
Silence). Its characteristic architecture of schist walled houses with woo
balconies and slate tile-stone roofs, remains intact. The village has growr
around the Mozarabic **Iglesia de Santiago**, a church which is all that remains of a
monastery. Note the portal with its paired horseshoe arch set off by an a
There are fine views from the belfry of the village and the valley beyond.

Las Médulas

★ **Las Médulas** – *22km/14mi southwest. Declared a World Heritage Site in 199*
The northwest slopes of the Aquilianos mountains on the left bank of the Sil ha
been transformed into a magic landscape of rocky crags and strangely shap
hillocks of pink and ochre by debris from a gold-mine worked in Roman time
Over the ages this has been covered by a vegetation of gnarled old chestnut tre

PONTEVEDRA ★

Galicia – Population 75 148

Michelin map 441 E 4

Local map see RÍAS BAJAS

Pontevedra was once a busy port lying sheltered at the end of its *ría*; fisherme
merchants, overseas traders lived there as did sailors and explorers such as Ped
Sarmiento, skilled navigator of the 16C, wise cosmographer and author of *Voyage
the Magellan Straits.* The Lérez delta, however, silted up so that by the 18
Pontevedra had begun to decline and the new port at Marín was taking its place.

★ BARRIO ANTIGUO (OLD QUARTER) *1hr 30min*

In spite of extensive development, the new town has respected the old,
kernel tucked into the area between calles Michelena, del Arzobispo Malvar ar
Cobián, and the river, where life continues peacefully in the shadow of glaze
house fronts, squares occasionally adorned with a Calvary (**Plaza de la Leña** .

PONTEVEDRA

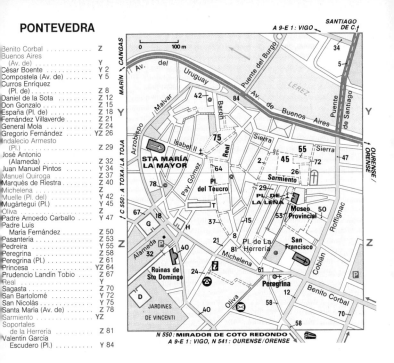

Benito Corbal . . . . Z
Buenos Aires
  (Av. de) . . . . Y
César Boente . . . . Y 2
Compostela (Av. de) . . . . Y 5
Curros Enríquez
  (Pl. de) . . . . Z 8
Daniel de la Sota . . . . Z 12
Don Gonzalo . . . . Z 15
España (Pl. de) . . . . Z 18
Fernández Villaverde . . . . Z 21
General Mola . . . . Z 24
Gregorio Fernández . . . . YZ 26
Indalecio Armesto
  (Pl.) . . . . Z 29
José Antonio
  (Alameda) . . . . Z 32
Juan Manuel Pintos . . . . Y 34
Manuel Quiroga . . . . Z 37
Marqués de Riestra . . . . Z 40
Michelena . . . . Z
Muelle (Pl. del) . . . . Y 42
Mugártegui (Pl.) . . . . Y 45
Oliva . . . . Z
Padre Amoedo Carballo . . . . Y 47
Padre Luis
  Maria Fernández . . . . Z 50
Pasanteria . . . . Z 53
Pedreira . . . . Y 55
Peregrina . . . . Z 58
Peregrina (Pl.) . . . . Z 61
Princesa . . . . YZ 64
Prudencio Landín Tobio . . . . Z 67
Real . . . . Y
Sagasta . . . . Z 70
San Bartolomé . . . . Z 72
San Nicolás . . . . Y 75
Santa Maria (Av. de) . . . . Z 78
Sarmiento . . . . YZ
Soportales
  de la Herrería . . . . Z 81
Valentín García
  Escudero (Pl.) . . . . Y 84

del Teucro Z; de Mugártegui Y 45) and streets near the Lérez (Pedreira Y 55, Real Y, San Nicolás Y 75). The town comes to life in **calle Sarmiento** (Z) on market days.

Plaza de la Leña (Z) – This is a delightful square with its asymmetrical shape, its Calvary and the beautiful façades that surround it. Two 18C mansions on the square have been converted into a museum.

Museo Provincial ⊘ (Z) – The ground floor of the museum contains prehistoric collections, in particular the Celtic **treasures**★ from A Golada and Caldas de Reis which date from the Bronze Age, and that of Foxados from the 2C and 1C BC, as well as the pre-1900 silverware collection of Fernández de la Mora y Mon, containing over 600 hand-worked pieces from a number of countries. The first floor, which is dedicated to paintings, has several 15C Aragonese Primitives on display.

The second mansion includes a reconstruction of a stateroom from the *Numancia*, the frigate captained by Admiral Méndez Núñez during the disastrous Battle of Callao (Peru's chief sea port) in 1866. When told that it was folly to attack a port so well defended, the admiral replied "Spain prefers honour without ships to ships without honour." On the museum's upper floor are an interesting antique kitchen and 19C Sargadelos ceramics. A large collection of interesting trinkets is also on display in this building.

Iglesia de Santa María la Mayor ⊘ (Y) – Old alleyways and gardens surround this delightful Plateresque church which was built by the mariner's guild in the fishermen's quarter between approximately the late 15C and 1570. The **west front**★ is carved like an altarpiece, divided into separate superimposed registers on which are reliefs of the Dormition and Assumption of the Virgin and the Trinity. At the summit is the Crucifixion at the centre of an openwork coping finely carved with oarsmen and fishermen hauling in their nets. A sculpture of Saint Jerome can be seen to one side.

The **interior** is a generally successful mingling of Gothic (notched arches), Isabelline (slender cabled columns) and Renaissance (ribbed vaulting) styles. The back of the west façade is covered in naive low reliefs of scenes from Genesis (Adam and Eve, Noah's Ark) and the New Testament.

San Francisco (Z) – The church's simply styled Gothic façade looks onto the gardens of plaza de la Herrería. The interior features timber vaulting.

Capilla de la Peregrina (Pilgrim's Chapel) ⊘ (Z) – This small church, with its scallop-shaped floor plan and convex façade, dates from the end of the 18C. Its interior contains a statue of the patron saint of Pontevedra.

> The **Cafetería Carabela** in the lively Praza da Ferrería, with its attractive view of both the Iglesia de San Francisco and the Capilla de la Peregrina, is a pleasant place for a drink or a bite to eat.

Ruinas de Santo Domingo (Santo Domingo Ruins) ⊙ (Z) – These ruins are a per
example of medieval romanticism. The church's Gothic east end still remains
tall bays overgrown with ivy. Arranged inside is a lapidary museum of Ro◼
steles, Galician coats of arms and tombs, in particular, tombs of craftsɪ
showing the tools they used, and tombs of noblemen.

EXCURSION

★★ **Mirador Coto Redondo** – *14km/9mi south on N 550*. The hill climb through ◼
and eucalyptus woods, with occasional good views, is pleasant. The **panoram**
from this viewpoint extends over both the Pontevedra and Vigo *rías*.

PORT AVENTURA★★★

Catalunya (Tarragona)

Michelin map 443 I 33

The 115ha/627 acres of the Port Aventura theme park occupy the localities of S◼
and Vilaseca, at the heart of the Costa Dorada. Port Aventura is a huge amusem
park that takes you on a fascinating and entertaining world tour. It is divided ◼
five different geographical zones, each focusing on a particular theme: Mediterran
Polynesia, China, Mexico and the Far West.

Besides the performances and demonstrations, each country has its own souv◼
shops and a great many places where you can sample local cuisine.

The car park for visitors gives access to the 20 gates where you will be given a g◼
to the park.

Practical Information

The park is open from 17 March to 1 November
For information, call: ☎ 902 20 22 27

Access

Port Aventura, located 10km/6mi from Tarragona and 113km/70mi from
Barcelona, can be reached by motorway A 7 (exit 35) and by N 340. If you are
coming by train, the theme park has its own stop. Otherwise, the closest
railway stations are Salou, Reus and Tarragona, from which there are regular
bus services to Port Aventura.

Nearest airports: Reus (15km/9mi) and Barcelona (120km/75mi).

Tickets

Adults (aged 12-60): 4 100 pts a day (6 250 pts for two days running).

Children aged 5-12 and adults over 60: 3 100 pts a day (4 850 pts for two days
running).

Children under 5: admission free.

Tickets can be bought at the gates and through the services of Servi-
Caixa.

Opening hours

From 17 March to 19 June and from 14 September to 1 November: 10am to
10pm.

From 20 June to 13 September: 10am to midnight.

Parking facilities

6 000 parking places for tourist vehicles and 250 for coaches.

Cars: 500 pts a day; motorcycles: 200 pts a day; caravans: 800 pts a
day.

Services

Automatic exchange machines and cash dispensers.

Toilets and facilities for changing babies.

Wheelchairs for hire: hand-driven 1 000 pts a day; electrically-driven 2 000 pts
a day.

Pushchairs for hire: 500 pts a day.

Left luggage office: 300 pts.

Pet-sitting facilities (cats and dogs, vaccinated pets only): 500 pts a
day.

TOUR

The park features a great many attractions, of which we have listed only some of the most interesting.

Mediterrània - *Located at the main entrance to the park, where all the services are concentrated (exchange, facilities for hiring wheelchairs and video cameras, souvenir shops etc).*
Mediterranean culture and atmosphere are encapsulated in this small coastal town, illustrated by its white streets and sunlit houses, the bustling activity of boats and the evocative whiff of freshly-caught fish... Here you will discover the fascinating secrets of the sea, like for instance, how to tie sailors' knots or how to understand the movements of the tide. On the pier of this small bay, the shops sell more than 40 articles with Port Aventura motifs (ties, T-shirts, pencils, swimming suits etc).

★ **Polynesia** - Beyond the Estación Norte (North Station), a path winds its way among tropical vegetation, brilliantly-coloured exotic birds and mini paradise islands. Grass-skirted musicians and dancers perform along the way. An outdoor stage is the setting for the **Makamanu Bird Show**, where parrots, cockatoos and magpies perform amazing acrobatic acts while they squawk amusing sentences.

★ **Tutuki Splash** - The Polynesian barge travels into the entrails of a volcano before hurtling into a cataract at a speed of over 55kph/35mph, splashing the adventurous sailors with water. However, they will soon recover from their emotional turmoil by sipping a refreshing glass of exotic fruit juice.

★ **China** - The heart of the theme park, this area symbolises all the magic, mystery and fantasy of a millenary civilization. The Chinese town of **Ximpang** houses **Jing Chou Temple**, where you can admire the **Magic Fantasy of China** show. It's a never-ending succession of attractions: butterflies, multicoloured fish, shadows that turn into the most unexpected shapes etc. Other interesting features are the **Imperial Cobra**, a revolving dragon that will delight small children, and the **Tea Cup roundabout**. The **Great Wall of China** encloses this whole area but beyond it lies the most exciting attraction of all.

★ **Dragon Khan** - Shaped as a large hook, this is the star attraction of Port Aventura. Only the bravest visitors risk a ride on the world's most spectacular roller coaster and its eight gigantic loops... Whizzing along at a speed of 110kph/69mph, climbing to the top the right way up and then zooming towards the ground upside down... this unforgettable experience is reserved for those with nerves of steel and a head for heights!

★ **México** - Treat yourself to a picturesque tour of Mexico, spanning centuries of culture. Admire the ruins of the legendary Maya civilization or the sights of colonial Mexico, enjoy the lively strains of Mariachi music and sample the spicy dishes of traditional Mexican cuisine... The imposing replica of the **Chichen-Itzá Pyramid** houses the **Gran Teatro Maya**, where ritual pre-Colombian dances are performed.

★ **Tren del Diablo** - Visitors' shouts and laughs mingle with the creaking of the carriages of this outdoor mining train that rushes through tunnels and along bridges and ravines.

★ **Far West** - **Penitence**, an old, faded village of the American West is the setting for all your dreams come true: playing the lead role in a western, becoming a seasoned cowboy, dancing in the local saloon amid a bunch of pretty girls and reckless adventurers: everything is possible in this fantasy world. Do not miss a ride on the **Union Pacific Steam Engine** which will take you on a tour round the park until you reach Mediterranea.

★ **Stampede** - Two wagons compete with each other on a high-speed wooden roller-coaster ride. An exhilarating white-knuckle experience.

★ **Grand Canyon Rapids** - The round boats like pressure cookers pop up and down in a frenzied rafting movement, the tiny vessels rocked by the Colorado defile and its rapids. This attraction is for dedicated water sports lovers who must hold on tight and surrender to a breathtakingly exciting ride.

> ### "The Biggest Stage in Port Aventura is the Street"
>
> Groups of actors enact small scenes in the various streets and avenues of the theme park. Moreover, each geographical zone has theatres and stages where shows are performed, lasting no more than 20min. Altogether, you can see over 70 different performances every day.

PRIEGO DE CÓRDOBA ★

Andalucía (Córdoba) – Population 20 823
Michelin map 446 T 17

This lovely town is situated on a plain in the heart of the Subbética Cordobesa ran
It reached its economic and artistic zenith in the 18C as a result of the silk indust

SIGHTS

★ **Fuentes del Rey y de la Salud (Fountains of the King and Health)** – *At the end of 1
calle del Río*. The sight created by these two fountains, the most well-known
the town, is a surprising one. The older, the **Fuente de la Salud**, is a Manner
frontispiece built in the 16C. Next to it is the lavish **Fuente del Rey** which w
completed at the beginning of the 19C. Both the dimensions and the richness
its design evoke the gardens of a Baroque palace. It has a total of 139 jets spout
water from the mouth of the same number of masks. The central displ
represents Neptune's chariot and Amphitrite.

Parroquia de la Asunción (Parish Church of the Assumption) ⊙ – *At the end of the Pas
del Abad Palomino*. This 16C church was remodelled in Baroque style in the 18

★★ **El Sagrario** – The chapel, which opens on to the Nave del Evangelio, is a masterpie
of Andalusian Baroque. It comprises an antechamber leading into an octago
space surrounded by an ambulatory. Light plays an important part in the effect
the scene; intensified by the whiteness of the walls and ceiling, it shimmers over t
extensive and lavish **yeserías** (plasterwork decoration), creating a magical atm
sphere. In spite of this excessive adornment, the overall effect is one of delicac

★ **Barrio de la Villa** – This charming quarter, dating back to medieval and Moori
times, has narrow, winding streets and flower-decked whitewashed houses.

El Adarve – This delightful balcony which looks out onto the Subbética mount
range encircles the Barrio de la Villa to the north.

PUEBLA DE SANABRIA

Castilla y León (Zamora) – Population 1 969
Michelin map 441 F 10

Puebla de Sanabria is an attractive mountain village near the Portuguese border
short distance from Galicia and the province of León. Its white-walled houses wi
tile-stone roofs and the occasional emblazoned façade are dominated by the 1!
castle of the Count of Benavente. The **church** is a late-12C, reddish granite co
struction with a west door simply outlined with a large bead motif. The view fro
the castle esplanade takes in the Río Tera and part of the lake.

EXCURSION

Valle de Sanabria – *19km/12mi northwest*.
The valley, now a nature reserve, was hollowed out northwest of Puebla by glac
erosion at the feet of the Sierras de Cabrera Baja and Segundera. It is a delight
area, well-known for its hunting and fishing, that owes much of its appeal to t
many streams running through the light bush vegetation.
Lago de Sanabria – Sanabria, the largest glacial lake in Spain, lies at an altitude
1 028m/3 373ft. It is used for all types of water sports, and salmon-trout fishin
San Martín de Castañeda – There are attractive **views**★ of the rushing stream of the Te
and the mountain encircled lake all the way to this Galician looking village. The fir
distinguishable sight of this is the east end of its noble 11C Romanesque **church**

PUEBLOS BLANCOS DE ANDALUCÍA ★

WHITE VILLAGES OF ANDALUCÍA
Michelin map 446 V 12-14

The mountainous region between Ronda and Arcos de la Frontera is formed by t
Sierras de Grazalema, Ubrique and Margarita. In these often weirdly shape
mountains, ranging from desolate heights to lush green valleys, are the remains
the *pinsapos* forest of native pines dating from the beginning of the Quaterna
period.
The area is well-watered on account of its proximity to the Atlantic; some years t
rainfall exceeds 3m/118in. This abundant precipitation is borne out by the region
many dams and reservoirs, among them Bornos, Arcos and Guadalcacín.
The beauty of the countryside is set off by the delightful white villages (*puebl
blancos*) often perched on rocky crags or stretched out along escarpments, the
narrow streets of whitewashed houses dominated by a ruined castle or a church. Th
inhabitants make a living from farming, stock raising and local crafts.

FROM RONDA TO ARCOS DE LA FRONTERA

By the southern route; 104km/65mi – about 3hr

★ **Ronda** – *See RONDA.*

★ **Grazalema** – The village, set in a mountain cirque, is one of Andalucía's most beautiful. Its natural-coloured woollen blankets woven on long looms are famous. The lonely road between Grazalema and Ubrique cuts its way through grey and pink countryside deeply scoured by erosion into fantastic shapes.

Grazalema

Ubrique – The town nestling in the mountains is an industrial centre for leather goods (bags and shoes).
After climbing to El Bosque the road crosses a cultivated area of orchards and olive groves to Arcos de la Frontera.

★ **Arcos de la Frontera** – *See ARCOS DE LA FRONTERA.*

FROM ARCOS DE LA FRONTERA TO RONDA

By the northern route; 102km/63mi – about 3hr

The road skirts the white village of Bornos which stands out against the vast reservoir of the same name. As you approach Algodonales, a beautiful **view**★ opens up of **Zahara** village, built on a rocky height dominated by the ruins of its castle.

Olvera – The village houses stretch out along a ridge amid rows of olive trees. Once past **Torre-Alháquime**, look back for a fine view of the village with Olvera in the background.

Setenil – The village lies huddled in a gorge cut by the Guadalporcún river with many of its houses nestled under the overhanging rock ledge.

The star ratings are allocated for various categories: regions of scenic beauty with dramatic natural features; cities with a cultural heritage; elegant resorts and charming villages; ancient monuments and fine architecture, museum and picture galleries.

PUENTE VIESGO ★

Cantabria – Population 2 464
Michelin map 442 C 18

The **cuevas** (caves) - El Castillo, Las Chimeneas, Las Monedas, La Pasiega - hollow out of the limestone mountainsides all round Puente Viesgo provide ample proof their habitation in prehistoric times.

★ **Cueva del Castillo** ⊘ - Cave dwellers began engraving and painting the wa towards the end of the Paleolithic Age (from the Aurignacian to the Magdaleni period). The many designs - 750 have been counted - outlines only a sometimes incomplete, are widely scattered and some are difficult to get to. Ma remain enigmatic, particularly the hands dipped in ochre and pressed against t wall, or outlined in red, to form negatives. They are thought, perhaps, symbolise man's superiority or to possess magical powers. Of the almost discovered only three are right hands.

The meaning of the parallel lines and point alignments also remains obscure. The may refer to weapons or traps for catching animals.

EXCURSION

Castañeda - 6km/4mi northeast.
The **antigua Colegiata** ⊘, a former collegiate church dating from the end of the 12 stands in the small, pleasant valley through which the Pisueña runs. The unusual deep doorway is given considerable elegance by a simple decoration of alterna convex and concave covings.
Inside, the central area has retained its original plan with semicircular arches the nave and the cupola on squinches.

The PYRENEES

See PIRINEOS ARAGONESES and PIRINEOS CATALANES

REINOSA

Cantabria – Population 12 852
Michelin map 442 C 17

Reinosa, built on the southern slopes of the Montes Cantábricos, in the vas depression formed by the Ebro basin, really belongs to the Castilian landscape wit its vast expanses of tableland and cereals. In the 18C its position on the road linkin Castilla with the port of Santander encouraged commercial development.
It is becoming a tourist centre as it is near the **embalse del Ebro** (a reservoir which i navigable for 20km/12mi) and the winter sports resort of Alto Campóo.

EXCURSIONS

Retortillo - 5km/3mi south of C 6318.
All that remains in the small **church** of the Romanesque period are th oven-vaulted apse and the triumphal arch with two finely carved capital illustrating warriors. A few yards away are the ruins of a villa which stood in the Roman city of **Julióbriga**.

★ **Cervatos** - 7km/4mi south on N 611.
The **antigua colegiata**★ ⊘, a former collegiate church with an unusually pure Romanesque style, is remarkable for the richness and imaginativeness of its carved **decoration**★. The portal tympanum is meticulously patterned with a tight openwork design. There is a frieze of lions back to back while varied and audacious figures decorate the cornice modillions and those beneath the capitals of the south apsidal window. Inside there are harmonious blind arcades in the apse and, again, the carving on the capitals and the consoles supporting the arch ribs is both dense and sophisticated with entangled lions, eagles with spread wings, plant motifs and strapwork. The nave was raised with intersecting ribbed vaulting in the 14C.

★★★ **Pico de Tres Mares** - 26km/16mi west on C 628.
On the way, paths from the village of Fontibre lead to a greenish pool, the **source of the Ebro** (Fuente del Ebro), the greatest Iberian river.
Access to the Pico de Tres Mares by chair-lift.
The peak (2 175m/7 136ft), one of the summits of the Sierra de Peña Labra, got its name as the source of three rivers which flow from it to three different seas (sea: *mar* in Spanish) - the Híjar, tributary of the Ebro which flows into

the Mediterranean; the Pisuerga, tributary of the Duero which flows into the Atlantic, and the Nansa, which flows directly into the Cantabrian sea. From the crest there is a splendid circular **panorama**★★★: to the north, of the Nansa and the embalse de la Cohilla (Cohilla dam) at the foot of Monte Cueto (1 517m/4 977ft), and circling right, the embalse del Ebro, the Sierra de Peña Labra, the embalse de Cervera de Pisuerga and the Montes de León; due west, the central range of the Picos de Europa including the 2 618m/8 589ft Peña Vieja, and linked to it by a series of high passes, the eastern range which includes the Peña Sagra (2 042m/6 699ft). In the foreground is the eroded mass of the Peña Labra (2 006m/6 581ft).

RÍAS ALTAS★

Galicia (Lugo, La Coruña)
Michelin map 441 A 5-7, B 4-8, C 2-5, D 2

hough indented by *rías* – inlets made by the Atlantic into the coastline, like the lochs of Scotland or the *fjords* of Norway – the northern coast of Galicia from adeo to Cabo Finisterre is generally low-lying. The rocks, bare and smooth, the nite houses with slate roofs, give the impression that the climate must be grim et holidaymakers arrive with the fine season, attracted by the scenery and small dy creeks. Galicia's *rías* are described below from east to west.

Ría de Ribadeo – The ría de Ribadeo is formed by the estuary of the Eo. After a headlong course, the río Eo, forming the border between Galicia and Asturias, slackens its pace to wind gently between the wide green banks of its lower valley. There is a beautiful **view**★ up the estuary from the bridge across the mouth of the river.
The old port of **Ribadeo** is now an important regional centre and summer resort.

Ría de Foz – **Foz**, at the mouth of its *ría*, is a small port with a coastal fishing fleet. Its two good Atlantic beaches are popular in summer.

Iglesia de San Martín de Mondoñedo ⊘ – *5km/3mi west*. Standing almost alone on a height is the church, once part of a monastery of ancient foundation and an episcopal seat until 1112 when this was transferred to Mondoñedo. The style of the church is archaic and, most unusually in this region, shows no sign of Compostelan influence. The east end, decorated with Lombard bands, is supported by massive buttresses; inside, the transept **capitals**★ are naively carved and rich in anecdotal detail: the one illustrating the parable of the rich man who allows Lazarus to die of hunger, shows the table overflowing with food while a dog beneath it is licking Lazarus's feet as he lies stretched out on the ground. The capitals, believed to date from the 10C, bear Visigothic influence in the plant motifs.

Ría de Viveiro – Sea, countryside and mountain combine in a varied landscape, a coastline of white sand beaches and lofty headlands sung by **Nicomedes Pastor Díaz**, 19C politician and poet. All **Viveiro** retains of its town walls is the Puerta de Carlos V (Charles V Gateway), emblasoned with the emperor's arms. In the summer months the port is transformed into a holiday resort. On the fourth Sunday in August, visitors from all over Galicia come for the local Naseiro Romería.

Ría de Santa María de Ortigueira – The *ría* is deep and surrounded by green hills while **Ortigueira** port has quays bordered by well kept gardens.

Ría de Cedeira – A small, deeply enclosed *ría* with beautiful beaches. The road gives good **views** of **Cedeira** (summer resort) and the surrounding countryside.

Ría de Ferrol – The *ría* forms a magnificent natural harbour entered by way of a narrow 6km/4mi channel guarded by two forts. In the 18C, on account of its exceptional site and favourable position for trade with America, King Ferdinand VI and King Charles III decided to make the port of **Ferrol** a naval base. The symmetry of the town plan evident in the old quarter dates from the same period.
Ferrol today is one of Spain's major naval bases and is also a dockyard.

Ría de Betanzos – *See BETANZOS*.

Ría de La Coruña – *See A CORUÑA*.

Costa de la Muerte (Coast of Death) – The landscape between La Coruña and Cabo Finisterre is of a wild, harsh and majestic coast. It has long been whipped by stormy weather and owes its inhospitable name to the many ships that have run aground or been smashed to pieces against its rocks. Tucked away in its more sheltered coves, however, are small fishing villages like **Malpica de Bergantiños**

Costa de la Muerte

which is protected by the Cabo de San Adrián (opposite the Islas Sisargas, isla on which there is a bird sanctuary) or **Camariñas** which is famous for bobbin-lace.

★ **Cabo Finisterre or Fisterra** (Cape Finisterre) – **Corcubión**★, near Cabo Finisterre, i attractive old harbour town of emblazoned houses with glassed-in balconies. coast **road**★ to the cape looks down over the Bahía de Cabo Finisterre, a bay w is enclosed by three successive mountain chains. The lighthouse on the head commands a fine **panorama**★ of the Atlantic and the bay.

RÍAS BAJAS★★

Galicia (La Coruña, Pontevedra)

Michelin map 441 D 2-3, E 2-3, F 3-4

The Rías Bajas, a coastline well supplied by the sea (renowned for its seafood) with deep inlets affording safe anchorages, is Galicia's most privileged and attrac region. In the season, holidaymakers, Spanish for the most part, come to enjoy beaches and resorts like those of A Toxa.

★★ RÍA DE MUROS Y NOIA

① From Muros to Ribeira

71km/44mi – about 1hr 15min

The *ría* is especially delightful for its wild scenery. The coastline, lower tha other *rías*, is strewn with rocks. The wooded northern bank is particul attractive.

Muros is a seaside town with a harbour and typical local style houses, while is notable for its main square looking out to sea, upon which stands the Go **Iglesia de San Martín**★ with a magnificently carved portal and rose window.

RÍA DE AROUSA

② From Ribeira to A Toxa

115km/71mi – about 3hr

Ría de Arousa, at the mouth of the río Ulla, is the largest and most indente the inlets.

Ribeira – A large fishing port with vast warehouses.

★★★ **Mirador de la Curota** – *10km/6mi from Puebla del Caramiñal, taking LC . west towards Oleiros and after about 4km/2.5mi turning right onto a nar road up to the viewpoint.*

From a height of 498m/1 634ft there is a magnificent **panorama★★★** of the four inlets of the Rías Bajas. On a clear day the view extends from Cabo Finisterre to the río Miño.

Padrón – It was to this village that the legendary boat came which brought St James to Spain. The boat's mooring stone (*pedrón*) can be seen beneath the altar in the **iglesia parroquial** ⊘ (parish church) near the bridge. The town, renowned for its green peppers, is also home to the residence in which the poet **Rosalía de Castro** (1837-85) lived. Her house has now been converted into a **museum** ⊘.

Vilagarcía de Arousa – A garden bordered promenade overlooking the sea gives the town the air of a resort. The Convento de Vista Alegre, founded in 1648, stands on the outskirts on the Cambados road. It is an old *pazo* with square towers, coats of arms and pointed merlons.

★ **Mirador de Lobeira** – *4km/2mi south. Take a signposted forest track at Cornazo.* The view from the lookout takes in the whole *ría* and the hills inland.

★ **Cambados** – Cambados has retained an old quarter of alleyways bordered by beautiful houses. At the town's northern entrance is the magnificent, square **Plaza de Fefiñanes★**, lined on two sides by the emblazoned Fefiñanes *pazo*, on the third by a 17C church with lines harmonising with the *pazo*, and on the fourth by a row of arcaded houses. Also worthy of note on the other side of the village are the romantic ruins of **Santa Mariña de Dozo**, a 12C parish church which is now a cemetery. Cambados is the place to try the local white Albariño wine which has a light fruity flavour.

Aquariumgalicia ⊘ – *From O Grove head towards San Vicente and turn off at Reboredo.* This, the only aquarium in Galicia, has over 15 000 exhibits representing more than 150 species on display in 18 tanks which recreate different marine habitats. The complex also includes a marine farm where species of commercial interest, such as the unusual turbot and the gilthead, are bred.

★ **A Toxa** – A sick donkey abandoned on the island by its owner and later recovered cured, was the first living creature to discover the health-giving properties of the spring on A Toxa. The stream has run dry but the pine-covered island in its wonderful **setting★★** remains an ideally restful place. It is the most elegant resort on the Galician coast with luxury villas and an early 20C palace. There is a small church covered in scallop shells.

The seaside resort and fishing harbour of **O Grove** on the other side of the causeway is renowned for its seafood.

The A Toxa-Canelas **road★** affords a succession of views of sand dunes and extensive, rock enclosed beaches like that of La Lanzada.

★ **RÍA DE PONTEVEDRA**

③ **From A Toxa to Hío**

62km/39mi – about 3hr

Sanxenxo – A very lively resort in summer with one of the best climates in Galicia.

Monasterio de Armenteira ⊘ – In Samieira a small road leads to this Cistercian monastery, where a 12C church and 17C Classical-style cloister can still be visited.

* **Combarro** – This small, typical fishing village with winding alleyways has a good many Calvaries and is famed for its **hórreos**★ (drying sheds) on the seafront.

* **Pontevedra** – *See PONTEVEDRA.*

  Marín – Headquarters of the Escuala Naval Militar or Naval Academy.

  Hío – The village at the tip of the Morrazo headland has a famous and intricately carved **Calvary**★.

★★ RÍA DE VIGO

⁴ **From Hío to Baiona**
70km/43mi – about 3hr

Although smaller than the ría de Arousa, the Vigo inlet is deeper and better protected, remarkably sheltered inland by hills and out to sea by islands, the Islas Cíes. In addition, by Domaio, where

A hórreo *in Combarro*

the steep, wooded banks draw together and the narrow channel is covered in mus
beds, it becomes really beautiful. From Cangas and Moaña you can see the wh
town of Vigo covering the entire hillside on the far side of the inlet.

Vigo – Vigo, Spain's principal transatlantic port, is the country's leading fish
port and one of its most important industrial and commercial centres. Legend l
it that treasure dating from the time of Philip V lies at the bottom of the in
Vigo's **setting**★ is outstanding: built in an amphitheatre on the south bank of
ría and surrounded by parks and pinewoods. There are magnificent **views**★★
Vigo and its bay from El Castro hill behind the town. Berbés, Vigo's oldest quar
and home to fishermen and sailors, is a picturesque part of town. Beside it is
unusual A Pedra market where fishwives sell the oysters which may be tastee
the many bars nearby.

Islas Cíes – Boats from Vigo harbour take passengers to the islands *(about 1*
The beautiful archipelago of crystalline water and immaculate white sand gua
the entrance to the ría de Vigo. The islands, a sanctuary to birds, were decr
a nature reserve in 1980.

★★ **Mirador la Madroa** – *6km/4mi. Follow signs to the airport and then to the z*
The esplanade commands a fine **view**★★ of Vigo and the *ría*.

The Alcabre, Samil and Canido beaches stretch down the coast south of Vig

Panxón – A seaside resort at the foot of Monte Ferro.

Playa América – A very popular, elegant resort in the curve of a bay.

* **Baiona** – *See BAIONA.*

La RIOJA★

La Rioja, Navarra, Álava
Michelin map 442 E 20-23, F 20-24

La Rioja, a fertile area in the Ebro Valley called after a tributary, the Río Oja, cov
an area of 5 000km²/1 931sq mi comprising La Rioja province and parts of Álava a
Navarra. **Rioja Alta** – Upper Rioja – to the west around Haro, is devoted principally
wine-growing while **Rioja Baja** – Lower Rioja – with **Logroño** and Calahorra as its m
towns, has unusual tableland relief and is given over to extensive vegetable growi
La Rioja flourished culturally and economically early in its history thanks to
position on the pilgrim route to Santiago de Compostela. Since then it has becc
famous for its wine.

The all-important **vineyards** of La Rioja cover an area of 43 000ha/106 260 acr
Although the vine has long held pride of place – Rioja wines are mentioned i
document as early as 1102 and they were already being exported to France, Fland

Italy in the 16C – the wine trade really began to develop in the 19C when French ⁣e-growers ruined by phylloxera came to try their luck in La Rioja. Today, La Rioja is ⁣ain's leading producer of quality wines, in particular the reds (11°-12°), which, ⁣ugh light and smooth, have some body. The Rioja mark of guaranteed origin covers ⁣e from Rioja Alta and Álava but also includes the stronger wines from Rioja Baja. ⁣s part of the province, however, specialises more in early vegetables – asparagus, ⁣chokes, peppers and tomatoes – for the important local canning industry.

SIGHTS

Logroño – The capital of the Rioja region is situated on the banks of the Ebro in a fertile valley which has become an important centre for the production of vegetables. Pilgrims on their way to Santiago de Compostela would have entered this pleasant town through the stone gateway, which still retains an attractive view over the old town with its Baroque tower of the cathedral, the spired tower of **Santa María del Palacio** and the Mudéjar tower of **San Bartolomé**.

Santa María la Redonda ⓥ – The church of Santa María dates from 1435, but has only been the town's cathedral since 1959. It has three naves, three polygonal apses and chapels in its side aisles. These include the Plateresque-style Chapel of Our Lady of Peace (Nuestra Señora de la Paz), founded in 1541 by Diego Ponce de León. The extraordinary grille enclosing the choir is particularly worthy of note.

Museo de la Rioja ⓥ – This regional museum is housed in a fine 18C Baroque palace in which General Espartero lived during the last century. The collection mainly originates from disentailments during the 19C. The Romanesque carvings and Gothic retable from Torremuña are particularly interesting, as is a superb Hispano-Filipino marble sculpture representing an expiring Christ from the Baroque period.

Ezcaray – This delightful village, situated at the foot of the Sierra de la Demanda range close to Logroño and surrounded by superb natural countryside on the banks of the Oja river, has become a summer resort and a popular ski area. It has preserved its quaint mountain style, its stone and wood porticoes, seignorial mansions, the church of **Santa María la Mayor** as well as the buildings of a former tapestry factory founded by Charles III in 1752. Today the tradition lives on in the manufacture of blankets.

Santo Domingo de la Calzada – *See SANTO DOMINGO DE LA CALZADA*.

Haro – This small but prosperous farming and commercial centre is famous for its wines. There are countless cellars and taverns in the old quarter where seignorial mansions with elegant 16C and 18C façades recall the town's prestigious past. In **plaza de la Paz** the simple lines of the neo-Classical town hall (Ayuntamiento), built by Juan de Villanueva in 1769, are particularly impressive, as is the Baroque tower of the **Iglesia de Santo Tomás** behind it. This church, which was constructed by Felipe Birgany in 1516, has preserved its fine Renaissance doorway.

Rioja Wine

Rioja is the only Spanish appellation with the Denominación de Origen Calificada (DOC) quality label. The wine is the result of over seven centuries of tradition and a superb position in the Ebro Valley between the Sierra de la Demanda and the Sierra de Cantabria. The wine region is traditionally divided into three sub-zones: Rioja Alavesa, Rioja Baja and Rioja Alta. Although seven grape varieties are permitted, the two most commonly used are Tempranillo and Grenache. Red wine accounts for 75% of production and is produced according to two different processes: **carbonic maceration** and **ageing**. The first produces  young, fresh wines which are best consumed in the year of production, whereas the ageing process, in Bordeaux oak barrels, results in three different wines, classified according to the time spent in the barrel and the time which has elapsed between the harvest and the moment the wine leaves the cellars: **Crianza** (12 months in the barrel, one year in the bottle), **Reserva** (12 months in the barrel, two years in the bottle) and **Gran Reserva** (24 months in the barrel, three years in the bottle).

Museo del Vino de la Rioja ⊙ – Without doubt, wine is one of the biggest attract of the Rioja region. This small museum is entirely devoted to this art v descriptions and explanations on wine production from cultivation all the through to the bottling process. An interesting and worthwhile visit for w lovers.

★ **Laguardia** – With its situation on a hill at the foot of the Sierra de Cantal Laguardia is perhaps the most attractive town in Rioja Alavesa. Its forti appearance from the main road is enhanced as you approach, as its two impo towers, San Juan to the south, and the tower of the abbey to the north, come view. The latter dates from the end of the 12C; in the past it was connecte the attractive parish church of **Santa María de los Reyes** ⊙ with its superb late-**portal** which has completely preserved its 17C polychrome decoration. tympanum is divided into three scenes relating events from the life of the Vir Note the figure of Christ holding a small child in his hands representing the of the Virgin. The interior is a strange mix of Gothic and Renaissance styles; Renaissance vault in the central nave is of particular interest.

The walkway around the village commands views over vast sweeps of viney. The **panorama** from the **Balcón de Rioja**★ or Rioja Balcony 12km/8mi northw of Laguardia near the Puerto de Herrera (Herrera Pass) (1 100m/3 60S is incredibly extensive, particularly along the length of the Ebro Valley, and arid in appearance apart from the winding silver thread of the river's course.

Nájera – See SANTO DOMINGO DE LA CALZADA.

San Millán de la Cogolla – See SANTO DOMINGO DE LA CALZADA.

★ **Valle del Iregua (Iregua Valley)** – 50km/31mi south of Logroño on N 111. For 15km/9mi the road skirts orchards and market-gardens in the Ebro pl until, near Isllallana, appear the first **rock faces**★ of the Sierra de Came overlooking the Iregua from a height of more than 500m/1 640ft. Two tun later, the valley narrows, squeezed between massive reddish-coloured bould It opens out into an island of greenery and narrows again upstream with torrent running at the bottom of a deep ravine while the mountain road domin the site of Torrecilla en Cameros. In the village of **Villanueva de Cameros** half-timbered houses are roofed with circular tiles.

RIPOLL★

Catalunya (Girona) – Population 11 204
Michelin map 443 F 36
Local map see PIRINEOS CATALANES

While Ripoll is the capital of an industrial region (ironworks, textiles and pa making) its main interest lies in its Benedictine monastery founded in the 9C **Wilfred the Hairy**, Count of Barcelona. The monastery was the pantheon of the cou of Barcelona, Besalú and Cerdaña until the 12C.

The monastery as a centre of learning – The library at Ripoll was one of the ricl in Christendom: not only did it possess texts of the scriptures and theolog commentaries but also works by pagan authors such as Plutarch and Virgil as as scientific treatises. The learning of Antiquity was restored by the Arabs, treasured and disseminated the works of the Greeks which they discovered w they captured Alexandria and, with it, its incredible library. Ripoll, previously ovel by the Moors, became, under Abbot Oliba, a link between Arab and Chris civilizations, a centre of culture, ideas and exchange to which came such mel Brother Gerbert, the future Pope **Sylvester II** (999).

Abbot Oliba – Oliba, son of a Count of Cerdaña and Besalú, a learned man and a l leader, held the appointments simultaneously from 1008 of Abbot of Ripoll St-Michel-de-Cuxa in the French Pyrenees (Roussillon) and from 1018 also of Bis of Vic. He lived until 1046 and thus had time to impress his mark deeply on the re both intellectually and as a great builder. He favoured the basilical type plan prominent transepts and a dome over the crossing as in the Collegiate Churcl Cardona.

★ANTIGUO MONASTERIO DE SANTA MARIA ⊙

All that remains of the original monastery are the church portal and the cloist

★ **Iglesia** – The 9C monastery church soon had to be enlarged. In 1032, the fam Abbot Oliba consecrated another church, a more majestic edifice, and a jewe early Romanesque art. An earthquake in 1428, various remodellings over the a and a fire in 1835, all destroyed the building. It was rebuilt at the end of the according to the original plan, with a nave and four aisles cut by a great transept on which seven apses abutted. The south transept contains the 12C tomb of Ramón Berenguer III, the Great, while in the north is the funerary monument to Wilfred the Hairy.

Portada (Portal) – The 12C portal, built a century after the church, is weather worn in spite of the late-13C overhang, and the figures are difficult to decipher. The portal design, comprising a series of horizontal registers, has been compared to that of a triumphal arch crowned by a large frieze. The carving may be seen to illustrate the glory of God and his people, victorious over his enemies (Passage of the Red Sea), a symbol of special significance at the time of the Reconquest.

The low reliefs cover not only the doorway but also the surround. The result is an exceptionally intricate series of carvings illustrating Biblical personages and events.

Claustro (Cloisters) – Only the gallery abutting the church dates back to the 12C. It was the only gallery until the 14C when the others were added, their later date being betrayed only by the carving on some of the capitals.

A - **Vision of the Apocalypse**
1) The Eternal Father enthroned
2) Angels
3) A winged man, the symbol of St Matthew
4) An eagle, the symbol of St John
5) The 24 Elders of the Apocalypse
6) A lion, the symbol of St Mark
7) A bull, the symbol of St Luke

B - **Exodus**
1) The crossing of the Red Sea
2) Manna descending from Heaven
3) Flight of quail guiding the People of God
4) Moses bringing forth water from the rock
5) Moses keeping his arms uplifted to ensure victory for his people
6) Foot soldiers and cavalry in combat

C - **The Book of Kings**
1) David and the musicians
2) Transporting the Ark of the Covenant
3) The plague of Zion
4) Gad (standing) speaks to David (seated) before the crowd
5) David declares Solomon his heir
6) Solomon, riding David's mule, is aceclaimed by the people
7) The judgment of Solomon
8) Solomon's dream

9) Elijah rises to heaven in a chariot of fire

D - David and the musicians
E - Monsters fighting
F - St Peter
G - St Paul
H - The life and martyrdom of St Peter (left) and St Paul (right)
I - The story of Jonah (left) and Daniel (right)
J - (at the arch centre - reading simultaneously right and left) - at the centre the Creator - two angels - above, the sacrifice of Cain and Abel - below, the killing of Abel; the death of Cain
K - (inner sides of the doorway pillars): the months of the year

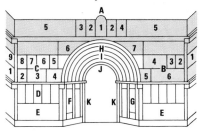

RONCESVALLES★

See ORREAGA

RONDA★★

Andalucía (Málaga) – Population 35 788

Michelin map 446 V 14

e town was built at the edge of the serranía de Ronda on a platform **site**★★ cut by e Guadalevín ravine. The ravine (*tajo* in Castilian Spanish) actually divides Ronda o two: the **Ciudad** or old town and the Mercadillo, now extended by the modern vn. There is an impressive bird's-eye **view**★ from the bridge, **Puente Nuevo**, down the er rock face. The road (Camino de los Molinos) to the power station, which passes ng the foot of the cliffs, affords another good **view**★ – this time up the ravine cut the bridge.

e cradle of bullfighting – Born in Ronda in 1695, **Francisco Romero** laid down the es of bullfighting, which until then had been only a display of audacity and agility. became the father of modern bullfighting by his introduction of the cape and the eta. His son Juan introduced the *cuadrillo* or supporting team and his grandson, ro Romero (1754-1839), became one of Spain's greatest bullfighters. He founded e **Ronda School**, known still for its classicism, strict observance of the rules and ocada a recibir.

SIGHTS

★ Plaza de Toros (Bullring) (Y) – The bullring, built in 1785, is one of the ol‹ in Spain. It is entered through an elegant gateway and is surrounded by arcades inside. Traditional *Corridas Goyescas*, fights in period costumes f the time of Goya, are held annually. The bullring was used in Rosi's film *Car* in 1984.

The **Museo Taurino** (Bullfighting Museum) ⊘ contains sumptuous costumes various mementoes and photographs of generations of Ronda matadors inclu‹ the Romero family and Ordóñez.

★ La Ciudad (YZ) – The old walled town, a vestige from the Moorish occupa which lasted until 1485, is a picturesque enclave of narrow alleys and white ho‹ with ironwork balconies.

Colegiata (Z) ⊘ – This collegiate church was built between the 15C and on the site of a former mosque of which it has retained a 13C horses‹ arch and the Mudéjar minaret which was converted into a belfry in 16C.

A two-tiered balcony on the church façade served as a gallery from w notables could watch events in the square below. Inside are three diffe architectural styles: Gothic in the aisles, Plateresque in the chancel and Barc in the stalls.

Palacio de Mandrágon (Z) – The palace's noble Renaissance façade is surmou‹ by twin Mudéjar turrets. The square nearby commands a **view** over ravine.

Palacio del Marqués de Salvatierra (Y E) – The Marquis, a great Renaissance trave adorned his palace with the strange figures of two Inca Indian couples holdin the triangular pediment. A wrought-iron balcony and detailed low reliefs comp the decoration.

Baños árabes (Moorish Baths) ⊘ **(Z)** – A reminder that Ronda was once the ca of a *taifa* kingdom.

EXCURSIONS

★★ Ronda to San Pedro de Alcántara road – *49km/30mi southeast on C 3: about 1hr.*

For 20km/12mi the road travels through a bare mountain landscape; it ‹ climbs steeply into a **corniche★★** above the Guadalmedina valley and its sm tributary valleys. The route is deserted, there's not a single village.

Puente Nuevo and the ravine (El Tajo), Ronda

RONDA

Armiñán . . . . .YZ
Capitán Cortés . . . . Y 3
Carmen Abela (Pl. de) . . . . Y 5
Cerrillo . . . . Y
Descalzos (Pl. de los) . . . Y
Doctor Fleming (Av.) . . . . Y 6
Duquesa de Parcent
  (Pl. de la) . . . . Z 8
España (Pl. de) . . . . Y 12
Espinel (Carrera de) . . . . Y
González Campos . . . . . . Z 15
Las Imágenes . . . . Z 18
María Auxiliadora (Pl.) . . . Z 20
Marqués de Salvatierra . . . Z 21
Merced (Pl. de la) . . . . . . Y 24
Padre Mariano
  Soubirón . . . . Y 26
Prado . . . . Z
Peñas . . . . Y
Real . . . . Y
Ruedo Alameda (Pl.) . . . . Z
Ruedo de Gameros . . . . . Z 27
Santa Cecilia . . . . Y 30
Santo Domingo . . . . Y 33
Sevilla . . . . Y
Tenorio . . . . .YZ
Virgen de la Paz . . . . Y
Virgen de los Dolores . . . . Y

E   Palacio del Marqués
    de Salvatierra

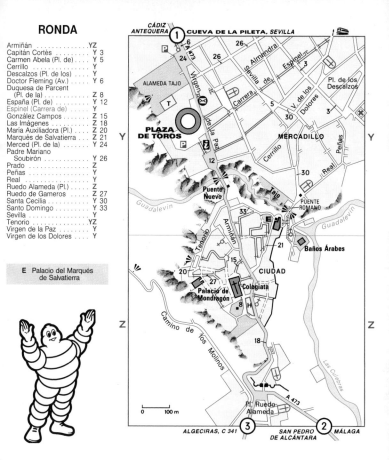

Ronda to Algeciras road – *118km/73mi southwest on C 341, C 3331 and N 340 – about 3hr.*
The Ronda-Gaucín section is particularly interesting when the road climbs steeply to overlook the Genal valley. It then continues, winding around the foot of Jimena de la Frontera perched on a hill. 22km/14mi further on, a narrow road on the right leads to **Castellar de la Frontera**, a village of flower-filled alleyways huddled within the castle grounds.

The White Villages of Andalucía – *See PUEBLOS BLANCOS DE ANDALUCÍA.*

Cueva de la Pileta (Pileta Cave) ⊙ – *27km/17mi – about 1hr plus 1hr 30min sightseeing. Take the northerly C 339 (towards Sevilla) and turn left after 14km/9mi.*
There is a striking **view**★★ when you come upon the Montejaque dam. The cave is interesting archeologically: lamplight reveals beautiful natural concretions of draperies and hangings but more importantly, rock paintings, antedating those of Altamira and which are believed to date back at least 25 000 years. There are figures of goats and panthers, symbolic drawings and a giant fish measuring 1.25m/49in.

SAGUNT/SAGUNTO

Comunidad valenciana (Valencia) – Population 55 957
Michelin map 445 M 29

agunto lies surrounded by a *huerta*; the town itself is backed up against a wide hill owned by the ruins of an ancient citadel. The port 5km/3mi away is also an dustrial centre.

legendary siege – Sagunto has a place in Spain's heroic history. In 218 BC e Carthaginian general, **Hannibal**, besieged Sagunto, then a small seaport allied Rome – the harbour and surrounding countryside have since silted over. gunto was abandoned by Rome, and the inhabitants, seeing only one alter-tive, to surrender, lit a huge fire. They fed the fire until the flames were gh, then women and children, the sick and the old, threw themselves into

309

the furnace while soldiers and menfolk made a suicidal sortie against the enemy. The event marked the beginning of the Second Punic War. Five years later, Scipio Africanus Major rebuilt the city which became an important Roman town.

Ruinas ⊙ – The ruins are reached through the upper part of town, through the narrow alleyways of the old Jewish quarter.

Teatro – The ancient Roman theatre was built on the hillside.

Acrópolis – Ruins and remains can be seen superimposed and juxtaposed: ramparts, temples and houses built by Iberians, Phoenicians, Carthaginians, Romans, Visigoths and Moors. In 1811, in the War of Independence, the French general Suchet besieged the town, leaving major works on the west side to mark yet another period in Sagunto's history. A vast **panorama**★ spreads out on all sides of the Acropolis of the town, *huerta*, Palancia Valley and the sea.

EXCURSIONS

Grutas de San José (San José Caves) ⊙ – *27km/17mi north. First take N 340 and then head for La Vall d'Uixo.*
The caves have been hollowed out by an underground river along which you go by boat for about 1 100m/1 200yd.

Segorbe – *33km/21mi northwest on N 234.*
The cathedral is chiefly important for its museum **(museo)** ⊙ which contains a large collection of altarpieces painted by the Valencia school★. There are several paintings by Juan Vicente Macip (d 1550) who was influenced by the Italian Renaissance style. An *Ecce Homo* by his son **Juan de Juanes** bears the touch of gentleness favoured by Leonardo da Vinci. There are also works by Rodrigo de Osona and Jacomart and a 15C marble low relief of a Madonna by Donatello.

Michelin on the Net: **www.michelin-travel.com**

Our route planning service covers all of Europe – twenty-one countries and one million kilometres of highways and byways – enabling you to plot many different itineraries from wherever you are. The itinerary options allow you to choose a preferred route, for example, quickest, shortest, or Michelin-recommended.

The network is updated three times weekly, integrating ongoing road works, detours, new motorways, and snowbound mountain passes.

The description of the itinerary includes the distances and travelling times between towns, selected hotels and restaurants.

SALAMANCA★★★

Castilla y León (Salamanca) – Population 166 322
Michelin map 441 and 444 J 12-13

Salamanca is a lovely university city of golden stone, narrow streets, splendid buildings and exuberant rich façades; it is a city of domes and spires with a long tradition of learning still youthfully alive.

HISTORICAL NOTES

The tumultuous past – Iberian in origin, Salamanca was conquered by Hannibal in the 3C BC, flourished under the Romans who built the **Puente Romano** (Roman bridge) **(AZ)** across the Tormes, and invaded repeatedly by the Moors. Alfonso VI took the city from the Moors in 1085. It recovered only to be troubled in the 14C and 15C by rivalry among the nobility whose younger members formed factions known as **Los Bandos**. Such was the vendetta spirit that when two Monroy brothers of the Sant Tomé Bando were killed by Manzano brothers of the San Benito Bando after an argument at a game of *pelota*, their mother, Doña María, and the Santo Tomé faction immediately took their revenge, planting the decapitated Manzano heads triumphantly on the Monroy tomb – after which the mother was known as **María La Brava**. Her 15C house, which remains to this day **(BY Q)**, can be found in the lively Plaza de los Bandos with its numerous 19C buildings. The *bandos* remained active until 1476.

Salamanca was occupied by the French during the War of Independence; when the French evacuated the town, Wellington entered it in June 1812 but within days had moved south to the **Arapiles Valley** where, on 22 July, he won the resounding Victory of Salamanca which proved to be a major turning point in the war.

La Universidad – The university was founded in 1215 (Oxford University, c 1167) and grew under the patronage of kings of Castilla, high dignitaries and learned men such as the antipope Benedict XIII. Its teaching was soon widely renowned (it took part in the reform of the Catholic Church) and by the 16C it numbered 70 professors of studies and 12 000 students.

Its great and famous members include the Infante Don Juan, son of the Catholic Monarchs; St John of the Cross and his teacher, the great humanist **Fray Luis de León** (1527-91); and **Miguel de Unamuno** (1864-1936), Professor of Greek, University Rector and philosopher of international standing.

The artistic flowering – In the late 15C and early 16C, two major painters were working in Salamanca: **Fernando Gallego**, one of the best Hispano-Flemish artists (much influenced in precision of line and realism by Dirk Bouts) and **Juan of Flanders** (b 1465), who settled in the city in 1504 and whose elegant and gentle work is outstanding for the subtle delicacy of its colours.

The 15C also saw the evolution of the original Salamanca *patio* arch, a mixtilinear arc in which the line of the curve, inspired by Mudéjar design, is broken by counter curves and straight lines. The 16C brought decoration to an ebullient climax in Plateresque art, the purest examples of which may be seen in Salamanca.

A secular tradition

The red inscriptions which appear on most of the town's monuments, in particular those of the university, are part of an old tradition that dates back to the 15C: on graduating, students would take part in a bullfight and, with the blood of the bull they had killed, write the word Victor and the date on a wall. Today the same is done with paint.

WHERE TO STAY

BUDGET HOTELS

Hotel Emperatriz (BY ❺) – *Compañía, 44.* ☎ *923 21 92 00/01/02, fax 923 21 92 01. 61 rooms.*
The name of the street refers to the Society of Jesus, as the Clerecía is located just a few yards from this hotel, which caters mainly to students. The façade has a noble appearance, yet the interior is somewhat simple in style.

Hostal Plaza Mayor (BY ❻) – *Plaza del Corrillo, 20.* ☎ *923 26 20 20, fax 923 21 75 48. 19 rooms.*
Ideal if you want to stay in the centre of Salamanca as it is situated just behind Plaza Mayor, opposite the Romanesque church of San Martín. The hotel's interior design highlights the main features of the house, such as its attractive wooden beams.

OUR SELECTION

Hotel Residencia Rector (BZ ❷) – *Rector Esparbé, 10.* ☎ *923 21 84 8* *fax 923 21 40 08. 14 rooms.*

A small luxury hotel with spectacular views of the cathedral and elega well-appointed rooms.

Palacio Castellanos (BZ ❶) – *San Pablo, 58.* ☎ *923 26 18 19, fax 923 26 18* *62 rooms.*

A combination of the modern comforts of the NH hotel chain and charm of a 15C palace. The Hispano-Flemish *patio* in the reception a is from this period, while the eclectic façade dates from the last th of the 19C. The contemporary paintings on the walls are in sh contrast to this, as is the modern design of the hotel's bedrooms. Hig recommended.

EATING OUT

Restaurants

Mesón Cervantes – *Plaza Mayor, 15.* ☎ *923 21 72 13.*

A bar with typical Castilian decor and fine views of plaza Mayor serv modern, innovative cuisine. Popular with Salamanca's young crowd night.

Río de la Plata – *Plaza del Peso,1.* ☎ *923 21 90 05.*

This is a small restaurant which has been steadily gaining in popularity. If y have to wait, why not take advantage of the bars nearby to enjoy some tap or perhaps have a drink in the restaurant bar.

Chez Victor – *Espoz y Mina, 26.* ☎ *923 21 31 23.*

Fine French cuisine in the heart of Castille. An elegant setting.

Tapas

La Covachuela – *Portales de San Antonio, 24.*

One of the best places for tapas in Salamanca, located behind plaza Mayor. its address would suggest, it is a tiny bar full of history where you can typical Salamanca dishes such as *chanfaina* (a liver and lung stew) and *hue farinatos* (eggs with sausage).

La Galería del Vino – *Plaza del Peso, 8-9.*

A modern bar where you can enjoy a pleasant glass of wine and var tapas.

Restaurante Río Tormes – *Plaza del Corrillo, 20.* ☎ *923 21 13 23.*

Excellent tapas in this Castilian-style restaurant.

La Tostita – *Plaza de San Marcos.* ☎ *923 26 25 98.*

A new generation of bar specializing in wines and toasted snacks. Why enjoy some delicious tapas on its pleasant terrace in summer ?

Prada a Tope – *Arco, 12-14.* ☎ *923 26 17 98.*

A shop with simple decor offering tastings of a wide range of products fr the Bierzo region. A paradise for tapas fans.

Cafés

Café Novelty – *Plaza Mayor, 2.*

A famous Salamanca café where Miguel de Unamuno used to meet his frier and colleagues. The wooden chairs and marble tables conjure up images of philosopher engaged in animated discussion. Its terrace on plaza Mayor off a wonderful view of one of Spain's finest squares.

Café Tío vivo – *Clavel, 5.*

The name originates from the *tío vivo* (merry-go-round) on the bar. cine-camera, spotlights and the objects decorating the bar give it an Americ feel.

Capitán Haddock – *Concejo, 13-15.*

The entrance is through a narrow passageway which gives us no hint of stylish decor and subdued lighting inside.

La Posada de las Almas – *Plaza de San Boal, 7.*

A journey back to the childhood of our grandparents. A café with a predilect for dolls' houses.

La Regenta – *Espoz y Mina, 19.*

An older feel than the previous four. A typical café with a 19C atmosphe

MONUMENTAL CENTRE

1 day. Follow the itinerary on the town plan.

Plaza Mayor (BY) – Plaza Mayor is unquestionably the life and soul of Salamanca. All the city's major streets converge on the square, where locals and visitors alike meet for a drink at its lively café terraces or for an evening stroll. It was built for the city by Philip V between 1729 and 1755 in gratitude for its support in the War of Succession, is among the finest in Spain. It was designed as a homogeneous unit principally by the Churriguera brothers: four ground level arcades with rounded arches decorated by a series of portrait medallions of the Spanish kings from Alfonso XI to Ferdinand VI and famous men such as Cervantes, El Cid, Christopher Columbus and Cortés support the three storeys which rise in perfect formation to an elegant balustrade. On the north and east sides are the pedimented fronts of the Ayuntamiento (town hall) and the Pabellón Real (Royal Pavilion), the latter distinguished by a bust of Philip V.

Plaza Mayor

Iglesia de San Martín (BY) – The Romanesque church has a north door with dog-tooth covings in the Zamora style.

Casa de las Conchas (House of Shells) (BY) – This 15C house with its 400 scallop shells, carved in the same golden stone as the wall, its line of highly decorative Isabelline windows and lower down, beautiful wrought-iron window grilles, composes a timelessly decorative and unique façade. its interior now house a public library. The *patio* has delicate mixtilinear arches, openwork balustrades, carved lions' heads and coats of arms. The view of the Clerecía from the top of the stairs is particularly attractive.

Clerecía ⓥ (BY) – This impressive Jesuit College was begun in 1617 and was only finished with the completion of the Baroque towers by Andrés García de Quiñones in 1755. There are Baroque cloisters beside the church.

Patio de las Escuelas (Schools' Square) (BZ) – This small square, off the old Calle Libreros, is surrounded by the best examples of Salamanca Plateresque. A bronze statue of Fray Luis de León stands in the middle of the square. The former university principals' residence is now home to the **Museo Unamuno** ⓥ, a museum dedicated to this famous philospher.

Universidad ⓥ (U) – The university's sumptuous **entrance**★★★ of 1534 is a brilliant piece of sculpture, composed with the utmost care for detail, as in the goldsmith's art. Above the twin doors, covered by basket arches, the carving is in ever greater relief as it rises through the three registers, to compensate for the increasing

313

distance from the ground. A central medallion in the first register shows
Catholic monarchs who presented the doorway; in the second, above crow
escutcheons and medallions, are portrait heads in scallop shell niches; in the th
flanking the Pope supported by cardinals, are Venus and Hercules (in sqi
frames) and the Virtues (in roundels). The most famous motif in this outstandi
ensemble is the death's head surmounted by a frog (on the right pilaster, half-
up) symbolising the posthumous punishment of lust.

The lecture halls are located around the **patio**: the **Paraninfo** or Large Hall, wl
official functions were held, is hung with 17C Brussels tapestries and a porti
of Charles IV from Goya's studio; the hall where Fray Luis de León lecture
theology, is as it was in the 16C with the professor's desk and sounding-bc
overlooking the rough-hewn students' benches – a luxury in days when stude
usually sat on the floor. Fray Luis' ashes are buried in the chapel (1767).

The grand staircase rises beneath star vaulting, its banister carved with foli
scrollwork and imaginary scenes and, at the third flight, a mounted bullfig
A gallery on the first floor has its original, rich, coffered ceiling with stalac
ornaments and a delicate low relief frieze along the walls. A still Gothic style d
with a fine 16C grille opens into the 18C library which contains 40 000 16C-
volumes as well as incunabula and manuscripts, some of which date back to the 1

Hospital del Estudio (Students' Hospice) – Now the University Rectorate.
hospice, completed in 1533, has an interesting Gothic entrance with
basket-handle arches. Visible on its upper part are two escutcheons of Sp
made before 1492 given that the pomegranate, the symbol of the Catl
monarchs, does not feature on them, and a trefoil arch framed by an *alfiz*.

Escuelas Menores (Minors' Schools) ⊙ (**U¹**) – Standing to the right of the hospital
crowned by the same openwork Renaissance frieze, is the entrance to the Min
Schools – a Plateresque portal decorated with coats of arms, roundels
scrollwork. The typical Salamanca **patio★★** (1428) inside, has lovely lines. To
right of the entrance is a new exhibition room with a fine Mudéjar ceiling;
University Museum opposite exhibits what remains of the ceiling painted
Fernando Gallego for the former university library. This section of the **Ciel
Salamanca★** (Salamanca Sky) illustrates constellations and signs of the zodiac.
interest of this remaining part gives an idea of what the whole must have b
like in the 15C. Several works by Juan of Flanders and Juan of Burgundy st
out in the museum.

★★ **Catedral Nueva (New Cathedral)** ⊙ (**BZ**) – Construction, begun in 1513, was larg
completed by 1560, although additions continued to be made until the 18
hence the variety of architectural styles: Gothic, Renaissance and Baroque.
The **west front★★★** is divided below the windows into four wide bays wl
correspond to the ground plan. The bays are outlined by pierced stonewc
carved as minutely as the keystones in the arches, the friezes and pinna
balustrades. The Gothic decoration of the central portal, which in retable s
includes scenes such as a Crucifixion shown between St Peter and St P
overflows the covings and tympanum.

The north doorway, facing the Colegio de Anaya, is adorned with a delicate
relief of Christ's entry into Jerusalem (Palm Sunday). The lower section of the
archivolt contains the somewhat surprising figure of a small astronaut.

The **interior**, in particular the pattern of the vaulting, the delicacy of the
nices and the sweep of the pillars, strikes one immediately on entering.
eight windows in the lantern are given added effect by a drum on wl
scenes from the Life of the Virgin were painted in the 18C by the Churrig
brothers who also designed the ornate Baroque stalls in the *coro*, the *trascoro*
organ loft above the stalls on the north side; the south loft is Plateresque (15

★★★ **Catedral Vieja (Old Cathedral)** ⊙ (**BZ**) – *Enter through the first bay off the sc
aisle in the new cathedral.* Fortunately the builders of the new cathedral respec
the fabric of the old which, nevertheless, is almost totally masked outside by
larger descendant. It was built in the 12C and is a good example of
Romanesque, the pointed arching being a legitimate, if unusual, innovation;
cimborrio (lantern), or Torre del Gallo, with two tiers of windows and ribbing
outstanding. High up beneath the vaulting, the capitals are carved with scene
tournaments and imaginary animals. The Capilla de San Martín (St Mart
Chapel) at the base of the tower is covered in 13C frescoes by Antón Sanche:
Segovia.

The **altarpiece★★** in the central apsidal chapel was painted by Nicholas of Flore
in 1445 and comprises 53 compartments decorated in surprisingly fresh cold
in vivid detail – an interesting testimony to the architecture and dress of the ti
– beneath a Last Judgement in which the dark background enhances the brillia
of the Risen Christ. The Virgin of the Vega at the retable centre is a 12C woc
statue, plated in gilded and enamelled bronze.

Recesses in the south transept contain French influenced 13C recumbent fig
and frescoes.

SALAMANCA

Álvaro Gil . . . . BY 3
Anaya (Pl.) . . . . BZ 4
Ángel (Pl.) . . . . BY 6
Azafranal . . . . CY
Bandos (Pl. de los) . . . . . . BY 7
Bordadores . . . . BY 9
Caldereros . . . . BZ 10
Calderón de la Barca . . . . . BY 12
Carmen (Cuesta del) . . . . . BY 13
Casas (Pl. de las) . . . . BY 15
Comuneros (Av. de los) . . . CY 16
Concilio de Trento . . . . BZ 18
Condes de Crespo Rascón . BY 19
Constitución (Pl. de la) . . . . CY 21

Corrillo (Pl.) . . . . BY 22
Dr. Torres Villarroel
 (Paseo del) . . . . BY 25
Espoz y Mina . . . . BY 28
Estación (Paseo de la) . . . . CY 30
Federico Anaya (Av. de) . . . CY 31
Filiberto Villalobos (Av. de) . AY 33
Fray Luis de Granada . . . . . BY 34
Fuente (Pl. de la) . . . . BY 36
Juan de la Fuente . . . . BZ 37
Libertad (Pl. de la) . . . . BY 39
Libreros . . . . BZ 40
Maria Auxiliadora . . . . CY 42
Marquesa de Almarza . . . . . CZ 43
Maléndez . . . . BY 45
Mayor (Pl.) . . . . BY
Monterrey (Pl. de) . . . . BY 46
Palominos . . . . BZ 51

Patio Chico . . . . BZ 52
Peso (Pl. del) . . . . BY 57
Pozo Amarillo . . . . BY 58
Ramón y Cajal . . . . AY 60
Reina (Pl. de la) . . . . CY 61
Reyes de España (Av.) . . . . BZ 63
San Blas . . . . AY 64
San Isidro (Pl. de) . . . . BYZ 66
San Julián (Pl.) . . . . CY 67
Santa Eulalia (Pl.) . . . . CY 69
Santa Teresa (Pl. de) . . . . . BY 70
Santo Domingo (Pl.) . . . . . . BZ 72
Sancti Spiritus (Cuesta) . . . CY 75
Serranos . . . . BZ 76
Toro . . . . BCY
Tostado . . . . BZ 78
Wences Moreno . . . . BY 79
Zamora . . . . BY

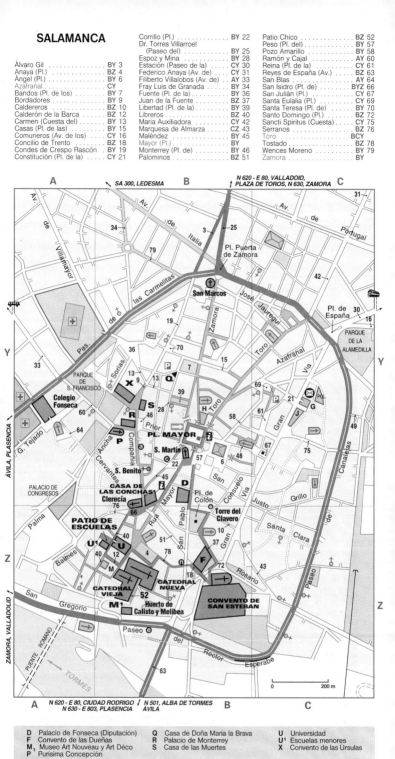

D Palacio de Fonseca (Diputación)
F Convento de las Dueñas
M₁ Museo Art Nouveau y Art Déco
P Purisima Concepción
Q Casa de Doña Maria la Brava
R Palacio de Monterrey
S Casa de las Muertes
U Universidad
U¹ Escuelas menores
X Convento de las Úrsulas

Claustro – Some of the capitals from earlier Romanesque galleries destroyed during the Lisbon earthquake in 1755 remain in these cloisters, forming a surprising contrast to the Plateresque decoration. The adjoining **Capilla de Talavera** with a Mudéjar dome on carved ribs was where the ancient Mozarabic rite was celebrated – the altarpiece is in the style of Pedro Berruguete. The Capilla de Santa Barbara was formerly used for university examinations. A museum occupying three rooms and the Capilla de Santa Catalina contains works by Fernando Gallego and his brother Francisco as well as others by Juan of Flanders (St Michael altarpiece).

315

The **Capilla Anaya** contains the outstanding 15C alabaster **tomb**★★ of Diego de Anaya, archbishop first of Salamanca and then of Sevilla. The sides are decorated with saints and their emblems. Surrounding the tomb is a magnificently wrought Plateresque grille. There is also a 15C **organ**★ and the superb 16C recumbent statues of Gutierre de Monroy and Constancia de Anaya.

From the **Patio Chico** (**BZ 52**) you can see the old cathedral apse and the scallop tiling on the **Torre del Gallo** (Cock Tower). From here, calle Arcediano leads to the delightful **Huerto de Calixto y Melibea** ⓥ (**AZ**).

Museo Art Nouveau y Art Déco ⓥ (**BZ M¹**) – This modern art museum is housed in the Casa Lis, a Modernist building dating from the beginning of the century. It is one of the few museums in Spain devoted to Art Nouveau and Art Deco. Its collection includes works by R Lalique, vases by E Galle and small sculptures by Hagenauer. The view of the building from the Tormes river is particularly impressive.

★ **Convento de San Esteban** (St Stephen's Monastery) ⓥ (**BZ**) – Gothic and Renaissance styles are mingled in this 16C and 17C building, so that while typically Gothic pinnacles decorate the side buttresses, nothing could be more Plateresque in style than the sculpture of the impressive **façade**★★. The low relief of the Martyrdom of St Stephen is by Juan Antonio Ceroni (1610).

★ **Claustro** – In these cloisters, note the prophets' heads in **medallions** and the grand staircase (1553).

Iglesia – The large church has star vaulting in the gallery and a central altarpiece by José Churriguera with an abundance of carving and gilt decoration. Crowning it is a painting The Martyrdom of St Stephen, by Claudio Coello.

Convento de las Dueñas

Convento de las Dueñas ⊘ (BZ F) – The Renaissance **cloisters**★★ of this convent have profusely carved capitals which are extraordinarily forceful in spite of their small size. Among the sculptures are the figures of symbolic animals, distorted human shapes as well as medallions decorated with the heads of majestic old men or delicately featured women.

Torre del Clavero (BYZ) – The tower, all that remains of a castle built in 1450, is an octagonal keep, crowned with sentry turrets decorated underneath with Mudéjar trellis-work.

Palacio de Fonseca or **Diputación** (Fonseca Palace or Council) (BY D) – The **patio**★ of this Renaissance palace combines Salamanca mixtilinear arches at one end with a corbelled gallery – supported by distorted atlantes – on the right and an arcade on the left in which the capitals resemble those in the Convento de las Dueñas. The view of the palace is particularly pleasant at night.

ADDITIONAL SIGHTS

Plaza de San Benito (San Benito Quarter) (BY) – Surrounding this delightful square, at the centre of which stands the **Iglesia de San Benito** (BY), are the mansions of Salamanca's old noble rival families. The church itself, dating from 1490, was the Maldonado family pantheon.

Iglesia de la Purísima Concepción (Church of the Immaculate Conception) ⊘ (BY P) – The church contains works by Ribera, including one of his most famous paintings, the **Immaculate Conception**★, which hangs above the high altar.

Palacio de Monterrey (BY R) – The typical Renaissance palace (1539), has an openwork balustrade crowning a long top floor gallery, between corner towers.

Casa de las Muertes (House of Death) (BY S) – The early-16C façade, one of the first examples of Plateresque, is attributed, complete with its design of medallions, foliated scrollwork and decorative putti, to Diego de Siloé.

Convento de las Úrsulas (Ursuline Convent) ⊘ (BY X) – The 16C church contains the **tomb**★ of Alonso de Fonseca on which the incredibly delicate carved low reliefs are attributed to Diego de Siloé. The **museum**, with its *artesonado* and coffered ceilings, houses panels and fragments of an altarpiece by Juan de Borgoña, one of which illustrates *St Ursula and the Virgins*. There are also two noteworthy works by Morales the Divine, an *Ecce Homo* and a *Pietà*.

Colegio Fonseca ⊘ (AY) – The college was built to plans by Diego de Siloé for Irish students in the 16C. A beautifully carved Plateresque door leads into a Gothic chapel with star vaulting. This contains a fine altarpiece by Alonso Berruguete. The **patio**★ is an elegant example of the Renaissance style.

Iglesia de San Marcos (St Mark's Church) (BY) – The 12C church's round shape was no doubt originally designed as protection against possible Moorish attack. Inside are fragmentary frescoes.

EXCURSIONS

Alba de Tormes – *23km/14mi southeast on N 501 and C 510.*
The small town stands on the banks of the wide Río Tormes. Only the massive keep remains of the castle of the dukes of Alba. The town boasts of possessing the mortal remains of St Teresa of Ávila in the church of the Carmelite Convent. The **Iglesia de San Juan**, a church with a Romanesque-Mudéjar east end, contains an outstanding 12C **sculpture**★ in the apse. It illustrates Christ and the Disciples seated in a semicircle, all equally noble in expression and stance.

Castillo del Buen Amor ⊘ – *21km/13mi north on N 630 then bear right onto a signposted private road.*
This fortified castle served as the Catholic monarchs' base in the early years when they were fighting supporters of La Beltraneja. Alonso II, Archbishop of Toledo, converted it into a palace, adding a pleasant Renaissance *patio* as a suitable setting for his mistress! Inside, note a Mudéjar fireplace and *artesonado* ceilings.

On the cover of Michelin Green Guides,
the coloured band on top indicates the language:
    blue for French
    pink for English
    yellow for German
    orange for Spanish
    green for Italian, etc.

SANGÜESA★

Navarra – Population 4 447

Michelin map 442 E 26

Sangüesa stands in arable country (mostly cereals) on the left bank of the Arag
river. It still seems to guard the bridge which in the Middle Ages brought the to
prosperity.

Sangüesa and the pilgrim way – Fear of the Moors compelled Sangüesans to l
until the 10C on the **Rocaforte** hillside; by the 11C, however, the citizens had mov
down to defend the bridge and clear a safe passage for pilgrims. In 1122, Alfons
of Aragón, the Battler, granted a *fuero* or charter to the town which then gr
rapidly. Sangüesa reached its climax at the end of the Middle Ages when, in contra
to the austere **Palacio del Príncipe de Viana** (Palace of the Prince of Viana), residence
the kings of Navarra, now the Ayuntamiento (town hall), with its façade (se
through the gateway) flanked by two imposing battlemented towers, prosperc
citizens began to build elegant residential mansions. The main street, the former F
Mayor which was once part of the pilgrim road, is lined with comfortable brick hous
with the Classical carved wood eaves and windows with rich Gothic or Plateresc
surrounds. In the second street on the right coming from the bridge can be seen t
Baroque front of the **Palacio de Vallesantoro**, a palace protected by monumen
overhangs carved with imaginary animals.

★ **Iglesia de Santa María la Real** – The church, begun in the 12C, was complet
in the 13C with the construction of the splendid south portal, the octagonal tow
and its spire.

★★ **Portada Sur** (South Portal) – Late-12C to 13C. The portal is so crowded wi
sculpture that one stands amazed at the number of subjects depicted and t
variety of ways in which they have been illustrated. At least two artists work
on the masterpiece: the Master of San Juan de la Peña and a certain Leodegari
The **statue columns**, already Gothic, derive from those at Chartres and Autun.
the **tympanum**, God the Father at the centre of a group of angel musicians receiv
at his right, the chosen, but with his down-pointing left arm reproves the sinne
In a corner weighing souls is St Michael.
The **covings** swarm with motifs; the second innermost shows the humbler trade
clogmaker, lutemaker and butcher.
The older **upper arches**, marked by an Aragonese severity of style, show G
surrounded by the symbols of the four Evangelists, two angels and the
disciples.

CASTILLO DE JAVIER ⊘ (JAVIER CASTLE)

7km/4mi northeast on NA 541.

St Francis Xavier, patron saint of Navarra, was born here in 1506. At 22, in Par
he met his Basque compatriot, Ignatius Loyola, with whom he was later
formulate the principles of the Society of Jesus. Xavier was sent by t
Portuguese who had considerable and well-established commercial interests wi
the Far East, as a missionary first to Goa and then to Japan. He died in 1552,
his way to China. He was canonised in 1622.

Castillo – The fortress, birthplace of the saint, was in part destroyed by Cardir
Cisneros in 1516. The visit includes the Patio de Armas (Parade Ground), the O
torio (Oratory), which contains a 13C Christ in walnut and an unusual 15C fresco
the Dance of Death, the Sala Grande (Great Hall) and, among the oldest parts of t
castle dating from the 10C-11C, the Cuarto del Santo (Saint's bedroom).

Santuario de SAN IGNACIO DE LOYOLA

País Vasco (Guipúzcoa)

Michelin map 442 C 23

A **santuario** (sanctuary) ⊘ was built by the Jesuits to plans by the Italian architect Ca
Fontana around the Loyola family manor-house near Azpeitia at the end of the 17
It has since become an important place of pilgrimage where large crowds attend t
solemnities held annually on St Ignatius day (31 July).

The Soldier of God – **Ignatius de Loyola** was born in 1491 in the Castillo de Loyola
an old family of the lesser nobility. He was bred to arms. It was while recovering fro
wounds received at the siege of Pamplona, that he heard the call of God and eig
months later, in 1522, left the Loyola manor to go on a pilgrimage to Arantzazu a
Montserrat. He next withdrew to a cave near Manresa in Catalunya where he beg
to write his **Spiritual Exercises**. In 1523 he set off in pilgrimage to Jerusalem fro
where, before returning to Spain, he journeyed to Paris (1528) and London (153c

ter further wanderings and attendance at various universities, he and the
mpatriots he had met in Paris, Diego Laínez and Francis Xavier, were ordained
537) and repaired to Rome. In 1540, the Pope recognised the **Society of Jesus** which
yola had conceived and for which he had drawn up the constitution.

natius of Loyola died in 1556 and was canonised in 1622 at the same time as
ancis Xavier and Teresa de Ávila.

SIGHTS

Santa Casa – The basement casemates of the 15C tower are vestiges of the
original Loyola manor-house. The rooms in which Ignatius was born, convalesced
and converted have been transformed into profusely decorated chapels.

Basílica – The Baroque basilica is more Italian than Spanish in style. It is
circular and surmounted by a vast cupola (65m/213ft high) attributed to
Churriguera.

Monasterio de SAN JUAN DE LA PEÑA★★

Aragón (Huesca)
Michelin map 443 E 27
Local map see JACA

ter a long climb through wild countryside in the Sierra de la Peña, the monastery
pears minute, in a hollow under overhanging rocks. The **site**★★ itself is spectacular.
e monastery, symbol of the continued existence of the Christian faith in the
rrenees at the time of the Muslim invasion, was chosen by the kings and nobles of
agón-Navarra as their pantheon. The community had been founded in the secluded
e in the 9C. In the 11C the order adopted the Cluniac reform. Generous royal
nations attracted many monks, some foreign, to the house.

the 17C, a second monastery was built higher up the mountainside.

TOUR ⊙ about 45min

Because of its age and extraordinary site lodged in the side of the mountain, the
monastery plan is unique.

Lower storey – This is partially underground and is believed to have been built
in the time of King Sancho Garcés in about 922.

Sala de Concilios – This council chamber, also known as the dormitory, has been built
in a massive architectural style.

Iglesia Baja (Lower Church) – This, the original church which later served as a crypt,
is one of the rare Mozarabic constructions still existing in the region. It consists
of two adjoining aisles divided by wide arches and ending in twin niche-apses
hollowed out of the living rock. Traces of mural painting can be seen on the walls
and on the undersides of the arches.

Upper storey – On reaching the upper storey, you enter the court of the pantheon
of the nobles.

Pantéon de Nobles Aragoneses (Pantheon of the Aragón nobility) – 11C-14C. Funerary
niches line the left wall in surrounds of moulded billets or pearls, each emblasoned
with a coat of arms, Chi-rho (sacred monogram) or a cross with four roses,
emblem of Iñigo Arista, founder of the Kingdom of Navarra. On one of the niches
an angel is shown carrying the soul of the deceased. A door opposite leads into
a **museum** which contains finds from the monastery excavations.

Iglesia Alta (Upper Church) – Late-11C. Rock roofs part of the single aisle, while the
three apsidal chapels, decorated with blind arcades, are hollowed out of the cliff
face.
The **Pantéon de Reyes** or Royal Pantheon, where the kings of Aragón and Navarra
were buried for 500 years, opens off the north wall. The present decor is 18C.

Claustro – 12C. A Mozarabic door serves as an entrance. The cloisters, cornered
between the precipice and the cliff face, which provides an unplanned roof, now
consist of two galleries only with historiated capitals and a third gallery in a poor
state of preservation.
The original column arrangement, alternating single, double or quadruple columns is reproduced in miniature between the capital abacuses and the arch billets.
The mason who carved the **capitals**★★ developed a personal style and Symbolism,
apparent in his chronological survey of man from the Creation to the coming of
the Evangelists, which was to influence sculpture throughout the region for years
to come.

EXCURSION

★ **Santa Cruz de la Serós** – *5km/3mi north.*
This famous convent, founded late in the 10C, was richly endowed by roy
princesses. The religious abandoned the convent in the 16C.
Only the **Romanesque church**, surrounded by small, typically Aragonese house
remains. The stout belfry, crowned by an octagonal turret abuts on the lanter
The portal with its Chi-rho (sacred monogram) decorated tympanum recalls th
of Jaca Cathedral.
Inside, a column and capitals have been assembled to form an unusual stoup

San Caprasio, the small church at the entrance to the village, has a nave adorn
with Lombard bands and a low apse, typical of the 11C. The belfry is la
12C.

SAN MARTÍN DE VALDEIGLESIAS

Madrid – Population 5 428
Michelin map 442 or 444 K 16

The old market town dominated by its castle walls serves as a departure point
local excursions.

EXCURSIONS

Toros de Guisando – *6km/4mi northwest.*
The *Bulls of Guisando*, as they are called, four rudimentarily carved figures
granite, stand in an open field. Similar figures may be seen throughout the p
vince of Ávila. They are,
however, obviously an-
cient and remain an
enigma in spite of the
possible theory that
they represent a com-
memorative monu-
ment, a Celtiberian
idol. They have certain
similarities to the
stone sows or *porcas*
that may be seen in vil-
lages in the Trás-os-
Montes region of
Portugal.

★ **Embalse de Burguillo**
(Burguillo Reservoir) –
20km/12mi northwest.
The man-made lake
on the Alberche river,
amid hills covered in

One of the Bulls of Guisando

sparse vegetation, provides a fine setting for water sports enthusiasts.

Pantano de San Juan – *8km/5mi east.*
As the road descends to this artificial lake there are attractive **views**★ of the narr
part of the Alberche reservoir where the banks are deeply indented and cover
in pine trees. The area is popular with Madrileños in summer on account of
water sports facilities.

Safari Madrid ⊘ – *27km/17mi southeast at* **Aldea del Fresno.**
This is one of Spain's largest game parks, where wild animals from the wo
over may be observed. The main attraction is a demonstration by birds
prey.

SAN SEBASTIÁN★★

See DONOSTIA

Monasterio de SANTA MARÍA DE HUERTA★★

Castilla y León (Soria)

Michelin map 442 I 23

In 1144, on the request of Emperor Alfonso VII, a Cistercian community came to settle in what was to become the Soria region on the border between Castilla and Aragón. Monks settled in Huerta in 1162 and shortly afterwards laid the foundations of the present buildings. The main initiators of the work, which continued until the late 13C, were the Abbot Martín de Finojosa and Rodrigo Jiménez de Roda. The sober Cistercian style was slightly modified by Renaissance innovations.

From 1835 to 1930 the monastery buildings stood empty before being re-inhabited and restored.

TOUR ⏱ *about 1hr*

The monastery is entered through a 16C **triumphal arch**.

Claustro herreriano (Herreran Cloisters) – 16C-17C. The buildings surrounding the cloisters are the monks' living quarters.

★ **Claustro de los Caballeros (Knights' Cloisters)** – 13C-16C. The cloisters owe their name to the many knights who lie buried there. The two storeys of the cloisters have very different styles: the arches at ground level are elegant, pointed and purely Gothic while above, the gallery added in the 16C has all the exuberance and imagination of the Plateresque *(it is a copy of the gallery in the Palacio de Avellaneda in Peñaranda de Duero)*. The decorative medallions are of prophets, Apostles and Spanish kings.

Sala de los Conversos (Laybrothers' Hall) – 12C. This is divided down its length by stout pillars, crowned with stylised capitals.

Cocina – The kitchen has a monumental central chimney.

★ **Refectorio** – The refectory, a masterpiece of 13C Gothic, impresses by its sheer size – it has sexpartite vaulting rising 15m/50ft above the 35m/115ft long hall – and the amount of light shining through the windows, in particular, the wonderful rose window in the south wall. Leading up to the **reader's lectern** is a beautiful staircase carved out of the wall with small arches supported by slender columns.

Iglesia – The church has been restored to its original state although the royal chapel has kept its sumptuous Churrigueresque decoration. Between the narthex and the aisles there is an intricate 18C wrought-iron screen.

Coro Alto – The choir is beautifully decorated with Renaissance panelling and woodwork. The Talavera *azulejos* on the floor are very old.

SANTANDER★

Cantabria – Population 196 218

Michelin map 442 B 18

Santander has a beautiful site along the north shore of a great bay closed by the narrow Magdalena headland and the sandy Somo point. The added advantage of extensive sand beaches makes it one of Cantabria's most sophisticated resorts. Its famous International University courses held in the summer and its music and dance festival make it all the more prestigious.

The new town – A tornado struck Santander on 15 February 1941: the sea swept over the quays and a fire broke out, devastating the entire centre of the town. Reconstruction was undertaken to a street plan of blocks of no more than four or five storeys; space was allocated to gardens beside the sea and promenades such as the Paseo de Pereda which skirts the pleasure boat harbour known as Puerto Chico. The heart of the town is around the Avenida de Calvo Sotelo, with its shops, and Plaza Porticada. The port developed from the natural advantage of the immense sheltered bay. Trade diversified over the centuries as local industries developed, particularly steel, chemicals and shipbuilding in **El Astillero**.

SIGHTS

Catedral ⊙ – The edifice at the top of the rise looks more like a fortress, eve
after the rebuilding in Gothic style following the 1941 tornado. Inside, the **font**
the right of the ambulatory is obviously a Muslim ablutionary basin.
The 12C **crypt** *(access through the south portal)* has three low aisles separated b
solid cruciform pillars. The Gothic cloisters have been considerably restored.

★ **Museo Regional de Prehistoria y Arqueología** ⊙ – The archeological museu
in the basement of the Diputación consists mainly of finds excavated
prehistoric caves in Cantabria (particularly El Castillo and El Pendo). The riche:
period is the Upper Paleolithic Era from which there are bones engraved wit
animal silhouettes and **batons**★ made of horn and finely decorated for a purpos
still unknown. The best specimen, made from an antler, was discovered at l
Pendo.
Among the Neolithic axeheads, note the particularly high polish on those o
diorite. Four large steles are representative of the apogee of the Cantabria
culture (Bronze Age). Finally, one gallery is devoted to remains of the Roma
occupation. The finds are mostly from Julióbriga *(see REINOSA: Excursions)* ar
Castro Urdiales and include coins, bronzes and pottery figurines.

Biblioteca Menéndez y Pelayo ⊙ – Marcelino Menéndez y Pelayo (1856-1912
Spanish and universal savant, amassed this fabulous collection of near
45 000 books, including manuscripts by great Castilian authors. The librar
bequeathed by the writer to his native town and since enlarged, is opposite h
house.

Museo de Bellas Artes (Fine Arts Museum) ⊙ – Works by Goya including a portra
of *Ferdinand VII*, some of his *Disasters of War*, *La Tauromaquia* and *Caprichc
etchings, are displayed along with works by regional painters.

★★ EL SARDINERO

At the end of the 19C the Spanish royal family took to sea bathing at Santande
making both the pastime and the town highly fashionable. The town went so fa
as to build the **Palacio de Magdalena** on the point of the same name for Alfonso XI
– now the International University annexe. Summer visitors have the choice
several beaches along the promontory, along the Magdalena headland an
bordering El Sardinero, three areas divided at high tide by tongues of land brillia
with flower gardens but when the tide recedes, linked by a long sand bank. Wat
sports, theatrical and other entertainments, the casino and golf course (
Pedreña, across the bay) are supplemented in July by further events, including th
great Santiago festival of bullfighting and throughout August by a festival
drama, music and dance.

The beach at El Sardinero

EXCURSIONS

Cabo Mayor - *7km/4mi north.* Good view from the lighthouse on this cape.

Murriedas - *7km/4mi south on the Burgos road.* The house of Pedro Velarde, hero of the War of Independence, has been restored and is now the home of the **Museo Etnográfico de Cantabria** (Cantabrian Ethnographic Museum) ⊙. A typical, Cantabrian gateway opens onto grounds in which may be seen a *hórreo* (squat drying shed) from the Liébana region and a Cantabrian stele. The 17C residence contains furniture, utensils and tools from all parts of the province. Mementoes of Velarde are displayed in his former bedroom and another large room on the first floor.

Parque de la Naturaleza de Cabárceno (Cabárceno Nature Reserve) ⊙ - *17km/11mi south, at El Astillero.* An old iron mine in the Sierra de Cabarga that had been worked from Roman times until 1989, is now part of an environmental rehabilitation project which includes a **game park** where animals from the world over may be seen.

Monasterio de SANT CUGAT DEL VALLÈS★★

Catalunya (Barcelona) – Population 38 834

Michelin map 443 H 36

The town is named after the Benedictine **monastery** ⊙ established in the Middle Ages on the site of an earlier chapel. This had been built very early to contain the relics of St Cucufas whose throat had been cut by Diocletian's legionaries on this spot eight Roman miles along the road from Barcelona around AD 304. Of the former walls there remain the church, at present used as a parish church, the cloisters and the chapter-house, now serving as a chapel, the Capilla del Santísimo. The rectory, formerly the Abbot's residence, is a Gothic building that was converted in the 18C.

★ **Iglesia** – This is a telling example of the transitional period between Romanesque and Gothic. The oldest part of the church is the 11C belfry decorated with Lombard bands incorporated into the main building when the side chapels were built (15C). A chancel had already been added in the 12C. The façade was completed in 1350. The flat, crenellated wall supported by thrusting buttresses was relieved by a radiating rose window as vast as the doorway below with its smooth covings. There are three apses, polygonal outside and with engaged pillars inside; the central one was given radiating vaulting, a feature which was to mark an alteration in style, reflected in the ogival vaulting in the lantern and above the three aisles. Among the works of art, note the 14C **All Saints Altarpiece★** by Pere Serra.

★ **Claustro** – The cloisters are among the largest Romanesque cloisters in Catalunya. During the 11C-12C a double row of columns (144 in all) was built around a close; in the 16C an upper gallery was added above a blind arcade decorated with sculpted modillions. The skilfully carved **Romanesque capitals★** are Corinthian (acanthus leaves), ornamental (strapwork), figurative (birds) and historiated (biblical scenes); these last ones are grouped largely in the south gallery which abuts the church. The most interesting of all, however, is the one over the northeast corner column on which the sculptor, Arnaud Cadell, portrayed himself at work and then cut his name.

Monasterio de SANTES CREUS★★★

Catalunya (Tarragona)

Michelin map 443 H 34

Approached from the south, the Monasterio de Santes Creus appears as a vast complex of buildings set in undulating countryside. The monastery, pendant to Poblet, was founded shortly after the latter in the 12C. It was placed in the care of Cistercians from Toulouse, came under the protection of the great families of Catalunya and into the favour of the kings of Aragón who appointed the abbot royal chaplain. The splendours of the Middle Ages were followed, as at Poblet, by the ravages of the 19C with the difference that at Santes Creus, worship never ceased in the church. Santes Creus hosts an interesting Festival of Classical and Sacred Music as well as an International Competition for Gregorian Chant.

TOUR ⓥ *2hr*

The monastery plan is similar to that of Poblet in that it has three perimete
walls. A Baroque gateway leads to the principal courtyard where the monast
buildings, enhanced with fine sgraffiti, now serve as shops and priva
residences. To the right is the abbatial palace, with its attractive *patio*, whic
is now the town hall; at the end stands the 12C-13C church. The façade is pla
apart from a rounded doorway, a large Gothic window and battlements adde
a century later.

*** **Gran Claustro (Great Cloisters)** – Construction began in the year 1313 on top c
earlier cloisters, of which there remain a fountain as well as the chapter-hous
The ornamentation, consisting of capitals and bands, is a perfect illustration c
Gothic motifs: plants and flowers, animals, biblical, mythological and satiric
themes. The scenes are executed with remarkable refinement and creativenes
The **Puerta Real** or Royal Gate on the south side of the church opens onto cloiste
with Gothic bays which, although much restored, still have lively carvings – not
the illustration of Adam and Eve on the first corner frieze where Eve
shown emerging out of Adam's rib, and the fine tracery of the arches. I
contrast, the transitional style of the **lavabo**, which incorporates a marble basi
appears almost clumsy. Carved tombs of the Catalan nobility fill the galler
niches.

The Great Cloisters

Sala capitular – This chapter-house is an elegant hall with arches supported on four pillars. The pure, sober lines of the walls, vaulting and arches create an overall impression of harmony. Abbots' tombstones have been inlaid in the pavement.

Dormitorio – Stairs next to the chapter-house lead to the 12C dormitory, a long gallery divided by diaphragm arches supporting a timber roof presently used as a concert hall.

Iglesia – The church, begun in 1174, closely follows the Cistercian pattern of a flat east end and overall austerity; the square ribbed ogive vaulting, replacing the more usual broken barrel vaulting, does nothing to soften its severity. The lantern (14C), the stained glass in the great west window, and the superb apsidal **rose window**★, partially hidden by the high altar retable, do, however, relieve the bareness. The ribbed vaults rest on pillars which extend back along the walls and end in unusual consoles with rich corbelling. Gothic canopies at the transept openings shelter the **royal tombs**★★: on the north side that of Peter the Great (c 1295, III of Aragón, II of Barcelona – 14C) and on the south, that of his son, James II, the Just, and his Queen, Blanche d'Anjou. The Plateresque decoration below the crowned recumbent figures in Cistercian habits, was added in the 16C.

Claustro Viejo – Although they were built during the 17C, these "old cloisters" occupy the site of former cloisters dating back to the 12C. The design of the old cloisters is simple with a small central fountain and four cypresses in the close, imparting a cool, contemplative atmosphere. Leading off the cloisters are the cellar *(right of the entrance)*, kitchens and refectory and beyond, the royal palace (note the splendid 14C **patio**★).

SANTIAGO DE COMPOSTELA★★★

Galicia (La Coruña) – Population 105 851

Michelin map 441 D 4

the Middle Ages, Santiago de Compostela, the third most important city of grimage after Jerusalem and Rome, attracted pilgrims from all parts of Europe ee *The Way of Saint James below)*. It remains one of Spain's most remar- ble cities with old quarters, churches, conventual buildings and an air at once cient, mystical and, on account of the 32 000 or so students at the University, ely.

ntrary to all expectations, the style of architecture that edominates is not Romanesque but Baroque and neo- assical which lends an air of solemnity to the town. is can be best appreciated from the Paseo de la rradura.

gend and history – The Apostle James the Greater, own as the Thunderer on account of his temper, ossed the seas, so the legend goes, to convert Spain to ristianity. His boat was cast ashore at the mouth of the la and he preached for seven years throughout the land fore returning to Judaea where he fell an early victim to rod Agrippa. His disciples, forced to flee, returned to ain with his body which they buried near the earlier nding place. Invasions by the Barbarians and later the abs caused the grave to be lost to memory.

rly in the 9C a star is believed to have pointed out the ave to some shepherds. This legend was to reinforce e theory that Compostela derived from *campus stellae* field of stars although a more recent thesis, following e discovery of a necropolis beneath the cathedral, holds at the derivation is from *compostela*, the Latin for metery.

844 Don Ramiro I was leading a handful of Spaniards in bold attack against the Moors grouped at **Clavijo** near groño, when a knight in armour mounted on a charger d bearing a white standard with a red cross upon it, is said have appeared on the battlefield. As he beat back the fidels the Christians recognised St James, naming him om that time *Matamoros* or Slayer of the Moors. The conquest and Spain had found a patron saint. During the usade the Lord of Pimentel, it is said, had to swim across a a. He emerged from the sea covered in shells which were en adopted as the pilgrim symbol.

J.Hidalgo – C.Lopesino/MARCO POLO

Saint James the Greater

325

WHERE TO STAY

BUDGET HOTELS

Hostal Pico Sacro (V ❸) – *San Francisco, 22.* ☎ *981 58 44 66. 12 rooms.*
Small, modest *hostal* with the major advantage of being just a stone's thr
from the Plaza del Obradoiro.

Casa do Cruceiro – *Raíces, Ames.* ☎ *981 54 85 96, fax 981 54 85*
6 rooms.
This country house 7km/4mi from Santiago is the perfect answer for the
in search of peace and tranquility. The service is excellent, the deco
combination of rustic and English touches. The hotel also has a pleasant po
and a small swimming pool.

OUR SELECTION

Hogar San Francisco (V ❻) – *Campillo del Convento de San Francisco,*
☎ *981 57 25 64/57 27 64, fax 981 57 19 16. 71 rooms.*
The hotel is located in what used to be the Monasterio de San Francisco.
location and price make it a good choice for your stay in the city. Comfortab
simply furnished rooms. The Museo de Tierra Santa (Holy Land Museum
housed inside the convent.

TREAT YOURSELF!

Hostal de los Reyes Católicos – *Pr. do Obradoiro, 1.* ☎ *981 58 22*
fax 981 56 30 94. 130 rooms.
The former Royal Hospital founded by the Catholic monarchs in 1499 has n
been converted into a luxury parador. Particularly worthy of note are its in
patios which trace the typology of hospitals in the 16C.

EATING OUT

Toñi Vicente – *Rosalía de Castro, 24.* ☎ *981 59 41 00.*
The gastronomic symbol of Santiago. A sober design, pastel shades a
excellent cuisine. Popular with personalities from the world of politics.

San Clemente – *San Clemente, 6.* ☎ *981 58 08 82.*
Very close to the cathedral but in a quiet part of the city off the tourist tra
Excellent fish.

Mesón A Lareira – *Rúa do Vilar, 11.* ☎ *981 57 62 28.*
A modern style and decor in one of Santiago's most colourful streets. Pleasa
terrace during the summer months.

0'42 – *Franco, 42.* ☎ *981 58 10 09.*
One of the city's famous addresses, located in a street with more restaura
than any other in Santiago. Rustic decor and an ideal place for tapas.

Prada a Tope – *La Troya, 10.* ☎ *981 58 19 09.*
A restaurant specializing in dishes from the Bierzo. The Prada pri
itself on the fact that all its products are fresh. An excellent address
enjoy dishes such as *boteiro*
(a local stew), washed
down with some excellent
house wines.

Bars and Cafés

Cafetería Paradiso – *Rúa do
Vilar, 29* – A café with a 19C
atmosphere.

Café Derby Bar – *Rúa das
Orfas, 29* – A timeless bar
said to be popular with Valle
Inclán.

Café Literario – *Praza da
Quintana* – A stylishly-deco-
rated café with a young clientele, located at the top of
a flight of steps with a fine
view of both the square and
the cathedral.

Café Universal – *Plaza de la
Universidad* – Opposite the
university's Faculty of
History. Student ambience.

Rúa do Vilar

Vinatería Don Pinario – *Plazuela de San Martín* – A combination of interesti
designs and a good selection of wines in this delightful square.

PRACTICAL INFORMATION

ourist Office - *Rúa do Vilar, 43*, ☎ 981 58 40 81.

Municipal Tourist Office - *Praza de Galicia s/n*, ☎ 981 58 44 00.

antiago 7 días - A free monthly publication with information on shopping, ntertainment, cultural events and leisure activities. Available from the ourist office.

Transport

irport - Labacolla, at Km 11 on the Santiago-Lugo road. ☎ 981 54 75 00. bus service operates to the airport from the junction of calle General ardiñas and calle República del Salvador, ☎ 981 58 18 15. **IBERIA**, ☎ 981 59 75 50; **AIR EUROPA**, ☎ 981 59 49 50; **SPANAIR**, ☎ 902 13 14 15.

rains - The **RENFE** station is on the Calle del Hórreo, ☎ 981 52 02 02.

ter-city buses - There are several bus stations in Santiago. The main ones re as follows: **Estación Central**, San Caetano, ☎ 981 58 77 00; **INTERCAR/ALSA** om where buses depart for Madrid, Santander, Bilbao, San Sebastián and road, including Portugal, France, Belgium and Germany.

ocal buses - Contact Trapsa, ☎ 981 58 18 15.

axis - Always available at the airport and at the bus and train stations. There also a 24h stand in Praza de Galicia ☎ 981 59 59 64.

ar hire - The main car hire companies have offices at the airport and in the ty centre. **AVIS**, República del Salvador, 10 ☎ 981 57 37 18; **HERTZ**, Avenida e Lugo, 145, ☎ 981 58 34 66.

HE WAY OF SAINT JAMES

ne relics of St James (Santiago) discovered early in the 9C soon became the object f a local cult and then of pilgrimage. In the 11C devotion spread abroad until a urney to St James' shrine ranked equally with one to Rome or Jerusalem, articularly perilous since the invasion of the Holy Land by the Turks. St James d a particular appeal for the French who felt united with the Spanish in face of e Moorish threat but English, Germans and even Scandinavians made e long pilgrimage travelling for the most part through France along the routes ganised to a considerable degree, by the Benedictines and Cistercians of Cluny d Cîteaux and the Knights Templars of the Spanish Order of the Red Sword who sured the pilgrims' safety in northern Spain, provided them with funds and agged the route with cairns. Hospitals and hospices in the care of the Hospitallers ceived the sick, the weary and the stalwart alike who travelled almost all in the lgrims' uniform of heavy cape, 8ft stave with a gourd attached to carry water, out sandals and broad-brimmed felt hat, turned up in front and marked with three four scallop shells. A Pilgrim Guide of 1130, the first tourist guide ever written, robably by Aimeri Picaud, a Poitou monk from Parthenay-le-Vieux, describes e inhabitants, climate and customs of different regions, the most interesting utes and the sights on the way - the pilgrim in those days was in no hurry and equently made detours which took weeks or months to complete, to visit a nctuary or shrine. Churches, therefore, both on and off the way, benefited, as d the associated towns, from the pilgrims who numbered between 500 000 and vo million a year.

1175, Pope Alexander III recognised the statutes of the Military Order of Santiago, awn up to ensure the protection of pilgrims.

f those who "took the cockleshell", the English, Normans and Bretons often came art of the way by boat, embarking from Parson's Quay in the Plymouth estuary, the case of the English, then disembarking at Soulac and following the French lantic coast south through Bordeaux to the Pyrenees, or they landed directly in ain at La Coruña, on the north coast or in Portugal. Mediterranean pilgrims landed Catalunya and Valencia and crossed the peninsula. The land routes through France gan at Chartres, St-Denis and Paris, and joining at Tours, continued south to rdeaux, at Vézelay and Autun to go through Limoges and Périgueux and at Le Puy d Arles.

ne stopping places along the way formed a main street or Calle Mayor around which village would develop. Farming communities grew into towns and some were ttled by foreigners or minority groups (often French or Jewish), who consolidated e recovered territory and brought with them a wealth of culture.

ith the passage of time, however, the faith that made people set out on pilgrimages gan to diminish; those seeking gain by trickery and robbery, and known as false lgrims, among whom was the poet Villon, increased; the Wars of Religion, when

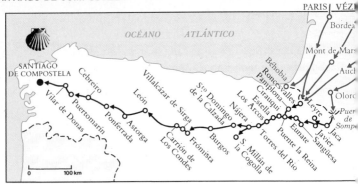

THE WAY OF ST JAMES

Christians fought among themselves, reduced the faithful even more. Finally
1589, Drake attacked La Coruña and the bishop of Compostela removed the re
from the Cathedral to a place of safety. They were lost and for 300 years
pilgrimage was virtually abandoned. In 1879 they were recovered, recognised by t
Pope and the pilgrimage recommenced. In Holy Years, when the feast day of
James (25 July) falls on a Sunday, there are jubilee indulgences and thousands
pilgrims once more visit the shrine.

THE WAY IN SPAIN – MAIN HALTS

The diverse ways through France met at Roncesvalles, Behobia and Somport
cross the Pyrenees and continued through northeastern Spain as two routes o
– the Asturian, from Roncesvalles, which until the 15C was considered extrem
dangerous because of possible attack by brigands, and a more (southerly rou
from Somport, known as the **Camino francés** or French Way on account of t
number of French pilgrims who followed it. It became marked over the centur
by churches and monasteries in which French architectural influence is obvio
The two routes converged at Puente la Reina.
The route from **Roncesvalles** to Puente la Reina was the shorter of the two w
only one main stop: **Pamplona**, while the longer Somport-Puente la Reina w
stopped at **Jaca, Santa Cruz de la Serós, San Juan de la Peña**, the **Monasterio de Leyre** a
Sangüesa.

* **Puente la Reina** – The venerable humpbacked bridge which spans the
 Arga and gives the town its name, was built in the 11C for the pilgrims on th
 way to Santiago. Standing at the entrance to the town, on the Pamplo
 road, is a bronze pilgrim, marking the point at which the two *camin*
 converged.
 The wide N 111 circles the old town outside whose walls stands the **Iglesia**
 Crucifijo (Church of the Crucifix) ⊘. The porch communicated with the pilgrim
 hospice. A second nave was added to the existing 12C main aisle in the 14C a
 now contains the famous Y-shaped Cross with the profoundly Expression
 Christ* carved in wood and said to have been brought from Germany by a pilg
 in the 14C. Leave the church to walk along the narrow but extremely elegant m
 street, the Calle Mayor, fronted by houses of golden brick and carved wood eav
 to the bridge. On the way you will see the **Iglesia de Santiago** (Church of St James)
 with its **doorway*** crowded with carvings, by now almost effaced. Inside, the na
 remodelled in the 16C, was adorned with altarpieces. Note also the two stat
 placed facing the entrance: St James the Pilgrim in gilded wood, and St Bart
 lomew.

* **Eunate** – 5km/3mi east of Puente la Reina. The origin of this **Romanesque** cha
 so harmonious in proportion and design, remains unknown. The finding
 human bones supports the theory of the building having been a funer
 chapel on the pilgrim road like that of Torres del Río. The outside gallery, n
 exposed, formerly led to adjoining buildings and was used by the pilgrims
 a shelter.

* **Cirauqui** – The village's winding alleys are lined by steps and closely crow
 by houses, their lower walls whitewashed, with rounded doorways, and th
 upper fronts adorned with iron balconies and further embellished with coats
 arms and carved cornices. At the top of the village *(difficult climb)* stands
 Iglesia de San Román with a multifoil 13C **portal*** similar to that of San Pedro
 la Rúa in Estella.

Estella and the Monasterio de Irache – *See LIZARRA.*

Los Arcos – The **Iglesia de Santa María de los Arcos** (Church of St Mary of the Arches), visible from a distance by its high tower, is Spanish Baroque inside. The effect is overwhelming: stucco, sculpture and painting cover every available space. Particularly noteworthy are the transept walls decorated in imitation Córdoba leather. Above the high altar, pure Baroque in style, rises a 13C polychrome wood statue of the Black Virgin of Santa María de los Arcos. The cloisters with Flamboyant bays illustrate the elegance and lightness of 15C Gothic.

Torres del Río – The **Iglesia del Santo Sepulcro★** (Church of the Holy Sepulchre) is an unusual Romanesque building, tall in height, octagonal in plan and dating from about 1200. Its resemblance to the chapel in Eunate has given rise to speculation that it is also a funerary chapel. Inside, vertical lines predominate; the magnificent Mudéjar inspired, star-shaped cupola is geometrical perfection. The decoration is sparse, consisting only of minute windows at the points of the star, modillions and historiated capitals.

Nájera and **Santo Domingo de la Calzada** – *See SANTO DOMINGO DE LA CALZADA.*

Burgos – *See BURGOS.*

Iglesia de Frómista – *See Iglesia de FRÓMISTA.*

Villalcázar de Sirga – The vast Gothic **Iglesia de Santa María la Blanca** ⊘ has a fine carved **portal★** on its south front and inside, in the south transept, two outstanding Gothic **tombs★**. The recumbent statues of the brother of Alfonso X, who had him murdered in 1271, and his wife Eleanor, have been delicately carved with an eye for detail (the costumes in particular) as has the tomb of the prince showing the funeral procession.

Carrión de los Condes – The counts of Carrión, attracted by the rich dowries promised to the daughters of El Cid, married but then mistreated them, and were executed for their sins.

Monasterio de San Zoilo ⊘, rebuilt during the Renaissance, has **cloisters★** designed by Juan de Badajoz with distinctive vaulting. The keystones and bosses are adorned with figurines and medallions.

The **Iglesia de Santiago** has beautiful 12C carvings on the façade including, on the portal's central coving, an architect with his compass, a barber with his scissors, a potter at his wheel, a cobbler, and so on. The high reliefs on the upper part show a Gothic influence.

Eunate chapel

★★ **León** - *See LEÓN.*

Astorga - *See ASTORGA.*

Ponferrada - *See PONFERRADA.*

Cebreiro - Cebreiro, not far from the Puerto de Piedrafita (Piedrafita pa (1 109m/3 638ft), is one of the places where one can best imagine the hardshi pilgrims underwent on their long tiring journey. The unusual drystone thatched houses *(pallozas)*, inhabited until recently, go back in constructio ancient Celtic huts, one of which houses an **Ethnographic Museum** (Mu Etnográfico). Still offering shelter to the traveller is an inn beside the small mountain church where pilgrims venerated the relics of the miracle of the H Eucharist which took place in c 1300, when the bread was turned to flesh the wine to blood. The holy relics are preserved in silver caskets presented Isabel the Catholic and may be seen together with the miraculous chalice paten.

Portomarín - The village of Portomarín had stood for centuries beside a bri spanning the Miño when modern civilization required the construction of a d at Belesar. Before the old village was drowned, however, the **church**★ of Knights of St John of Jerusalem was taken down and re-erected stone by st on the new site. It is square in shape, fortified and ornamented with n sive supporting arches and Romanesque doors with delicately carved covi The west door depicts Christ in Majesty with the 24 old musicians of Apocalypse.

Vilar de Donas - *6.5km/4mi east of Palas de Rei.* The **church**, slightly off the n road, is entered through a Romanesque doorway. Lining the walls **inside**, are tombs of the Knights of the Order of St James, slain in battle against the infid 15C **frescoes**★ still decorate the apse, illustrating Christ in Majesty with St Paul St Luke on his left and St Peter and St Mark on his right and, on the chancel w the faces of the elegant young women who gave the church its name – (*dona* Galician).

★★★ THE TOWN OF SANTIAGO *see town plan p 333*

★★★ **Plaza del Obradoiro** (Plaza de España) (V) – The size of the square and architectural quality of its surrounding buildings make it a fitting setting for cathedral. See photo, p 332.

★★★ **Catedral** ⊙ (V) – The present cathedral, built upon the same site as the f basilica erected over the Apostle's tomb shortly after its discovery, and tha Alfonso III destroyed by Al-Mansur in 997, dates almost entirely from the 1 12C and 13C, although from the outside it looks more like a Baroque build

★★★ **Obradoiro façade** – This Baroque masterpiece (its name means work of gold **Fernando Casas y Novoa** has adorned the cathedral entrance in magnificence s 1750. The central area, richly sculptured and given true Baroque movemen the interplay of straight and curved lines, rises to what appears almost to be a tongue of flame. The upward triangular lines are emphasised by high flank towers, slender and slightly in recess but sumptuously ornate.

★★★ **Pórtico de la Gloria** (Doorway of Glory) – Behind the Baroque façade stands narthex and the Pórtico de la Gloria, a late-12C wonder by **Maestro Mateo**, lead to the nave. The statues of the triple doorway are exceptionally beautiful bot a composition and in detail, for the master used all his artistry to give variet expression, style and colour.
The doorway is slightly more recent than the rest of the Romanesque cathe and shows features of the Gothic style. Mateo, who also built bridges, had crypt below reinforced to bear the weight of the portico. The central port dedicated to the Christian Church, the one on the left to the Jews, that on the r to the Gentiles or pagans. The central portal tympanum shows the Sav surrounded by the four Evangelists while on the archivolt are the 24 Elders of Apocalypse. The engaged pillars are covered in statues of Apostles and proph Note the figure of Daniel with the hint of a smile, a precursor to the fam Smiling Angel in Reims Cathedral in France. The pillar beneath the seated fig of St James, bears finger marks upon the stone; traditionally, on entering cathedral, exhausted pilgrims placed their hands here in token of safe arrival the other side of the pillar, the statue known as the saint of bumps is believe impart memory and wisdom to whoever bumps his forehead against it.

Interior – The immense Romanesque cathedral into which pilgrims crowded in Middle Ages has remained intact with all the characteristics of pilgrim churc at the time: a Latin cross floor plan, vast proportions, an ambulatory an triforium. The nave and transept, complete with aisles, are plain yet maje aesthetic yet functional. Galleries open onto the aisles through twin bays ben a supporting arch. The side aisles are covered with 13C groin vaults. At m

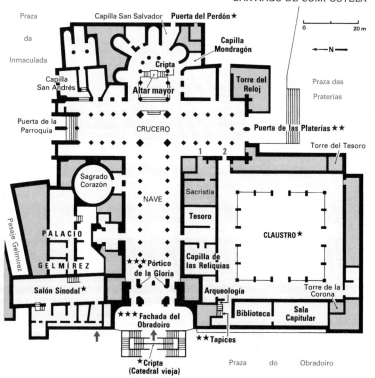

festivals a huge incense burner, the **botafumeiro** *(displayed in the library)*, is hung from the transept dome keystone and swung to the eaves by eight men pulling on a rope.

The decoration in the sanctuary is surprisingly exuberant for a Romanesque setting. The **Altar Mayor** or High Altar, surmounted by a sumptuously apparelled 13C statue of St James, is covered by a gigantic baldachin. (Pilgrims mounting the stairs behind the altar may kiss the saint's mantle).

Beneath the altar is the **cripta**, a crypt built into the foundations of the 9C church which contained St James' tomb and now enshrines the relics of the saint and his two disciples, St Theodore and St Athanasius.

Particularly beautiful among the cathedral's many outstanding features is the Gothic vaulting of the Capilla Mondragón (1521), and the 9C Capilla de la Corticela, which at the time of its construction was separate from the cathedral. The Renaissance doors to the **sacristía** (sacristy) (1) and *claustro* (cloisters) (2) on the right arm of the transept are also worthy of note.

Museo ⊙ – The museum consists of three distinct parts. Access to the **tesoro** (treasury), occupying a Gothic chapel to the right of the nave, is via the inside of the cathedral. Exhibits on display include a gold and silver monstrance by Antonio de Arfe (1539-66). To visit the **cripta★** (crypt), built in the 11C to compensate for differences in floor level and to support the Pórtico de la Gloria, exit the Plaza del Obradoiro. The entrance to the crypt is partially obscured by the large staircase beneath the Obradoiro façade. This is in fact a small Romanesque church with a Latin cross plan and attractive columns and sculpted capitals. Access to the rooms devoted to the cathedral's archeological excavations, the **biblioteca** (library), where the *botafumeiros* are displayed, the **sala capitular** (chapter-house) with its impressive granite vault and walls hung with 16C Flemish tapestries, and the balcony rooms, displaying **tapestries★★** by Goya, Bayeu, Rubens and Teniers, is via a side entrance.

Claustro – *Access via the museum.* This Renaissance cloister was designed by Juan de Álava who, in line with architectural trends at the beginning of the 16C, combined a Gothic structure with Plateresque decoration. The cloister was completed by Rodrigo Gil de Hontañón and Gaspar de Arce.

Puerta de las Platerías (Goldsmiths' Doorway) – This is the only 12C Romanesque doorway to have been preserved. Not all of the entrance we see today is original, as many of the sculptures were taken from the Puerta de la Azabachería. The most impressive figure is without doubt that of David playing the viola on the left door. Adam and Eve can also be seen being driven out of the Garden of Eden; the Pardoning of the Adulterous Woman is also distinguishable on the right hand

331

corner of the left tympanum. The **Torre del Reloj** (Clock Tower), on the right, was added at the end of the 17C. To the left, stands the **Torre del Tesoro** (Treasury

For one of the best views of the cathedral, descend the steps in Avenida de Rajoy, to the left of the town hall.

Tower). The façade of the **Casa del Cabildo**, opposite the *fuente de los caballos* or ho trough, is a Baroque feature built in the 18C.

Palacio Gelmírez ⓥ (V A) – This is the bishops' palace, to the left of the cathed 12C and Gothic style apartments are open to the public, including the vast S **Sinodal★** (Synod Hall) which is more than 30m/98ft long and has sculptured o vaulting. Carved in high relief on the bosses are scenes from the wedding banq of Alfonso IX de León.

★ **Hostal de los Reyes Católicos (Hostelry of the Catholic Monarchs)** (V) – The hoste founded by Ferdinand of Aragón and Isabel of Castilla as a pilgrim inn and hosp and now a parador, has an impressive **façade★** adorned with a splendid Plateres doorway. The hospital's plan of a cross within a square, which affords four eleg Plateresque *patios*, was common to hospitals of the period.

Plaza del Obradoiro

Ayuntamiento (town hall) (V H) – Opposite the cathedral is the severely Class 18C façade of the former Palacio de Roxoy by the French architect Cha Lemaur. Today, the building serves as the town hall and the Presidency of Xunta de Galicia.

Colegio de San Jerónimo (VX) – The college, a 17C building on the square's so side, has an elegant 15C gateway with a strong Romanesque influence.

★★ Barrio Antiguo (Old Town)

Present-day Santiago is the result of superimposing a medieval structure v Renaissance rationale and Baroque theatricality. Despite this, the old part of city continues to be a maze of delightful narrow streets which open out onto li squares such as Fonseca, Platerías, Feijóo, San Martín and San Roque.

SANTIAGO DE COMPOSTELA

Acibechería	V 2
Algalia de Arriba	V 5
Arco de Palacio	V 9
Caldeirería	X 17
Camino (Porta do)	V 20
Castrón Douro	X 22
Cervantes (Pr. de)	V 25
Faxeiras (Porta da)	X 37
Ferradura (Paseo da)	X 40
Galeras	X 42
Galicia (Pr. de)	X 45
Gelmírez	X 47
Inmaculada (Pr. da)	V 58
Nova (R.)	X
Orfas	X 70
Patio de Madres	X 72
Pena (Porta de la)	X 75
Praterías (Pr. das)	VX 77
Preguntoiro	V 80
Rodrigo de Pardón (Av. de)	X 90
San Francisco	V 98
San Martiño (Pr. de)	V 101
San Roque	X 104
Senra	X 113
Trinidade	V 116
Troia	V 119
Vilar (R. do)	X

A	Palacio Gelmírez
H	Ayuntamiento
M¹	Museo de las Peregrinaciones
M²	Centro Gallego de Arte Contemporáneo
P	Casa de la Parra
R	Casa de la Canónica

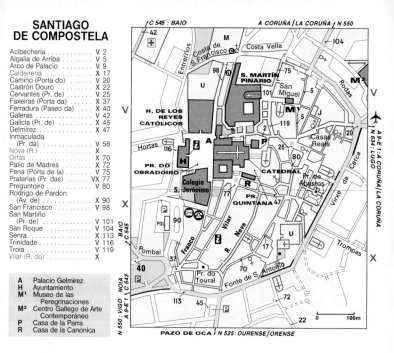

Rúa do Franco (X) – This is a picturesque street with old colleges (such as Fonseca), shops and cafés.

Rúa do Vilar (X) – The street leading to the cathedral is bordered by arcaded and ancient houses, as is the **Rúa Nova** (X) which runs parallel, although this has more shops.

Plaza de la Quintana (VX) – The square surrounding the east end of the cathedral bustles with lingering students. The lower part is bordered by the former **Casa de la Canónica** (Canon's Residence) (**R**) with a plain but harmonious arcade and, at right angles, by the 17C Monasterio de San Pavo de Anteltares, whose windows barred by beautiful old wrought ironwork embellish an otherwise austere construction. Opposite, the doorway in the cathedral's east end, known as the **Puerta del Perdón**★ (Door of Pardon) or Puerta Santa (Holy Door), designed by Fernández Lechuga in 1611 and opened only in Holy Years (when the feast day of St James, 25 July, falls on a Sunday), incorporates all the statues of the prophets and patriarchs carved by Maestro Mateo for the original Romanesque *coro*. At the top of a large flight of stairs is the **Casa de la Parra**, House of the Bunch of Grapes (**P**), a fine late-17C Baroque mansion.

Museo de las Peregrinaciones (Pilgrimage Museum) ⊘ (V **M¹**) – This small museum, devoted to the origins and history of pilgrimages to Santiago, occupies what is said to have been the house of King Don Pedro I (14C). Due to its heavy restoration, hardly any of its original medieval features remain.

Monasterio de San Martín Pinario ⊘ (V) – The monastery church overlooking plaza San Martín, preceded by a double flight of stairs, has an ornate front composed like a Plateresque altarpiece.

The interior consists of a surprisingly wide single aisle covered by coffered barrel vaulting. It is lit by a Byzantine-style lantern without a drum. The high altar retable, in the most ornate Churrigueresque manner, is by the great architect Casa y Novoa (1730). On either side are Baroque pulpits canopied by cottage-loaf-shaped sounding boards. A grand staircase beneath an elegant cupola leads to three 16C-18C cloisters, one of which is the Claustro de las Procesiones (Processions Cloister).

The monastery façade overlooking plaza de la Inmaculada is colossal in style with massive Doric columns in pairs rising from the ground to the roof. Plaza de la Azabachería opposite is so named because of the guild of jet ornament craftsmen (*azabacheros*) who had their workshops in this square.

Museo do Pobo Galego (Museum of the Galician people) ⊘ – This regional museum is housed in the former Convento de Bonaval (17-18C). It provides visitors with a general introduction into Galician culture, with the emphasis on its diversity. Rooms are devoted to the sea, crafts, musical instruments and dwellings. The building has a particularly impressive triple **spiral staircase**★, which provides access to the exhibition rooms. The **Centro Gallego de Arte Contemporáneo** (Galician Contemporary Art Centre) (V **M²**) is situated opposite this museum.

Additional Sights

Paseo da Ferradura (Herradura) (X 40) – The wooded hill rising from the old tow
makes a pleasant walk with a good **view**★ of the city and the cathedral.

★ **Colegiata de Santa María del Sar** ⊘ – *Calle Castrón de Ouro* (X 22). The 12
Romanesque collegiate church appears anachronistic by the addition in the 18
of its buttresses. The strength of the latter, however, is not superfluous when o
looks inside at the astonishing slant of the pillars caused by the pressure of tl
vaulting. The only cloister gallery to remain abuts the church and is exceeding
elegant, with paired **arches**★ richly decorated with carved floral and leaf moti

EXCURSIONS

★ **Pazo de Oca** ⊘ – *25km/16mi south on N 525.*
This austere Galician **manor** or *pazo*, with a crenellated tower, surrounds, on tw
sides, a vast square in which stands a Calvary. The romantic **park**★★ behind com
as a complete surprise. There are shady arbours, terraces covered with ru
coloured lichen, pools, and a silent lake on which a stone boat floats idly.

Monasterio de Sobrado Dos Monxes ⊘ – *60km/37mi northeast. Leave Sa
tiago along N 634, then take N 547 until Arzua. Proceed to Sobrado along LC 2:
and LC 232.*
Sobrado is one of Galicia's vast monasteries, built between the Renaissance a
Baroque periods. It is badly weatherworn but is in the process of restoration wi
the Cistercian community now living within its walls. Preoccupation with si
brought a certain severity in the decoration of the church façade. On the oth
hand, the interior displays fertile imagination in the design of the cupolas in t
transept, the sacristy and the Capilla del Rosario (Rosary Chapel) as well as in t
Claustro de los Medallones (Medallion Cloisters).
Of the monastery's medieval buildings, there remain a kitchen with a monumen
fireplace, a chapter-house and the Capilla de la Magdalena (Mary Magdale
Chapel).

SANTILLANA DEL MAR★★

Cantabria – Population 3 839
Michelin map 442 B 17

Santillana del Mar has kept almost intact its ancient buildings and traditions;
nightfall farmers still return with their beasts to stable them in age-old byres abo
which rise the fine stone façades of *casonas* or seignorial mansions with coats
arms. It is just the soft setting described by the 18C French writer Lesage for I
unpretentious hero **Gil Blas**.
Santillana grew up around a monastery which sheltered the relics of St Juliana, w
was martyred in Asia Minor – the name Santillana is a contraction of Santa Juliar
Throughout the Middle Ages, the monastery was famous as a place of pilgrimage a
was particularly favoured by the Grandees of Castilla. In the 11C it became power
as a collegiate church; in the 15C, the town, created the seat of a marquisate, w
enriched by the fine mansions which still give it so much character.
The famous **Cuevas de Altamira** (Altamira Caves) are 2km/1mi from the village.

★★ THE VILLAGE *1hr 30min*

The village has two main streets, both leading to the collegiate church. Betwe
the two lies a network of communicating alleys. Most of the noblemer
residences, with plain façades of massive rough stone, date from the 15C, 1
and 17C. Almost all have wrought-iron balconies or wooden galleries *(solanas)* a
the majority sport traditional crests or coats of arms.

Calle Santo Domingo – **Casa de los Villa** is distinguishable by its semicircular bal
nies. The device on the armorial bearings shows an eagle with spread wings pierc
by an arrow and the motto "A glorious death crowns a whole life with honour".
Turn left at the fork into calle de Juan Infante.

Plaza de Ramón Pelayo or Plaza Mayor – The vast triangular square is border
on the right by the **Parador Gil Blas** and the 14C **Torre de Merino** (Merino Tower) w
crenellations visible beneath the roof. The **Torre de Borja-Barreda** opposite has
elegant doorway with a pointed arch. On the left is the Ayuntamiento (town ha
in an 18C building.

Calle de las Lindas *(at the end of the square on the right)* runs between massi
looking houses with austere façades to join calle del Cantón and Calle del Río wh
lead to the collegiate church.

As you approach the church, you will see several noblemen's residences: on the right is the **Casa de los Hombrones**, named after the two knights supporting the Villa coat of arms. Further along, the **Cossío** and **Quevedo** houses both have magnificent coats of arms. Calle del Río is named after the stream that feeds the village drinking fountain and disappears beneath Quevedo House. On the left, the house of the Archduchess of Austria, the former **Casa de los Abades** (Abbot's House), is adorned with three coats of arms.

Plaza de las Arenas – The much restored but still impressive **Torre de los Velarde** behind the collegiate church, was originally the keep of the 15C palace.

★ **Colegiata** ⊘ – The collegiate church dates from the 12C and 13C. While the design of the east end is pure Romanesque, that of the west to some extent lacks unity, although the harmonious placing of the windows and towers and the golden colour of the stone make it blend in well with the overall architecture of the square. Above the portal, which was remodelled in the 18C, is a niche with a statue of St Juliana.

Colegiata

★ **Claustro** ⊘ – Although the Romanesque east gallery has disappeared, these late-12C cloisters still have great appeal. Each pair of twin columns is covered by a capital carved by a master craftsman. Though plant and strapwork motifs predominate, the **capitals**★★ in the south gallery, which do illustrate a scene, often in allegory, are very expressive: look out for Christ and six of the disciples, Christ's baptism, the beheading of John the Baptist and Daniel in the lions' den.

Interior – The vaulting in the aisles was rebuilt at the end of the 13C when it was given intersecting ribs, but that above the transept and apses is original. The aisles and apses are out of line and the cupola, unusually, is almost elliptical. The pillars are crowned by highly stylised capitals. St Juliana's memorial sarcophagus, carved in the 15C, stands at the centre of the nave. The chancel contains a 17C Mexican beaten silver altarfront and Romanesque stone figures of **four Apostles**★ carved in the Byzantine hieratic style. The 16C Hispano-Flemish **altarpiece**★ has the original polychrome wood predella which is carved to show the Evangelists in profile.

Convento de Regina Coeli – *On the other side of the village.* The **Museo Diocesano** ⊘ now occupies the restored 16C Convento de Clarisas (Convent of the Poor Clares). On display are popular religious art objects found in the province.

A large coat of arms adorns the fine 18C **Casa de Los Tagle** at the end of the street.

Catalunya (Girona) – Population 3 898

Michelin map 443 F 36
Local map see PIRINEOS CATALANES

Coming from Ripoll, when you enter the old city of the Abbesses, you can admire the pretty **medieval bridge**★ spanning the Ter river. This 15C construction was built on top of a former Romanesque bridge. The town has been named after the Monasterio de Sant Joan.

★★ **Monasterio** ⊘ – The monastery was founded in the 9C by Count Wilfred the Hairy, whose daughter Emma was the very first Abbess of this Benedictine monastery. However, it soon closed its doors to women and was subsequently occupied by male religious orders.

★ **Iglesia** – Before entering, note the east end with its three storeys. The arches and columns with carved capitals recall those of southwest France.

Interior – Originally, the east end which crowned the nave and transept had an ambulatory, above which rose a cupola supporting the belfry. In 1428, this part of the building was destroyed by an earthquake. Local masons repaired the church by extending the nave, placing columns where previously the ambulatory had been. The decoration of the apses echoes that of the east end, the motifs on the richly carved capitals those of oriental fabrics.

A magnificent **Descent from the Cross**★★, a group in polychrome wood carved in 1251, presides over the central apse. The artist departed from the traditional scene by introducing additional figures and greater Realism – note St John's sad gestures and the Virgin receiving her son. In 1426 an unbroken host was discovered on the Christ figure's head, which has made the statue an object of particular veneration to this day.

Descent from the Cross

Among the church's other treasures are the lovely 14C Gothic altarpiece in alabaster of Santa María la Blanca and the tomb of Miró de Tagamanent.

Claustro – These cloisters are simple and elegant; the sweeping arches and slender columns with capitals decorated with plant motifs replaced those of an earlier Romanesque cloister in the 14C. The **museum** houses an interesting collection of embroidered fabric.

Antiguo Palacio de la Abadía – Opposite the church on the square stands the 14C former Abbatial Palace. Note the small *patio* and its carved capitals.

SANTO DOMINGO DE LA CALZADA★

La Rioja – Population 5 308

Michelin map 442 E 21

s historical town, an important staging post on the Way of St James, was founded he banks of the Oja river in the 11C and owes its name to a hermit, Dominic, who t a bridge to help pilgrims on their way to Santiago de Compostela, a causeway *zada*: road, causeway) to Burgos, a hospice and a hospital. Parts of the 14C parts can still be seen.

plourful **medieval market** is held every year in the old town to coincide with fes- ties commemorating the Constitution and the Immaculate Conception (6 and ecember).

OLD TOWN

The old town is huddled around the **Plaza del Santo**, dominated by the cathedral and the former hospital, which has now been converted into a parador. The streets around the square, particularly the Calle Mayor, have preserved a number of 16C and 17C stone houses with fine doorways. The 18C Ayuntamiento (town hall), the major monument in the nearby plaza de España, is crowned by an impressive escutcheon.

Catedral ⊘ – The church is Gothic, apart from the ambulatory and one of the apsidal chapels which are Romanesque (second half of the 12C). The saint's tomb 13C), beneath a 1513 canopy, is in the south transept, and opposite is a sumptuous Gothic cage. This contains a live white cock and hen in memory of a miracle attributed to the saint. According to legend, a pilgrim was unjustly accused of theft and hanged. After a month on the gallows, he was still alive and, on seeing his parents, said "Tell the judge to let me down; St Dominic has protected me". The judge, on hearing the news just as he was about to begin a meal of roast chicken, declared "He must be as alive as this bird" whereupon the cockerel stood up and, fully feathered, crowed aloud to proclaim the pilgrim's innocence.

The **retable**★★ at the high altar (1538) is an unfinished work by Damian Forment. The artist has used the human body as a decorative element, making this an original work and one of the 16C's major sculptures. The second chapel off the north aisle contains a fine 15C Hispano-Flemish altarpiece.

The cathedral contains other works of great interest, including the **Capilla de la Magdalena**★ *(Evangelist's nave)* with its fine Plateresque decoration and mag- nificent screen. Note the delicate 15C Flemish statue of La Verónica. In the Epistle nave, opposite the Capilla de la Magdalena, the **Capilla de San Juan Bautista or Santa Teresa** contains an impressive screen, interesting noble tombs and a magnificent etable with Hispano-Flemish paintings. A large imperial escutcheon crowns the Plateresque decoration in the Capilla de la Inmaculada.

On the exterior, a Baroque-style 18C **tower** can be seen. In the same square, opposite the cathedral, the small **Ermita del Santo** (Saint's Hermitage) has an attractive Gothic interior.

EXCURSIONS

Nájera – *20km/12mi east.* Nájera stands on the pilgrim road to Santiago de Compostela. It was reconquered by Sancho Garcés I in 920 and became the capital of the Kingdom of Navarra until 1076, when La Rioja – and Nájera with it – was incorporated into Castilla.

Monasterio de Santa María la Real ⊘ – The monastery was founded by Don García III, King of Navarra, in 1032. According to legend, the site is that of a cave which the king stumbled upon (while following a vulture and a partridge) and where he found a statue of the Virgin. It fell into total ruin in the 15C, but was rebuilt in the same century.

Claustro – The cloisters abut a strangely purple-coloured cliff. The bays in the lower gallery are filled with Plateresque stone tracery (1520), each to a different arabesque pattern.

* **Iglesia** – Beneath the gallery, two soldiers bearing the colours of King García [and] his Queen, Estefanía of Barcelona, guard the entrance to the **Panteón Real**★ (R[oyal] Pantheon) of princes of Navarra, León and Castilla of the 11C and 12C. [The] recumbent statues were carved in the 16C. At the centre, between the knee[s of the] figures of the founders, is the entrance to the cave where the Virgin [was] found. The present polychrome figure is 13C. Among the royal sarcopha[gi in] the south aisle is the **tomb of Doña Blanca de Navarra**★, a jewel of Romane[sque] sculpture.

Coro Alto – Note the beautiful carving and infinite variety of the miseric[ords] and armrests in the **choir stalls**★ (1495) and particularly the central seat on w[hich] the founder king is depicted majestically in full armour beneath a deli[cate] canopy.

San Millán de la Cogolla – *19km/11mi southeast.* This site, which was decl[ared] a World Heritage Site in December 1997, was already famous in the 5C w[hen] Millán or Emilian de Berceo and his followers settled here as hermits. In the [?] a monastery and Mozarabic church were built in the mountains (Suso) and t[hen,] in 1053, another monastery was built in the valley (Yuso). The first kn[own] manuscripts in Castilian Spanish, the *Glosas Emilianenses*, were written at [San] Millán. **Gonzalo de Berceo**, the first cult Castilian poet, who wrote *La Vida de [San] Millán* (The Life of St Millan and *Los Milagros de Nuestra Señora* (The Miracle[s of] Our Lady), was educated here.

* **Monasterio de Suso** ⊙ – The monastery stands on a hillside overlooking [the] Monasterio de Yuso and the Cárdenas Valley. It is a magnificent Mozar[abic] building partly hollowed out of the rock with a cubic apse and large carved cor[bels] The church has two aisles separated by three horseshoe-shaped arches. The a[isles] were extended westwards in the Romanesque era. A cave necropolis for the b[odies] of the monks was discovered near the church.

Monasterio de Suso

Monasterio de Yuso ⊙ – The monastery was built between the 16C and 18[C in] Renaissance style in the case of the church, neo-Classical and Baroque respect[ively] for the portals and sacristy. In the treasury are splendid **ivories**★★ from two [?] reliquaries. These were robbed of their gold mounts and precious stones by Fr[ench] soldiers and are now shown as sets of ivory plaques – San Millán's (1067[–?] consisting of 24 Romanesque pieces, is carved with great human expres[sion] while San Felices' (1090), consists of five pieces with a distinctly Byzar[tine] hieratic style.

Monasterio de Cañas ⊙ – *16km/10mi southeast.* This monastery has [been] inhabited by Cistercian monks since its foundation in 1170. The 16C church [and] chapter-house are extraordinary examples of the purity and simplicit[y of] Cistercian art, with elegant pointed arches, floral decoration and simple [?] vaulting. A museum is scheduled to open in the former granary during the co[urse] of 1999.

Castilla y León (Burgos)

Michelin map 442 G 19

Monasterio de Santo Domingo de Silos ⊘ is named after an 11C monk, Dominic, who instructed the conventual buildings of a former 6C-8C Visigothic abbey that was polished by Al-Mansur. The new buildings were abandoned in 1835 but were upied by Benedictine monks from Poitou, in France, in 1880, who planted the nificent cypress in the cloisters and a huge sequoia in front of the portal. The astery is also renowned for its concerts of Gregorian chant.

laustro – These are among the most beautiful cloisters in Spain. Countless pets have been inspired by the atmosphere of spirituality that emanates from e well-proportioned lleries, the lone press and the lovely oloured vaulting.

F. Bouillot/MARCO POLO

he cloisters are very g for a Romanesque uilding and comprise vo superimposed, archi-cturally similar galle-es. The ground floor lleries have about 60 unded arches supported paired columns and, in the iddle of each gallery, by a roup of five columns. The eight w reliefs on the corner pillars e masterpieces of Romanes-

e sculpture. Careful study reveals that several major sculptors worked on the stone. he first and most original craftsman (mid to late 11C) was primarily a linear artist ho favoured hieratic postures and preferred Symbolism to Realism – his work tends along the east, north and part of the west galleries and includes the low reliefs the southeast, northeast and northwest corner pillars. The second artist (early 2C) was more partial to volume than line and personified his figures. The third ason, again using a completely different style, carved the southwest pillar (12C). he **capitals**, apart from those which are historiated, illustrate a fantastic bestiary hich derives from the Mudéjar use of animal and plant motifs. *The most teresting have been numbered in the description of the galleries that follows.*

utheast pillar – Carved like an ivory diptych; Ascension *(left)*, Pentecost *(right)*.

st gallery – (1): strapwork, (2): entwined plants, (3): harpies defended by dogs.

ortheast pillar – This shows the Descent from the Cross and on the upper register, e earth and the moon on the point of being clouded over; on the other side is original representation of the Entombment and the Resurrection as a single mposition. Opposite the pillar is the fine doorway known as the **Puerta de las rgenes** (4) which led to the former Romanesque abbey church. Its horseshoe arch flanked by columns with interesting capitals.

orth gallery – (5): entwined plants, (6): the Elders of the Apocalypse, (7): harpies tacked by eagles, (8): birds. The gallery also contains St Dominic's 13C tomb

(9): three Romanesque lions bear the recumbent figure of the saint.

Northwest pillar – This pillar, concerned with the doubts on the Resurrection in the minds of some disciples, shows Christ on the road to Emmaus and before St Thomas.

West gallery – (10): strapwork, (11): birds with necks entwined, (12): perfectly curved flamingoes, (13): birds and lions ensnared by plant tendrils. The capitals that follow are by the second sculptor.

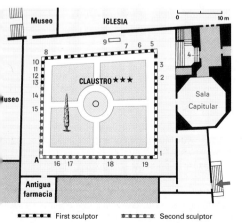

Museo · IGLESIA · 0 10 m

9 7 6 5
8
10 5
11 3
12 CLAUSTRO ★★★
13 4 2
useo
14 Sala
15 Capitular

A 1
16 17 18 19

Antigua farmacia

▪▪▪▪▪ First sculptor   ▪▪▪▪▪ Second sculptor

(14): the birth of Jesus, (15): scenes of the Passion. Note the well-preserved *artesonado* ceiling.

Southwest pillar (A) – By the third artist. On the left is an admirable Annunciat' which the Virgin Mary appears crowned by two angels; on the right is a Tr Jesse.

South gallery – (16) and (17): plant tendrils ensnaring birds in the first and in the second, (18): eagles clutching hares, (19): grimacing monster heads

Museo – The museum displays some very old pieces, including an 11C chal St Dominic's with filigree decoration, an enamel reliquary, a 10C-11C manus of the Mozarabic rite and the tympanum from the portal of the original ch

Antigua Farmacia (Old Pharmacy) – Fine collection of Talavera ceramic jars

Iglesia – The present church (1756-1816), which is agreeably proporti combines the rounded volume of Baroque with the plain grandeur of the Her style.

EXCURSION

Garganta de la Yecla – *3km/2mi southwest; allow 20min.*
A footpath follows a deep narrow gorge cut into a thick layer of grey limes

SARAGOSSA★★

See ZARAGOZA

SEGOVIA★★★

Castilla y León – Population 57 617
Michelin map 444 J 17
Local map see Sierra de GUADARRAMA

The noble Castilian city of Segovia, former residence of King Alfonso X the Wis King Henry IV, was an important economic and political centre in the Middle Age was to play a decisive role in the history of Castilla. Segovia has an extraord site★★ that is best appreciated if approached from the east. The centre of the which is circled by ramparts, appears perched on a triangular rock at an altitu 1 000m/3 280ft. To the left is the Roman aqueduct, to the right are the cath domes and spires and further right still, at the tip of the triangle, the Alc 100m/328ft above the confluence of the Eresma and Clamores rivers. For a overall view, drive along Cuesta de los Hoyos and Paseo de la Alameda.

HISTORICAL NOTES

Segovia was an important military town in Roman times; under the Moors Middle Ages it became a wool town and industrial centre – by the 15C it num 60 000 citizens and had entered its golden age.

Isabel the Catholic, Queen of Castilla – On the death of Henry IV in 1474 grandees refused to recognise the legitimacy of his daughter, Doña Juana, k as **La Beltraneja** after her mother's favourite, Beltrán de la Cueva. In Segovia i stead, the grandees proclaimed Henry's half-sister, Isabel, Queen of Castilla – preparing the way for Spain's unification since Isabel was already marrie Ferdinand, heir apparent of Aragón. La Beltraneja, aided by her husband, Alfor of Portugal, pressed her claim, but renounced in 1479 after the defeats at Tor Albuera.

The "Comuneros" – The Spanish were incensed at the beginning of Charles V's by the emperor's Flemish court and companions, his attempt to impose absolut and new taxes. Town forces *(comunidades)* under the leadership of the Toledan, de Padilla and the Segovian, Juan Bravo, rose in revolt but were crushed fina Villalar in 1521 and their leaders beheaded in Segovia.

Architecture – Picturesque streets have 15C-16C Castilian type entrances sur ded by *alfiz* and plaster façades with Mudéjar geometrical designs or *esgraf* Segovia's main treasures, however, are her Romanesque churches.

Romanesque churches – These beautiful churches of golden stone have con architectural features: well rounded apses, frequently a tall square belfry besid east end and a covered gallery where weavers' or merchants' guilds used to

Segovia today – Segovia is famous for its outstanding monuments as well gastronomic specialities like the exquisite suckling-pig *(cochinillo asado).*

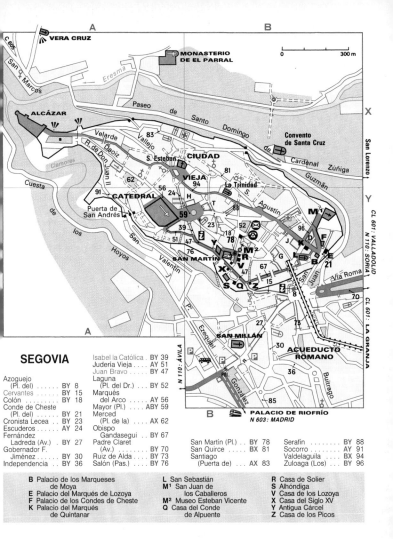

SEGOVIA

Azoguejo
  (Pl. del) ...... BY 8
Cervantes ...... BY 15
Colón .... BY 18
Conde de Cheste
  (Pl. del) ...... BY 21
Cronista Lecea .. BY 23
Escuderos ...... AY 24
Fernández
  Ladreda (Av.) . BY 27
Gobernador F.
  Jiménez ...... BY 30
Independencia .. BY 36

Isabel la Católica . BY 39
Judería Vieja .... AY 51
Juan Bravo ..... BY 47
Laguna
  (Pl. del Dr.) ... BY 52
Marqués
  del Arco ..... AY 56
Mayor (Pl.) .... ABY 59
Merced
  (Pl. de la) .... AX 62
Obispo
  Gandasegui .. BY 67
Padre Claret
  (Av.) .... BY 70
Ruiz de Alda .... BY 73
Salón (Pas.) .... BY 76

San Martín (Pl.) .. BY 78
San Quirce ..... BX 81
Santiago
  (Puerta de) ... AX 83

Serafin .... BY 88
Socorro .... AY 91
Valdelaguila .... BX 94
Zuloaga (Los) ... BY 96

B Palacio de los Marqueses
    de Moya
E Palacio del Marqués de Lozoya
F Palacio de los Condes de Cheste
K Palacio del Marqués
    de Quintanar

L San Sebastián
M¹ San Juan de
    los Caballeros
M² Museo Esteban Vicente
Q Casa del Conde
    de Alpuente

R Casa de Solier
S Alhóndiga
V Casa de los Lozoya
X Casa del Siglo XV
Y Antigua Cárcel
Z Casa de los Picos

ACUEDUCTO ROMANO (BY)

This Roman aqueduct is one of the finest still in existence and it is still operating. The simple, elegant structure, was built during the reign of Trajan in the 1C to bring water from the río Acebeda in the Sierra de Fuenfría to the upper part of the town. It is 728m/2 388ft long, rises to a maximum height of 28m/92ft in plaza del Azoguejo where the ground is lowest and consists throughout of two tiers of arches.

CIUDAD VIEJA (OLD TOWN) *4hr. Follow the itinerary on the plan.*

Plaza Mayor (ABY 59) – Dominated by the impressive cathedral, the arcaded square with its terrace cafés is a popular meeting place with Segovians. Among the buildings surrounding the square are the Ayuntamiento (town hall) and the teatro Juan Bravo.

Catedral ⊘ **(AY)** – This was built during the reign of Emperor Charles V to replace the cathedral that had been destroyed during the Comuneros' Revolt in 1511. It is an example of the survival of the Gothic style in the 16C when Renaissance architecture was at its height. The beautiful golden stone, the stepped east end with pinnacles and delicate balustrades and the tall tower, bring considerable grace to the massive building. The width of the aisles combines with the decorative lines of the pillars and ribs in the vaulting, to make the interior both light and elegant. Among the chapels, which are closed by fine wrought-iron screens, the first off the south aisle contains as altarpiece an *Entombment* by Juan de Juni. The first chapel on the left contains a Corpus Christi monstrance. The *coro* stalls, in the late-15C Flamboyant Gothic style, are from the earlier cathedral.

★ **Claustro** ⊘ – The 15C cloisters from the former cathedral, which stood near Alcázar, were transported stone by stone and rebuilt on the new site. The S Capitular (chapter-house) has beautiful 17C Brussels **tapestries**★ which illustr the story of Queen Zenobia.

★ **Plaza de San Martín (BY 78)** – The square in the heart of the old aristocr quarter is the most evocative of historic Segovia. It is formed of two small squa joined by a flight of steps. The statue is of Juan Bravo. Around the square st the **Casa del Siglo XV** (15C House) (**X**), also known as Juan Bravo's house, wit gallery beneath the eaves, the 16C tower of the **Casa de los Lozoya** (**V**) as a remin of the family's power in former times, the Plateresque façade of the **Casa de S** (Solier Mansion, also known as Casa de Correas) (**R**) and the ornate entrance big houses. In the middle of the square is the 12C **Iglesia de San Martín**★, a chu framed on three sides by a covered gallery on pillars with carved strapwork animal figures on the capitals.
The 17C **antigua Cárcel** (Old Prison) (**BY Y**) has a decorative Baroque pediment

Museo Esteban Vicente ⊘ (**BY M²**) – The museum is housed in the palace Enrique IV in the so-called Hospital de Viejos (Old People's Hospital). The only tr of the original building is the fine chapel with a Mudéjar ceiling which has b converted into an auditorium. The museum was created following a donatio the artist Esteban Vicente and exhibits his work from 1925 to 1997.

Alhóndiga (BY S) – This 15C granary has been transformed into an exhibit room.

Casa del Conde de Alpuente (BY Q) – The elegant façade of this 15C Gothic ho is adorned with *esgrafiado* designs.

Casa de los Picos (BY Z) – The house, faced closely with diamond pointed stor is the most original of Segovia's 15C mansions.

★★★ **Acueducto Romano (Roman Aqueduct) (BY)** – *See above.*

Iglesia de San Sebastián (BY L) – Small Romanesque church on a quiet squa

Plaza del Conde de Cheste (BY 21) – On the square stand the palaces of the **Mar** **de Moya** (**B**), the **Marqués de Lozoya** (**E**), the **Condes de Cheste** (**F**) and the **Marqué** **Quintanar** (**K**).

★ **Iglesia de San Juan de los Caballeros (BY M¹)** – This is Segovia's old Romanesque church (11C). Its outstanding feature is the portico (taken from church of San Nicolás) with its carvings of portrait heads, plant motifs animals. The church, which was almost in ruins at the turn-of-the-century, bought by Daniel Zuloaga, who converted it into his home and workshop. To it houses the **Museo Zuloaga** ⊘, exhibiting drawings by the artist and paintings his nephew, Ignacio Zuloaga.

Iglesia de la Trinidad (Holy Trinity Church) (BY) – This somewhat austere Ro nesque church has a decorated apse where there is blind arcading and capi carved with imaginary beasts and plant motifs.

Iglesia de San Esteban (St Stephen's Church) ⊘ (**AX**) – One of the latest (13C) most beautiful of Segovia's Romanesque churches. The porticoes running al two of its sides have finely carved capitals.
The five-storey **tower**★ has elegant bays and slender columns on the corners. interior is in Renaissance style. Inside, the altar in the south transept has a 1 Gothic figure of Christ in polychrome wood.

★ **Alcázar** ⊘ (**AX**) – The Alcázar, standing on a cliff overlooking the valley, was b in the early 13C and modified in the 15C and 16C. Its keep is flanked by corbe turrets. Several rooms have retained their magnificent *artesonado* ceilings display medieval armoury, period pictures and furnishings. The Sala del Cordón terrace command a fine **panorama** of the fertile Eresma Valley, the Monasterio d Parral, the Capilla de la Vera Cruz and the meseta beyond. The **Real Colegio de Artill** (Royal Artillery School) now houses a museum reminding visitors of importance of the chemical laboratory established here in the 18C and the Fre chemist **Louis Proust**, who formulated his law of constant proportions in Segovia. views from the keep *(152 steps)* stretch across the city to the Sierra de Guadarran

SIGHTS OUTSIDE THE WALLS

★ **Iglesia de San Millán** ⊘ (**BY**) – The early-12C church stands in the middle c large square which allows a full view of its pure, still primitive Romanesque li and two porticoes with finely carved modillions and capitals. Inside, the th aisles have alternating pillars and columns as in Jaca Cathedral. The apse has bl arcading and a decorative frieze which continues throughout the church. transept has Moorish ribbed vaulting.

Monasterio de El Parral ⊙ **(AX)** – The monastery was founded by Henry IV in 1445 and later entrusted to the Hieronymites. The **church**, behind its unfinished façade, has a Gothic nave with beautifully carved doors, a 16C altarpiece by Juan Rodríguez and, on either side of the chancel, the Plateresque tombs of the Marquis and Marchioness of Villena.

Capilla de la Vera Cruz ⊙ **(AX)** – The unusual polygonal chapel was erected in the 13C, probably by the Templars; it now belongs to the Order of Malta. A circular corridor surrounds two small chambers, one above the other, in which the order's secret ceremonies were conducted. The Capilla del Lignum Crucis contains an ornate Flamboyant Gothic altar. There is a good **view** of Segovia.

Convento de Santa Cruz (BX) – The convent pinnacles, the decorated Isabelline **entrance** with a Calvary, a *Pietà* and the emblems of the Catholic monarchs, can be seen from the road.

Iglesia de San Lorenzo (BX) – The Romanesque church with its unusual brick belfry stands in a picturesque square surrounded by corbelled half-timbered houses.

EXCURSIONS

Palacio de La Granja de San Ildefonso – *See La GRANJA DE SAN ILDEFONSO.*

Riofrío – *11km/7mi south on N 603.*
The Palacio Real (Royal Palace) can be seen through the holm oaks where deer roam, below the Mujer Muerta (the Dead Woman), a foothill of the Sierra de Guadarrama.

Palacio ⊙ – Riofrío was planned by Isabel Farnese as the equal of La Granja which she had to vacate on the death of her husband, Philip V. Construction began in 1752 but though it was very big – it measures 84m × 84m (276ft × 276ft) –

Alcázar, Segovia

S.Mason/STOCK PHOTOS

it was nothing more than a somewhat pretentious hunting lodge. This pala[
construction was never completed and Isabel Farnese never lived in it.
furniture belongs to the period of Francisco de Asís de Borbón, the husban[
Isabel II, and Alfonso XII, both of whom spent considerable periods of time in
palace.

It is built around a Classical style grand courtyard and monumental staircase v
double flights lead to sumptuously decorated apartments. The green and [
façade reveals the Italian origins of the wife of Philip V.

A **Museo de Caza** (Hunting Museum) illustrates the development of hunting meth[
since prehistoric times with the aid of paintings and display cases of anima[
their natural habitat.

La SEU D'URGELL/SEO DE URGEL★

Catalunya (Lleida) – Population 11 195
Michelin map 443 E 34
Local map see PIRINEOS CATALANES

This onetime city of prince-archbishops, stands in peaceful countryside where
Valira, which rises in the mountains of Andorra, joins the Segre river. Since 1278
duties of the archbishop have included those of joint ruler of Andorra with the Fre
President, until the 1993 constitution granting Andorra full independence.

The former county capital now lives on trade and agriculture which includes st
farming and dairy produce, particularly cheese.

★★ **Catedral de Santa Maria** ⊙ – The cathedral, whose construction was starte[
the 12C, shows strong Lombard influence. The west face with two differ[
colours of stone, is divided into three parts corresponding to the three ai[
inside. The central part is typically Italian with its pediment crowned by a sr
campanile.

Inside, the elevation is spectacular, the nave rising on cruciform pillars, surr[
ded, in the French style, by engaged columns. A most effective twin arched gal[
decorates the east transept wall and then reappears outside to circle the a[

★ **Claustro** – The cloisters are 13C, although the east gallery had to be rebuilt in 16[
The granite capitals illustrating human figures and animals were carved v[
consummate artistry and humour by masons from the Roussillon. The Sa[
Maria door (southeast corner) opens into the 11C **Iglesia de Sant Miquel**★, the o[
remaining building of those constructed by St Ermangol.

★ **Museo Diocesano** ⊙ – The Diocesan Museum has a wonderful collection of work[
art from the region, dating from the 10C to the 18C. The most precious wor[
a beautifully illuminated 11C **Beatus**★★, one of the best preserved copies
St John's Commentary on the Apocalypse written in the 8C by the priest, Bea[
of Liébana.

Of note also are an interesting **papyrus**★ belonging to Pope Sylvester II, the 1[
enamelled Romanesque crucifix from the Monasterio de Silos which show[
Byzantine influence, the 14C **Abella de la Conca**★ altarpiece by Pere Serra also w[
a Byzantine influence as well as characteristics from the Siena School, and [
14C *St Bartholomew Altarpiece* in coloured stone which illustrates scenes w[
great realism. The crypt contains church plate and the 18C funerary urn [
St Ermangol.

SEVILLA★★★

SEVILLE – Andalucía – Population 704 857

Michelin map 446 T 11-12

Plan of the conurbation on Michelin map 446

villa, standing in the plain of the Guadalquivir, is capital of Andalucía and Spain's
urth largest city. It has all the characteristics of a bustling metropolis but has many
oods and facets which may escape the visitor in too much of a hurry. It is well worth
king the time to stroll along the narrow streets of old quarters like Santa Cruz or
le slowly through the city's peaceful parks and gardens in a horse-drawn carriage.
e great festivals, when vast crowds flock to the city from all over Spain and
erseas, reveal the provincial capital in many guises. During the **Semana Santa**, or **Holy
ek**, *pasos* processions are organised nightly in each city quarter by rival brother-
ods. *Pasos* are great litters sumptuously bejewelled and garlanded with flowers on
ich are mounted religious, polychrome wood statues; these constructions are
rne through the crowd on the shoulders of between 25 and 60 men. Accompanying
e statues are penitents, hidden beneath tall pointed hoods; from time to time a
ice is raised in a *saeta*, an improvised religious lament. During the **April Fair** or **Feria**
st week in April) the city becomes a fairground with horse and carriage parades.
e women in flounced dresses and the men in full Andalusian costume ride up to
ecially erected canvas pavilions to dance the *sevillana*.
villa is also the great centre of *flamenco* and *tablaos* (tableaux), famous too for its
llfights held in the 18C **Plaza de la Maestranza** (AX), and finally for its many little bars
d cafés where the merrymaking continues around *copas* (drinks) and tapas.

STORICAL NOTES

villa's history is neatly summed up by the lines carved long ago on the Puerta de
rez (Jerez Gate): "Hercules built me; Caesar surrounded me with walls and towers;
e King Saint took me." Sevilla, known as Hispalis under the Iberians, was chief city
 Roman Baetica and, before Toledo, became the capital of the Visigothic Kingdom.
 712 the Moors arrived; in the 11C, on the fall of the Córdoban caliphs, the city was
eated capital of a kingdom which gained in prosperity a century later under the
mohads. In 1195 **Sultan Yacoub al-Mansur** (1184-99), builder of the famous Giralda,
on victory over the Christians at the Battle of Alarcos.
 19 November 1248, **King Ferdinand III of Castilla**, the Saint, as he was known (and
 referred to in the lines above) and who was cousin to St Louis of France, delivered
e city from the Moors who were all expelled.
e discovery of America in 1492 brought new prosperity to Sevilla. Expeditions to the
w World set out from the port: **Amerigo Vespucci** (1451-1512), the Florentine who
termined to prove that Columbus's discoveries were not the Indies
t a new continent to which his own name was ultimately given;
gellan, who set out in 1519 to circumnavigate the world. By 1503
e city's trade with ports far and near had become such that Isabel
e Catholic created the *Casa de contratación* or Exchange to
courage and also to control all trade with America. This mono-
ly lasted until 1717 when the silting up of the Guadalquivir
ought about the transfer of the Casa concession to Cádiz.

t and architecture in Sevilla – The ramparts on the north
le of the town, the lofty Alcázar, the Torre del Oro (*Gold
wer*) (BY) – built in 1220 on the banks of the Guadalquivir
 guard the port which could be closed by a chain stretched
ross the river to another tower, since vanished, on the
r bank – and finally, the Giralda, are all reminders of
villa's Moorish occupation.
terestingly, Sevilla was, in fact, Christian at the time
e Nasrids were building the Alhambra in Granada and
 the use of the **Mudéjar style**, that mixture of Moorish
d Christian, long after the reconquest of the town in
?48, reflected their fascination for Arab design – as
emplified in the Alcázar built under Peter the Cruel,
e Casa de Pilatos, the **Palacio de las Dueñas** (BCV) and the
rre de San Marcos (San Marcos Belfry) (CV).

Spain's Golden Age, the **Seville School** of painters bro-
ht renown to the city. Three generations of artists
rresponded to the three reigns: under Philip III (1598-
521) **Roelas** and **Pacheco**, portraitist and Velázquez'
aster; under Philip IV (1621-65) **Herrera the Elder**, whose
intings have an epic touch, and **Zurbarán** (1598-1664)
o after having studied in the city remained here and
rtrayed motionless figures with rare spiritual inten-
ty. Finally under Charles II (1665-1700) there was
rillo (1618-82), a Baroque artist, author of numerous

The Giralda

J.Hidalgo - C.Lopesino/MARCO POLO

345

gently radiant Immaculate Conceptions and, also, of brilliantly depicted every scenes, particularly those including young women, children and characters commo every town and village, such as the water carrier. Also of this period was **Valdés** (1622-90), who had a violent Baroque technique, and whose best work can be see the Hospital de la Caridad (Hospital of Charity). **Velázquez** (1599-1660) was bor Sevilla; he entered Pacheco's Academy and later became his son-in-law; on movin Madrid he became court portraitist and, laden with honours, spent the rest of his painting the royal family.

Sevilla's statues, many the work of the 17C sculptor, **Martínez Montañés**, are disper throughout the city's churches. The best-known are the **Cristo del Gran Poder** (Chris Great Power) by **Juan de Mesa** in **San Lorenzo** (AV), the **Cachorro** by Francisco Antonio G in the **Capilla del Patrocinio**, calle Castilla (AX), named after the gypsy who served as sculptor's model, and finally, the **Macarena Virgin**, the most popular figure in Sev which stands, when not in procession, in a special chapel (CV).

Sevilla today – Sevilla is an important industrial town (textiles, food processi farm machinery, aeronautics) and the centre of an agricultural region (cere cotton, sugar beet) as well as the only river port in Spain.

The **1992 World Fair** was held on the **Isla de la Cartuja** (Island of the Carthusian Monaste between two branches of the Guadalquivir. This great event, which has left indelible mark on Sevilla, not only resulted in a large-scale urban modernizat programme for the city (bridges, communications etc), but also involved incorporation of the land on the Isla de la Cartuja into the urban structure of Sevi This is also where the **Isla Mágica** theme park, which retraces the discovery of the N World by the Spanish, taking as its point of departure 16C Sevilla, and the **Ce Andaluz de Arte Contemporáneo**, housed in the former Cartuja monastery, are locat

RESTAURANTS

Albahaca – *Pl. Santa Cruz, 12.* ☎ *95 422 07 14.*
e colourful rooms of this former mansion house are the perfect setting for
ner in this famous part of the city. Excellent fish dishes and a delightful terrace.

ral del Agua – *Callejón del Agua, 6.* ☎ *95 422 48 41.*
leasant, refreshing surprise awaits you in this quiet, atmospheric alley. The
race, with its abundant vegetation, is delightful in the heat of summer.
ssic Andalusian cuisine.

erna del Alabardero – *Zaragoza, 20.* ☎ *95 456 06 37.*
e of the best tables in Sevilla. Seven rooms also available for guests. Home
the Sevilla's School of Hotel Management.

TAPAS

popular are tapas in Sevilla that customers are often forced out onto the
eet with a glass in their hand. The city now offers visitors a range and
ality of tapas without equal, with most bars to be found in the Santa Cruz
CX), Arenal (**AX**) and Triana (**AY**) districts. Sunday is the traditional day for
aperitif in the Plaza del Salvador (**BX**).

Santa Cruz

Teresas – *Ximénez de Enciso, 16.*
ypical tavern which takes its customers back to the turn-of-the-century. One
Santa Cruz's legendary bars.

Gitanilla – *Ximénez de Enciso on the corner of the Mesón del Moro.*
mediately opposite Las Teresas. A good choice for fried tapas and a quick
ass of wine to start you off on the tapas trail.

dega Santa Cruz – *Rodrigo Caro con Mateos Gago.*
ually full of young people enjoying tapas on large barrels in the street.

eipiriña – *Rodrigo Caro, 3.*
bar renowned for its chorizo and a wide range of Sevillian tapas specialities.

rvecería La Giralda – *Mateos Gago, 1.*
e simple exterior conceals one of Santa Cruz's most typical bars. Decorated
th *azulejos* and prints of the Giralda. Delicious *raciones*.

dega Belmonte – *Mateos Gago, 24.*
new tavern simply decorated with bottles and prints. You must try the *lomo
pimienta* (spicy pork).

Triana

osco de las Flores – *Betis, next to the Puente de Triana.*
is bar's major plus is undoubtedly its terrace, from where there is a
agnificent view of the Guadalquivir and the Torre del Oro. Fish specialities.

s Columnas – *San Jacinto, 29.*
new bar but with a traditional ambience and a huge choice of tapas.

l y Sombra – *Castilla, 149-151.*
s tapas are a Sevilla institution. Legs of ham, a huge choice of wines, and
llfighting posters offer the perfect backdrop for a selection of tapas,
cluding *solomillo al ajo* (sirloin with garlic).

sa Cuesta – *Castilla, 1.*
the other end of the same street. Tables outside in fine weather.

Arenal and Plaza Nueva

fanta Sevilla – *Arfe, 36.*
recently-opened bar with a traditional atmosphere. Barrel tables and a
riety of typically Sevillian tapas.

sablanca – *Zaragoza, 50.*
ways extremely lively. This narrow tapas bar is a popular meeting place for
cals.

deguita Romero – *Harinas, 10.*
is bar serves one of Sevilla's best *pringá*, a local meat stew, washed down
th wine from the barrel.

Santa Catalina

Rinconcillo – *Gerona, 40.*
ell worth a detour, if only to have a look at the city's oldest tavern. Founded
1764, although its current decor takes us back to the 19C.

Alfalfa

odega Extremeña – *Águilas, on the corner of Candilejo.*
bar specializing in products from Extremadura on a corner of the lively and
mospheric Plaza de la Alfalfa. A wide selection of cheeses, including the
ouse speciality, the *torta del casar*. While you're here, why not try the bar's
xcellent pork, ham and blood sausage tapas ?

347

SHOPPING

Most of the city's smartest shops and large department stores
located in and around the following streets: Sierpes, O'Donnell and San Pa
A less upmarket shopping area can also be found behind San Salva
church.

The trendiest boutiques are in the Calle de la Asunción, in **Los Remedios** (A
Antique-lovers are best advised to wander through the historic centre of
city, particularly through the Santa Cruz district.

The **Jueves** (Thursday) is an interesting small market which takes place one
week along the calle Feria. On Sundays there are other local markets on
Alameda de Hércules.

Arts and crafts – Sevilla has a rich tradition of arts and crafts. Potters
still be found in the Santa Cruz and **Triana (AY)** districts; the latter contains
aptly named Calle Alfarería, literally Pottery Street. The "La Cartuja" fact
is the heir to this tradition which dates back to Roman times and the per
of Moorish occupation of the city. Other typical products from Sevilla inclu
inlaid woodwork, shawls, fans, flamenco costumes, wrought iron, harness
guitars and castanets.

The Jueves market

PRACTICAL INFORMATION

Tourist office – Avda. de la Constitución, 21 B, ☎ 95 422 14 04.

Municipal tourist office – Paseo de Las Delicias, 9 ☎ 95 223 44 65.

Sevilla Information Centre – Arjona, 28 ☎ 95 450 56 00. **Intern**
http://www.sevilla.org

Publications – Two free bilingual publications (Spanish-English) are pub
shed for tourists every month. These brochures, **Welcome Olé** and **The Touri**
can be obtained from major hotels and tourist sites around the city. Sevi
City Hall's Department of Culture **(NODO)** also publishes a monthly brochu
listing all the city's cultural events. A monthly publication covering the who
of Andalucía, **El Giraldillo**, contains information on the region's fai
exhibitions and theatres, as well as details on cinemas, restaurants a
shops. **Internet:** http://www.giraldillo.es

Transport

...port – Aeropuerto de San Pablo, 14km/9mi towards Madrid on the N IV ...torway, ☎ 95 451 25 78. A bus service operates from in front of the Hotel ...onso XIII, by the Puerta de Jerez.

...ains – Estación de Santa Justa, ☎ 95 441 41 11. The high-speed **AVE** (Tren ... Alta Velocidad) departs from this station, taking just 45min to Córdoba and ...r 30min to Madrid. For bookings, call ☎ 95 454 03 03. For **RENFE** (Spanish ...ate Railways) information, call ☎ 95 454 02 02.

...ter-city buses – Sevilla has two bus stations: **Estación Plaza de Armas** ... 95 490 77 37 and **Estación del Prado de San Sebastián**, Manuel Vázquez ...gastizábal, ☎ 95 441 71 11.

...cal buses – Sevilla has an extensive network of daytime bus services, as well ... six night-time bus routes, all of which leave from Plaza Nueva. Daytime ...ses generally run from 6am to midnight, while night-time routes operate ...ery hour until 6am. Various types of tickets are available, including ...-journey *Bonobus* booklets, 10-journey transfer tickets (enabling passen-...rs to use the same ticket for 1hr) and a monthly pass (*bono mensual*). For ...formation, call ☎ 95 441 11 52.

...xis – **Radio Taxi** ☎ 95 458 00 00/457 11 11 and **Tele Taxi** ☎ 95 462 22 22/...2 14 61.

...r hire – **Avis** ☎ 95 463 33 00; **Hertz** ☎ 95 457 00 55.

...rse-drawn carriages – It is well worth taking a trip on one of the numerous ...rse-drawn carriages operating in the city. They can normally be hired by the ...thedral, in the María Luisa park and by the Torre del Oro.

Boat trips on the Guadalquivir

For a different perspective of the city, why not take to the Guadalquivir, which is navigable as far as Sevilla ? Boat trips last 1hr during the day and 1hr 30min at night. Departures every half-hour from the Torre del Oro. ☎ 95 456 16 92.

THE GIRALDA AND CATHEDRAL *1hr 30min*

Giralda ⊘ (**BX**) – The Giralda – 98m/322ft high – was once a minaret; its name, literally weather vane, comes from the revolving bronze statue of Faith at its summit. When the Giralda was built in the 12C, it resembled its Moroccan sisters, the Koutoubia in Marrakesh and the Hassan Tower in Rabat, and was surmounted by four decorative gilded spheres. The top storey and Renaissance style lantern were added in the 16C. The delicate ornament is typical of the style of the Almohads, a dynasty of strict religious belief, opposed to ostentation, whose members created monumental grandeur in exact accordance with their ideals of utter simplicity. A gently sloping ramp, interrupted at intervals by platforms, leads to the top at 70m/230ft from which there are excellent **views**★★ of the town. The **Patio de los Naranjos** (Orange Tree Court) also remains from the ancient mosque; the Puerta del Perdón on the court's north wall (best viewed from the street), built in 1552, is a fine example of the Mudéjar style.

Catedral ⊘ (**BX**) – "Let us build a cathedral so immense that everyone, on beholding it, will take us for madmen", the chapter is said to have declared when they were knocking down the mosque. They succeeded, for Sevilla's cathedral is the third largest in Europe after St Peter's in Rome and St Paul's in London. The exterior is massive.

As one of the last to be built in the Gothic style, the cathedral shows obvious Renaissance influence. The main portals are modern though harmonising with the whole, however, the Puerta de la Natividad (Nativity Doorway) on the right and the Puerta del Bautismo (Baptism) on the left, on either side of the west door, include beautiful sculptures by Mercadante de Bretaña or Brittany (c 1460) while the Gothic Puerta de Los Palos and Puerta de las Campanillas, on either side of the rounded Capilla Real (Royal Chapel) (1575) at the east end, have Renaissance style tympana in which Maestro Miguel Perrin (1520) has made full play of perspective in true Renaissance style.

The interior is striking in size and richness. The massive column shafts, supporting huge arches, appear slender because they are so tall; the magnificent Flamboyant vaulting rises 56m/184ft above the transept crossing.

Enter through the Lonja or Puerta de San Cristóbal in the south transept.

SEVILLA

Alemanes . . . . BX 12
Alfaro (Pl.) . . . . CXY 15
Alférez Provisional
  (Glorieta) . . . . BZ 18
Almirante Apodaca . . . . . CV 20
Almirante Lobo . . . . BY 22
Álvarez Quintero . . . . . . BX 23
Amparo . . . . BV 25
Aposentadores . . . . BV 28
Argote de Molina . . . . . . BX 30
Armas (Pl. de) . . . . AX 31
Banderas (Patio de) . . . BXY 35
Capitán Vigueras . . . . . . CY 42
Cardenal Spínola . . . . . . AV 47
Castelar . . . . AX 55
Chapina (Puente) . . . . . . AX 59
Conde de Urbina (Av.) . . CZ 65
Covadonga (Glorieta) . . CZ 67
Cruces . . . . CX 75
Doctor Pedro Castro . . . CZ 90
Doña Elvira . . . . BX 95
Doña Guiomar . . . . AX 97
Ejército Español . . . . . CZ 105
Escuelas Pías . . . . CV 114
Farmacéutico E.
  Murillo Herrera . . . . . AY 115
Feria . . . . BV 123
Francisco Carrión
  Mejías . . . . CV 126
Francos . . . . BX
Fray Ceferino
  González . . . . BX 127
García de Vinuesa . . . . . BX 130
General Polavieja . . . . . BX 135
Hernán Cortés (Av.) . . . CZ 140
Jesús de la Vera Cruz . . AV 147
José María Martínez
  Sánchez Arjona . . . . . AY 150
Julio César . . . . AX 152
Luis Montoto . . . . CX 160
Marcelino Champagnat . AY 172
Marineros Voluntarios
  (Glorieta) . . . . BZ 180
Martín Villa . . . . BV 190
Mateos Gago . . . . BX 192
Murillo . . . . AV 202
Museo (Pl.) . . . . AV 205
Navarros . . . . CVX 207
O'Donnell . . . . BV 210
Pascual de Gayangos . . AV 220
Pastor y Landero . . . . . AX 222
Pedro del Toro . . . . BX 227
Pizarro (Av.) . . . . CZ 232
Ponce de León (Pl.) . . . CV 234
Puente y Pellón . . . . . . BV 239
Puerta de Jerez . . . . . . BY 242
Presidente
  Carrero Blanco . . . . . BZ 243
República Argentina
  (Av.) . . . . AY 255
Reyes Católicos . . . . . . AX 260
Rodríguez Caso (Av.) . . CZ 262
San Gregorio . . . . BY 272
San Juan de la Palma . . BV 277
San Pedro (Pl.) . . . . . . BV 286
San Sebastián (Pl.) . . . . CY 287
Santa María
  La Blanca . . . . CX 297
Santander . . . . BY 300
Santiago Montoto
  (Av.) . . . . BZ 301
Saturno . . . . CV 302
Sierpes . . . . BVX
Tetuán . . . . BX
Triunfo (Pl.) . . . . BX 307
Velázquez . . . . BV 310
Venerables . . . . BX 312
Virgen de África . . . . . . AZ 314
Virgen del Águila . . . . . AZ 315
Virgen de Fátima . . . . . AZ 317
Virgen de Loreto . . . . . . AZ 320
Virgen del Valle . . . . . . AZ 325
Viriato . . . . BV 329

B	Hospital de los Venerables
E	Archivo General de Indias
H	Ayuntamiento
U	Universidad

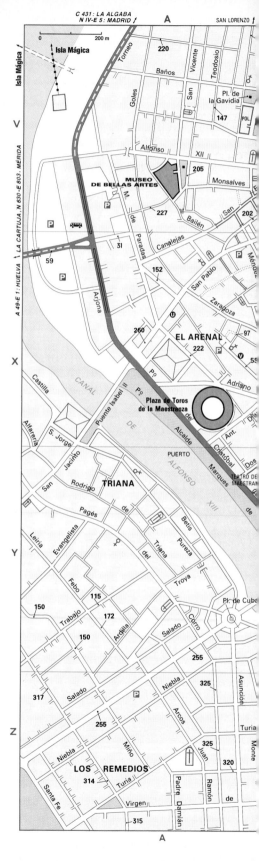

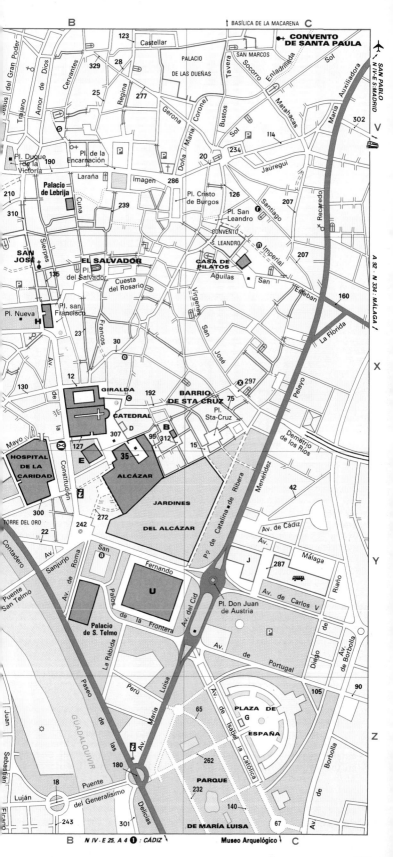

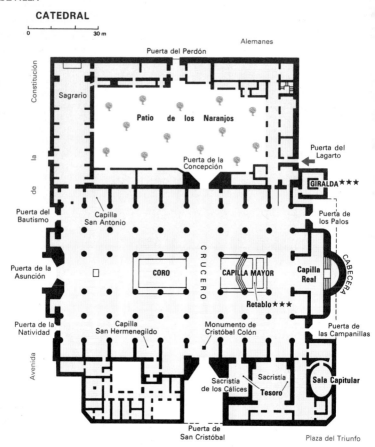

CATEDRAL

Columbus' tomb lies in the south transept; the 19C monument shows the discoverer's coffin being borne by four kings symbolising León, Castilla, Navarra and Aragón.

Capilla Mayor (Chancel) – The chancel is unbelievably rich. Splendid Plateresque grilles (1518-33) precede the immense Flemish **altarpiece★★★**, profusely but delicately carved with scenes from the life of Christ and gleaming with gold leaf (1482-1525).

Coro – Partly hidden by a grille (1519-23) by Brother Francisco of Salamanca, are 15C and 16C choir stalls. The **trascoro**, a screen of multicoloured marble, jasper and bronze, is 16C.

Tesoro – The treasury is in 16C rooms; the sacristy contains the cathedral plate including a Renaissance **monstrance** (custodia) by Juan de Arfe and the Tenebrario or Plateresque candelabrum with 15 branches used in Holy Week.

The **Sacristía de los Cálices** (Chalice Sacristy) displays painting and sculpture including canvases by Goya (*Santa Justa and Santa Rufina*), Valdés Leal and Murillo. The rooms adjoining the chapter-house contain collections of chasubles, lecterns and antiphonaries. One of them displays the pages' costumes of the *Seises*, a group of choristers who dance before the high altar at Corpus Christi and on 8 December, perpetuating a secular tradition of unknown origin.

Sala Capitular – The vast 16C Renaissance chapter-house has an elliptical dome and an *Immaculate Conception* by Murillo.

★★ **Capilla Real** (Chapel Royal) – The Chapel Royal opens through an arch so high that the decoration can only be appreciated from a distance. It is covered by an elegant, richly ornamented Renaissance dome with carved busts decorating the cells. On either side are the tombs of Alfonso X of Castilla (d 1284) and his mother, Beatrice of Swabia. At the centre of the high altar is the robed figure of Our Lady of the Monarchs, patron of Sevilla, given, according to legend, by St Louis of France to his cousin St Ferdinand of Spain, who lies buried in a silver gilt shrine below the altar. The chapel screen dates from 1771.

Numerous works of art are displayed in the periphery chapels: the tomb of Cardinal Juan de Cervantes in the Capilla de San Hermenegildo (St Hermenegild's Chapel) on the south side and paintings by Murillo in that of San Antonio (north side).

★★ ALCÁZAR AND BARRIO SANTA CRUZ 2hr 30min

★★ **Alcázar (Reales Alcázares)** ⊘ **(BXY)** – The palace visible today is the result of several phases of construction. All that remains of the 12C Alcázar of the Almohads are the Patio de Yeso and the section of wall dividing the Patio de la Montería from the Patio del León. The rest of the building dates from the Christian period. In the 13C, Alfonso X the Wise built a palace on top of the Almohad remains, known today as **Charles V's rooms**. Then, in the 14C, **Peter the Cruel** (1350-69) erected the main nucleus of the building on view today. This part, which is known as **Peter the Cruel's Palace**, was built in 1362. It is a masterpiece of Mudéjar art, built by masons from Granada; as a result, the decoration is highly influenced by the Alhambra which dates from the same period, making the building, in spite of later modifications under Juan II, the Catholic monarchs, Charles V and Philip II, one of the purest examples of the Mudéjar style.

Cuarto del Almirante (Admiral's Apartments) – *Right side of the Patio de la Montería.* It was here that Isabel the Catholic founded the Casa de Contratación. The Sala de Audiencias (Audience Chamber) contains a model of Columbus's vessel *Santa María* and an altarpiece, the **Virgin of the Navigators**★ (1531-36), painted by Alejo Fernández.

★★ **Palacio de Pedro el Cruel** (Peter the Cruel's Palace) – The narrow façade, sheltered by a carved polychrome pine overhang, is strongly reminiscent of the Patio del Cuarto Dorado (Golden Room Court) in the Alhambra. From here, a small passageway leads to the **Patio de las Doncellas** (Court of the Maidens), a beautifully proportioned, Moorish arched *patio* which is still exquisite in spite of the upper storey added in the 16C. A number of Mudéjar rooms open onto this *patio*. On the right-hand side, an elevated round arch leads to the **Dormitorio de los Reyes Moros** (Bedroom of the Moorish Kings), two rooms decorated with blue toned stucco and a magnificent *artesonado* ceiling. Pass through a small room with a flat ceiling to reach the **Patio de las Muñecas** (Dolls' Court) with its delicate, Granada-influenced decoration. The gallery on the upper floor dates from the 19C. On the arch to the left of the north side two medallion faces can be seen which according to legend give the patio its name. The Catholic Monarch's bedroom leads to the **Salón de Felipe II** (Philip II's Saloon), with its magnificent Renaissance coffered cedar ceiling; this in turn connects, via the **Arco de los Pavones** (Peacocks' Arch), with the **Salón de Embajadores** (Ambassadors' Hall), the most sumptuous room in the Alcázar, with its remarkable 15C half-orange cedarwood **cupola**★★. The tour is completed around the Patio de las Doncellas with the **Sala de Infantes**, leading to the Prince's Gardens (Jardines del Príncipe) and the **Sala de Carlos V** (Charles V's Room), the palace's former chapel.

Come out of the palace into the Patio de la Montería and through a vaulted passage on the right.

Salones de Carlos V (Charles V's Rooms) – These rooms correspond to the Gothic palace built under the reign of Alfonso X. The structure and groin vaults date from this period. It was here that Charles V married Isabel of Portugal. The rooms house a magnificent collection of Brussels **tapestries**★★ (1554) illustrating Emperor Charles V's conquest of Tunis in 1535.

★ **Jardines (BCY)** – These gardens are one of the best examples of this magnificent Moorish art. Leave Charles V's rooms and pass by the Jardín de las Danzas (Dancing Garden) and the Mercurio pool to reach the 17C **Galería del Grutesco**★ *(see overleaf)*, from where there is an impressive view of the gardens, laid out in terraces with numerous ornamental basins. The most enchanting parts of the garden are **Charles V's pavilion**, the Jardín de la Cruz, recreating the myth of Daedalus, and the English garden.

An alleyway leads to the Patio de Banderas or Flag Court.

Patio de Banderas (Flag Court) **(BXY 35)** – The small enclosed square is bordered by elegant façades which stand out against the background of the cathedral and the Giralda tower.

★★ **Barrio de Santa Cruz (Santa Cruz Quarter) (BCX)** – This former Jewish quarter or Judería was the quarter favoured by Sevilla nobility in the 17C; it remains well worth visiting for its character, its alleys, wrought-iron grilles, flower-filled *patios* and squares shaded by orange trees and palms. It is even more delightful in the evenings when cafés and restaurants overflow into the squares like those of Doña Elvira, los Venerables Sacerdotes, Alfaro, Santa Cruz and Las Cruces.

★ **Hospital de los Venerables** ⊘ **(BX B)** – This building, located in the lively Plaza de los Venerables, is one of the best examples of 17C Sevillian Baroque art. It now serves as the headquarters for the Cultural Focus Foundation. Its fine **church** is covered with frescoes painted by Valdés Leal and his son Lucas Valdés.

Galería del Grutesco

ADDITIONAL SIGHTS

★★ **Museo de Bellas Artes (Fine Arts Museum)** ⊘ **(AV)** – This excellent museum in the former Convento de la Merced (Merced Friary) was built in the 17C by Juan d Oviedo around three beautiful *patios*. It houses an important collection of paintings covering Spain's Golden Age. The Baroque doorway was added in the 18C.

The first of the museum's 14 rooms contains examples of medieval art. **Room I** once the refectory, is dedicated to Renaissance art, in particular a fine sculpture of *St Jerome* by Pietro Torrigiani, a contemporary of Michelangelo. Other work of note include Alejo Fernández's *Annunciation*, with its Flemish and Italian influence clearly evident, a diptych of *The Annunciation and Visitation* by Coffermans, and a *Holy Family* by Villegas. Two magnificent portraits of *A Lady and a Gentleman* by Pedro Pacheco are the highlight in **Room III** while severa Baroque style pictures of the Infant Jesus are on display in **Room IV**.

Room V★★★ is undoubtedly the museum's star attraction. The church, its wall decorated with paintings by the 18C artist Domingo Martínez, provides stunning backdrop to an outstanding collection of work by Murillo and one of Zurbarán's masterpieces *The Apotheosis of St Thomas Aquinas* (in the nave), with its skilfully executed play between light and shade. **Murillo**, a master of both the pictorial technique and the use of light in his canvases, is the great painter of religious subjects and idealized figures, such as beggar children, with a stron popular appeal; his style is characterised by soft forms, delicate colouring an sweetness of mood, earning it the label *estilo vaporoso*. His works can be foun in the transept and in the apse where his monumental *Immaculate Conception* with its energetic movement, holds pride of place. It is surrounded by severa notable paintings of saints: *Santa Rufina and Santa Justa*, clutching the Giralda and *San Leandro and San Buenaventura*. On the right-hand side of the transep a kindly *Virgen de la Servietta* is particularly interesting (admire the effect of th Child moving towards you). Note also *St Francis embracing Christ on the Cros* and a further *Immaculate Conception*, also known as *The Child*. Among severa paintings on its left-hand side, *St Anthony and Child, Dolorosa* and *St Felix o Cantalicio and Child* are all worth a closer look.

Upper Floor: Room VI (a gallery) displays a fine, richly decorated collection of Saints (anonymous, though some painted by followers of Zurbarán), two saints and a *Christ* by Zurbarán himself, and a powerful portrait of *St James the Apostle* by Ribera. **Room VII** contains further works by Murillo and his disciples while **Room VIII** is entirely devoted to the other great Baroque artist Valdés Leal. European Baroque is represented in **Room IX** with, among others, canvases by Brueghel and the supreme *Portrait of a Lady* by Cornelis de Vos. **Room X**★★ merits special attention, with its walls mostly set aside for **Zurbarán** (1598-1664). He had a particular skill for painting the shades of white of the monks' habits and the pure cloth of Christ, as admired in the fine *Christ on the Cross* (in this same room), in which the body of Christ, painted against a dark background, almost appears as if sculpted in relief. Zurbarán's compositions are both simple and peaceful. A certain lack of concern for perspective is apparent in some of his work, resulting in one or two inaccuracies, as can be seen in *St Hugh and Carthusian Monks at Table* which is otherwise quite outstanding. His preoccupation with the treatment of the canvas, as already seen in the Fathers of the Church in *The Apotheosis of St Thomas Aquinas*, can equally be admired in the splendid velvet brocade in *San Ambrosio*. In addition to his paintings of saints, his *Virgin of the Caves* and *San Bruno's visit to Urbano II* are also of interest. On display in the same room are various sculptures, including *San Bruno* by Martínez Montañés. The ceiling of the inner room should not be missed. **Room XI** (a gallery), with its collection of 18C works, is enlivened by Goya's *Portrait of Canon José Duato*. The following two rooms **(XII and XIII)** display 19C art, in particular, there are some superb portraits by Esquivel, while the final room **(XIV)** shows several 20C canvases (Vázquez Díaz, Zuloaga).

★ **Casa de Pilatos** (Pilate's House) ⊙ (CX) – The palace, built between the late 15C and early 16C by Don Fadrique, the first Marquis of Tarifa, is thought to be based on Pontius Pilate's house in Jerusalem. It is a mixture of Mudéjar, Renaissance and Flamboyant Gothic styles.
The large *patio*, in which the Mudéjar style predominates, resembles an elegant Moorish palace with finely moulded stuccowork and magnificent lustre **azulejos**★★. The statues, some Antique and the rest 16C, portray, among others, Roman emperors and Athena. The ground floor rooms with *artesonado* ceilings, the chapel with Gothic vaulting and *azulejo* and stucco decoration on the altar, and the remarkable wood **dome**★ over the grand **staircase**★ illustrate the vitality of the Mudéjar style in civil architecture during the Renaissance. Among the painted ceilings on the first floor is that by Francisco Pacheco (1603) illustrating the Apotheosis of Hercules.

★★ **Parque de María Luisa** (BCZ) – The 19C park with its beautiful trees, pools and fountains, once formed the grounds of the Palacio de San Telmo. Several buildings remain from the 1929 Ibero-American Exhibition including the semicircular edifice surrounding the vast **Plaza de España**★ (CZ). Each of the 58 benches around the square with their *azulejo* decoration, represents a province of Spain and illustrates an episode from its particular history. There is rowing in the canals on the square.

Plaza de España, Sevilla

B. Brillion/MICHELIN

Museo Arqueológico (Archeological Museum) ⊙ (CZ) – The museum in the n₪ Renaissance palace on Plaza de América houses interesting collections of objec from prehistoric through to Phoenician, Punic and Roman times. The 7C ₪ **Carambolo Treasure★** includes gold jewellery from the ancient Tartessos civilizatic as well as a statue of Astarte with a Phoenician inscription and the Ebora Treasu dating from the period of Phoenician colonisation, the 8C to the 5C BC. T Roman section, with part of its finds from Itálica *(see below)*, consists of statue Venus, Diana the Huntress, Trajan, a head of Alexander the Great, a beautif₪ Hispania, as well as mosaics and bronzes.

★ **Hospital de la Caridad (Hospital of Charity)** ⊙ (BY) – The hospital was found₪ in 1625 by Miguel de Mañara who called upon the great Sevillian artists of t₪ time to decorate the church with the themes of Death and Charity. Valdés Le₪ illustrated the first with a striking sense of the macabre, Murillo the seco₪ in two large paintings: *The Miracle of the Loaves and Fishes* which faces *Mos₪ Smiting Water from the Rock*, as well as in *St John of God* and *St Isab₪ of Hungary caring for the Sick*. Pedro Roldan's *Entombment* adorns the hi₪ altar.

★ **Convento de Santa Paula** ⊙ (CV) – This 15C convent is one of the most beautif and lavish in the city. The church's breathtaking **portal★** (1504) is adorned wi₪ ceramics. Despite the obvious mix of styles (Mudéjar, Gothic and Renaissance the overall effect is a harmonious one. Inside, the nave is covered by a 17C ro₪ and the chancel by a Gothic vault covered with attractive frescoes. The church al₪ contains sculptures and paintings of interest.

Museum – *Entrance through no 11 on the plaza.* It has some fine works on displa by important artists such as Ribera, Pedro de Mena, Alonso de Cana etc.

★ **Iglesia del Salvador** ⊙ (BX) – This 17C-18C church rises majestically on one si₪ of the square which gives it its name. The sensation of vastness pervades t₪ whole of the interior. It contains some of the city's most impressive 18C **Baroq₪ retables★**.

Palacio de Lebrija ⊙ (BV) – The structure of the building is a typical example ₪ an Andalucian palace-residence, with a *patio* and interior garden. The decoratic is perhaps more of a surprise with Roman mosaic floors from nearby Itálic₪ Mudéjar *artesonado* ceilings and 16C and 17C *azulejos*.

Archivo General de Indias (The Indies Archives) ⊙ (BXY E) – The building, dating fro₪ 1572, was designed by Juan de Herrera, architect of the Escorial, as an Exchang₪ *(lonja)*. It now houses a unique collection of documents on America at the time ₪ its discovery and conquest including maps and charts, plans of South America₪ towns and their fortifications as well as the autographs of Columbus, Magellar Cortés and others.

★ **Capilla de San José (St Joseph's Chapel)** ⊙ (BX) – The profusely gilded, Baroqu₪ chapel, gleams at night by the lights of evening service. The overpowerin₪ altarpiece, organ and ornate galleries are typical of the period (1766).

Ayuntamiento (town hall) (BX H) – The hall's **east face★**, dating from 1527 to 1534 is attractively Renaissance in style with delicate scrollwork decoration. Sta vaulting covers the vestibule.

Palacio de San Telmo (BY) – The palace (1682-1796), once a naval academy an₪ residence of the dukes of Montpensier and now a seminary, has a grand Baroqu₪ **entrance**, three storeys high, by Leonardo de Figueroa. It now serves as th₪ headquarters of the Presidencia de la Junta de Andalucía.

Universidad (BY U) – The university with its harmonious Baroque façades an₪ elegantly laid-out *patios*, is in the old tobacco factory (18C).

★ **Isla Mágica (Magic Island)** ⊙ (AV) – Cross the symbolic Puente de La Barqueta t₪ reach this theme park which takes visitors on an adventurous journey back to th₪ century of the discoveries. The 40ha/99 acre site is divided into six theme area₪ **Sevilla, the Gateway to the Indies; The Gateway to America; Amazonia; The Pirates' Den; The Fountain of Youth; and El Dorado**. Theatrical performances are held throughout th₪ park, which also offers some impressive attractions such as the **Anaconda**, ₪ breathtaking water ride, "The Rapids of the Orinoco", for rafting enthusiasts, and **The Jaguar**, the most exciting attraction of them all. Other spectacular rides include the **Flight of the Falcon**, a merry-go-round with a difference. The park also has a whole host of restaurants and shops to help you catch your breath as you continue along your magical journey.

La Cartuja–Centro Andaluz de Arte Contemporáneo ⊙ – This contemporary art museum is housed in the former Monasterio de la Cartuja. In the 19C, the monastery was used as a ceramics factory, the ovens and chimneys of which can still be seen today. The museum is now used for temporary exhibitions.

EXCURSION

Itálica ⊘ – *9km/6mi northwest on N 630 towards Mérida.*
Standing on a cypress-covered hillside overlooking the Guadalquivir plain, are the remains of a **Roman town**, the birthplace of the emperors Hadrian and Trajan and the poet Silius Italicus. The great size of the amphitheatre illustrates the importance of the town at the time. By following the network of streets covering the hillside you see mosaics, among others of birds and Neptune, in their original sites.

Anfiteatro – This amphitheatre was one of the largest in the Roman Empire with seating for 25 000 spectators. Parts of both the seating area and the pit beneath the stage remain from its original elliptical design.
The Itálica theatre, on the far side of the old road leading to the N 630, has now been restored.

SIGÜENZA★

Castilla-La Mancha (Guadalajara) – Population 5 426
Michelin map 444 I 22

The pink and ochre coloured town of Sigüenza, dropping in tiers from the hilltop on which it is built, is dominated by its imposing cathedral fortress and castle (parador).
The old town is a maze of narrow streets bordered by stylish mansions. In the centre, the **plaza Mayor**, which extends from the south wall of the cathedral, is a delightful square with its 16C arcaded gallery and Renaissance town hall (Ayuntamiento).

★ **Catedral** ⊘ – The nave, begun to a Cistercian plan in the 12C, was only completed in 1495, the end of the Gothic period; the ambulatory and cloisters are slightly later. The roof and transept dome were rebuilt after the bombings of 1936.
The façade appears more like that of a fortress than a church as it stands flanked by crenellated towers and powerful buttresses until you notice its great rose and Romanesque windows with their old stained glass.

Interior – The nave with sober lines and high vaulting supported on massive pillars graced by slender engaged columns, conveys an impression of solid strength.
In the **north aisle**, the **doorway★** into the Capilla de la Anunciación (Chapel of the Annunciation) is decorated with Renaissance pilasters, Mudéjar arabesques and Gothic cusping. The 15C triptych beside it by the Castilian School is dedicated to Sts Mark and Catherine.
In the **north transept** is a fine **sculptured unit★★**: a 16C **porphyry doorway** opening onto the cloisters of multicoloured marble. The 16C **Santa Librada altar** designed by Covarrubias as a retable features a central niche containing an altar surmounted by painted panels of the martyrdom of the saint and her eight sisters, all born, according to legend, on the same day. Beside it, note the 16C **sepulchre of Dom Fadrique of Portugal**, a more ornate monument adorned with Plateresque decoration.
The **sacristy** by Covarrubias has an amazing **ceiling★** – a profusion of heads and roses between which peer thousands of cherubim; the panelling and woodwork of doors and furniture are delicately carved in ornate Plateresque. The 16C **Capilla de las Reliquias** (Reliquary Chapel) is covered with a **dome★**.
A chapel off the **ambulatory** contains a 16C wooden **Crucifix**.
The **chancel** (Presbiterio) has a beautiful 17C wrought-iron grille framed by two alabaster pulpits, one Gothic (on the right), the other Renaissance (on the left). The altarpiece is 17C.
The Capilla del Doncel in the south transept was designed for the **Doncel tomb★★** commissioned by Isabel the Catholic for her young page, Don Martín Vázquez de Arce, who died at the gates of Granada in 1486. The figure, considered a major work of sepulchral art in Spain, shows the youth reclining on one elbow and reading serenely; it is extraordinarily realistic. In the centre of the room is the mausoleum of the Doncel's parents.

Claustro – The 16C Gothic cloisters are surrounded by chapels with Plateresque doors, among them the 16C-17C Puerta de Jaspe (Jasper Doorway) which communicates with the transept.
The **Sala Capitular** (chapter-house) displays books, manuscripts and a collection of 17C Flemish tapestries.

Museo de Arte Antiguo (Museum of Ancient Art) ⊘ – *Opposite the cathedral.* Among the many works displayed are sculptures by Pompeo Leoni (Room C), a *Pietà* attributed to Morales, an *Immaculate Conception* by Zurbarán (Room E) and a fiery statue of the *Prophet Elijah* by Salzillo (Room N).

EXCURSION

Atienza - *31km/19mi northwest on C 114.*

Atienza is a typical Castilian village built at the foot of a castle of which only t
keep remains proudly upright on its rock. **Plaza del Trigo**, surrounded by portico
is attractively medieval. The town, an important commercial enclave during t
Middle Ages, was granted protection by Alfonso VIII of Castilla in recognition f
the support its citizens gave him in 1162 when, as a child, he sought refuge fr
his uncle, Ferdinand II of León who hoped to secure the Castilian throne. The eve
is commemorated annually in the Whitsun **Caballada** festival.

Atienza once had seven churches but since the Civil War all that remains of intere
are the Churrigueresque altarpiece in the **parish church** on Plaza del Trigo and t
Rococo chapel in the **Iglesia de la Trinidad** (Holy Trinity Church) near the cemete

SITGES★★

Catalunya (Barcelona) – Population 13 096
Michelin map 443 I 35

Situated south of Barcelona, Sitges has become a popular holiday resort famous f
its two lovely, carefully-kept beaches. Its 2km/1m long Passeig Marítim, an aven
that joins up with the beach at Ribera, is dotted with hotels, luxury residences a
various other establishments. During the Modernist movement Sitges was
important cultural centre and many examples of architecture dating from those da
can be seen in the city. Sitges is well known too for its carpet of flowers on the Sund
following Corpus Christi, the International Catalunya Film Festival in October, a
the International Festival of Theatre in June.

★★ VILA VELLA (OLD TOWN) *1hr 30min*

Dominating the breakwater of La Punta, sheltering the fishing harbour, stan
the parish church. All around are the streets of the old town lined wi
white-walled houses, their balconies brilliant with flowers. Local museums hous
in neo-Gothic mansions contain canvases from the late 19C, when Rusiñol a
Miguel Utrillo (official father of the French painter) painted in this quarter.

★★ **Museo del Cau Ferrat** ⊙ - The painter **Santiago Rusiñol** (1861-1931) convert
two 16C fishermen's houses, adding some Gothic features, into a home f
himself and an art centre which was inaugurated in 1884, at the same time as t
Casa de la Vila opposite, a neo-Gothic mansion. The collections left to the tow
by Rusiñol, and which are displayed in this museum, include ceramics, painting
sculptures and wrought-iron works.

Painting - Note two remarkable works by El Greco: *Penitent Mary Magdalene* a
The Repentance of St Peter. The gallery also contains canvases by Picasso, Casa
Nonell, Llimona, Zuloaga and Rusiñol himself *(Poetry, Music and Painting).*

Wrought-iron - This collection, which has given its name to the museum *(c*
ferrat), consists of various exhibits of different styles and periods. A Romanesq
brazier and Gothic door handles are among the most interesting objects
display.

Sculpture - Modern works by Manolo Hugué, Gargallo and Clarassó are exhibit
alongside ancient sculptures.

Ceramics - A great many ceramic objects (dishes, vases, figurines) decorate t
exhibition rooms. Note the large blue jar painted with country scenes.

★ **Museo Maricel del Mar** ⊙ - The museum is in the former 14C hospital t
American Charles Deering had converted under the supervision of Miguel Utri
in 1913. It is linked by a footbridge to another mansion, the Maricel de Terr
The collections displayed are of medieval and Baroque works of art. At t
entrance is a fine Gothic high relief of the Three Wise Men in a Hispano-Flemi
style.

★ **Casa Llopis** ⊙ - This bourgeois house built at the end of the 18C in the then ne
part of the town illustrates the considerable wealth accumulated by the city in t
19C and gives a good idea of the life of the middle and upper classes during t
Romantic period with frescoes on the walls, English furniture, various mechanic
devices and musical boxes. Dioramas on the ground floor supplement the pictu
with scenes of private, social and popular activities
The museum also houses the **Lola Anglada Collection**, an outstanding display of 17
18C and 19C dolls from all over Europe made of wood, leather, papier mâché a
china.

EXCURSION

★ **Vilanova i la Geltrú** - *7km/4mi west.*
Situated in a small bay, this locality is both an important fishing harbour and a popular holiday resort for tourists. Its fine sandy beaches and shallow waters are its main attraction.

★ **Museu Romàntic Casa Papiol** ⊙ – The large mansion built by the Papiol family between 1780 and 1801 gives a good idea of the values cherished by the devout yet well to do industrial middle classes in the 19C. A certain austerity reigns in the library with its 5 000 or so 16C to 19C volumes, in the Deputy's office, the chapel with its strange relic of St Constance and in the reception rooms where the walls are covered in biblical scenes executed in grey monochrome. On the other hand, the opulence of the house is evident in the rich furnishings, the ballroom and the Louis XVI apartment where the French General, Suchet, once stayed. The kitchen is spick and span, gleaming with ceramic tiles.
Workrooms and annexes on the entresol and ground floors contain equipment and stores: the stove, olive oil reserve, servants' kitchen and the stables.

★ **Biblioteca-Museu Balaguer** ⊙ – Set up in a curious building of Egyptian inspiration, this library-museum was founded at the instigation of the poet, historian and politician **Víctor Balaguer** (1824-1901). The library boasts around 40 000 titles. The museum houses an impressive **contemporary art collection**, with works from the 1950s and 1960s by Catalan artists, the **Legado 56** collection, with small works outlining the evolution of painting from the end of the 14C to the beginning of the 20C, and an interesting collection of **16C and 17C paintings**, including one **Annunciation** by El Greco, along with contemporary pictures (Fortuny, Casas, Rusiñol), archeological artefacts and examples of Oriental art.

★ **Museu del Ferrocarril** ⊙ – The museum houses one of the most impressive collections of railway engines in Spain.

SOLSONA★

Catalunya (Lleida) – Population 6 601
Michelin map 443 G 34

Narrow winding streets with the occasional medieval house in the shadow of the castle ruins give the town character.
Corpus Christi is the occasion for young men, dressed in ancient costumes, to parade through the streets firing salvoes from blunderbusses, for giant pasteboard figures to appear and children to dance the Ball de Bastons in the streets.

★ **Catedral** ⊙ – Only the belfry and the apse, decorated with Lombard bands and carved modillions, remains of the Romanesque church, the rest is Gothic with Baroque additions such as the portals and the Capilla de la Virgen (Lady Chapel) off the south transept. The latter was designed to shelter within its ornate marble walls the **Mare de Déu del Claustro★**, a beautifully carved Romanesque figure of the Virgin Mary in black stone.

★★ **Museo Diocesano y Comarcal (Diocesan and Regional Museum)** ⊙ – The Romanesque and Gothic style **paintings★★** in the museum housed in the Palacio Episcopal (Episcopal Palace, an 18C Baroque building), are excellent examples of Catalan art. The fresco collection of works from throughout the province includes a painting from the **Sant Quirze de Pedret church★★★**, discovered beneath an overpainting done 100 years later. This fresco, executed in an archaic style, shows God, with arms outstretched, in a circle which represents heaven, surmounted by a phoenix symbolising immortality. Another circle features a peacock proudly pecking at a bunch of grapes. The narrative talent of the 12C Maestro de Pedret can be seen in the theme of the Apocalypse, painted in a style obviously of Byzantine influence in a reconstituted Mozarabic apse. Totally different are the thinly outlined, elegant 13C paintings from **Sant Pau de Caserres★** - in particular, some wonderful angels of the Last Judgement – and the already Gothic style, 14C works from Cardona.
The museum is also known for its collection of **altar fronts** which includes a frontal from Sagars, in which all decoration is omitted to heighten the symbolism of the scenes illustrated, and a realistic painting of the Last Supper, **La Cena de Santa Constanza★** by Jaime Ferrer (15C).
The **Museo de la Sal** (Salt Museum), another department, is possibly unique. Everything displayed on the table has been carved out of rock salt from Cardona: the setting, the repast and the weird, pinnacled centrepiece.

Use the key at the beginning of this guide to get the most out of your Michelin guide.

SORIA★

Castilla y León – Population 35 540
Michelin map 442 G 22

Soria stands at an altitude of 1 050m/3 445ft on the banks of the Duero, the riv
that waters and cools the vast, windswept, russet coloured Castilian plateau. Tl
desolate scenery and medieval atmosphere of the old town have been sung by poe
over the ages including the Sevillian **Antonio Machado** (1875-1939), who wrote *Camp*
de Castilla.

"Soria pura, cabeza de Extremadura" – The motto in the city arms recalls even
in the 10C when Soria and its dependent countryside marked the limits of Castile
the face of the Muslim conquered south. Gradually the Christians built a **fortified li**
along the Duero reinforced by bastions such as **Soria, Berlanga, Gormaz, Peñaranda ar
Peñafiel**.

In the Middle Ages, the town grew prosperous partly through its role in the **Mest**
a powerful association of sheep farmers that organised the seasonal migration o
flocks between Extremadura, Castilla and pastures in the north of the country.

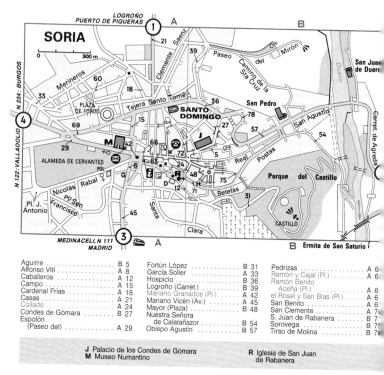

Aguirre	B 5	Fortún López	B 31	Pedrizas	A 6
Alfonso VIII	A 8	García Solier	A 33	Ramón y Cajal (Pl.)	A 6
Caballeros	A 12	Hospicio	B 36	Ramón Benito	
Campo	A 15	Logroño (Carret.)	B 39	Aceña (Pl.)	A 6
Cardenal Frías	A 18	Mariano Granados (Pl.)	A 42	el Rosel y San Blas (Pl.)	A 6
Casas	A 21	Mariano Vicén (Av.)	A 45	San Benito	A 6
Collado	A 24	Mayor (Plaza)	B 48	San Clemente	A 7
Condes de Gómara	B 27	Nuestra Señora		S. Juan de Rabanera	B 7
Espolón		de Calatañazor	B 54	Sorovega	B 75
(Paseo del)	A 29	Obispo Agustín	A 57	Tirso de Molina	B 76

J Palacio de los Condes de Gómara
M Museo Numantino
R Iglesia de San Juan de Rabanera

SIGHTS

★ **Iglesia de Santo Domingo (A)** – The attraction of this church's west front lies in
its two tiers of blind arcades, its window and richly carved **portal★★**. The overall
French air is explained by the fact that the church's founders were Alfonso VIII
and his queen, Eleanor Plantagenet, on either side of the portal. The carving on
the tympanum is less cluttered than that of the archivolt where the figures have
been carved with great attention to detail. The scenes so realistically illustrated
include the early chapters of Genesis (on the capitals of the jamb shafts), the
24 Elders of the Apocalypse playing stringed instruments, the Massacre of the
Innocents, and Christ's childhood, Passion and Death (in ascending registers on
the archivolt).

Palacio de los Condes de Gómara (Palace of the Counts of Gómara) **(B J)** – The long
façade, part Renaissance, part Classical, the bold upstanding tower and double
patio are a proud example of late-16C opulence.

Iglesia de San Juan de Rabanera (A R) – The Romanesque portal taken from a
ruined church dedicated to St Nicholas, recalls the events of the saint's life in the
capitals on the slender columns on the right and on the tympanum. The unusual
decoration at the church's east end shows both Byzantine and Gothic influences.
Inside are two interesting Crucifixes – a Romanesque one over the altar and a
Baroque one in the north transept.

Museo Numantino (Numantia Museum) ⊘ **(A M)** – The collections in the recently restored museum illustrate the historical development of Soria from the Paleolithic Age to modern times. Most of the items displayed come from local excavations – note the artefacts from Celtiberian necropolises and the coloured pottery from Numantia *(see below)*.

Catedral de San Pedro ⊘ **(B)** – The 16C Gothic cathedral is light and spacious; the **cloisters**★ are older, possessing three Romanesque galleries. The capitals have been delicately re-sculpted in a pure Romanesque style that recalls the work in Santo Domingo de Silos. In the gallery walls are the funerary niches in which the monks are buried.

Monasterio de San Juan de Duero ⊘ **(B)** – The monastery founded by the Hospitallers of St John of Jerusalem stands in a rustic setting on the far bank of the Duero. Only the graceful gallery arcading, with four different orders, remains of the 12C-13C **cloisters**★. The intersecting, overlapping arches owe much to Moorish art. The church contains a small lapidary museum. Two small chambers with beautiful historiated capitals stand at the entrance to the apse; the ciborium effect is unusual, more like in an Orthodox church.

Parque del Castillo (Castle Park) (B) – The lines of the poet, Machado, on the Soria countryside come alive on this hillside: ...violet mountains, poplars beside green waters...

Ermita de San Saturio (San Saturio Hermitage) ⊘ **(B)** – A shaded path beside the Duero leads to the cave where the holy man sat in meditation. The octagonal chapel built into the rock and covered with frescoes is 18C.

EXCURSIONS

Ruinas de Numancia ⊘ – *7km/4mi northeast via ① on the town plan; take N 111 as far as Garray and then a little road sharp right heading south.* There are few signs of the events which took place in Numancia in 133 BC. The Romans were in Spain at the time and thought that having pacified the peninsula their legions would suffer little opposition; Numancia, however, resisted them. **Scipio Aemilianus**, who had destroyed Carthage, directed the siege against Numancia. After eight months the Numantines could resist no more but, unwilling to submit, they burned their city and perished one and all.
The present ruins are of the Numancia rebuilt by the Romans.

★ **Sierra de Urbión** – *Roads are liable to be blocked by snow between November and May.* It seems surprising that this part of the Sistema Ibérico mountain range which at one point rises to 2 228m/7 310ft and is so close to the Soria plateau and the flat ochre coloured Ebro Valley, should be hilly and green, filled with streams rushing through pinewoods and meadows. One of these streams is the source of the Duero, one of Spain's longest rivers *(910km/565mi)*.

Laguna Negra de Urbión

J.Hidalgo – C.Lopesino/MARCO POLO

★★ **Laguna Negra de Urbión** – *53km/33mi northwest by ④ on the plan and N234* *about 1hr. At Cidones bear right towards Vinuesa; continue for 18km/11mi befo* *turning onto the Montenegro de Cameros road. After 8km/5mi bear left onto t* *Laguna road (9km/6mi).* The **road**★★, after skirting the Cuerdo del Pozo reserve *(embalse)*, which is ringed by tall stone cliffs, rocks and holm oaks, continu through pines to the **Laguna Negra** (alt 1 700m/5 577ft). The lagoon is a small glac lake at the foot of a semicircular cliff over which cascade two waterfalls.

★★ **Laguna Negra de Neila** – *About 86km/53mi northwest by ④ and the plan a* *N234. At Abejar turn right towards Molinos de Duero; continue to Quintana de Sierra where you bear right for Neila (12km/7mi) and then left for Huerta Arriba; 2km/1mi on the left is the road to Laguna Negra.* The **road**★★ throug green, picturesque countryside commands changing views of the valley and Sier de la Demanda. The lake lies at an altitude of 2 000m/6 562ft.

SOS DEL REY CATÓLICO ★

Aragón (Zaragoza) – Population 974
Michelin map 443 E 26

It was in this town in the **Palacio de los Sada** (Sada Palace) that Ferdinand the Cathol who was to unite Spain, was born in 1452. The houses, palaces, walls and doorwa which line the narrow cobbled streets and alleys leading to the keep and the chur give the town a medieval air.
On the **Plaza Mayor**, an irregularly shaped square, stand the imposing 16C Ayunt miento (town hall), which like the Palacio de los Gil de Jaz has large carved woo overhangs, and the Lonja (Exchange) with wide arches.

★ **Iglesia de San Esteban (St Stephen's Church)** ⊙ – The church is reached through vaulted passageway. The 11C **crypt**★ beneath the church is dedicated to Our La of Forgiveness (Virgen del Perdón). Two of the three apses are decorated with fi 14C **frescoes**. The central apse contains outstanding capitals carved with t figures of women and birds.
The statue columns at the **main door** have the stiff and noble bearing of those Sangüesa. The church itself, built in the transitional style, has a beautiful Renaissan **gallery**★. A chapel contains a 12C Romanesque figure of Christ with eyes open wid

EXCURSIONS

Uncastillo – *21km/13mi southeast.*
The Romanesque **Iglesia de Santa María** has an unusual 14C tower adorned wi machicolations and pinnacle turrets. The **south portal's**★ rich and delicate carvin of imaginary beasts for the most part, makes it one of the most beautif doorways of the late Romanesque period. The church gallery with Renaissan **stalls**★ and the **cloisters**★ are 16C Plateresque.

TALAVERA DE LA REINA

Castilla-La Mancha (Toledo) – Population 69 136
Michelin map 444 M 15

The name Talavera, like that of Manises and Paterna, has been associated since t 15C with the **ceramic tiles** used to decorate the lower walls of palaces, mansions ar chapels. Talavera *azulejos* were always recognisable by their blue and yellow design today tiles have been largely replaced by the manufacture of domestic and pure decorative ware such as plates, vases and bowls. Green indicates that an object wa made in **El Puente del Arzobispo**, a small village *(34km/21mi southwest)* which no specialises in the mass production of pottery drinking jars – *cacharros*.

Basílica de la Virgen del Prado (Basilica of the Prado Virgin) ⊙ – *In a park at t entrance to the town coming from Madrid.* The church, which is virtually a *azulejos* museum, gives a good idea of the evolution of the local style. The olde tiles, dating from the 14C to 16C, yellow coloured and with geometric design are in the sacristy *(access through the north door)*; 16C to 18C tiles, blue coloure and with narrative designs, are in the church proper and the portal.

EXCURSION

Oropesa – *32km/20mi west.*
Two churches and a castle rise above the town. The **castle**★ retains its prou bearing of 1366; the annexes were built in 1402 and are now a parador. A plaq in the stairwell recalls that a Count of Oropesa, **Francisco de Toledo**, was Viceroy Peru from 1569 to 1581.
The village of **Lagartera**, 2km/1mi west of Oropesa, has been known for sever centuries for the embroidery done by its women who, during the summer month may be seen sitting at their front doors working. They embroider long skirts ar vivid coloured bonnets in peasant style, tablecloths and subtly toned silk hangin with scatterings of flowers – every cottage has its own display.

TARRAGONA★★★

Catalunya – Population 112 801

Michelin map 443 I 33

arragona, a city rich in reminders of Antiquity and the Middle Ages, is also a modern
own with wide avenues and prosperous commercial streets. Its seafront, rising in
ers up the cliffside and brilliant with flowers, skirts the old city and circles the Palace
f Augustus, before following the line of the perimeter enclosing the cathedral.
arious industries, in particular petrochemicals, are developing in the outskirts along
ith the expansion of the port.

apital of Tarraconensis - The history of Tarragona dates back many centuries. The
nposing ramparts built of enormous Cyclopean blocks of stone, indicate that it was
ounded by peoples from the eastern Mediterranean early in the first millennium BC.
due course it suffered occupation by the Iberians. The Romans, who by 218 BC
ad control of the larger part of the peninsula, developed Tarraconensis into a major
ty and overseas capital. Although it could never equal Rome, it enjoyed many of the
ame privileges as the imperial capital and Augustus, Galba and Hadrian did not
isdain to live in it.

onversion to Christianity, it is said by St Paul, brought it appointment as a
netropolitan seat, its dignitaries, the primacy of Spain, an honour it retained
hroughout the Barbarian invasions of the 5C and the devastations of the Moors in
he 8C but lost finally to the ambition of Toledo in the 11C. The city was then
bandoned until the 12C, when it reverted to the Christians.

★ROMAN TARRAGONA *2hr 30min*

The best preserved monuments lie outside the city limits: the Mausoleo de
Centcelles (Centcelles Mausoleum) and the Acueducto de las Ferreres (Ferreres
Aqueduct), Scipios tower and the Arco de Triunfo de Berá (Berá Triumphal Arch).

★ **Passeig Arqueològic (Archeological Promenade)** ⊘ **(DZ)** - It was the Scipios, according to Livy and Pliny, who built Tarragona's city walls in the 3C BC. They were
erected on existing Cyclopean bases, the great boulders being held in position by

TARRAGONA

Angels (Pl.)	DZ 2	
Baixada de Misericòrdia	DZ 3	
Baixada de Toro	DZ 5	
Baixada Roser	DZ 8	
Cavallers	DZ 9	
Civaderia	DZ 10	
Coques (Les)	DZ 12	
Enginyer Cabestany	CZ 14	
López Peláez	CZ 19	

Mare de Deu del Claustre	DZ 22	
Nova (Rambla)	CDZ	
Pau Casals (Av.)	CZ 27	
Pla de la Seu	DZ 29	
Pla de Palau	CZ 32	
Ponç d'Icart	CZ 33	
Portalet	CZ 34	
Ramón i Cajal (Av.)	CZ 40	
Roser (Portal del)	CZ 43	
Sant Agustí	DZ	
Sant Antoni (Portal de)	DZ 46	
Sant Hermenegild	DZ 49	

Sant Joan (Pl.)	DZ 52	
Unió	CZ	
William J. Bryant	DZ 55	

B	Fòrum Romà
D	Fòrum Provincial
E	Antic Hospital
M	Museu Arqueològic
M¹	Recinte Monumental del Pretori i del Circ Romà
M²	Museu d'Art Modern
M³	Museu Casa Castellarnau

their sheer size. They were so massive that they were for a long time thought have been barbaric or pre-Roman. The medieval inhabitants extensively raised a rebuilt the ramparts; the 18C citizens remodelled them but still left us with wa bearing the marks of 2 000 years of history. A pleasant walk has been laid c through the gardens at the foot of the walls.

The outer perimeter was built by the English in 1707 during the War of t Spanish Succession.

★★ **Museu Nacional Arqueològic de Tarragona** (Archeological Museum) ⓥ (**DZ M**) – T exhibits are all from Tarragona or its immediate environs; most date from t Roman period.

Roman Architecture – *(Room II, ground floor)*. Gathered here are vestiges of the mc imposing buildings in Tarraco.

★★ **Roman Mosaics** – The museum presents the finest collections in Catalunya. The ex bits displayed in Rooms III *(first floor)* and Room VIII *(second floor)* testify to t high degree of craftsmanship achieved by the Romans in this field. The most extra rdinary piece is unquestionably the **Mosaic of the Medusa**★★, with its penetrating gaz

★ **Roman Sculpture** – *(Rooms VI to X, second floor)*. The **funerary sculptures** *(Room I* are superb and extremely well preserved. Note *(Room VI)* the **bust of Lucius Verus** executed in the 2C, a perfect example of the art of that period, and the small vot **sculpture of Venus**★, whose tiny proportions in no way detract from its over beauty and grace.

★ **Recinto Monumental del Pretorio y Circo Romano** (Praetorium and Roman Circus) (**DZ M'**) – This site includes a tall square tower from the 1C BC which has sin undergone heavy restoration. You can visit the **vaulted underground galleries**★ or el go to the top and enjoy the sweeping **view**★★ of the ruins and the town.

The most important exhibit is **Hippolyte's sarcophagus**★★, which was discovere virtually intact on the bed of the Mediterranean sea in 1948 and whose sculptur ornamentation is at once lively, varied and finely executed.

Roman Circus – Designed originally for chariot races, this vast building (325 × 115m/1 066ft × 378ft) is now reduced to a few terraces, the vaul supporting them, sections of the outer façade and some doorways.

The Roman amphitheatre

★★ **Amfiteatre** ⓥ (**DZ**) – Shaped as an ellipse, the amphitheatre is situated at th water's edge, in a naturally sloped **site**★ which was put to good use when the tier were built.

It was here that Bishop Fructuosus and his deacons, Augurius and Eulogius, wer martyred in 259.

Traces of the commemorative Visigoth basilica have been discovered within th Romanesque walls of the Iglesia de Santa María del Miracle, a church which replaced the original Visigoth basilica in the 12C and is itself now in ruins.

Forum Romà ⓥ (**CZ B**) – This used to be the Roman Forum, the core of the city': political, religious, commercial and legal activities. Today all that remain are the 24 columns that once supported the portico.

Museo y Necrópolis Paleocristiana ⊙ – The necropolis walls enclose an open-air excavation site, covered by a metal structure, the building housing the museum, a number of funerary crypts and a large landscaped area where a great many sarcophagi are displayed. The whole ensemble provides an interesting insight into the different burial methods in existence between the 3C and the 6C: simple tombs made with amphorae or tiles, sarcophagi and graves belonging to wealthy, influential families.

CIUDAD MEDIEVAL (MEDIEVAL CITY) 1hr

The city walls enclose a network of ancient alleys. A wide flight of steps leads up to the cathedral.

Catedral ⊙ (DZ) – *Access is through the door leading to the cloisters, at the end of the calle Mare Déu del Claustre.* Construction began in 1174 on top of the former site of Jupiter's Temple. The cathedral was built in transitional Gothic, although the side chapels are both Plateresque and Baroque.

Front – Approached by a flight of steps, the façade can be divided into three parts: a typical Gothic central section flanked by two Romanesque side sections. The **main doorway**★ represents the Final Judgement, with highly expressive relief work. The archivolts are carved with Apostles and Prophets and, on the pier, the Virgin (13C) receives the Faithful. Note the large Gothic rose window.

Interior – It is based on the plan of a Latin cross, with three naves and a transept crossing. The Romanesque apse has semicircular arches. Each end of the transept crossing opens onto rose windows with stained glass dating from the 14C. The three naves were built mostly in the Gothic style.

The cathedral interior houses many works of art but the finest piece is undoubtedly the **altarpiece of Santa Tecla**★★★ (1430), closing off the central apse, which is reached by two Gothic doorways open on either side. Santa Tecla (St Thecla) is the city's patron saint. Converted to Christianity by St Paul, she was persecuted on many occasions but was spared torture and death through divine intervention. This work by Pere Joan shows a marked talent for detail, ornamentation and picturesqueness, as is clearly demonstrated in the predella, engraved with the skill of a goldsmith (note the flies settling on the gaping wound of the ox). To the right of the altar lies the 14C **Tomb of the Infante Don Juan de Aragón**★★, attributed to an Italian master.

The Capilla de la Virgen de Montserrat *(second chapel in the nave of the Gospel)* houses a **retable**★ by Luis Borrassà (15C) and **reliefs**★ recounting the life story of the city's saint can be admired in the Capilla de Santa Tecla *(third chapel in the nave of the Epistle)*. The **Capilla de los Sastres**★★ *(to the left of the Capilla Major)* is one of the most impressive in all the cathedral, featuring intricate ribbed vaulting, a pretty altarpiece and paintings. This superb ensemble is further enhanced by the sumptuous tapestries hanging from the ceiling, most of which are decorated with allegorical motifs.

Claustro – The cloisters are very unusual and large – each gallery is 45m/148ft long. They were built in the 12C and 13C and the arches and geometric decoration are clearly Romanesque, but the vaulting is Gothic, as are the large supporting arches which divide the bays into groups of three.

Moorish influence is evident in the *claustra* of geometrically patterned and pierced panels filling the oculi below the arches, the line of multifoil arches at the base of the cathedral roof and the octagonal lantern which can be seen from the northeast corner of the cloisters. Inlaid in the west gallery is a *mihrab*-like stone niche, dated 960.

Note the remarkable **Romanesque doorway**★, dominated by a *Christ in Majesty*, which links the cathedral to the cloisters.

Museo Diocesano ⊙ – The museum occupies four rooms in the capitular outbuildings. These contain religious vestments, paintings, altarpieces and reliefs of a very high standard. The fine collection of tapestries in Room III includes **La Buena Vida**★, a Flemish work dating back to the 15C. The same room houses a 17C **pall**★ from Rome. In Room II, devoted to the Corpus Christi, one of the most beautiful exhibits is no 105, a richly ornate **monstrance**★, and a polychrome alabaster relief work depicting St Jerome (16C).

ADDITIONAL SIGHTS

Museu-Casa Castellarnau ⊙ (DZ M³) – During a visit to Tarragona, the Emperor Charles V is said to have stayed in this wealthy 14C-15C residence, which became the property of the Castellarnau family in the 18C. It features a pretty Gothic *patio* and many fine examples of 18C furniture.

El Serrallo – This popular seaside district, founded in the late 19C, has many restaurants offering tasty seafood and fish dishes. It is also known for the lively fish market held every day.

EXCURSIONS

★★ **Acueducto de Las Ferreres** – *Leave by Rambla Nova* (**CZ**). 4km/2.5mi fr
Tarragona you will see the Roman aqueduct up on your right. It is a well preser
two-tier structure, 217m/712ft long, known as the Puente del Diablo (De
Bridge). You can walk *(30min)* through the pines to the base.

★ **Mausoleo de Centcelles** ⊘ – *5km/3mi by Ramón i Cajal Avenue* (**CZ**). *Take*
Reus road; bear right after crossing the Francolí. Turn right in Constanti into
calle de Centcelles; continue a further 500yd along an unsurfaced road. J
before the village of Centcelles make a right-angle turn to the left.
The mausoleum, which now stands in a vineyard, takes the form of t
monumental buildings faced with pink tiles. They were built in the 4C by a weal
Roman near his summer residence which was also vast and included priv
thermal baths. The first chamber in the mausoleum is covered by an imme
cupola (diameter: 11m/36ft), decorated with **mosaics★★** on themes favoured
the early Christians such as hunting scenes, Daniel in the lions' den etc.
adjoining chamber, which is the same size only square, has an apse on either si
The group of buildings is obviously outstanding although its symbolism rema
obscure.

★ **Torre de los Escipiones** – *Leave Tarragona east on N 340 and after 5km/3mi t*
left. This square, sober-looking funerary tower (1C) is made up of three sectio
The upper and central parts both present reliefs portraying two characters. It
first thought, mistakenly, that these were the Escipion brothers, after whom
tower was named. However, it later transpired that they in fact portrayed A
a Phrygian divinity associated with death rituals.

★ **Villa Romana de Els Munts** ⊘ – *12km/7.5mi east. Leave Tarragona on*
Augusta (N 340). Nestling in the locality of Altafulla, in a privileged **site★★** perc
on top of a hillock gently sloping towards the sea, stands this old Roman villa.
can visit the L-shaped arcaded passage that was flanked by gardens and the **Ro**
baths★, whose complex plan are proof of the city's former prosperity.

★ **Arco de Berà** – *Situated in the locality of Roda de Berà, 20km/12mi east leav*
on Via Augusta (N 340). The Via Augusta used to pass under this imposi
well-proportioned arch (1C). It features a single opening and eight groo
pilasters crowned by Corinthian capitals.

Consult the Places to Stay map at the beginning of this guide to select the a stop
or holiday destination. The map offers the following categories:
   Short holidays
   Weekend breaks
   Overnight stops
   Resorts

Depending on the region, this map also shows marinas, ski areas, spas, centres
mountain expeditions, etc.

TERRASSA/TARRASA

Catalunya (Barcelona) – Population 157 442
Michelin map 443 H 36

An important industrial city located near Barcelona, Terrassa is one of the countr
leading manufacturing centres for textiles. Its origins date back to the Ror
municipium of Egara. It has kept the impressive ensemble of churches known as
Conjunto Monumental de Iglesias de Sant Pere, a splendid example of pre-Rom
esque religious architecture.

SIGHTS

★★ **Conjunto Monumental de Iglesias de Sant Pere** ⊘ – This fine cluster
churches, a reminder of the former bishopric of Egara (5C), constitutes a sooth
haven of peace in the midst of the bustling city. These three buildings (9C-12
of unquestionable artistic value, show Pyrenean influence but also feature a gr
many Roman and Visigoth ruins.

★ **Sant Miquel** – Sant Miquel, a former baptistry of square design with a heptago
apse, was built in the 9C using late Roman remains. The dome above the for
supported on eight pillars; four have Roman capitals, four have Visigot
Alabaster windows in the apse provide a filtered light by which to see the 9C-1
pre-Romanesque wall paintings. Below is a crypt, abutted by three small ap
with horseshoe-shaped arches.

★ **Santa Maria** - The church is a good example of the Romanesque Lombard style. Before the façade are the remains of a 5C mosaic from the original church. The present edifice is in the shape of a Latin cross, with a *cimborrio* (lantern) and an octogonal cupola. Inside, the 11C apsidal vaulting features vestiges of mural paintings but a 13C wall fresco in the south transept, illustrating the martyrdom of Thomas Becket of Canterbury, has preserved its bright colours. Among the superb 15C altarpieces, note the one in the north transept by Jaime Huguet of **St Abdon and St Sennen**★★.

Sant Pere - A rustic church whose construction began in the 6C, it was built according to a trapezoid plan and has a Romanesque transept crossing. Embedded in the apse is a curious **stone altarpiece**★.

★ **Masia Freixa** - This strange-looking Modernist bourgeois mansion (1907), which presently houses the Academy of Music, is situated inside the Sant Jordi Park. Visitors' attention will be attracted by the repeated use of parabolic arches.

★ **Museu de la Ciencia y la Tècnica de Catalunya** ⊘ - The museum occupies the premises of an old 1909 steam works (Aymerich, Amat i Jover) that is an interesting example of industrial architecture under the Modernist movement. It offers a retrospective of the various technological advances which have occurred in connection with industrialisation.

Museu Tèxtil (Textile Museum) ⊘ - Oriental materials, including rare Coptic fabrics from the 4C and 5C, Merovingian fabrics and brocades provide an excellent panoramic history of textile and manufacture.

TERUEL★

Aragón – Population 31 068
Michelin map 443 K 26

..e capital of Bajo (Lower) Aragón, at an altitude of 916m/3 005ft, occupies a ..bleland separated from the surrounding plateau by a wide divide through which ..ws the Turia. A landscape of ravined brown ochre heights provides a unique ..tting★.

Mudéjar town - Old Mudéjar towers rise above the tawny brick of the town. The ..eat richness of Mudéjar architecture in Teruel arises because Christians, Jews and ..uslims all lived peacefully together in the town until the 15C - the last mosque was ..osed only in 1502.

..e legend of the Lovers of ..eruel - In the 13C, **Diego de ..arcilla** and **Isabel de Segura** were .. love and wished to marry ..t Isabel's father had set his ..ghts on a richer suitor. Diego ..ereupon went to the wars to ..in honour and riches. The ..y of his return, five years ..ter, was Isabel's wedding ..y to his rival. He died before ..r in despair and the follo- ..ng day Isabel was overcome ..th grief and died in her turn. ..is drama inspired many ..5C poets and dramatists ..cluding **Tirso de Molina**.

SIGHTS

Plaza del Torico (7), in the heart of the town, is the traditional local meeting place. The square lined with Rococo style houses, gets it name from the small statue of a bull calf on a pillar at its centre.

★ **Mudéjar towers** - There are five in all. They were built between the 12C and 16C, in each case to a three-

Torre de San Martín

TERUEL

Abadía	Z 2
Amantes	Y 3
Amantes (Pl. de los)	Z 4
Ambeles (Ronda de)	Z 5
Bretón (Pl.)	Z 6
Carlos Castel (Pl.) o Pl. del Torico	YZ 7
Catedral (Plaza de la)	Y 8
Chantría	Y 10
Comte Fortea	Z 9
Cristo Ray (Plaza de)	Y 12
Dámaso Torán (Ronda de)	Y 13
Fray Anselmo Polanco	Y 14
Joaquín Costa	Y 15
Miguel Ibáñez	Y 16
Monjes (Pl. de los)	Y 17
Óvalo (Paseo)	Z 18
Pérez Prado (Pl. de)	Y 19
Pizarro	Z 20
Ramón y Cajal	Z 22
Rubio	Y 23
Salvador	Z 24
San Francisco	Z 25
San Juan (Pl.)	Z 27
San Martín	Y 28
San Miguel	Y 29
Temprado	Z 30
Venerable F. de Aranda (Pl.)	Y 35
Yagüe de Salas	Y 37

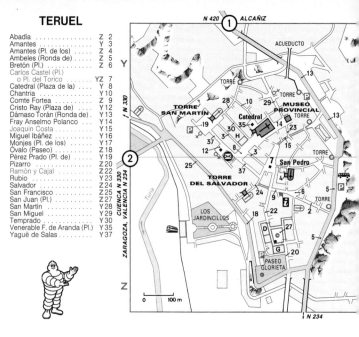

storey plan: at the base an arch provided access to the street; the centre, pier
only by narrow Romanesque openings, was decorated with Moorish influen
ornamental brickwork and ceramics, while at the top was a belfry, pierced by b
in pairs below and quadruples above. The two best examples, the **Torre de San Ma**
and the **Torre del Salvador**, are both 13C.

★ **Museo Provincial** ⊘ – The museum, housed in a mansion with an eleg
Renaissance façade crowned by a gallery, displays ethnological and archeolog
collections. The former stables in the basement house tools and other every
objects from the region; note the reconstitution of a forge and the 15C Got
door knocker.
The first floor is given over to ceramics, an industry for which Teruel has b
renowned since the 13C. Green and purple designs adorn the oldest pieces, b
those produced in the 18C (as is the case for pots and jars from a pharmacy
Alcalá).
The upper floors contain archeological collections from different periods: pr
storic (an Iron Age sword from Alcorisa), Iberian, Roman (a catapult) and Arab
11C censer).

Catedral ⊘ – The cathedral, originating in the 13C with the tower, was enlar
in the 16C and further increased by a lantern and ambulatory in the 17C.
late-13C **artesonado ceiling**★, hidden in the 17C beneath star vaulting and
preserved, has now once more been revealed and is a precious example of Mudé
painting. Its cells, beams and consoles are painted with decorative motifs, pec
at court and hunting scenes.
The cathedral possesses a 15C **altarpiece** of the Coronation of the Virgin (no
transept) in which the scenes depicted along the second band are showr
perspective suggesting Flemish influence. The **retable at the high altar**, carved in
16C, is by **Gabriel Joli**. Joli was known for his powerful portraits and his skilful v
of illustrating movement by a marked turn of the body.

Iglesia de San Pedro – In spite of 18C reconstruction, the church has kept
original Mudéjar style in its tower and east end.
The **Mausoleo de los Amantes de Teruel** (The Teruel Lovers' Mausoleum) ⊘ adjoins
church. They are shown in an alabaster relief by Juan de Ávalos (20C). Throu
the glass walls of the tomb, also in the chapel, the lovers' actual skeletons car
seen.

Michelin Green Guides *to European destinations:*

Austria – Belgium and Luxembourg – Berlin – Brussels – Europe – Franc
Germany – Great Britain – Greece – Ireland – Italy – London – Netherla
– Portugal – Rome – Scandinavia and Finland – Scotland – Sicily – Sp
– Switzerland – Tuscany – Venice – Vienna – Wales – The West Country
England... and the collection of regional guides to France

TOLEDO★★★

Castilla-La Mancha – Population 63 561
Michelin map 444 M 17

ledo stands out dramatically against the often luminously blue Castilian sky: a
lden city rising from a granite eminence, encircled by a steep ravine filled by the
een waters of the Tajo (Tagus). It is as spectacular as it is rich in history, buildings
d art; every corner has a tale to be told, every aspect reflects a brilliant period
Spanish history when the cultures of east and west flourished and fused: one
constantly aware of this imprint of Christian, Jewish and Moorish cultures which,
in Granada, productively co-existed during the Middle Ages. Within its **walls**, the
y shelters beautiful sights amid old winding alleys which provide a splendid
tting for the **Corpus Christi** procession, held on the first Sunday following Corpus
risti.

ledo is renowned for its **damascene** ware (black steel inlaid with gold, silver and
pper thread) as well as its culinary specialities including braised partridge and
rzipan.

e site – The city's incomparable site can be seen particularly well from
e carretera de circunvalación, a ring-road which for a couple of miles parallels,
 the far bank, the almost circular loop of the Tajo which flows all
e way round from the Puente de Alcántara (Alcántara Bridge) to the Puente de
n Martín.

r truly memorable views of the city, couched between the Alcázar and the
onasterio de San Juan de los Reyes (Monastery of St John of the Kings), it is
orth going to the **lookout points** on the surrounding heights. These are covered by
tensive olive groves *(cigarrales)* in which white houses stand half concealed. The
ador terrace (**BZ P**) set above the carretera de circunvalación commands a good
norama.

Toledo

The Burial of the Count of Orgaz, by El Greco

HISTORICAL NOTES

Roman town to Holy Roman city – The Romans, appreciating the site's advanta
strategically and geographically at the centre of the peninsula, fortified and built
the settlement into a town they named Toletum. It passed, in due course, into
hands of the Barbarians, and in the 6C to the Visigoths who ultimately made
monarchial seat. The Visigoths, defeated at Guadelete in 711, abandoned the to
to the Moors who incorporated it in the Córdoba Emirate, until the successful re
of the *taifas* in 1012 raised it to the position of capital of an independent kingdo

El Greco – Domenikos Theotokopoulos, the Greek – El Greco – one of the
great figures in Spanish painting, was born in Crete in 1541. After an
apprenticeship painting icons, he went to Italy where he worked under Titian
and studied Michelangelo before journeying to Spain in 1577 and settling in
Toledo where he remained until he died in 1614. Although he didn't always
succeed in pleasing Philip II he found favour and fortune with Toledans. His
work, with its acquired Italian techniques, retained considerable Byzantine
influence which appeared as a lengthening of forms – a mannerism which
increased as the painter aged. A recurring feature in illustrated scenes was the
division of the canvas into two – earth and heaven – demonstrating El Greco's
belief that this life was but preparation for an exalted hereafter. The
supernatural is a constant preoccupation, figures convey an intense spiritual
inner power – all is seen with the eye of the visionary and portrayed sometimes
by means of apparent distortion, by brilliant, occasionally crude colours, often
by violent, swirling movement so that some pictures have the aspect of
hallucinations. But the portraits by contrast are still, the colours deep,
expressions meditative in religious, watchful in the worldly.

085 Toledo was conquered by Alfonso VI de León. Two years later, the king
ed his capital to it from León. It is to Alfonso VII, crowned emperor there, that
do owes its title of imperial city. Toledo, with its mixed Moorish, Jewish and
stian communities, began to prosper richly. The Catholic monarchs gave it the
astery of St John but lost interest in the city when they began to compare it with
nada, reconquered under their own aegis in 1492. Emperor Charles V had the
zar rebuilt. Also during his reign the city took part in the Comuneros' Revolt led
uan de Padilla, a Toledan.

gress was halted in 1561 when Philip II named Madrid as Spain's capital, leaving
do as the spiritual centre, the seat of the primacy. The events of 1936 within and
out the Alcázar, brought it briefly into the limelight of history.

edo and the Visigoths – Toledo played a key role during the Visigothic supremacy
e peninsula which began in 507. By 554 they had made it their capital and Councils
tate, which had met in Toledo as early as 400, were resumed; that of 589, following
n the conversion of King Reccared two years previously, established Visigothic
emony and the religious unification of Spain. The Visigoths, torn by internal strife,
ever, were unable to resist the Moors and abandoned Toledo in 711; it took Pelayo
a small band of Christians to reinstate the dynasty.

edo and the Jews – Toledo would appear to have been by far the most important
ish town in Spain: in the 12C the community numbered 12 000.
der Ferdinand III (1217-52), a tolerant monarch who encouraged the intermingling
he races which brought about a cultural flowering, the city developed into a great
llectual forum. This well-being reached its climax under his son, **Alfonso X, the Wise**
52-84), who gathered round him a court of learned Jews and established the
ool of Translation. Jewish prosperity and immunity suddenly and brutally ceased
355 with a pogrom instigated by the supporters of Henry IV of Trastamara; at
same time many conversions followed the preaching of the Dominican, **San Vicente**
er. The final blow came in 1492 with the Catholic Monarch's decree of expulsion.

WHERE TO STAY

DGET HOTELS

lmazara – 3.5km/2mi on Cuerva road. ☎ 925 22 38 66, fax 925 25 05 62.
rooms.
mall hotel occupying a 16C country house with a spectacular view of the
y from its terrace. The construction is typical of Toledo with a mixture of
ourful brickwork, tiles and wooden beams. Although a little on the spartan
e, the rooms are both clean and comfortable.

R SELECTION

tal el Cardenal (BX ❸) – Paseo de Recaredo, 24. ☎ 925 22 49 00,
x 925 22 29 91. 27 rooms.
e former residence of Cardenal Lorenzana has been converted into an
ractive restaurant with 27 rooms. The garden is delightful on a summer's
ernoon. Excellent cuisine.

ría Cristina (CX ❹) – Marqués de Mendigorría, 1. ☎ 925 21 32 02,
x 925 21 26 50. 73 rooms.
uated next to the Tavera Hospital and with a similar style (colourful
ckwork). Its interior has preserved a Mudéjar apse, from which the hotel's
taurant takes its name. Spacious rooms.

tor el Greco (AY ❺) – Alamillos del Tránsito, 13. ☎ 925 21 42 50,
x 925 21 58 19. 33 rooms.
7C building in the heart of the Judería which has managed to retain several
tails from this period. Very close to El Greco's house and museum. The
estrooms and lounges are simply furnished.

EATING OUT

olfo – La Granada, 6. ☎ 925 22 73 21.
cated behind the cathedral in an historical building with attractive coffered
ilings. The cuisine imaginatively combines tradition and modern ideas.
cellent game dishes.

relio – Plza del Ayuntamiento, 4. ☎ 925 22 77 16.
typically Castilian atmosphere. Perhaps lacking refinement, but with
tractive wooden beams and check tablecloths. The cuisine includes local
ledo dishes such as stuffed partridge, as well as a selection of fresh fish.

són de los López Toledo – Sillería, 3. ☎ 925 5 47 74.
used in a large 16C house, this restaurant offers the very best in La Mancha
oking along with several dishes from outside the region. The interior
cludes Mudéjar designs and a simple, but elegant, patio.

Mudéjar art in Toledo - Toledo, which for centuries had numbered citizen
different races and religions, became the ideal setting under Christian rule fo
development of the Mudéjar style which appears not only in palaces (Taller del M
but also in synagogues (Tránsito, Santa María la Blanca) and churches. Thus i
13C and 14C most Toledan churches were given Romanesque semicircular **east**
but blind arcades with variations unknown elsewhere; bricks were used in plac
stone and **belfries** squared and decorated until they appeared strongly reminisce
minarets. The edifices often have a nave and two aisles – a Visigothic influen
tripartite apses – a Romanesque souvenir – and wood vaulting carved in the Mod
style.

★★★ TOLEDO ANTIGUO (OLD TOLEDO) *1 day*

There is something to see and enjoy at every step in Toledo. Walking along
maze of narrow, winding lanes you pass churches, old houses and palaces.

★★★ **Catedral** ⊙ (BY) - Construction began in the reign of Ferdinand III (St Ferdin
in 1227, under Archbishop Rodrigo Jiménez de Rada. Unlike other churches i
vicinity, the design was French Gothic but as building continued until the en
the 15C, plans were modified and the completed edifice presents a conspectu
Spanish Gothic, although considerably masked by additions. The church, ne
theless, remains of outstanding interest for its sculptured decoration
numerous works of religious art.

Exterior - The **Puerta del Reloj** (Clock Doorway), in the north wall, is the old entra
dating from the 13C although modified in the 19C. The west front is pierce
three tall 15C portals of which the upper registers were completed in the 16C
17C. At the centre is the **Puerta del Perdón** (Pardon Doorway), crowded with sta
and crowned with a tympanum illustrating the legend according to which
Virgin Mary, wishing to reward San Ildefonso, Bishop of Toledo in the 7C, fo
devotion, appears, at Assumption, in the episcopal chair, to present him wi
magnificent embroidered chasuble.
The harmonious tower is 15C; the dome, which replaces the second tower,
designed by El Greco's son in the 17C. In the south wall, the 15C **Puerta de los Le**
(Lion Doorway) designed by Master Hanequin of Brussels and decorated by J
Alemán was flanked in 1800 by a neo-Classical portal.
*Enter through the Puerta del Mollete, left of the west front, which opens onto
cloisters.*

Interior - The size and sturdy character of the cathedral rather than its eleva
are what strike one as one gazes up over the five unequal aisles and the g
supporting pillars. A wonderful collection of stained glass (1418-1561) colo
the windows; magnificent wrought-iron grilles enclose the chancel, *coro*
chapels. The attention is also drawn to the cardinals' hats hanging from the va
above the tombs of those cardinals who were primates of Spain.

Capilla Mayor - The chancel, the most sumptuous part of the cathedral,
enlarged in the 16C by Cardinal Cisneros.
The immense polychrome **retable**★★, carved in Flamboyant style with the Lif
Christ depicted in detail on five registers, is awe inspiring. The silver statue of
Virgin at the predella dates from 1418. The marble tomb of Cardinal Mendoz
Plateresque style on the left is by Covarrubias. The recumbent figure is the w
of an Italian artist.

Coro - A series of 14C high reliefs and wrought-iron enclosed chapels form
perimeter of the choir which is itself closed by an elegant iron screen (15
Within are magnificent 15C and 16C **choir stalls**★★★ of which the lower parts
wood, were carved by Rodrigo Alemán to recall, in 54 beautifully detailed
picturesque scenes, the conquest of Granada; the 16C upper parts, in alabas
portraying Old Testament figures, are by Berruguete *(left)* and Felipe Viga
(right). The central low relief, the Transfiguration, is also by Berruguete. The s
of his work creates the impression of movement while that of Vigarny is m
static. The pipes of a sonorous organ dominate the central area, occupied by
bronze lecterns and a Gothic eagle lectern. The 14C marble White Virgin is Fre

Girola - The double ambulatory, surmounted by an elegant triforium with mult
arches, is bordered by seven apsidal chapels separated by small square chap
The vaulting is a geometrical wonder.
There is little room to step back for a good look at the **Transparente**★,
contentious but famous work by Narciso Tomé which forms a Baroque islan
the Gothic church. Illuminated by the sun's rays which pour through an open
in the ambulatory roof (made to allow light to fall on the tabernacle),
Transparente appears as an ornamental framework of angels and swirling clo
and rays surrounding the Virgin and the Last Supper. The **Capilla de San Ildefo**
(Chapel of San Ildefonso) contains tombs, of which the one in the centre
Cardinal Gil de Albornoz (14C) is the most notable. The **Capilla de Santiago** (St Jam
is a mausoleum for Don Álvaro de Luna, Constable of Castilla, and his famil

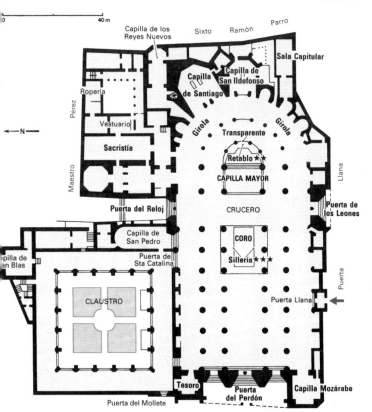

Sala Capitular (chapter-house) – The antechamber is adorned with an impressive Mudéjar ceiling and two Plateresque carved walnut wardrobes. Remarkable Mudéjar stucco doorways and carved Plateresque panels precede the chapter-house where there is a particularly beautiful multicoloured **Mudéjar ceiling★**. Below the frescoes by Juan de Borgoña, are portraits of former archbishops including two by Goya painted in 1804 and 1823.

Sacristía (Sacristy) – The first gallery, with its vaulted ceiling painted by Lucas Jordán, includes a powerful group of **paintings by El Greco★** of which **El Expolio** (the Saviour stripped of His Raiment), painted soon after the artist's arrival in Spain, is outstanding. It conveys a dominating, exalted personality, set against the swirling folds of robes in vivid, often acidic tones, which establish a rhythmical movement akin to Baroque, on the canvas. Also among the collection is one of El Greco's series of portraits of the Apostles. Works by other artists in the sacristy include a remarkable portrait of *Pope Paul III* by Titian, a *Holy Family* by Van Dyck, a *Mater Dolorosa* by Morales and the *Taking of Christ* by Goya which displays to advantage his skill in composition, in the use of light and portraying individuals in a crowd. There is also one of Pedro de Mena's (17C) most characteristic and famous sculptures, *St Francis of Assisi* (in a glass case). In the vestry are portraits by Velázquez *(Cardinal Borja)*, Van Dyck *(Pope Innocent XI)* and Ribera.

The old laundry *(ropería)* contains liturgical objects dating back to the 15C. Continuing on from the sacristy you reach the **Nuevas Salas del Museo Catedralicio** (Cathedral Museum's New Galleries), installed in the Casa del Tesorero (Treasurer's House). The rooms display works by Caravaggio, El Greco, Bellini and Morales.

Tesoro (Treasury) – A Plateresque doorway by Covarrubias opens into the chapel under the tower. Beneath a Granada style Mudéjar ceiling note the splendid 16C silver-gilt **monstrance★★** by Enrique de Arfe, which, although it weighs 180kg and is 3m high (just under 400lb and 10ft high), is paraded through the streets at Corpus Christi. The pyx at its centre is fashioned from gold brought from America by Christopher Columbus.

There is also a 13C Bible given by St Louis of France to St Ferdinand (Ferdinand III of Castilla).

TOLEDO

Alcántara (Puente de) . .	CX
Alfileritos	BY
Alfonso VI (Pl. de)	BX
Alfonso X El Sabio	BY 2
Alfonso XII	BY 3
América (Av. de)	AX
Angel	AY
Ave María	BZ
Ayuntamiento (Pl. del) . .	BY 4
Azarquiel (Puente de) . .	CX
Cabestreros (Paseo de) . .	CZ
Cadenas	BY 7
Campana (Travesía) . . .	BY 8
Cardenal Lorenzana	BY 9
Cardenal Tavera	BX
Carlos III (Av. de)	AX
Carlos V (Cuesta de) . . .	BY 13
Carmelitas	AY 14
Cava (Av. de la)	AX
Cervantes	CY
Circo Romano	
(Paseo del)	AX
Colegio de Doncellas . . .	AY 17
Comercio	BY
Conde (Pl. del)	AY 18
Consistorio (Pl. del) . . .	BY 19
Cordonerías	BY 20
Cruz Verde	
(Paseo de la)	BZ
Duques de Lerma	
(Av. de los)	BX
El Salvador	BY 22
Esteban Illán	BY 24
Gerardo Lobo	BX
Hombre de Palo	BY 27
Honda	BX 28
Juanelo (Ronda de) . . .	CY
Mas del Ribero (Av. de) . .	AX
Matías Moreno	AY
Merced	BY
Nuncio Viejo	BY 29
Nuñez de Arce	BX 32
Padilla (Pl. y Calle de) .	ABY 33
Padre Mariana (Pl.)	BY 34
Pascuales	
(Cuesta de los)	CY 36
Plata	BY
Pozo Amargo	BZ
Real del Arrabal	BX
Recaredo (Paseo de) . . .	AX
Reconquista	
(Av. de la)	ABX
Reyes Católicos	AY
Rosa (Paseo de la)	CX
San Cristóbal (Paseo) . .	BZ 38
San Juan de Dios	AY 40
San Justo (Cuesta) . . .	CY
San Justo (Pl.)	BY 41
San Marcos	BY 42
San Martín (Puente) . . .	AY
San Román	BY 44
San Sebastián	
(Carreras de)	BZ
San Torcuato	BZ
San Vicente (Pl. de) . . .	BY 45
Santa Leocadia	
(Cuesta de)	AY
Santo Tomé	ABY
Sillería	BX
Sixto Ramón Parro	BY 46
Sola	BZ
Taller del Moro	BY 48
Toledo de Ohio	BY 49
Tornerías	BY 50
Tránsito (Paseo del) . . .	AYZ 52
Trinidad	BY
Venancio González	CX 53
Zocodover (Pl. de)	CY

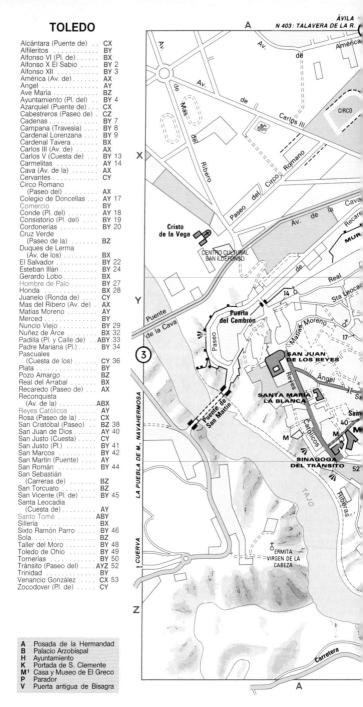

A	Posada de la Hermandad
B	Palacio Arzobispal
H	Ayuntamiento
K	Portada de S. Clemente
M¹	Casa y Museo de El Greco
P	Parador
V	Puerta antigua de Bisagra

Capilla mozárabe (Mozarabic Chapel) – The chapel beneath the dome was buil[t]
Cardinal Cisneros (16C) to celebrate mass according to the Visigothic
Mozarabic ritual which had been threatened with abolition in the 11C.

Claustro (Cloisters) – The architectural simplicity of the 14C lower gallery contra[sts]
with the bold mural decoration by Bayeu of the Lives of Toledan saints (Sa[nta]
Eugenia and San Ildefonso).

Ringing the square before the cathedral are the 18C **Palacio Arzobispal** (Archbisho[p's]
Palace) (**BY B**), the 17C **Ayuntamiento** (town hall) (**BY H**) with its classical façade [and]
the 14C **Audiencia** (Law Courts) (**BY**).

Iglesia de Santo Tomé ⊙ (**AY**) – The church, like that of San Román, ha[s a]
distinctive 14C Mudéjar tower. Inside is El Greco's famous painting **The Buria[l of]
the Count of Orgaz**★★★ executed for the church in about 1586. The intermen[t is]
transformed by the miraculous appearance of St Augustine and St Step[hen]

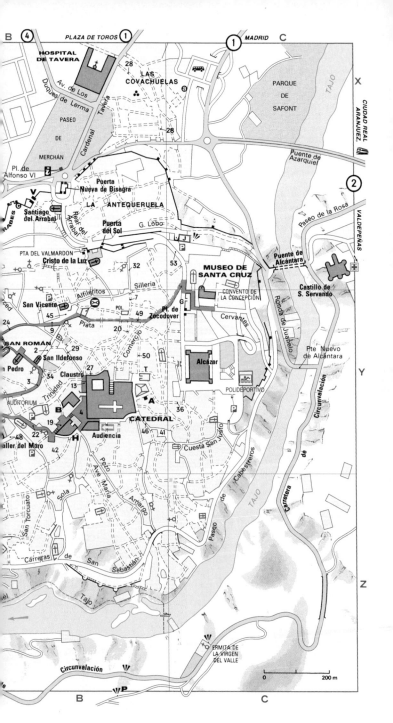

waiting to welcome the figure from earth, symbolised by a frieze of figures in which, as he highlighted faces and hands and painted vestments with detailed biblical references, El Greco made every man an individual portrait – he is said to have painted a self-portrait in the sixth figure from the left.

★ **Casa y Museo de El Greco** (El Greco House and Museum) ⊙ (**AY M¹**) – In 1585, El Greco moved into a house similar to this attractive 16C Toledan **house**. In the first floor studio hang a *St Peter Repentant*, a version of the painting in the cathedral and, in what would have been the artist's workroom, a signed *St Francis and Brother León*.

Museo – On the first floor of the museum are an interesting View and Plan of Toledo (including a likeness of his son, one of various differences from the version in the Prado) and the complete series of individual portraits of the Apostles and Christ (a later, more mature series than that in the cathedral). The **capilla** on the ground floor, with a multicoloured Mudéjar ceiling, has a picture in the altarpie█ of *St Bernardino of Siena* by El Greco. *The Crowning of Thorns* is Hispan█ Flemish.

★★ **Sinagoga del Tránsito** ⓥ **(AYZ)** – Of the 10 synagogues of the old Jewish quart█ (Judería), this and Santa María la Blanca are the only ones to remain. Money f█ its construction was provided in the 14C by Samuel Ha-Levi, treasurer to Kin█ Peter the Cruel. In 1492 it was converted into a church and dedicated so█ afterwards to the Dormition (Tránsito) from which it gets its name.

It appears from the outside as a small unpretentious building but inside █ amazing **Mudéjar decoration**★★ covers the upper part of the walls and all the ea█ end. Above the rectangular hall is an *artesonado* ceiling of cedarwood; just belo█ are 54 multifoil arches, some blind, others pierced with delicate stone trace█ Below again runs a frieze, decorated at the east end with *mocárabes* and on t█ walls, bearing the arms of Castilla, with inscriptions in Hebrew to the glory █ Peter the Cruel, Samuel Ha-Levi and the God of Israel. The three arches at t█ centre of the east wall are surmounted by a panel in relief of roses surrounded █ magnificent strapwork and, at either side, by inscriptions describing t█ synagogue's foundation. The women's balcony opens from the south wall.

The adjoining rooms, at one period a Calatrava monastery, have been convert█ into a **Museo Sefardí** (Sephardic Museum) displaying tombs, robes, costumes a█ books. Several are presents from Sephardim or descendants of the Jews expell█ from Spain in 1492.

★ **Sinagoga de Santa María la Blanca** ⓥ **(AY)** – This was the principal synagog█ in Toledo in the late 12C; in 1405, however, it was given to the Knights █ Calatrava who converted it into a church and gave it its present name. Subseque█ vicissitudes, including modification of the east end in the 16C, incredibly left t█ Almohad-style mosque unharmed so that the hall appears as before with f█ tiered aisles, separated by 24 octagonal pillars supporting horseshoe-shap█ arches. The plain white of the pillars and arches is relieved by the intricately carv█ **capitals**★ adorned with pine cones and strapwork. Above, the decoration is equa█ outstanding. The polychrome wood altarpiece is 16C.

Inside Santa María la Blanca

★ **Monasterio de San Juan de los Reyes (St John of the Kings Monastery)** ⓥ **(AY)** – █ monastery was built by the Catholic monarchs in thanksgiving to God for th█ decisive victory over the Portuguese at Toro in 1476. It was entrusted to █ Franciscans. The overall architecture is typically Isabelline, that style wh█ includes in the Flamboyant Gothic style, touches of Mudéjar and even Renaissa█ art, particularly in this case since construction continued until the early 17C. █ exterior is somewhat austere despite the ornamental pinnacles and sto█ balustrade which crown the edifice and, in the latter instance, circles the octago█ lantern. Covarrubias designed the north portal during the later stages █ construction, including in the decoration the figure of John the Baptist flank█ by Franciscan saints. The fetters from the façade were taken from Christ█ prisoners freed from the Muslims in Andalucía.

Claustro – Although restored, the cloisters remain extremely attractive with Flamboyant bays and the original Plateresque upper galleries (1504) crowned with a pinnacled balustrade. The upper gallery has Mudéjar *artesonado* vaulting.

Iglesia – The church, rebuilt after being fired by the French in 1808, has the single wide aisle typical of Isabelline churches; at the crossing are a dome and a lantern. The **sculptured decoration★** by the church's Flemish architect, Juan Guas, provides a delicate stone tracery *(crestería)* which at the transept forms twin tribunes for Ferdinand and Isabel. The transept walls are faced with a wonderful frieze of royal escutcheons, supported by an eagle, the symbol of St John. Other decoration includes Mudéjar *mocárabes* on the bosses in the transept vaulting and heads in picturesque high relief on the triumphal arches. The original altarpiece has been replaced by a 16C Plateresque retable.

Not far away are a Visigothic palace and gateway, which were once part of the town perimeter. The gateway was rebuilt in the 16C. The **Puerta del Cambrón (AY)** is named after the *cambroneras* or hawthorns which once grew around it.

Turn left out of calle Santo Tomé onto the picturesque Travesía de Campana alley.

Before you, in the small shaded Plaza del Padre Mariana, stands the monumental Baroque façade of the **Iglesia de San Ildefonso (BY)** and higher up, that of the **Iglesia de San Pedro (BY)**.

★ **Iglesia de San Román: Museo de los Concilios de Toledo y de la Cultura Visigoda (Museum of the Councils of Toledo and Visigothic Culture)** ⊘ **(BY)** – The 13C Mudéjar church, at the highest point in the town, has a fine upstanding tower closely resembling that of Santo Tomé. Inside, the three aisles divided by horseshoe-shaped arches are reminiscent of Santa María la Blanca. The walls are covered in 13C frescoes of the raising of the dead, the Evangelists and, on the far wall, one of the Councils of Toledo. The apse was modified in the 16C when a cupola was built over it by Covarrubias. Note the 18C altarpiece.

The Visigothic collections include, in glass cases, fine bronze jewellery and copies of votive crowns decorated with cabochon stones from Guarrazar (originals in the Museo Arqueológico, Madrid). On the walls are steles, fragments from capitals, balustrades from the choir and pilasters decorated with geometric motifs or scrollwork.

The Plateresque **doorway** *(portada)* opposite the church belongs to the Convento de San Clemente **(BY K)**.

In plaza de San Vicente, note the Mudéjar east end of the **Iglesia de San Vicente (BY)** before continuing up calle de la Plata with its houses with carved entrances.

Plaza de Zocodover (BCY) – This bustling triangular square is the heart of Toledo. It was rebuilt after the Civil War as was the Arco de la Sangre (Arch of Blood) which opens onto calle de Cervantes.

★ **Museo de Santa Cruz (Santa Cruz Museum)** ⊘ **(CXY)** – Cardinal Pedro González de Mendoza, Archbishop of Toledo, died before fully realising his ambition to build a hospital for the sick and orphaned, but his project was completed by Queen Isabel. The result is a fine group of Plateresque buildings begun by Enrique Egas and completed by Covarrubias who was responsible for the **façade★★**. On the gateway tympanum Cardinal Mendoza kneels before the Cross supported by St Helena, St Peter, St Paul and two pages; on the arches are the cardinal virtues while above two windows frame a high relief of St Joachim and St Anne.

Inside, the architecture is outstanding for the size of the nave and transept – forming a two-tiered Greek cross – and for the beautiful coffered ceilings.

The museum which is large but well arranged, is known for its **collection of 16C and 17C pictures★** which includes **18 paintings by El Greco★**.

Ground floor – The first part of the nave contains 16C Flemish tapestries, **Primitive paintings★**, and the *Astrolabios* or *Zodiac* tapestry, woven in Flanders in the mid 15C for Toledo cathedral, which fascinates still by its originality and modern colouring. Note, in the south transept, the *Ascension* and the *Presentation of Mary in the Temple* by the Maestro de Sijena. In the second part of the nave hangs the immense pennant flown by Don Juan of Austria at the Battle of Lepanto. Before it is a 17C Crucifix, recalling the one believed to have been present at the battle and which is now in Barcelona Cathedral. The north transept contains a *Christ at the Column* by Morales.

First floor – A staircase leads to the upper gallery of the north transept which displays the **paintings by El Greco★**. There are gentle portraits of the *Virgin* and *St Veronica* as well as a version of the *Expolio (original in the Cathedral Sacristy)*, later than that in the cathedral. The most famous painting in the collection is the **Altarpiece of the Assumption★**, which dates from 1613, the artist's final period. The figures are particularly elongated, the colours rasping.

The south transept contains a *Holy Family at Nazareth* by Ribera, the specialist in tenebrism (term applied to paintings in dark tones) who here showed himself to be a master of light and delicacy.

In the first part of the nave are 16C Brussels tapestries illustrating the life
Alexander the Great. There are also 17C statues from the studio of Pascual
Mena of a *Mater Dolorosa* and an *Ecce Homo*.

The **Plateresque patio**★ has bays with elegant lines complemented by the openwo
of the balustrade and enhanced by beautiful Mudéjar vaulting and, even more,
the magnificent **staircase**★ by Covarrubias. Adjoining rooms house a museum
archeology and decorative arts.

ADDITIONAL SIGHTS

Within the city walls

Alcázar ⊙ **(CY)** – The Alcázar, destroyed and rebuilt so many times, stand
massive and proud as ever, dominating all other buildings. It was Charles V wi
decided to convert the 13C fortress of which El Cid had been the first governo
into an imperial residence. The conversion was entrusted first to Covarrubi
(1538-51) and subsequently to Herrera, who designed the austere south fron
The siege and shelling of 1936 left the fortress in ruins. From 21 July for eig
weeks, infantry cadets under Colonel Moscardó, resisted the Republicans. The
families, about 600 women and children, took refuge in the undergroui
galleries.

Reconstruction has restored the Alcázar to its appearance at the time of Charles
– an innovation is the Victory Monument by Ávalos in the forecourt. Inside, ye
see the underground galleries which sheltered the cadets' families, and the offi
above in which Colonel Moscardó was ordered by phone to surrender or see h
son shot. His son died on 23 August; the Alcázar was relieved on 27 Septembe
Weapons and uniforms are displayed in museum rooms off the *patio*.

Posada de la Hermandad (House of Brotherhood) (BY A) – A 15C building which use
to be a prison.

Puerta del Sol (BX) – The Sun Gate in the town's second perimeter, rebuilt in th
14C, is a fine Mudéjar construction with two circumscribing horseshoe arches. A
the centre a later low relief shows the Virgin presenting San Ildefonso with
chasuble. At the top, the brick decoration of blind arcading incorporates a
unusual sculpture of two girls bearing the head of the chief *alguazil* (officer
justice) of the town on a salver; he had been condemned for raping them, the stoi
goes.

Cristo de la Luz (Christ of the Light) (BX) – In AD 1000 the Moors built a mosque c
the site of a ruined Visigothic church; in the 12C this mosque was converted in
a Mudéjar church. Legend has it that the church was named Christ of the Ligl
because when Alfonso VI was making his entry into Toledo, El Cid's horse in th
royal train suddenly knelt before the mosque in which, inside a wall, a Visigoth
lamp was discovered lighting up a Crucifix. Three series of arches of differei
periods, intersecting blind arcades and a line of horizontal brickwork surmounte
by Cufic characters make up the façade. Inside, pillars, for the most pa
Visigothic, support superimposed arches, similar in design to those in the mosqu
in Córdoba. Nine domes, each different, rise from square bays.

The adjoining gardens lead to the top of the Puerta del Sol from which there
an interesting view of the city.

Taller del Moro ⊙ **(BY)** – This workshop *(taller)*, used by a Moor as a collectin
yard for building material for the cathedral is, in fact, an old palace. The Mudéja
decoration can still be seen in rooms lit by small openwork windows, intercoi
nected through horseshoe-shaped openings ornamented with *atauriques* c
Almohad style stucco.

Iglesia de Santiago del Arrabal (St James on the Outskirts) (BX) – This beautifu
restored Mudéjar church contains the ornate Gothic Mudéjar pulpit from whic
San Vincente Ferrer is said to have preached. The altarpiece is 16C.

Beyond the city walls

★ **Hospital de Tavera** ⊙ **(BX)** – The hospital, founded in the 16C by Cardinal Tavera
was begun by Bustamante in 1541 and completed by González de Lara and th
Vergaras in the 17C.

After the Civil War, the Duchess of Lerma rearranged certain **apartments**★ in 17
style, where paintings of great artistic value may be seen.

Ground floor – In the vast library, the hospital archives contain volumes bound i
leather by Moorish craftsmen. Among the paintings displayed, El Greco's *Hoi
Family* is arresting, the portrait of the *Virgin* perhaps the most beautiful the artis
ever painted. Note also the *Birth of the Messiah* by Tintoretto, the *Philosophe*
by Ribera and, in an adjoining room, his strange portrait of the *Bearded Womar*

First floor – The reception hall contains another El Greco, the sombre portrait c
Cardinal Tavera, painted from a death mask. Beside it are *Samson and Delilah* b
Caravaggio and two portraits of the *Duke and Duchess of Navas* by Antonio Morc

A gallery to the **church** leads off from the elegant twin *patio*. The Carrara marble portal is by Alonso Berruguete who also carved the tomb of Cardinal Tavera. The retable at the high altar was designed by El Greco whose last work, a **Baptism of Christ**★ is displayed in the church. It is an outstanding painting in which the artist's use of brilliant colours and elongated figures is at its most magnificent.

Giving onto the *patio* is the hospital's former pharmacy, which has been restored.

Puerta Antigua de Bisagra (Old Bisagra Gate) (BX V) – This gate in the former Moorish ramparts is the one through which Alfonso VI entered the city in 1085.

Puerta Nueva de Bisagra (New Bisagra Gate) (BX) – The gate was rebuilt by Covarrubias in 1550 and enlarged during the reign of Philip II. Massive round crenellated towers, facing the Madrid road, flank a giant imperial crest.

Puente de Alcántara (CX) – The 13C bridge ends respectively to west and east in a Mudéjar tower and a Baroque arch. On the far side of the Tajo, behind battlemented ramparts, the restored 14C **Castillo de San Servando** (San Servando Castle), an advanced strongpoint in medieval times, can be seen.

A plaque on the town wall by the bridge recalls how **St John of the Cross** (1542-91) escaped through a window from his monastery prison nearby.

Puente de San Martín (AY) – The medieval bridge, rebuilt in the 14C following damage by floodwaters, is marked at its south end by an octagonal crenellated tower; the north end is 16C.

Cristo de la Vega (AX) – The Church of Christ of the Vega, formerly St Leocadia, stands on the site of a 7C Visigothic temple, the venue of early church councils and, according to legend, the site of St Leocadia's apparition before San Ildefonso and the king. Although considerably modified in the 18C, it still has a fine Mudéjar apse. Inside, a modern Crucifix now stands in place of the one around which many legends had gathered including one in which the figure offered an arm to a jilted girl who had come to seek comfort.

EXCURSION

Guadamur – *15km/9mi southwest. Leave Toledo by* ③ *on the map, bearing left onto CM 401.*

The **castillo** (castle) ⊙ overlooking the village was built in the 15C and restored in the late 19C. The apartments, occupied for a period by Queen Juana the Mad and her son, the future Emperor Charles V, have been furnished with Spanish period furniture.

TORDESILLAS

Castilla y León (Valladolid) – Population 7 637

Michelin map 442 H 14-15

e historic town, massed upon the steep bank of the Duero, gave its name to the nous **Treaty of Tordesillas**. In 1494, the kings of Spain and Portugal, under the itration of the Borgia Pope Alexander VI, signed the treaty dividing the New World tween them. All lands west of a line of longitude 370 leagues west of Cape Verde re to be Spanish, all to the east, Portuguese – a decision which gave Spain all Latin erica except Brazil.

na the Mad locked herself away here on the death of Philip the Fair in 1506. On her ath 46 years later, she was buried in the Convento de Santa Clara. Her body was er removed to Granada.

Convento de Santa Clara ⊙ – The old palace, built by Alfonso XI in 1350 in commemoration of his victory at the Battle of Salado, was converted into a convent by his son, Peter the Cruel, who installed María de Padilla here, to whom he may have secretly been married in spite of Blanche de Bourbon being his queen. For María, who in this distant heart of Castilla was homesick for the beauty of Sevilla, he commissioned Mudéjar decoration.

The **patio**★, with multifoil and horseshoe-shaped arches, has strapwork decoration and multicoloured ceramic tiles. The **Capilla Dorada** (Gilded Chapel) with a fine Mudéjar cupola, exhibits mementoes and works of art including Juana's organ, Charles V's virginal, Philip II's clavichord and a 13C altarfront.

The **church** is on the site of the former throne room; the choir has a particularly intricate **artesonado ceiling**★★. In the Flamboyant Gothic **Capilla de los Saldaña** (Saldaña Chapel) are the founders' tombs and a 15C retable, originally a travelling altar.

EXCURSIONS

Medina del Campo - *24km/15mi southeast on N 6.*
The town was famous for its fairs in the Middle Ages. Isabel the Catholic died h
in 1504. Today, Medina del Campo is a major railway junction and b
agricultural centre where a large market is held on Sundays (*shops close*
Thursdays to open instead on Sundays).

★ **Castillo de la Mota** – The impressive brick castle overlooking the town is flanked
one side by a massive keep. Juana the Mad often stayed here and Cesare Bor
was imprisoned in the keep for two years.

TORO

Castilla y León (Zamora) – Population 9 649
Michelin map 441 or 442 H 13

Toro stands beside the Duero at the centre of a vast clay soil plain. Wheat is gro
north of the river (Tierra del Pan) and vines to the south (Tierra del Vino).
Most of the town's Romanesque churches, built in brick with interesting Mudé
decoration, have sadly deteriorated with age. The collegiate church, on the ot
hand, is built of limestone and has survived better.

★ **Colegiata** ○ – Construction of the collegiate church began in 1160 with
elegant transept lantern and ended in 1240 with completion of the west por

Exterior – The Romanesque **north portal** illustrates typical themes: above, the
Men of the Apocalypse and below, angels linked together by a rope symbolis
the unity of Faith.
The Gothic **west portal**★★, repainted in the 18C, is the church's great treasure
is dedicated to the Virgin; the Celestial Court is shown on the archivolt,
expressive Last Judgement on the coving. The statues on the jambs of the
and tympanum, although a little stiff, have very youthful faces.

Interior – Start beneath the **cupola**★, one of the first of its kind in Spain, with t
tiers of windows in the drum. Polychrome wood statues stand against the pill
at the end of the nave on consoles, one of which is carved with an amusing vers
of the birth of Eve (below the angel). In the sacristy is the **Virgin and the Fly**★
magnificent Flemish painting by either Gerard David or Hans Memling.

Iglesia de San Lorenzo ○ – This is the best preserved of Toro's Romanes
churches made of local brick. With its stone base, blind arcading and dog-to
decoration on the upper cornice, it has much of the Mudéjar style of Castilla
León. Inside, the Gothic **altarpiece** flanked by Plateresque tombs, was painted
Fernando Gallego.

EXCURSIONS

San Cebrián de Mazote - *30km/19mi northeast on C 519.*
The 10C **Iglesia de San Cebrián de Mazote** ○, built to a cruciform plan with three ai
divided by horseshoe-shaped arches, is a rare Mozarabic church. The modilli
are typical but some of the capitals and low reliefs bear traces of an earl
Visigothic style.

TORTOSA ★★

Catalunya (Tarragona) – Population 29 717
Michelin map 443 J 31

Tortosa, for centuries the last town before the sea, was charged in those times v
guarding, from the heights overlooking the Ebro, the region's only river brid
Today it is an agricultural town prospering from the olives planted on the hillsi
terraced and divided by low drystone walls and, lower down, from the e
vegetables, the maize, oranges and peaches sheltered from the sea wind by line
cypresses and flourishing in the rich alluvial soil brought down by the Ebro. From
Castillo de la Suda, a castle which has been converted into a parador, there is a
view of the town, the Ebro and the valley.

HISTORICAL NOTES

Tortosa was first Roman then Visigothic; in 714 it was seized by the Moors who b
the Fortaleza de la Suda (fortress). It was reconquered by Ramón Berenguer I\
1148. For several centuries Catalans, Moors and Jews lived peacefully toget
providing a wonderful setting in which different cultures flourished side by si
During the Battle of the Ebro in July 1938, the Republicans lost 150 000 me
Tortosa.

View of Tortosa from Castillo de la Suda

CIUDAD ANTIGUA (OLD TOWN) *3hr*

Catedral ⊙ – The cathedral was built in pure Gothic style even though construction, begun in 1347, continued for 200 years. The 18C **façade**★ built in the Baroque style is lavishly decorated: capitals with plant motifs, curved columns and outstanding reliefs. In Catalan tradition the lines of the **interior**★★ are plain, the arches high and divided into two tiers only in the nave. Note the double ambulatory. The chancel is framed by radiating chapels which, as was originally planned, should be divided by fenestration like that at the north entrance to the ambulatory.

The retable at the high altar has a large wood **polyptych**★ painted in the 14C, illustrating the Life of Christ and the Virgin Mary. Another interesting work is the 15C **altarpiece of the Transfiguration**★, attributed to Jaime Huguet, presenting lavish ornamentation and delicately carved figures.

The two stone 15C **pulpits**★ in the nave are beautifully carved with low reliefs: those on the left illustrate the Evangelists and their symbols, those on the right the Doctors of the Roman church, Saints Gregory, Jerome, Ambrose and Augustine.

Capilla de Nuestra Señora de la Cinta (Chapel of Our Lady of the Belt) – *Second chapel off the south aisle*. This was built in the Baroque style between 1642 and 1725 and is decorated with paintings and local jasper and marble; at its centre is the relic, the belt of Our Lady *(services of special veneration: first week in September)*.

Font – *First chapel off the south aisle*. The stone basin is said to have stood in the garden of the antipope Benedict XIII, Pedro de Luna and bears his arms. A great many funerary steles and reliefs can be found in the austere cloisters (14C) adjoining the right side of the temple.

Palacio Episcopal (Bishop's Palace) ⊙ – The 14C Catalan *patio* of this palace, built in the 13C-14C, is memorable for the straight flight of steps which completely occupies one side and the arcaded gallery, lined with slender columns. On the upper floor, the **Gothic chapel**★, entered through a carved doorway from a well-proportioned ante-room, has ogive vaulting in which the ribs descend on to figured bosses. The final decorative touch is given by the false relief windows built into the walls on either side.

Reales Colegios de Tortosa ⊙ – In 1564 the Emperor Charles V founded this lovely Renaissance ensemble, consisting of the Colegio de Sant Lluís and the Colegio de Sant Jordi y Sant Domingo.

The **Colegio de Sant Lluís**★ was at one time used for educating newly-converted Muslims: the door of the main façade features two sphinxes symbolising knowledge, flanked by the imperial coat of arms. In the section above are sculptures of St James and St Matthew, who were the patrons of the College. fine oblong **patio★★** is curiously decorated with characters in relief, represent an incredibly wide range of expressions and attitudes. The college now houses **Arxiu d'Història Comarcal de les Terres de l'Ebre★** ⊘, which contains an extens collection of documents about the town, along with an unusual display of sto and coins.

The Renaissance façade of the **Colegio de Sant Jordi y de Sant Domingo** bears a La inscription (*Domus Sapientiae* meaning House of Knowledge), indicating vocation of this institution.

Iglesia de Sant Domingo ⊘ – Built in the 16C, this church was once part of Reales Colegios. It is the home of the **Museo Municipal**, with its large collectior coins.

★ **Llotja de Mar** – A fine Gothic building (16C) with two rectangular naves separa by semicircular arches. The old maritime exchange was moved to its curr premises in 1933.

EXCURSION

★★ **Parque Natural del Delta del Ebro (Ebro Delta Nature Reserve)** ⊘ – *25km/16mi e* There are boat trips between Deltebre and the river mouth (*45min there back*). The reserve, covering an area of 7 736ha/19 116 acres, was create 1983 to protect the birds that shelter there and to encourage local econo development. The vast delta, closed by the Isla de Buda (Buda Island), is a swar stretch of alluvium deposits collected by the Ebro from the Montes Cantábri range, the Pyrenees and the Aragón plateaux. Three-quarters of the land is gi over to the growing of rice and early fruit and vegetables.

TRUJILLO★★

Extremadura (Cáceres) – Population 8 919
Michelin map 444 N 12

The modern town gives little idea of the originality and charm of the old town, b on a granite ledge higher up the hillside. This was hastily fortified by the Moor the 13C against attack by the Christians and, as the centuries passed, superimposed on its Arabic appearance, noble mansions built in the 16C and 17C the Indianos – those who had journeyed across the Atlantic and returned wit fortune.

The land of the Conquistadores – "Twenty American nations", it is s "were conceived in Trujillo". Accurate or not, it is certainly true that the city claim to have fathered numbers of conquerors and colonisers of the New Wo **Francisco de Orellana** who left in 1542 to explore the legendary country of Amazons; **Diego García de Paredes**, nicknamed the Samson of Extremadura account of his Herculean strength, and the most famous of all, **Francisco Piz** (1475-1541), the conqueror of Peru. This swineherd, who married an princess, followed what had been Cortés' policy in Mexico of seizing and execut the ruler, in this case the Emperor Atahualpa, plundering his riches and occupy his capital, Cuzco (1533). The early discovery of the Potosí silver mines made F the most important colony in the Spanish Empire but an implacable rivalry betw Pizarro and his companion in arms, Almagro, brought about the death first Almagro in 1538 and then of Pizarro, murdered amid untold riches in his o palace.

★★ PLAZA MAYOR (Z)

Plaza Mayor, like all the old quarter of Trujillo, is less austere than Cáce the mansions generally having been built later in the 16C and 17C, decorated with arcades, loggias and corner windows. The widespread use whitewash on house fronts and the more steeply inclined alleys bring additic interest to the town. Those visiting Trujillo in late spring or at any t throughout the summer will hear the flapping wings and see the outline of m a high perched stork.

The square is unusual for its irregular shape and different levels linked by v flights of steps and the great variety of seignorial mansions overlooking it. Wc examining in detail, it evokes a way of life long gone and at night its appeara is positively theatrical.

Equestrian statue of Pizarro (YZ) – 1927 bronze by the American sculpt Charles Runse and Mary Harriman.

R.Mazin/DIAF

Plaza Mayor

Iglesia de San Martín (Y) – 16C. The rubble and freestone walls of the church enclose a vast nave chequered with funerary paving stones. The south parvis served in the past as a public meeting ground.

Palacio de los Duques de San Carlos (Palace of the Dukes San Carlos) (Y) – 17C. Now an enclosed convent. The tall granite façade, decorated in the transitional Classical Baroque style has a corner window surmounted by the double-headed eagle crest of the Vargas. Visitors have access to the **patio** with two tiers of rounded arches and a fine staircase of four flights.

Palacio del Marqués de Piedras Albas (Palace of the Marquis of Piedras Albas) (Z) – The Renaissance loggia has been accommodated into the original Gothic wall.

Palacio des Marqués de la Conquista (Palace of the Marquis de la Conquista) (Z L) – The palace was built by Hernando Pizarro, the conquistador's brother. It has an exceptional number of windows with iron grilles and a Plateresque **corner window**★, added in the 17C with, on the left, the busts of Francisco Pizarro and his wife, and on the right Hernando and his niece, whom he married. Above is the family crest. Crowning the façade is a series of statues representing the months of the year.

Ayuntamiento Viejo (Former town hall) (Z J) – 16C. Three tiers of Renaissance arcades from a nearby *patio* have been reconstructed to form the façade of what is now the Palacio de Justicia (Law Courts).

Casa de las Cadenas (House of Chains) (Y R) – The chains are said to have been brought by Christians freed from Moorish serfdom.

Torre del Alfiler (Alfiler Tower) (Y) – The so-called needle tower is a Mudéjar belfry and a favourite spot with storks.

ADDITIONAL SIGHTS

Palacio de Orellana-Pizarro (Z) – 16C. This palace has a beautiful Plateresque upper gallery.

Iglesia de Santiago (Y) – This church's 13C Romanesque belfry and the tall seignorial tower belonging to the Palacio de los Chaves stand on either side of the Arco de Santiago (St James' Arch), one of the town's seven original gateways. The nave of the church was modified in the 17C.

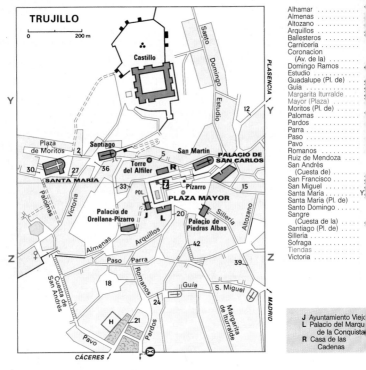

TRUJILLO

0   200 m

Castillo

Alhamar . . . .
Almenas . . . .
Altozano . . . .
Arquillos . . . .
Ballesteros . . . .
Carnicería . . . .
Coronacion
  (Av. de la) . . . .
Domingo Ramos . . . . .
Estudio . . . .
Guadalupe (Pl. de) . . .
Guia . . . .
Margarita Iturralde . . . .
Mayor (Plaza) . . . .
Moritos (Pl. de) . . . . . .
Palomas . . . .
Pardos . . . .
Parra . . . .
Paso . . . .
Pavo . . . .
Romanos . . . .
Ruiz de Mendoza . . . . .
San Andrés
  (Cuesta de) . . . .
San Francisco . . . .
San Miguel . . . .
Santa María . . . . .Y
Santa María (Pl. de) . . .
Santo Domingo . . . . . .
Sangre
  (Cuesta de la) . . . . .
Santiago (Pl. de) . . . . .
Silleria . . . .
Sofraga . . . .
Tiendas . . . .
Victoria . . . .

J Ayuntamiento Viejo
L Palacio del Marqu
   de la Conquista
R Casa de las
   Cadenas

★ **Iglesia de Santa María** ⊙ (Y) – 13C. This Gothic church, in which the netwo
vaulting was reconstructed in the 15C, is the pantheon of Trujillo's great men
the *coro alto*, lit by a wide rose window, are the two stone seats in which
Catholic monarchs sat during Mass when in residence in the city. The 24 pan
of the Gothic **retable**★ at the high altar are attributed to Fernando Gallego.
From the top of the belfry there is a delightful **view** of brown tile roofs, the Pl
Mayor arcades and the castle.

Castillo (Y) – The castle stands out prominently on the granite ledge from wh
the blocks were hewn for its construction. The massive crenellated curtain v
is reinforced by numerous heavy square towers. Above the keep the patron
Trujillo, Our Lady of Victory, can still be seen keeping vigil. The view from the w
takes in the town and its Plaza Mayor.

TUDELA ★

Navarra – Population 26 163

Michelin map 442 F 25

Tudela is the centre of the Ribera, a well irrigated, prosperous horticultural reg
growing and canning asparagus, haricot beans, artichokes and peppers.
In the 9C, the town was a dependency of the Córdoba Caliphate. From that time
later periods, it has preserved a large Moorish quarter, the Morería, and old Mud
style houses.
St Anne's feast day (26 July) is celebrated annually, as at Pamplona, with sev
days of great rejoicing including *encierros* and bullfights. During Holy Week, an ev
known as the Descent of the Angel, takes place on the picturesque **Plaza de los Fue**
which served as a bullring in the 18C.

SIGHTS

★ **Catedral** ⊙ – The 12C-13C cathedral is an excellent example of the transitic
Romanesque-Gothic style. The **Last Judgement Doorway**★ (Portada del Juicio Fin
difficult to see through lack of space, is an incredibly carved unit with nea
120 groups of figures illustrating the Last Judgement.
The **interior**, Romanesque in the elevation of the nave, is Gothic in its vaulting
clerestory. Excepting the *coro* enclosure and several side chapels, which
Baroque, the church is rich in Gothic works of art including early 16C choir sta
the retable at the high altar and the stone reliquary statue of Byzant
appearance dating from about 1200 of the *White Virgin*. Just beside it, the **Ca
de Nuestra Señora de la Esperanza**★ (Chapel of our Lady of Hope) has several 1
masterpieces including the sepulchre of a chancellor of Navarra and the cen
altarpiece.

The 12C-13C **cloisters**★★ *(claustro)* are exceedingly harmonious with Romanesque arches resting alternately on groups of two or three columns with historiated capitals. Most of them relate scenes from the New Testament and the lives of the saints in a style inspired by the carvings of Aragón. A door of the mosque which once stood on the site has been preserved in one of the gallery walls.

Iglesia de San Nicolás – When the church in calle Rúa in the old quarter was rebuilt in the 18C a tympanum of Romanesque origin was placed in the façade built of brick in the Mudéjar style. God the Father is shown seated, holding his Son and surrounded by the symbols of the Evangelists.

EXCURSIONS

Tarazona – *21km/13mi southwest on N 121.* (Aragón). In the Middle Ages, Tarazona was for a time, the residence of the kings of Aragón. Round the former royal mansion, now the **Palacio Episcopal** (Episcopal Palace), an old quarter still remains with narrow streets overlooking the quays of the río Queiles.

Catedral ⊙ – The cathedral was largely rebuilt in the 15C and 16C. Several architectural styles may be seen: Aragón Mudéjar in the belfry tower and lantern, Renaissance in the portal and, in the **second chapel**★ as you walk left round the ambulatory, delicately carved Gothic **tombs** of the two Calvillos cardinals from Avignon.
The **Mudéjar cloisters** have bays filled with 16C Moorish plasterwork tracery.
Not far away, a small enclosed square surrounded by houses, the 18C **Plaza de Toros Vieja**, was once a bullring.

★ **Monasterio de Veruela** ⊙ – *39km/24mi south from Tudela and 17km/11mi from Tarazona. From Tarazona, take N 122 towards Zaragoza then bear right onto Z 373.*
Cistercian monks from southern France came in the middle of the 12C to this spot where they founded a monastery and surrounded it with a fortified perimeter wall. Seven centuries later the Sevillian poet **Bécquer** was to stay while writing his *Letters from my Cell* in which he described the Aragón countryside much in the manner of later guide books!

★ **Iglesia** – The church, built in the transitional period between Romanesque and Gothic, has a sober but attractive façade with a single oculus, a narrow band of blind arcades strangely lacking a base line and a doorway decorated with friezes, billets and capitals.
The interior, with pointed vaulting, is an amazing size. The vault groins are pointed over the nave and horseshoe-shaped over the aisles and ambulatory. A Plateresque chapel with a multicoloured carved door was built onto the north transept in the 16C. Opposite, the sacristy door is in a surprising Rococo style.

★ **Claustro** – The cloisters are ornate Gothic. At ground level the brackets are carved with the heads of men and beasts; above are three galleries with Plateresque decoration. The **Sala Capitalar**★ (chapter-house), in pure Cistercian style, contains the tombs of the monastery's first 15 abbots.

TUI/TUY★

Galicia (Pontevedra) – Population 15 346
Michelin map 441 F 4

Tui stands just across the border from Portugal in a striking **setting**★. Its old quarter, facing the Portuguese fortress of Valença, stretches down the rocky hillside to the right bank of the río Miño. The **Parque de Santo Domingo** (Santo Domingo Park), in which stands a Gothic church of the same name, commands a good view of the site.
Discoveries on monte Alhoya confirm that a settlement existed on the site in ancient times. The town was then occupied successively by Romans, Arabs and Northmen and grew rapidly in the Middle Ages.
Since 1884, when a bridge was built by Gustave Eiffel across the Miño, Tui has served as a gateway to Portugal.

SIGHTS

The historic town is one of the oldest of Galicia's four provinces; its emblasoned houses and narrow stepped alleys climbing towards the cathedral testify to its rich past.

★ **Catedral** ⊙ – The low-lying cathedral, fringed with crenellations and flanked by towers, still resembles the fortress it was for so long. It was consecrated in 1232 having been built, for the most part, in Romanesque Gothic, a style perfectly suited in its simplicity to the building's military role. The Romanesque north door, marked only by arches cut into the wall stone, is almost austere. In contrast the west front is adorned with a 14C porch which, while remaining defensive in character, is highly decorative with equilateral arches preceding a richly sculp-

tured **portal**★. The tympanum, beneath the carved covings, glorifies the Mother
God; above the Adoration of the Magi and Shepherds are the towers of heave
Jerusalem rendered ethereal by the interplay of mass and void.

Inside are the impressive reinforcing beams the cathedral was given in the 15C a
18C to compensate for the slant of the pillars. The transept plan of three ais
is Compostelan and, in Spain, is found only in this church and that of Santia
de Compostela. Modifications were made to the chapels from the 16C to the 1
The choir stall carvings recount the life and miracles of San Telmo, patron of T
The sentry path over the wide **cloister** galleries, soberly decorated in Cisterc
style, commands good views of the river valley.

Capilla de San Telmo (San Telmo Chapel) – A Portuguese style reliquary shrine
been built below the cathedral on the site of the house of **San Pedro González Tel**
a Dominican who lived in Tuy and died in 1240. Pilgrims visit the alcove in
crypt where the saint died (*entrance: Rúa do Corpo Santo*).

ÚBEDA★★

Andalucía (Jaén) – Population 31 962

Michelin map 446 R 19

Úbeda was, at one time, very prosperous. It was recaptured from the Moors in 12
and became a base in the Reconquest campaign. It is now one of the best examp
in Spain of homogeneous construction, dating principally from the time of
Renaissance.

Traditional craftsmen, chiefly potters, are to be found in calle Valencia (**BY**).

During Holy Week, a solemn evening procession is held on Good Friday.

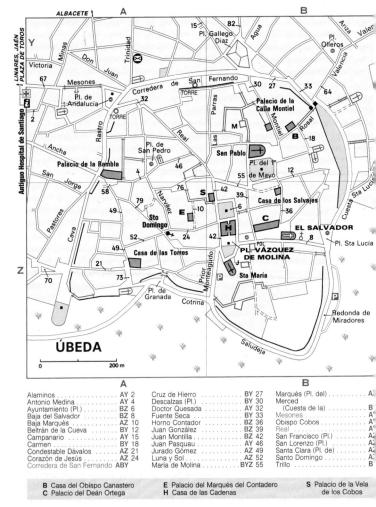

Alaminos	AY 2	Cruz de Hierro	BY 27	Marqués (Pl. del)	A
Antonio Medina	AY 4	Descalzas (Pl.)	BY 30	Merced
Ayuntamiento (Pl.)	BZ 6	Doctor Quesada	AY 32	(Cuesta de la)	B
Baja del Salvador	BZ 8	Fuente Seca	BY 33	Mesones	A
Baja Marqués	AZ 10	Horno Contador	BZ 36	Obispo Cobos	A
Beltrán de la Cueva	BY 12	Juan González	BZ 39	Real	A
Campanario	AY 15	Juan Montilla	BZ 42	San Francisco (Pl.)	A
Carmen	BY 18	Juan Pasquau	AY 46	San Lorenzo (Pl.)	A
Condestable Dávalos	AZ 21	Jurado Gómez	AZ 49	Santa Clara (Pl. de)	A
Corazón de Jesús	AZ 24	Luna y Sol	AZ 52	Santo Domingo	A
Corredera de San Fernando	ABY	María de Molina	BYZ 55	Trillo	B

B Casa del Obispo Canastero	**E** Palacio del Marqués del Contadero	**S** Palacio de la Vela
C Palacio del Deán Ortega	**H** Casa de las Cadenas	de los Cobos

BARRIO ANTIGUO (OLD QUARTER) *1hr 30min*

Plaza Vázquez de Molina (BZ) – The square, the monumental centre of Úbeda, is lined with old, historic buildings like the **Palacio del Deán Ortega** (BZ C), which has been converted into a parador.

Casa de las Cadenas (House of Chains) (BZ H) – The mansion, now the Ayuntamiento (town hall), named after the chains round the forecourt, was designed in 1562 by Vandelvira, who was also responsible for the construction of Jaén Cathedral.

The majestic but not overly ornate façade is relieved by alternating bays and pilasters and decorated above with caryatids and atlantes.

The *patio*, bordered by delicate arcades, opens onto plaza del Ayuntamiento.

The archives room on the second floor, covered by *artesonado* decoration the entire length of the façade, commands fine views of the square and the town.

Iglesia de Santa María (BZ) – The church's architecture is varied: the main door and that of Consolada *(left side)* are 17C, the cloisters 16C. The **chapels**★, set in sculptured surrounds, are closed by beautiful **grilles**★, most of which were wrought by Maestro Bartolomé.

Iglesia de El Salvador ⊙ (BZ) – *If visiting outside service times, enter by the north door.* Diego de Siloé designed this homogeneous and sumptuous church in 1536. Its massive façade combines the most characteristic ornamental motifs of the Renaissance.

The **interior**★ is frankly theatrical: the nave has vaulting outlined in blue and gold and is closed by a monumental wrought-iron grille. Beyond, the Capilla Mayor (chancel) forms a kind of rotunda in which an immense 16C altarpiece includes a baldachin with a sculpture by Berruguete of the Transfiguration (only the figure of Christ remains).

The **sacristy**★★, by Vandelvira, is ornamented with coffered decoration, medallions, caryatids and atlantes with all the splendour of the Italian Renaissance style.

Casa de los Salvajes (House of the Savages) (BZ) – Two very odd savages, dressed in animal skins held together with belts of blackberry branches, may be seen on the façade, supporting a bishop's crest.

Casa de los Salvajes – détail

F. Bouillot/MARCO POLO

Iglesia de San Pablo (BY) – The church is a harmonious mixture of Gothic architecture, as seen in the west door, and the Isabelline style, to be seen in the **south door** (1511). The **chapels**★, adorned in several instances with fine wrought-iron grilles, are the church's chief interior feature: the Capilla de las Calaveras (Chapel of the Skulls) was designed by Vandelvira; the Capilla de las Mercedes is in the Isabelline style and richly carved.

Palacio de la Calle Montiel (BY) – This palace was one of the town's first Renaissance buildings and has a monumental gate flanked by twisted columns.

Casa del Obispo Canastero (Bishop Canastero's Mansion) (BY B) – Among the figures decorating the mansion's diamond pointed stone façade are two soldiers bearing the owner's coats of arms.

Palacio del Marqués del Contadero (Palace of the Marquis of Contadero) (AZ E) – late-18C façade, crowned by a gallery, is Renaissance, a testimony to the l◼ survival of the style in Úbeda.

Palacio de la Vela de los Cobos (ABZ S) – The palace's distinguished faça◼ surmounted by an arcaded gallery, is most unusually L-shaped.

ADDITIONAL SIGHTS

Casa de las Torres (Tower Mansion) (AZ) – The mansion front, closely flanked◼ two square towers, is profusely decorated in the Plateresque style, with delicat◼ carved sculpture.

Antiguo Hospital de Santiago (Former St James' Hospital) – *Take calle Obispo Co* (AY). A high relief of St James Matamoros stands over the entrance to the form◼ hospital, now a cultural centre. Inside are an arcaded *patio* and a grand stairc◼ with multicoloured vaulting (1562-75).

Palacio de la Rambla (AY) – The portal includes the figures of soldiers bearing ◼ palace's coat of arms.

Iglesia de Santo Domingo (AZ) – The church's south door, overlooking a sm◼ picturesque square, is a delicate Renaissance work decorated with foliage mot◼ and roses.

UCLÉS

Castilla-La Mancha (Cuenca) – Population 297
Michelin map 444 M 21

The massive castle-monastery *(castillo-monasterio)* of Uclés stands impressively ◼ a hill overlooking the village. From 1174 to 1499 it was the headquarters of the Ord◼ of Santiago.
Because of its strategic value, the little village was the scene of a good deal ◼ fighting, including the Battle of Uclés in 1108 when the Almoravids defeated t◼ army of Alfonso VI of Castilla.

Castillo-monasterio ⊘ – The present building was begun in 1529 in t◼ Plateresque style, but the greater part of the work was undertaken by Herrera◼ disciple, **Francisco de Mora** (1560-1610) who tried to build his own Escorial – t◼ building is, in fact, known as the Little Escorial. Two successful Baroq◼ sculptures are immediately evident: the courtyard fountain and the main gat◼ The ramparts command an extensive panorama.

The chapter on art and architecture in this guide gives an outline of artistic creation ◼ the region, providing the context of the buildings and works of art described in the Sig◼ section.

This chapter may also provide ideas for touring.

It is advisable to read it at leisure/before setting out.

UJUÉ★

Navarra – Population 209
Michelin map 442 E 25

Ujué, perched on a summit overlooking the Ribera region, remains, with its tortuo◼ streets and picturesque façades, much as it was in the Middle Ages.
Its **romería** (pilgrimage) is famous: the procession, dating back to the 14C, sets o◼ annually on the Sunday after St Mark's Day (25 April), when penitents dressed ◼ black capes and hoods and bearing a Cross gather from far and wide to implore th◼ mercy of the Virgin of Ujué.

Iglesia de Santa María – A Romanesque church was built on the site at the e◼ of the 11C. In the 14C, Charles II, the Bad, undertook the building of a Goth◼ church but work must have been interrupted for the Romanesque chancel remai◼ to this day. The central chapel contains the venerated **Santa María la Blanca**, a woode◼ Romanesque statue, plated in silver.

Fortaleza (Fortress) – The church towers, invariably used for military purpose◼ command a view which extends to Olite, the Montejurra and the Pyrenees. Of th◼ medieval palace there remain lofty walls and a covered watch path circling th◼ church.

VALDEPEÑAS

Castilla-La Mancha (Ciudad Real) – Population 25 067

Michelin map 444 P 19

depeñas, which stands at the southern tip of the vast wine-growing area of La
ancha, is the production centre of a well-known table wine.
e in the town centres around plaza de España where blue and white coloured
uses rise above shady porticoes. On one side stands the Late Gothic façade of the
esia de la Asunción (Church of the Assumption), with a harmonious tower and a
ateresque upper gallery.

EXCURSIONS

San Carlos del Valle - *22km/14mi northeast.*
The small village of San Carlos has a delightful 18C **Plaza Mayor**★ set off by the
warm colour of its brick houses. A former hospice, at no 5, has a stone entrance
and a typical *patio*. Overlooking all is the Baroque village church, crowned by a
dome and four lantern turrets.

Las Virtudes - *24km/15mi south.*
The village claims that its **bullring** *(plaza de toros)* is the oldest in Spain (1641). It
is square and is blocked along one side by the wall of the 14C **Santuario de Nuestra
Señora de las Virtudes** (Sanctuary of Our Lady of Holy Virtue) ⊘ which inside has a
Mudéjar ceiling over the nave and a Churrigueresque altarpiece.

VALENCIA★★

Comunidad valenciana – Population 777 427

Michelin map 445 N 28

lencia, Spain's third largest city, has all the character of a large Mediterranean
wn and is notable for its pleasant, mild climate and the quality of its light. Its wide
enues (Grandes Vías), lined with palms and fig trees, encircle the old quarter with
 fortified gateways, churches and narrow streets with quaint, old-fashioned shop
nts and Gothic houses, of which some have attractive *patios*. However, Valencia
also a city in the process of change, with projects such as the **Ciudad de las Ciencias
e las Artes** (Arts and Science City), **Calatrava bridge** and **Palacio de Congresos** (Conference
ntre) by Norman Foster propelling the city to the forefront of architectural design.
lencia is the capital of a fertile agricultural province as well as a prosperous
dustrial centre with shipyards, metallurgical and chemical plants, furniture, paper
d textile factories. Its produce for export, including the citrus fruit, early
getables and wine from the surrounding *huerta*, is handled by its busy port, **El Grao**.
urism has developed rapidly along the poetically named **Costa del Azahar** (Orange
ossom Coast) which stretches in a wide fringe of sand to the north and south of
lencia. The city itself has two beaches, **Levante** and **La Malvarrosa**, both of which are
nnected to the city centre by modern tram. On account of its sunshine and the fact
at it is sheltered from Meseta winds by nearby sierras, the immediate coast has
come one of Spain's major summer tourist centres with resorts such as **Benicàssim**,
opesa, **Peñíscola**, **Benicarló** and **Vinarós** to the north and **El Saler**, **Cullera** and **Gandía** and **Oliva**
 the south. Apartment blocks have sprung up to form an unusual urban landscape
tween the long sandy beaches and the orange groves inland.

000 years of history - The city, founded by the Greeks in 138 BC, passed
ccessively into the hands of the Carthaginians, Romans, Visigoths and Arabs. In
94 it was reconquered by **El Cid**, who was titled Duke of Valencia but lived only five
ars in the city before dying there in 1099. The Moors recaptured it three years later
d held it until 1238 when it was repossessed, this time by James the Conqueror,
o declared it the capital of a kingdom which he allied to Aragón. Valencia then
joyed a long period of prosperity until the end of the 15C when, following the
scovery of America and the development of ports in Andalucía, it began to decline.
silk renaissance in the 17C renewed its fortunes.
er the past two centuries, Valencia has been involved in every war and insurrection
Spain. During the War of the Spanish Succession (1701-14), the city sided with
e Archduke, Charles of Austria but found itself stripped of its privileges; in 1808,
ebelled against the French and was then taken by Suchet in 1812; in 1843 it rose
der **General Narváez** to restore the regency of María Cristina of Naples; finally during
e Civil War in March 1939, after the fall of Catalunya, the city became the last
fuge of the Republican forces.

t in Valencia - Valencia enjoyed a period of brilliance, both economically and
tistically, in the 15C. Examples of Gothic architectural flowering are to be seen in
e old city's palaces, mansions, gates, the cathedral and the Lonja (Exchange). In
inting, several artists won renown: **Luis Dalmau**, influenced by Flemish painting, who
veloped a Hispano-Flemish style; **Jaime Baço**, known as **Jacomart**, and his fellow artist
an Reixach who were both influenced by Flanders and Italy; and the **Osonas**, father
d son, who also showed Flemish austerity in their work.

Valencia craftsmen of the 15C were also outstanding in the decorative arts: wrou€ ironwork, gold and silversmithing, embroidery and particularly ceramics, for wh special centres were established at Paterna and Manises *(see the Museo de Cerám below).*

The Valencia huerta and Albufera – The city lies along the banks of the Turia at heart of fertile countryside known locally as **La Huerta**. On this expanse, watered an irrigation system laid down by the Romans and improved by the Moors, are countless citrus trees and market gardens which produce the fruit and ea vegetables exported throughout Europe.

South of Valencia, a vast lagoon, the **Parque Natural de La Albufera** (from the Ara meaning Small Sea), separated from the Mediterranean by an offshore bar, Dehesa, has, since the 13C, been planted with paddy fields. It is also a fishing ar its eels appear on typical menus in restaurants in **El Palmar** *(18km/11mi south)* wh also serve Valencia's famous dish, **paella**. *For further details on the park, contact* **Centro de Interpretación del Racó de l'Olla** ⊙; ☎ *961 62 73 45.*

Tribunal de las Aguas (Water Tribunal) – Since the Middle Ages disputes in the *hue* have been settled by the Tribunal de las Aguas: every Thursday at noon, repres tatives of the areas irrigated by the eight canals, accompanied by an *alguazil* (offi of justice), meet in front of the Portada de los Apóstoles (Apostle's Door) of cathedral; the offence is read out, judged (the judges all in black) and the sente pronounced immediately (a fine, deprivation of water) by the most senior judge. proceedings are oral and there is no appeal.

The *huerta* has found its place in literature in the realistic, dramatic novels of **Vic€ Blasco Ibáñez** (1867-1928) including *La Barraca (The Cabin)* and *Entre Narar* (Among the Orange Trees). The small **Museo Blasco Ibáñez** ⊙, in a chalet built by writer at the Playa de la Malvarrosa, can also be visited.

Las Fallas – Valencia holds a week-long carnival every year during week preceding 19 March. The custom goes back to the Middle Ages wl on St Joseph's Day, the carpenters' brotherhood, one of the town's traditio crafts, burned their accumulated wood shavings in bonfires known as *Fa* (from the Latin *fax*: torch). The name became synonymous with a festival which, in time, objects were made solely for burning – particularly effigies of I popular members of the community! In the 17C single effigies were replaced pasteboard groups or floats produced by quarters of the town – rivalry is s that the figures today are fantastic in size, artistry and satirical implication. Pri are awarded during the general festivities which include fireworks, processio bullfights etc before everything goes up in the fires or *cremá* on the evening 19 March. Figures dating from 1934 to the present day which have been spared from the bonfires are on display in an interesting museum, the **Museo Fallero** ⊙.

★ CIUDAD VIEJA

(OLD TOWN) *2hr*

★ **Catedral** ⊙ **(EX)** – The cathedral stands on the site of a former mosque. Although work began in 1262, the major part of the building dates from the 14C and 15C. The Gothic style was completely masked in the late 18C by a neo-Classical renovation which has since been removed.

★ **El Miguelete** ⊙ – Abutting the façade, El Miguelete, or El Micalet as the Valencians call it, an octagonal tower, owes its name to the large bell consecrated on St Michael's Day. From the top there is a bird's-eye view of the cathedral roofs and the town with its countless glazed ceramic domes.

El Miguelete

Exterior – The early-18C west face, which is elegant in spite of being narrowly confined, is in imitation of the Italian Baroque style, after plans by a German architect. The Assumption on the pediment is by Ignacio Vergara and Esteve.

The south door, the Puerta del Palau (Palace Door), is Romanesque, the north, the **Portada de los Apóstoles** (Apostles' Door), Gothic, decorated with numerous, but timeworn sculptures. The statue of the Virgin and Child, which once stood against the pier, is now on the tympanum surrounded by angel musicians.

Interior – Although the elevation of the Gothic vaulting is not very great, a great deal of light filters in through the alabaster windows in the beautiful Flamboyant Gothic **lantern**.

The high altar retable, painted early in the 16C by Fernando de Llanos and Yáñez de la Almedina, illustrates the Lives of Christ and the Virgin in a style markedly influenced by Leonardo da Vinci.

In the ambulatory, behind the high altar, a Renaiassance portico hides a translucent alabaster relief of the Resurrection (1510). Opposite is the 15C Virgen del Coro (Chancel Virgin) in polychrome alabaster and, in a chapel, a Crucifixion known as the Cristo de la Buena Muerte (Christ of Good Death).

Capilla del Santo Cáliz or Sala Capitular (Chapel of the Holy Grail or Chapter-house) ⊘ – The chamber, which in the 14C served as a reading room, has elegant star vaulting. Behind the altar, twelve alabaster low reliefs by the Florentine sculptor, Poggibonsi, are part of a fine Gothic structure in the centre of which can be seen a magnificent 1C carnelian agate cup, said to be the Holy Grail (the vessel traditionally used by Our Lord at the Last Supper and in which a few drops of his blood are said to have fallen). The cup, according to legend, was brought to Spain in the 3C and belonged first to the Monasterio de San Juan de la Peña then to the crown of Aragón which, in the 15C, presented it to Valencia Cathedral. This chapel provides access to the **museum**, which contains a monumental monstrance made after the Civil War and two large paintings by Goya of San Francisco de Borja.

Museo de la Ciudad (City Museum) ⊘ (EX M²) – This museum is housed in the 19C Palacio del Marqués de Campo. It contains the city's art gallery and a small section devoted to the history of Valencia from its foundation through to the Christian period.

Cripta Arqueológica de la Cárcel de San Vicente (San Vicente Gaol Archeological Crypt) ⊘ (EX) – A small Visigothic chapel with a sepulchre surrounded by four finely-decorated screens and two Visigothic stone sarcophagi.

Almudín (EX E) – This is a 14C to 16C granary with popular style frescoes covering the walls and two 19C *azulejos* altars. It is now used as a venue for temporary exhibitions.

Iglesia de Nuestra Señora de los Desamparados ⊘ (EX B) – Beneath the church's painted cupola stands the venerated statue of the patron of Valencia: the Virgin of the Abandoned *(desamparados)*.

Palacio de la Generalidad ⊘ (EX) – This fine 15C Gothic palace to which one tower was added in the 17C and a second identical one added in the 20C, was until 1707 the meeting place of the Valencia Cortes charged with the collection of tax.

Visitors enter an attractive Gothic *patio* decorated with a sculpture by Benlliure of Dante's *Inferno* (1900). Then they see a golden saloon with a wonderful gilt and multicolour **artesonado ceiling**★ and a large painting of the Tribunal de las Aguas or Water Tribunal *(see above)*. On the first floor are the Sala de los Reyes (Royal Hall) displaying portraits of the Valencian kings, the Oratorio (Oratory) with its altarpiece by the local 16C painter, Juan Sariñena, and the Gran Salón de las Cortes Valencianas (Valencian Government Grand Council Chamber). The *azulejos* frieze and the coffered ceiling are 16C. Members of the Cortes are portrayed in several 16C canvases.

Calle de Caballeros (DEX) – Some of the houses along the main street of the old town have kept their Gothic *patios* (no 22).

Iglesia de San Nicolás ⊘ (DX) – This, one of the town's oldest churches, has been completely renovated in the Churrigueresque style. Among the 16C paintings are an altarpiece by Juan de Juanes *(chapel to the left on entering)* and a *Calvary* by Osona the Elder *(by the font)*.

Lonja (Silk Exchange) ⊘ (DY) – The present building was erected on the request of the Valencia silk merchants in the 15C to replace an earlier commodities exchange similar to those of Barcelona and Palma. The prosperity which required a larger building was well reflected in the style of the new edifice: Flamboyant Gothic.

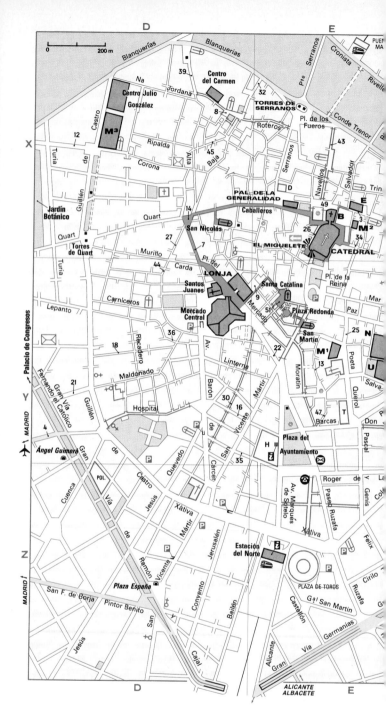

The Lonja, topped by a crenellated roof ridge, has an impressive Gothic entrance. The left wing, separated from the entrance by a tower, is crowned by a gallery decorated with a medallion frieze. The old commercial silk hall★★ is lofty, with ogival arches supported on elegantly cabled columns; the bays in the walls are filled with delicate tracery.

Iglesia de los Santos Juanes ⊘ **(DY)** – This is a vast church with a Baroque façade. The single aisle, originally Gothic, was modified in the 17C and 18C by the addition of exuberant Baroque stuccowork. The small tower crowning the Baroque façade can be seen to best effect from the Lonja.

Mercado Central (Central Market) (DY) – The enormous metal and glass construction, built in 1928, is a good example of Modernist architecture. Try going there in the mornings when it is at its busiest with stalls of glistening fish and great piles of fruit and vegetables fresh from the *huerta*.

Map labels:

Jardines del Real

MUSEO DE BELLAS ARTES SAN PIO V

Av. Blasco Ibáñez

U

Jardín de Monforte

Pío V

Llano del Real

Pl. del Temple

Puente del Real

Micer

Masco

Paseo

Pl. de Tetuán

Convento de Santo Domingo

Alameda

Puente Calatrava

Ciudadela

Paz

Gta de Gómez Ferrer

Pl. Alfonso el Magnánimo

Av. Navarro Reverter

Plaza Porta de la Mar

Sorolla

Colón

Conde Salvatierra de Álava

Grabador

Plaza América

Jorge

Isabel la Católica

Cirilo

Juan

Turia

Altea

Puente de Aragón

Sorni

Amorós

Estève

Av. Jacinto Benavente

Cortés

Marqués

Joaquín

de

Císcar

Salamanca

Maestro

Conde

Almirante

Burriana

Costa

Doña

Germana

Regne

Gozalbo

Cadarso

Reina

de

València

F

TARRAGONA ALICANTE ↓

PLATJA DE MALVA-ROSA
L'Hemisfèric

Almirante	EX	2
Almudín	EX	3
Ángel Guimerá	DY	4
Ayuntamiento (Pl. del)	EY	
Bolsería	DX	7
Carmen (Pl. del)	DX	8
Dr. Collado (Pl.)	EY	9
Dr. Sanchis Bergón	DX	12
Embajador Vich	EY	13
Esparto (Pl. del)	DX	14
Garrigues	DY	16
General Palanca	FY	17
Guillém Sorolla	DY	18
Maestres	FX	20
Maestro Palau	DY	21
María Cristina (Av.)	EY	22
Marqués de Dos Aguas	EY	25
Marqués de Sotelo (Av.)	EZ	
Micalet	EX	26
Moro Zeit	DX	27
Músico Peydro	DY	30
Nápoles y Sicilia (Pl.)	EX	31
Padre Huérfanos	EX	32
Palau	EX	34
Pascual y Genis	EYZ	
Paz	EFY	
Periodista Azzati	DY	35
Pie de la Cruz	DY	36
Poeta Quintana	FY	38
Salvador Giner	DX	39
San Vicente Ferrer (Pl.)	EY	40
Santa Ana (Muro)	EX	43
Santa Teresa	DY	44
Santo Tomás	DX	45
San Vicente Mártir	DY	
Transits	EY	47
Universidad	EY	48
Virgen (Pl. de la)	EX	49
Virgen de la Paz (Pl.)	EY	51

B	Nuestra Señora de los Desamparados
E	Almudín
M¹	Museo de Cerámica
M²	Museo de la Ciudad
M³	Centro de la Beneficencia, Museo de Prehistoria Y Etnología
N	Colegio del Patriarca
U	Universidad

Iglesia de Santa Catalina (EY) – The church is notable for its 17C Baroque belfry which is best seen from Plaza de Zaragoza.

Plaza Redonda (EY) – A passageway leads to this unusual little round square, more like a *patio*, surrounded by stalls selling lace and haberdashery.

Iglesia de San Martín (EY) – The west door is decorated with a group of bronze figures by the Flemish Gothic School, which illustrates St Martin on horseback dividing his cloak.

ADDITIONAL SIGHTS

★ **Museo de Cerámica (Ceramics Museum)** ⊘ (EY M¹) – The former **Palacio del Marqués de Dos Aguas**★★ has an amazing Churrigueresque façade: the alabaster doorway, carved in the 18C by Ignacio Vergara after a cartoon by the painter, Hipólito Rovira, shows two atlantes pouring water from amphorae in illustration of the

Palacio del Marqués de Dos Aguas – Museo de Cerámica

marquis' name. The painter covered the façade with frescoes which w
destroyed in the 19C. The marquis' impressive carriage may be seen on
ground floor.

The **museo** (museum), housed in the exuberantly decorated palace rooms, conta
over 5 000 ceramic exhibits dating from the Iberian period to the present day.
collection was donated in large part by González Martí. Most of the pieces
display were made locally. The oldest, going back to the 13C, are from **Pate**
(6km/4mi northwest of Valencia). The green and white ware, in which bro
manganese streaks can be seen, and the alternative blue and white, w
supplanted in popularity in the 14C by lustreware from **Manises** *(8km/5mi we*
This, in turn, fell from favour in the 17C, when the colours of Talavera ceram
were found more pleasing. In the 18C potteries were set up in **Alcora** and the cr
was revived locally in Valencia and the surrounding area. Manises has resum
production and is now manufacturing on a fairly large scale. Paterna ware
displayed in a gallery on the ground floor. On the first floor are galleries show
Alcora ceramics, 17C and 18C Manises lustreware, Oriental porcelain from Ch
and Japan and *socarrats* or the tiles which, in the 14C and 15C, were used to f
the areas between beams in ceilings. On the second floor a **Valencian kitchen** *(coci*
has been reconstituted.

★ **Museo de Bellas Artes San Pío V** ⊘ (**FX**) – This Fine Arts museum near the Jardi
del Real (Royal Gardens) is especially interesting for its **collection of Vale**
Primitives★★. Countless altarpieces prove the vitality of the Valencia School of
15C.

Among the many artists are Jacomart, Reixac and the Osonas Elder and Young
Some of the retables are by less well-known artists such as Gonzalo Pérez,
author of the Flemish influenced altarpiece of San Martín, or by anonymo
artists like that of Fray Bonifacio Ferrer. The triptych of the *Passion*
Hieronymous Bosch is an extraordinarily expressive work; the central panel i
copy of *Los Improperios* – the Mocking of Christ – in El Escorial.

Representing the Renaissance are Macip, Juan de Juanes, Yáñez de la Almed
and Fernando de Llanos whose use of colour recalls that of Leonardo da Vir
Tenebrism (term applied to paintings in dark tones) made its first appearance

Spain at the beginning of the 17C in the works of Ribalta and came to full fruition in those of Ribera *(St Sebastian)*. Spain's Golden Age is also represented with works by El Greco, Morales and Velázquez. Goya's mastery of portrait is also evident in his pictorial portrayal of *Francisco Bayeu*.

Valencian art from the 19C and 20C is comprehensively covered with works by Joaquín Sorolla, Pinazo and Muñoz Degrain. Various sculptures by Mariano Benlliure are also exhibited throughout the museum.

Jardines del Real (Royal Gardens) (FX) – The city's biggest park is close to the pleasant **Jardín de Monforte**. The **Puente del Real** (Royal Bridge), which crosses the **Jardín del río Turia**, is 16C.

Convento de Santo Domingo (FY) – The monastery's Classical style entrance, with statue niches for saints, was designed by Philip II (1527-98).

Colegio del Patriarca (Patriarch or Corpus Christi College) ⊘ **(EY N)** – This former seminary, founded by the Blessed Juan de Ribera, Archbishop of Valencia and Patriarch of Antioch, dates back to the 16C.

The *patio*, which is architecturally harmonious and decorated with *azulejos* friezes, has, at the centre, a statue of the founder by the modern sculptor Benlliure. The **church** is one of the few examples of Renaissance churches in Spain with frescoes painted on the walls. In the Capilla de la Purísima hang four 15C Flemish tapestries.

The **museum** has an interesting collection of 15C to 17C pictures includes paintings by Juan de Juanes, a precious **triptych of the Passion**★ by Dirk Bouts, a portrait (on pasteboard) of the founder, Ribera, by Ribalta, and other works by Ribalta, Morales and El Greco (one of the many versions of the *Adoration of the Shepherds*). There is also an admirable 14C Byzantine Cross from the Monasterio de Athos.

Facing the college is the **Universidad** (University) **(EY U)**, its buildings grouped round a vast Ionic quadrangle.

Plaza del Ayuntamiento (EY) – This bustling square in the centre of modern Valencia, with the Ayuntamiento (town hall) overlooking it on one side, holds a spectacular flower market.

Estación del Norte (EZ) – The **railway station**, built between 1909 and 1917, was designed by an admirer of Austrian Modernist *(Sezession)* architecture. It is an interesting example of early-20C architecture and decoration with its wood counters and *azulejos* panels decorated with scenes of the *huerta* and *Albufera (in the cafeteria)*.

Torres de Serranos ⊘ **(EX)** – The towers, now considerably restored, are, nevertheless, a good example of late-14C military architecture; they guarded one of the entrances to the medieval city. The defensive features all face outwards. Note the flowing lines of the battlements and the delicate tracery above the gateway.

Torres de Quart (DX) – These 15C towers, again a fine example of military architecture, guard another entrance to the city.

Instituto Valenciano de Arte Moderno (Valencian Institute of Modern Art) ⊘ – The institute comprises two separate buildings standing at some distance from each other:

– the **Centro Julio González (DX)**, a vast modern building devoted to contemporary art, displays a permanent collection of works by the Valencian sculptor Julio González. Most of its galleries, however, are used for temporary exhibitions, often featuring the institute's own collection of paintings by Tàpies, Saura, Millares, Chillida and the Equipo Crónica group.

– the **Centro del Carmen (DX)**, a former Carmelite convent, architecturally a mixture of the Gothic, Renaissance and Classical styles, provides a wonderful setting for works by contemporary artists.

Centro de la Beneficencia ⊘ **(DX M³)** – This former Augustinian convent was converted into a welfare centre in 1840. Today, it is a cultural complex comprising the Museo de Prehistoria, Museu d'Etnologia and Sala Parpalló, a room used to host temporary exhibitions.

Museo de Prehistoria – An attractive presentation of the most important archeological discoveries found in the region from the Paleolithic to Roman periods. Exhibits include reproductions of Parpalló cave paintings, a collection of Neolithic ceramics and rooms devoted to Iberian art.

Museu d'Etnologia – This ethnographic museum is dedicated to increasing the awareness of Valencian culture.

Jardín Botánico ⊘ **(DX)** – Valencia was one of the first cities to adopt the 16C Italian trend of creating gardens for botanical study. The present garden dates from 1802 and is still used for research purposes.

L'Hemisfèric ⊙ – This building was the first to be built as part of the large-sc
Ciudad de las Artes y de las Ciencias cultural project, which now includes the Museo
las Ciencias, Palacio de las Artes and Parque Oceanográfico Universal. Design
by the architect **Santiago Calatrava** in the shape of a human eye, it now include
cinema-planetarium with Omnimax screenings.

EXCURSION

El Puig - *18km/11mi north on N 340* (FX).
The **Monasterio de la Virgen del Puig** ⊙, occupied by the Order of Mercy, overlooks
village. The monastery's foundation in the 13C was prompted by the discove
in 1237, of a 6C Byzantine style marble low relief of the Virgin which had
hidden in the earth beneath a bell since the barbarian invasion. James
Conqueror chose the Virgin as patron of the Kingdom of Valencia and ordered
building of a convent in her honour.
In the church, the Gothic vaulting has been freed of its 18C stucco overlay.
Byzantine Virgin is to be seen at the high altar. The present monastery was b
between the 16C and 18C; paintings from the Valencia School are displayed in
upper 18C cloisters.

VALLADOLID ★

Castilla y León – Population 345 891
Michelin map 441 H 15

Valladolid, one of the former capitals of Castilla, is rich in decorated buildings, a
in art. It is also a modern industrial (engineering, automobiles, food production) a
commercial (trade fairs) centre. The Holy Week *(Semana Santa)* ceremonies
splendid.

HISTORICAL NOTES

As from the 12C, Castilla's kings frequently resided at Valladolid and the Cor
(Parliament) often assembled there. Peter the Cruel married there in the 1
Ferdinand and Isabel in 1469; it was the birthplace of Philip IV and his sister An
of Austria, mother of Louis XIV.
The city was also deeply involved in the 16C Comuneros Revolt during the reign
Emperor Charles V *(see SEGOVIA)*.

Castillo de Simancas *(11km/7mi southwest)* – This castle was converted by Empe
Charles V into a repository for state archives. The collection represents a compl
history of Spanish administration from the 15C to the 19C.

The Isabelline style – The Isabelline style, which emerged in the late 15C, i
mixture of Flamboyant Gothic and Mudéjar tradition, the ultimate stage bef
Plateresque. The decorative focus on entrances produced rectangular panels wh
eventually extended from ground level to cornice and were compartmented like
altarpiece.
The most characteristic examples of the style in Valladolid are the Colegio de S
Gregorio and the façade of the Iglesia de San Pablo.
Whereas the Salamanca Plateresque fronts, abundantly and delicately decora
with a hint of the Renaissance, are outstanding, those of Valladolid, being earl
demonstrate a less sophisticated but more vigorous art.

★ ISABELLINE VALLADOLID 1hr 30min

★★★ **Museo Nacional de Escultura Policromada** (National Museum of Polychrome Sc
ture) ⊙ (CX) – The museum is housed in the **Colegio de San Gregorio**, the city's great
Isabelline monument, founded in the 15C by Fray Alonso de Burgos, confessor
Isabel the Catholic.
The **entrance**★★, attributed to Gil de Siloé and Simon of Cologne, is one of
marvels of Spanish art. The decoration is unbelievably rich; every fantasy fr
savages to interwoven branches of thorns, is somehow felicitous in its inclusi
in the strongly hierarchical composition which focuses first on the doorway a
then rises to the magnificent heraldic motif above.

Museo – From the 16C to the 17C Valladolid was one of Spain's major centres
sculpture. This museum is a reflection of this with its wonderful collection
religious statues in polychrome wood, a material which, because both carved a
painted, was particularly well suited to the expression of the dramatic. On t
ground floor are the remarkable altarpiece designed by Alonso Berruguete for
church of San Benito, shown here dismantled, and the *Martyrdom of
Sebastian*, one of his major works. Some of the galleries on the first floor ha

kept their *artesonado* ceilings. The walnut stalls from San Benito (1525-29) are the combined work of Andrés de Nájera, Diego de Siloé, Felipe Vigarny and Juan de Valmaseda.

A door opens into an extraordinary **patio★★**. At ground level, tall cabled columns support basket arches; above the theme is repeated but with an infinitely delicate, dense decoration: twin bays, their arches and tympanums adorned with lacework tracery, rise above a magnificent balustrade. A cornice frieze, evenly interspersed with escutcheons, completes the stonework fantasy. Exhibits in the remaining rooms include the *Entombment* by Pedro de Juni, in which the figures display a certain mannerism, and works by Pompeo Leoni and Pedro de Mena (*Mary Magdalene*).

A Plateresque staircase leads down to the ground floor where the outstandingly natural **Christ Recumbent** by Gregorio Fernández and a painting by Zurbarán of the *Holy Shroud* are displayed.

A **chapel★**, designed by Juan Guas, contains an altarpiece by Berruguete, a tomb by Felipe Vigarny and carved choir stalls.

Iglesia de San Pablo (St Paul's Church) (CX) – The lower **façade★★**, by Simon of Cologne, consists of a portal with an ogee arch all framed within a seg-mental arch, and above, a large rose window and two coats of arms supported by angels.

The upper façade, from a later date, is a less exuberant composition in the Plateresque style, divided into panels adorned with inset statues and armorial bearings.

Iglesia de San Pablo – detail of the façade

ADDITIONAL SIGHTS

★ **Catedral** ⊙ (CY) – The cathedral project, commissioned in about 1580 by Philip II from Herrera, was only realised very slowly and was distorted to some degree by the architect's 17C and 19C successors – as in the upper part of the façade, filled with Baroque ornament by Alberto Churriguera, and in the octagonal section of the tower.

Although never completed, the **interior** remains one of Herrera's major successes. The altarpiece (1551) in the central apsidal chapel, where the interplay of perspective and relief makes the figures come to life, is by Juan de Juni.

Museo ⊙ (CY) – In the old Gothic Iglesia de Santa María la Mayor at the east end of the cathedral, are a 15C altarpiece, two paintings by the Ribera School, two portraits attributed to Velázquez and a silver monstrance by Juan de Arfe (16C).

Iglesia de Santa María la Antigua (CY) – The only Romanesque features in this otherwise Gothic church, are its tall slender Lombard tower and its portico with triple columns along the north wall.

Iglesia de las Angustias ⊙ (CY L) – The church, built by one of Herrera's disciples, contains in its south transept Juan de Juni's masterpiece, the **Virgen de los Siete Cuchillos★** (Virgin of the Seven Knives).

Universidad (CY U) – The university's Baroque façade is by Narciso and Anto
Tomé.

Colegio de Santa Cruz (CY) – The college, built at the end of the 15C, is one
the first truly Renaissance buildings in Spain; the finely carved decoration at
entrance, in fact, is still Plateresque but the rusticated stonework and wind
design are of entirely Classical inspiration.

Iglesia de San Benito (St Benedict's Church) (BY) – The 15C church's generally rob
simplicity and massive, monumental porch, give it a fortress-like air. T
Herreran style *patio* is magnificent in its simplicity.

Museo Oriental ⊙ (BZ M¹) – The museum, located in a neo-Classical college (18
designed by Ventura Rodríguez, houses a collection of Chinese (bronze, porcela
lacquerware, coins and silk embroidery) and Philippine art (ivory pieces a
numerous reminders of the Spanish presence on these islands).

Casa de Cervantes ⊙ (BY R) – The house belonged to Cervantes in the last ye
of his life and looks much as it did at that time (17C) with whitewashed walls a
some of his own simple furnishings.

VALLADOLID

Arco de Ladrillo		
(Paseo del)	BZ	2
Arzobispo Gandásegui	CY	3
Bailarin		
Vicente Escudero	CY	5
Bajada de la Libertad	BCY	6
Cadenas		
de San Gregorio	CX	8
Cánovas del Castillo	BCY	9
Cardenal Mendoza	CY	10
Chancillería	CX	13

Claudio Moyano	BY	14
Doctrinos	BY	16
Duque de la Victoria	BY	17
España (Pl. de)	BY	18
Fuente Dorada		
(Pl. de)	BY	20
Gondomar	CX	21
Industrias	CY	24
Maldonado	CY	25
Marqués del Duero	CXY	26
Miguel Iscar	BY	29
Pasión	BY	30
Portillo de Balboa	CX	32
San Agustin	BXY	35

San Ildefonso		BY
San Pablo (Pl. de)		BX
Santa Cruz (Pl. de)		CY
Santiago		BY
Santuario		CY
Sanz y Forés		CXY
Teresa Gil		BY
Zorrilla (Paseo de)		BZ

L	Iglesia de las Angustias
M¹	Museo Oriental
R	Casa de Cervantes
U	Universidad

VALLE DE LOS CAÍDOS★★

Madrid

Michelin map 444 K 17

he Valle de los Caídos, the Valley of the Fallen, built between 1940 and 1958, is a
triking monument to the dead of the Civil War (1936-39) commissioned by Franco
a beautiful **setting**★★ deep in the Guadarrama mountains. The valley, formerly the
uelgamuros, is dotted with granite outcrops and pine trees. The road leads to the
ot of the esplanade in front of the basilica, which is hollowed out of the rock face
self and is dominated by a monumental Cross.

★ **Basílica** ⊙ – The basilica's west door in its austere granite façade is a bronze work
carved by Fernando Cruz Solís, crowned by a *Pietà* by Juan de Ávalos. At the
entrance to the vast interior is a fine wrought-iron screen with 40 statues of
Spanish saints and soldiers. The 262m/860ft nave (St Peter's, Rome:
186m/610ft; St Paul's, London: 152m/500ft) is lined with chapels between
which have been hung eight copies of 16C Brussels tapestries of the Apocalypse.
Above the entrances to the chapels are alabaster copies of the most famous
statues of the Virgin Mary in Spain. A **cupola**★, 42m/138ft in diameter, above the
crossing, shows in mosaic the heroes, martyrs and saints of Spain approaching
both Christ in Majesty and the Virgin Mary. On the altar stands a painted wood
figure of Christ Crucified, set against a tree trunk; it is the work of the sculptor
Beovides. At the foot of the altar is the funerary stone of José Antonio Primo de
Rivera, son of the dictator and founder of the Falangist Party, and that of Franco.
Ossuaries contain coffins of 40 000 soldiers and civilians from both sides in the
Civil War.

★ **La Cruz** ⊙ – The Cross by the architect Diego Méndez, is 125m/410ft high
(150m/492ft including the base), the width from fingertip to fingertip,
46m/150ft. The immense statues of the Evangelists around the plinth and the
four cardinal virtues above are by Juan de Ávalos. There is a good **view** from the
base *(access by funicular)*. The great building showing Herreran influence on the
far side of the valley from the basilica is a Benedictine monastery, seminary and
social studies centre.

VERÍN

Galicia (Orense) – Population 11 018

Michelin map 441 G 7

erín, built between the wide vine-covered slopes of the Támega Valley *(viñedos del
alle)*, was already well known in the Middle Ages; today it lies off the main road and
lively and picturesque with narrow paved streets, houses with glassed-in balconies,
rcades and carved coats of arms.

hermal springs with curative qualities rise in the neighbourhood, notably those of
ontenova and, further on, Cabreiroa, Sousas and Villaza.

Castillo de Monterrei – *6km/4mi west.* There is a parador next to the castle. It
played an important role throughout the Portuguese-Spanish wars, having been
strategically built on the frontier for the purpose. It was more than a castle since
included within the perimeter were a monastery, a hospital and a town which was
abandoned in the 19C.
The approach is up an avenue of lime-trees which commands a full **panorama**★ of
the valley below. To enter the castle you pass through three defence walls, the
outermost dating from the 17C. Inside, at the centre, stand the square 15C Torre
del Hamenaje (Keep) and the 14C Torre de las Damas (Lady's Tower); the palace
courtyard is lined by a three-storey arcade and is less austere. The 13C church has
a **portal**★ delicately carved with a notched design and a tympanum showing Christ
in Majesty between the symbols of the Evangelists.

VIC★★

Catalunya (Barcelona) – Population 29 113
Michelin map 443 G 36

Since ancient times there has always been a village on the site now occupied by th
commercially and industrially thriving town of Vic (leather goods, food processin
and textiles). The city is renowned for its *salchichones* (salami-type sausages), i*
butifarras* (Catalan sausages) and its *fuets*.

SIGHTS

★ **Catedral** ◯ – The elegant Romanesque belfry and the crypt, both built in the 11(
are all that remain of the present church's forerunners.
The cathedral was built in the neo-Classical style between 1781 and 180:
In 1930 the famous Catalan artist **José María Sert** decorated the **interior**★ with wa
paintings which were lost when the church was set on fire at the beginning of th
Civil War in 1936. Sert took up his brushes again and by 1945, when he died, th
walls were once more covered with vast murals.
The **paintings**★ have an intensity, a power reminiscent of Michelangelo and also
profound symbolism. They evoke the mystery of the Redemption *(chance*
awaited from the time of Adam's original sin *(transept)* and prophesied by th
martyrs *(nave)*. Three scenes on the back of the west door illustrate the triump
of human injustice in the Life of Christ and in the history of Catalunya: agai
an architectural background which includes the cathedral in ruins after the fir
Jesus chases the moneylenders from the temple *(right)* but is himself condemne
to crucifixion *(left)*, while *(in the centre)* Pilate washes his hands and the crow
hails Barabbas, symbol of the vandals of revolution. The monochrome golds ar
browns in the murals tone with the fluted pillars, likewise the scale of the mura
with the vastness of the nave.
The former high altar **retable**★★, at the end of the ambulatory, is a 15C alabast
work which escaped the cathedral's many restorers. Its 12 panels, divided b
statues of the saints and by mouldings, are devoted to the glorification of Chris
the Virgin and St Peter. Opposite, lies the canon who commissioned the retab
in a Gothic tomb by the same sculptor.

Claustro (Cloister) – Wide, tracery-filled 14C arches surround the small close
which stands the monumental tomb of the philosopher, **Jaime Balmes** (1810-48
native of Vic. In a cloister gallery one can see the tomb of the painter JM Ser
surmounted by his last and unfinished work, a *Crucifixion*, intended by the arti:
to replace the one in the cathedral.

★★★ **Museu Episcopal** ◯ – *Closed for restoration. A selection of the museum's worl
are on display in the Hospital de la Santa Creu.*
The museum contains works from local churches. Its rich collections, particular
of Romanesque altar fronts painted on wood and Gothic altarpieces, provide
comprehensive survey of the development of Catalan art.

As the building which houses the museum is being completely rebuilt, until 2001 a selection of 200 works,
including the *Retable of Santa Clara* by the great colour-
ist **Luis Borrassá**, who introduced the international style
to Spain, the *Retable of Seu d'Urgell* by **Ramón Mur** and
the *Retable of Verdú*, an exceptional work by **Jaime Ferrer
II**, will be exhibited in the Hospital de la Santa Creu.

★ **Plaça Major** – The pretty neo-Classical façades add a
touch of class to this arcaded square where the many
bars and café terraces attract a lively crowd. A popular market is held in the square every Saturday.

EXCURSION

★ **Monasterio de Santa Maria de L'Estany** ◯
– *24km/15mi southwest.* The small village
of L'Estany grew up around this medieval
Augustinian monastery. There remain the
12C Romanesque church, whose cupola was
rebuilt in the 15C, and the beautiful **cloisters**★: the arcades are supported by matching columns and decorated with 72 remar
kable **capitals**★★. The north gallery is
Romanesque and narrative in style (New
Testament); the west, decorative with palm
fronds and gaunt griffons; the south, geometrical and interlaced although the sophisticated execution and heraldic positions
of the animals indicate a later date; the east
is profane with wedding scenes and musicians after ceramics from Paterna which
drew on Moorish motifs for their design.

Romanesque statue of the Virgin
Museo Episcopal

VILAFAMÉS

Comunidad valenciana (Castellón) – Population 1 399

Michelin map 445 L 29

here is a lovely view of this charming town with its cobblestone streets from the
astle ruins. A good many artists have made Vilafamés their home.

Museo Popular de Arte Contemporáneo (Contemporary Art Museum) ⊘ – The
museum, housed in a 15C palace, is the centre of a very active cultural scene. Many
of the works it displays are by famous artists including Miró, Barjola, Serrano and
Genovés.

VILLENA

Comunidad valenciana (Alicante) – Population 31 141

Michelin map 445 Q 27

n the Middle Ages the region of Villena was a powerful feudal domain guarded by
utpost strongholds, invariably perched on rocky heights: Chincilla, Almansa, Biar,
ax and La Mola. The **castillo** (castle) with its majestic keep, had several owners,
mong them two well-known men of letters: **Don Juan Manuel** in the 14C, and, in the
5C, **Enrique de Aragón** (1384-1434).

Museo Arqueológico (Archeological Museum) ⊘ – The museum is in the town hall
(Ayuntamiento) which has a fine Renaissance façade. It displays two solid gold
collections dating from the Bronze Age (1500-1000 BC) of which one is the
outstanding **Villena Treasure★★** with gold jewellery and gourds decorated with sea
urchin shell patterns.

Iglesia de Santiago ⊘ – The vaulting in this 15C-16C church is supported in an
unusual way upon spiral pillars which continue above the carved imposts as turned
engaged columns. The overall effect gives the nave great elegance.

EXCURSION

Bocairent – *26km/16mi northeast* on C 3316. The church in this small market
town where **Juan de Juanes** died (1523-79) has an interesting **Museo Parroquial** (Parish
Museum) ⊘ with several paintings by the artist – known as the Spanish Raphael
– and his school (a 14C *Last Supper* by Marcial de Sax), as well as a collection of
church plate.

VITORIA★

See GASTEIZ

XÀTIVA/JÁTIVA

Comunidad valenciana (Valencia) – Population 24 586

Michelin map 445 P 28

Játiva, set amid vine and cypress covered hillsides, can be seen from a distance
because of its crenellated ramparts which ring the two highest hills.
The town was the birthplace of two members of the Borja family who became
popes, Calixtus III (1455-58) and Alexander VI, and, in 1591, of the painter José
de Ribera.

El Españoleto

José (Jusepe) de Ribera studied in Valencia, probably with Ribalta, before going
to Italy where he settled in Naples in 1616. Lo Spagnoletto, or the Little
Spaniard, as Italians called him on account of his small stature, became
accredited to successive Spanish viceroys of Naples, notably the Duke of
Osuna, and won early and equally widespread fame in Italy and Spain. He died
in Italy in 1652.
A robust and realistic style, reminiscent of Caravaggio in its technique of
chiaroscuro, characterises his early work: the religious figures, the monks and
saints, have a somewhat coarse energy; the faces are portrayed with
painstaking detail; the composition emphasises the dramatic, often dwelling
upon the atrocious. However, some of his works, more serene and in mellower
colours, reveal a different and surprisingly sensitive artist.

SIGHTS

Plaza de Calixto III – The 16C **cathedral**, modified in the 18C, faces the hospi which has an ornate Gothic and Plateresque style façade.

Museo ⊘ – The Almudin, which used to be a granary, now houses a collection paintings.
In the *patio* is an 11C **Moorish fountain** or *pila*, one of the most interesting remai of Moorish sculpture in Spain as it depicts human figures, which is extremely ra in Islamic art.

Ermita de Sant Feliu (Sant Feliu Hermitage) ⊘ – *On the road to the castle*. A gro of 15C Valencia **Primitives** hangs in the chapel. At the entrance is a white mark **stoup**★ hollowed out of a former capital.

Castillo ⊘ – What remains of the castle – it was demolished under Philip V stands on the site of the original town. It commands extensive **panoramas** of t town, the surrounding countryside, the *huerta* and the sea in the distanc Among the Castillo Mayor's distinguished prisoners was the Count of Urg pretender to the throne of Aragón, who was defeated by his rival, Ferdinan in 1412.

ZAFRA

Extremadura (Badajoz) – Population 14 065
Michelin map 444 Q 10

A 15C *alcázar* (now a parador) stands guard at the entrance to this white-walled tow one of the oldest in Extremadura. It was built by the dukes of Feria with nine rou towers crowned by pyramid shaped merlons. The white marble *patio* is Renaissan and the delightful gilded saloon Mudéjar.
Zafra's cattle fairs are famous locally, especially the Feria de San Miguel (St Michae Fair) during the week of 5 October.

★ **The squares** – The town's two squares, the large 18C **Plaza Grande** and t adjoining and much smaller 16C **Plaza Chica**, with their fine arcaded houses, for an attractive precinct.

Iglesia de la Candelaria ⊘ – The 16C church in transitional Gothic-Renaissan style can be identified by its massive red-brick belfry. In the shallow sou transept there stands an **altarpiece** by Zurbarán painted in 1644.

EXCURSION

Llerena – *42km/26mi southeast.*
The **Plaza Mayor** of this modest country town is one of the most monumental in Extremadura. On one side stands the **Iglesia de Nuestra Señora de Granada** (Church Our Lady of Granada) in which the composite façade is harmonised by t colourful interplay of white limestone and brick; the delicacy of two superimpos arcades contrasts with the mass of a great Baroque belfry. A pomegranate *granada* in Spanish – decorates the escutcheon on the tympanum over the ma door.

ZAMORA★

Castilla y León – Population 68 202
Michelin map 441 H 12

Only traces remain of the walls which made Zamora the westerly bastion of t fortified Duero line during the Reconquest. The town played its part in the repeat struggles for the throne of Castile: in the 11C when Sancho III's sons fought for h kingdom, and in the 15C, when La Beltraneja unsuccessfully disputed the rights Isabel the Catholic.

Semana Santa (Holy Week) – Zamora's Holy Week solemn celebrations are renown for the numbers who attend and for the spectacular *pasos* street processions. C Palm Sunday a children's procession escorts a *paso* of Christ's entry into Jerusaler on Maundy Thursday evening a totally silent, torchlight procession follows t poignant *Dead Christ*, a sculpture by Gregorio Fernández, borne by white-rob penitents through the streets in imitation of the walk to Golgotha. Most of the *pasos* may be seen in the **Museo de la Semana Santa** ⊘ (B **M**¹).

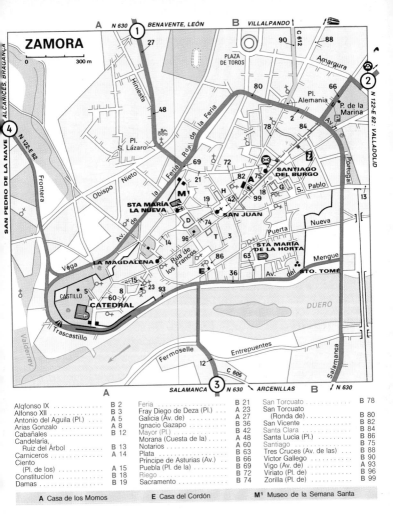

A			
Alqfonso IX	B 2	Feria	B 21
Alfonso XII	B 3	Fray Diego de Deza (Pl.)	A 23
Antonio del Aguila (Pl.)	A 5	Galicia (Av. de)	A 27
Arias Gonzalo	A 8	Ignacio Gazapo	B 36
Cabañales	B 12	Mayor (Pl.)	B 42
Candelaria,		Morana (Cuesta de la)	A 48
Ruiz del Árbol	B 13	Notarios	A 60
Carniceros	A 14	Plata	B 63
Ciento		Príncipe de Asturias (Av.)	B 66
(Pl. de los)	A 15	Puebla (Pl. de la)	B 69
Constitucion	B 18	Riego	B 72
Damas	B 19	Sacramento	B 74

San Torcuato	B 78
San Torcuato	
(Ronda de)	B 80
San Vicente	B 82
Santa Clara	B 84
Santa Lucia (Pl.)	B 86
Santiago	B 75
Tres Cruces (Av. de las)	B 88
Victor Gallego	B 90
Vigo (Av. de)	A 93
Viriato (Pl. de)	B 96
Zorilla (Pl. de)	B 99

| A Casa de los Momos | E Casa del Cordón | M¹ Museo de la Semana Santa |

SIGHTS *Town plan above*

★ **Catedral** ⊘ (A) – The cathedral was built between 1151 and 1174 and was subsequently given additions and alterations.

The north front is neo-Classical in keeping with the square it overlooks; it contrasts, however, with the Romanesque **bell-tower** and the graceful cupola covered in scallop tiling which recalls the Torre del Gallo in Salamanca. The south front, the only original part of the building, has blind arcades and a Romanesque portal with unusual covings featuring openwork festoons.

The aisles are transitional Romanesque-Gothic, the vaulting ranging from broken barrel to pointed ogive. Slender painted ribs support the luminous **dome**★ on squinches above the transept. At the end of the Gothic period, master wood carvers and wrought-iron smiths worked in the church – there are fine **grilles** enclosing the *coro*, two 15C Mudéjar pulpits and **choir stalls**★★, decorated with Biblical figures on their backs and with allegorical and burlesque scenes on armrests and misericords.

Museo Catedralicio (Cathedral Museum) ⊘ – The museum, off the Herreran-style cathedral cloisters, displays a collection of 15C Flemish **tapestries**★★ illustrating the life of Tarquin and the Trojan War; others, dating from the 17C, are of Hannibal's campaigns.

The **Jardín del Castillo** (Castle Garden) (A) behind the cathedral, commands fine **views** of the Duero river below.

★ **Romanesque churches** – The 12C saw a series of originally designed Romanesque churches built in Zamora province. Particular features included portals without tympana, surrounded by multifoil arches and often possessing heavily carved archivolts; the larger churches also had domes on squinches over the transept crossing. The best examples of the style in Zamora are the **Magdalena** (A), **Santa María la Nueva** (B), **San Juan** (B), **Santa María de la Orta** (B), **Santo Tomé** (B) and **Santiago del Burgo** (B).

Seignorial mansions – **Casa del Cordón** (B E) and **Casa de los Momos** (B A) have elegant Isabelline windows.

Cupola with scallop tiling, Catedral de Zamora

EXCURSIONS

★ **San Pedro de la Nave** – *19km/12mi northwest. Leave Zamora by ④ on the to* *plan. Follow N 122 for 12km/7mi then turn right.*
The Visigothic church **(iglesia)** ⊘, in danger of being submerged on account the damming of the Esla, has been rebuilt at El Campillo. It is late 7C and artistically remarkable for the carving on the transept **capitals** with its stro sense of composition: Daniel in the lions' den, the sacrifice of Isaac etc. T frieze, halfway up the wall, presents Christian symbols including grapes a doves.

Arcenillas – *7km/4mi southeast on C 605* (B).
In the village church **(iglesia)** ⊘, 15 **panels**★ depicting the Life, Death and Res rection of Christ have been reassembled from the great Gothic altarpiece design for Zamora Cathedral by late-15C artist **Fernando Gallego**, one of the greate Castilian painters of this age, who adopted a Hispano-Flemish style in which the are echoes of Van der Weyden, but with stronger colours and softer fac expressions.

Benavente – *66km/41mi north. Leave Zamora by ① on the town plan and ta* *N 630.*
During the Middle Ages the town was a prosperous commercial centre. Seve fine monuments remain from that period.
The Renaissance style **Castillo de los Condes de Pimentel** (Castle of the Counts Pimentel), now a parador, has preserved its 16C Torre del Caracol (snail-sh tower). From the terrace are **views** of the valley.
The transitional **Iglesia de Santa María del Azogue** is a church with a wide east end wi five apses and two Romanesque portals typical of the local Zamora style. Insi a beautiful 13C *Annunciation* stands at the transept crossing.
The **Iglesia de San Juan del Mercado** has a 12C carving on the south portal illustrati the journey of the Magi.

ZARAGOZA★★

SARAGOSSA – Aragón – Population 622 371
Michelin map 443 H 27

Zaragoza is a warm brick agglomeration lying between its two cathedrals a spreading down into the Ebro basin of which it is the capital. It occupies a privileg position at the centre of the vast depression, once an arid desert and now a fert plain, watered by the three rivers which meet in it and the nearby imperial canal n used for irrigation. Sugar refining and textiles are staple industries in the lo economy which is being developed and diversified.
The city was largely rebuilt in the 19C after the War of Independence and althou not especially striking, pleases on account of its historic monuments and the bustli life along its modern boulevards.

aragoza is both a major university and religious centre, veneration of the Virgen del
lar (Virgin of the Pillar) making it the leading Marian shrine in Spain.

he **Pilar festivals** – In the week of 12 October, Zaragozans extol their Virgin with
credible pomp and fervour: on the 13th at about 7pm the **Rosario de Cristal** procession
oves off by the light of 350 carriage-borne lanterns. Other festivals during the week
clude the **Gigantes y Cabezudos** procession (cardboard giants and dwarfs with massive
ads), *jota* dancing and the famous bullfights.

ISTORICAL NOTES

aesaraugusta-Sarakusta – Salduba, well situated at the confluence of the Ebro
d its tributaries, the Gállego and the Huerva, became, in the year 25 BC, a Roman
lony named Caesaraugusta after the Emperor Caesar Augustus. On 2 January in
D 40, according to tradition, the Virgin appeared miraculously to St James, leaving
proof of her apparition the pillar around which the **Basílica de Nuestra Señora del Pilar**
as later built. In the 3C the city is said to have suffered persecution at the hands
Diocletian – it still honours from that time the memory of the Uncounted Martyrs,
terred in the crypt of **Santa Engracia** (Z).

our centuries of Muslim occupation would appear to have left the city, renamed
arakusta, with but a single major heirloom. From the brilliant but shortlived *taifa*
ngdom established under the Benihud dynasty in the 11C, there remains the
Jafería, a palace, built by the first monarch of the line and a unique and very precious
xample of Hispano-Muslim art.

aragoza, capital city – The Aragón kings, after freeing the city from the Moors,
roclaimed Zaragoza, the great agricultural town on the Ebro, as capital. The city,
owever, jealous of its autonomy, voted itself the most democratic *Fueros* in the
hole of Spain and increased its prosperity through wise administration and the
stablishment of the **Lonja** (Commodities Exchange). Tolerant by tradition, it
rotected its Muslim masons, so that the Mudéjar style could be used to embellish
s churches: the apse of **La Seo** (Cathedral), **San Pablo** (Y) and **Magdalena** (Z) towers.
ouses in the old town with elegant *patios* and *artesonado* ceilings give a good idea
f the city's prosperity in the 16C.

wo heroic sieges – Zaragoza's resistance before Napoleon's army in the terrible
ears 1808-1809 shows the Spanish people's desire for independence and the
etermination of those of Aragón in particular.
June 1808 the city was invested for the first time by the French, the siege only
eing lifted on 14 August. The exultant Zaragozans sang "The Virgin of Pilar will
ever be French." Alas! On 21 December General Lannes appeared with his men who
emained until the town capitulated on 20 February. By the end, half the inhabitants,
ome 54 000, had died. From that appalling siege there remains the shrapnel pitted
uerta del Carmen (Carmen Gate) (Z).

SIGHTS

La Seo ⊙ (Y) – The Cathedral of Zaragoza, La Seo, is remarkable for its size and
includes all the decorative styles from the Mudéjar to the Churrigueresque,
although it is basically Gothic in design. In the 17C, the tall belfry which
harmonises with those on the Pilar Cathedral nearby, was added; in the 18C the
Seo was given a Baroque façade.
Walk into Calle del Sepulcro to see the Mudéjar decoration on the **east end**.
The interior is impressive with its five aisles of equal height. Above the high
altar is a Gothic **retable**★ with a predella carved by the Catalan, Pere Johan, and
the three central panels of the Ascension, Epiphany and the Transfiguration
sculpted by Hans of Swabia (the stance of the figures and the modelling of the
faces and robes strike a German note).
The **surrounding wall of the chancel** *(trascoro)* and some of the side chapels were
adorned in the 16C with groups of carved figures, clear evidence of the vitality of
Spanish sculpture during the Renaissance. Other chapels, ornamented in the 18C,
show the all too excessive exuberance of the Churrigueresque style; one exception
is the **Parroquieta**, a Gothic chapel containing a 14C tomb influenced by the
Burgundian style and, in particular, a **cupola**★ in the Moorish style, in polychrome
wood with stalactites and strapwork (15C).

★ **Museo Capitular** – *In the sacristy.* Exhibited are paintings, an enamel triptych,
religious objects and a large amount of church plate including silver reliquaries,
chalices and an enormous processional monstrance made up of 24 000 pieces.

★ **Museo de Tapices** – An outstanding collection of Gothic hangings. All were woven in
Arras or Brussels; titles include the *Sailing Ships*, the *Crucifixion* and the *Passion*.

★ **Lonja** ⊙ (Y) – Zaragoza, like the other major trading towns of Valencia, Barcelona
and Palma de Mallorca in the Kingdom of Aragón, founded a commercial exchange
as early as the 16C. These buildings, in a transitional style between Gothic and
Plateresque, include some of the finest examples of civil architecture in Spain. In

		Capitán Portolés	Z 13	Magdalena	Z
		César Augusto (Av.)	Z 15	Manifestación	Y
		Cinco de Marzo	Z 18	Sancho y Gil	Z
		Conde de Aranda	Z	San Pedro Nolasco (Pl. de)	Z
Alfonso I	YZ	Coso	Z	San Vicente de Paul	YZ
Alfonso V	Z 6	Don Jaime I	YZ	Teniente Coronel	
Candalija	Z 10	Independencia (Av.)	Z	Valenzuela	Z

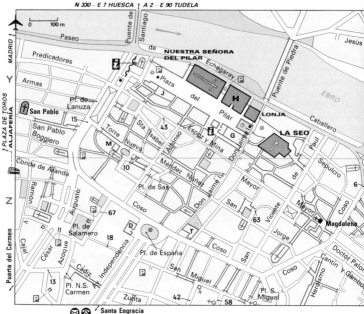

this instance the vast hall is divided into three by tall columns, their shaft
ornamented with a carved band of grotesques. Coats of arms supported
cherubim mark the start of the ribs which open out into star **vaulting**.
The **Ayuntamiento** (town hall) (**Y H**) has been rebuilt in traditional Aragón style wi
ornate eaves. Two modern bronzes stand at the entrance.

★ **Basílica de Nuestra Señora del Pilar** ⊙ (**Y**) – Several sanctuaries have been bu
successively on this site to enshrine the miraculous pillar. The present buildin
Zaragoza's second cathedral, was designed by Francisco Herrera the Younger
about 1677. It takes the form of a buttressed quadrilateral lit by a central dom
The cupolas, with small lantern towers, whose ornamental tiles may be se
reflected in the waters of the Ebro, were added by Ventura Rodríguez
the 18C.
The interior is divided into three aisles by giant pillars with fluted pilasters. Som
of the frescoes decorating the cupolas were painted by Goya as a young man
The **Capilla de la Virgen** (Lady Chapel) by Ventura Rodríguez is, in fact, virtually
miniature church on its own. It contains in a niche on the right, the pillar and
Gothic wood statue of the Virgin. The Virgin's mantle is changed every day exce
on the 2nd of the month, the anniversary of the apparition (2 January) and t
12th of the month, that of the Hispanidad (12 October). Pilgrims go to kiss t
pillar through an opening at the rear.
The **high altar** in the centre of the church is surmounted by a **retable**★ carved
Damián Forment of which the predella is outstanding. The **coro** is closed by a hi
grille and adorned with Plateresque stalls.

★ **Museo Pilarista** ⊙ – Displayed are the sketches made by Goya, González Velázqu
and Bayeu for the cupolas of Our Lady of the Pillar, a model by Ventura Rodrígu
and some of the jewels which adorn the Virgin during the Pilar festivals. Amo
the very old ivory pieces are an 11C hunting horn and a Moorish jewellery bo

★ **Aljafería** ⊙ – Access by calle Conde de Aranda (**Z**). The Aljafería, a Moorish pala
built in the 11C by the Benihud family, was rearranged to serve as a palace f
the Aragón kings and Catholic monarchs before being taken over by t
Inquisition and later converted into a barracks. The enormous building, so close
resembling the Muslim-style mansions of Andalucía, comes as a surprise so f
north.
The Moorish palace is centred around a rectangular patio bordered by portico
with delicate tracery and carved capitals. The **musallah**, a form of private mosq
for the emirs, has been restored complete with mihrab and all the accustome
Moorish fantasy of multifoil arches and floral decoration. The stuccowork
brightly painted.

The first floor and the staircase transport the visitor 400 years ahead to the sumptuous style of the Catholic monarchs when Flamboyant Gothic reigned supreme. Only the ornate **ceiling**★, its cells divided by geometric interlacing and decorated with fir cones, remains, however, of the throne room. Another *artesonado* ceiling can be seen in the room in which **Santa Isabel**, daughter of Pedro III of Aragón and future Queen of Portugal, was born in 1271.

EXCURSION

Fuendetodos – *45km/28mi southwest. Take N 330 and after 21km/13mi bear left onto A 2101.*
It was in a modest house (**Casa-Museo de Goya** ⊘ – *open to the public*) in this village that the great painter **Francisco Goya y Lucientes** was born in 1746. The **Museo de Grabados** ⊘ next door displays a collection of his work in the field of engravings.

Cala Macarella, Menorca

The Islands

Balearic Islands★★★

The Balearic Archipelago covers a land area of 5 000km²/1 900sq mi and is made of three large islands – Mallorca, Menorca and Ibiza – each with a character distin from the others, two small ones – Formentera and Cabrera, as well as many isle The Comunidad Autónoma Balear (Balearic Autonomous Community) is one Spain's 50 provinces, with Palma as administrative capital. The language, Balea is derived from Catalan but has kept ancient roots (such as the articles Se, Sa a Ses from the Latin Ipse).

WHERE TO STAY

Mallorca

OUR SELECTION

Ses Rotges (Cala Ratjada) – *Rafael Blanes, 21.* ☎ *971 56 31 (fax 971 56 43 45. 24 rooms.*
This small hotel is situated in a quiet setting and has spacious, tastefu decorated and reasonably priced rooms.

Born (Palma) **(AY ➊)** – *Sant Jaume, 3.* ☎ *971 71 29 42, fax 971 71 86 30 rooms.*
A good central option in Palma itself. The hotel occupies a former 16C pal which was subsequently restored in the 18C. A delightful Ibizan-style pat

San Lorenzo (Palma) **(AY ➋)** – *San Lorenzo, 4.* ☎ *971 72 82 (fax 971 71 19 01. 6 rooms.*
Small 17C palace in a pedestrian area near the centre of La Palma. Peace and tastefully decorated.

León de Sineu (Sineu) **(BZ ➌)** – *Dels Bous, 129.* ☎ *971 52 02 fax 971 85 50 58. 8 rooms.*
A small hotel in an old house with a charming landscaped patio.

TREAT YOURSELF!

Palacio Ca Sa Galesa (Palma) – *Miramar, 8.* ☎ *971 71 54 00, fax 971 72 15 12 rooms.*
A former 17C palace next to the cathedral.

La Residencia (Deià) – *Finca Son Canals.* ☎ *971 63 90 11, fax 971 63 93 62 rooms.*
This small hotel occupies a 17C ancestral home in the attractive small town Deià. Ibizan-style architecture.

La Reserva Rotana (Manacor) – *4km/2.5mi north on the s'Avali ro. ☎ 971 84 56 85, fax 971 55 52 58. 25 rooms.*
On a large country estate. The property also has a delightful annexe w slightly cheaper rooms.

Ibiza

OUR SELECTION

Montesol (Ibiza) **(Y ➊)** – *Passeig Vara de Rey, 2.* ☎ *971 31 01 (fax 971 31 06 02. 55 rooms.*
One of Ibiza's best-known hotels with a very popular cafeteria and terra Well-appointed rooms in a building dating from the turn-of-the-century.

La Colina (Santa Eulalia de Río) – *5.5km/3.5mi southeast towards Ibi ☎ 971 33 27 67, fax 971 33 27 67. 16 rooms.*
Small, basic family-style hotel with tastefully decorated rooms which are bc clean and comfortable. Reasonably priced in relation to others on the isla A recommended address, given its location in the tourist area of Santa Eula close to Ibiza's only river.

El Corsario (Ibiza) – *Ponent, 5.* ☎ *971 39 32 12, fax 971 39 19 53. 14 room*
Located in the old part of Ibiza town, the Ciudad Alta, at the foot of t fortress, was built by order of Charles V. The hotel occupies an old 17C hou with all its peculiarities, irregular walls and high ceilings. Some of its roo enjoy a spectacular view of the port and the Mediterranean.

TREAT YOURSELF!

La Ventana (Ibiza) **(Z ➋)** – *Sa Carrossa, 13.* ☎ *971 39 08 57, fax 971 39 01 4 13 rooms.*
The simplicity of the hotel's exterior in is sharp contrast to its tastef charming interior which is Ibizan in style, decorated in natural colours, a includes beds covered by old-fashioned veils. A real treat!

llage (San José) – *Cala Vedella – 8km/5mi southeast towards Ibiza.* ☎ *971 80 80 81, fax 971 80 80 27. 19 rooms.*
truly peaceful location in the middle of a pine grove. Spacious, carpeted ooms, all with a terrace.

acienda (San Miguel de Balansat) – *Na Xamena.* ☎ *971 33 45 00,* x *971 33 45 14. 56 rooms.*
a delightful location with spectacular views. The predominantly white uildings contrast pleasantly with the blue of the swimming pools and sea. pacious, elegant rooms. The perfect hotel for those seeking peace and quiet.

Menorca

UDGET HOTELS

Engolidor (Migjorn Gran) – *Major, 3.* ☎ *971 37 01 93. 4 rooms.*
s family home appearance gives a hint of the warm, friendly welcome waiting guests. The restaurant has a pleasant summer terrace and some of e rooms have dormer windows.

UR SELECTION

nali (San Luis) – *On the S'Ullastrar-Binibèquer road, no 50.* ☎ *971 15 17 24,* x *971 15 03 52. 9 rooms.*
hotel situated in a pleasant country house with comfortable, individually rnished rooms.

amontana Park (Fornells) – *Urbanización Playa de Fornells.* ☎ *971 37 67 42,* x *971 37 67 48. 87 apartments.*
complex of apartment buildings rising up above the beach. The terraces have ne views out to sea.

REAT YOURSELF

rt Mahón (Mahón) – *Av. Fort de l'Eau, 13.* ☎ *971 36 26 00,* x *971 35 10 50. 80 rooms.*
luxury hotel in front of Mahón's marina. Colonial in style with a magnificent arden-terrace, pool and solarium facing out to the port.

PRACTICAL INFORMATION

ETTING TO THE BALEARICS

y ferry – **Trasmediteránea** has services to Mahón, Palma and Ibiza from arcelona and Valencia. For information and bookings, call ☎ 902 45 46 45 Internet http://www.trasmediterranea.es; **Baleària** operates ferries between enia and Ibiza (4hr) and Palma (9hr). For information, call ☎ 902 160 180 ` 971 40 53 60. **Internet:** http://www.eurolineas.com

y plane – **Iberia** ☎ 902 400 500; **Spanair** ☎ 902 13 14 15; **Air Europa** ☎ 902 40 15 01.

Mallorca

formation and tourist offices – **Palma:** Santo Domingo, 11 – ☎ 971 72 40 90; **Alcudia:** Ctra. Artá, 68 – ☎ 971 89 26 15. **Cala Rajada:** Plaça els Pins – ☎ 971 56 30 33.

ransport around the island – Public buses operate between Palma and the ther main towns on the island: Alcudia, Andratx and Deià.

oller train – A charming old electrically-powered train which covers the 7km/17mi between Palma and Soller.

Menorca

formation and tourist offices – **Mahón:** Plaça de la Esplanada, 40 – ☎ 971 36 37 90; **Ciudadela:** Plaza de La Catedral – ☎ 971 38 26 93.

Ibiza

formation and tourist offices – **Ibiza:** Paseo Vara de Rey, 13 – ☎ 971 30 19 00; **San Antonio:** Paseig de ses Fonts. ☎ 971 34 33 63; **Santa làlia:** Mariano Riquer Wallis, 4 – ☎ 971 33 07 28.

Formentera

formation and tourist offices – Puerto de la Savina – ☎ 971 32 20 57.

ransport – **Ferries: Baleària** operates services between the islands of Ibiza and ormentera (25min) from 7.45am to 7pm. For information on Ibiza, call ☎ 971 31 40 05. Because of its small size (the maximum distance on ormentera is 20km/12mi), the best way to see the island is by moped or cycle.

MALLORCA★★★

MAJORCA – Area 3 640km²/1 405sq mi – Population 602 074

Michelin map 443 M, N, O 36-40

Mallorca is the largest of the Balearic Islands, measuring some 75km/47mi from north to south and 100km/62mi from east to west. The beautiful scenery, the m climate and the hotel infrastructure make the island a major European tourist cent

Landscape – A relief map of Mallorca shows three different zones:

The **Sierra de Tramuntana** in the northwest rises in limestone crests – the highest is P **Major** (1 445m/4 740ft) – running parallel to the coast. In spite of its low altitu the chain, its cliffs plunging spectacularly into the sea, forms a solid rock barr against offshore winds from the mainland. Pines, junipers and holm oaks cover slopes, interspersed here and there by the gnarled and twisted trunks of Mallorc famous olive trees. Villages, perched halfway up hillsides, are surrounded by terra planted with vegetables and fruit trees.

The central plain, **El Pla**, is divided by low walls into arable fields and fig and almc orchards; the market towns, with outlying windmills to pump water, retain regular plan of medieval fortress towns.

The **Sierras de Levante** to the east have been scoured by erosion, hollowed out i wonderful caves. The coast is rocky and indented with sheltered, sand-carpet coves.

The short-lived Kingdom of Mallorca (1262-1349) – On 5 September 1229, Jame (Jaime I) of Aragón set sail from Salou to recapture Mallorca, an importa commercial bastion in the Mediterranean, from the Muslims, hoping to quell unr among his nobles by offering them land. The decisive battle took place in the Bay Palma on 31 December 1229.

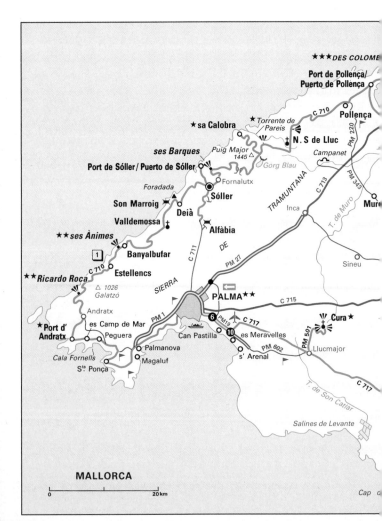

irty years later the Conqueror united Mallorca-Baleares, Roussillon and Montpel-
r in a single independent kingdom which he presented to his son, James II. He and
s successor, Sancho, brought prosperity to the island, founding new towns,
ilding strongpoints and peopling the territory with Catalan immigrants. Nor did
apparently suffer when Pedro IV seized the archipelago in 1343, killing the young
ince at Llucmajor, to reunite it to the crown of Aragón.

urches were built, a merchant navy was established which brought local prosperity
d a school of cartography founded which rapidly became famous.

e Mallorcan Primitives (14C-15C) – Gothic Mallorcan painting, characterised by a
arked gentleness of expression, was wide open to external influences: the so-called
ster of Privileges (Maestro de los Privilegios) showed, even in the 14C, a Sienese
eference for miniaturisation and warm colours; later, both **Joan Daurer** and the
ented **Maestro de Obispo Galiana** became inspired by Catalan painting; the end of the
ntury saw the assertion of personal characteristics in **Francesch Comes**, whose
annerism was to portray figures with full lips.

the 15C, artists on the island included some who had studied in Valencia such as
briel Moger, the suave **Miguel de Alcanyis** and **Martí Torner**. The **Maestro de Predelas** is
tinguishable by his attention to detail, **Rafael Moger** by his realism. There were also
o master painters, both from abroad, **Pedro (Pere) Nisart** and **Alonso de Sedano**, who
roduced the Flemish style which was to dominate Mallorcan painting in the 16C
e Palma; Museo de Mallorca).

mous Mallorcans and illustrious visitors – **Ramón Llull** (1232-1316) is a good
ample of the cosmopolitan outlook of Mallorca in the 13C. A reformed libertine,
became a great humanist, learning foreign languages and studying philosophy,
eology and alchemy. A defender of the Christian faith, he travelled widely and was
er beatified.

Fray Junípero Serra (1713-83) left to do missionary work in California, where he founded a number of missions including those of San Francisco and San Diego. He was beatified in 1988.

Among the foreign writers, poets and savants to visit the island in the 19C, were **Frédéric Chopin** and **George Sand** who spent the winter of 1838 in the Cartuja de Valldemossa (Valldemosa Carthusian Monastery).

Robert Graves (1895-1985), the strongly individualistic English poet, novelist and critic whose works include *I, Claudius*, *Good-bye to All That* and *The White Goddess*, lived (as of 1929) and died here.

The Austrian archduke, **Ludwig Salvator** (1847-1915), spent most of his 53 years' stay on the west coast where he compiled the most detailed study ever made of the archipelago. He was patron to the French speleologist, EA Martel, who explored many of the island's caves in 1896.

Economy – Tourism is the major force in the economy, with shoe manufacturing second and an artificial pearl industry at Manacor now finding foreign outlets.

Horticulture supplies the fresh fruit canning and dried fruit industries (figs and apricots) while the almond crop is largely exported.

Ensaimada, a light spiral roll dusted with sugar, and **sobrasada**, a hot pork sausage, are the tasty, local specialities.

Map labels:
Cap de Formentor ★
atja de Formentor
lcúdia
Port d'Alcúdia
ollentia
Can Picafort
Cala Agulla
C 712
Capdepera
Artà
Cala Rajada
C 715
ARTÀ ★★★
LEVANTE
PM 404
T. de s'Avalls
C 715
Manacor
DE Hams
Portocristo
DRACH ★★★
2
SIERRAS
PM 401
Sant Salvador
C 717
Cala d'Or ★
Santanyí
★ Cala
antanyí
Cala Figuera ★
es Salines

ALCÚDIA Population 8 004

Alcúdia, still encircled by 14C ramparts, guards access to the promontory wh
divides the bays of Pollença and Alcúdia. The **Puerta del Muelle** or **Xara** (Quai Gat
which led to the harbour, and the **Puerta de San Sebastián** or **Puerta de Mallorca** on
other side of town, remain of the early fortified walls and were reconstructed a
incorporated into the ramparts when they were strengthened in the 14C. T
streets in the shadow of the walls have a distinctive medieval air as have
town's houses, brightened by Renaissance surrounds to their windows.
About a mile south is the site of the ancient Roman town of **Pollentia** founded
the 2C BC. All that remains of the city are the theatre ruins.

Museo Monográfico de Pollentia (Pollentia Monographic Museum) ⊘ – A chapel
Alcúdia's old quarter houses the museum with its collections of statues, oil lam
bronzes and jewellery from the site of the ancient city of Pollentia.

Excursions

Puerto de Alcúdia – *2km/1mi east.*
The port of Alcúdia overlooks a vast bay built up with hotels and tower blocks
long beach stretches away to the south as far as Can Picafort. The mars
hinterland of La Albufera is a nature reserve.

Cuevas de Campanet ⊘ (Campanet Caves) – *17km/11mi southwest along C 7
and a secondary, signposted road.*
The caves were discovered in 1947. About half the caves along
1 300m/1 500yd long path have ceased formation, their massive concretic
now totally dry. In the area which is still waterlogged, the most common featu
are straight and delicate stalactites.

Muro – *Take C 713 southwest for 11km/7mi and then bear left for anoth
7km/4mi via Sa Pobla.*
The road crosses countryside bristling with windmills.

Sección Etnológica del Museo de Mallorca ⊘ – The ethnological section of the Mallo
Museum, in a large 17C nobleman's residence, displays collections of traditio
furniture, dress and farm implements as well as an old pharmacy and isla
ceramics including *Xiurels* whistles.
An annexe houses exhibitions on various craftsmen: a blacksmith, cabinetmak
gilder, engraver, welder, goldsmith and cobbler.

★★ PALMA Population 308 616

The visitor who has the good fortune to arrive in Palma by boat discovers a c
spread across the curve of a wide bay, its proud cathedral standing guard as
foregone days of maritime glory. The town's many ancient buildings testify to
former heyday. The city's residential quarters with their hotels stretch out
either side of the historic centre and along the seafront, in Avinguda Gabriel Ro
shaded by palms, which leads to the harbours. The old harbour, bordered
Passeig Sagrera, serves both passenger and merchant ships. The new harbour
the southern tip of El Terreno quarter, accommodates the largest liners.

The Bahía de Palma – The bay, protected from north and west winds by the P
Major range, has a mild climate all the year round. Hotels and tourist apartm
blocks stretch along the seafront for 20km/12mi. To the west, the hotels sta
along the indented Bendinat coastline where there is little sand, except at the t
beach areas of **Palmanova** and **Magaluf**. The coast to the east is less sheltered, be
straight, but has mile upon mile of fine sand with a series of resorts – **Can Past
ses Meravelles** and **s'Arenal** whose beaches are known collectively as the Platjas
Palma.

The "Ciutat de Mallorca" – This was the name by which the city was known af
its liberation on 31 December 1229 and during its most prosperous period wh
trade links were forged with Barcelona, Valencia, the countries of Africa and
kingdoms of northern Europe; Jews and Genoese established colonies in
town, the latter even founding an exchange, and James II (Jaime II) and
successors endowed the city with beautiful Gothic buildings. Finally, the Arag
policy of expansion in Naples and Sicily enabled Palma to extend her commer
interests also.

Palma's old mansions – In the 15C and 16C, the great families of Palm
descended from rich merchants and members of the aristocracy, favoured
Italian style. They built elegant residences with stone façades, relieved
windows with Renaissance style decoration. It was only in the 18C tha
characteristic Mallorcan *casa* (house) appeared with an inner court of mass
marble columns, wide shallow arches and incorporating stone steps to a high a
graceful loggia. Balustrades of stone or wrought iron completed the decorati
The same families built themselves luxurious summer villas in the mountains
the north of Palma.

Modern Palma – The city, in which more than half of the island's population lives, has the greatest number of visitors of any town in Spain (more than 15 million in 1996).

Tourists congregate in and around the **Terreno** – especially in Plaza Gomila – and **Cala Major** quarters in the west of town, but the native heart of the city remains the Passeig des Born. This wide *rambla*, known as **El Born** (AY), followed the course of the Riera river before this was diverted in the 16C to run outside the walls on account of its devastating floodwaters. The shops selling pearls, glassware, leather goods, clothes and local craftwork are in the old town east of El Born in pedestrian streets around Plaça Major and in avinguda Jaume III.

Barrio de la Catedral (Cathedral Quarter) *3hr*

Catedral ⊘ (AZ) – The bold yet elegant cathedral, its tall buttresses surmounted by pinnacles, rises above the seafront. The Santanyi limestone of its walls changes colour according to the time of day: ochre, golden or pink. The cathedral, which was begun in the early 14C on the site of a former mosque, is one of the greatest constructions of the late Gothic period.

Cathedral, Palma

The west face was rebuilt in neo-Gothic style in the 19C after an earthquake but its 16C Renaissance portal has remained intact. The south door, known as the **Portada del Mirador** (Viewpoint Doorway), overlooks the sea, the delicate Gothic decoration dating from the 15C preserved beneath a porch. On the tympanum is a scene of the Last Supper while the statues of Saints Peter and Paul on either side prove that Sagrera, architect of the Llotja (Exchange), was also a talented sculptor.

The **interior** is both large and light, measuring 121m × 55m (397ft × 180ft) with a height of 44m/144ft to the top of the vaulting above the nave. Fourteen tall, incredibly slender octagonal pillars divide the nave from the aisles. The lack of adornment increases the impression of spaciousness. The Capilla Mayor or Real (Royal Chapel), itself the size of a church, contains at its centre an enormous wrought-iron baldachin by Gaudí (1912) with Renaissance choir stalls on either side. The tombs of the kings of Mallorca, Jaime II and Jaime III, lie in the Capilla de la Trinidad (Trinity Chapel).

Museo-Tesoro (Treasury Museum) ⊘ – The Gothic chapter-house contains the Santa Eulàlia altarpiece by the Maestro de los Privilegios (1335). In the oval, Baroque chapter-house are a number of reliquaries including that of the True Cross, decorated with precious stones. There are also two Baroque candelabra in embossed silver by Joan Matons.

La Almudaina ⊘ (AZ) – This ancient Moorish fortress, dating from the Walis' caliphate, was converted in the 14C and 15C by the kings of Mallorca into a royal palace. Today, as one of the official residences of the King of Spain, several

PALMA

Antoni Maura (Av.) . . . . AZ 2
Born (Passeig des) . . . . . . AY
Bosseria . . . . BY
Can Savellà . . . . BY 8
Can Serra . . . . BZ 10
Constitució . . . . AY 12
Corderia . . . . BY 15

Jaume III (Av.) . . . . AY
Mercat (Pl.) . . . . AY 18
Palau . . . . BZ 22
Pont i Vic . . . . BZ 25
Portella . . . . BZ 27
Puresa . . . . BZ 30
Ramon Llull . . . . BZ 32
Rei Joan Carle I
(Pl.) . . . . AY 35
Reina (Pl. de la) . . . . AY 37
Riera . . . . BY 40

Sant Francesc . . . . B
Sant Gaietà . . . . A
Sant Pere Nolasc . . . . B
Santa Eulàlia (Pl.) . . . . B
Temple . . . . B

C Antiguo Consulado del Ma
H Ayuntamiento
M¹ Museo del Mallorca
M² Museo Diocesano

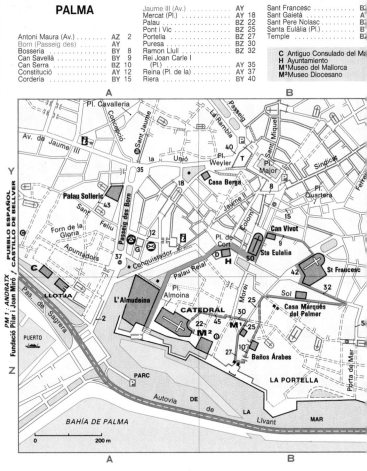

rooms have recently been restored and elegantly furnished with Flem
tapestries, clocks and paintings. In the courtyard, note the carved overhang
eaves and the doorway of the Iglesia de Santa Ana (St Anne's Church), one
the rare examples of Romanesque architecture in the Balearics. There is a 1
altarpiece inside.

Ayuntamiento (BY H) – Carved wooden eaves overhang the 17C façade of
town hall.

Iglesia de Santa Eulàlia ⊘ **(BY)** – 13C-15C. The tall nave is unusually b
for a Gothic church. The first chapel off the south aisle contains a 1
altarpiece.
Between the churches of Santa Eulàlia and Sant Francesc, at no 2 Carrer Save
is the 18C **Can Vivot**, its beautiful *patio* decorated with marble columns.

Iglesia de Sant Francesc ⊘ **(BY)** – 13C-14C. The church's façade, rebuilt in
late 17C, has an immense Plateresque rose window and a Baroque portal wit
beautifully carved tympanum by Francisco Herrera. The interior consists of a v
single aisle. The first apsidal chapel on the left contains the tomb of Ram
Llull: a recumbent statue of the philosopher lies upon a frieze of imagin
beasts supported by seven Gothic niches.
The **cloisters★** *(claustro)*, begun in 1286 and completed in the 14C, are extrem
elegant. Apart from one side of trefoil openings, the architect divided
remaining galleries into multifoil bays supported on groups of slender colum
which he varied in diameter together with the decoration on the capitals
achieve diversity and grace. The ceiling is painted throughout.

Casa Marqués del Palmer (BZ) – In the middle of the aristocratic Carrer
Sol stands the impressive Casa Marqués del Palmer, a mansion built in 15
in stone and now blackened by age. Renaissance decoration around the up
floor windows mellows the austerity of its Gothic wall. The upper galle
protected by the traditional deep eaves, is a replica of the one adorning
Llotja.
The former old Jewish quarter, **La Portella**, lies close against the town wall.

Baños árabes ⊘ (**BZ**) – The Moorish baths are the only relic to have remained intact from the time of the caliphate in Palma. The baths, beneath their small circular windows and classical dome, supported on 12 columns with rudimentary capitals, were used after the Reconquest by Jews and Christians alike.

Museo de Mallorca ⊘ (**BZ M¹**) – The museum consists of three sections: Archeological, Fine Arts (Bellas Artes) and Ethnographical *(for this last section, see Sección Etnológica del Museo de Mallorcathis, Muro, p 414)*.

Muslim Archeology – Palma was occupied by the Muslims from the 8C to 1229 when it was known as Madina Mayurqa. The only architectural vestiges from the 12C, when it was one of the most important towns in all *Al-Andalus*, are the Almudaina, Arco de la Almudaina (Almudaina Arch) and the Baños árabes. The ground floor displays capitals, *artesonado* ceilings and ceramics from this period.

Fine Arts – *(See The Mallorcan Primitives, p 413)*. This section of the museum has an excellent collection of Mallorcan Gothic paintings from the 14C and 15C. Works from the early 14C show a clear Italian influence; among them is the Santa Quiteria altarpiece by the Maestro de los Privilegios. Catalan works begin to appear after 1349 when Mallorca was annexed by Aragón: the *Crucifixion* by Ramón Destorrents, interesting for its composition and expression, was to influence other paintings. In Room 2 are the *Annunciation, St Lucy* and *Mary Magdalene* by Maestro del Obispo Galiana (late 14C). Room 3: Francesh Comes, one of the most prestigious of the early-15C painters, is represented here by his **St George**★, remarkable for the depth and detail of the landscape. There is also a 15C *San Onofre Altarpiece* by the Maestro de Predellas. In the rooms devoted to 16C, 17C and 18C art, note the paintings of St Michael and St John by Juan de Juanes.

Museo Diocesano (**Diocesan Museum**) ⊘ (**BZ M²**) – *On the square behind the cathedral.* Among the many Gothic works displayed is Pere Nisart's outstanding **St George**★ (1568) which shows the saint slaying the dragon against a backdrop of the town of Palma, as it was in the 16C.

A walk west of El Born *1hr*

Llotja ⊘ (**AZ**) – The designer of this 15C commodities exchange was **Guillermo Sagrera**, a famous architect who was a native of Mallorca. The Llotja's military features are only for the sake of appearances: the openwork gallery made to look like a sentry path never served as one; the merlons and turrets are not for defence but decoration. But such devices distract the eye from the inevitable buttresses and the austerity of the outer walls which were further modified by Gothic windows with delicate tracery. The interior, in which cross vaults outline the pointed arches which descend onto six beautiful, spirally fluted columns, is exceptionally elegant.

Antiguo Consulado del Mar (**Former Maritime Consulate**) (**AY C**) – The early-17C building adorned with a Renaissance balcony was the meeting place of the Tribunal de Comercio Marítimo (Merchant Shipping Tribunal). Today it is the presidential seat of the Comunidad Autónoma de las Islas Baleares (Autonomous Community of the Balearic Islands).

Walk up the Passeig des Born.

Palau Solleric ⊘ (**AY**) – The decoration of the front of this 18C palace overlooking the Born, is completed by an elegant loggia; behind this front *(follow the narrow covered way round the building)* is the most perfect **patio**★ in Palma, complete with a beautifully proportioned double flighted staircase set off by delicate wrought ironwork. Exhibitions are held in the palace rooms.

Additional sights

Casa Berga (**BY**) – The mansion dating from 1712 now houses the Palacio de Justicia (Law Courts). The façade is encumbered uncharacteristically with stone balconies but the inner courtyard, although vast, is a typical Mallorcan *patio*.

Pueblo Español (**Spanish Village**) ⊘ – *Off the town plan, along Passeig de Sagrera* (**AZ**). This model village, where the most typical houses of every region of Spain have been reconstructed, differs from the village of this kind built in Barcelona, in that here the buildings are exact reproductions of actual famous houses or monuments: the Patio de los Arrayanes (Myrtle Court) from Granada, the Casa de El Greco in Toledo, the Plaza Mayor in Salamanca etc. Craftsmen at work in the alleys and folk dancing and singing in the streets bring the village to life. Features of all the major Roman constructions in Spain have been incorporated in the monumental **Palacio de Congresos** (Congressional Hall) facing the village.

Castillo de Bellver ⊘ – *Leave Palma by Passeig de Sagrera* (**AZ**). The castle, built by the Mallorcan kings of the 14C as a summer residence, was converted not long afterwards into a prison, which it remained until 1915.

Among those incarcerated was the poet, dramatist and politician **Jovellanos**, kno
also, at the time, for his progressive system of education. He was released
1808, just as French officers captured by the Spanish at the Battle of Bai
arrived.

The castle's circular perimeter, round buildings and circular inner court are hig
original; a free-standing keep dominates all. The arcade on the ground floor is
off by a series of tall Roman statues. These were donated by Cardinal Desp
together with his Italian collections, and belong to the Museo Municipal de Hist
(Municipal History Museum). Also displayed in the museum are finds fr
excavations in Pollentia.

A full **panorama**★★ of the Bahía de Palma can be seen from the terrace.

Fundació Pilar i Joan Miró (Pilar and Joan Miró Foundation) ⊙ – *Leave the town ce*
via the Passeig de Sagrera (**AZ**). The museum was born from the desire of
artist and his wife to provide the city of Palma with a lively cultural and arti
centre. In the shadow of Son Abrines, Miró's private residence since 1956,
works donated by the artist are displayed in a part of the building called
Espacio Estrella, a satellite section of Moneo, an amalgam of the Museo de A
Romano, Mérida, and the Museo Thyssen-Bornemisza in Madrid. Visitors to
foundation are also provided with an introduction to one of the most wide-rang
and original artists in contemporary art. The large studio provided for him by
friend JL Sert and the San Boter studio are also shown.

★★★ LA COSTA ROCOSA (THE ROCKY COAST) *itinerary* 1 *map p 412*

Mallorca's west coast, known as the Rocky Coast, is dominated by the limest
barrier of the Sierra de Tramuntana which reaches an altitude of 1 436m/4 71
at Puig Major. The mountain range, its wild terrain softened only by the occasic
pinewood, drops dramatically to the deep, translucent sea. In the south, aro
the villages of Estellencs and Banyalbufar, the slopes have been terraced i
marjades where olives, almonds and vines are grown. In the more fertile val
further inland, *fincas* or large estates with seignorial mansions such as Granja
Alfàbia were established from the 17C to the 19C.

From Palma to Sóller *125km/78mi – allow 1 day*

The indented coast between Palma and Port d'Andratx with its wide sandy cre
and coves has been built up into a series of resorts: **Palmanova, Santa Ponça** wh
a Cross commemorates the landing of James I of Aragón in 1229, **Peguera,**
Fornells and **es Camp de Mar.**

★ **Port d'Andratx** – The small fishing port now also used by pleasure craft lies
sheltered in the curve of a narrow harbour. The town of Andratx surrounded
almond plantations some distance behind the harbour, is scarcely distinguisha
against the grey mountain background, dominated by the 1 026m/3 366ft h
Galatzó peak.

The C 710 between Andratx and Sóller is an extremely winding **scenic road**★
cutting mostly along the edge of the cliff that extends all the way to the inden
northwest coast. It commands outstanding views and is shaded along its len
by pine trees.

★★ **Mirador Ricardo Roca** – The view from this lookout point drops sheer to t
coves below, lapped by the wonderfully limpid sea.

Estellencs – The village is surrounded by terraces of almond and apricot tre

Banyalbufar – The tall stone village houses stand in terraces surrounded by fie
of tomatoes and vines. There is swimming in the harbour.

★★ **Mirador de Ses Ánimes** – The panorama from the watchtower stretches al
the coast from the Isla de Dragonera to the south and as far as Port de Sól

Real Cartuja de Valldemossa (Valldemossa Carthusian Monastery) ⊙ – The mc
stery, set in the heart of Valldemossa village, was made famous by the v
George Sand and Chopin paid in the winter of 1838-1839. The bad weather
local hostility to their unorthodox way of life left George Sand disenchant
although the beauty of the countryside did evoke enthusiastic passages in
book, *A Winter in Majorca*, and Chopin regained his inspiration during the st
There are pleasant views of the village's surrounding olive groves, carob trees
almond orchards from their cells.

An 18C **pharmacy**, built into one of the cloister galleries, has a fine collection of j
and boxes. A small **museum** displays xylographs (wood engravings).

The road beyond Valldemossa runs along cliffs more than 400m/1 300ft hi

Son Marroig ⊙ – The former residence of Archduke Ludwig Salvator include
exhibition of archeological finds and Mallorcan furniture collected by the aut
and his volumes on the Balearic Islands. A small marble belvedere in the gar
affords a view of the locally famous, pierced rock rising out of the sea,
Foradada.

Deià

R.Drexel/STOCK PHOTOS

Deià – The village of reddish-brown houses perched on a hillside amid olive and almond trees has attracted a number of writers and painters. All around are higher hills, covered in holm oaks and conifers giving it almost a mountain setting. There is a pleasant walk from the village down to a creek with a small beach.

Sóller – The town lies spread out in a wide basin where market gardens, oranges and olives grow.

Port de Sóller – Port de Sóller lies in the curve of an almost circular bay, its sheltered harbour ideal for pleasure boats. With the advantages of a sand beach and low mountain hinterland, it is now the major seaside resort of the west coast. A small train runs between Port de Sóller and Sóller. Boat trips along the coast set off from the harbour.

Take C 711 from Sóller to Alfàbia.

The road twists steeply up the hillside commanding views westwards of Sóller, the harbour and the sea before descending the range's southern slopes towards the plain.

Jardines de Alfàbia (Alfàbia Gardens) ⊙ – The estate was originally a Moorish residence although all that now remains of the 14C period is the *artesonado* ceiling over the porch.
Follow the signposted path through the gardens with their bowers, fountains and luxuriant palms, bougainvillaeas and clumps of bamboo.
A visit to the **library** and grand saloon conveys the atmosphere of a traditional seignorial residence.

Return to Sóller.

From Sóller to Alcúdia *130km/80mi – allow 1 day*

Take the narrow mountain road from Sóller via the picturesque villages of Biniaraix and Fornalutx, their ochre-coloured stone houses set off by green shutters, to join C 710.

Mirador de Ses Barques – From this viewpoint there is an interesting panorama of Port de Sóller.
The road leaves the coast to head inland through mountainous countryside. It runs through a long tunnel before following the upper valley of the Pareís. All the while the landscape is dominated to the west by the impressive **Puig Major** *(military base on the summit)*.

After skirting Gorg Blau reservoir, take the Sa Calobra road.

Sa Calobra road – The magnificently planned road plunges towards the Mediterranean, dropping 900m/2 953ft in 14km/9mi. It drops vertiginously through a weird and desolate landscape of steep, jagged rocks, above which towers the Puig Major.

* **Sa Calobra** – Pleasure boats from Port de Sóller are often to be seen moor
the rocky creek beside which stand the few houses of Sa Calobra village. Ne
is the mouth of the **Pareís river**★, its clear water pouring over the beach of r
white shingle which lies in its path to the sea. The river bed is accessible
couple of hundred yards along a track which passes through two undergr
galleries; a 2-3km/1.5-2mi walk along the course gives an idea of how encl
the stream is.

Return to C 710.

About 800m/875yd north of the Sa Calobra fork, a small **mirador**★ *(lookout
664m/2 178ft)* gives a good view over a length of the cleft hollowed out by
Pareís. The road then passes through a lovely forest of holm oaks.

Monasterio de Nuestra Señora de Lluc ⊙ – The origin of the monastery c
back to the 13C when a young shepherd found a statue of the Virgin on the
and a shrine was subsequently built. The present buildings date from the
(church) and early 20C (hostelry). *La Moreneta*, as the dark stone Gothic st
of the Virgin is known, is patron of Mallorca and venerated by a great n
pilgrims.

*From a pass 5km/3mi north of Lluc, you can see right across to the Bah
Pollença.*

Pollença – The town stands between two hills, the Puig (333m/1 092ft) to
east, and a hill to the west crowned by a Calvary *(access up a long flight of s
bordered by cypresses)*. The streets are picturesque, lined with low ochre-colo
houses with rounded arches over the entrances.

Port de Pollença – This large resort has a perfect **setting**★ in a sheltered
between the Cabo Formentor headland to the north and the Cabo del Pinar t
south, and provides a vast expanse of calm water for water-skiing and sai
There are moorings in the harbour for pleasure craft and a pleasant prome
skirts the beach.

* **Cabo de Formentor road** – The road commands spectacular views as it twists
turns, rising several times to the edge of the clifftops and, at one point, follo
a narrow jagged crest. The **Mirador des Colomer viewpoint**★★★ *(access along a ste,
path)* overlooks, in an impressive, vertical drop, what is known as Mallorca's C
Brava where great rock promontories plunge to the sea.
The **Platja de Formentor** is a well sheltered beach facing Pollença bay. It is fu
enhanced by the flowered terraces of the grand Hotel Formentor, built in 1
and once famous for its casino and millionaire guests. The road continues tow
the cape and once through the tunnel which temporarily hides the Cala Fig
to the north, it passes through a steep and arid landscape. The **Cabo de Formen**
dominated by a lighthouse, is the most northerly point of the island. It drops s
to the sea, 200m/650ft, in a formidable rock wall.

Return to Port de Pollença, then skirt the bay until you reach Alcúdia.

Alcúdia – *See Alcúdia.*

★★ **EAST COAST AND CAVES** *itinerary* ② *map p 412*

From Artà to Palma *165km/103mi – allow 1 day*

Artà – The town of Artà with its narrow streets may be distinguished fro
distance by its high rock site crowned by the Iglesia de Sant Salvador (
Salvador Church) and the ruins of an ancient fortress. The Artà region is ri
megalithic remains *(see MENORCA)*, particularly *talayots* which sometimes ca
seen over the low walls dividing the fields.

Take C 715 east.

Capdepera – *Access to the fortress: by car, along narrow streets; on foo
steps.* The remains of a 14C fortress still girding the hilltop give Capdeper
angular silhouette of crenellated walls and square towers. The buttre
ramparts now enclose only a restored **chapel**, but it is still possible to walk th
sentry path, **viewing**★ the sea and the nearby *calas*.

Cala Rajada – Cala Rajada with its delightful fishing village and pleasure
harbour, has grown into a seaside resort on account of the creeks which li
either side of it.

Casa March ⊙ – The gardens of this vast residence on the hillside facing the
have become an outdoor museum of modern sculpture. Over 40 sculpt
blending in perfectly with the vegetation, are the works of famous artists
as Henry Moore, Sempere, Otero Besteiro, Berrocal, Barbara Hepworth, Edu
Chillida and Arman.

By crossing the pinewood towards the lighthouse, you come to two rocky inlets, so far relatively wild, but 2km/1mi further north, is **Cala Agulla**, well known for its sandy beach.

Return to Capdepera and follow the signs to the Coves d'Artà.

Coves d'Artà ⊘ – The caves, magnificently sited in the cape closing Canyamel bay to the north and accessible by a cliff road, were largely hollowed out by the sea - the giant mouth overlooks the sea from a height of 35m/115ft. The chambers themselves are impressively lofty and contain massive concretions. The vestibule is blackened by smoke from 19C visitors' torches but the caves that follow are varied and equally impressive, containing the **Reina de las Columnas** (Queen of Columns) 22m/72ft tall, Dantesque surroundings cleverly highlighted in the **Sala del Infierno** (Inferno Chamber) and a fabulous decoration of concretions in the **Sala de las Banderas** (Hall of Flags), 45m/148ft high.

Return to PM 404 and bear left. At Portocristo, take the Manacor road off which you soon turn for the Coves dels Hams.

Coves dels Hams ⊘ – The caves, following the course of a former underground river, communicate directly with the sea, so that the water level in several of the small clear pools rises and falls with the slight Mediterranean tide. The concretions are delicate and some, such as the stalactites in the **Sala de los Anzuelos**★ (Fish-hook Chamber), are as white as snow.

Return to Portocristo and bear right.

Coves del Drach ⊘ – Four chambers succeed one another over a distance of 2km/1mi, their transparent pools reflecting richly decorative concretions. The marine origins of the caves seem unquestionable in spite of their size: the French speleologist, **EA Martel**, who first explored them in 1896, believed that infiltration through the limestone subsidence and faults had caused the cavities in which several pools are slightly salty. Rainfall dissolved the soft Miocene limestone, forming as it did so, countless concretions. In the words of Martel: "On all sides, everywhere, in front and behind, as far as the eye can see, marble cascades, organ pipes, lace draperies, pendants of brilliants hang suspended from the walls and roof." It is the **roofs**, above all, which are amazing, glittering with countless, sharply pointed icicles. The tour ends with a look at the limpidly translucent **lago Martel**. The vast chamber in which the lake lies has been converted into a kind of concert hall; musicians in boats rise up seemingly from the depths and, in a dreamlike atmosphere, glide across the water as they play.

Continue along the road towards Santanyí and turn right onto PM 401.

Monasterio de Sant Salvador ⊘ – The monastery perched on a rise 500m/1 640ft above the plain *(tight hairpin bends)*, commands a wide **panorama**★★ of the eastern part of the island.

It was founded in the 14C although the **church** and buildings, now used for pilgrims, were rebuilt in the 18C. In the church behind the Baroque high altar is a deeply venerated **Virgin and Child**, while in the south chapels are three **cribs** set in dioramas and a multicoloured stone **altarpiece** carved in the 14C in low relief with scenes of the Passion.

Return to C 717 and head south to Santanyí.

Secondary roads lead off C 717 to a series of resorts built up in the creeks along the coast, namely **Cala d'Or**★, with fully developed tourist facilities, **Cala Figuera**★, which is still a delightful little fishing village, and **Cala Santanyí**★.

Take the Palma road from Santanyí. At Llucmajor, bear right onto PM 501.

Santuario de Cura ⊘ – The road climbs from Randa up tight hairpin bends to the monastery high on the hillside. The buildings have been restored and modernised by the Franciscans who have occupied them since 1913. You may visit the 17C **church**, the Sala de Gramática (Grammar Room) and a small **museum**.

From the terrace on the west side of the monastery there is a **panorama**★★ of Palma, the bay, the Puig Major chain and, in the northeast, Cabo de Formentor headland, the northernmost point on the island.

Return to Llucmajor and continue west along C 717 to Palma.

Palma – *See PALMA.*

MENORCA★★

MINORCA – Area 669km²/258sq mi – Population 65 109

Michelin map 443, M 41-42

Menorca, the most northerly of the Balearic Islands, ranks second in terms of
(48km/30mi long and 15km/9mi wide) and population. The island has, so
remained out of the tourist mainstream, its 189km/117mi of coastline escaping
the most part, overdevelopment. Nevertheless, the windswept plateau and heath
more akin to a mist-enveloped Atlantic countryside, have a certain, if somev
melancholy, charm.

Menorca divides into two distinct zones, determined by relief and geological or
The island's highest point, monte Toro, 358m/1 174ft, is in the northern part of
island, known as the Tramuntana, where there are outcrops of dark slate rock f
the Primary and Secondary geological periods. Along the coast, these ancient, erc
cliffs have been cut into a saw's edge of *rías* and deep coves. The second zone, so
of the Maó-Ciutadella dividing line, is the Migjorn limestone platform of li
coloured rock which forms tall cliffs along the coast cut by creeks.

The vegetation is typically Mediterranean with pinewoods, wild olives battered
gnarled and twisted shapes by the north wind, together with mastic trees, hea
and aromatic herbs such as rosemary, camomile and thyme.

Throughout the island, fields are divided by drystone walls punctuated by gates m
from twisted olive branches.

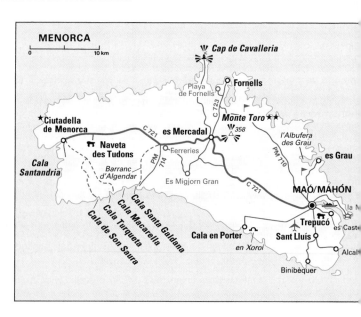

HISTORICAL NOTES

After settlement by prehistoric peoples, whose monuments may be seen through
the island, Menorca was colonised by the Romans, conquered by Vandals in 427
then came under Muslim control. In the 13C, Alfonso III de Aragón invaded the isla
made Ciutadella capital and encouraged settlers from Catalunya and Aragón. In
16C, Barbary pirates attacked first Maó and then Ciutadella, leaving both citie
virtual ruin.

In 1713, Menorca, which had begun to prosper through sea trade in the late 17C,
ceded to the English crown by the Treaty of Utrecht. Maó became Englar
economic stronghold in the Mediterranean. Apart from a short period of French
from 1756 to 1763, the island remained throughout the 18C under the British w
built houses and, under an enlightened governor, Kane, roads. The island's first ro
between Maó and Ciutadella, still exists (north of C 721) and is known as Can
Kane. At the beginning of the 19C, Menorca was restored definitively to Spain
The island's economy has gradually been oriented towards the leather industry
jewellery making while cattle raising provides the island with dairy produ
particularly its well-known cheeses.

The Megalithic monuments – In the second millennium BC, at the end of the Bro
Age, the Balearics were populated by settlers similar to those who inhabited Sard
during the same period. The cavernous nature of the Minorcan countryside offe
natural shelter both for the living and the dead; some of the caves, such as Calasco
are even decorated. At the same time, **talayots** began to appear (over 200 have b
identified). They take the form of great cones of stones possibly covering a fune

mber and forming, it is believed, the base for a superimposed wooden house. ...er characteristic monuments of the civilization include **taulas**, consisting of two ...e stone blocks placed one on top of the other in the shape of a T, possibly serving ...ltars, and **navetas**, single monuments which take the form of upturned boats and ...tain funeral chambers.

...more detailed information on local archeology, a map may be bought on the island ...wing the sites of the monuments: Mapa Arqueológico de Menorca, by J Mascaró ...arius.

...norcan architecture – The walls and even the roofs of Minorcan houses are ...ghtly whitewashed; the low dividing walls so typical of the island also have a white ...d along the top. Tiles are used for roofing, chimneys and guttering. Houses are ...t facing south, their fronts characterised by wide, open bays while the northern ...ls, exposed to fierce *tramontana* winds, have very small windows.

...lish influence on architecture is evident in the towns where many of the houses ...e sash windows and some of the seignorial mansions are in the Palladian style ...hionable in Britain in the 18C.

... fields around Ciutadella are scattered with curious stone constructions shaped ... ziggurats (the pyramidal stepped towers of ancient Mesopotamia); these ...racas, vaulted inside with false ceilings, served as shelters for shepherds.

CIUTADELLA/CIUDADELA Population 20 707

...n the Middle Ages, Ciutadella, the citadel, and capital of Menorca, was ringed with ...walls. The ramparts were demolished in 1873 but their layout can still be ...distinguished in the circle of avenues around the old quarter. The fortified aspect ...of the city becomes evident when viewed from the harbour.

...After being sacked by Turkish pirates in the 16C, Ciutadella was partly rebuilt in ...the late 17C and 18C. Today, the atmosphere in the alleys of the old quarter and ...in the harbour, give the town a calm and indefinable charm.

...Each year the **Midsummer's Day** or **Fiestas de San Juan**, are celebrated with traditional ...rejoicing. On the preceding Sunday, a man representing John the Baptist, dressed ...n animal skins and carrying a lamb, runs through the town to the sound of *fabiols* ...(small flutes) and *tambourins*. On 24 and 25 June, over 100 horsemen take part ...n jousting tournaments and processions.

Tour *about 1hr*

Barrio Antiguo (Old Quarter) – **Plaza del Born**, the former parade ground, is flanked ...by the eclectic 19C façade of the **Ayuntamiento** (town hall) and the early-19C **Palacio ...de Torre-saura**, a palace with side loggias. In the centre of the square is an obelisk ...commemorating the townspeople's heroic stand against the Turks in the 16C.

Catedral ⊘ – The late-14C fortified church has kept part of the minaret of the ...mosque which once stood on the site. Inside, the single aisle is ogival and the apse ...pentagonal. You will be able to see the church's Baroque doorway from Calle del ...Rosario facing the cathedral.

J.Hidalgo - C.Lopesino/MARCO POLO

At the end of the street, turn left into calle del Santísimo where two fine late-
mansions may be seen on opposite sides of the street: **Palacio Saura** has a Baro
façade adorned with a cornice, while **Palacio Martorell** is of a more sober desi≀
By way of calle del Obispo Vila, in which stand the Claustro de Socorro (Socc
Cloisters) and the Iglesia de Santo Cristo (Santo Cristo Church), you come to
main street which leads to **Plaza de España** and the arcaded **Carrer de Ses Voltes.**

Puerto (Harbour) – *(See photo, p 423).* The ramp approach to the harbour, wl
is well sheltered and serves mainly pleasure craft, is along a former countersc;
The buildings along the quays are bustling with cafés and restaurants.
esplanade beyond, Pla de Sant Joan, is bordered by boat shelters hollowed ou
the living rock. The whole area comes alive at night.

Excursions

Nau or **Naveta des Tudons** – *5km/3mi east of Ciutadella.*
This funerary monument, shaped like an upturned ship, is notable for the vast ;
of the stones in the walls and more particularly, those lining the floor insid

Cala Santandria – *3km/2mi south.*
This is a small sheltered beach in a creek.

Cala Torre-saura, Cala Turqueta, Cala Macarella – *Ask on the spot
directions.*
The three beaches are set in small, beautifully unspoilt creeks fringed
sweet-smelling pines.

MAÓ/MAHÓN Population 21 814

Maó's **site**★ is most striking when approached from the sea: it appears high a
a cliff in the curve of a deep, 5km/3mi long roadstead or natural harbour.
Maó reached its height during the English occupation from 1713 to 1782 w
it was endowed with Palladian style mansions.
On the north side of the harbour is the Finca de San Antonio – the Golden F;
– where Admiral Nelson lived during a brief stay on the island, and where he
the finishing touches to his book, *Sketches of My Life* (October 1799).
The town gave its name to the famous *mahonnaise* sauce which we now kno∎
mayonnaise.
Most of the town's shops are in the network of streets between **Plaza del Ejér**
a large, lively square lined with cafés and restaurants, and the quieter **Plaz**
España with its two churches: **Santa Maria**, with a beautiful Baroque organ,
Carmen, whose cloisters have been converted to hold the municipal market.

Museo de Menorca ⊘ – The museum occupies a former Franciscan monast∢
The rooms are laid out around a sober 18C cloister and display prehistoric
other objects relating to Menorcan history, including a room dedicated to the l
talayot culture.

Puerto (Harbour) – Walk down the steep ramp from carrer de Ses Voltes, cu
a majestic flight of steps, and follow the quay to the north side of the roadst∢
Look across the water for a view of the town at its most characteristic, witl
larger buildings lining the top of the cliff and below, the open-air dance halls,
restaurants, shops and coloured fishermen's cottages, snug against the foc

Excursions

★ **La Rada (Roadstead)** – The south side consists of a series of coves and villa∢
among them Cala Figuera with its fishing harbour and restaurants. **Es Cas**
further along, was built as a garrison town by the English when it was c;
Georgetown. It has a grid plan, with the parade ground at its centre. The isla
in the natural harbour include Lazareto and, beside it, Cuarentena, which, a∎
name suggests, was a quarantine hospital for sailors. A road follows the nortr
shore to the Faro de la Mola (Mola Fort) affording views of Maó.

Talayot de Trepucó – *1km/0.6mi south of Maó.*
This megalithic site is famous for its *taula* which is 4.80m/16ft high.

Sant Lluís – *4km/2mi south.*
The town with its narrow streets was founded by the French during t
occupation of the island.
Small resorts have grown up nearby: at **Alcalfar** where the houses stand a l
distance inland beside a creek between two rocky promontories, and **Binibè**
a small, completely new village which, with its alleyways, small squares,
dazzling white houses, has been made to look like a fishing hamlet.

Es Grau – *8km/5mi north.*
Beside the attractive white village with its long beach is a vast lagoon, **Albufe**
es Grau, 2km/1mi long and 400m/437yd wide. It is an ideal spot to watch the
migrant bird life (rails, ducks and herons).

Cala en Porter - *12km/8mi west.*
High promontories protect a narrow estuary inlet, lined by a sandy beach. Houses stand perched upon the left cliff. From their lofty position, ancient troglodyte dwellings, the **Coves d'en Xoroi**, overlook the sea. A bar has been installed in one of them.

MERCADAL Population 2 601

Mercadal, a small town of brilliantly whitewashed houses halfway between Maó and Ciutadella, is the point where roads to the coast meet on the north-south axis.

Excursions

Monte Toro - *3.5km/2mi along a narrow road.*
On a clear day, the **view** from the church crowned summit (358m/1 175ft) is of the entire island. You can see the indented Bahía de Fornells (Fornells Bay) to the north, the straight line of the coastal cliffs to the south and Maó to the southeast.

Fornells - *8.5km/5mi north on C 723.*
Fornells, a small fishing village of whitewashed houses with green shutters, lies at the mouth of a deep inlet, surrounded on all sides by bare moorland. The village lives off crawfish fishing, as can be seen from the single-sail craft moored in the harbour. The local speciality, crawfish soup or *caldereta*, is a food-lover's delight.

Cap de Cavalleria - *12km/8mi north along PM 722.*
The drive to the cape, the northernmost point on the island, is through windswept moorland, battered by the *tramontana* from the north, with large, white, elegant country houses, like that at Finca Santa Teresa. The **view** from the lighthouse is of a rocky, indented coast, more Atlantic than Mediterranean.

Cala Santa Galdana - *16km/10mi southwest via Ferreries.*
The beauty of this magnificent cove set in a limpid bay flanked by tall cliffs, has been somewhat marred by the construction of large hotels.
It is also possible to walk to the cove from **the Algendar ravine** *(on leaving Ferreries, take the track left towards Ciutadella).* The path *(3hr there and back)* winds through a ravine beside a stream which is enclosed in places by cliffs up to 50m/160ft tall.

IBIZA★

Area 572km²/221sq mi – Population 74 001
Michelin map 443 O, P 33-34

...za, the **Isla Blanca** or White Island, as it has been called, is the largest of the Pityuses ...nds (the name given to Ibiza and Formentera by the ancient Greeks). It lies 52 ...tical miles from the peninsula and 45 southwest of Mallorca, and is 41km/25mi ...g.

...zzling white house walls, flat roof terraces, tortuous alleys and an atmosphere ...ilar to that of a Greek island give Ibiza a unique character within the Balearics. ...za's history dates from the beginnings of trade development throughout the ...diterranean: in the 10C BC, Phoenicians made the island a staging post for ...os loaded with Spanish metal ores returning to Africa; in the 7C BC, Carthage ...w all powerful and founded a colony on the island; under the Romans the capital ...w in size and prosperity to judge from the necropolis discovered at Puig des ...lins.

...**dscape** – Ibiza is a mountainous island where the muddled lines of relief leave ...le space for cultivation between the limestone hills. Among pines and junipers on ...hillsides stand the cube-shaped houses of many small villages. The shore appears ...d and indented, guarded by high cliffs; promontories are marked by rocks out to ..., some standing as high as the amazing limestone needle known as **Vedrá★** (almost ...0m/300ft).

...**ditional architecture** – While the architecture inland has managed to preserve ...traditions, that on the coast tends to have suffered from overdevelopment to ...et the demands of tourism.
...e typical Ibizan cottage, or **casament**, is made up of several white cubes with few ...dows; each represents a single room and opens off a central common room. The ...aded porches provide shade and a sheltered area for storing crops.

Country churches are equally plain with gleaming white exteriors and dark interiors. façades are square, surmounted by narrow bell gables and pierced by wide porch In the days of pirate attacks, the island's inhabitants took refuge in the fortif churches of villages such as Sant Carles, Sant Joan, Sant Jordi, Sant Miquel and F de Missa.

Folklore and traditional costume – Ibiza's uncomplicated folklore lives on in everyday practices of its modern inhabitants. Women are still to be seen wearing traditional long gathered skirt and dark shawl. At festivals the costume is brighter with fine gold filigree necklaces or *emprendades*. The island dances are perform to the accompaniment of flute, tambourine and castanets, by groups whose s becomes evident as they perform the steps faster and faster.

Economy – Ibiza's main resource is its tourism, an industry that has unfortunat marred some of the island's sites. The **salt-pans** *(salinas)* in the south, exploited si Carthaginian times, produce about 50 000t of salt a year.

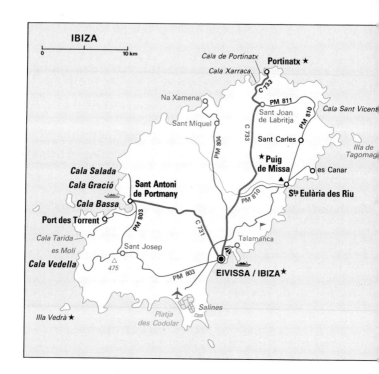

★ EIVISSA/IBIZA Population 30 376

Eivissa's colourful beauty and impressive **site★★** are best appreciated for the fir time if seen from the sea; alternatively take the **Talamanca** road out of town ar look back *(3km/2mi northeast)*. The town, built on a hill overlooking the se consists of an old quarter ringed by walls, the lively Marina district near th harbour, and, further out, residential and shopping areas. All along the shorelir are large hotels.

★ Dalt Vila (Upper Town) (Z) *1hr 30min*

The Dalt Vila, enclosed by the 16C walls built under Emperor Charles V, is the hea of the old city and retains even today a certain rustic, medieval character. Ther remain many noble houses worth looking at particularly for their vast *patios* ar Gothic windows.
Enter the quarter through the **Porta de Taules** (YZ), a gateway which is surmounte by Philip II's crest, and either continue by car up a steep slope to the cathedr square or take a leisurely stroll through the quiet meandering streets with the shops and art galleries.

Catedral ⊙ (Z) – The cathedral's massive 13C belfry, which closely resembles keep but for its two storeys of Gothic bays, totally dominates the town. The nav was rebuilt in the 17C. An ancient bastion behind the east end has been converte into a lookout point from which you can get a good **panoramic view★** of the tow and harbour.

D. Clément/EXPLORER

Dalt Vila (Upper Town), Eivissa

Museo Arqueológico de Ibiza y Formentera ⊘ (z **M**¹) – The museum's most impressive exhibits are those from Punic art, which developed around the Mediterranean from the 7C BC to the 3C AD. Particularly impressive are the ex-votos discovered on Ibiza and Formentera, predominantly from excavations at Illa Plana and the Es Cuiram cave. The cave is believed to have been a temple to the goddess Tanit, who was venerated there from the 5C to the 2C BC. Also worthy of note are the examples of polychrome moulded glass, ostrich eggs, and Punic, Roman and Moorish ceramics.

Additional Sights

Museu Monogràfic de Puig des Molins (Puig des Molins Monographic Museum) ⊘ (z) – The Puig des Molins hillside necropolis was a burial-ground for the Phoenicians from the 7C BC and then for the Romans until the 1C AD. There is a model of the site in Room IV and some of the hypogea or underground funerary chambers, of which over 3 000 have been discovered, may be visited.
The objects displayed were found in the tombs and include articles from everyday life as well as items used in funerary rituals which represented symbols of resurrection.
The outstanding, partly coloured, 5C BC **bust of the goddess Tanit**★, a Punic version of the Phoenician Astarte, is a perfect example of Greek beauty. A second bust is more Carthaginian.

La Marina (Y) – The Marina district near the municipal market and the harbour, with its restaurants, bars and shops, stands in lively contrast to the quieter Dalt Vila.

Sa Penya (Y) – The former fishermen's quarter, now the centre of Ibiza's nightlife, is built on a narrow rock promontory at the harbour mouth and is quite different from the rest of the town. Within the limited space available, white cubic houses overlap and superimpose on one another in picturesque chaos, completely blocking streets in places and compelling them to continue by means of steps cut out of the rock.

SANT ANTONI DE PORTMANY/SAN ANTONIO ABAD
Population 14 663

Sant Antoni with its vast, curved bay has been extensively developed by the tourist industry. The old quarter, hidden behind modern apartment blocks, centres around a fortified 14C church rebuilt in the 16C. There is a large pleasure boat harbour. Several coves and creeks are within easy distance of the town.

Excursions

Cala Gració – *2km/1mi north.*
A lovely, easily accessible, sheltered creek.

Cala Salada – *5km/3mi north.*
The road descends through pines to a well sheltered beach in a cove.

Port des Torrents and Cala Bassa – *5km/3mi southwest.*
Port des Torrents is all rocks; Cala Bassa a long, pine fringed beach. In this part of the coast the rocks are smooth and separate and just above or just below the water line, providing perfect underwater swimming conditions.

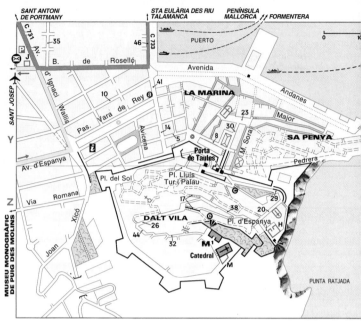

EIVISSA
IBIZA

		Comte de Rosselló	Y 14	Obispo Torres	
		Costa Vella	Z 17	Pere Francés	
		General Balanzat	Z 20	Perre Tur	
		Joan Román	Z 26	Ramón	
		Josep Verdera	Y 23	i Tur	
Aníbal	Y 5	La Corrossa	Z 29	Sant Ciríac	
Antoni Palau	Y 8	Maestro		Sta Eulàlia	
Bartomeu Vicent Ramón (Av.)	Y 10	J. Mayans	Y 30	des Riu	

Cala Vedella – *15km/9mi south.*

A road skirts the shoreline through pine trees between the beaches of Cala Ta⋯ (rather built-up), Es Molí (unspoiled) and Cala Vedella in its enclosed creek. You can return to Sant Antoni along a mountain road cut into the cliffs as fa⋯ Sant Josep.

SANTA EULÀRIA DES RIU/SANTA EULALIA DEL RÍO

Population 15 545

Santa Eulària des Riu, standing in a fertile plain watered by Ibiza's only river, grown into a large seaside resort with modern buildings. Beaches in the vicin⋯ like that at **Es Canar**, have also been developed.

★ **Puig de Missa** – *Bear right off the Eivissa – Ibiza road 50m/55yd after the pe⋯ station (on the left).* The minute, fortified town crowning the hilltop ⋯ remarkable conspectus of the island's traditional peasant architecture; the t⋯ is a surviving example, in fact, of those easily defended hills, where, in cas⋯ danger, the church (16C) served as a refuge.

Excursion

★ **Portinatx** – *27km/17mi north on PM 810, PM 811 and C 733.*

The road passes through **Sant Carles** which has a fine church and is a departure p⋯ for quiet local beaches. It then descends to the vast **Sant Vicent** creek *(cala)* ⋯ a beautiful sandy beach and opposite, the Isla de Togomago, before crossing ⋯ almost mountainous landscape covered in pines. The last section of the appro⋯ road is picturesque as it threads its way between holm oaks and almond tr⋯ looking down on **Cala Xarraca**. Creeks sheltered by narrow cliffs with pine tr⋯ fringing the sandy beaches, make **Cala de Portinatx** one of the island's m⋯ attractive areas.

Help us in our constant task of keeping up-to-date.
Send us your comments and suggestions to

Michelin Tyre PLC
38 Clarendon Road – WATFORD Herts WD1 1SX
Tel: (01923) 415000/ANG

Web site: www.michelin-travel.com

FORMENTERA

Area 115km²/44sq mi – Population 4 760

Michelin map 443 P 34, Q 34

mentera, the Wheat Island of the Romans (*frumentum*: wheat in Latin) lies barely n/3.5 nautical miles south of Ibiza, the sea between them being dotted with small ts. It is the fourth largest of the Islas Baleares with an overall west to east length 14km/9mi although it is in fact really two islets joined by a sandy isthmus. The pital" Sant Francesc de Formentera, the passenger port, Cala Savina, the t-pans, Cabo de Barbaria and the dry open expanse on which cereals, figs, almonds a few vines are grown, are on the western islet; the island's 192m/630ft high ountain", its slopes covered in dwarf pines, rises from the **Mola** promontory on the tern islet. Rock cliffs and sand dunes alternately line the shore.

mentera's inhabitants arrived comparatively recently, the island having been ndoned in the Middle Ages in the face of marauding Barbary pirates and only opulated at the end of the 17C. Most of the present population are fishermen and sant farmers, shipping figs and fish to Ibiza and salt to Barcelona.

The beaches (Playas or Platjas) – The white sandy beaches with their clear water are the island's main attraction. Long beaches stretch along either side of the isthmus, the rocky Tramuntana to the north and the sheltered, sandy Migjorn to the south. Other, smaller beaches around the island include Es Pujòls (the most developed), Illetas and Cala Saona.

Cala Savina – Your landing point on the island is in the main harbour: a few white houses stand between two big lagoons, salt-marshes glisten in the distance on the left.

Sant Francesc (San Francisco Javier) – Chief and only town on the island. Its houses are clustered around the 18C church-fortress.

El Pilar de la Mola – The hamlet at the centre of the Mola promontory has this geometrically designed church which is similar to those on Ibiza, only smaller.

Faro de la Mola – The lighthouse overlooks an impressive cliff. There is a monument to Jules Verne who mentioned this spot in one of his books.

Canary Islands★★★

The Canary Islands lie slightly north of the Tropic of Cancer – average lati**
28ºC/82ºF – in the Atlantic, 10 times nearer to the coast of Africa (115km/7C
than to Spain to which they belong (1 150km/700mi). The total surface area of
seven islands together with six smaller islets is 7 273 km²/2 808sq mi (compare **
Madrid province: 7 995 km²/3 086sq mi); the population numbers over 1 600 0
The archipelago is divided into two provinces : the eastern, called **Las Palmas**, cons
of Gran Canaria, Fuerteventura and Lanzarote; the western, called **Santa Cru**
Tenerife, consists of Tenerife, La Palma, La Gomera and El Hierro. The Canary Isla
are one of Spain's autonomous communities, in which Santa Cruz de Tenerife
Las Palmas de Gran Canaria share the status of capital. Each island has its own l
council (Cabildo Insular), which, in reality, acts as its own governing body.

The Conquest... – The islands are alluded to in Greek literature, referred to n
exactly by Plutarch and described in some detail by Pliny the Elder who called t**
the Isles of the Blest or the Fortunate Islands. Many explorers landed in
archipelago but none stayed, not even **Lancelloti Malocello** from Genoa, altho
Lanzarote took its name from him. The first expedition worthy of the name
made in 1402. The native population put up a fierce resistance and after several y**
of effort, **Jean de Bethencourt** and **Gadifer de la Salle** had subdued only four isla**
Lanzarote, Fuerteventura and, to a lesser degree, La Gomera and El Hierro.
archipelago finally came under the control of Spain at the end of the century with
conquest of Gran Canaria by **Pedro de Vera** in 1483, of La Palma in 1492 and Tene
in 1496 by **Alonso Fernández de Lugo**.
The origin of the name "Canaries" remains obscure, although some think it is der
from the Latin *canis* (dog), alluding to the very large dogs to be found on the isla**

... and the Guanches – When they arrived in the islands in 15C the explorers fo
that the native population was still living in the Stone Age. The **Guanches** (the na
of the inhabitants of Tenerife was extended to the rest of the archipelago) grew cr
and kept cattle. They lived in caves in the volcanic rock, wore goats' skins and
meal **(gofio)**, made from grilled cereals, and cheese made from goats' or sheep's n

Parque Nacional del Teide

ir utensils were rudimentary. Only the way in which they buried their dead, almost
ays mummified and sewn up in goat skins, showed any sign of sophistication.
le is known about the origins of these people. From a study of their dead they
ear to have belonged to the Cro-Magnon type of man; certain traits are typical
the Berbers of North Africa. No explanation has been found for the presence
ong them of fair-skinned, blond people. Conquest and more particularly natural
sters (plague, famine and volcanic eruptions) have left few survivors.

canic creation – The islands were thrust up from the Atlantic seabed by volcanic
ptions well before the Tertiary Era. La Gomera and Gran Canaria have the typical
ic silhouette and most of the islands, except for Fuerteventura and Lanzarote, are
y hilly and end in steep cliffs on the coast. The height of the Pico del Teide, at
18m/12 195ft the highest point in the archipelago and indeed in all Spain, slightly
eeds the average depth of the sea round the islands, 3 000m/16 640 fathoms.
pite its small area, La Palma reaches a height of 2 426m/7 959ft. Erosion and
cessive eruptions (the most recent was on La Palma in October 1971) have altered
islands' configuration; lava streams (of the Hawaian type), slag deserts (of the
omboli type) and fields and cones of cinder (of the Vulcanian type) form what is
wn locally as the **malpaís** which is most extensive on Lanzarote.

Fortunate Islands – Every year over 10 million tourists visit the islands to enjoy
ir wonderful climate and magnificent scenery. Although the Canary Islands are
ated in a sub-tropical zone, they enjoy a mild climate because of two characteri-
s: the persistence of trade winds and the presence of a cold current watering their
res. Without their influence, the Islands would be far hotter and far drier. While
Teide is snow-capped for several months in the year, the coasts bask in a very
asant climate; the average temperature rarely drops below 18°C/65°F.

Getting to the Canary Islands

By plane – All the islands except La Gomera have an airport (Tenerife has two),
offering easy, rapid access to the Spanish mainland and the rest of Europe,
which is where most of the tourists to the islands come from. Naturally, there
are also many air routes linking the various islands. The two airports with the
greatest number of regular flights are Tenerife and Gran Canaria, whereas the
airport at El Hierro schedules flights between the different islands.
Iberia ☎ 902 400 500.
Binter Canarias: Inter-island flights only. Contact Iberia for information and
reservations.
Spanair ☎ 902 13 14 15 (flights to Gran Canaria, Tenerife and Lanzarote).
Air Europa ☎ 902 40 14 01 (flights to Gran Canaria, Tenerife and Lanzarote).

By ferry – For those intending to visit the Canary Islands from mainland
Spain, there is a two-day boat trip leaving from Cádiz and travelling to Santa
Cruz de Tenerife and Las Palmas de Gran Canaria. There are also ferry, jet-foil
and hydrofoil services to travel from one island to the other.
Trasmediterránea ☎ 902 45 46 45. Internet:http:// www.trasmediterranea.es

The time – Clock times on the Canary Islands are the same as Greenwich Mean
Time (so one hour behind mainland Spain).

Accommodation – Consult the current **Michelin Red Guide España & Portugal**.
Visitors must bear in mind that on these islands the high season runs from
1 November to 30 April. During this period tourists come here to enjoy the
wonderful climate and forget their cold, continental winters and springs. The
more touristy areas feature big hotels belonging to well-known hotel chains.
It has become difficult for people to book rooms independently, as most of the
hotels cater to clients on package tours sent by travel agents. On the two larger
islands, the south coast boasts particularly pretty beaches and a very sunny
climate. La Palma, El Hierro and La Gomera are perfect resorts for those
seeking a quiet, secluded spot.

Local cuisine – Canary Island gastronomy is renowned for its *papas arrugadas*
(literally wrinkled potatoes: tiny potatoes cooked in their skins in a small
amount of heavily salted water so that a salt crust is formed around the
potatoes as the water evaporates) and for its sauces made with olive oil, *mojos
verdes* (flavoured with coriander) or *mojos rojos* (flavoured with paprika). Fish
is also a popular dish and is caught locally – *sama*, sea bass, grouper, *vieja* –
and cooked in a variety of manners (on one side, in a stew, with cooking salt
etc). Two traditional dishes are *potaje* (a vegetable stew) and *sancocho* (stewed
grouper with bananas, potatoes and a spicy sauce). The islands are also
renowned for the variety and quality of their fruit: besides the tasty banana,
try their delicious papayas, guavas and mangoes.

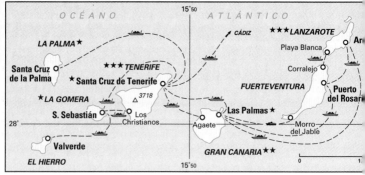

The temperature rises closer to Africa but does not exceed 30°C/86°F thanks to
cold Canary current. Rain is practically unknown in the archipelago; the eas'
islands sometimes experience whole years of drought.

The vegetation on the main islands and on the south side of the smaller islands, w
is protected from the wind (sotavento), consists mainly of xerophils, plants adap
to dry conditions: cactus (cardón) and **nopal** (tunera), a type of Barbary fig whic
attractive to the cochineal fly from which a popular red dye is extracted. On the
north coasts, however, which are exposed to the northeast trade winds (barlover.
the humidity in the atmosphere sustains a luxuriant vegetation (laurel and g
ericas). The volcanic soil is rich in natural minerals and very fertile. Irrigation ena
a great variety of plants to be grown. Water draining from the mountain peak
stored in huge cisterns. Banana plantations now cover the lowland in the nort
Gran Canaria and Tenerife while tomatoes are cultivated in the south. In the eas
islands peasant ingenuity makes up for the absence of surface water.

The only species of the original flora to survive is the age-old **dragon tree** (dracae
of which there are many fine specimens on the islands. The tree sap was used
medicinal purposes by the Guanches.

Barely thirty or forty years ago, the economy of the Canary Islands was pred
nantly agricultural, specializing in export crops (bananas, oranges, tomatoes
tobacco), but today only 8% of the population live off farming. In fact, the isla
main source of income is tourism. The expansion of this area of activity has brou
about an increase in the services sector, which employs 60% of the worl
population.

TENERIFE★★★

Area 2 053km²/792sq mi – Population 685 583
Michelin map 222

Tenerife, the largest of the Canary Islands, takes its name from the Guanche w
meaning snow-capped mountain. Indeed the dominant feature of the island with
long mountain spine is a gigantic volcanic cone 3 718m/12 195ft high, the Pico
Teide. Past volcanic activity is everywhere apparent on Tenerife, one of the m
spectacular examples being the Cañadas crater which rings El Teide. As in C
Canaria, the south is arid, the north lush with banana trees. Although steep cliffs e
the shore, the major resort of Puerto de la Cruz is at the island's north end, toge'
with one of the finest landscapes in the Canaries – the sea of Orotava ban
plantation rippling below the great snow-capped El Teide.

LA LAGUNA Population 117 718

La Laguna, once the island's capital and now home to its university, was foun
by Lugo in 1496 on the edge of a lagoon which has since disappeared. The orig
quadrilateral plan is still evident. On the feast of Corpus Christi the streets
carpeted with flowers; on 14 September the Crucifix from San Frans
monastery, dedicated to the town's patron, is venerated in a massive proces:
and general festivities which include Canary Island wrestling, a sport which g
back to Guanche times.

Plaza del Adelantado – This pleasant, tree-lined square is the heart of La Lagu
It is fronted by several interesting buildings: the old **Convent of Santa Catalina**, wl
has retained its original upper gallery, a local feature rarely seen nowadays
once common enough in the islands; the 17C **Palacio de Nava** with its stone faç.
reminiscent in style of the bishop's palace, and the town hall or **Ayuntamient**
with its neo-Classical façade (entrance for visits on calle Obispo Rey Redondo).

latter is in fact a combination of several buildings. The 16C and 18C portals on the Calle Obispo Rey Redondo, a street lined with some delightful houses, are particularly impressive.

Follow the calle Obispo Rey Redondo.

Catedral ⊘ – The elegant neo-Classical façade was erected in 1819 but the nave and four aisles were rebuilt in neo-Gothic style in 1905. Of particular note is the retable in the Capilla de los Remedios *(right transept)*, which also contains a 16C Virgin and 17C Flemish panels. The treasury houses rich liturgical objects.

Iglesia de la Concepción ⊘ – The 17C grey stone tower stands over this church, built at the beginning of the 16C, but with later modifications. It is typical of the sanctuaries built at the time of the conquest. In contrast to the sober style of the architecture, the interior has retained several Mudéjar ceilings, a ceiling with Portuguese influence, a Baroque pulpit and choir stalls, and a beaten silver altar *(Capilla del Santísimo).*

Take calle Belén, then head down calle San Agustin.

Palacio Episcopal or Antigua Casa de Salazar – The bishop's palace, also known as the House of Salazar, has a beautiful stone façade dating from the 17C and an attractive flower-decked patio.

Museo de Historia de Tenerife ⊘ – The late-16C **Casa Lercano**, with its fine patio, is home to this interesting museum. Its exhibits provide an overview of the island's social, economic, religious and institutional history from the 15C to the present day.

Santuario del Cristo ⊘ – *At the end of calle Nava Grimón*. The church contains a much venerated 15C Crucifix at the centre of a typical beaten silver altarpiece.

Monte de Las Mercedes *Round tour of 49km/30mi – allow 3hr*

The mountainous Anaga headland is high enough to trap the clouds from the north so that the area is sufficiently humid for woodlands of tree laurel, giant heather and fayas, a local species, to flourish. The winding roads which carve their way through this part of the island offer some superb views.

Mirador de Cruz del Carmen ⊘ – A good view of La Laguna Valley can be enjoyed from this viewpoint which is situated inside the Parque Rural de Anaga. The Visitors' Centre has an interesting exhibition on the park.

Mirador del Pico del Inglés – An impressive panorama spreads out form the 1 024m/3 360ft peak of the Anaga headland to the distant Pico del Teide.

El Bailadero – The road crossing this pass commands good views in both directions.

Taganana – On the way downhill there are magnificent **views**★★ of the village's picturesque setting between two ravines. It is worth visiting the **Iglesia parroquial de Nuestra Señora de Las Nieves** ⊘ for its Hispano-Flemish altarpiece.

Almáciga – View of the coast and the Anage headland from the hermitage.

San Andrés – Small fishing village; nearby is the golden sand beach of Las Teresitas.

PICO DEL TEIDE

This volcanic peak, which is snow-capped for much of the year giving it an other-worldly atmosphere, towers to 3 718m/12 195ft above sea level, making it the highest summit on Spanish territory. In the foreground to the west is the secondary crater of Pico Viego, otherwise known as Montaña Chahorra, while to the southeast stretches the **Cañadas**★★★ plateau at the foot of El Teide.

There are four routes up to the top of El Teide, of varying degrees of interest and quality of road. Perhaps the least interesting is that from **Guía de Isora**, along a wide road through stands of pine trees across the lava streams of Pico Viejo. The other three routes are a lot prettier.

La Esperanza Approach – The road climbs to the crest which divides the island into two, looking down on the north and south coasts alternately.

Pinar de la Esperanza – The road runs for several miles through this extensive pinewood.

In the centre of the clearing, at a place known as **Las Raíces**, an obelisk commemorates the alliance of the local military chiefs in July 1936 under General Franco, then Captain-General of the Canary Islands, against the Spanish Republican Government. (Franco was posted to the Canaries in February 1936 after the triumph of the Popular Front.)

Belvederes – The road is punctuated by a series of belvederes (Montaña Grande, Pico de las Flores, Ortuño, Chipeque). When the mass of cloud which frequently surrounds El Teide disperses, admire the stark contrast between the lushness of the north coast and the aridity of the Güimar Valley to the south.

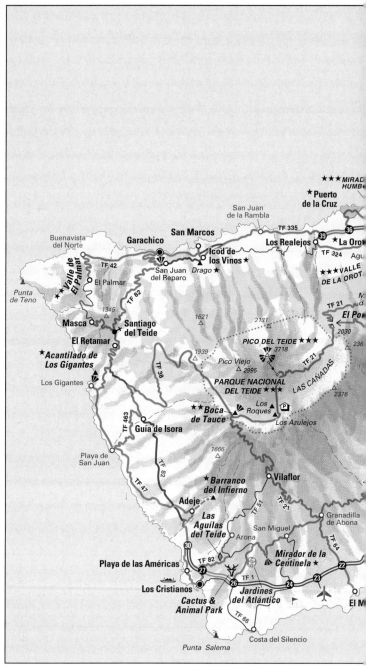

After La Crucita, the road enters into a high-mountain landscape. The Astro‐
mical Observatory at Izaña is visible to the left.

El Portillo – *Alt 2 030m/6 660ft*. The pass, which joins up here with the TF 21 r‐
from La Orotava, is the gateway to the mineralogically extraordinary world of
Cañadas.

★★★ **Parque Nacional del Teide** ⊘ – *At the entrance to the park is the El Portillo vis‐
centre which contains an informative exhibition on volcanism, as well
information on the network of local paths; the Cañada Blanca centre is loca‐
next to the parador. About 350m/1 150ft below the summit of El Teide
Las Cañadas plateau, a spectacular volcanic crater at an altitude of o
2 000m/6 560ft which had fallen in on itself before El Teide was created.*

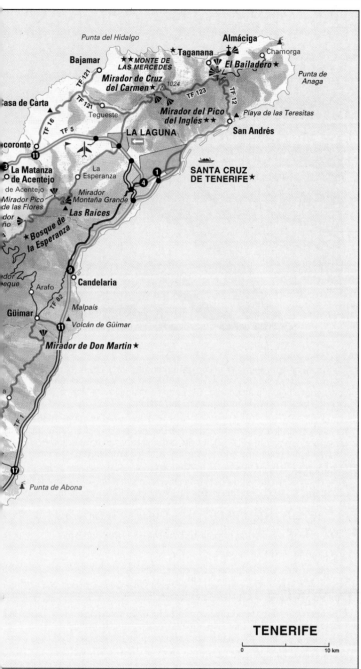

Pico del Teide rises up from its northern side. In the centre of the park, opposite the hotel (parador), are a few boulders of lava **(Los Roques)**, laid bare by erosion. Other rocks **(Los Azulejos)** are covered with copper oxide which glints blue-green in the sun.

Pico de Teide – *Ascent by cable-car from La Rambleta (2 356m/7 728ft): not suitable for those with respiratory or heart problems (the cable-car climbs 1 199m/3 932ft in 8min).* From the top (3 555m/11 660ft), a steep 30min walk across loose volcanic scree leads to the summit *(the path to the summit is currently closed).* The top of the cone is occupied by a crater, almost 25m/82ft deep and 50m/164ft in diameter, swathed in wisps of sulphurous smoke. On a clear day, the view covers the whole of the Canaries archipelago.

El Teide

★ **La Orotava Approach** - The vegetation on the north coast (bananas, fruit tr corn, potatoes and vines) is clearly visible during the climb. The exter pinewoods begin in **Aguamansa**. Beyond the village at the side of the road the a huge basalt daisy, a natural rock formation.

Guía Approach - The climb via Guía is more mountainous. The narrow crosses two Pico Viejo defiles, Las Narices del Teide (last eruption in 1798) the Chinyero volcano (1909). As the last volcanoes to have erupted, the con between the pinewood and the defiles is more pronounced.

Vilaflor Approach - **Vilaflor** is the highest town on the island (1 466m/4 8C The road passes through a beautiful pinewood and then, at the **Boca de Tauce pa** (2 055m/6 742ft), reveals a striking view of Las Cañadas dominated by El T

TOUR OF THE ISLAND *310km/194mi - about 3 days*

The North Coast *La Laguna to Garachico - 100km/62mi*

La Laguna - *See La Laguna.*

Bajamar - Large resort on a picturesque stretch of rocky coast with natural p

Casa de Carta - The property is a typical Canary Island farm. An 18C bui houses the **Museo de Antropología de Tenerife** ⊙.

Tacoronte - Here the lordly summit of El Teide comes into view. In the **Igle** **Santa Catalina** ⊙ there is a fine Mudéjar roof in the chancel.

Tacoronte is home to a handsome specimen of the dragon tree.

La Matanza de Acentejo - Here in 1495 Lugo and his troops were soundly be by the Guanches; soon afterwards, however, Lugo got his revenge at La Vic de Acentejo.

★★★ **Mirador de Humboldt** - The lookout point is named after the German natur Alexander Humboldt, who visited Tenerife in 1799 and was especially struc the **Orotava Valley**★★★. This immense depression at the foot of El Teide exten the way to the sea, covered by a dense green carpet of banana trees broken by gleaming water and the buildings of La Orotava town and Puerto de la C

★ **La Orotava** - *See La Orotava.*

★ **Puerto de la Cruz** - *See Puerto de la Cruz.*

Los Realejos - From the town hall terrace of the upper village, there is a vie the villages along the coast; the nearby **Iglesia de Santiago Apóstol** ⊙ has intere vaulting. There is a dragon tree growing in the cemetery, which is perched tall rock spike.

Icod de los Vinos – The town of Icod, which dates from the conquest (15C), is at the centre of a wine-producing area (*vinos* means wines). It boasts a **dragon tree**★ which is several thousand years old, the oldest and the most imposing in the Canary Islands (*signposted once you enter the town*). The **Iglesia de San Marcos** is as interesting as the nearby landscaped square which is surrounded by elegant houses with wooden balconies.

San Marcos – The road runs through banana plantations to reach this seaside resort which is sited in a rocky creek and backed by jagged black cliffs.

Garachico – Before the volcanic eruption in 1716 Garachico was an important town on the north coast. Little remains: a cluster of old houses and a fortress, the **Castillo de San Miguel**. A promenade has been built on the rough pointed rocks.

Valle de El Palmar – Take TF 42 to the west of Garachico. Just beyond the El Palmar Valley, there is a tiny village built on a volcanic chimney in the centre of a crater which is neatly terraced for cultivation.

The West Coast *Garachico to Los Cristianos – 77km/48mi*

Garachico – *See above.*

Drive south to **San Juan del Reparo** for a good **view**★ of Garachico.

Santiago del Teide – Picturesque domed church.

Masca – Very dangerous road in poor state of repair. Remote but charming hamlet set in delightful **countryside**.

El Retamar – South of the village the road begins a long descent through lava fields produced by the eruption of the Chinyero volcano in 1909.

Acantilado de Los Gigantes – The Teno mountain range ends here in enormous black cliffs which are rightly called Los Gigantes, the giants, because of their 400m/1 300ft vertical drop.

Adeje – Within walking distance of the village (*2km/1mi east*) lies the grandiose beauty of Hell Valley, **Barranco del Infierno**★, an enormous open crevice with a small water course running through it.

Playa de las Américas – Hotel Jardín Tropical

Playa de las Américas – A large resort with beaches of black sand and a multitude of hotels, apartments, restaurants, bars, nightclubs etc.

Los Cristianos – Once a fishing village, it is now one of the island's largest and busiest resorts. The Playa de las Vistas, in the centre of Los Cristianos, is one of its best beaches, with an attractive promenade running along it.

The South Coast *Los Cristianos to Santa Cruz – 133km/83mi*

Los Cristianos – *See above.*

Parque Ecológico de Las Águilas del Teide ⊙ – *3km/2mi on the Los Cristianos-Arona road*. This wildlife park has a large number of exotic birds and other animals on display across 75 000m²/89 700sq yd of lush gardens. The park also organizes parrot shows and birds of prey demonstrations.

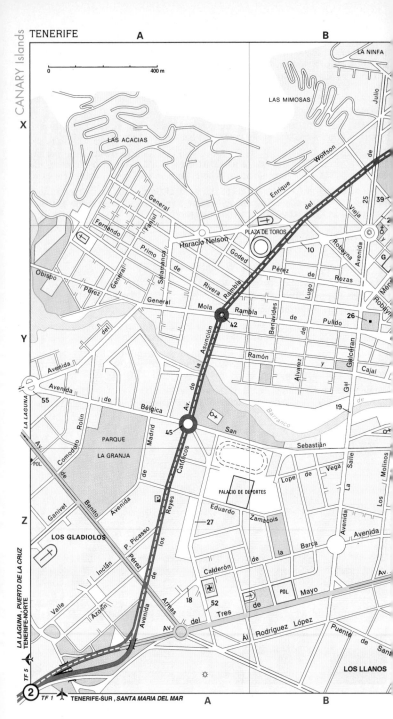

Cactus & Animal Park ☉ – *Motorway exit 26 (Guaza), then take the signpos[t] road to the left.* These cactus gardens are laid out in a desert-like setting. The p[ark] also contains a small animal area and an interesting reptilarium.

Jardines del Atlántico ☉ – *4km/2.5mi on the Guaza-Valle de San Lorenzo ro[ad]; the turn-off is indicated to the right.* A stroll through this estate provides visit[ors] with an introduction to the indigenous flora and traditional crops on the isla[nd] (bananas, tomatoes, papayas, avocados etc). The gardens also display[a] collection of agricultural and domestic tools.

Follow TF 82 in the Valle de San Lorenzo. Although longer and more winding th[an] the motorway, the inland road (TF 82) is more beautiful and punctuated by ma[ny] fine views.

SANTA CRUZ DE TENERIFE

Alférez Provisional (Plaza) . . .	**CY** 3
Bethencourt Alfonso	**CY** 5
Bravo Murillo (Av. de)	**DY** 6
Candelaria (Pl. de la)	**DY** 8
Castillo	**CY**
Costa y Grijalba	**BY** 10
Doctor Guigou	**CX** 12
Doctor José Naveiras	**CX** 13
Domínguez Alfonso	**CY** 15
Fragata Danmark	**AZ** 18
General Galcerán (Puente)	**BY** 19
General Gutiérrez	**DY** 20
General O'Donnell	**BX** 23
General Serrador (Puente)	**CY** 24
General Weyler (Pl. del)	**BY** 26
Heliodoro Rodríguez López . .	**AZ** 27
Iglesia (Pl. de la)	**DY** 30
Imeldo Serís	**CY** 31
José Murphy	**CY** 34
Numancia	**BX** 39
Paz (Pl. de la)	**AY** 42
Pérez Galdós	**CY** 43
República Dominicana (Pl.) . .	**AY** 45
Saludo	**DX** 46
San Francisco (Pl.)	**DY** 49
San Isidro	**DX** 50
Santo Domingo (Pl.)	**CY** 51
Tomé Cano	**AZ** 52
Valentín Sanz	**CY** 53
29 de Mayo (Pl. del)	**AY** 55

★ Mirador de la Centinela – Like a sentinel, the viewpoint is positioned on a rocky projection commanding a vast area of the plain pitted with craters.

El Médano – *Take TF 614.* The beach, one of the best on the island for windsurfing, lies in the shelter of an eroded volcanic cone and is bordered by an attractive promenade.

Return to the inland road.

★ Mirador de Don Martín – The belvedere provides a view of the Güimar rift valley, the slopes of which are mainly covered in tropical fruit plantations. Between the town and the sea stands the imposing Güimar volcano.

Güimar – A major town on the south coast.

Candelaria – This coastal town is a well-known place of pilgrimage. In 1390 t Guanche shepherds found a statue of the Virgin Mary washed up on the bea It was set up in a cave but in 1826 a storm swept it away. A **basílica** ⊘ (19! houses the new statue of the patron and the archipelago to which islanders m; a pilgrimage on 14 and 15 August. In the square outside are nine statues of Menceyes, the ancient Guanche chiefs of Tenerife.

★ SANTA CRUZ DE TENERIFE Population 202 674

The capital of the island began life as a small port serving La Laguna, develo; further in the 19C and has since become the island's maritime and indust centre. It is a port of call for ocean liners and cargo vessels, a role it shares w Las Palmas. An oil refinery, tobacco factory and other industrial plants contrib to the local economy.

From the harbour breakwater there is an interesting **view**★ of the town: a stepp semicircle of high-rise buildings against the backdrop of the Pico del Teide and Anage massif.

The Guimera theatre, new auditorium (under construction) and exhibit buildings bear witness to the city's cultural interests and tradition.

This quiet, peaceful town takes on quite a lively, even frenzied appearance during **Carnival**. That of Santa Cruz de Tenerife is probably the most famous and colourful in all of Spain. The whole city takes part in this hugely popular celebration. Children and grown-ups alike dress up and join the mounted procession that involves many groups of performers and onlookers.

Queen of the Santa Cruz Carnival

Iglesia de la Concepción ⊘ **(DY)** – The few houses with balconies built around the 16C-18C church are all that remains of the old city. The most impressive features of the church's exterior are the high tower and balconies; its interior contains some fine Baroque retables.

★ **Museo de la Naturaleza y el Hombre** (Museum of Nature and Man) ⊘ **(CY)** – This interesting museum is housed in the former Hospital Civil, a large neo-Classical building. Its exhib include well-presented collections from the fields of archeology and natu science.

Palacio de Carta (CY) – This 18C palace is situated on the Plaza de la Candelar close to the monumental Plaza de España. Although it has now been convert into the headquarters of a bank, it retains its delightful patio with wooden arch and galleries.

Iglesia de San Francisco ⊘ **(CDY)** – The church was built in the 17C and 18C a displays the typical characteristics of Canary Island churches from this peric naves with wooden roofs and cylindrical pillars. The chancel contains a Baroq retable.

★ **Parque Municipal García Sanabria (BCX)** – This alluring tropical and Medit ranean garden is close to La Rambia, a large landscaped boulevard and one of t city's main arteries.

Museo Militar ⊘ **(DX)** – It was when attacking the town and castle on 24 J 1797 that Nelson lost both the battle ... and his right arm. Among the cannon view is one known as the Tiger, which fired the fatal ball.

★ **Parque marítimo César Manrique** ⊘ – Leave by ② on the town plan. This lar leisure complex by the sea is a series of swimming pools and restaurants. Bas on a design by César Manrique, it successfully combines water, volcanic rock a vegetation.

PUERTO DE LA CRUZ Population 39 549

The mushroom growth of Puerto de la Cruz at the heart of the banana region on the north coast, is due not to the fishing on which it once relied but to tourism. The sun and the Pico del Teide look down on an exuberant proliferation of high-rise buildings going up side by side along the rock-strewn and reef-outlined coast. A pleasant, lively **seafront promenade★**, lined with outdoor terraces, shops and flower-hung viewpoints, and which includes the small 18C San Telmo hermitage, provides the main attraction of Tenerife's premier resort. The old part of the town (the pedestrian area between the Plaza de la Iglesia and Plaza del Charco) has preserved the typical architecture of the 17C and 18C with its balconied houses and attractive churches.

Lago Martiánez (Martiánez Lake) ⓒ – This large complex of swimming pools by the sea is surrounded by vegetation and volcanic rock. It is a fine example of the successful combination of aesthetics and leisure which characterises many of the works of its creator, the artist César Manrique.

Jardín de Aclimatación de la Orotava ⓒ – *Follow signs to Jardín Botánico.* The botanical gardens, which cover only 2ha/5 acres, contain an extraordinary profusion of all sorts of trees and flowers from the Canary Islands and elsewhere in the world. The garden was created in 18C by the Marquis of Villanueva del Prado on the orders of Carlos III. It contains a wide variety of palm trees, although its most impressive exhibit is the rubber plant, which is over 200 years old and perches on adjacent roots as if on stilts.

Playa Jardín (Garden Beach) – *To the west of the town; follow signposts.* This attractive, black sandy beach is surrounded by well-tended gardens. The **Castillo de San Felipe**, an old watchtower which is now used for cultural functions, can be seen to its eastern end.

Loro Parque ⓒ – *West of Playa Jardín; well signposted.* This sub-tropical 50 000m²/59 800sq yd garden has a comprehensive collection of parrots and animals (gorillas, monkeys, crocodiles etc), as well as a dolphinarium. Parrot and dolphin shows are regularly held for visitors.

LA OROTAVA

This ancient town, arranged in terraces at the foot of the mountain, dominates the fertile valley of the same name. It has preserved an interesting **historic centre** with fine mansions from different periods. Some of its pinewood *(tea)* balconies are some of the most beautiful in the Canary Islands.

On the Thursday after Corpus Christi, the streets are strewn with flowers and the main square is decorated with a gigantic variegated sand and pebble picture. On the second Sunday after the feast the people of the neighbouring villages meet for an excursion *(romería de San Isidro)* dressed in traditional costume and riding in bullock carts (St Isidore was a farm labourer). Their attractive costumes and colourful carts add a picturesque note to this festival, which has been declared an event of national tourist interest.

Leave your car in plaza de la Constitución and continue your visit on foot.

Plaza de la Constitución – The square, which is fronted by the 17C Baroque church of San Agustin and the Liceo Taoro cultural centre, acts as an interesting viewpoint.

Follow calle Carrera, then descend the street to the right.

Iglesia de la Concepción – The 18C church, built on the site of an earlier construction, has a graceful Baroque façade between flanking towers. The treasury is open to the public.

Return to calle Carrera.

Calle Carrera – The street passes in front of the **Plaza del Ayuntamiento**, with its neo-Classical style Palacio Municipal. The **Hijuela del Jardín Botánico** behind it, a lush park created in the 19C, used to act as a nursery for the Botanical Gardens in Puerto de la Cruz.

At no 17, a 16C residence is now home to the **Museo Etnográfico Guanche** ⓒ

Calle de San Francisco – This street is adorned with some of the town's most beautiful balconies.

La Casa de los Balcones – Despite the title, this is in fact two 17C houses (nos 3 and 5), both with magnificent balconies and delightful patios. A craftwork shop *(ground floor)* and a small **Museo** ⓒ *(first floor)* which shows the inside of a traditional bourgeois house have been created inside no 3.

La Casa Molina – Another craftwork shop has been established in this 16C-17C Renaissance-style house, which offers a fine view from its terrace.

Return to calle Carrera, then follow calle Tomás Zerolo to the left.

Museo de Artesanía Iberoamericana ⓒ – The museum is housed in the former Convento de Santo Domingo (17C). It displays a varied collection of Spanish and Latin-American handicrafts, including musical instruments, ceramics, textiles etc.

GRAN CANARIA★★

1 532km²/592sq mi – Population 715 611

Michelin map 220

The island is shaped like a limpet and rises to its highest point, the Pozo de
Nieves, at the centre. The surrounding slopes are cut by dry ravines (barranc
from which swift streams have been diverted to man-made lakes and irrigat
channels.

The island relief is more or less uniform but the contrast in climate is marked:
north is fertile, humid and the kingdom of the banana tree; the south is an arid reg
where the cultivation of tomato plants is being introduced.

The north and west coasts consist of steep cliffs; the south is fringed by wi
accessible beaches and is being rapidly developed to provide facilities
tourists.

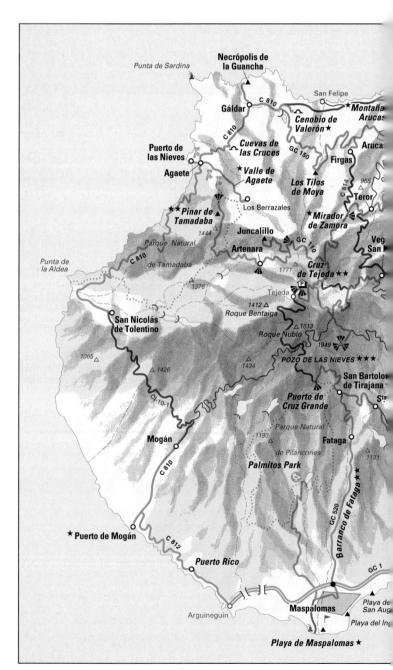

THE NORTH COAST

Las Palmas to San Nicolás de Tolentino

128km/79mi – about 1 day

Leave Las Palmas by GC 2, ④ on the plan. Take exit 8 and head towards Arucas.

Arucas – After Las Palmas and Telde, Arucas is the third largest town on the island. A narrow road leads from the north wall of the main church to the top of **Montaña de Arucas**, which is shaped like a sugar loaf, offering a vast **panorama**★ as far east as Las Palmas de Gran Canaria. At the foot of the mountain the town's black cathedral stands out against the white houses of the town.

Take C 813. At Buenlugar, 6km/4mi beyond Arucas, turn left.

GRAN CANARIA

0 ———————— 10 km

Firgas – This is the source of a sparkling mineral water which is very popular throughout the archipelago. The Paseo de Gran Canaria, next to the landscaped Plaza de San Roque, which is fronted by a church and Ayuntamiento (town hall), pays a picturesque homage to the island's local communities.

Return to the main road.

Los Tilos de Moya – The winding road runs to the side of the mountain, passing Moya 2km/1mi to the left. Los Tilos is a protected area with a wood of wild laurel trees.

At Guía, turn right to join C 810. Head toward Las Palmas for a few metres, then turn off to Cenobio de Valerón.

★ **Cenobio de Valerón** ⊘ – In a remarkable location on the edge of a ravine some caves have been hollowed out of the volcanic tufa; they are protected by a layer of basalt. Although it is thought that in the time of the Guanches the caves were a type of convent *(cenobio)* where daughters prepared for their role as Sacred Virgins, they were in fact used as a large collective granary. On the top of the mountain the chiefs met in council *(Tagoror)*.

Return to C 810 and head towards Gáldar.

Gáldar – At the foot of Mount Gáldar the Guanche king held his court *(guanarteme)*; there are a few precious traces of this mysterious civilization.

A cave **(Cueva Pintada)** ⊘ was discovered in 1881 containing some **mural paintings**★ which have not yet been interpreted. Various Guanche objects are on display.

Necrópolis de la Guancha ⊘ – *On the coast 2km/1mi north of Gáldar.*

Excavations in the archeological area have brought to light the remains of a Guanche settlement and necropolis. The burial ground consists of circular constructions built of great blocks of lava and a large burial mound.

Return to Gáldar and take C 810 south.

Cuevas de las Cruces – *Halfway between Gáldar and Agaete.* Attractive natural cave formations in the volcanic tufa.

Agaete – This charming white-walled village is situated in the heart of a fertile region. On 4 August the village celebrates the **Fiesta de la Rama**, one of the island's most popular festivals.

★ **Los Berrazales road** – *Southeast of Agaete.* The road runs parallel to the **Agaete Valley**★, which is sheltered by high mountains and covered in lush vegetation.

Puerto de las Nieves – *West of Agaete*. This little fishing harbour was also us for shipping bananas in the days when land transport to Las Palmas de G Canaria was difficult. From the quay there is a good view in front of the clifr the famous Finger of God (Dedo de Dios), a pointed rock which resembles a fing The hermitage **(ermita)** ⊘ contains some interesting 15C Flemish paintings.

San Nicolás de Tolentino – A highly spectacular road, which follows the ste cliffs along the coast and crosses several ravines, leads to San Nicolás, a villa in a fertile basin growing sugar cane and tomatoes.

THE CENTRE OF THE ISLAND

Las Palmas de Gran Canaria to Cruz de Tejeda

156km/97mi – about 1 day

Leave Las Palmas de Gran Canaria by C 811, ② on the plan

Tafira – A holiday resort favoured by the inhabitants of Las Palmas. The towr also home to the island's university.

★ **Jardín Canario** ⊘ – The tropical garden, which is arranged in terraces, make pleasant walk.

In Monte Lentiscal turn left.

★★ **Mirador de Bandama** – A road leads to the top of Bandama (569m/1 867ft). T summit provides a superb view of the enormous volcanic crater of the same nam with its eruption formations intact, inside of which can be seen a small cultivat area. The **panorama** is impressive, taking in Tafira, the Montaña de Arucas and L Palmas to the north, the crater, Las Palmas golf club (the oldest in Spain) a Telde to the south, and the island's mountainous centre to the west.

Return to C 811.

Santa Brígida – This residential settlement sits close to a ravine planted wi palm trees. An interesting plant and flower market is held at weekends.

Vega de San Mateo – The village is situated in an important agricultural area. large fruit and vegetable market is held here on Saturdays and Sundays. T **Casa-Museo Cho Zacarías** ⊘, which is housed in a series of traditional houses, two which date from the 17C, displays a comprehensive ethnographic collection whi includes pottery, furniture, textiles, traditional implements etc.

Continue along C 811 for 6km/4mi, then bear left.

★★★ **Pozo de las Nieves** – From the summit (1 949m/6 394ft), which is sometim snow-capped, there is a spectacular **panorama**★★★ of the whole island. To the sou the view stretches as far as the Playa de Maspalomas, with San Bartolomé d Tirajana in the foreground; to the west, the unusual shapes of the Roque Nub to the left and the Roque Bentayga to the right are also visible. On a clear day Mount Teide (Tenerife) stands out on the horizon.

★★ **Cruz de Tejeda** – *Northeast of Pozo de las Nieves*. Near the hotel (parador) whic has been built at the top of the pass (1 450m/4 757ft) lies the village of Tejed in a huge volcanic basin. From the chaotic landscape, which Unamuno, a Spanis writer, described as a "petrified tempest", rise two volcanic necks: Roqu Bentaiga and Roque Nublo which was thought to be an object of veneration amon the indigenous people of the Canary Islands.

Bear west to Artenara along GC 110.

The drive includes attractive **views**★ of the troglodyte village of **Juncalillo** wher most of the people live in caves formed by a lava flow.

Artenara – This small, well-kept village is the highest on the islan (1 230m/4 035ft). The enchanting **Ermita de la Cuevita**, a hermitage dug into th rock, contains a statue of the Virgin with Child. From here, the **panorama**★ of th Bentaiga and Nublo peaks, Tejeda and Pozo de las Nieves is particularl impressive. From the restaurant (Mesón de la Silla), which is housed in a cave o the edge of the village, there is an interesting **view**★ of Roque Bentaiga.

★★ **Pinar de Tamadaba** – The road passes through this magnificent wood of Canar pines which extends to the edge of a cliff which drops sheer to the sea. *After a lefthand bend, continue to the end of a tarred road, following signs to the Zona de Acampada, then park the car and walk 200m/220yd through the pin trees to the edge.* On a clear day, the **view**★★ of Agaete, Gáldar and the coast, with the Pico del Teide on the horizon, is superb.

Return by the same road and turn left onto GC 110 to Vallesseco.

★ **Mirador de Zamora** – Just north of Vallesseco there is an attractive **view**★ of Teror nestled in a wide valley surrounded by impressive mountains.

Teror – The majesty of the façade of the 18C **Iglesia de Nuestra Señora del Pino** ⊘ perfectly befits a town which has such a distinguished air and retains many fine mansions with wooden balconies. The church houses a statue of Our Lady of the Pine Tree, the island's venerated patron, who is said to have appeared in the branches of a pine tree in 1481.

The treasury contains various embroidered cloaks belonging to the statue and other rich gifts.

There is an extraordinary atmosphere at the annual pilgrimage (8 September) when thousands of islanders gather in Teror to present their gifts and join in worship.

On Sundays a lively market attracts a large crowd.

THE SOUTH COAST

Las Palmas de Gran Canaria to Maspalomas

59km/37mi – about 2hr

Leave Las Palmas de Gran Canaria by GC 1, ① on the plan, and then take exit 8 (Telde).

Telde – Like Gáldar, this city was the capital of the island's indigenous people. In the lower town stands the **Iglesia de San Juan Bautista** ⊙, a 15C church, subsequently rebuilt in the 17C and 18C, which contains a 16C Flemish retable depicting the Life of the Virgin. The figure of Christ *(above)* was made in Mexico out of reeds and a light, paper-based paste.

From the square in front of the church take calle Inés Chimida.

The road leads to the quiet **San Francisco district** which has retained its old-fashioned character with its narrow paved streets and whitewashed houses. For centuries this district has been known for its traditional craftwork.

Follow C 813 towards Ingenio. Beyond the junction with C 816 turn left, immediately after some cottages, into a rough track; the last 250m/270yd is on foot.

★ **Cuatro Puertas** – The cave, which has four openings or doors *(cuatro puertas)*, is where the council for the indigenous population of the island *(Tagoror)* used to meet. The east face of the mountain is riddled with caves where the Guanche embalmed their dead. The view over the east coast is impressive. The summit (to the east) is a sacred site.

Ingenio – Famous for its embroidery.

MASPALOMAS

The largest resorts are situated along the flat, sandy coastline to the south: **Maspalomas, Playa del Inglés** and **Playa de San Agustín**. These tourist centres are home to countless hotels, apartments, chalets, shopping centres, restaurants, night-clubs, outdoor cafés, water parks and a whole host of other leisure facilities for the huge numbers of visitors who come here to enjoy the superb beaches and wonderful climate in this part of the island.

Maspalomas has developed around its spectacular dunes and **beach★**, which are part of a 400ha/990 acre protected zone. Other attractions in this area include natural pools and a palm grove.

Dunes of Maspalomas

Palmitos Park  – *13km/8mi north.* The arid ravine contains an oasis where exotic birds from Australia and South America can be seen at liberty. The park also contains an interesting aquarium, a cactus garden and a greenhouse with myriad butterflies.

Mogán – *38km/24mi northwest.* The road (C 812) runs northwest along the steep, built-up coast, passing through **Puerto Rico**, a resort with apartment buildings clinging to the slopes of a ravine, and **Puerto de Mogán**★, a picturesque resort and fishing centre built around an attractive marina and port. The road then turns inland up a ravine *(barranco)* to Mogán.

Puerto de Mogán

★ **San Bartolomé de Tirajana** – *48km/30mi north by GC 520.*
The way up to San Bartolomé passes through the **Barranco de Fataga**★★, an impressively beautiful ravine, a sort of grandiose canyon. The road passes close to Arteara, in an oasis at the bottom of a ravine, and then through Fataga, a picturesque village surrounded by orchards, before reaching San Bartolomé which is set in a magnificent green mountain cirque at the foot of tall cliffs probably the inner walls of an old volcanic crater.

Puerto de Cruz Grande – Fine view of the mountains south of Roque Nublo.

Return to San Bartolomé and take C 815 going southeast.

Santa Lucía – The small **Museo Guanche**  displays objects excavated to the east the village in a hill which has been shaped by erosion to look like a fortress *(fortaleza)*.

LAS PALMAS DE GRAN CANARIA

Alfonso XII		AU 2
Ansite (Av.)		AT 4
Cornisa (Paseo)		AT 12
Doctor Márañón		AU 14
Don Benito (Plaza de)		AU 17
Fernando Guanarteme		AS 20
Ingeniero Léon y Castillo (Pl.)		AU 28
Juan Réjón		AS 36
Juan XXIII (Av.)		AT 37
La Naval		AS
León y Castillo		AT 40
Lugo (Paseo de)		AT 44
Luis Correa Medina		AU 46
M. González Martin		AT 49
Marítima del Sur (Av.)		AU 52
Mata (Carret. de)		AU 53
Ortiz de Zárate		AT 59
Pérez Muñoz		AS 63
Pino Apolinario		AU 65
Pío XII		AU 66
San José (Paseo)		AU 76
Secretario Padilla		AT 80
Simancas		AT 81
Tecen		AS 83
Tomás Morales (Paseo)		ATU 85
Zaragoza		AU 90

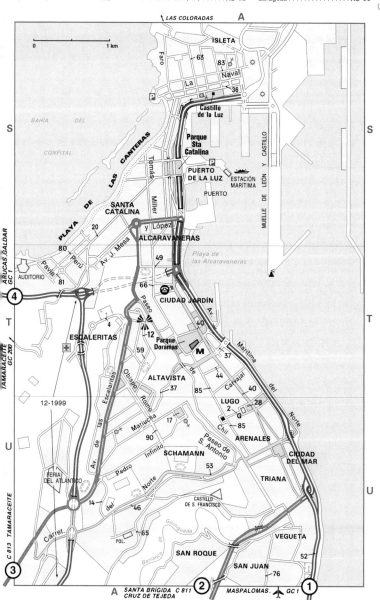

★ **LAS PALMAS DE GRAN CANARIA** Population 360 483

Las Palmas de Gran Canaria was founded in a palm grove in 1478 by Juan Rejón; it is now capital of the province of Las Palmas de Gran Canaria and is one of Spain's major ports.

The city is the largest in the archipelago, extending for nearly 10km/6mi between the Guiniguada Ravine (south) and the Isleta Peninsula (north) which forms a natural breakwater to the harbour.

Las Palmas de Gran Canaria comprises three districts: the old city, Vegueta, dates from the time of the conquest; Puerto de la Luz, the tourist district, is flanked by the harbour and Alcaravaneras beach on the east side and Canteras beach on the west; between them lies the residential garden city, Ciudad Jardín. Beyond the cliff which once formed the western limit to the city, new housing developments are proliferating.

The airport *(25km/16mi)* and Las Palmas harbour are on the air and sea route between Europe and South America and bring the island many visitors.

Christopher Columbus – It is often maintained that, but for the Canary Islands, Columbus (1451-1506) would never have reached America. His persistence in trying to convince the sovereigns of Portugal, England, France and Castile of the existence of a westerly passage to Asia is well known. Eventually their Catholic Majesties of Castile provided him with three ships – the *Niña*, the *Pinta* and the *Santa María* – for an expedition to the Indies.

He set sail westwards from Palos in August 1492 but was forced to put into Las Palmas and La Gomera for repairs to the *Pinta*. On 12 October 1492 he spied land and set foot for the first time on the American continent – on the Antilles Island of San Salvador.

On each of his three subsequent voyages he landed at Las Palmas or on La Gomera before going on to discover the other islands of the Antilles (1493), the Orinoco delta (1498) and the shores of Honduras (1502).

★ Vegueta – Triana *2hr*

These two districts form the historic centre of Las Palmas. It was only from the 19C onwards that the city began to extend beyond these areas with the development of Puerto de La Luz.

Plaza de Santa Ana – The pleasant palm-bordered square is overlooked by the fine façade of the town hall (1842) on one side, and by the cathedral on the other. The bronze dogs recall the possible derivation of the name of the archipelago *(see p 430)*. To the side are the Bishop's Palace (Palacio Episcopal), with an *alfiz*-decorated portal showing clear Mudéjar influence, and the Renaissance-style Casa del Regente. During the Corpus Christi procession, the square and adjacent streets are carpeted with flowers, sawdust and salt.

Catedral ⊘ – The cathedral was begun at the beginning of the 16C but not completed until the 19C. The façade is strictly neo-Classical; the interior, however, is more Gothic. It has three elegant aisles with tierceron vaulting and several side chapels. In the transept are statues by the Canary Island sculptor, José Luján Pérez (1756-1815): St Joseph and the *Mater Dolorosa (right)* and the Virgin and Child *(left)*.

Museo Diocesano de Arte Sacro ⊘ **(M')** – *Entrance in calle Espíritu Santo.* The museum, which is dedicated to sacred art, is housed in cathedral buildings around the 16C Patio de los Naranjos. It contains a collection of 16C-19C engravings and pieces of gold and silverwork. The chapter-house contains a mosaic from Manises (Valencia).

★ **Casa de Colón** ⊘ – *Entrance in calle Colón.* The palace of the island's first governors, where Columbus himself stayed in 1502, now houses a museum in a typical Canary Island setting: maps and navigational instruments evoke Columbus' expeditions. Note the fine *artesonado* ceilings. The upper floor contains a collection of 16C-19C paintings.

Casa de Colón

VEGUETA, TRIANA

Balcones (de los)	CZ 5	Las Palmas (Muelle de)	CY 38	San Antonio (Paseo)	BY 73
Cano	CY 8	López Botas	CZ 41	San Pedro	CZ 78
Doctor Chil	CZ 13	Luis Millares	CZ 47	T. Massieu	CZ 84
Domingo J. Navarro	BY 16	Malteses	CZ 50	Viera y Clavijo	BY 88
General Bravo	BY 23	Mayor de Triana	CY		
General Mola	CZ 24	Ntra Sra del Pino (Pl.)	BY 56		
Juan de Quesada	CZ 31	Obispo Codina	CZ 57		
Juan E. Doreste	CZ 33	Pelota	CZ 60		
		Pérez Galdós	BY 62		
		Ramón y Cajal	BZ 69		

E   Centro Atlántico de Arte Moderno (CAAM)
M¹   Museo Diocesano de Arte Sacro

Nearby is the **Iglesia de San Antonio Abad** ⓥ on the site of the chapel in which Columbus attended Mass. The present church has an elegant Baroque interior.

Centro Atlántico de Arte Moderno ⓥ **(E)** – The **Calle de los Balcones (CZ 5)** has preserved several 18C buildings with fine doorways. The centre is housed in one of these and has been completely converted by the architect Sáenz de Oíza. It was originally founded with the aim of fostering cooperation between Europe, Africa and America and providing strong links between these three continents. It hosts interesting temporary exhibitions. Its collections present works by 20C artists from the Canary Islands, the Spanish mainland and abroad. The centre will soon be extended to an annexe.

★ Museo Canario ⓥ – The isolation of the Canary Islands prolonged their prehistory until the end of the Middle Ages. This interesting museum displays a collection of anthropological and archeological artefacts from the islands' prehispanic culture, including mummies, idols, skins, ceramics etc. Particularly interesting is the collection of terracotta seals *(pintaderas)* found only on Gran Canaria, whose purpose remains a mystery (were they for body paint, branding or sealing harvests?), and a recreation of the cave, Cueva Pintada, in Gáldar.

Two squares – **Plaza del Espíritu Santo** and Plaza de Santo Domingo – are worth visiting for their picturesque charm.

Casa-Museo Pérez Galdós ⓥ **(CY)** – Manuscripts, photographs, drawings and personal objects belonging to the writer, Pérez Galdós (1843-1920), are displayed in the house where he was born.

> ### Puerto de la Luz
>
> The port of Las Palmas de Gran Canaria is the engine behind the city's development and is one of the largest in Spain. Its privileged position on the transatlantic routes between Europe, Africa and America has resulted in the development of an international port with a high volume of passenger and goods traffic. It is also one of the largest fishing ports in the region, given its proximity to the rich fishing grounds off the African coast, and the leading distribution centre for goods in the Canary Islands. The port area also includes a large naval repair centre which is able to offer a full range of services to vessels calling into the port.

Parque de San Telmo (CY) – The street starting in the southwest corner of th pleasant park, Calle Mayor de Triana, is the bustling main shopping street in th old town. The interior of the small **Iglesia de San Bernardo** ⊘ is full of character wi its Baroque altars and paintings on the walls of the east end. An unusual Moderni kiosk stands in another corner of the park.

The Modern Town 2hr

Drive along Avenida Marítima del Norte. The road skirts the town on lar reclaimed from the sea.

Parque Doramas (AT) – This large central park encloses the Santa Catalina Hot with its casino, and the **Pueblo Canario** ⊘ (**M**), a Canary Island village created by th painter Néstor de la Torre (1888-1938). The complex includes several craftwor shops and the **Museo Néstor** ⊘.
Folk festivals are held in the village.

Parque Santa Catalina (AS) – The park is at the centre of the tourist district in Puer de la Luz and the neighbouring streets are lined with restaurants, bars and nightclul thronged with tourists. Equally numerous are the Indian bazaars selling all sorts Asian goods, and particularly cameras, radios, tapes and videos at low pric because the port of Las Palmas enjoys privileged customs regulations.

★ **Playa de las Canteras** – This superb broad curving beach slopes gently into th water; it is sheltered from rough seas by a line of rocks offshore and backed b a pleasant 3.5km/2mi promenade with a multitude of popular restaurants ar outdoor cafés.
At its southeastern end stands the **Auditorio Alfredo Kraus**, a building designed b Oscar Tusquets. The auditorium, which was opened in 1998, hosts an ope season and other major concerts.

Castillo de la Luz ⊘ (AS) – The fort, which was built at the end of the 15C protect the town against pirates, organises temporary exhibitions.

Paseo Cornisa (AT 12) – This avenue in the modern Escaleritas district above th garden city provides a fine **panorama**★ of Puerto de la Luz and La Isleta.

Playa de las Canteras

FUERTEVENTURA

1 731km²/670sq mi – Population 49 542

Michelin map 221

erteventura, the largest island after Tenerife in the Canary Archipelago, is also the
ast densely populated after El Hierro with 28 people per km² or about 73 per sq mi.
is an arid land, a "skeletal island" in the words of the Spanish writer, Unamuno,
otted with countless bare crests, mostly extinct volcanoes. Only goats can graze
uch terrain. The sites of villages scattered in the vast plains and in the ravines are
arked by palm trees and numerous windmills, drawing water from the subsoil for
e cultivation of cereals and tomatoes.

erteventura shares the climate of its near neighbour, Africa; the continent's sand,
own across the sea, gave the island its present form by building up an isthmus, El
ble, between the originally separate islets of Maxorata and Jandía. The endless
eaches are also due to wind-borne African sand. The island's attraction lies in the
eauty of its bare landscape, in the immense beaches of white sand with turquoise
ater which make up almost the entire shoreline, in the rocks which provide good
nderwater fishing and in the open sea fishing in the channel between the island and
frica which yields good catches. A mild climate, moderate winds and a calm sea
pecially on the east coast, make this tranquil island the ideal resort for sailing,
ving, fishing and, in particular, windsurfing. To prove the point, the world
indsurfing championships are held here in July and August.

he great humanist, **Miguel de Unamuno**, was exiled to the island in 1924.

PUERTO DEL ROSARIO Population 16 883

Both in the capital and at the airport there are taxis and cars for hire for touring.
South of Puerto del Rosario there is a long beach, **Playa Blanca**.

Excursions

Corralejo - *39km/24mi to the north on FV 10 and FV 101.*

La Oliva - Take the path starting by the church. The **Casa de los Coroneles**, an 18C
house, which used to be the official residence of the Governor of the Island, is
surmounted by two crenellated towers and ornamented with attractive wooden

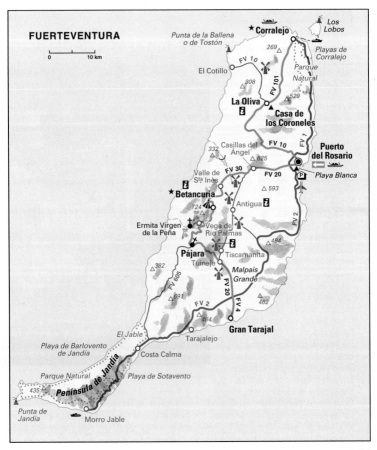

451

Centros de Turismo y Ocio ⊘

These leisure and tourist centres are housed in buildings with typical island architecture and introduce visitors to the traditional ways of life, culture and gastronomy of the island.

La Cilla "Museo del Grano", in La Oliva – The museum has been installed in an old granary and provides explanations on traditional agriculture.

Mirador de Morro Velosa, in Betancuria – A belvedere with a superb view of the centre of the island. The restaurant serves typical dishes from the Canary Islands.

Centro de Artesanía Molino de Antigua, in Antigua – This arts and crafts centre is housed in an old mill encircled by a garden of palm and cactus trees. It also contains a craftwork shop and a general information centre providing details on the island.

Centro de Interpretación de los Molinos, in Tiscamanita – A traditional cottage alongside a mill is the setting for this information centre which explains the history of mills *(molinos)* on Fuerteventura.

---

balconies. Nearby *(right)* stands the **Casa del Capellán**, a minute house enclos within a drystone wall; the motifs decorating the door and window are very simi to those in Pájara church.

★ **Corralejo** – The fishing village and tourist resort is situated at the northern end the island beyond the *malpaís*, or lava fields. Crystal clear water laps at t immense white dune beaches of the Parque Natural Dunas de Corralejo and t Isla de Lobos, a paradise for underwater fishing which can be reached by boa Lanzarote is visible to the north.

Gran Tarajal – *67km/42mi south. Leave Puerto del Rosario by FV 20. Beyo Casillas del Angel, turn right onto FV 30.*

South of Valle de Santa Inés there is a fine view of Betancuria.

★ **Betancuria** – This quiet town in the valley was founded in 1404 by Bethencourt who chose this remote spot in the heart of the mountains as the capital of the island. Betancuria retains not only a certain urban style from the early years of the conquest but also a ruined Franciscan monastery and an ancient **cathedral** with white walls and a picturesque wooden balcony now called the **Iglesia de Santa María la Antigua** ⊘. The interior consists of a nave and two aisles; the baptistery contains an interesting crucifix; the sacristy has retained its attractive ceiling with panel ornament. On the south side of the town there is a small **Museo Arqueológico** ⊘ which displays several Guanche exhibits.

Betancuria

The road south provides an attractive contrast between the wide horizon of bare rose-tinted peaks and the village of Vega de Río Palmas nestling in its gre valley-oasis. Not far away stands the hermitage of the Virgen de la Peña, a place pilgrimage, where the islanders gather every year on the third Saturday September to venerate Fuerteventura's patron saint.

Pájara – The carvings on the church doorway betray signs of Aztec inspiration (plumed heads, pumas, snakes and suns).

In Pájara take FV 20 to the left.

Gran Tarajal – Tamarisk trees surround the port which exports its tomato production and which is the second largest town on the island.

Península de Jandía – *Morro del Jable: 54km/34mi southeast of Gran Tarajal.* This natural park is famous for its magnificent beaches; half of the island's total can be found within it. On the windward side of the island the beaches are wilder, while those on the leeward side tend to be wider and flatter.

The length of time given in this guide
   – for touring allows time to enjoy the views and the scenery;
   – for sightseeing is the average time required for a visit.

LA GOMERA★

378km²/146sq mi – Population 15 858
Michelin map 222

his round island (378km²/146sq mi) rises steeply from coastal cliffs cut by deep vines to a meseta with a single peak, Mount Garajonay (alt 1 487m/4 879ft). The rrain made communication from valley to valley so difficult that until recently local eople used a system of whistling invented by the Guanches. Few traces remain of rly volcanic activity apart from the blocks of solidified volcanic material known cally as *roques* and the basalt cliffs, Los Órganos, visible only from the sea. The rtile red soil is carefully husbanded: even the steepest hillsides are industriously rraced.

Gomera is the ideal island for visitors seeking peace and quiet, contact with nature d outdoor activities such as hiking, mountain-biking, horse-riding and water orts.

San Sebastián de la Gomera – Christopher Columbus stopped off here, in what is now the administrative centre of the island, before going on to discover America in 1492. His route can be traced down the main street from the corner house where he took on water *(ask to see the well (el pozo) in the country courtyard – patio)*, past the **Iglesia de la Asunción** where he heard Mass, to the two-storey white house, a little before the post office where he is said to have slept. In 1488 Doña Beatriz de Bobadilla took refuge in the **Torre del Conde de Gomera** to escape from the Guanches who had just killed her husband because of his cruelty and for seducing one of their women. The countess was only delivered from attack by the arrival of Pedro de Vera who massacred the besiegers.

★ **Parque Nacional de Garajonay** ⊙ – *15km/9mi. Leave San Sebastian de la Gomera by TF 711.* The road emerges from the first tunnel into the **Hermigua valley★★**: the white houses, palm trees and banana plantations at the foot of the high cliffs make a picturesque scene.

★ **Agulo** – Very picturesque site beside the sea in the north of the island. Tenerife is visible on the horizon.

F. Brocal/MICHELIN

Banana trees

LA GOMERA

0   6 km

★★ Parque Nacional de Garajonay – *A visit to the Juego de Bolas Visitors' Centre ⊙ is recommended.*

The national park, created in 1981, is covered by a thick forest of laurels, traces of the Tertiary Era, and giant heathers, punctuated by rocks (*roques*). The almost permanent mist, caused by the trade winds, lends the region an air of mystery.

★★ Valle Gran Rey – *55km/34mi from San Sebastian de Gomera by TF 713.* The road ascends the slopes to the south of the island; the climb up to the central *meseta* inside the national park is less steep.

Chipude – A potters' village in an attractive setting.

Arure – From the far side of the bridge there is a good **panorama★** of Taguluche.

★★ Barranco del Valle Gran Rey – The ravine, at the end of which are the village houses, is the most spectacular on the island.

El HIERRO

278km²/108sq mi – Population 6 995

Michelin map 222

Although the smallest of the Canary Islands, El Hierro is not the flattest. It consists of a half crater open to the north with a rim more than 1 000m/3 280ft high (Malpaso 1 501m/4 925ft). This remote island has few inhabitants but they speak a remarkably pure Castilian. Apart from fishing from La Restinga, the people raise sheep and goats (they make delicious cheeses) and farm and cultivate vines from which they produce an excellent white wine. El Hierro has a varied landscape and a rocky coast which is ideal for underwater swimming.

EXCURSIONS FROM VALVERDE

Valverde – The administrative centre of the island is situated at an altitude of 571m/1 873ft.

Tamaduste – *8km/5mi northeast.* A large sandbank has dammed the sea inlet by the small seaside resort and formed a quiet lagoon.

★★ El Golfo – *8km/5mi west.* There is an excellent **view★★** of El Golfo from the **Mirador de La Peña**. The depression is probably an ancient crater. The rim is covered with laurels and giant heather while the level floor is cultivated. La Fuga de Gorreta, near the Salmor rocks (*northeast*), is the habitat of a primeval lizard.

EL HIERRO

0   5 km

La Dehesa – *Round trip of 105km/65mi. Leave Valverde by TF 912 going south.*

Tiñor – Until 1610, when it was blown down in a storm, a Garoé tree stood on the northeast side of the village. It was venerated by the Bimbaches since its leaves collected water by condensation and the tribesmen made use of the supply.

Sabinosa – The village has a spa-hotel where

The Sacred Tree of El Hierro

In his book *Historia de los Reyes Católicos*, Andrés Bernáldez marvels at the presence of the Island of El Hierro of the **Garoé**: this tree with evergreen leaves strongly resembles the poplar, although it is smaller and bushy enough to hide two men; it also produces small acorns as bitter as gall that possess medicinal properties. "The bark continually oozes drops of water, which are collected in a basin placed at the foot ot the tree."

This species was so dramatically threatened with extinction that, on 12 June 1610, the Island's Council voted a ruling aimed at heightening public awareness of the problem, encouraging the population to take better care of their land and to water it more often...

---

diseases of the skin and the digestion are treated. Three kilometres further on begins a track which crosses the arid pastoral region called La Dehesa and provides **extensive views**★ of the south coast of the island where the fiery red earth, pitted with craters, slopes steeply to the sea, which has been named Mar de las Calmas in view of its still waters.

Punta de Orchilla – Orchilla Point was designated as the original meridian in 2C AD long before Greenwich. Beyond the lighthouse lies a wood of sabine trees, conifers with twisted trunks which are found only on El Hierro.

Ermita de Nuestra Señora de los Reyes ⊘ – The Hermitage of Our Lady of the Kings, the partron saint of El Hierro, contains statues of the three Wise Men (los Reyes) and one of the Virgin Mary which is carried in procession every four years to Valverde. Dancers from the villages it passes through take turns to carry the Virgin along the route.

El Pinar – A pleasant **pine forest**★ extends all over this region.

LANZAROTE★★★

836km²/323sq mi – Population 88 475
Michelin map 221

Lnzarote is the most unusual of the Canary Islands. Seaside resorts have been built ong its fine white sand beaches but usually visitors allow at least a couple of days o see its unique scenery, which has resulted in its designation as a Biosphere eserve. The island's black earth landscape, dotted with oases of vegetation and ops, is full of contrasting textures and colours. Over the centuries, Lanzarote has ad to adapt to the difficult natural conditions which have shaped the character and tivities of its inhabitants.

rom the 14C to the present – The island owes its name to Lancelloti Malocello from enoa, who landed here in the 14C. Actual conquest came in 1401 with the arrival f the Normans, **Gadifer de la Salle** and **Jean de Bethencourt**, who met little resistance with e result that before long Bethencourt was able to present the island to the King of astile. Lanzarote then became the base for expeditions against the other islands hich met with no success until finally Fuerteventura was also subdued. When ethencourt left Lanzarote in 1416, much mourned by the local inhabitants, to turn to his native France, he entrusted the government of the island to his cousin, aciot.

nce the main islands had been conquered, Lanzarote was largely left to its wn devices and, as its coast was open and its mountains low, it became a prey marauding pirates in search of slaves... Calamity of a different nature occurred 1730 in the form of a massive volcanic eruption. Near the village of Timanfaya flaming mountain range, the **Montañas del Fuego**, suddenly appeared. The eruption sted six years and covered one third of the island in a sea of lava. In 1824 ere was another eruption in the north where a new volcano, Tinguatón, spewed olten lava over the southwest part of the island engulfing the fields and ouses.

radually the people re-established themselves in the lunar landscape; the lava fields *malpaís*) and the thick black layers of ash and pebbles are pitted with over 100 aters. In **La Geria**, where volcanic pebbles (lapilli) are plentiful, vines have been anted and low semicircular walls have been built to protect them from the northeast ind. The grapes produce an excellent light white wine – Malvasía – with a distinctive uquet. Throughout the island the fields are covered with a deep layer of the lapilli *picón* in the local dialect) as they retain moisture, a precious attribute on an island here it scarcely ever rains. Another feature of this arid land is the dromedary; its umpbacked silhouette is an integral element in the landscape.

THE CENTRE OF THE ISLAND

Round trip of 62km/39mi from Arrecife

Arrecife – The administrative centre is on the coast facing offshore ree
it was defended by the **Castillo de San Gabriel** which was built in the 16C
an islet and linked to the town by two bridges, one of which, the Puente
Bolas, is a drawbridge. The fort now houses the small **Museo Arqueológico
Etnográfico** ⊘.
Arrecife has a pleasant beach and a picturesque maritime lagoon, the Charca
San Ginés, where fisherman tie up their small boats. To the north, at the end
the avenue bordering the sea, the 18C **Castillo de San José** stands on a sm
promontory. The castle has been restored by César Manrique and now houses t
Museo Internacional de Arte Contemporáneo ⊘. The gallery's cafeteria-restaurant offe
fine views of the Puerto de Naos and Arrecife to the right, and the Los Mármol
quay to the left.

★ **Taro de Tahíche: Fundación César Manrique** ⊘ – The Foundation w
set up in 1968 in a house that was built on top of five volcanic bubb
formed during the eruptions of 1730 to 1736. César Manrique was an origin
artist who deliberately chose this location for his Foundation to demonstra
the bond between architecture and nature. Besides his own work, visitors c
admire an exhibition of contemporary art (Miró, Tàpies, Mompó, Guerrer
Chirino etc).

Monumento al Campesino ⊘ – This monument near **Mozaga**, in the centre
the island, has been erected as a homage to the peasant farmers of Lanzarot
Next to it, the **Casa-Museo del Campesino** is an example of the island's typi
architecture.

★ **Tiagua: Museo Agrícola El Patio** ⊘ – This agricultural museum is housed in
old farm. Its outbuildings display ethnographic and ethnological exhibits whi
provide an overview of the traditional way of life and culture of the islan
farmers. A tasting of Malvasía wine is also offered to visitors.

Museo del vino El Grifo ⊘ – The 18C El Grifo wine storehouses have be
converted into a museum explaining traditional wine production methods.

★★ **La Geria** – La Geria lies between Yaiza and Mozaga in a weird landscape of black
desert pockmarked with craters. The village is an important centre for w
production.

César Manrique (1920-92)

César Manrique is intimately linked to Lanzarote and its tourist development; it was towards the latter that he channelled the very best of his artistic talent, promoting a new standard to regulate property speculation and urban growth in order to avoid the disastrous consequences of uncontrollable development.

Manrique was born on Lanzarote, and everywhere on the island visitors can see the importance of the work he carried out. He was responsible for the Island Council's Art, Culture and Tourism Centres, in which he introduced his ideas on the integration of art and nature. These centres and the Fundación César Manrique bear witness to the passion he felt for Lanzarote and for his concerns for the preservation of its natural heritage. In total, seven centres have been created: the Museo de Arte Contemporáneo Castillo de San José; the El Diablo restaurant in the Parque Nacional de Timanfaya; the Casa-Museo and the Monumento al Campesino (Peasants' Monument); the Cueva de Los Verdes; the Jameos del Agua; the Mirador del Río and the Jardín de Cactus *(see descriptions in the text)*.

THE SOUTH OF THE ISLAND

Round trip of 124km/77mi from Arrecife – about 1 day

Parque Nacional de Timanfaya ⊘ – The range, which emerged during the eruptions of 1730-1736, stands out sometimes red, sometimes black, in a lunar landscape of volcanic cinder and slag. The **Montañas de Fuego** form the central part of this massif.

5km/3mi north of Yaiza, dromedaries wait by the roadside; they provide an exotic if somewhat swaying and jolting ride up the mountainside, from where there is a good view of the next crater.

Although the volcanoes have not erupted since 1736, their inner fires burn and bubble still. At **Islote de Hilario** some strange phenomena still occur: twigs dropped into a hole in the ground 50cm/20in deep catch fire; water poured into a pipe set into the lava evaporates immediately into steam because of the high temperature of the subsoil (140ºC/254ºF at 10cm/4in, over 400ºC/752ºF at 6m/20ft). From the El Diablo restaurant, where the kitchen uses the heat of the earth for its cooking, there are some fine views of the surrounding area. Buses leave Islote to follow the **Ruta de los Volcanes**, a special 14km/9mi road through the lava fields and craters, providing extraordinary views of the landscape.

El Golfo

From a natural lookout point there is a view over an immense lava field pitted wi volcanoes stretching to the sea. The road passes through the Valley of Tranqu lity, a region of ashes. In the inhospitable solitude of these mountains lichens a the only sign of life.

Los Hervideros – In the caverns at the end of the tongue of lava, the sea bo *(hervir: to boil)* in a endlessly fascinating spectacle.

★★ **El Golfo** – A lagoon, retained by a sandbank in the crater, is filled with viv emerald green water; a steep cliff of pitted black rock forms an impressi backdrop.

★ **Salinas de Janubio** – To form these saltpans, the sea has entered a disused crat producing myriad contrasts in colour and form – the gleaming white pyramids salt, the deep blue still water and the geometrically square pans in the semicircu lagoon.

Playa Blanca de Yaiza ⊘ – This pleasant resort has a pedestrianiz promenade which separates the old fishermen's houses from the attracti white sandy beach. Ferries operate regularly to Fuerteventura, which is visib in the distance.

★ **Punta del Papagayo** – The **Rubicón** region was where Bethencourt origina settled. The only trace of the conquest is the Castillo de las Colaradas, an old tow standing on the edge of the cliff. From "parrot" point *(access along a road at t entrance to Playa Blanca de Yaiza, through which you enter into the **Espa protegido de los Ajaches** ⊘, a protected area)*, with its magnificent rocky creek there are good **views**★ of the Playa Blanca and Fuerteventura.

Return to Arrecife on LZ 2.

THE NORTH OF THE ISLAND

Round trip of 77km/47mi from Arrecife – about half a day

Arrecife – *See above.*

★ **Guatiza: Jardín de Cactus** ⊘ – This cactus garden has been aesthetical designed to display a large selection of species from the Canary Islands, Ameri and Madagascar. It is laid out in terraces in an old quarry; an old windmill has al been added to the site. It is situated in an area with an abundance of prickly pear a cactus which attracts cochineals; in the past these insects were crushed to obta a crimson colourant.

★★★ **Cueva de los Verdes** ⊘ – At the foot of the Corona volcano are undergrou galleries where the Guanches used to take refuge from marauding pirates. Th galleries were formed during successive eruptions when lava streams cooled ar

Dromedaries in the Montañas del Fuego

hardened into dense basalt layers, diverting or allowing subsequent streams to flow around or over earlier flows. There are 2km/1mi of galleries at different levels, illuminated to show the kaleidoscope of colours and shapes in the underground phantasmagoria.

Jameos del Agua ⊘ – This attractive leisure complex has a restaurant, bar, dance floor and auditorium. A *jameo* is a cavity which is formed when the top of a volcanic tube collapses. The natural lagoon in the cave is the habitat of a minute, albino millenary crab which is born blind. The **Casa de los Volcanes** on the upper level contains interesting information on volcanism.

Mirador del Río ⊘ – At the north end of the island, a steep headland, **Riscos de Famara**, stands isolated above the waves. The belvedere blends superbly into the cliff and commands a superb **panorama**★★ across the azure waters of the **El Río** strait to La Graciosa and its neighbouring islands (Montaña Clara, Alegranza, Roque del Oeste and Roque del Este); immediately below are the local saltpans. A passenger ferry operates from Orzola to La Graciosa.

Tropical Park ⊘ – The park contains 45 000m²/53 820sq yd of tended gardens devoted to exotic birds. Regular events are held for visitors, including the ever-popular parrot shows.

Haría – As on all the islands, the northern end is the least arid. Some 5km/3mi south of the village there is a fine **view**★ from a lookout point of the lush Haría Valley with its hundreds of palm trees. In the distance rises the Corona volcano.

Teguise – Teguise, once the island's capital, is the home of the *timple*, a miniature guitar which is a vital element in Canary Island folklore. Nearby is the **Castillo de Santa Bárbara**, built in the 16C on the Guanapay volcano, which houses the **Museo del Emigrante** ⊘, containing an interesting collection of documents and mementoes relating to the emigration of Canary Islanders to America.

From the summit there is a vast **panorama**★ including Teguise in the foreground and the island of La Graciosa on the horizon.

LA PALMA★

706km²/273sq mi – Population 75 577
Michelin map 222

Palma, which rises to 2 426m/7 949ft at its centre, is the highest island in the world on account of its small size. The huge central crater, the **Caldera de Taburiente**, with a diameter of over 10km/6mi and a depth of 1 500m/4 920ft, was probably produced by the volcano which created the island. A chain of peaks, Las Cumbres, extends south; deep ravines cut into the steep slopes producing an indented coastline. In the mountains, where the rainfall is plentiful, the water is collected to irrigate the lower terraces.

Local products

Cigars – Tobacco was first introduced to the islands by Cuban Indians. The handmade palm cigars have a deserved reputation and are highly appreciated by cigar connoisseurs the world over.

Silk – La Palma's textile tradition dates back to the 17C. Today, a number of local artisans still work with natural silk.

Cheese – Smoked white goats' cheese is one of La Palma's specialities. The island's goat population now numbers some 30 000.

SANTA CRUZ DE LA PALMA Population 17 069

The administrative centre of the island was founded by Lugo in 1493 at the foot of a tall cliff which is, in fact, a half-eroded crater, the Caldereta. In the 16C, with rising cane sugar exports and the expansion of the dockyards using local hardwood timber, Santa Cruz was one of Spain's major ports; nowadays, it is a peaceful city where mansions with elegant façades and great wooden balconies line the seafront promenade.

At Playa de Los Cancajos, 5km/3mi to the south, the beach and rocks are black.

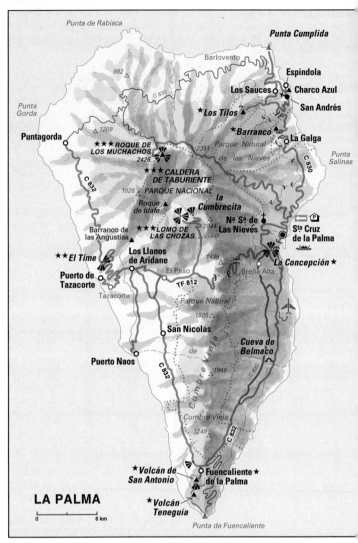

LA PALMA

Plaza de España – Several of the buildings date from the Renaissance. The 1
Iglesia de El Salvador ⊙ has beautiful ceilings with **artesonado ornament**★; the sacri
has Gothic vaulting. Opposite stand the 16C town hall and a line of houses in ▮
colonial style.

Walk uphill to the delightful **Plaza de Santo Domingo**. Next to a further educati
college stands the **chapel** ⊙ of a former monastery; it is furnished with so▮
beautiful Baroque altars.

THE NORTH OF THE ISLAND

★★★ **Observatorio Roque de los Muchachos** ⊙ – *36km/22mi. About 1hr 45min*
the ascent. Laurel bushes and pine trees line the winding road which off▮
extensive views as it climbs to 2 432m/7 949ft; at the top is one of the worl▮
most important astrophysical observatories. From the Roque de los Muchach▮
there is an impressive **panorama**★★★: in fine weather this takes in the Caldera, L▮
Llanos de Aridane, the island's mountain chain and the island of El Hierro (*sout▮*
the Pico del Teide on Tenerife (*east*) and the island of La Gomera (*southeast*▮

Punta Cumplida – *36km/22mi north along C 830.* There are very fine views▮
the coast from the cliff road which crosses some deep ravines (*barrancos*) wh▮
are part of the Los Tiles Biosphere Reserve. Note also the impressive number▮
craters.

La Galga – North of the village, on emerging from the tunnel, the road crosse▮
steep and well-wooded **ravine**★.

San Andrés – In the church there is a beautiful Mudéjar ceiling in the chancel.

Charco Azul – Natural seawater pools.

Espíndola – A tiny fishing village where the boats are drawn up onto a shingle beach in a breach in the cliff face.

Punta Cumplida – Walk round the lighthouse on the promontory to see the waves breaking on the basalt rock piles. The attractive Fajana swimming pools are located north of here.

Los Sauces – The main agricultural centre in the north of the island.

Los Tilos – Make a detour up the Agua ravine to reach the forest of lime trees which covers the picturesque ravine. The **Centro de Investigación e Interpretación de la Reserva de la Biosfera de Los Tilos** ⊘, provides interesting details on the flora to be found in the Biosphere Reserve.

THE SOUTH OF THE ISLAND

Via Los Llanos and Fuencaliente

Round trip of 190km/118mi from Santa Cruz

North of Santa Cruz ravine take the first turning on the left. Ahead is the **Barco de la Virgen** ⊘, a cement reproduction of Columbus' Santa María, which houses a small naval museum. The road passes the Fuerte de la Virgen, a fortress which defended the town in the 16C.

Las Nieves – At the foot of Pico de las Nieves, shaded by the great laurel trees in the square, stands the **Santuario de Nuestra Señora de las Nieves** ⊘ which houses the statue of the island's patron saint. Every five years the figure is carried in procession to the boat built in her honour and then to the Iglesia de El Salvador in Santa Cruz.

Mirador de la Concepción – The summit of the Caldereta commands a wonderful **bird's-eye view**★ of Santa Cruz de la Palma, the harbour and the mountains.
Take TF 812 west.

Parque Nacional Caldera de Taburiente ⊘ – *4km/2.5mi west of the tunnel on the right is the* **Centro de Visitantes** ⊘, *containing information on the waymarked footpaths within the park (length, timings, difficulty etc). A little further on, turn right towards La Cumbrecita.* **Cumbrecita pass** (1 833m/6 014ft) *and* **Lomo de las Chozas pass** *(1km/0.6mi further on)* provide a splendid **panorama**★★★: the depths of La Caldera de Taburiente, dotted with Canary Island pines and crowned by rose-tinted peaks (Roque de los Muchachos – opposite). Standing up from the sharp stone spine dividing the crater floor is a rock spike, Roque de Idafe, which was sacred to the Guanches.

Los Llanos de Aridane – The island's second largest town lies at the centre of an attractive plain which is planted with banana palms and avocado trees.

El Time – From the top of El Time cliff there is a remarkable **panorama**★★ of the Aridane plain, a sea of banana palms, and of the Barranco de las Angustias, an impressive rock fissure which is the only outlet for the water which collects in the Caldera de Taburiente.

Puntagorda – The beauty of the landscape makes this drive particulary worthwhile.
Return to El Time.

Puerto de Tazacorte – Small harbour where Lugo landed in 1492. The beach is popular on Sundays with the citizens of La Palma.

Puerto Naos – A picturesque descent first through the lava fields which date from the eruption in 1949 and then through the banana plantations. A seaside resort has developed beside the vast black sandy beach.

San Nicolás – The lava stream from the Nambroque volcano which cut the village in two in 1949 still scars the landscape.

Fuencaliente – Before reaching Fuencaliente, look back from the Mirador de las Indias for a **glimpse**★ of the coast through the pines. The sunny village was a spa until its hot water spring disappeared during the eruption of the **San Antonio volcano**★ in 1677. Circle the volcano to see the impressive craters of the **Teneguía volcano**★ which appeared in October 1971 and the lava stream which flowed towards the sea and separated the lighthouse from the village. The surrounding land, which is now covered in ash, is cultivated as before and glass houses have been erected at the very foot of the new volcano.

Cueva de Belmaco – *5km/3mi from the airport fork.* At the back of the cave are several rocks engraved with enigmatic labyrinthine Guanche inscriptions.

Cloisters, San Juan de Duero, Soria

J. Hidalgo/Campesino/MARCO POLO

Practical
Information

Travelling to Spain

Optimum seasons for travelling, depending on the region

Spring and autumn are the best seasons for a general tour but there is a region Spain for every season:

Spring – Andalucía, Extremadura, Castilla, the Balearic and Canary Islands and Mediterranean coast.

Summer – By the sea: País Vasco (Basque Country), Cantabrian coast and Gali in the mountains: Pyrenees, Picos de Europa, Sierra Nevada, Sierra de Gredos Sierra de Guadarrama.

Autumn – The whole of Spain.

Winter – Mediterranean and the Balearic and Canary Islands; winter spor Pyrenees and Sierra Nevada.

Temperature chart:

	J	F	M	A	M	J	J	A	S	O	N	D
Barcelona	13	14	16	18	21	25	28	28	25	21	16	13
	6	7	9	11	14	18	21	21	19	15	11	
Madrid	9	11	15	18	21	27	31	30	26	19	13	9
	1	2	5	7	10	14	17	17	14	9	5	
Santander	12	12	15	15	17	20	22	22	21	18	15	12
	7	6	8	9	11	14	16	16	15	12	9	
Sevilla	15	17	20	23	26	32	36	36	32	26	20	16
	6	6	9	11	13	17	20	20	18	14	10	
Valencia	15	16	18	20	23	26	29	29	27	23	19	16
	5	6	8	10	13	16	19	20	17	13	9	

Maximum temperatures in red; minimum temperatures in black.

Formalities – Despite the law which came into force on 1 January 1993 authoris the free flow of goods and people within the EU, it is nonetheless advisable t travellers should be equipped with some valid piece of identification such as a **passp** Holders of British, Irish and US passports do not need a visa for a visit to Spain less than 90 days. Visitors from some Commonwealth countries or those plann to stay longer than 90 days should enquire about visa requirements at their lc Spanish consulate. US citizens should obtain the booklet *Your Trip Abr* (US$ 1.25) which provides useful information on visa requirements, custo regulations, medical care etc for international travellers. Apply to the Superintend of Documents, PO Box 371954, Pittsburgh, PA 15250-7954, ☎ 202-512-180

Customs regulations – Tax-free allowances for various commodities within the have increased with the birth of the single European market. The HM Customs Excise Notice 1, *A Guide for Travellers*, explains how recent changes affect travel within the EU. The US Customs Service (PO Box 7407, Washington DC 200 ☎ 202-927 6724) offers a publication *Know Before You Go* for US citizens.

Pets (cats and dogs) – A general health certificate and proof of rabies vaccination sho be obtained from your local vet before departure.

By air – The various national and other independent airlines operate services Spain's international airports (Madrid, Alicante, Barcelona, Bilbao, Málaga, Palr Sevilla and Valencia). Information, brochures and timetables are available from airlines and from travel agents.
Iberia Airlines: 27-29 Glass House St, London, W1R 6JU, ☎ (0171) 830 00 Fax (0171) 413 1262. Website: http://www.iberia.com
Reservations within the US and Canada: ☎ 800-772-4642 (calls to this toll-f number are charged at the usual international rate for callers outside the US).

By sea – Brittany Ferries operates a ferry service between Plymouth and Santan (leaves Plymouth on Mondays and Wednesdays, returns from Santander on Tu days and Thursdays; *journey time: 24hr*). For reservations, contact:
Millbay Docks, Plymouth PL1 3EW, Devon, ☎ (0990) 360 360.
Estación marítima, Santander, Spain, ☎ 942 36 06 11.
Website: http://www.brittanyferries.com

By sea then on through France – There are also numerous cross-Channel servi (passenger and car ferries, hovercraft, SeaCat) from the United Kingdom and E to France.

e two major frontier posts on the French-Spanish border are at either end of the
renees - Irún in the west and La Jonquera in the east. You may also cross (from
st to east) at Vera de Bidasoa, Echalar, Dancharia, Erratzu, Ochagavía, Valcarlos,
ba, Canfranc, Sallent de Gállego, Bielsa, Les Puente del Rey, Bossòst, Andorra,
igcerdà, Collado d'Ares and Cerbère.

der the Channel then on through France - An alternative to the cross-Channel
ry services is the **Channel Tunnel**. The high-speed undersea rail link carries passen-
rs (without cars) from London to Paris, from where it is possible to travel on by
in *(see below)*. It also ferries motorists and their cars through the tunnel (35min)
specially designed double-decker wagons. The Calais terminal is linked by
o-roads to the French motorway network (the distance to Madrid by road is about
500km/1 000mi; a possible route is via Bordeaux, Biarritz, San Sebastián, either
bao or Vitoria, and Burgos).
r information, contact Le Shuttle passenger enquiries: ☎ (0990) 353 535.
ebsite: http://www.eurotunnel.com

rail - British Rail offers a wide range of services to the Channel ports and French
ilways (SNCF) operates an extensive network of lines including many high-speed
ssenger trains and motorail services throughout France. Information and boo-
gs from:
itish Rail International, Ticket and Information Office, PO Box 303, Victoria
ation, London SW1V 1JY, ☎ (08705) 848 848, Fax (0171) 633 9900.
lgo trains - the Spanish version of the French TGV or high-speed trains - operate
ernight between Paris (leaving at about 9pm) and Barcelona and Madrid (journey
ne about 12-13hr). Alternatively, travellers can take a TGV from Paris to
ontpellièr and pick up a connecting train south there.

coach - Regular coach departures are operated from London to Madrid and to
ger provincial towns.
rolines, 52 Grosvenor Gardens, Victoria, London SW1W OAU,
(0171) 730 8235.

ravelling in Spain

cuments - An **international driving licence** (obtainable in the UK from the AA or the
C or in the US from the American Automobile Association for US$ 10) is required
en driving in Spain.
r the vehicle it is necessary to have the **registration papers** (log-book) and a **nationality
te** of the approved size.

surance - An International Insurance Certificate (Green Card) is compulsory. Third
rty insurance is also compulsory in Spain. Certain UK motoring organisations (AA,
C) run accident insurance and breakdown service schemes for members and
otorists should check available schemes with their own insurance company. Bail
nds are no longer necessary, although travellers may still wish to take this
ecaution (consult your insurance company). Members of the American Automobile
sociation should obtain the free brochure *Offices to Serve You Abroad* (which gives
tails of affiliated organisations in Spain).
the driver of the vehicle is not accompanied by the owner, he or she must have
itten permission from the owner to drive in Spain.

iving regulations and general information - The minimum driving age is 18.
affic drives on the right. It is compulsory for passengers in both front and rear
ats to wear **seat belts**. Motorcyclists (on all sizes of machine) must wear safety
lmets.
e **maximum speed** permitted is:
kph/31mph in built-up areas;
kph/56mph on the open road (without a hard shoulder);
0kph/62mph on the open road with a hard shoulder of at least 1.5m/5ft;
0kph/75mph on dual carriageways/motorways *(autovía/autopista)*.
1991 the Spanish road network included over 2 000km/1 250mi of motorways.
st of the Spanish motorways have **tolls** *(peajes)*.
per (97-96 octanes), normal (92-90 octanes) and diesel are generally available but
t all petrol stations sell unleaded petrol *(sin plomo)*.

ad maps - Michelin map 990 at a scale of 1: 1 000 000 covers the whole of
ain, while the 441-446 series at 1: 400 000 covers the different regions. The
0-222 series (1:125 000, 1:150 000 and 1:175 000) covers the Canary Islands.
e the back cover of this guide for the map numbers and their corresponding
gions.

Route planning – Michelin has created a website to help motorists prepare th journey. The service enables browsers to select their preferred route (faste shortest etc) and to calculate distances between towns and cities: **www.michelin-vel.com**

Car hire – The major car hire firms such as Avis (☎ 901 13 57 90), Europ (☎ 901 10 20 20) and Hertz (☎ 901 10 10 01) have offices in all large towns. C may be hired from branches at airports, main stations and large hotels. minimum age to qualify for car hire is 21. Tourists driving vehicles with rental pla are advised to leave no valuables in the car. Fly-drive schemes are operated by ma airlines. The Spanish Royal Automobile Club (RACE) provides roadside assistance can be contacted on ☎ 900 11 22 22 or 91 593 33 33.

By train – Spanish Railways, RENFE (☎ 91 328 90 20), have a 13 000km/8 08(rail network offering first and second class travel. They have a variety of special ra and tourist fares including discounts for travel on "Blue Days" (*días azules*), or Youthpass and non-resident Eurailpass holders. Mention should be made of t particularly comfortable trains, the Al-Andalus Express in Andalucía and the Tra cantábrico in the north, designed to give the traveller a cultural, scenic introduct to the country. Lastly, in 1992 (to coincide with Expo '92), RENFE inaugurated AVE (Alta Velocidad Española – Spanish High Speed Train) on the Madrid-Córd(Sevilla route. This train (similar to the French TGV) has reduced travel time betw Madrid and Córdoba to 1hr 45min and Madrid and Sevilla to 2hr 15min. Trains le Madrid from Atocha station and Sevilla from the newly opened Santa Justa stati For further information, call ☎ 91 534 05 05.

Tourist trains

El Expreso Al Andalus – A 5-day trip across Andalucía including excursions. meals and accommodation. The service operates from April to June and September to December; ☎ 91 571 66 96.

El Transcantábrico – This narrow-gauge train skirts the coastline of Canta bria from San Sebastián (Donostia) to Santiago de Compostela. The trip lasts one week and combines rail and coach travel. The service operates from June to October; ☎ 91 571 66 96.

El Tren de la Fresa – A historic train linking Madrid and Aranjuez between April and October (*see ARANJUEZ*); ☎ 902 22 88 22.

By ferry – For information on ferries to the Islas Baleares (daily sailings fr Barcelona and Valencia), the Islas Canarias (a weekly service from Cádiz) or to Nc Africa (sailings from Almería, Málaga and Algeciras) contact the state-ow shipping company Trasmediterránea at:
c/o Southern Ferries, 1st floor, 179 Piccadilly, London W1, ☎ (0171) 491 49(or Alcalá 61, 28014 Madrid, ☎ 91 423 85 00.
The company also has a website at http://www.trasmediterranea.es

Balearia operates services to and from the Balearics. For information, contact company at calle Jaime el Conquistador 6, Madrid; ☎ (91) 473 20 55. Balear website is at http://www.eurolineas.com

By air – Spain has 39 airports (10 of which are on the islands). The largest ar(follows:

Madrid-Barajas ☎ (91) 393 60 00.
Barcelona ☎ (93) 298 38 38.
Bilbao ☎ (94) 486 93 00.
Sevilla ☎ (95) 444 90 00.
Málaga ☎ (95) 204 84 084.
Valencia ☎ (96) 370 95 00.
Palma ☎ (971) 78 90 99.

Main airline companies offering domestic flights:

Iberia and **Aviaco:** información Madrid ☎ (91) 329 57 67; información Barcel ☎ (93) 412 56 67; Inforiberia ☎ 902 400 500 (information and reservation:

Air Europa: ☎ (902 401 501.

Spanair: ☎ 902 13 14 15.

This guide, which is revised regularly, incorporates tourist information provided at the of going to press. Changes are however inevitable owing to improved facilities fluctuations in the cost of living.

General information

...ency – The unit of currency in Spain is the peseta, written as pts. In early 1999, ...xchange rates were about 235 pts to the pound (143 pts to the US dollar). Coins ...e in the following denominations: 1, 5, 10, 25, 50, 100, 200 and 500 pts, with ...s in 1 000, 2 000, 5 000 and 10 000 values. Visitors should be aware of the ...easing variety of Spanish coins (over 15 different ones) and that several ...minations (5, 25, 100 and 200 pts) are represented by several different coins. ...e are no restrictions on the amount of currency (Spanish or other) that ...igners may bring with them into Spain. They may leave Spain with the currency ...valent of up to 500 000 pts.

...owing the launch of the Euro at the beginning of 1999 and in preparation for its ...introduction in Spain in 2002, many prices are beginning to appear in both ...tas and euros. As a guideline, in January 1999 1 Euro was worth 168 pts.

...nging money, credit cards – Banks, airports and some stations have exchange ...es. International credit cards are accepted in most shops, hotels and restau-...s. An increasing number of *cambios* (bureaux de change) are also available ...ughout the country.

...ks – Banks are generally open Mondays to Fridays 9am to 2pm and on Saturdays ...n 9am to 12.30pm. These times are subject to change, especially in summer. ...t banks have cash dispensers which accept international credit and debit cards.

...erences in time – Spain is 1hr ahead of GMT.
...Spanish keep very different hours from either British or Americans. As a general ...restaurants serve lunch from 1.30pm to 3.30pm and dinner from 9pm to 11pm.

...t Offices (Correos) – Post offices are open weekdays from 9am to 2pm. The main ...: offices in large towns and those in international airports have a 24-hour service. ...nps *(sellos)* are sold in post offices and tobacconists *(estancos)*. The **Michelin Red** ...**e España & Portugal** gives the post code for every town covered. ...National **Girobank**'s postcheque allows British customers to withdraw cash on their ...accounts from main post offices in Spain. Check with your local Girobank office.

...phones (Teléfonos) – Telephones in new public booths take 5, 25, 50, 100 and ...peseta coins (older booths only take 5, 25 and 100 peseta coins), as well as ...necards. For **international calls**, dial 00, wait for the dialling tone and then dial the ...ntry code (44 for the United Kingdom, 353 for Ireland, 1 for the United States), ...area code and the number. Telephone cards *(tarjeta telefónica)* in 1 000 and ...00 pts denominations can be purchased in *tabacos* and are particularly recom-...ded for international dialling.

...**internal calls**, dial the 9-digit number (composed of the old area code plus the ...ting correspondent's number, as of April 1998).
...international dialling code for Spain is 34, after which you should dial the full ...git number.

...ps – These are generally open weekdays 10am to 1.30pm and 5pm to 8pm (some ...artment stores stay open during the lunch hour). Some shops are closed on ...urday afternoons and most all day Sunday.

...numents, museums and churches – Monuments and museums are generally ...n 10am to 1.30pm and 4pm to 7pm. Some churches are only open during services ...y in the morning or in the evening.

...ertainment – When there are two performances scheduled, matinées begin at ...n (4.30pm on Sundays and holidays) and the evening performances at 10pm or ...30pm.

...lic holidays – The dates in italics are holidays in some, but not all, autonomous ...munities.

...anuary	*(2nd Thursday after Whitsun)*
...anuary	*25 July*
...anuary	15 August
...March	12 October
...undy Thursday	1 November
...d Friday	*6 December*
...lay	8 December
...pus Christi	25 December

...ddition each town celebrates the feast day of its patron saint. For local holidays ...tact the Tourist Information centres *(Oficina de Turismo* or simply *Turismo)*.

...dical treatment – British citizens should apply for **Form E 111**, issued by the post ...ce, which entitles the holder to urgent treatment for accident or unexpected ...ss in EU countries. This form should be presented to the relevant medical services ...r to receiving treatment. For further information in the UK, contact the ...artment of Health and Social Security; ☎ (0191) 218 7777.

Since medical insurance is not always valid out of the United States, traveller
advised to check with their insurance companies about taking out suppleme
medical insurance with specific overseas coverage.

Electric current – 220 volts AC (some of the older establishments may still
110 V). Plugs are two-pin.

Water – Water is generally safe to drink although it may be a little salty alon
Mediterranean coast – this is true of Barcelona – in which case you may p
mineral water *(agua mineral)*.

Accommodation

Travellers' addresses – This new section, which has been added to several town
cities in this guide, offers a choice of hotels in three categories to suit all bud
Prices are based on a double/twin room.
– The **Budget** category offers rooms at less than 11 000 pts. These are usually s
simple hotels with a basic level of comfort.
– **Our Selection** covers hotels with rooms at between 11 000 and 20 000 pts v
certain amount of character.
– In the **Treat Yourself** category we have included hotels with particular charm, off
a high degree of comfort and ensuring a memorable stay. Naturally, the cost of
hotels is in keeping with the high level of facilities provided.

The **Michelin Red Guide España & Portugal** is revised annually and is an indispen
complement to this Green Guide with additional information on hotels and re
rants including category, price, degree of comfort and setting. Towns underlir
red on Michelin maps 441–446 are listed in the current Red Guide with a choi
hotels and restaurants.

The Spanish Tourist Board also publishes a hotel guide with hotel categories rar
from one-star to five-star establishments.

Bear in mind that hotel prices do not include the 7% VAT and that they may
according to the season.

Paradors – Most of these are extremely comfortable, restored historic monun
(castles, palaces and monasteries) in beautiful sites. For further information, co
Paradores de Turismo, Carretera Requena 3, 28013, Madrid, ☎ 91 561 66 66
official UK representative is Keytel International, 402 Edgware F
London W2 1ED, ☎ (0171) 616 0300, Fax (0171) 616 0317. Parador:
indicated on Michelin maps 990 and 441 – 446 *(see Key on p 4 for symbol)*.

Tipping – Bar, restaurant and café bills always include service in the total ch
Nevertheless, it is customary to leave an extra 10 %. Porters, doormen, taxi dr
and cinema usherettes will also generally appreciate a tip.

Youth Hostels (Albergues Juveniles) – Spain's 160 youth hostels are ope
travellers with an International Card. For further information, contact the Inst
de la Juventud, calle Ortega y Gasset 71, 28006 Madrid, ☎ 91 347 7
Fax 91 401 81 60. Information about facilities for students may be obtained
TIVE Jose Ortega y Gasset 71, 28006 Madrid.

Camping – Details on camping and caravanning are supplied by the Feder
Española de Campings, calle San Bernardo 97-99, Edificio Colomina, 3° pl
puerta C-B, 28015 Madrid, ☎ 91 448 12 34. It is advisable to book in advanc
popular resorts during summer.

The chapter on art and architecture in this guide gives an outline of artistic creation
region, providing the context of the buildings and works of art described in the Sights se

This chapter may also provide ideas for touring.

It is advisable to read it at leisure/before setting out.

Useful addresses

Spanish embassies and consulates

Spanish Embassy, 39 Chesham Place, London SW1X 8SB, ☎ (0171) 235 5555, (0171) 259 5392.

Spanish Consulate, 20 Draycott Place, London SW3 2RZ, ☎ (0171) 589 8989, (0171) 581 7888, consulates also in Manchester and Edinburgh.

Embassy of Spain, 2375 Pennsylvania Avenue NW, Washington DC 20037, ☎ 202-452-0100, Fax 202-833-5670, consulates in Boston, Chicago, Houston, Los Angeles, Miami, New Orleans, New York and San Francisco.

Foreign embassies and consulates in Spain

American embassy: Serrano 75, 28006 Madrid, ☎ 91 587 2200.

American consulates: Paseo Reina Elisenda de Montcada 23, 08034 Barcelona, ☎ 93 280 2227

In addition there are consular agencies in Málaga (☎ 952 47 48 91), Sevilla (☎ 95 423 18 85), Valencia (☎ 96 351 69 73), Las Palmas (☎ 928 27 12 59), La Coruña (☎ 981 21 32 33) and Palma de Mallorca (☎ 971 72 50 51).

Australian embassy: Pl. Descubridor Diego de Ordas 3, 2°, 28003 Madrid, ☎ 91 441 9300.

Australian consulates: Barcelona (☎ 93 330 94 96); **Sevilla** (☎ 95 422 0971).

British embassy: Calle Fernando el Santo 16, 28010 Madrid, ☎ 91 700 82 00.

British Consulate-General: Centro Colón, Marqués de la Ensenada 16, 2a, 28004 Madrid, ☎ 91 308 52 01.

British consular offices: Alicante (☎ 965 21 60 22); **Barcelona** (☎ 93 419 90 44); **Bilbao** (☎ 94 415 76 00); **Ibiza** (☎ 971 30 18 18); **Las Palmas**, Canary Islands (☎ 928 26 25 08); **Málaga** (☎ 952 21 75 71); **Menorca**, Menorca (☎ 971 36 33 73); **Palma de Mallorca**, Mallorca (☎ 971 71 24 45); **Santa Cruz de Tenerife**, Canary Islands (☎ 922 28 68 63); **Santander** (☎ 942 22 00 00); **Sevilla** (☎ 954 22 88 75); and **Vigo** (☎ 986 43 71 33).

Canadian embassy: Calle Núñez de Balboa 35, 28001 Madrid, ☎ 91 431 43 00.

Canadian consulate: Barcelona (☎ 93 215 07 04); **Málaga** (☎ 95 221 64 69).

Embassy of Ireland: Paseo de la Castellana 46, 4ª, 28046 Madrid, ☎ 91 576 3500.

Honorary Irish consulates: Barcelona (☎ 93 491 50 21); **Bilbao** (☎ 94 491 25 75); **La Coruña** (☎ 981 35 64 85); **Málaga** (☎ 95 247 51 08); **Palma de Mallorca**, Mallorca (☎ 971 722 504); **Sevilla** (☎ 95 421 63 61); and **Santa Cruz de Tenerife**, Canary Islands (☎ 922 245 671).

Tourist information

Spanish National Tourist Offices:

London: 22-23 Manchester Square, London W1M 5AP, ☎ (0171) 486 8077, (0171) 486 8034/8043.

New York: 666 Fifth Avenue, New York, NY 10103, ☎ 212-265-8822, Fax 212-265-8864.

Chicago: Water Tower Place, Suite 915 East, 845 North Michigan Avenue, Chicago, IL 60611, ☎ 312-642-1992, Fax 312-642-9817.

Los Angeles: 8383 Wilshire Blvd, Suite 960, Beverly Hills, CA 90211, ☎ 213-658-7188/7192, Fax 213-658-1061.

Useful Telephone Numbers

Tourist Information (in English) – ☎ 901 300 600; available daily 10am to 8pm. This service is only available within Spain.

Spanish Directory Enquiries – ☎ 1003.

International Directory Enquiries – ☎ 1025.

Emergency Services – ☎ 061.

Miami: 1221 Brickell Avenue, Miami, FL 33131, ☎ 305-358-1992, Fax 305-8223.

Toronto: 2 Bloor St West, 34th Floor, Toronto, Ontario M4W 3E2, ☎ 416-961-3 Fax 416-961-1992.

Madrid: Secretaría General de Turismo, c/José Lázaro Galdeano 6, 28036 Ma ☎ 91 343 3500.

Tourist Information Centres – All Spanish towns have a Tourist Informa Centre, known as the Oficina de Turismo or simply Turismo, marked on Mic town plans with an **🛈**. The addresses and telephone numbers of these centres ca found in the Admission times and charges section in this guide, as well as in **Michelin Red Guide España & Portugal**.

Eating Out

Travellers' addresses – The restaurants listed in this section have chosen for their surroundings, ambience, typical dishes or unusual chara For a wider selection of restaurants and more detailed gastronomic i mation, consult the **Michelin Red Guide España & Portugal**. Restaurants classified under three categories: "Budget" (a meal for less than 3 000 pts), Selection" (between 3 000 pts and 6 000 pts) and "Treat Yourself" (6 000 pts).

Sports

Winter sports – There are 31 ski resorts in Spain including 17 in the Pyren 6 in the Cordillera Cantábrica, 4 in the Cordillera Central, 3 in the Cordillera Ibé and 1 in the Sierra Nevada (near Granada). Details may be obtained from Federación Española de Deportes de Invierno, c/Infanta María Teresa 14, 28 Madrid, ☎ 91 344 09 44 or from ATUDEM (Asociación Turística de Estacic de Esquí y Montaña) at calle Padre Damian, 43 2, puerta 26A, 28036 Mac ☎ 91 359 15 57. A map showing the major resorts, their altitude and facili (ski-lifts, downhill and cross-country runs) is available from the Spanish Tou Office.

Sailing – There are numerous pleasure boat harbours and sailing clubs in Spair season it is possible to hire boats with or without crew. Apply to the Real Federa de Vela, calle Luis de Salazar 12, 28002 Madrid, ☎ 91 519 50 08.

ıba-diving – Foreigners should either obtain a diving permit from the head office the Spanish Merchant Navy or have an equivalent document from their own ıntry. They should also obtain a temporary permit from the local municipal or rine authorities.

ındsurfing – Although this sport can be practised all around the coast the principal ıas are Punta de Tarifa (Cádiz), the Islas Canarias, Mundaka and Sopelama beaches zcaya). Boards can be hired on all major beaches.

ıter-skiing – Spain's east coast and inland lakes and reservoirs provide good ıditions for water-skiing. Enquire at the local Oficina de Turismo or at the resort. ıeración Española de Esquí Náutico, calle Sabino de Arana 30, 08028 Barcelona, (93) 330 89 03.

ınting and fishing – Hunting and fishing permits may be obtained from local onomous community authorities. For details of these and the calendar of hunting sons, contact the Federación Española de Caza, c/Francos Rodríguez 70, 2º,)39 Madrid, ☎ 91 311 14 11.

rse-riding – A wide choice of options is available to horse-riding enthusiasts, ging from short excursions to treks lasting several days. Every autonomous ımunity has a large number of companies and organisations offering equestrian ıvities. For further information, contact the Federación Hípica Española, calle nte Esquinza 8, 28010 Madrid, ☎ 91 319 02 32.

ıuntaineering – For lists of qualified instructors and local guides apply to the cina de Turismo or the Federación Española de Montañismo, calle Alberto Aguilera !8015 Madrid, ☎ 91 445 13 82.

ıf – Spain is now recognised as one of Europe's foremost golfing nations with ıld-class players such as Seve Ballesteros and José-María Olazabal and a wide ection of golf courses to choose from. Several of the many golf courses are of ımpionship standard. Details may be obtained from the Real Federación Española Golf, calle Capitán Haya 9-5º, 28020 Madrid, ☎ 91 555 26 82. ıf courses and their telephone numbers are listed in the current **Michelin Red Guide aña & Portugal** under the nearest town. A map showing the golf courses, the number holes, addresses and telephone numbers is available from the Spanish Tourist ıce.

El Mas Nou golf club, Platja d'Aro

Fr. Turc/GC (DICT)

Further reading

General – History

Contest of Christian and Muslim Spain – Reilly (Blackwell Publishers)
Fire in the Blood – Ian Gibson (Faber)
Franco – Paul Preston (Fontana Press)
Hispanic World in Crisis and Change – Lynch (Blackwell Publishers)
Imperial Spain (1469-1716) – JH Elliott (Pelican; Penguin)
Living in Spain in the Eighties – John Reay Smith (Robert Hale Ltd)
Moorish Spain – Richard Fletcher (Weidenfeld and Nicolson)
Roman Spain – SJ Keay (British Museum)
Spain and the Jews – edited by Elie Kedourie (Thames & Hudson)
Spain: Change of a Nation – Robert Graham (1984)
Spanish History – S Ortiz-Carboneres (O Wolff Publishers Ltd)
The Basques – Collins (Blackwell Publishers)
The Sephardim – Lucien Gubbay and Abraham Levy (Carnell Ltd)
The Spaniards – John Hooper (Viking)
The Spanish Civil War – Alun Kenwood (O Wolff Publishers Ltd)
The Spanish Labyrinth – Gerald Brenan (Cambridge University Press)

Christopher Columbus

Admiral of the Ocean Sea – Samuel Eliot Morison (Little, Brown)
Columbus: For Gold, God and Glory – John Dyson (Hodder & Stoughton)
Columbus, His Enterprise – Hans Koning (Latin American Bureau)
In Search of Columbus – Hunter Davies (Sinclair-Stevenson)
The Columbus Myth – Ian Wilson (Simon and Schuster)
The Mysterious History of Columbus – John Noble Wilford (Knopf)
The Spanish Seaborne Empire – JH Parry (University of California Press)

Travel

Andalusia – Michael Jacobs (Penguin)
A Stranger in Spain – HV Morton (Methuen)
A Visit to Spain – Hans Christian Andersen (Peter Owen)
Barcelona – Robert Hughes (Harvill)
Barcelonas – Manuel Vázquez Montalbán (Verso)
Castile – J Bentley (George Philip)
Charm of Majorca – Charles Moore (Venton Educational Ltd)
Cities of Spain – David Gilmour (John Murray)
Contrasting Spain – Charles Moore (Venton Educational Ltd)
Guide to the Wines of Spain – Jan Read (Mitchell Beazley; Reed Int)
Iberia – Spanish Travels and Reflections – James A Michener (Secker & Warbu
Jogging Round Majorca – Gordon West (Black Swan)
Madrid – M Jacobs (George Philip)
Madrid and Southern Spain – A Launay and M Pendered (BT Batsford)
Not Part of the Package – Paul Richardson (Pan)
On the Shores of the Mediterranean – Eric Newby
Pilgrim's Road – Bettina Selby (Abacus)
South from Granada – Gerard Brenan (Cambridge University Press)
Spain – Jan Morris (Penguin Travel Library)
Spanish Journeys: A Portrait of Spain – Adam Hopkins (Viking)
The Face of Spain – Gerald Brenan (Penguin)
The Pillars of Hercules – Paul Theroux (Penguin)
Wild Olives – William Graves (Hutchinson)

Art – Literature

A Moment of War – Laurie Lee (Viking)
A Rose for Winter – Laurie Lee (Penguin)
As I Walked Out One Midsummer Morning – Laurie Lee (Penguin)
Fiesta, The Sun Also Rises – Ernest Hemingway (Grafton Books)
For Whom The Bell Tolls – Ernest Hemingway (Penguin)
Goya – José Gudiol (Thames & Hudson)
Homage to Catalonia – George Orwell (Penguin)
Miró – R Penrose (Thames & Hudson)
Picasso – Timothy Hilton (Thames & Hudson)
Salvador Dalí – Dawn Ades (Thames & Hudson)
Spanish Design and Architecture – Emma Dent Coad (Cassell Plc)
Spanish Short Stories 1 – edited by Jean Franco (Penguin)
The House of Bernarda Alba – Federico García Lorca
The Literature of the Spanish People – Gerald Brenan
The Prado – Sánchez Cantón (Thames & Hudson)
Velasquez – Joseph Emile Muller (Thames & Hudson)

Vocabulary

rms of address

s, no	sí, no
od morning	buenos días
od afternoon	buenas tardes
odbye	hasta luego, adiós
ease	por favor
w are you?	¿qué tal?
ank you (very much)	(muchas) gracias
cuse me	perdone
on't understand	no entiendo
, Mr, you	señor, Usted
adam, Mrs	señora
ss	señorita

me

en?	¿cuándo?
at time?	¿a qué hora?
day	hoy
sterday	ayer
morrow morning	mañana por la mañana
morrow afternoon	mañana por la tarde

opping

w much?	¿cuánto (vale)?
o) expensive	(demasiado) caro
ot, little	mucho, poco
ore, less	más, menos

big, small	grande, pequeño
credit card	tarjeta de crédito

Correspondence

post box	buzón
post office	Correos
telephone	teléfono
letter	carta
post card	(tarjeta) postal
poste restante	lista (de Correos)
stamp	sello
telephone call	conferencia
tobacco shop	estanco, tabacos

On the road, in town

car	coche
petrol	gasolina
on the right	a la derecha
on the left	a la izquierda
road works	obras
danger, dangerous	peligroso
beware, take care	cuidado
to go round, tour	dar la vuelta a
after, beyond	después de
to go round, to circle	girar

OOD AND WINE

r further useful hotel and restaurant vocabulary, consult the current Michelin Red ide España & Portugal.

, olives	aceite, aceitunas	egg: fried eggs	huevo: huevos al plato
	agua con gas/senza	ham	jamón
arkling/still water	gas	French beans	judías verdes
rlic	ajo	(king) prawns	langostino
tichoke	alcachofa	milk	leche
n allergic to...	alergia: tengo alergia a	vegetables	legumbres
ans	alubias	lemon	limón
chovies	anchoas	butter	mantequilla
e	arroz	apple	manzana
na	atún	seafood	mariscos
ultry	ave	orange	naranja
gar	azúcar	nut(s)	nuez (nueces)
d	bacalao	bread	pan
bergine/	berenjena	potatoes	patatas
gplant		fish	pescados
ffee with hot	café con leche	(black) pepper	pimienta (negra)
lk		(red/green) pepper	pimiento (rojo/verde)
ck coffee	café solo		
uid	calamares	banana	plátano
b	cangrejo	chicken	pollo
eat	carne	dessert	postre
ion	cebolla	soup	potaje
rk	cerdo	cheese	queso
er	cerveza	salt	sal
icy sausages	chorizos	sausages	salchichas
tton (lamb)	cordero (lechal)	water-melon	sandía
eam	crema (de leche)	mushrooms	setas/hongos
een salad	ensalada	veal	ternera
rs-d'œuvre	entremeses	omelette	tortilla
d cooked	fiambres	trout	trucha
eats		beef	vaca/buey
awns	gambas	vegetarian	vegetariano/a
ick peas	garbanzos		vino
rden peas	guisantes	white/rosé/red wine	blanco/rosado/tinto
cream	helado	carrot	zanahoria
er	hígado	fruit juice	zumo de frutas

SITES AND SIGHTS

See also architectural terms in the Introduction.
Words in italics are in Catalan.

where is?	¿dónde está?	entrance, exit	entrada, salida
may one visit?	¿se puede visitar?	apply to	dirigirse a
key	llave	wait	esperar
light	luz	beautiful	bello, hermoso
sacristan	sacristán	storey, stairs, steps	piso, escalera
guide	guía	religious statue/	imagen
porter, caretaker	guarda, conserje	sculpture	
open, closed	abierto, cerrado	island, isle	isla
Muslim fortress	alcazaba	lake	lago, *estany*
Muslim palace	alcázar	mosque	mezquita
environs, outskirts	alrededores		monasterio,
pass, high pass	alto	monastery	*monestir*
town hall	ayuntamiento	mount, mountain	monte
	ajuntament	belvedere,	mirador
audience, court	audiencia	viewpoint,	
spa	balneario	lookout point	
gully, ravine	barranco	museum	museo, *museu*
quarter	barrio, *barri*	source, birthplace	nacimiento
wine cellar/store	bodega		palacio (r…
cape, headland	cabo, *cap*	(royal) palace	*palau*
street	calle, *carrer*	artificial lake	pantano
main street	calle mayor	avenue, esplanade,	paseo, *passeig*
road, track	camino	promenade	
belfry	campanario	sculptured figures:	paso
chapel	capilla	the Passion	
capital	capitel	manor-house	pazo
main road	carretera	(Galicia)	
Carthusian	cartuja	square	plaza, *plaça*
monastery		main square	plaza mayor
house	casa	bullring	plaza de toros
town hall	casa consistorial	portal, west door	portada
castle	castillo	portal, porch	pórtico
Celtic village	castro	dam	presa
town, city	ciudad, ciutat	village, market	pueblo, *poble*
cloister	claustro	town	
college, collegiate	colegio, colegiata	bridge	puente, *pont*
church		door, gate,	puerta
pass, high pass	collado, *coll*	entrance	
monastery,	convento	pass, harbour,	puerto
convent		port	
cross, Calvary	cruz	estuary	ría
picture	cuadro	river, stream	río
cave, grotto	cueva, gruta, cava	Roman:	romano; románi…
defile, cleft	desfiladero	Romanesque	
reservoir, dam	embalse	church	santuario
hermitage, chapel	ermita	century	siglo
station	estación	carved wood	talla
excavations	excavaciones	tapestries	tapices
property, domain	finca	ceiling	techo
fountain	fuente	treasury, treasure	tesoro
gorges	gargantas	tower, belfry	torre
cavern, grotto	gruta	keep	torre del homen…
defile, narrow	hoz	mountain stream,	torrente
pass, gorge		torrent	
vegetable/	huerto, huerta	valley	valle, *vall*
market garden		fertile plain	vega
church	iglesia	window: plain or	vidriera
no entry,		stained glass	
not allowed	prohibido	view, panorama	vista

Calendar of events

ain's major festivals are mentioned in the list below. To confirm details, which
y vary slightly, and for smaller events, apply to the local Spanish tourist office
ficina de Turismo) which will have a revised calendar with details of places and
es.

ek before Ash Wednesday

**diz, Santa Cruz de
nerife** .... Carnival festivities; processions

nival Sunday (1st Sunday in March)

ges .... International Vintage Car Rally

Sunday in Lent

stellón de la Plana .... Feast of the Magdalen; bullfights, processions

-19 March

lencia .... St Joseph's Day "Fallas"

y Week

**rtagena, Cuenca, Málaga,
ırcia, Sevilla, Valladolid,
mora** .... Solemn processions

st week after Easter

ırcia .... Spring Festival

ril

villa .... Feria

24 or 24-26 April

coi .... St George's Festival: "Moros y Cristianos"

Fiesta de San Jorge (St George's Festival), Alcoi

st Sunday in April

dújar (Jaén) .... Romería (pilgrimage) to the Virgen de la Cabeza

ril or May

rez de la Frontera .... Feria del Caballo (Horse show)

475

1st fortnight in May
Córdoba .... *Patios* festival and national flamenco comp‹
ons

15 May
Madrid .... San Isidro Festival: several days of bullfight‹

Whitsun
El Rocío (Huelva) .... Gypsy pilgrimage to the Nuestra Señora del R‹
shrine
Atienza (Guadalajara) .... Caballada festival

2nd Sunday after Whitsun: in celebration of Corpus Christi
Puenteareas (Pontevedra) .... Streets carpeted with flowers
Sitges .... Streets carpeted with flowers; competitions
Toledo .... Solemn processions

24 June
Alacant .... "Hogueras" Midsummer's Day (St John) Fes‹
Ciutadella (Menorca) .... Midsummer's Day (St John) Festival

4-6 July
A Estrada (Pontevedra) ..... "A Rapa das Bestas" Festival

"A Rapa das Bestas" Festival

6-14 July
Pamplona .... "Sanfermines" bull-running

1st or 2nd Saturday in August
Arriondas-Ribadesella
(Asturias) .... Kayak races down the río Sella

14-15 August
Elche .... Elche Mystery Play

7-17 September
Albacete .... Feria

September
edo .... America Day in Asturias

September
edo .... St Matthew's (San Mateo) Festival

26 September
roño .... La Rioja Wine Harvest Festival

September
rcelona .... Festival of Our Lady of Mercy (Virgen de la Merced)

October
adalupe .... Hispanidad Festival: solemn processions

ek of 12 October
agoza .... Pilar Festival

Admission times and charges

As admission times and charges are liable to alteration, the information belo
given only as a general guideline.
The following list details the opening times and charges (if any) and other rele
information concerning all sights in the descriptive part of this Guide accompa
by the symbol ⊙. The entries below are given in the same order as in the alphabe
section of the Guide.
The prices quoted apply to individual adults with no reduction. Special condition.
both times and charges are generally granted to groups if arranged beforehar
Charges for admission are given in pesetas: pts.
Given the great wealth of Spanish painting and sculpture, museums are c
re-arranging their exhibitions or undergoing restoration so it is always worth
while to telephone ahead of time to confirm admission times.
Opening times for churches are only given if the interior is of special interest.
general rule, avoid visiting a church during a service; however, some are only c
at these times in which case you are expected to be as discreet as possible.
For information on public holidays see the Calendar of events. Details on local f
days and festivals may be obtained from the Tourist Information Centre.
Telephone: From 4 April 1998 all Spanish telephone numbers have 9 digits: add
old area code to the existing number.

A

AGUILAR DE CAMPÓO
🄱 Plaza de España 32 – 34800 – ☎ 979 12 2

Monasterio de Santa María la Real - Open 10am-2pm and 4-8pm; 200 pts to
the museum; ☎ 979 12 50 00.

Colegiata de San Miguel - Guided tours available by prior arrangement f
noon-1pm and 4-5pm; in summer from 10.30am-1.30pm and 4-5
☎ 979 12 22 31.

AIGÜESTORTES I ESTANY DE SANT MAURICI

Parque Nacional - It is advisable to start your visit at the Casa del Parque Naci
L'Estudi (west), Plaza del Treio 3, Boi; ☎ 973 69 61 89; or the Casa del Pa
Nacional (east), Calle Prat del Guarda 2, Espot; ☎ 973 62 40 36; open f
9am-1pm and 3.30-7pm (9am-1pm Sun and public holidays Oct-Mar); closed 1
and 25 Dec; tickets for the park cost 500 pts (1 000 pts Rtn).

ALACANT/ALICANTE
🄱 Explanada de España 2 – 03002 – ☎ 96 520 (

Catedral de San Nicolás - Open 7am-noon and 6-8pm; Sun and public holi‹
8.30am-1pm; no charge ☎ 96 521 26 62.

Ayuntamiento: Capilla - Open 9am-2pm; closed Sat-Sun and public holid
☎ 96 514 91 10.

Iglesia de Santa María - Closed for restoration; ☎ 96 521 60 26.

Museo de la Asegurada - Open 10am-1pm and 5-8pm; Sun and public holi‹
10am-1pm; 1 May-30 Sept 10.30am-1.30pm and 6-9pm; Sun and public holi‹
10.30am-1.30pm; closed Mon, 1 Jan and 25 Dec; no charge; ☎ 96 314 07 (

Castillo de Santa Bárbara - Open 21 Sept-21 Mar 9am-7pm; 22 Mar-22 ‹
10am-8pm; last visit 30min before closing time; 300 pts for use of the lift, no ch‹
for those driving or on foot; ☎ 96 526 31 31.

Cuevas de Canalobre - Guided tours (40min) 11am-5.50pm; 21 June-30 ‹
10.30am-7.50pm (same times during Holy Week); closed 1 Jan and 25 Dec; 550‹
☎ 96 569 92 50.

ALBACETE
🄱 Tinte 2. Edificio Posada del Rosario – 02001 – ☎ 976 58 (

Museo de Albacete - Open 10am-2pm and 4.30pm-7pm; Sun and public holi‹
9am-2pm; closed Mon, Maundy Thur, Good Fri, 1 Jan and 25 Dec; 200 ‹
☎ 967 22 83 07.

ALBARRACÍN
🄱 Catedral, 5 – 44100 – ☎ 978 71 02 51 or ☎ 978 70 (

Catedral - Guided tours (30min) 10.30am-2pm and 4-6pm (8pm Apr-S‹
300 pts (includes a visit to the museum); ☎ 978 71 00 84.

CALÁ DE HENARES 🛈 Callejón de Santa María 1 – 28801 – ☎ 91 889 26 94

tigua Universidad o Colegio de San Ildefonso - Guided tours (40min) .30am-1.30pm and 6-7pm; Sat, Sun and public holidays 11am-2pm and 0-5.30pm; 1 June-30 Sept 11.30am-1.30pm and 6-7pm; Sat-Sun and public idays 11am-2pm and 5-8pm; closed 1 Jan and 25 Dec; 300 pts (combined ticket uding the Capilla de San Ildefonso); ☎ 91 889 26 94.

pilla de San Ildefonso - Same opening times as for the Antigua Universidad.

CÁNTARA 🛈 Av. de Mérida 21 – 10980 – ☎ 927 39 08 63

nvento de San Benito - Guided tours (30min) 10am-2pm and 4-6pm; Sat .30am-2pm and 4-6pm; in summer 10am-2pm and 6-8pm; Sun and public idays 11.30am-1.30pm; closed over Christmas; ☎ 927 39 00 80.

CAÑIZ

legiata - Open daily 10.30am-1.30pm and 4.30-7.30pm; in winter am-1.30pm and 4.30-6pm; closed Mon and Wed mornings; 200 pts; 978 83 12 13.

ICANTE
e ALACANT

MAGRO 🛈 Bernardas 2 – 13270 – ☎ 926 86 07 17

rral de Comedias - Open 10am-2pm and 4-7pm; Sat 10am-2pm and 4-6pm; n and public holidays 11am-2pm and 4-6pm; 1 Apr-30 June and in Sept am-2pm and 6-9pm; Sat 10am-2pm and 6p-8pm; Sun and public holidays am-2pm and 6-8pm; closed Mon; 400 pts; 100 pts on Sat-Sun; ☎ 926 86 07 17.

nvento de la Asunción - Open 11am-1pm and 5-6pm; Sun and public holidays am-noon; ☎ 926 86 03 50.

MERÍA 🛈 Parque de Nicolás Salmerón s/n – 04002 – ☎ 950 27 43 55

azaba - Open 9.30am-1.30pm and 3.30-6.30pm; 16 June-30 Sept am-2pm and 3-8pm; closed 1 Jan and 25 Dec; 250 pts (no charge for citizens the European Union); ☎ 950 27 16 17.

tedral - Open 10am-5.30pm; tourists may not visit the church on Sun and public lidays; 300 pts; ☎ 989 67 90 03.

stillo de ALMODÓVAR DEL RIO

ng the bell; the guard will show you around; ☎ 957 71 36 02 (Town Hall).

QUÉZAR

legiata - Guided tours daily except Tues 11am-1pm and 4-6pm (11am-1pm and 0-7.30pm in summer); 200 pts; ☎ 974 31 82 67.

Jevas de ALTAMIRA

ided tour - The number of visitors is restricted in order to preserve the paintings the caves. Write well in advance (a year) for permission to Centro de Investigación Museo de Altamira, 39 330 Santillana del Mar, (Cantabria); ☎ 942 81 80 05.

useo - Open daily 9.30am-2.40pm; closed Mon, 1 Jan, 1 May, 28 June, 16 Aug, , 25 and 31 Dec; ☎ 942 81 80 05.

incipat d'ANDORRA 🛈 Carrer Docteur Vilanova 1 – Andorra la Vella – ☎ (376) 82 02 14

e also entry in alphabetical section of guide for practical information.

sa de les Valls - Guided tours (30min) weekdays 10am-1pm and 3-6pm; it is cessary to book your visit one month in advance; closed 1 Jan, 8 Sept, 25 and 26 ec; ☎ (376) 82 91 29.

lesia de Sant Joan de Caselles - Visits by prior arrangement; ☎ (376) 85 14 34.

NTEQUERA 🛈 Pl. de San Sebastián 7 – 29200 – ☎ 95 270 25 05

useo Municipal - Guided tours (40min) 10am-1.30pm; Sat 10am-1pm; Sun am-1pm; closed Mon and public holidays; 200 pts; ☎ 95 270 40 21.

lesia del Carmen - Open 10am-2pm; Sat 10am-2pm and 4-7pm; closed Mon; 0 pts; ☎ 95 270 25 05 or 909 53 97 10.

s Dólmenes - Open 10am-2pm and 3-5.30pm; Sat and Sun open mornings only; sed Mon and public holidays; ☎ 95 270 25 05.

RACENA 🛈 Pl. de San Pedro s/n – 21200 – ☎ 959 11 03 55

uta de las Maravillas - Guided tours (45min) hourly 10.30am-1.30pm and 6pm; every 30min on Sat, Sun and public holidays; 875 pts; ☎ 959 12 83 55.

ARANJUEZ

🛈 Puente de Barcas – 28300 – ☎ 91 891 0

Palacio Real - Guided tours 10am-5.15pm; 1 Apr-30 Sept 10am-6.15pm; cl
Mon, 1 and 6 Jan, 2 and 30 May, 15 Aug, 5 Sept, 25 and 26 Dec; may also close du
official ceremonies; 650 pts (no charge Wed for citizens of the European Uni
☎ 91 542 00 59.

Parterre and Jardín de la Isla - Open 8am-6.30pm; 1 Apr-30 Sept 8am-8.30
closed Mon, 1 and 6 Jan, 2 and 30 May, 15 Aug, 5 Sept and 25 and 26
☎ 91 542 00 59.

Jardín del Príncipe - Same opening times as for the Parterre and Jardín de la

Casa del Labrador - Guided tours available; same opening times as for the Pa
Real; 425 pts (600 pts for combined ticket including the Casa de Marinos); no cha
Wed for citizens of the European Union.

Casa de Marinos - Guided tours available; same times and charges as for the C
del Labrador; 325 pts (600 pts for combined ticket including the Casa del Labrad
no charge Wed for citizens of the European Union.

ARCOS DE LA FRONTERA

🛈 Cuesta de Belén, s/n – 11630 – ☎ 956 70 2

Iglesia de Santa María - Open 2 Sept-30 Nov 10am-1pm and 4-6.30pm; 1 M
1 Sept 10am-1pm and 5-6.30pm; Sat 10am-2.30pm; closed Sun and pu
holidays as well as Dec, Jan and Feb; 150 pts; ☎ 956 70 22 64.

ASTORGA

🛈 Pl. Eduardo de Castro (Iglesia Santa Marta). 24700. ☎ 987 61 6

Catedral - Open 9am-noon and 4.30-6pm; in summer 9am-noon and 5-6.30
☎ 987 61 58 20.

Museo de la Catedral - Open 11am-2pm and 3.30-6.30pm; in sum
10am-2pm and 4-8pm; closed Jan; 250 pts (400 pts combined ticket including
of the Palacio Episcopal); ☎ 987 61 58 20.

Palacio Episcopal - Open 11am-2pm and 3.30-6.30pm; 21 Apr-20 S
10am-2pm and 4-8pm; closed Sun and public holidays Oct-Mar, 1 and 6 Jan
25 Dec; 250 pts; ☎ 987 61 68 82.

Museo de los Caminos - Same opening times as for the Palacio Episcopal; 400
(combined ticket including visit of the Museo de la Catedral).

ÁVILA

🛈 Pl. Catedral 4 – 05001 – ☎ 920 21 1

Catedral - Open 10.30am-1.30pm and 3.30-5.30pm; 15 Apr-15
10.30am-1.30pm and 3.30-6pm; closed 1 and 6 Jan, Maundy Thur, 15 Oct
25 Dec; 250 pts; ☎ 920 21 16 41.

Museo - Open 10am-1.30pm and 3.30-5.30pm (in summer 4-6pm); last
30min before closing time; closed 1 and 6 Jan, Corpus Christi, 15 Oct and 25
250 pts; ☎ 920 21 16 41.

Basílica de San Vicente - Open 10am-2pm and 4-7pm; visitors are requested
to interrupt religious services; 100 pts; ☎ 920 25 52 30.

Monasterio de Santo Tomás - Open 10am-1pm and 4-7pm; entrance to clois
100 pts; ☎ 920 22 04 00.

Iglesia de San Pedro - Open 9.30am-12.30pm and 6-8.30pm; no sightseeing vi
during religious services; ☎ 920 22 93 28.

B

BADAJOZ

🛈 Pl. Libertad 3 – 06005 – 924 22 2

Catedral - Open 10am-noon and 6-8pm (it is not possible to visit the church
Sun); visits to the museum Fri and Sat only 11am-1pm; 300 pts (including Mus
☎ 924 22 39 99.

Museo Arqueológico Provincial - Open 10am-3pm; closed Mon and pu
holidays; 200 pts (no charge for citizens of the European Union); ☎ 924 22 23

Museo Provincial de Bellas Artes - Open 10am-2pm and 4-6pm; Sat-S
10am-2pm; closed Mon and public holidays; no charge; ☎ 924 21 24
or 924 24 80 34.

BAEZA

🛈 Pl. del Pópulo s/n – 23440 – 953 74 0

Catedral - Open daily 10.30am-1pm and 4-6.30pm; 1 June-30 S
10.30am-1pm and 5-8pm; ☎ 953 74 04 44.

Iglesia de San Andrés - Open 6-9pm (during services only); ☎ 953 74 04 44

olegiata - Visits by prior arrangement; ☎ 986 35 51 65.

nterreal - Open 8am-11pm; 100 pts and 500 pts per car; ☎ 986 35 50 00.

RBASTRO   🖪 Pl. Aragón – 22300 – ☎ 974 31 43 13

edral - Open daily 10am-1pm and 6pm-8pm; ☎ 974 31 16 82.

reciudad - Open 10am-2pm and 4-7pm; 1 May-15 June 10am-2pm and
7.30pm; Sat 10am-2pm and 4-8.30pm; Sun and public holidays 9am-2pm and
3.30pm; 16 June-15 Sept 10am-2pm and 4-8.30pm; Sun and public holidays
n-2pm and 4-8.30pm; ☎ 974 30 40 25.

RCELONA   🖪 Plaza de Catalunya, 17-S – 08002 – ☎ 93 304 31 34
            🖪 Paseo de Gràcia, 107 (Palau Robert) – 08008 – ☎ 93 238 40 00
            🖪 Sants Estació – 08014 – ☎ 93 491 44 31

seu del Barça - Open 10am-6.30pm; Sun and public holidays 10am-2pm;
ed 1 and 6 Jan and 25 Dec; 475pts; ☎ 93 496 36 08.

erinto de Horta - Open 10am-6pm (7pm Mar and Oct, 8pm Apr and Sept, 9pm
y and Aug); 275 pts; no charge on Wed and Sun; ☎ 93 428 25 00.

edral - Open daily 8am-1.30pm and 4-7.30pm (except during religious
vices); the terrace and the *coro* open daily except Sat afternoons and Sun
0 pts); ☎ 93 315 15 54.

seo Diocesano de Barcelona - Open 11am-2pm and 5-8pm; Sun 11am-2pm
y, closed Mon; 300 pts; ☎ 93 315 22 13.

ustro: Museu - Open daily 11am-1pm and 4-7pm; closed Sat afternoons;
) pts; ☎ 93 315 15 54.

seu del Calçat - Open daily except Mon 11am-2pm; 200 pts; ☎ 93 301 45 33.

seu d'Història de la Ciutat - Open 10am-2pm and 4-8pm; 1 July-30 Sept
am-8pm; Sun and public holidays all year 10am-2pm; closed Mon, 1 Jan, Good
, 1 May, 24 June, 25 and 26 Dec; 500 pts (no charge the first Sat of each month);
93 315 11 11.

seu Frederic Marès - Open 10am-5pm; Sun and public holidays 10am-2pm;
sed Mon, 1 Jan, Good Fri, 1 May, 24 June, 25 and 26 Dec; 300 pts;
93 310 58 00.

seu d'Art Contemporàni de Barcelona - Open 10am-8pm; Sun and public
idays 10am-3pm; 25 June-30 Sept 10.30am-8pm; Sun and public holidays
am-3pm; closed Tues, 1 Jan and 25 Dec; 700; ☎ 93 412 08 10.

ntre de Cultura Contemporàni de Barcelona - Open 11am-2pm and 4-8pm;
d and Sat 11am-8pm; Sun and public holidays 11am-7pm; closed Mon, 1 Jan and
Dec; 600 pts; ☎ 93 481 10 69.

esia de Santa Maria del Pi - Open 8.30am-1pm and 4.30-8.45pm; Sun and
lic holidays 9am-2pm and 5-9pm (no visits during religious services);
93 318 47 43.

au Güell - Open 10am-2pm and 4-8pm; closed Sun and public holidays; 300 pts;
93 319 74.

nvento de Santa Mònica - Open 10am-2pm and 5-8pm; Sun and public holidays
am-2pm; closed 1 and 6 Jan, Good Fri and 25 Dec; ☎ 93 412 22 79.

seo de Cera - Open 10am-1.30pm and 4-7.30pm; Sat-Sun and public holidays
am-1.30pm and 4.30-8pm; 900 pts; ☎ 93 317 26 49.

assanes y Museu Marítim - Open 10am-7pm; 1 Oct-1 Apr from 10am-6pm;
n and public holidays from 10am-3pm; last visit 1hr before closing time; closed
n, 1 Jan, Good Fri, 1 May, 24 June, 25 and 26 Dec; 800 pts; ☎ 93 301 18 71.

ax - Check times and prices; ☎ 93 225 11 11.

uarium - Open 9.30am-9pm 1 Oct-31 May (9.30pm in Sept and June; 11pm in
y and Aug); last visit one hour before closing; 1 400 pts; ☎ 93 221 74 74.

sílica de la Mercè - Open 10am-1pm and 6-8pm; Sat 10am-1pm and
8.30pm; Sun and public holidays 10am-2pm and 7pm-8.30pm;
93 310 50 51.

rc de la Ciutadella - Open daily 8am-8pm; 1 Apr-30 Sept 8am-9pm; 200 pts;
93 424 38 09.

seu Zoologia - Open 10am-2pm. Closed Mon, 1 Jan and 25 Dec. 400 pts (no
arge the first Sun of the month). ☎ 93 319 69 12.

rc Zoològic - Open May-Aug from 9.30am-7.30pm; Apr and Sept from
am-7pm; Mar from 10am-6pm; Jan, Feb, Oct and Dec from 10am-5pm. Closed
Dec. 1 400 pts. ☎ 93 221 25 06.

Museu d'Art Modern - Open 10am-7pm; Sun and public holidays 10am-2.30
closed Mon, 1 Jan, 1 May and 25 Dec; 500 pts (no charge the first Thur of
month); ☎ 93 319 57 28.

Museo d'Historia de Catalunya - Open Mon-Thur 10am-7pm; Fri and
10am-8pm; Sun and public holidays 10am-2.30pm; 500; ☎ 93 225 47 00.

Museu Tèxtil i d'Indumentària - Open 10am-8pm; Sun and public holi
10am-3pm; closed Mon, 1 Jan, Good Fri, 1 May, 24 June, 25 and 26 Dec; 400
no charge the first Sat of the month; ☎ 93 310 45 16.

Museu Picasso - Open 10am-8pm; Sun 10am-3pm; closed Mon, 1 Jan, Good
1 May, 24 June, 25 and 26 Dec; 500 pts; no charge the first Sun of the mo
☎ 93 319 63 10.

Museu Barbier-Mueller d'art precolombí - Open 10am-8pm; Sun and p
holidays 10am-3pm; closed Mon, 1 Jan, Good Fri, 1 May, 24 June, 25 and 26
500 pts; ☎ 93 319 63 10.

Iglesia de Santa Maria del Mar - Open daily 9.30am-1.30pm and 4.30-6pm;
8.30am-2pm and 4.30-8.30pm; ☎ 93 310 23 90.

Museu Nacional d'Art de Catalunya - Open 10am-7pm; Thur 10am-9pm; Sun
public holidays 10am-2.30pm; closed Mon, 1 Jan, 1 May and 25 Dec; 800 pts
charge the first Thur of each month); ☎ 93 426 53 86.

Poble Espanyol - Open Mon 9am-8pm; Tues-Thur 9am-2am; Fri and
9am-4am; Sun 9am-midnight; last visit 1hr before closing time; closed 1 Jan
25 Dec at noon; 950 pts; no charge on Sun from 8pm-midnight; ☎ 93 325 78

Museo de Artes, Industrias y Tradiciones Populares - Visits by prior arrangem
☎ 93 423 69 54.

Olympic Stadium - Guided tours (1hr) by prior arrangement, providing there ar
sporting events held at the same time; closed Aug; ☎ 93 426 20 89.

Palau Sant Jordi - Open daily 10am-1pm; ☎ 93 426 20 89.

Galería Olímpica - Open 1 Oct-31 Mar 10am-1pm and 4-6pm; Sat, Sun and p
holidays 10am-2pm; 1 Apr-30 June 10am-2pm and 4-7pm; Sun and p
holidays 10am-2pm; 1 July-30 Sept 10am-2pm and 4-8pm; Sun and p
holidays 10am-2pm; closed Mon, 1 Jan and 25 Dec; 390 pts; ☎ 93 426 06

Fundació Joan Miró - Open 11am-7pm; Thur 11am-9.30pm; Sun and p
holidays 10.30am-2.30pm; 1 July-30 Sept 10am-8pm; Thur 10am-9.30pm;
and public holidays 10am-2.30pm; last visit 30min before closing time; closed N
1 and 6 Jan, 25 Dec; 700 pts; ☎ 93 329 19 08.

Museu Arqueològic - Open 9.30am-7pm; Sun 10am-2.30pm; closed Mon; 200
(no charge on Sun); ☎ 93 424 65 77.

La Sagrada Familia - Open Jan and Feb 9am-6pm; Mar, Sept and Oct 9am-7
Apr-Aug 9am-8pm; 1 Jan and 25 Dec 9am-1pm; 800 pts; ☎ 93 455 02 47

La Pedrera or Casa Milà - Open 10am-8pm; 500 pts; ☎ 93 484 59 95.

Casa Milà (La Pedrera)

sa Quadras: Museu de la Mùsica - Open 10am-2pm; Wed 10am-8pm (except in
mmer); closed Mon, 1 Jan, Good Fri, 1 May, 24 June, 25 and 26 Dec; 300 pts (no
arge on the first Sun of each month); ☎ 93 416 11 57.

rc Güell - Open Nov-Feb 10am-6pm; May-Aug 10am-9pm; Mar and Oct
am-7pm; Apr and Sept 10am-8pm; ☎ 93 424 38 09.

sa-Museu Gaudí - Open Nov-Feb 10am-6pm; May-Aug 10am-9pm; Mar and
t 10am-7pm; Apr and Sept 10am-8pm; ☎ 93 284 64 46.

lau de la Mùsica Catalana - Guided tours only (1hr) on Tues and Thur by prior
rangement in Catalan, Spanish, English and French; closed on public holidays and
Aug; 500 pts; ☎ 93 268 10 00.

ndació Antoni Tàpies - Open 11am-8pm; closed Mon, 1 and 6 Jan, 25 and
Dec; 500 pts; ☎ 93 487 03 15.

onastir de Santa Maria de Pedralbes - Open 10am-2pm; last visit 30min before
sing time; closed Mon, 1 Jan, Good Fri, 1 May, 24 June, 25 and 26 Dec; 400 pts (no
charge the first Sun of each month); ☎ 93 203 92 82.

lau de Pedralbes: Museu de les Artes Decoratives - Open 10am-3pm; closed Mon,
Jan, Good Fri and 25 Dec; 400 pts each museum; 700 pts for both (no charge the
st Sun of each month); ☎ 93 280 16 21. Museu de Ceràmica - Same opening times
the Museu de les Artes Decoratives; ☎ 93 280 16 21.

useu de la Ciència - Open 10am-8pm; closed Mon, 1 and 6 Jan, 25 Dec; 500 pts
50 pts for planetarium); ☎ 93 212 60 50.

LMONTE

stillo - Open 10am-1pm and 3.30-6pm; in summer 10am-1.30pm and 4-8pm;
0 pts; ☎ 967 17 00 08.

TANZOS

lesia de Santa María del Azogue - Open daily 10.30am-2pm and 4-7.30pm (no
its during religious services); ☎ 981 77 07 02.

lesia de San Francisco - Open daily 10.30am-2pm and 4-7.30pm.

LBO/BILBAO   🚹 Pl. Arriaga, 1 – 48005 – ☎ 94 416 00 22

useo Guggenheim - Open from 10am-8pm; closed Mon; 700 pts;
94 435 90 00.

useo de Bellas Artes - Open 10am-1.30pm and 4-7.30pm; Sun 10am-2pm;
sed Mon and public holidays, 1 and 6 Jan, Holy Week, 25 and 31 July, 15 and 23
g, 12 Oct, 1 Nov, 6, 8 and 25 Dec; 400 pts; no charge on Wed; ☎ 94 439 60 60.

useo Vasco - Open 10.30am-1.30pm and 4-7pm; Sun 10.30am-1.30pm; closed
on and public holidays; 300 pts; ☎ 94 415 54 23.

useo Diocesano de Arte Sacro - Open from 8am-1.30pm and 4-7 pm; Sun
.30am-1.30pm; closed Mon and public holidays; no charge; ☎ 94 441 01 25.

sílica de Begoña - Open 8am to 1.30pm and 4.30-8.30pm (9pm on Sat); Sun
d public holidays 9.30am-2pm and 5.30-9pm; 15 Aug 4am-10pm;
94 412 70 91.

BURGO DE OSMA

tedral and Museo - Open 9.30am-1pm and 4-7pm; Sun and public holidays
on-2pm and 4-7pm; 2 Nov-31 Dec only open on Sun and public holidays; 200 pts
useum); ☎ 975 34 01 96.

rlanga de Duero: Colegiata - To visit the collegiate church, follow the instructions
itten on the church door; ☎ 975 34 30 49.

sillas de Berlanga: Iglesia de San Baudelio de Berlanga - Open 1 July-31 Aug from
.30am-2pm and 5-9pm; 1 Apr-30 June and 1 Sept-31 Oct from 10.30am-2pm
d 4-7pm; 1 Nov-31 Mar from 10.30am-2pm and 4-6pm. On Sun and public
lidays all year round open from 10.30am-2pm. Closed on Mon, Tues, 1 Jan and
Dec. 100 pts (no charge at Sat-Sun). ☎ 975 22 13 97.

ñón de río Lobos - For information on visits, call ☎ 975 36 35 64.

JRGOS   🚹 Pl. Alonso Martínez 7 – 09003 – ☎ 947 20 31 25

tedral - Open daily 9.30am-1pm and 4-7pm (except Sun mornings and during
ligious services and celebrations); 400 pts; ☎ 947 20 47 12.

co de Santa María - Open 11am-2pm and 5-9pm; Sun 11am-2pm; closed Mon
d public holidays; no charge; ☎ 947 26 53 75.

BURGOS

Iglesia de San Nicolás - Open daily 6.30-7.30pm; Mon open all day; public holid 9am-2pm and 5-6pm; 15 June-15 Sept 9am-2pm and 4-8pm; closed dur religious services; ☎ 947 20 70 95.

Iglesia de San Esteban: Museo del Retablo - Open June-Oct 10.30am-2pm a 4.30-7pm; open by prior arrangement the rest of the year; closed Mon; 200 p

Iglesia de San Gil - Open from 10am-2pm and 5-8pm; in summer by pr arrangement; closed Mon; ☎ 947 26 11 49.

Real Monasterio de Las Huelgas - Guided tours (50min) 11am-1.15pm a 4-5.15pm (Sat 5.45pm); Sun and public holidays 10.30am-2.15pm; 1 Apr-30 S 10.30am-1.15pm and 4-5.45pm; Sun and public holidays 10.30am-2.15p closed Mon and public holidays; 650 pts (no charge Wed for citizens of the Europe Union); ☎ 947 20 16 30.

Cartuja de Miraflores - Open daily 10.15am-3pm and 4-6pm; Sun and pu holidays 10.15am-11am, 11.30am-12.30pm, 1.15-3pm and 4-6.15pm; charge.

Museo de Burgos - Open 10am-2pm and 4.15pm-7pm; Sat and Sun 10am-2p closed Mon and public holidays; 200 pts (no charge Sat and Sun); ☎ 947 26 58

Museo Marceliano Santa María - Open 10am-1.50pm and 5pm-7.50pm; ! 10am-1.50pm; closed Mon and public holidays; 25 pts; ☎ 947 20 56 87.

C

CÁCERES
☐ Pl. Mayor 10 – 10003 – ☎ 927 24 63

Iglesia de Santa María - Open 10am-2pm and 5-7.30pm (6-8.30pm 1 Ma 30 Sept); Sun and public holidays 9.30am-2pm and 5-7.30pm (6pm-8.30 1 May-30 Sept); 100 pts (museum); ☎ 927 21 53 13.

Palacio de Carvajal - Open Mon-Fri 8am-3pm; Sat, Sun and public holid 10am-2pm; ☎ 927 25 55 97.

Casa de las Veletas: Museo de Cáceres - Open 9am-2.30pm; Sun 10.15am-2.30p closed Mon and public holidays; 200 pts (no charge for citizens of the Europe Union); ☎ 927 24 72 34.

Iglesia de Santiago - Open 9am-noon and 6-8pm; ☎ 927 24 49 06.

Santuario de la Virgen de la Montaña - Open daily 8.30am-2pm and 4-8p closed 22 Apr until the first Sun in May; ☎ 927 22 00 49.

Museo Vostell Malpartida - Open from 10am-1.30pm and 4-6.30pm; in summ 10am-1.30pm and 4-9pm, in spring from 10am-1.30pm and 5-7.30pm; clo Sun and public holidays; 200 pts; no charge on Wed; ☎ 927 27 64 92.

CÁDIZ
☐ Calderón de la Barca 1 – 11003 – ☎ 956 21 13

Museo Provincial de Cádiz - Open Tues-Sun 9.30am-2pm (2.30pm in wint closed Mon and public holidays; 250 pts (no charge for citizens of the Europe Union); ☎ 956 21 22 81.

Museo Histórico Municipal - Open 9am-1pm and 4-7pm (5-8pm from June-15 Sept); Sat-Sun 9am-1pm; closed Mon, 1 and 6 Jan, 28 Feb, 1 May, 15 A 7 and 12 Oct, 1 Nov, 6, 8, 24, 25 and 31 Dec; ☎ 956 22 17 88.

Iglesia de San Felipe Neri - Open weekdays 8.30am-10am and 7.30pm-10pm; ! 5.30-10pm; Sun 10.30am-2pm; ☎ 956 21 16 12.

Catedral and Museo - Open noon-1pm; closed Sun and public holidays; 100 p Museum open 10am-noon; closed Sun and public holidays; 400 p ☎ 956 28 61 54.

Medina Sidonia: Iglesia de Santa María - Open daily 10am-7pm; ☎ 956 41 03 2

Castillo-Convento de CALATRAVA

Open 10am-2pm and 4-7pm; 1 Apr-30 Sept 10am-2pm and 6-9pm; closed M and public holidays; ☎ 926 62 35 48.

CANGAS DE NARCEA

Corias: Monasterio - Open 9.30am-12.30pm and 3.30-7.30pm; ☎ 98 581 01 !

CARAVACA DE LA CRUZ

Castillo-Iglesia de la Santa Cruz - Guided tours (45min) 11am-1.30pm a 5-7pm; 10am-1pm and 4.30-8.30pm during Aug); closed 1-5 May and 14 Se 400 pts; ☎ 968 70 77 43.

ARDONA
🛈 Av. del Rastrillo s/n – 08261 – ☎ 93 869 27 98

Colegiata de Sant Vincenç - Open 10am-1pm and 3-5.30pm (6.30pm from July-30 Sept); Sun and public holidays 10am-1.30pm; last visit 30min before closing time; closed Mon, 1 Jan and 25 Dec; 300 pts; no charge on Tues; ☎ 93 868 41 69.

ARMONA
🛈 Arco de las Descalzas – 41410 – ☎ 95 414 22 00

Iglesia de Santa María - Open daily 9am-noon and 6-9pm; ☎ 95 419 09 55.

Necrópolis Romana - Open 10am-2pm and 4-6pm; 15 June-15 Sept 10.30am-2pm; Sat-Sun 10am-2pm (except Sun from 15 July-15 Sept); closed Mon and public holidays; 250 for citizens not belonging to the European Union; ☎ 95 419 09 55.

ARTAGENA
🛈 Pl. Ayuntamiento – 30202 – ☎ 968 50 64 83

Museo Nacional de Arqueología Marítima - Open 10am-3pm; closed Mon, 1 and Jan, 1 May, 24, 25 and 31 Dec as well as local public holidays; 400 pts (no charge on Sun); ☎ 968 50 84 15.

ELANOVA

Monasterio - Guided tours (45min) at noon, 1pm, 5pm and 6pm; June-Sept at 11am, noon, 1pm, 5pm, 6pm and 7pm; 200 pts; ☎ 988 43 22 01.

CEUTA
🛈 Alcalde José Victori Goñalons s/n – 11701 – ☎ 956 51 40 92

Museo Municipal - Open 10am-1pm and 5-8pm; 1 June-31 Aug 10am-1pm and 5-9pm (until 2pm Sat all year); closed Sun and public holidays; no charge; ☎ 956 51 73 98.

Parque marítimo del Mediterráneo - Open 11am-7pm (8pm in winter); closed Thur in winter; 300 pts Mon, 600 pts Tues-Sat, 800 pts Sun and public holidays; ☎ 956 51 69 89.

CIUDAD RODRIGO
🛈 Pl. de las Amayuelas 6 – 37500 – ☎ 923 46 05 61

Catedral - Open daily 10am-1pm and 4-6pm (no visits during religious services); 200 pts to visit the cloisters; ☎ 923 48 14 24.

COCA

Castillo - Guided tours (30min) 10.30am-1.30pm and 4.30-6pm; Sat, Sun and public holidays 11am-1.30pm and 4-6pm; 1 July-30 Sept 10.30am-1.30pm and 4.30-8pm (7pm in May and June); Sat, Sundays and public holidays 10am-1.30pm and 4.30-8pm (7pm in May and June); last visit 30min before closing time; closed the first Tues of each month; 300 pts; ☎ 921 58 66 22.

CÓRDOBA
🛈 Torrijos 10 – 14003 – ☎ 957 47 12 35
🛈 Plaza Judá Levi – 14003 – ☎ 957 20 05 22

Mezquita-Catedral - Open Jan and Dec 10am-5.30pm; Feb and Nov 10am-6pm; Mar and July-Oct 10am-7pm; Apr-June 10am-7.30pm; last visit 30min before closing time; closed on 1 Jan, 25, 26 and 27 May, 24, 25 and 31 Dec (afternoons); 750 pts; ☎ 957 47 05 12.

Sinagoga - Open 10am-1.30pm and 3.30-5.30pm; Sun and public holidays 10am-2pm; closed Mon, 1 and 6 Jan, 24, 25 and 31 Dec; 50 pts; (no charge for citizens of the European Union); ☎ 957 20 29 28.

Palacio de Viana - Guided tours (1hr) 10am-1pm and 4-6pm; Sun and public holidays 10am-1.30pm; 16 June-30 Sept 9am-2pm; closed Wed, 1 Jan, Good Fri, 1 May, 1st fortnight in June, 24 Oct and 25 Dec; 400 pts (no charge on Thur); ☎ 957 48 22 75.

Museo Arqueológico Provincial - Open 10am-2pm and 5-7pm; Sun and public holidays 10am-1.30pm; 15 June-15 Sept 10am-2pm and 6-8pm; Sun and public holidays 10am-1.30pm; closed Mon, 1 and 6 Jan, 24, 25 and 31 Dec; 250 pts for citizens not belonging to the European Union; ☎ 957 47 40 11.

Alcázar - Open 10am-2pm and 4.30-6.30pm; (6pm-8pm 1 May-30 Sept); Sun and public holidays all year 9.30am-3pm; closed Mon, 1 Jan, Good Fri, 25 Dec; 425 pts (no charge on Fri); ☎ 957 48 50 01.

Torre de la Calahorra - Guided tours (1hr) from 10am-6pm; 1 May-30 Sept 10am-2pm and 5.30-8.30pm; 500 pts; ☎ 957 29 39 29.

Museo Municipal Taurino - Open 10am-2pm and 5-7pm; 1 May-30 Sept 10am-2pm and 6-8pm; Sun and public holidays all year 9.30am-3pm; closed Mon, 1 Jan, Good Fri, 25 Dec; 425 pts (no charge on Fri); ☎ 957 48 50 01.

CÓRDOBA

Posada del Potro - Open 9am-2pm and 5-8pm; closed Sat, Sun, public holidays a throughout Aug; no charge; ☎ 957 48 50 01.

Museo Julio Romero de Torres - Same opening times as Museo Municipal Tauri ☎ 957 48 50 01.

Museo de Bellas Artes - Open 10am-2pm and 5-7pm; 16 June-30 S 10am-1.30pm and 6-8.30pm; Sun and public holidays all year mornings on closed Mon, 1 and 6 Jan, Good Fri, Maundy Thur, 24, 25 and 31 Dec; 250 pts (charge for citizens of the European Union); ☎ 957 47 33 45.

Medina Azahara - Open 10am-2pm and 4-6.30pm (1 May-15 June 6-8.30pr Sun and public holidays open mornings only; 16 June-30 Sept 10am-1.30pm a 6-8.30pm; Sun and public holidays open mornings only; closed Mon, 1 and 6 Jan, 2 25 and 31 Dec; 250 pts (no charge for citizens of the European Union); ☎ 952 91 3

CORIA

Catedral - Open daily 9.30am-1pm and 4-7pm; ☎ 927 50 39 60.

A CORUÑA/La CORUÑA   🛈 Dársena de la Marina s/n – 15001 – ☎ 981 22 18

Colegiata de Santa María del Campo - Open daily 9.30am-1.30pm and 5.30-7p in summer 8.30am-1pm and 5.45-7pm (no visits during religious services); charge; ☎ 981 20 31 86.

Iglesia de Santiago - Open daily 9.30am-1pm and 6.30-8.30pm (no visits duri religious services); ☎ 981 20 56 96.

Castillo de San Antón: Museo Arqueológico e Histórico - Open 10am-7pm (9pm in Ju and Aug); Sun and public holidays 10am-2.30pm (1pm in July and Aug); closed Mc 300 pts; ☎ 981 20 59 94.

Museo de Bellas Artes - Open Tues 10am-3pm; Wed-Fri 10am-8pm; S 10am-2pm and 4.30-8pm; Sun 10am-2pm; closed Mon; 400 pts, no charge on S afternoons; ☎ 981 22 37 23.

Domus-Casa del Hombre - Open daily 10am-7pm (9pm in summer); 30 ☎ 981 22 89 47.

Torre de Hércules - Open daily 10am-6pm (7pm in summer); Fri and Sat evenin 10pm-midnight; 250 pts; ☎ 981 22 10 54.

Cambre: Iglesia de Santa María - Open 9.30am-7.30pm; in summ 9.30am-9.30pm; ☎ 981 67 51 57.

Sant Pere de Rodes monastery ruins overlooking El Port de la Selva

COSTA BRAVA

Monasterio de Sant Pere de Rodes - Open 10am-12.15pm and 3-5.30pm (6.30pm Mar-Oct); last visit 20min before closing time; closed Mon, 1 Jan and 25 Dec; 400 pts (no charge on Tues); ☎ 972 20 34 04.

Cadaqués: Iglesia de Santa Maria - Open 1 June-30 Sept 10am-1pm and 4-8pm; other times of year prior arrangement; ☎ 972 25 80 84.

Cadaqués: Museu Perrot-Moore - Open 10.30am-1.30pm and 4-8pm; Sun and public holidays 10.30am-1.30pm; closed Sun and public holidays in winter; ☎ 972 25 83 12.

Casa-Museo Salvador Dalí - Visits by prior arrangement 10.30am-6pm; 10am-9pm 15 June-15 Sept; closed Mon; 1 200 pts; ☎ 972 25 80 63.

Castello d'Empúries: Iglesia de Santa Maria - Open 1 June-30 Sept 9.30am-1pm and 4-8pm; the rest of the year by prior arrangement; ☎ 972 25 05 19.

Islas Medes - Several companies organise boat trips around the islands. Apply to the Tourist Information Office; ☎ 972 75 19 10.

Calella de Palafrugell: Jardín Botànic del Cap Roig - Open 8am-5pm; 1 Apr-30 Sept 10am-2pm and 6-9pm; closed Mon and public holidays; ☎ 926 62 35 48.

Iglesia-Monasterio de Sant Feliu de Guíxols - Open 11am-2pm and 5-8pm; in summer 11am-2pm and 6-9pm; Sun and public holidays 11am-2pm; closed Mon, 1 Jan and 25 Dec; ☎ 972 82 15 75.

Tossa de Mar: Museu Municipal - Open 10am-1pm and 3-6pm; 1 June-30 Sept 10am-1pm and 3-7pm; closed Mon and 25 Dec; 200 pts; ☎ 972 34 07 09.

Blanes: Jardín Botánico de Marimurtra - Open 9am-6pm; 1 Nov-31 Mar 10am-5pm; Sat and Sun 10am-2pm; closed 1 and 6 Jan and 25 Dec; 300 pts; ☎ 972 33 08 26.

COSTA DE CANTABRIA

Santoña: Iglesia de Nuestra Señora del Puerto - Open 8-11am and 3.30-8.30pm; Sun and public holidays 8.30am-1pm and 6.30-7pm; ☎ 942 66 01 55.

Careyo: Iglesia de Santa María - Visits by prior arrangement; 25 pts; ☎ 942 62 11 67.

COSTA DE LA LUZ

Monasterio de la Rábida - Guided tours (40min) 10am-1pm and 4-6pm; Sun and public holidays 10.45am-1pm and 4-6pm (7pm from 1 May-31 Aug); closed Mon; ☎ 959 35 04 11.

Moguer: Convento de Santa Clara - Guided tours (45min) by prior arrangement at 11am, noon, 1pm, 5pm; 6pm and 7pm; Sun and public holidays at 11am, noon and 1pm; closed Mon and the first fortnight in Sept; 250 pts; ☎ 959 37 01 07.

Sanlúcar de Barrameda: Iglesia de Santo Domingo - Open 10am-noon and 6.30-8pm (no visits during religious services); ☎ 956 36 04 91.

COSTA DEL SOL

Cueva de Nerja - Open 10.30am-2pm and 4-6.30pm (8pm in July and Aug); 750 pts; ☎ 95 252 95 20.

COSTA VASCA

Zumaia: Casa-Museo de Ignacio Zuloaga - Open 4-8pm; closed Mon, Tues and 15 Sept-1 Mar; 400 pts; ☎ 943 86 23 41.

Cuevas de Santimamiñe - Guided tours (1hr) at 10am, 11.15am, 12.30pm, 4.30pm and 6pm; closed Sat, Sun and public holidays; no charge; ☎ 94 420 77 01 or 94 420 77 27.

Castillo de Butrón: Open 10.30am-5.30pm; Sat-Sun and public holidays 11am-6pm; Apr-Sept 10.30am-8pm; 700 pts (standard visit); 900 pts with planta noble; closed 1 Jan and 25 Dec; ☎ 94 615 11 10.

COSTA VERDE

Ribadesella: Cuevas de Tito Bustillo - Open 1 Apr-15 Sept; guided tours (45min) 10am-1pm and 3.30-5pm; closed Mon in Apr, May, June and Sept and Sun in July and Aug; 300 pts (no charge on Wed); ☎ 98 586 11 20.

Valdediós: Iglesia de San Salvador - Open 11am-1pm and 4.30-6pm; 1 Nov-30 Apr mornings only; closed Mon; ☎ 98 597 69 55.

Valdediós: Monasterio - Guided tours 11am-1pm; 1 May-31 Oct 11am-1pm and 4-6pm; closed Mon and one month a year (dates vary); ☎ 98 589 23 24.

COVADONGA

🖪 Pl. la Basilica s/n – 33589 – ☎ 98 584 60

La Santa Cueva - Open daily 8.30am-9pm; ☎ 98 584 60 26.

Basílica - Open daily 8.30am-9.30pm (no visits during religious services).

Museo de la Vírgen - Open daily 10.30am-1pm and 3-8pm; 200 p
☎ 98 584 60 35.

COVARRUBIAS

🖪 Manuel Ruiz Zorrilla – 09346 – ☎ 947 40 30

Colegiata and Museo-Tesoro - Guided tours (30min) 10.30am-7pm (Sun a
public holidays no visits at noon); closed Tues; 250 pts; ☎ 947 40 63 11.

Iglesia de Quintanilla de las Viñas - Open 9.30-2pm and 4-7pm; 1 Oct-31 M
9.30am-5.30pm; closed Mon, Tues, the last weekend of each month and dur
school holidays (dates vary); ☎ 947 28 15 70.

Lerma: Colegiata - Guided tours (1hr 15min) 10.30am-12.30pm and 5.30-6.30p
Sat 10.30am-12.30pm and 4.30-7pm; Sun and public holidays 11.30am-2pm;
winter by prior arrangement with the Tourist Office; closed Mon and 1 May; 200 p
☎ 947 17 01 43 (Tourist Office).

CUENCA

🖪 San Pedro 6 – 16001 – ☎ 969 23 21
🖪 Dalmancio Garcia Izcara, 8-1º – 16000 – ☎ 969 22 22

Catedral - Open 9am-2pm and 4.30-6pm (8pm Sat); Sun and public holida
9am-2pm; closed Mon; ☎ 969 21 24 63.

Museo Diocesano - Open 9am-2pm and 4.30-6pm (8pm Sat); Sun and pub
holidays 9am-2pm; closed Mon, 1 Jan, 25 Dec and for local festivities; 200 p
☎ 969 21 20 11.

Museo de Arte Abstracto Español - Open 11am-2pm and 4-6pm (8pm Sat); S
11am-2.30pm; closed Mon; 500 pts; ☎ 969 21 29 83.

Museo de Cuenca - Open 10am-2pm and 4-7pm; Sun and public holida
10am-2pm; closed Mon; 200 pts; ☎ 969 21 30 69.

D

DAROCA

🖪 Pl. de España 7 – 50360 – ☎ 976 80 01

Colegiata de Santa María - Open 11am-1pm and 5.30-7.30pm; Sun and pub
holidays 11.30am-1pm and 6-8pm (no visits during religious services at 12.30p
and 7pm); closed Mon; no charge; ☎ 976 80 07 61.

Museo Parroquial - Same opening times as above; 300 pts; ☎ 976 80 07 61.

Iglesia de San Miguel - Visits by prior arrangement; ☎ 976 80 01 29.

DONOSTIA/SAN SEBASTIAN

🖪 i Reina Regente – 20003 – ☎ 943 48 11

Monte Igueldo: Funicular - Open 1 Nov-31 Mar 11am-6pm; Sat, Sun and pub
holidays 11am-8pm; 1 Apr-30 June and in Sept 11am-8pm; in July and A
10am-10pm; closed Wed in winter; 105 pts (200 pts Rtn); ☎ 943 21 05 64.

Iglesia de Santa María - Open 8.30am-1.30pm and 4.30-8pm; ☎ 943 42 19 95.

Museo de San Telmo - Open 10.30am-1.30pm and 4-8pm; Sun 10am-2pm; last visit 15min before closing time; closed Mon, 1, 6 and 20 Jan, 1 May and 25 Dec; ☎ 943 42 49 70.

Aquarium-Palacio del Mar - Open 10am-1.30pm and 3.30-7.30pm; 1 July-15 Sept 10am-8pm; closed Mon (except in summer), 1 Jan and 25 Dec; 450 pts; ☎ 943 44 00 99.

Museo Naval - Open 15 Sept-15 June from 10am-1.30pm and 4-7.30pm; 16 June-14 Sept 10am-1.30pm and 5-8.30pm; Sun all year 11am-2pm; ☎ 943 43 00 51.

Parque Nacional de DOÑANA

Visitors' centres are open 8am-7pm (9pm June-Sept); closed 1 Jan, during the Romería del Rocío at Whitsun and 24, 25 and 31 Dec; it is possible to tour the park (4hr) in a Landrover if you book in advance (2 500 pts); ☎ 959 43 04 32. It is also possible to go on a river trip (4hr) if you book in advance (2 100 pts); ☎ 956 36 38 13. For further information, contact the National Park on ☎ 956 38 16 35 or ☎ 956 44 87 11.

E

ÉCIJA
🛈 Av. Andalucía – 41400 – ☎ 95 483 30 62

Iglesia de Santiago - Open daily 11am-1pm and 6-7pm; ☎ 95 590 29 33.

ELX/ELCHE
🛈 Pg. de l'Estació – 03202 – ☎ 96 545 38 31

Huerta del Cura - Open daily 9am-6pm (1 May-30 Sept 9am-8.30pm); 300 pts; ☎ 96 545 19 36.

Parque Municipal - Open daily 7am-9pm; no charge; ☎ 96 545 13 13.

Museo Arqueológico - Open 10am-1pm and 4-7pm; Sun and public holidays 10am-1pm; closed Mon, 1 Jan, 15 Aug and 25 Dec; 100 pts (no charge for Spanish visitors); ☎ 96 545 36 03.

EMPÚRIES/AMPURIAS

Neápolis - Open daily 10am-6pm; 1 Apr-30 Sept 10am-8pm; closed 1 Jan and 25 Dec; 400 pts; ☎ 972 77 02 08.

Biblioteca, Monasterio de El Escorial

J.Hidalgo – C.Lopestino/MARCO POLO

Monasterio de El ESCORIAL

⊞ Floridablanca 10 – 28200 – ☎ 91 890 15

Palacios, Panteones, Salas Capitulares, Basílica and Biblioteca - (The Bibliote is currently closed for repairs). Open daily 10am-6pm (10am-7pm 1 Apr-30 Sep last tickets sold 1hr before closing time; closed Mon, 1 and 6 Jan, 1 May, 10 Au 11, 13, 24, 25 and 31 Dec; 850 pts (no charge Wed for citizens of the Europe Union); ☎ 91 890 59 02.

Casita del Príncipe - Closed for repairs; ☎ 91 890 59 03.

Casita de Arriba - Open 10am-6pm during Holy Week (Tues-Sun) and Aug; clos the rest of the year; 350 pts (no charge Wed for citizens of the European Unio ☎ 91 890 59 03.

ESTELLA

See LIZARRA

F

FIGUERES/FIGUERAS

⊞ Pl. del Sol – 17600 – ☎ 972 50 31

Teatre-Museu Dalí - Open 10.30am-5.15pm; 1 July-30 Sept 9am-7.15pm; la visit 30min before closing time; in Aug also open evenings 10pm-0.15am; clos Mon (except July, Aug and Sept), 1 Jan and 25 Dec; 800 pts (1 000 pts in summe 1 200 pts late nights in Aug; ☎ 972 51 18 00.

Iglesia de Sant Pere - Open 8.15am-12.45pm and 3.30-9pm; ☎ 972 50 31 5

Museu de Joguets - Open 10am-1pm and 4-7.30pm; closed Tues, 1 Jan a 25 Dec; 600 pts; ☎ 972 50 45 85.

Museu de l'Empordà - Open 11am-1pm and 3-7pm; Sun and public holida 11am-1.30pm; 1 June-14 Sept 10am-1pm and 3-7pm; Sun and public holida 3-7pm; closed Mon; 300 pts; ☎ 972 50 23 05.

FRÓMISTA

⊞ Paseo Central – 34440 – ☎ 979 81 01

Iglesia de San Martín - Open daily 10am-2pm and 3-6pm; in summer 10am-2p and 4.30-8pm; ☎ 979 81 01 44.

G

GANDÍA

⊞ Marqués de Campo – 46700 – ☎ 96 287 77

Palacio Ducal - Guided tours (45min) 1 Nov-31 May at 11am and 5pm; 1 Ap 30 Sept at 11am and 6pm; Sat all year at 11am; closed Sun and public holiday 250 pts; ☎ 96 287 12 03.

GASTEIZ/VITORIA

⊞ Parque de la Florida s/n – 01008 – ☎ 945 13 13

Catedral de Santa María - Closed for repairs; ☎ 945 25 55 67.

Museo de Arqueología - Open 10am-2pm and 4-6.30pm; Sat 10am-2pm; S and public holidays 11am-2pm; closed Mon (except on public holidays, when t museum closes on the Tues), 1 Jan, Good Fri and 25 Dec; ☎ 945 18 19 18.

Museo "Fournier" de Naipes - Same opening times as for the Museo de Arqueolog above.

Museo de Bellas Artes - Same opening times as for the Museo de Arqueolog above.

Museo de Armería - Same opening times as for the Museo de Arqueología abov

Gaceo: Iglesia - To visit the church, ask for the keys from Señor Ignacio at house no 1 in Gaceo; ☎ 945 30 02 37.

Alaiza: Iglesia - It is possible to visit the church by prior arrangement or by aski for the keys at Casa no 26 in Alaiza; ☎ 908 90 16 70.

Santuario de Estíbaliz - Open 9.30am-8pm; 28 Apr-31 Oct 8am-8.30pm (n visits during religious services); ☎ 945 29 30 88.

Mendoza: Museo de Heráldica Alavesa - Open 10am-2pm and 4-6.30pm; S 10am-2pm; Sun and public holidays 11am-2pm; closed Mon, 1 Jan and Good Fr ☎ 945 23 17 77.

ee also entry in alphabetical section of guide for practical information.

pper Rock Nature Reserve - Nature reserve is open daily from 7am-10pm; sites
5t Michael's Cave, Apes' Den, Great Siege Tunnels, Military Heritage Centre,
Gibraltar: A City Under Siege" exhibition and Moorish Castle) are open daily from
.30am-7pm. Last tickets sold 1hr before closing time. Closed 1 Jan and 25-26 Dec
ubject to demand). £5 per person (includes entry to all the sites in the reserve); no
harge to disabled visitors (but check wheelchair access with staff, as some sites pose
fficulties). The only vehicles allowed on the Upper Rock are official ones, as space
at a premium. ☎ (+350) 42400.

ibraltar Museum - Open Mon-Fri from 10am-6pm, Sat from 10am-2pm. Closed
un. £2 (children under 12: £1).

lameda Gardens - Open daily from early morning (8-9am)-7pm. No charge.

GIRONA/GERONA   🛈 Rambla de la Llibertad 1 – 17004 – ☎ 972 22 65 75

atedral - Open 10am-2pm and 4pm-6pm; 1 Mar-30 June 10am-2pm and
pm-7pm; 1 July-30 Sept 10am-8pm; Sun and public holidays 10am-2pm; closed
1on and 7-31 Jan; ☎ 972 21 44 26.

esoro - Same opening times as for the Catedral; 400 pts ☎ 972 21 44 26.

1useu d'Art de Girona - Open 10am-6pm; 1 Mar-30 Sept 10am-7pm; Sun and
ublic holidays 10am-2pm; closed Mon, 1 and 6 Jan, Easter Sun, 25 and 26 Dec;
00 pts (no charge on Sun and public holidays); ☎ 972 20 38 34.

años árabes - Open 10am-2pm; 1 Apr-30 Sept 10am-7pm; Sun and public
olidays 10am-2pm; closed Mon between 1 Apr and 20 Sept, 1 and 6 Jan, Easter
un, 25-26 Dec; 200 pts; ☎ 972 21 32 62.

1onasterio de Sant Pere de Galligants: Museu Arqueològic - Open 10am-2pm and
-7pm; 1 June-30 Sept 10.30am-1.30pm and 4-7pm; Sun and public holidays
0am-2pm all year; closed Mon, 1 Jan, Easter Sun, 25-26 Dec; 200 pts (no charge
n Sun); ☎ 972 20 46 37.

1useu del Cinema - Open 1 May-30 Sept 10am-7pm (6pm from 1 Oct-30 Apr);
osed Mon (except on public holidays), 1 and 6 Jan, 25 Dec; ☎ 972 41 22 77.

úbol: Casa-Museu Castell Gala-Dalí - Open 15 Mar-30 June and 1-31 Oct
0.30am-6pm (closed Mon); 1 July-30 Sept daily 10.30am-7.30pm; last visit
0min before closing time; closed 2 Nov-14 Mar; 600 pts; ☎ 972 48 82 11.

anyoles: Museu Arqueològic Comarcal - Open 10.30am-1.30pm and 4-6.30pm; 1
uly-31 Aug 11am-1.30pm and 4-8pm; Sun and public holidays all year
0.30am-2pm; closed Mon; 500 pts; ☎ 972 57 23 61.

glesia de Santa María de Porqueres - Open daily 10am-8pm; ☎ 972 57 23 61.

Besalù: Iglesia de Sant Pere - Open daily 10am-2pm and 4-7pm; ☎ 972 59 12 40.

Besalù: "Mikwa" - Same opening times as for the Iglesia de Sant Pere; 50 pts; for
isits, contact the Tourist Office in Plaça Llibertat; ☎ 972 59 12 40.

lot: Iglesia de Sant Esteve - Open 7am-9am and 7-8pm; Sun and public holidays
0am-1pm and 7-9pm (no visits during religious services); ☎ 972 26 04 74.

lot: Museu Comarcal de la Garrotxa - Open 10am-2pm and 4-6pm; July-Sept
0am-2pm and 5-7pm; Sun and public holidays all year 10am-2pm; closed Tues,
Jan and 25 Dec; 300 pts (no charge the first Sun of each month); ☎ 972 26 67 62.

GRANADA   🛈 Pl. Mariana Pineda 10 – 18009 – ☎ 958 22 66 88
🛈 Calle de Mariana Pineda, s/n – 18009 – ☎ 958 22 59 90

he Alhambra and Generalife - Open 9am-6pm; Night visits (Palacios Nazaríes
nly) Sat 8-10pm: ticket office closes 1hr 15min (during the day) and 15min (at
ight) before last visit; in summer open 9am-8pm; night visit Tues, Thur and Sat
0pm-midnight: ticket office closes 1hr 15min before last visit; Sun all year
am-6pm; last visit 1hr before closing time; closed afternoons on 1 Jan, Easter Sat
nd 25 Dec; 725 pts (day and night visits) (no charge on Sun); ☎ 958 22 75 25.

apilla Real - Open daily 10.30am-1pm and 3.30-6.30pm; Sun and public holidays
1am-1pm and 3.30-6.30pm; 1 May-30 Sept 10.30am-1pm and 4-7pm; Sun and
ublic holidays 11am-1pm and 4-7pm; closed 2 Jan (morning), Good Fri and 12 Oct
morning); 250 pts (no charge Sun mornings); ☎ 958 22 78 48.

atedral - Open 10.30am-1pm and 3.30-6.30pm; Sun and public holidays
.30-6.30pm; 1 Apr-30 Sept 10.30am-1.30pm and 4-7pm; Sun 4-7pm; 300 pts;
☎ 958 22 29 59.

artuja - Open 10am-1pm and 3.30-6pm (4-8pm in summer); Sun and public
olidays 10am-noon and 3.30-6pm (4-8pm in summer); 250 pts (no charge on
un); ☎ 958 16 19 32.

Iglesia de San Juan de Dios - Open 8am-noon and 6-9pm; ☎ 958 27 57 00.

Monasterio de San Jerónimo - Open daily 10am-1.30pm and 3-4.30pm; 1 Apr-30 Sept 10am-1.30pm and 4-7.30pm; 250 pts; ☎ 958 27 93 37.

El Bañuelo - Open 10am-2pm and 5-7pm; Sat 9am-2pm; closed Sun, Mon and public holidays; ☎ 958 22 23 39.

Hospital Real - Open weekdays 9am-8pm; closed Sat, Sun and public holidays ☎ 958 24 30 60.

Museo Arqueológico - Open daily 9.30am-2pm; Sat and Sun 10am-2pm; closed Mon and public holidays; 250 pts for citizens not belonging-the European Union ☎ 958 22 56 40.

La GRANJA DE SAN ILDEFONSO

Palacio - Open 10am-1.30pm and 3-5pm; Sun and public holidays 10am-2pm; Sat, Sun and public holidays 1 Apr-31 May 10am-6pm; 1 June-30 Sept 10am-6pm; closed Mon all year, 1, 6 and 23 Jan, 24, 25 and 31 Dec; 650 pts, no charge on Mon; ☎ 921 47 00 19.

Jardines - Open daily 10am-6pm (9pm in summer); fountains operate at 5.30pm Sat, Sun and public holidays (except during periods of drought) from Holy Week middle of Aug; full display on 30 May, 25 July and 25 Aug; 325 pts (fountains ☎ 921 47 00 19.

Real Fábrica de Cristales - Open 11am-7pm (8pm from 1 Apr-30 Sept); closed Mon; 400 pts; ☎ 921 47 17 12.

Sierra de GREDOS

Cuevas de Águila - Guided visits (45min) 10.30am-1pm and 3-6pm from 21 May-21 Sept; 500 pts; ☎ 920 37 71 07.

GUADALAJARA 🛈 Pl. de los Caídos – 19001 – ☎ 949 21 16

Palacio del Infantado - Open 10.30am-2pm and 4.15-7pm; Sun and public holidays 10.30am-2pm; Sat, Sun and public holidays 1 July-31 Aug 10.30am-2pm; closed Mon, 1 Jan, Good Fri, 1 May, 24, 25 and 31 Dec, and during local festivities 200 pts (no charge on Sat afternoons and Sun mornings); ☎ 949 21 33 01.

Pastrana: Colegiata - Guided tours (1hr 30min) 10am-2pm and 4-6pm; Sun and public holidays 1pm-2.30pm and 4-6pm; 300 pts; ☎ 949 37 00 27.

GUADALUPE 🛈 Pl. Santa María de Guadalupe – 10140 – ☎ 927 15 41

Monasterio - Guided tours daily 9.30am-1pm and 3.30-6.45pm; 300 pts ☎ 927 36 70 00.

Sierra de GUADARRAMA

Real Monasterio de Santa María de El Paular - Guided tours at noon, 1pm and 5pm; Sun and public holidays at 1pm and 4-6.30pm; closed Thur afternoons ☎ 91 869 14 25.

GUADIX 🛈 Av. Mariana Pineda – 18500 – ☎ 958 66 26

Catedral - Open 9am-1pm and 4-6pm; 1 June-30 Sept 11am-1pm and 5-7pm ☎ 958 66 08 00.

Alcazaba - Open 9am-2pm and 4-7pm; Sat 9am-2pm; closed Sun; 100 pts ☎ 958 66 01 60.

La Calahorra: Castillo - Open Wed 10am-1pm and 4-6pm; ☎ 958 67 70 98.

H – I – J

HUESCA 🛈 Calle General Lasheras, 5 – 22003 – ☎ 974 22 57

Catedral - Open daily 10.30am-1pm and 4-6.30pm (no visits during religious services); ☎ 974 22 06 76.

Museo Arqueológico Provincial - Closed for repairs; ☎ 974 22 05 86.

Iglesia de San Pedro el Viejo - Open daily 10am-2pm; ☎ 974 22 23 87.

IRUÑEA/PAMPLONA 🛈 Duque de Ahumada 3 – 31002 – ☎ 948 22 07

Catedral - Open 9am-10.30am and 6-8pm; Sun and public holidays 11am-2pm and 6-8.30pm; ☎ 948 22 56 79.

Museo Diocesano - Open 10.30am-1.30pm and 4-6pm; 15 July-15 Sept 10.30am-6pm; Sat all year 10.30am-1.30pm; closed Sun and public holidays; 100 pts; ☎ 948 21 08 27.

Museo de Navarra - Open 10am-2pm and 5-7pm; Sun and public holidays 11am-2pm; closed Mon, 1 Jan, Good Fri, 7 July and 25 Dec; 300 pts (no charge Sat afternoons and Sun); ☎ 948 42 64 92.

Iglesia de San Saturnino - Open daily 8.30am-2pm and 6.30-7.30pm; ☎ 948 22 11 94.

Santuario de San Miguel de Aralar - Open 10am-2pm and 4pm-dusk; ☎ 948 39 60 28.

JACA   🛈 Av. Regimento de Galicia 2 – 22700 – ☎ 974 36 00 98

Catedral - Open daily noon-2pm and 4-7pm; ☎ 974 35 62 41.

Museo Diocesano - Open daily 11am-2pm and 4-7pm; closed Mon and in Nov; 100 pts; ☎ 974 35 51 30.

Castillo de Loarre - Open 15 Oct-15 Mar 11am-2.30pm; 16 Mar-31 May and 1 Sept-15 Oct 10am-1.30pm and 4-7pm (8pm 1 June-31 Aug); closed Mon (except in summer) and Tues; no charge; ☎ 974 38 26 27.

Ansó: Museo Etnológico - Open May-Oct 10.30am-7.30pm; Sat, Sun and public holidays 10.30am-1.30pm and 3-8pm; the rest of the year by prior arrangement; ☎ 974 37 00 22.

Siresa: Iglesia de San Pedro - Open in summer 10.30am-1pm and 4-8pm; in winter ask for the keys from the guard on the first floor of the Bar Pirineos.

JAÉN   🛈 Arquitecto Bergés 1 – 23007 – ☎ 953 22 27 37

Museo Provincial - Open 10am-2pm and 4-7.30pm; Sat and Sun 10am-2pm; 1 June-15 Sept 9am-2pm (Sun 10am-2pm); closed Mon and public holidays; 250 pts; (no charge for citizens of the European Union)☎ 953 25 06 00.

Catedral - Open daily 8.30am-1pm and 4.30-7pm; ☎ 953 22 27 37.

Museo de la Catedral - Open Sat and Sun 11am-1pm; 100 pts; ☎ 953 22 27 37.

Baños árabes - Open 9am-8pm; Sat and Sun 9.30am-2.30pm; last visit 30min before closing time; closed Mon and public holidays; no charge; ☎ 953 23 62 92.

JÁTIVA

See XÀTIVA

JEREZ DE LA FRONTERA   🛈 Larga 39 – 11403 – ☎ 956 33 11 50

Museo de los Relojes - Open 10am-2pm; closed Sat in Aug and Sun all year; 300 pts; ☎ 956 18 21 00.

Real Escuela Andaluza de Arte Ecuestre - Guided tours including visit of facilities and training sessions 11am-1pm; horse show on Thur only at noon; closed Sat, Sun and public holidays; 450 pts (general visit); 1 500 pts or 2 400 pts (show); ☎ 956 31 11 11.

Colegiata - Open 6.30pm-8pm; Sun and public holidays 11am-2pm and 7-8pm; ☎ 956 34 84 82.

Casa del Cabildo: Museo Arqueológico - Open 10am-2pm and 4-7pm (10am-2.30pm July and Aug); Sat, Sun and public holidays all year 10am-2.30pm; closed Mon, 1 and 6 Jan, Good Fri and 25 Dec; 250 pts (no charge the first Sun of each month and in Nov); ☎ 956 34 13 50.

Alcázar - Open 10am-2pm and 4-6pm; Sat 10am-2pm; closed Sun and public holidays; no charge; ☎ 956 33 73 06.

Iglesia de San Miguel - Visits by prior arrangement; ☎ 956 34 33 47.

LEÓN   🛈 Pl. de la Regla 3 – 24003 – ☎ 987 23 70 82

Catedral - Open 9.30am-1.30pm and 4-7pm; Sat 9.30am-2pm and 5-7pm; 1 June-30 Sept 9.30am-2pm and 4-7.30pm (7pm Sat); closed Sun and public holidays; ☎ 987 87 57 70.

Museo Catedralicio - Guided tours (30min) 9.30am-1.30pm and 4-7pm; Sat 9.30am-2pm and 5-7pm; 1 June-30 Sept 9.30am-2pm and 4-7.30pm; Sat 9.30am-2pm and 4-7pm; last visit 1hr before closing time; closed Sun and public holidays; 450 pts; ☎ 987 87 57 70.

Panteón Real and Tesoro - Guided tours (40min) 10am-1.30pm and 4-6.30p
(Sun and public holidays mornings only); closed Mon (except in July and Aug), 1 Ja
the first fortnight in Feb and 25 Dec; 400 pts (free Thur afternoons for Spani
citizens); ☎ 987 22 96 08.

Museo de León - Open 10am-2pm and 4.30-8pm; 1 May-30 Sept 10am-2pm ar
5-8.30pm; Sun and public holidays all year 10am-2pm; closed Mon; 200 pts (fr
Sat, Sun, 23 Apr, 18 May, 12 Oct and 6 Dec); ☎ 987 23 64 05.

San Miguel de Escalada: Iglesia - Open 10am-2pm and 4-6pm; Sun and publ
holidays 10am-3pm; 1 May-30 Sept 10am-2pm and 5-8pm; Sun and publ
holidays 10am-1pm; closed Mon; ☎ 987 23 70 82.

Cuevas de Valporquero - Guided tours (1hr 15min) 10am-5pm Sat-Sun and publ
holidays Apr and May (Fri, Sat and Sun in Oct); June, July, Aug and Sept open dai
10am-2pm and 4-7pm; 575 pts; ☎ 987 29 22 43.

Monasterio de LEYRE

Iglesia - Guided tours (35min) 10.30am-1.30pm and 4-6.30pm; 10 Dec-28 Fe
10.30am-1.30pm and 3-5.30pm; closed 1 and 6 Jan and 25 Dec; 225 pt
☎ 948 88 40 11.

LIZARRA/ESTELLA
🚹 San Nicolás 1 – 31200 – ☎ 948 55 40

Iglesia de San Pedro de la Rúa - Guided visits (30min) 10am-2pm and 5-7pm fro
Holy Week-Sept; the rest of the year (including Sun) by prior arrangement with th
Tourist Information Office; closed 1 and 6 Jan and 25 Dec; ☎ 948 55 40 11.

Monasterio de Irache - Open 10am-1.30pm and 5-7pm; Sat, Sun and publ
holidays 10am-1.30pm and 4-7pm; closed Mon, Tues afternoons, and in De
☎ 948 55 44 64.

Monasterio de Iranzu - Open all year except Christmas and Epiphany; 300 pt
☎ 948 52 00 47.

LLEIDA/LERIDA
🚹 Av. de Madrid 36 – 25002 – ☎ 973 27 09 9

Seu Vella - Open 10am-1.30pm and 3-5.30pm (10am-1.30pm and 4-7.30p
1 June-30 Sept); Sun and public holidays all year 10am-1.30pm; last visit 20m
before closing time; closed Mon, 1 Jan and 25 Dec; 300 pts (no charge on Tues
☎ 973 23 06 53.

Iglesia de Sant Llorenç - Open during religious services; ☎ 973 26 79 94.

LUGO
🚹 Pr. Maior 27 (Galerías) – 27001 – ☎ 982 23 13

Museo Provincial - Open 10.30am-2pm and 4.30-8.30pm (8pm Sat); Su
11am-2pm; 1 July-30 Aug 11am-2pm and 5-8pm (Sat 10am-1pm); closed Su
1 June-30 Aug; ☎ 982 24 21 12.

Santa Eulalia de Bóveda: paleo-Christian monument - Open 11am-2pm and 3.30-5pr
1 June-30 Sept 11am-2pm and 3.30-7.30pm; Sun and public holidays all ye
11am-2pm; closed Mon. ☎ 908 08 02 14.

M

MADRID
🚹 c/ Duque Medinaceli, 2 – 28014 – ☎ 91 429 49 5
🚹 Pl. Mayor, 3 – 28012 – ☎ 91 266 54 7
🚹 Madrid-Barajas airport – 28042 – ☎ 91 305 86 5

Pontificia de San Miguel - Open daily 10am-1.30pm and 5.30-8.20pm; close
public holidays and during religious services; ☎ 91 548 40 11.

Museo de San Isidro - Opening scheduled during 1999.

Iglesia de San Francisco El Grande - Guided tours (30min) 11am-1pm ar
4-6.30pm; last visit 30min before closing time; in summer 11am-1pm and 5-8pr
Sun and Mon open only for worship (daily service 8-11am); 50 pt
☎ 91 365 38 00.

Iglesia de San Isidro - Open daily 7am-1pm and 6-9pm; ☎ 91 369 20 37.

Palacio Real - Unaccompanied or guided tours (40min) 9.30am-5pm (9am-6p
1 Apr-30 Sept); Sun and public holidays 9am-2pm (3pm 1 Apr-30 Sept); close
1 and 6 Jan, during Holy Week, 1, 5 and 15 May, 24 July, 15 Aug, 9 Sept, 1 No
6, 8 and 25 Dec and during state receptions; 850 pts (no charge Wed for citizens
the European Union); ☎ 91 542 00 59.

mpo del Moro - Open 10am-6pm; closed Sun; ☎ 91 366 54 77.

useo de Carruajes Reales - Temporarily closed for repairs; ☎ 91 542 00 59.

onasterio de las Descalzas Reales - Temporarily closed for repairs; uided tours (45min) daily Tues, Wed, Thur and Sat 10.30am-12.45pm d 4-5.45pm; Fri 10.30am-12.45pm; Sun 11am-1.45pm; closed Mon, 1 Jan, ly Week from Wed-Sat, 1, 2 and 15 July, 15 Aug, 9 Sept, 1 Nov, 6, 8 and Dec; 650 pts; (no charge Wed for citizens of the European Union); 91 542 00 59.

al Monasterio de la Encarnación - Guided tours (45min) Tues, Wed, Thur and t 10.30am-12.45pm and 4-5.45pm; Sun 11am-1.45pm; closed Mon, Tues and i, 1 and 6 Jan, Holy Week from Wed-Sat, 1, 2 and 15 May, 25 and 27 July, 15 Aug, Oct, 1 Nov, 6, 8 and 25 Dec; 425 pts (no charge on Wed for citizens of the European ion); ☎ 91 542 00 59.

ro de la Moncloa - Open 10.30am-1.45pm and 4.30-7.15pm; in summer am-1.45pm and 5.30-8.45pm (Sat, Sun and public holidays 5pm-8.45pm); sed Mon, 1 Jan and 25 Dec; 200 pts; ☎ 91 544 81 04.

rque del Oeste: Teleférico - Consult timetables; 360 pts (515 pts Rtn); 91 541 11 18.

rque del Oeste: Amusement Park - Consult timetables; 450 pts (gives access-rounds), 2 200 pts (pass giving access-all entertainments - 1 225 pts for children der 7); combined ticket with Zoo-Aquarium 2 300 pts (1 600 pts for children under ; ☎ 91 463 29 00.

rque del Oeste: Zoo-Aquarium: Open daily in summer 10am-9pm; Nov-Feb .30am-6pm (6.30pm on Sat and public holidays); 1 590 pts (1 280 pts for ildren under 7); combined ticket with Amusement Park 2 300 pts (1 600 pts for ildren); ☎ 91 512 37 70.

useo del Prado and Casón del Buen Retiro - Open 9am-7pm; Sun and public lidays 9am-2pm; closed Mon, 1 Jan, Good Fri, 1 May and 25 Dec; 500 pts (no arge Sat afternoons 2.30-7pm and Sun); the Casón del Buen Retiro is currently sed for repairs; 91 330 28 25.

useo Thyssen-Bornemisza - Open daily 10am-7pm; last visit 30min before sing time; closed Mon, 1 Jan, 1 May, 24 (afternoon), 25 and 31 (afternoon) Dec; 0 pts; ☎ 91 369 01 51.

rdín Botánico - Open daily 10am-6pm Nov-Feb (7pm in Mar and Oct, 8pm in Apr d Sept, and 9pm in May, June, July and Aug); ticket office closes 30min before, e exhibition greenhouse closes 1hr before; closed 1 Jan and 25 Dec; 200 pts; 91 420 30 17.

useo Nacional Centro de Arte Reina Sofía - Open 10am-9pm (including public lidays); Sun 10am-2.30pm; closed Tues; 500 pts (no charge Sat after 2.30pm and n); ☎ 91 467 50 62.

useo del Ejército - Open daily 10am-2pm; closed Mon, 1 and 6 Jan, Maundy ur, Good Fri, 1 May, 24, 25 and 31 Dec; 100 pts; no charge on Sat; 91 522 89 77.

useo Nacional de Artes Decorativas - Open weekdays 9.30am-3pm; Sat and Sun 0am-2pm; 400 pts, no charge on Sun; ☎ 91 532 64 99.

useo Naval - Open daily 10.30am-1.30pm; closed Mon, 1 Jan, Maundy Thur and od Fri, 16 July, all through Aug and 25 Dec; no charge; ☎ 91 379 52 99.

rque del Buen Retiro - Open all day; ☎ 91 010.

useo Arqueológico Nacional - Open 9.30am-8.30pm; Sun and public holidays 30am-2.30pm; closed Mon and public holidays; 500 pts (no charge Sat after 30pm and Sun); ☎ 91 578 02 03.

useo de Cera - Open daily 10am-2.30pm and 4.30-8.30pm; last admission 0mins before closing; 900 pts; ☎ 91 319 26 49.

useo Lázaro Galdiano - Open daily 10am-2pm; closed Mon, 1 Jan, Maundy Thur, od Fri, 1 and 2 May, all through Aug, 1 Nov; 6, 24, 25 and 31 Dec; 400 pts (no arge on Sun); ☎ 91 561 60 84.

al Academia de Bellas Artes de San Fernando - Open 9am-7pm; Sat, Sun and blic holidays 9am-2.30pm; 1 July-31 Aug open 9am-6.30pm; Sat, Sun and blic holidays 9am-2pm; closed 1 and 6 Jan, Good Fri, 25 and 31 Dec and some cal public holidays (dates vary); 400 pts (no charge on Sat and Sun); 91 522 14 91.

Palacio de Cristal, Parque del Retiro

Museo de América - Open 10am-3pm; Sun and public holidays 10am-2.30p closed Mon, 1 and 6 Jan, 1 and 15 May, 9 Nov, 24, 25 and 31 Dec; 500 p ☎ 91 543 94 37.

San Antonio de la Florida - Open 10am-2pm and 4-8pm; Sat-Sun 10am-2p closed Mon and public holidays; 300 pts (no charge on Wed and Su ☎ 91 542 07 22.

Museo Cerralbo - Open daily 9.30am-2.30pm (Sun 10am-2pm); closed Mon a public holidays; 400 pts (no charge on Wed and Sun); ☎ 91 547 36 46.

Museo Sorolla - Open daily 10am-3pm; Sun and public holidays 10am-2pm; clos Mon, 24 and 31 Dec; 400 pts (no charge on 18 Mar, 12 Oct and 6 De ☎ 91 310 15 84.

Museo Taurino - Open daily 9.30am-2.30pm; Sun and public holidays 10am-1p closed Mon, Sat and all Sat-Sun and public holidays from 1 Nov-28 Fe ☎ 91 725 18 57.

Museo de la Ciudad - Open 10am-2pm and 4-6pm; 1 July-31 Aug 10am-2pm a 5pm-7pm; Sat and Sun all year 10am-2pm; closed Mon and public holida ☎ 91 588 65 99.

Museo Municipal - Open 9.30am-8pm; Sat and Sun 10am-2pm; in Aug op 9.30am-2pm; closed Mon and public holidays; 300 pts; no charge on Wed and S ☎ 91 588 86 72.

Museo Romántico - Open 9am-1pm; Sun and public holidays 10am-2pm; clos Mon; 400 pts; no charge on Sun; ☎ 91 448 10 71.

Museo del Ferrocarril - Open 10am-3pm; closed Mon; 500 pts; no charge on S ☎ 902 22 88 22.

Museo Nacional de Ciencia y Tecnología - Open 10am-2pm and 4-6pm; S 10am-2.30pm; in summer from 10am-1pm; closed Mon; no char ☎ 91 530 31 21.

MÁLAGA
🛈 Pasaje de Chinitas 4 – 29015 – ☎ 95 221 34

Alcazaba - Open daily except Tues 8.30am-7pm; ☎ 952 21 60 05.

Catedral - Open 10am-12.45pm and 4-6.45pm; closed Sun, 1 Jan and 25 D Museo Cardenalicio: 200 pts; ☎ 952 21 59 17.

El Sagrario - Open daily 9.30am-12.30pm and 6pm-7.30pm.

Museo de Bellas Artes - Currently closed; ☎ 952 21 83 82.

Museo-Casa Natal Picasso - Open daily 10am-2pm and 6-9pm (5-8pm in winte Sun all year 10am-2pm; no charge; ☎ 952 21 50 05.

Museo de Artes y Costumbres Populares - Open 10am-1.30pm and 4-7pm; closed Sun and public holidays; 200 pts; ☎ 952 21 71 37.

Finca de la Concepción - Guided tours (1hr 15min) 10am-6.30pm (spring), 7.30pm (summer), 5.30pm (autumn) and 4pm (winter); closed Mon, 1 Jan and 25 Dec; 425 pts; ☎ 952 25 21 48.

MEDINA DE RIOSECO

Iglesia de Santa María - Open 11am-2pm (1pm in winter); the visit includes the Iglesia de Santiago; closed Mon; 300 pts, ☎ 983 70 03 27.

Iglesia de Santiago - Same admission times as above; 300 pts; ☎ 983 70 03 27.

MELILLA �𝌆 Av. General Aizpuru 20 – 29804 – ☎ 95 267 40 13

Museo Municipal - Open 10am-2pm and 4.30-9.30pm; Sun and public holidays 10am-2pm and 4-9pm; 15 June-15 Oct 10am-2pm and 5.30-10pm; Sun and public holidays 10am-2pm and 6-10pm; closed Mon and public holidays; ☎ 95 268 13 39.

MÉRIDA ☒ Paseo José Alvarez Saénz de Buruaga – 06800 – ☎ 924 31 53 53

Museo Nacional de Arte Romano - Open 10am-2pm and 4-6pm; 1 June-30 Sept 10am-2pm and 5-7pm; Sun and public holidays all year 10am-2pm; closed Mon, 1 and 6 Jan, 1 May, 10, 24, 25 and 31 Dec; 400 pts (no charge Sat afternoons and Sun); ☎ 924 31 16 90 or 924 31 19 12.

Teatro Romano, Anfiteatro and Casa Romana - Open 1 Oct-31 Mar 9am-1.45pm and 4-6.15pm; 1 Apr-30 Sept 9am-1.45pm and 5-7.15pm; closed 8, 10, 24 and 31 Dec; 750 pts (combined ticket including Teatro, Anfiteatro, Casas Romanas, Alcazaba and Iglesia de Santa Eulalia); ☎ 924 31 20 24.

Alcazaba - Same opening times as for the Teatro Romano and the Anfiteatro; ☎ 924 31 53 53.

Iglesia de Santa Eulalia - Open daily 10am-1.45pm (2.45pm in summer) and 4-5.45pm (6.45pm in summer); 750 pts, (combined ticket including Teatro, Anfiteatro, Casas Romanas, Alcazaba and Iglesia de Santa Eulalia); ☎ 976 39 74 97.

MONDOÑEDO

Catedral - Open daily 9am-1.30pm and 4-7.30pm (7pm Sat); Sun and public holidays 9am-10am, 11am-noon, 12.30-2pm and 4-8pm; it is not possible to visit the cathedral during Holy Week; ☎ 982 52 10 06.

MONTBLANC ☒ Muralla de Santa Tecla 18 – 43400 – ☎ 977 86 12 32

Iglesia de Sant Miquel - Visits by prior arrangement; ☎ 977 86 22 91.

Iglesia de Santa Maria - Open 8am-8pm; ☎ 977 86 22 91.

Museu Comarcal de la Conca de Barberà - Open 10am-1pm and 4-7pm; 1 June-30 Sept 10am-2pm and 5-8pm; Sun and public holidays all year 10am-2pm; closed Mon, 1 Jan and 25 Dec; 300 pts; ☎ 977 86 03 49.

Museu Frederic Marès - Closed for repairs; ☎ 977 86 03 49.

Convento de la Serra - Same opening times as for the Iglesia de Santa María; ☎ 977 86 22 91.

Sierra de MONTSERRAT ☒ Monestir – 08199 – ☎ 93 835 02 51 ext. 186

Basílica - Open daily 7am-7.45pm (8.15pm Sat, Sun and public holidays); ☎ 93 835 02 51.

Funiculars: Sant Joan - Jan, Feb, Mar, Nov and Dec 11am-4pm; Sat, Sun and public holidays 10am-4pm; Apr, May and Oct 10am-5pm; June-Sept 10am-7pm; closed 6-21 Feb; 835 pts Rtn; service operates every 20min; ☎ 93 205 15 15.

Santa Cova - Jan, Feb, Mar, Apr, Oct, Nov and Dec open Sat, Sun and public holidays 10.10am-1pm and 3.30-4.20pm; June, July, Aug and Sept open 10.10am-1pm and 3.30-6.50pm; closed 23-28 Feb; 340 pts Rtn; service operates every 20min.

MORELLA ☒ Pl. de San Miguel 2 – 12300 – ☎ 964 17 30 02

Basílica de Santa María la Mayor - Open daily noon-2pm and 4-6pm; 1 July-30 Sept 11am-2pm and 4-7pm (avoid visiting during services); closed 1 and 6 Jan, the last week in Nov, 25 and 31 Dec; 150 pts (including museum); ☎ 964 16 07 93.

Catedral - Cathedral open daily 7am-1pm and 5-8pm; museum open da 10am-1pm and 5-7pm (8pm in summer); both closed during the Romería of t Virgen de la Fuensanta (dates vary); 200 pts (museum); ☎ 968 21 63 44.

Museo Salzillo - Open 9.30am-1pm and 3-6pm; 1 Apr-30 Sept 9.30am-1pm a 4-7pm; Sun and public holidays 11am-1pm (closed Sat and Sun in July and Au closed Mon (except in July and Aug); 250 pts; ☎ 968 29 18 93.

Alcantarilla: Museo de la Huerta - Open 10.30am-7pm; Sat, Sun and public holida 10am-2pm and 3.30-7pm; 30 Sept-30 Nov 10.30am-6pm; Sat, Sun and pub holidays 10am-1.30pm and 4.30-6pm; 1 Dec-28 Feb 10am-5.30pm; Sat, Sun a public holidays 10am-2pm and 4-5.30pm; closed Mon, 1 Jan, Good Fri, throughc Aug and on 25 Dec; ☎ 968 89 38 66.

Orihuela: Colegio de Santo Domingo - Open 9.30am-1pm and 4-6pm; in summ 9.30am-1pm; closed Sat-Sun and public holidays; no charge; ☎ 96 530 02 49

Catedral - Guided visits (35min) 10.30am-1.30pm and 4-6.30pm; S 10.30am-1.30pm; 1 Apr-30 Sept 10.30am-1.30pm and 4.30-7pm; closed S and public holidays; outside of normal hours visits by prior arrangement; 100 p ☎ 96 530 06 38.

Museo de la Catedral - Open 10am-1.30pm and 4-6.30pm (10am-1.30pm a 5-7pm in summer); Sat 10am-1.30pm; closed Sun and public holidays; 100 p ☎ 96 530 27 47.

Iglesia de Santiago - Open daily 10am-noon and 5.30-7pm; ☎ 96 530 27 47

N

Valle del NAVIA

Grandas de Salime: Museo Etnográfico - Open 11.30am-2pm and 4-6.30p (1 Sept-30 June closed afternoons Sun and public holidays); closed Mon; 250 pts (charge on Tues); ☎ 985 62 72 43.

O

Castillo de los Reyes de Navarra - Open 10am-2pm and 3.30-5.30pm; 1 May 30 Sept 10am-2pm and 4-7pm (8pm in July and Aug); Holy Week and lo weekends 10am-7pm; 350 pts; ☎ 948 74 00 35.

Iglesia de Santa María la Real - Visits by prior arrangement; ☎ 948 71 24 3

Monasterio de La Oliva - Open daily 8.30am-6.30pm; ☎ 948 72 50 06.

OLIVENZA

Museo Etnográfico González Santana - Open 11am-2pm and 4-6pm; closed Mo ☎ 924 49 02 22.

Antigua Universidad - Visits by prior arrangement; ☎ 943 78 34 53.

Iglesia de San Miguel - Visits by prior arrangement; ☎ 943 78 34 53.

Santuario de Arantzazu - Open daily 8am-1pm and 3.30-8pm; ☎ 943 78 09 5

Iglesia de la Real Colegiata - Open 1 July-30 Sept 10am-7.30pm; 1 Oct to 30 Ju open 10am-7.30pm (5.30pm on Sat, Sun and public holidays); closed Mon durir bad weather; 200 pts; ☎ 948 76 00 00.

Sala Capitular - Same opening times as above.

Museo - Open 10am-2pm and 4-8pm July-Sept; Sat, Sun and public holiday 11am-1.30pm (2pm Oct-Dec) and 4-6pm; at other times by prior arrangemen 200 pts; ☎ 948 76 00 00.

SEIRA

onasterio de Santa María la Real - Guided tours (45min) 9.30am-12.30pm and 5.30pm (6.30pm in spring and summer); Sun and public holidays a single visit at 2.30pm; 200 pts; ☎ 988 28 20 04.

SUNA

legiata and Sepulcro Ducal - Guided tours (45min) 1 Oct-30 Apr 10am-1.30pm d 3.30-6.30pm; 1 May-30 Sept 10am-1.30pm and 4-7pm; closed Mon, 1 and (afternoon) Jan, Maundy Thur, Good Fri, 24 (afternoon), 25 and 31 (afternoon) ec; 300 pts; ☎ 95 481 04 44.

URENSE/ORENSE
🛈 Curros Enríquez 1 – 32003 – ☎ 988 37 20 20

atedral - Cathedral open 7.45am-1.30pm and 4-8.30pm; Sun and public holidays 15am-1.30pm and 4.30-8.30pm; 100 pts (Capilla del Santísimo Cristo); Museum en noon-1pm and 4-7pm; Sun and public holidays 4.30pm-7pm; 150 pts; ☎ 988 22 09 92.

useo Arqueológico y de Bellas Artes - Open daily 9.30am-2.30pm and 9.30pm; Sun 9.30am-2.30pm; closed Mon; 400 pts; ☎ 988 22 38 84.

austro de San Francisco - Open daily 11am-2pm and 4-6pm; ☎ 988 38 81 40.

VIEDO
🛈 Pl. Alfonso II El Casto 6 – 33003 – ☎ 98 521 33 85

atedral - Open 10am-1pm and 4-6pm; 1 Mar-31 May 10am-1pm and 4-7pm; June-14 Sept 10am-8pm; Sat all year 10am-1pm and 4-6pm; no visits during ligious services on Sun and public holidays; ☎ 98 520 31 17.

ámara Santa - Open 10am-1pm (mornings); afternoons open 4-6pm 1 Nov- 3 Feb; 4-7pm 1 Mar-15 May and 14 Sept to 31 Oct; 4-8pm 16 May-13 Sept; Sat year 4-6pm; closed Sun and public holidays; 400 pts (no charge on Thur); ☎ 98 520 31 17.

useo de Bellas Artes de Asturias - Open 10.30am-1.30pm and 5-8pm; Sat 1.30am-2pm and 5-8pm; Sun and public holidays 11am-2pm; 1 June-30 Sept 0.30am-1.30pm and 5-8pm; Sat 11am-1.30pm; closed Mon, 1 and 6 Jan, Good ri, 8 Sept, 12 Oct; 1 Nov, 6 and 25 Dec; no charge; ☎ 98 521 30 61.

useo Arqueológico - Open 10am-1.30pm and 4-5pm; Sun and public holidays 1am-1pm; closed Mon; no charge; ☎ 98 521 54 05.

lesia de Santullano or San Julián de los Prados - Open daily noon-1pm and 5pm; 1 May-31 Oct 11am-1pm and 4-5pm; closed Mon; ☎ 98 528 25 18.

lesia de Santa María del Naranco - Open 10am-1pm and 3-5pm (Sun and public olidays mornings only); 1 May-15 Oct 9.30am-1pm and 3-7pm (Sun and public olidays mornings only); 200 pts; no charge on Mon; ☎ 98 529 56 85.

lesia de San Miguel de Lillo - Same opening times and charges as for Santa María l Naranco.

lesia de Santa Cristina de Lena - Open 10am-1pm and 4-6pm; closed Mon; ☎ 98 549 38 83.

olegiata de San Pedro de Teverga - Visits by prior arrangement; ☎ 98 576 42 75.

ALENCIA
🛈 Mayor 105 – 34001 – ☎ 979 74 00 68

atedral - Open 10.30am-1.30pm and 4-6.30pm Oct-June (7.30pm July-Sept); at open until 6pm (7pm July-Sept); Sun and public holidays single visit at 11.15am l year; 300 pts; ☎ 979 70 13 47.

useo - Same opening times as above; 300 pts; ☎ 979 70 13 47.

años de Cerrato: Basílica de San Juan Bautista - Guided tours (20min) 10am-1pm and 7pm; closed Mon; ☎ 988 77 03 38.

AMPLONA

ee IRUÑEA

PARDO

alacio Real - Guided tours (35min) 10.30am-5pm; Sun and public holidays 55am-1.40pm; 1 Apr-30 Sept Mon-Sat 10.30am-6pm; Sun and public holidays 25am-1.40pm; closed 1 and 6 Jan, 25 Dec and during state receptions; 650 pts o charge Wed for citizens of the European Union); ☎ 91 376 15 00.

El PARDO

Casita del Príncipe – Temporarily closed for repairs; ☎ 91 376 03 29.

La Quinta – Temporarily closed for repairs; ☎ 91 376 03 29.

Convento de Capuchinos – Open 7.30am–1pm and 4.30–8pm; ☎ 91 376 08 0

PEÑARANDA DE DUERO

Palacio de Avellaneda – Guided tours (30min) 10am–1.30pm and 4–7pm; last vi
30min before closing time; closed Mon; 1 Jan, 24, 25 and 31 Dec; ☎ 947 55 20 0

PEÑÍSCOLA
🛈 Paseo Marítimo – 12598 – ☎ 964 48 01

Castillo – Open 16 Oct–31 Mar 10am–1pm and 3.15–5.30pm; during Holy We
9am–2.30pm and 4–9.30pm; 15 June–15 Sept 10am–2.30pm and 5–9.30pm
1 Apr–14 June and 15 Sept–15 Oct 9am–8.30pm; closed 1 Jan, 22 May, 9 Sept,
Oct and 25 Dec; 150 pts; ☎ 964 48 00 21.

PICOS DE EUROPA

Iglesia de Nuestra Señora de Lebeña – In summer open 10am–8.30pm; in wint
visits by prior arrangement; ☎ 942 74 43 32.

Monasterio de Santo Toribio de Liébana – Open 9.30am–1pm and 3.30–7p
(8pm May–Sept); ☎ 942 73 05 50.

Fuente Dé: Teleférico – Operates 9.30am–5pm; in summer 9am–8pm; close
6 Jan–15 Mar; 1 300 pts; ☎ 942 73 66 10.

Cueva del Buxu – Guided tours (30min) 10am–12.30pm and 4–6.30pm; the dai
number of visitors is limited to 25; it is not possible to book in advance; closed Mo
Tues mornings, 1 Jan, in Nov, 24, 25 and 31 Dec; 200 pts (no charge on Wed
☎ 908 17 54 67.

Monasterio de PIEDRA

Parque y Cascadas – Open daily 9am–dusk; 1 000 pts; ☎ 976 84 90 11.

PIRINEOS ARAGONESES

Roda de Isábena: Catedral – Guided tours (20min) 11.15am–1.30pm and 4–6p
(4.30pm–5.30pm in summer); closed 1 Jan and 25 Dec; 200 pts; ☎ 974 54 45 35

PIRINEOS CATALANES

Beget: Romanesque church – Keys held by Sra. María Vila Sauquet, opposite the church

Camprodon: Monestir Sant Pere – Visits by prior arrangement; ☎ 972 74 01 24 an
972 74 01 36.

Vall de Núria: Rack railway – Consult timetables; 2 150 pts Rtn; ☎ 972 73 20 20

Llívia: Museu Municipal – Open 10am–1pm and 3–6pm (7pm 1 Apr–30 Sept); Sun an
public holidays 10am–2pm; closed Mon (except in July and Aug); 150 pts
☎ 972 89 63 13.

Tremp: Iglesia de Santa María – Open 9am–1pm and 5.30–7.30pm; ☎ 973 65 06 90

Salardú: Iglesia de Sant Andreu – Visits by prior arrangement; ☎ 973 64 12 91.

Vielha: Iglesia de Sant Miquèu – Open 8am–8pm (except during services)
☎ 973 64 12 91.

Bossòst: Iglesia de la Assumpció de María – Open 9am–8pm; ☎ 973 64 82 53.

Taüll: Iglesia de Sant Climent – Open July–Oct 10am–2pm and 4–8pm; Nov–June
10.30am–2pm and 4–6pm; at other times by by prior arrangement; 100 pts;
☎ 973 69 61 79.

Taüll: Iglesia de Santa María – Open daily; ☎ 973 69 40 00.

PLASENCIA

Monasterio de Yuste – Guided tours (30min) 9.30am–12.30pm and 3–6pm
(Apr–Oct 3.30–6.30pm); 100 pts (no charge Thur mornings); ☎ 927 17 21 30.

Monasterio de POBLET

Guided tours (1hr) 10am–12.30pm and 3–5.30pm; 1 Mar–31 Oct 10am–12.30pm
and 3–6pm; closed 25 Dec; 500 pts; ☎ 977 87 02 54.

T. Vidal/GC (DICT)

Monasterio de Vallbona de les Monges - Guided tours (45min) Tues-Sun from 10.30am (noon on Sun and public holidays)-1.30pm and 4.30-6.45pm (6pm from Nov-28 Feb); closed Mon, 1 Jan and 25 Dec; 250 pts; ☎ 973 33 02 66.

PONTEVEDRA 🛈 General Mola 1 bajo – 36002 – ☎ 986 85 08 14

Museo Provincial - Open 10am-1.30pm and 4.30-8pm; 1 June-30 Sept 10am-2.15pm and 5-8.45pm; Sun and public holidays all year 11am-1pm; closed Mon, 1 and 6 Jan and 25 Dec; 200 pts; (no charge for citizens of the European Union); ☎ 986 85 14 55.

Iglesia de Santa María la Mayor - Open 10am-noon and 5-7pm (no visits during religious services); ☎ 986 86 61 85.

Capilla de la Peregrina - Open daily 8am-1pm and 4.30-8pm; ☎ 986 85 68 85.

Ruinas de Santo Domingo - Open 1 June-30 Sept 10am-1.30pm; the rest of the year by prior arrangement with Don Manuel Castaño; closed Mon, Sat, Sun and public holidays; ☎ 986 85 14 55.

PRIEGO DE CÓRDOBA 🛈 c/ Real, 46 – 14800 – ☎ 957 59 44 27

Parroquia de la Asunción - Visits by prior arrangement 11am-1.30pm and 5.30-9.30pm; ☎ 957 54 07 13 (Sr. José Mateo Aguilera).

PUENTE VIESGO

Cueva del Castillo - Guided tours (40min) 1 Nov-31 Mar 10am-2.15pm; 1 Apr-21 Oct 10am-12.15pm and 3-6.15pm; closed Mon, 1 Jan, 1 May and 25 Dec; 350 pts for citizens not belonging to the European Union; ☎ 942 59 84 25.

Castañeda: Antigua Colegiata - To visit the Collegiate Church, contact the Museo Diocesano in Santillana del Mar; ☎ 942 81 80 04.

R

REINOSA

Cervatos: Antigua Colegiata - Keys held at the neighbouring house (D. Julio). ☎ 942 75 10 36.

RÍAS ALTAS

Foz: Iglesia San Martín de Mondoñedo - Open daily 11am-1pm and 4-7pm; ☎ 982 13 26 07.

RÍAS BAJAS

Padrón: Iglesia parroquial - Open daily 7-8.30pm; Sun and public holidays 9am-1pm and 7-8.30pm; in summer open 10.30am-1pm and 4.30-8.30pm; ☎ 981 81 03 50.

Museo Rosalía de Castro - Open 9.30am-2pm and 4-8pm; closed Mon, Sun afternoons and public holidays; ☎ 981 81 12 04.

O Grove: Aquariumgalicia - Open 11am-7pm (10am-9pm in summer); closed Mon and Tues in winter; 775 pts. ☎ 986 73 29 68.

La RIOJA

Logroño: Santa María la Redonda - Open 7.45am-1.15pm and 6.30-8.45pm; Sun 8.35am-2pm and 6.30-8.45pm; ☎ 941 25 76 11.

La RIOJA

Museo de la Rioja – Open 10am–2pm and 4–9pm; Sun 11.30am–2pm; closed Mo 1 and 6 Jan, Good Fri and 25 Dec; free admission; ☎ 941 29 12 59.

Haro: Museo del Vino de la Rioja – Open 10am–2pm and 4–8pm; Sun 10am–2pr 300 pts, no charge on Wed; ☎ 941 31 05 47.

Laguardia: Iglesia de Santa María de los Reyes – Open Sat only 10am–2pm; if the chur is closed, call the Tourist Office; ☎ 941 60 08 45.

RIPOLL
🛈 Pl. de l'Abat Oliba s/n – 17500 – ☎ 972 70 23

Antiguo Monasterio de Santa María – Open daily 8am–1pm and 3–8pm; cloiste open daily 10am–1pm and 3–7pm; closed Mon (except in summer); ☎ 972 70 02 4

RONCESVALLES
See ORREAGA

RONDA
🛈 Pl. de España 1 – 29400 – ☎ 95 287 12

Museo Taurino – Open daily 10am–6pm (8pm in summer); closed day of bullfigh and day before; 250 pts; ☎ 95 287 41 32.

Colegiata – Open daily 10am–6pm; 200 pts; ☎ 95 287 22 46.

Baños árabes – Open 9.30am–2pm and 4–6pm; Sun and public holiday 10.30am–1pm; closed Mon; no charge; ☎ 95 287 38 39.

Cueva de la Pileta – Guided tours (1hr) daily 10am–1pm and 4–6pm; 700 pt ☎ 95 216 72 02.

S

SAGUNT/SAGUNTO
🛈 Pl. Cronista Chabret – 46500 – ☎ 96 266 22

Ruinas – Open 10am–2pm and 4–6pm; Sun and public holidays 10am–2pm; close Mon, 1 Jan, Good Fri and 25 Dec; ☎ 96 266 22 13.

Grutas de San José – Guided tours (45min); consult timetables; closed 1 Jan an 25 Dec; 850 pts; ☎ 964 69 05 76.

Segorbe: Catedral and Museo – Open 10.30am–1.30pm; closed Mon, 1 and 6 Jan, 2 Dec and during local festivals at the end of Aug (Fiestas Patronales); 400 pts ☎ 964 71 10 14.

SALAMANCA
🛈 Rúa Mayor 70 – 37002 – ☎ 923 26 85 7

Clerecía – Open daily 1–2pm and 7–8pm; ☎ 923 26 46 60.

Universidad and Escuelas Menores – Open 9.30am–1.30pm and 4–7pm; Sun an public holidays 10am–1pm; ticket office closes 30min before last visit; 300 pts (n charge Mon mornings); ☎ 923 29 44 00.

Catedral Nueva – Open daily 10am–2pm and 4–8pm; 300 pts; ☎ 923 21 74 76

Catedral Vieja – Open 10am–1.30pm and 4–7.30pm; 300 pts; ☎ 923 21 74 76

Huerto de Calixto y Melibea – Open daily 10am–2pm and 4–7pm; no charge.

Museo Art Nouveau y Art Déco – Open 11am–2pm and 4–7pm (5–9pm in summer); Sat, Sun and public holidays 11am–8pm (11am–9pm in summer) 300 pts; no charge on Thur mornings; closed Mon, 1 Jan, 24, 25 and 31 Dec ☎ 923 12 14 25.

Convento de San Esteban – Open daily 9am–1pm and 4–8pm; 200 pts ☎ 923 21 50 00.

Convento de las Dueñas – Open daily 10.30am–1pm and 4.30–7pm; 200 pts; ☎ 923 21 54 42.

Iglesia de la Purísima Concepción – Open noon–1pm and 5–8pm; closed Sun; ☎ 923 21 27 38.

Convento de las Úrsulas and Museo – Open daily 11am–1pm and 4.30–6.30pm; closed the last Sun of each month; 100 pts; ☎ 923 21 98 77.

Colegio Fonseca – Open daily 10am–2pm and 4–7pm; 100 pts (no charge Mon mornings); ☎ 923 29 45 70.

Castillo del Buen Amor: Guided tours (30min) 9am–2pm and 4–6.30pm; May–Sept 9am–2pm and 4–8.30pm; closed Nov; 400 pts; ☎ 923 26 15 12.

SANGÜESA
🛈 Alfonso el Batallador 20 – 31400 – ☎ 948 87 03 29

Castillo de Javier – Guided tours 9am–1pm and 4–7pm; last visit 20min before closing time; closed 1 Jan and 25 Dec; ☎ 948 88 40 24.

SAN IGNACIO DE LOYOLA

Santuario - Open 10am-1pm and 3-7pm; ☎ 943 81 65 08.

Monasterio de SAN JUAN DE LA PEÑA

Open 10am-1.30pm and 4-7pm; closed Mon; open 1 June-31 Aug 10am-1.30pm and 4-8pm. 15 Oct-15 Mar 11am-2.30pm; closed Mon and Tues. ☎ 974 34 80 99.

SAN MARTÍN DE VALDEIGLESIAS

Safari Madrid - Open 10.30am-6pm; in summer 10.30am-8pm; 1 600 pts (children 850 pts); ☎ 91 862 23 14.

SAN SEBASTIÁN

See DONOSTIA

SANTA MARÍA DE HUERTA

Monasterio - Open 10am-1pm and 3-6.45pm; Sun and public holidays 12.30pm-1pm and 3-6.45pm; last visit 15min before closing time; 200 pts; ☎ 975 32 70 02.

SANTANDER ☐ Jardines de Pereda – 39004 – ☎ 942 21 61 20

Catedral - Open daily 10am-1pm and 4-7.30pm; Sat 10am-1pm and 4.30-9pm; Sun and public holidays 8am-2pm and 4.30-9pm (no visits during religious services); ☎ 942 22 60 24.

Museo Regional de Prehistoria y Arqueología - Open 9am (10am 16 June-15 Sept)-1pm and 4-7pm; Sun and public holidays all year 11am-2pm; closed Mon, 1 Jan, Good Fri, 1 May and 25 Dec; ☎ 942 20 71 09.

Biblioteca Menéndez y Pelayo - Guided tours (20min) by prior arrangement 9.30-11.30am (every 30min); closed Sat-Sun and public holidays; ☎ 942 23 45 34.

Museo de Bellas Artes - Open 10am-1pm and 5-8pm (Sat 10am-1pm only); 16 June-15 Sept 10.30am-1pm and 5.30-8pm (Sat 10.30am-1pm only); closed Sun and public holidays; ☎ 942 23 94 87.

Muriedas: Museo Etnográfico de Cantabria - Guided tours (40min) 10am-1pm and 4-6pm (7pm 21 June-20 Sept); Sun and public holidays all year 11am-2pm; last visit 30min before closing time; closed Mon, 1 Jan, Good Fri, 1 May and 25 Dec; ☎ 942 25 13 47.

Parque de la Naturaleza de Cabárceno - Open 9.30am-6pm (7pm 1 Apr-30 June; 8pm 1 July-12 Oct); 800 pts (500 pts for children); ☎ 942 56 37 36.

SANT CUGAT DEL VALLÈS

Monasterio - Open 10am-1.30pm and 3-5.30pm (6.30pm 1 June-30 Sept); Sun and public holidays all year 10am-1.30pm; closed Mon; 200 pts; no charge on Tues; ☎ 91 674 69 04.

SANTES CREUS

Monasterio - Open daily 10am-1.30pm and 3-7pm 16 Mar-15 Sept (6pm 16 Jan-15 Mar; 5.30pm 16 Sept-15 Jan); last visit 45min before closing time; closed Mon, 1 Jan and 25 Dec; 400 pts (no charge on Tues); ☎ 977 63 83 29.

SANTIAGO DE COMPOSTELA ☐ Vilar 43 – 15705 – ☎ 981 58 40 81

The Way of St James

Puente la Reina ☐ Ayuntamiento – 31100 – ☎ 948 34 00 07

Iglesia del Crucifijo - Open afternoons only; if the church is closed, apply-the convent opposite; ☎ 948 34 00 50.

Iglesia de Santiago - Open 10am-1.30pm and 5-8pm; if the church is closed, apply-the butcher's opposite; ☎ 948 34 01 32.

Villalcázar de Sirga: Iglesia de Santa María La Blanca - Visits by prior arrangement; ☎ 979 88 80 76.

Carrión de los Condes: Monasterio de San Zoilo - Open 10.30am-1.30pm and 4-7pm; 1 July-15 Sept 10am-2pm and 4-7.30pm (including Sat, Sun and public holidays); closed Mon, 1 and 6 Jan, 25 Dec and local festivals; 200 pts; ☎ 979 88 09 02.

Town of Santiago

Catedral – Open daily 7.30am–9pm; ☎ 981 58 11 55.

Museo and Tesoro – Open 11am–1pm and 4–6pm; 1 June–30 Sept 10am–1.30p▮ and 4–7.30pm; Sun and public holidays all year 10am–1.30pm; 400 p▮ ☎ 981 58 11 55.

Palacio de Gelmírez – Open 10am–1.30pm and 4.30–7.30pm; closed Mon; 200 p▮ ☎ 981 57 23 00.

Museo de las Peregrinaciones – Open 10am–8pm; Sat 10am–1.30pm and 5–8p▮ Sun 10am–1.30pm; closed Mon; no charge; ☎ 981 58 15 58.

Monasterio de San Martín Pinario – Open during exhibitions on▮ ☎ 981 58 40 81.

Museo do Pobo Galego – Open 10am–1pm and 4–7pm; closed Sun and pub▮ holidays; no charge; ☎ 981 58 36 20.

Museo do Pobo Galego

Colegiata de Santa María del Sar – Visits by prior arrangement 10am–1pm a▮ 4–7pm; the entrance is through the apse; closed Sun and public holidays; 50 pt▮ ☎ 981 56 28 91.

Pazo de Oca – Open 10am–2pm and 4–8pm (gardens only); 500 pts; no charge M▮ mornings until 12.30pm (except public holidays); ☎ 981 58 74 35.

Monasterio de Sobrado Dos Monxes – Open daily 10.15am–1.15pm a▮ 4.15–6.30pm; Sun and public holidays 12.15–1.15pm and 4.15–6.15pm; 100 pt▮ ☎ 981 78 75 09.

SANTILLANA DEL MAR
🄱 Pl. Mayor – 39330 – ☎ 942 81 82 ▮

Colegiata and Claustro – Open 9.30am–1pm and 4–6pm; 15 June–30 Se▮ 10.30am–1pm and 4–8pm; closed Wed in winter, 28 June, 16 Aug and all Fe▮ 300 pts (combined ticket including the Museo Diocesano); ☎ 942 81 80 04.

Convento de Regina Coeli: Museo Diocesano – Same opening times as abov▮ ☎ 942 81 80 04.

SANT JOAN DE LES ABADESSES
🄱 Rambla Comte Guifré 5 – 17860▮ ☎ 972 72 05 ▮

Monasterio – Open 1 Nov–28 Feb 10am–2pm; Sat, Sun and public holiday▮ 10am–2pm and 4–6pm; 1 Mar–30 Apr and 1–31 Oct 10am–2pm and 4–6pm (7p▮ 1 May–30 Sept); 1 July–31 Aug 10am–7pm; 200 pts; ☎ 972 72 00 13.

SANTO DOMINGO DE LA CALZADA

Catedral – Open Apr–Oct 10am–7pm; the rest of the year 9am–2pm and 4–8p▮ closed Sun and public holidays; 250 pts (guided tour); ☎ 941 34 00 33.

ájera: Monasterio de Santa María la Real – Open 10am-12.30pm and 4-6pm; un and public holidays 10am-12.15pm and 4-6.45pm; 1 Apr-30 Sept .30am-1.30pm and 4-7.30pm; Sun and public holidays 9.30am-12.15pm and -6.45pm; last visit 30min before closing time; closed Mon (in winter), 1 Jan, 7 Sept and 25 Dec; 200 pts; ☎ 941 36 36 50.

an Millán de la Cogolla – 🛈 Monasterio de San Millán. 26 226. ☎ 941 37 30 49

Monasterio de Suso – Open 10am-2pm and 4-6pm (7pm 1 June-30 Sept); closed Mon, 1 Jan and 25 Dec; ☎ 941 37 31 73.

Monasterio de Yuso – Guided tours (45min) 10.30am-1pm and 4-6pm; 5 May-15 Sept 10.30am-1.30pm and 4-6.30pm; closed Mon 14 Sept-14 May; 00 pts; ☎ 941 37 30 49.

Monasterio de Cañas – Open 10am-1pm and 3.30-6pm in summer (9.30am-2pm nd 4-7pm in winter); closed Sun during mass (12.30pm); 200pts; ☎ 941 37 90 83.

SANTO DOMINGO DE SILOS

Monasterio – Open 10am-1pm and 4.30-6pm; Mon, Sun and public holidays 1.30-6pm; closed Maundy Thur afternoon-Easter Mon at noon; 250 pts (no charge on Mon); ☎ 947 39 00 49.

SARAGOSSA

See ZARAGOZA

SEGOVIA
🛈 Plaza Mayor 10 – 40001 – ☎ 921 46 03 34

Catedral – Open 9.30am-6pm; 1 Nov-28 Feb 9am-7pm; closed 1 and 6 Jan and 25 Dec; ☎ 921 43 53 25.

Museo Esteban Vicente – Open 11am-2pm and 4-7pm; Sun and public holidays 11am-2pm; closed Mon; no charge; ☎ 921 46 20 10.

Iglesia San Juan de los Caballeros: Museo Zuloaga – Open 10am-2pm and 5-7pm; Sun 10am-2pm; closed Mon and public holidays; 200 pts; no charge at weekends; ☎ 921 146 33 48.

Iglesia de San Esteban – Ask for the keys at the Rectory; 1 July-30 Sept 11am-2pm and 2.30-7pm; ☎ 921 46 00 27.

Alcázar – Open daily 10am-6pm (7pm 1 Apr-30 Sept); closed 1 Jan and 25 Dec; 400 pts; ☎ 921 46 07 59.

Iglesia de San Millán – Open 8.30am-12.30pm and 7-9pm; closed Tues mornings and public holidays; ☎ 921 43 53 25.

Monasterio de El Parral – Open daily 10am-12.30pm and 4-6.30pm; Sun 10am-11.30am and 4-6.30pm (avoid visiting during religious services); ☎ 921 43 12 98.

Capilla de la Vera Cruz – Open 10.30am-1.30pm and 3-6pm (7pm in spring and summer); closed Mon and in Nov; 200 pts; no charge on Tues for Spanish citizens; ☎ 921 43 14 75.

Riofrío: Palacio – Open 10am-1.30pm and 3-5pm; 1 Apr-31 May 10am-1.30pm and 3-5pm; Sat, Sun and public holidays 10am-6pm; 1 June-30 Sept 10am-6pm; closed Mon, 1, 6 and 23 Jan, 25 and 31 Dec; 650 pts; no charge Wed for citizens of the European Union); ☎ 921 47 00 19.

La SEU D'URGELL/SEO DE URGEL
🛈 Av. Valls d'Andorra, 33 – 25700 – ☎ 973 35 15 11

Catedral de Santa María – Open 9.30am-1pm and 4-6pm; Sun and public holidays 9.30am-1pm; 150 pts (cloisters); ☎ 973 35 32 42.

Museo Diocesano – Open noon-1pm; 1 July-30 Sept 10am-1pm and 4-6pm; Sat, Sun and public holidays 11am-1pm; closed 1 and 6 Jan and 25 Dec; 300 pts; ☎ 973 35 32 42 (noon-1pm).

SEVILLA
🛈 Av. Constitución 21 – 41004 – ☎ 95 422 14 04
🛈 Paseo de las Delicias 9 – 41012 – ☎ 95 423 44 65

Giralda – Open 10.30am-6pm; Sun and public holidays 10am-1.30pm and 2-5pm (ticket office closes 1hr before); closed 1 and 6 Jan, 30 May, Corpus Christi, 15 Aug, 8 and 25 Dec; restricted opening times on Tues, Maundy Thur and Good Fri; 300 pts; ☎ 95 456 33 21.

Catedral – Open 10.30am-6pm; Sun and public holidays 2-5pm (ticket office closes 1hr before); closed 1 and 6 Jan, 30 May, Corpus Christi, 15 Aug, 8 and 25 Dec; restricted opening times on Tues, Maundy Thur and Good Fri; 600 pts; ☎ 95 456 33 21.

SEVILLA

Alcázar - Open 9.30am-6pm 1 Oct-31 Mar; Sun and public holidays 9.30am-2.30pm; 9.30am-8pm 1 Apr-30 Sept; last visit 1hr before closing time; closed Mon, 1 and 6 Jan, Good Fri and 25 Dec; 600 pts; ☎ 95 450 23 23.

Hospital de los Venerables - Guided tours (20min) daily 10am-2pm and 4-8pm; closed Good Fri and 25 Dec; 500 pts; ☎ 95 456 26 96.

Museo de Bellas Artes - Open 9am-3pm Wed-Sun; 3-8pm Tues; closed Mon and public holidays; 250 pts; ☎ 95 422 18 29.

Casa de Pilatos - Open daily 10am-6pm (7pm in summer); 500 pts for each floor; ☎ 95 422 52 98.

Torre del Oro, Sevilla

Museo Arqueológico - Open 9am-8pm; closed Mon, 1 and 6 Jan, 10 Apr, 1 May, 12 Oct, 2 Nov, 7, 24, 25 and 31 Dec; 250 pts (charge for citizens of the European Union); ☎ 95 423 24 01.

Hospital de la Caridad - Open 9.30am-1.30pm and 3.30-6.30pm; 9am-1pm S and public holidays; 400 pts; ☎ 95 422 32 32.

Convento de Santa Paula - Open daily 10am-12.30pm and 4.30-6.30pm; clos Mon and some public holidays (dates vary); ☎ 95 442 13 07.

Iglesia del Salvador - Open daily 9am-10am and 6.30-9pm; ☎ 95 421 12 3

Palacio de Lebrija - Open daily 5-7pm; closed on public holidays; ☎ 95 423 81 3

Archivo General de Indias - Visits by prior arrangement 10am-1pm; clos weekends and public holidays; ☎ 95 422 96 44.

Capilla de San José - Open 7-9pm; Sun 11am-noon; ☎ 95 422 32 42.

Isla Mágica - Consult opening times and prices on ☎ 95 448 70 00.

La Cartuja-Centro Andaluz de Arte Contemporáneo - Open 10am-8pm; S 10am-3pm; closed Mon; 300 pts, no charge on Tues; ☎ 95 448 06 11.

Itálica - Open 9am-5pm; Sun 10am-4pm; 1 Apr-30 Sept 9am-9pm; S 9am-3pm; closed Mon; 250 pts (no charge for citizens of the European Unio ☎ 95 599 73 76.

SIGÜENZA
🛈 Pl. Mayor 1 (Ayuntamiento) – 19250 – ☎ 949 39 32

Catedral - Open 11am-2pm and 4-7pm; Mar-Nov 10am-2pm and 5-7pm; guide visits available to rooms usually closed to visitors; 300 pts; ☎ 949 39 14 40.

Museo de Arte Antiguo - Open noon-2pm and 4.30-6pm; Sat, Sun and pub holidays 11am-2pm and 5-7pm; 1 Oct-31 Mar only open weekends and pub holidays noon-2pm and 4.30-6pm; closed Mon; 200 pts; ☎ 949 39 10 23.

SITGES
🛈 Sinia Morera 1 – 08870 – ☎ 93 884 50 04 or 93 884 50

Museu del Cau Ferrat - Open 9.30am-2pm and 4-6pm; Sat 9.30am to 8p 1 July-15 Sept 9.30am-2pm and 4-9pm; Sun and public holidays all ye 9am-2pm; closed Mon, 1 Jan, 24 June, 24 Aug, 23 Sept, 25 and 26 Dec; 500 p (no charge the first Wed of each month); ☎ 93 894 03 64.

Museu Maricel del Mar - Same opening times as above; ☎ 93 894 03 64.

Casa Llopis - Open 9.30am-2pm and 4-6pm (8pm on Sat); 1 July-15 Se 9.30am-2pm and 4-9pm; Sun and public holidays all year 9am-2pm; guided visi of museum (50min) at peak times; 500 pts (no charge the first Wed of each month ☎ 93 894 29 69.

Museu Romàntic Casa Papiol - Open 9.30am-1.15pm and 4-5.15pm; S 10am-1pm and 4-5pm; Sun 10am-1pm; closed Mon and public holidays; 200 p (no charge on Sun); ☎ 93 893 03 82.

blioteca-Museu Victor Balaguer - Open 10am-1.30pm and 4-6.30pm; Thur ternoons all year 6-9pm; 1 June-30 Sept 10am-1.30pm and 4.30-7pm; Sun and blic holidays all year 10am-1.30pm; closed Mon, 1 Jan, Holy Week, 1 May, 5 Aug d 25 and 26 Dec; 300 pts (no charge Thur afternoons and the first Sun of each onth); ☎ 93 815 42 02.

useu del Ferrocarril - Open 10am-5pm; 15 June-15 Sept 10am-2pm and -7pm; Sat, Sun and public holidays 10am-2pm; closed Mon, 1 and 6 Jan, 25 and 5 Dec; 500 pts; ☎ 93 815 84 91.

OLSONA   🖪 Carret. Basella 1 – 25280 – ☎ 973 48 23 10

atedral - Open daily 8am-1pm and 4-8pm; July and Aug 8am-1pm and 5-9pm; oid visiting during services on Sun and public holidays; ☎ 973 48 06 19.

useo Diocesano y Comarcal - Open daily 10am-1pm and 4-6pm (10am-1pm d 4.30-7pm 1 May-30 Sept); 10am-2pm Sun and public holidays all year; closed on (except public holidays), 1 Jan and 25 Dec; 300 pts; ☎ 973 48 21 01.

ORIA   🖪 Pl. Ramón y Cajal s/n – 42003 – ☎ 975 21 20 52

useo Numantino - Open 9am-2pm and 5-9pm; 1 Oct-30 Apr 9am-8.30pm; Sun d public holidays all year 9am-2pm; closed Mon, 1 Jan, 2 Oct, 25 Dec and during cal festivals in June (Jueves La Saca and Domingo de Calderas); 200 pts (no charge weekends); ☎ 975 22 13 97.

atedral de San Pedro - Open 10.30am-2pm and 4-6pm (5-9pm 1 May-30 Sept); un and public holidays all year 10am-2pm; closed Mon; ☎ 975 21 20 52.

onasterio de San Juan de Duero - Open 1 Nov-31 Mar 10am-2pm and 30-6pm; 1 Apr-31 May and 1 Sept-31 Oct 10am-2pm and 4-7pm; 1 June- Aug 10am-2pm and 5-9pm; Sun and public holidays all year 10am-2pm; closed on, 1 Jan, 26 June, 2 Oct and 25 Dec; 100 pts (no charge at weekends); ☎ 975 22 13 97.

rmita de San Saturio - Open 10.30am-2pm and 4-6.30pm; 1 May-30 Sept).30am-2.30pm and 5-9pm; ☎ 975 18 07 06.

uinas de Numancia - Open 1 Nov-31 Mar 10am-2pm and 3.30-6pm; 1 Apr- May and 1 Sept-31 Oct 10am-2pm and 4-7pm; 1 June-31 Aug 10am-2pm and -9pm; Sun and public holidays all year 10am-2pm; closed Mon, 2 Oct and the last un in June; 100 pts; ☎ 975 21 20 52.

OS DEL REY CATÓLICO

lesia de San Esteban - Open 10am-1pm and 3.30-5.30pm; Sun and public olidays 10am-noon and 3.30-5.30pm; Apr-Oct 10am-1pm and 4-6pm; Sun and blic holidays 10am-noon and 4-6pm; 100 pts; ☎ 948 88 82 03.

ALAVERA DE LA REINA   🖪 Ronda del Cañillo (Torreón). 45600. ☎ 925 82 63 22

asílica de la Virgen del Prado - Open 10am-11am and 4-5pm; closed Sun and blic holidays; ☎ 925 80 14 45.

ARRAGONA   🖪 Fortuny 4 – 43001 – ☎ 977 23 34 15
            🖪 Major, 39 – 43003 – ☎ 977 24 50 64

asseig Arqueològic - Open 1 Oct-31 Mar 10am-1.30pm and 3.30-5.30pm; Apr-31 May 10am-1.30pm and 3.30-6pm; 1 June-30 Sept 9am-midnight; Sun d public holidays 9am-2pm (3pm Apr-Sept); closed Mon, 1 and 6 Jan, 1 May, 1 Sept, 24, 25, 26 and 31 Dec; 450 pts; ☎ 977 24 57 96.

useu Nacional Arqueològic de Tarragona - Open 10am-1.30pm and 4-7pm; 5 June-15 Sept 10.30am-2pm and 4-7pm; Sun and public holidays all year 0am-2pm; closed Mon, 1 and 6 Jan, 1 May, 11 Sept, 24, 25 and 26 Dec; 300 pts; ☎ 977 23 62 09.

ecinto Monumental del Pretorio y Circo Romano - Open 10am-1.30pm and -6.30pm; Sun and public holidays 10am-2pm; 1 June-30 Sept 9am-8pm; Sun d public holidays 9am-3pm; closed Mon, 1 and 6 Jan, 1 May, 11 Sept, 25 and 5 Dec; 450 pts; ☎ 977 24 27 52.

mfiteatre - Open Oct-Mar 10am-1.30pm and 3.30-5.30pm; 1 Apr-31 May 0am-1.30pm and 3.30-6.30pm; Sun and public holidays 10am-2pm; 1 June- 0 Sept 9am-8pm; Sun and public holidays 9am-3pm; closed Mon, 1 and 6 Jan, May, 11 Sept and 25, 26 and 31 Dec; 450 pts; ☎ 977 24 25 79.

TARRAGONA

Forum Romà – Same opening times as for the Amphitheatre; ☎ 977 23 34 1

Museo y Necrópolis Paleocristiana – Same opening times and charges as the Mus Nacional Arqueològic; ☎ 977 21 11 75.

Catedral and Museo Diocesano – Open 16 Mar-30 June 10am-1pm and 4-7p 1 July-15 Oct 10am-7pm; 16 Oct-15 Nov 10am-12.30pm and 3-6pm; 16 N 15 Mar 10am-2pm; closed Sun and public holidays; 300 pts; ☎ 977 23 86 85

Catedral, Tarragona

Museu-Casa Castellarnau – Same opening times as for the Recinto Monumen ☎ 977 24 22 20.

Mausoleo de Centcelles – Open 10am-1.30pm and 3-5.30pm; 1 June-30 S 10am-1.30pm and 4-7.30pm; Sun and public holidays all year 10am-1.30p closed Mon, 1 and 6 Jan, 1 May, 11 Sept, 25, 26 and 31 Dec; 300 p ☎ 977 52 33 74.

Villa Romana de Els Munts – Open 10am-1.30pm and 3-5.30pm; 1 June-30 S 10am-1.30pm and 4-7.30pm; open Sun and public holidays all year 10am-1p last visit 20min before closing time; closed Mon, 1 Jan and 25 Dec; 300 pts (no cha on Tues); ☎ 93 412 11 40.

TERRASSA
🛈 Raval de Montserrat 14 – 08221 – ☎ 93 739 70

Conjunto Monumental de Iglesias de Sant Pere – Open 10am-1.30pm a 4-7pm; Sun 11am-2pm; closed Mon and public holidays; ☎ 93 739 70 19 93 789 27 55.

Museu de la Ciencia y la Tècnica de Catalunya – Open 10am-7pm; 1 July-31 A 10am-2.30pm; closed Mon, 1 Jan and 25 and 26 Dec; 400 pts (no charge the fi Sun of each month); ☎ 93 736 89 66.

Museu Tèxtil – Open 9am-6pm; Thur 9am-9pm; Sat and Sun 10am-2pm; clos Mon and public holidays; 300 pts (no charge the first Sun of each month and 18 Ma ☎ 93 731 49 80.

TERUEL
🛈 Tomás Nougués 1 – 44001 – ☎ 978 60 22

Museo Provincial – Open 10am-2pm and 4-7pm; Sat and Sun 10am-2pm; clos Mon and public holidays; no charge; ☎ 978 60 01 50.

Catedral – Open daily 9am-2pm and 5-9pm; ☎ 978 60 22 75.

Mausoleo de los Amantes de Teruel – Open 10am-2pm and 5-8pm; Sun and pub holidays 10.30am-2pm and 5-8pm; closed Mon; 50 pts; ☎ 978 60 21 67.

tedral - Open 10.30am-1pm and 3.30-6pm; Sun and public holidays .30am-1.30pm and 4-6pm; 1 May-30 Sept daily until 7pm; closed mornings of an, Palm Sun, Good Fri, Easter Sun, Corpus Christi and 15 Aug; closed afternoons Maundy Thur, Good Fri, and 24, 25 and 31 Dec; 500 pts (no charge Wed ternoons); ☎ 925 22 22 41.

esia de Santo Tomé - Open daily 10am-1.45pm and 3.30-5.45pm (6.45pm in mmer); closed 1 Jan and 25 Dec; 150 pts; ☎ 925 25 60 98.

sa y Museo de El Greco - Open 10am-2pm and 4-6pm; Sun and public holidays am-2pm; closed Mon, 1 Jan and 25 Dec; 400 pts (no charge Sat afternoons and n); ☎ 925 22 40 46.

nagoga del Tránsito - Same opening times as for the Casa y Museo de El Greco; 0 pts; ☎ 925 22 36 65.

nagoga de Santa María la Blanca - Open daily 10am-2pm and 3.30-6pm (7pm summer); closed 1 Jan and 25 Dec; 150 pts; ☎ 925 22 72 57.

onasterio de San Juan de los Reyes - Open daily 10am-1.45pm and 30-5.45pm (6.45pm in summer); closed 1 Jan and 25 Dec; 150 pts; 925 22 38 02.

esia de San Román: Museo de los Concilios de Toledo y de la Cultura Visigoda - Open am-2pm and 4-6.30pm; Sun and public holidays 10am-2pm; closed Mon, 1 Jan d 25 Dec; 100 pts (no charge Sat afternoons and Sun); ☎ 925 22 78 72.

useo de Santa Cruz - Open 10am-6.30pm; Sun and public holidays 10am-2pm; n 10am-2pm and 4-6.30pm; closed 1 Jan and 25 Dec; 200 pts (no charge Sat ternoons and Sun); ☎ 925 22 01 36.

cázar - Open 10am-1.30pm and 4-5.30pm (6.30pm in summer); closed Mon, Jan and 25 Dec; 125 pts; ☎ 925 22 30 28.

ller del Moro - Open 10am-2pm and 4-6.30pm; Sun and public holidays am-2pm; closed Mon, 1 Jan and 25 Dec; ☎ 925 22 71 15.

ospital de Tavera - Guided tours (30min) 10.30am-1.30pm and 3.30-6pm; sed Mon, 1 Jan and 25 Dec; 500 pts; ☎ 925 22 04 51.

adamur: Castillo - Closed for restoration.

nvento de Santa Clara - Guided tours (1hr) 10.30am-1pm and 4-5.30pm 0am-1pm and 3.30-6.30pm 1 Apr-30 Sept); Sun and public holidays all year .30am-1.30pm and 3.30-5.30pm; closed Mon, 1 and 6 Jan, Maundy Thur ternoon), Good Fri, 23 Apr, Corpus Christi, 2 fiestas in Sept (dates vary) and 24, and 31 Dec; 425 pts (no charge Wed for citizens of the European Union); 983 77 00 71.

legiata - Open 11am-1pm and 5-8pm; Oct-Dec 10am-1pm and 4-8pm; closed n, Fri mornings and in Jan; ☎ 980 69 03 88.

esia de San Lorenzo - Temporarily closed for repairs; ☎ 980 69 03 88.

esia de San Cebrián de Mazote - Visits by prior arrangement; ☎ 983 78 00 77.

tedral - Open daily 8am-1pm and 5-8pm (no visits during religious services); 977 44 17 52.

lacio Episcopal - Open daily 10am-2pm; closed Sun and public holidays; 977 44 07 00.

ales Colegios de Tortosa - Open Mon-Fri 9am-1.30pm and 4-7pm; first Sat of ery month 9am-2pm; closed second Mon of every month and public holidays; no arge; ☎ 977 44 15 25.

xiu Històric Comarcal de les Terres de l'Ebre - Same opening times as the Iglesia Santo Domingo; ☎ 977 44 15 25.

esia de Santo Domingo - Open 9am-1.30pm and 4-7pm; 1 June-14 Sept m-3pm; Sat all year 9am-2pm; closed Sun and public holidays; ☎ 977 44 15 25.

rque Natural del Delta del Ebro - Open all year; visitors are advised to apply to e Centro de Información del Delta, c/o Doctor Martín Buera 22, at Deltebre, open am-2pm and 3-6pm; Sat 10am-1pm and 3.30-6pm (7pm July and Aug); Sun d public holidays 10am-1pm; closed 1 Jan and 25 Dec; ☎ 977 48 96 79.

esia de Santa María - Open daily 10.30am-2pm and 4.30-7pm; May-Sept .30am-2pm and 5-8pm; 50 pts; ☎ 927 32 26 77.

TUDELA 🖼 Pl. Vieja 1 – 31500 – ☎ 948 82 1?

Catedral - Open daily 9am-1pm and 4-7pm (4.30-8pm in summer); Mu
Diocesano closed in winter; 200 pts (winter); 250 pts (summer) including Mu
Diocesano; ☎ 948 41 17 93.

Tarazona: Catedral - Temporarily closed for repairs.

Monasterio de Veruela - Open 1 Oct-31 Mar 10am-1pm and 3-6pm; 1 A|
30 Sept 10am-2pm and 4-7pm; 200 pts; ☎ 976 64 90 25.

TUI 🖼 Puente Tripes. Av. de Portugal – 36700 – ☎ 986 60 1?

Catedral - Open 10.30am-1.30pm and 4-7pm (in summer 4.30-8pm); the Mu
Diocesano remains closed in winter; 200 pts (in winter); ☎ 986 60 31 07.

U – V

ÚBEDA 🖼 Av. Cristo Rey 2 – 23400 – ☎ 953 75 0?

Iglesia de El Salvador - For visits, call the sacristy; ☎ 953 75 08 97.

UCLÉS

Castillo-Monasterio - Open daily 9.30am-8pm; 200 pts; ☎ 969 13 50 58.

VALDEPEÑAS

Santuario de Nuestra Señora de las Virtudes - Open 10am-6pm; 1 Apr-30 S
10am-9pm; closed Tues; ☎ 926 33 82 35.

VALENCIA 🖼 Pl. del Ayuntamiento 1 – 46002 – ☎ 96 351 0?
🖼 Av. Cataluña 5 – 46010 – ☎ 96 369 7?
🖼 c/ Paz 48 – 46003 – ☎ 96 394 2?

Centro de Interpretación del Racó de l'Olla - Open Mon, Wed and Fri 9am-2|
Tues and Thur 9am-2pm and 3.30-5.30pm; Sat, Sun and public holidays 9am-2
and 3-5.30pm; ☎ 96 162 73 45.

Museo Blasco Ibáñez - Open 9.15am-2pm and 4.30-8pm; Sun 9.15am-2|
closed Mon; no charge; ☎ 96 356 47 86.

Museo Fallero - Open 10am-2pm and 4-7pm; Sat, Sun and public holid
10am-2pm; closed Sun June-Oct, 1 and 6 Jan, 19 Mar and 25 Dec; 300 |
☎ 96 347 96 23.

Catedral - Open daily 10.30am-1pm and 4.30-6.30pm; ☎ 96 391 81 27.

El Miguelete - Open daily 10am-1pm and 4.30-7pm; 200 pts; ☎ 96 391 81

Capilla del Santo Caliz or Sala Capitular - Open 10am-1pm and 4.30-6pm (7
June-Sept); 10am-1pm Dec-Mar; public holidays all year 10am-1pm; closed S
200 pts. ☎ 96 391 81 27.

Museo de la Ciudad - Open 9.30am-2pm and 5.30-8pm; Sun 9.30am-2pm;
charge; ☎ 96 391 02 19.

Cripta Arqueológica de la Cárcel de San Vicente - Open 9.30am-2pm
5.30-8pm; Sun 9.30am-2pm; closed Mon; no charge; ☎ 96 394 14 17.

Iglesia de Nuestra Señora de los Desamparados - Open daily 7am-2pm |
4pm-9pm; ☎ 96 391 92 14.

Palacio de la Generalidad - Guided tours (45min) by prior appointment Mon-
9am-2pm; ☎ 96 386 34 61.

Iglesia de San Nicolás - Closed for restoration; ☎ 96 391 33 17.

Lonja - Open daily 9am-2pm and 5-7pm; Sun 9am-1.30pm; closed Mon, S
public holidays and days preceding the official opening of temporary exhibitic
☎ 96 352 54 78.

Iglesia de los Santos Juanes - Open 8am-1pm and 6-8pm; in summer o
7.30am-1pm and 6-8pm; ☎ 96 391 63 54.

Museo de Cerámica - Temporarily closed for repairs; ☎ 96 351 63 92.

Museo de Bellas Artes San Pío V - Open 10am-2pm and 4-6pm; Sun and pu
holidays 10am-2pm; closed Mon, 1 Jan, Good Fri and 25 Dec; ☎ 96 360 57 S

Colegio del Patriarca - Open daily 11am-1.30pm; 15-31 July and 1-15 S
5pm-7pm; closed Good Fri; ☎ 96 351 41 76.

Torres de Serranos - Open 9am-2pm and 4.15-8pm; Sat open mornings o
closed Sun, Mon and public holidays; ☎ 96 391 90 70.

stituto Valenciano de Arte Moderno (IVAM) - Centro Julio González open
am-7pm; Centro del Carmen open 11am-2.30pm and 4.30-7pm; closed Mon, 1
, Good Fri and 25 Dec; Centro Julio González: 350 pts (no charge on Sun); Centro
Carmen: no charge; ☎ 96 386 30 00.

ntro de Beneficiencia: Museo de Prehistoria - Open 9.15am-2pm and 4.30-8pm;
n and public holidays mornings only; closed Mon; ☎ 96 352 54 78 (ext. 1097).

seu d'Etnologia - Open 10am-2.30pm and 4-7pm; 15 June-15 Sept
am-2.30pm and 5-8pm; closed Mon, 1 Jan, 1 May and 25 Dec; ☎ 96 388 36 29.

rdín Botánico - Open 10am-6pm (7pm Mar and Oct; 8pm Apr-Sept; 9pm
ne-Aug); closed Mon; 50 pts; ☎ 96 391 16 57.

emisferic - For programme, prices and reservations, call ☎ 902 10 00 31.

onasterio de la Virgen del Puig - Open 10am-1pm and 4-7.30pm; closed Mon
ernoons; 300 pts; ☎ 96 147 02 00.

ALLADOLID   🖪 Pl. de Zorrilla 3 – 47001 – ☎ 983 35 18 01

seo Nacional de Escultura Policromada - Open 10am-2pm and 4-6pm; Sun
d public holidays 10am-2pm; last visit 15min before closing time; closed Mon,
and 6 Jan, 1 and 13 May, 8 Sept, 24, 25 and 31 Dec; 400 pts (no charge Sat
ernoons, Sun and public holidays, 18 May, 12 Oct and 6 Dec); ☎ 983 25 03 75.

tedral - Open 10am-1.30pm (11am-1.30pm in winter) and 4.30-7pm; Sat
am-2pm; Sun and public holidays 10am-2pm and 5.45-6.45pm; closed Mon;
983 30 43 62.

useo - Open 10am-1.30pm and 4.30-7pm; Sat, Sun and public holidays
am-2pm; closed Mon; 350 pts; ☎ 983 30 43 62.

esia de las Angustias - Open 9.30am-1pm and 5.30-8.30pm; Sun and public
lidays 10am-2pm.

useo Oriental - Open 4-7pm; Sun and public holidays 10am-2pm; during Holy
eek 11am-2pm and 4-7pm; 400 pts; ☎ 983 30 68 00.

sa de Cervantes - Guided tours (30min) 9.30am-3.30pm; Sun and public
lidays 10am-3pm; closed Mon, 1 and 6 Jan, 1 and 13 May, 8 Sept, 24, 25 and
Dec; 400 pts; ☎ 983 30 88 10.

ALLE DE LOS CAÍDOS

sílica and La Cruz - Open 10am-6pm; 1 Apr-30 Sept 9.30am-7pm; closed Mon,
and 6 Jan, 17 July, 10 Aug and 24, 25 and 31 Dec; 650 pts (350 pts ascent by
nicular railway); ☎ 91 890 56 11.

C   🖪 Pl. Major 1 – 08500 – ☎ 93 886 20 91

tedral - Open 10am-1pm and 4-7pm (no visits during religious services); closed
on; 300 pts (no charge Sun mornings); ☎ 93 886 01 18.

useu Episcopal - Open 10am-1pm; 15 May-14 Oct 10am-1pm and 4-6pm; Sun
d public holidays all year 10am-1pm; closed 25 Dec; 300 pts; ☎ 93 886 22 14.

onasterio de Santa Maria de L'Estany - Open 10am-1pm and 4-7pm (6.30pm
winter); 300 pts; ☎ 93 830 31 39.

LAFAMÉS

useo Popular de Arte Contemporáneo - Open 11am-1pm and 5-7pm; Sat-Sun
d public holidays 11am-2pm and 4-7pm; 15 June-15 Sept 11am-1pm and
8pm; Sat-Sun and public holidays 11am-2pm and 5-8pm; 200 pts;
964 32 91 52.

LLENA

useo Arqueológico - Open 10am-2pm and 5-8pm; Sat, Sun and public holidays
am-1.30pm; closed Mon, 1 Jan, 1 May, 15 Aug, 8 Sept and 25 Dec;
96 580 11 50 (ext. 50).

esia de Santiago - Open daily 8.30am-noon and 6.30-8pm; ☎ 96 581 39 19.

cairent: Museo Parroquial - Guided tours (1hr) by prior arrangement; Sun and public
lidays from 12.30pm; 100 pts; ☎ 96 235 00 62.

TORIA
e GASTEIZ

K – Z

ÁTIVA/JÁTIVA   🖪 Alameda Jaume I, 50 – 46800 – ☎ 96 227 33 46

useo - Open 10am-2pm and 4-6pm; 15 June-15 Sept 9.30am-2.30pm; Sat,
n and public holidays all year 10am-2pm; closed Mon, 1 Jan, 22 May, 24, 25, 26
d 31 Dec; 300 pts (no charge on Tues); ☎ 96 227 65 97.

XÀTIVA/JÁTIVA

Ermita de Sant Feliu - Open 10am-1pm and 3-6pm; Apr-Sept 10am-1pm
4-7pm; Sun and public holidays all year 10am-1pm; ☎ 96 227 33 46.

Castillo - Open 10am-1pm and 3.30-6pm (7pm in summer); Sat-Sun and pu
holidays 10am-6pm (8pm in summer); closed Mon, 1 Jan, 24, 25 and 31 [
300 pts (no charge on Tues); ☎ 96 227 33 46.

Iglesia de la Candelaria - Open 10.30am-1pm and afternoons during religi
services; ☎ 924 55 01 28.

Museo de la Semana Santa - Open 10am-2pm and 4-7pm (5-8pm in summ
Sun and public holidays all year 10am-2pm; 300 pts; ☎ 980 53 22 95.

Catedral and Museo Catedralicio - Cathedral open 9am-2pm and 4-6pm (/
-Sept 9am-2pm and 5-8pm); Museum open 11am-2pm and 4-6pm (Apr-S
9am-2pm and 5-8pm); Museum closed Mon mornings and Sun afternoons; 300
☎ 980 52 03 74.

San Pedro de la Nave: Iglesia - Open Mon-Fri 4.30-6.30pm; Apply to the bar nea
for the keys; ☎ 980 55 57 09.

Arcenillas: Iglesia - Open daily 9am-2pm and 4-6pm; ☎ 980 57 12 15.

La Seo - Guided visits noon-1pm and 5-8pm; unaccompanied visits 1-2pm;
10am-2pm; closed Mon; no charge; ☎ 976 39 74 97.

Lonja - Temporary exhibitions 10am-2pm and 5-9pm; Sun and public holid
10am-2pm; closed Mon, 1 Jan, 24 (afternoon), 25 and 31 (afternoon) Dec, as
as during the preparing and dismantling of exhibitions; ☎ 976 39 72 39.

Basílica de Nuestra Señora del Pilar - Open daily 6.45am-8.30pm (9.30pm
summer); ☎ 976 29 95 64.

Museo Pilarista - Open daily 9am-2pm and 4-6pm; 150 pts; ☎ 976 29 95

Aljafería - Open 10am-2pm and 4.30-6.30pm; 1 May-31 Oct 10am-2pm
4-8pm; Sun and public holidays all year 10am-2pm; ☎ 976 28 95 28.

Fuendetodos: Casa-Museo de Goya - Open 11am-2pm and 4-7pm; closed Mon (exc
public holidays), 1 Jan, 23 and 24 Aug, 12 Oct, 24, 25 and 31 Dec; 300
☎ 976 14 38 30.

Fuendetodos: Museo de Grabados - Same opening times as above; 300
☎ 976 14 38 30.

Balearic Islands

MALLORCA

Museo Monográfico de Pollentia - Open daily 10am-1.30pm and 4pm-6
1 Apr-30 Sept 10am-1.30pm and 5-7pm; Sat and Sun all year 10.30am-1
closed Mon and public holidays; 200 pts; ☎ 971 54 70 04.

Cuevas de Campanet - Guided tours (45min) daily 10am-6pm (7pm 26 A
25 Oct); closed 1 Jan and 25 Dec; 1 000 pts; ☎ 971 51 61 30.

Muro: Sección Etnológica del Museo de Mallorca - Open 10am-2pm and 4-7pm; Sun
public holidays 10am-2pm; closed Mon; 300 pts; ☎ 971 71 75 40.

Catedral and Museo-Tesoro - Open 10am-3pm (6pm Apr-Oct); Sat 10am-2
closed Sun and public holidays; 300 pts; ☎ 971 72 31 30.

La Almudaina - Open 10am-2pm and 4-6pm; 1 Apr-30 Sept 10am-6.30pm;
and public holidays all year 10am-2pm; Sun in Aug 10.30am-1.30pm; closed S
450 pts (no charge Wed for citizens of the European Union); ☎ 971 72 71 45